BGP
(Border Gateway Protocol)
from theory to practice

Flavio **LUCIANI**
Antonio **PRADO**
Tiziano **TOFONI**

First Issue: November 2023

Errata
We collect all the errata for this book at the following URL:
https://book.reissromoli.com

How to report errata
If you have errata to report, please send an e-mail to antonio@prado.it

CONTENTS

7 – TRAFFIC MANAGEMENT POLICIES 247

8 – BGP IN SERVICE PROVIDER NETWORKS 299

FOREWORD

Back in 2011, Reiss Romoli published the first edition of the book "*BGP: From Theory to Practice*", written by Tiziano Tofoni. Many years have gone by since then, and the author of the first edition deemed it necessary for it to undergo an extensive review, since, in the meantime, BGP – although quite consolidated – underwent its own evolution. New techniques significantly improved its security and convergence speed aspects – the two Achilles's heels of the first BGP versions.

Despite our different professional journeys, we all have a common denominator in BGP. According to our 'vision', BGP is the standard protocol without which the entire Internet would not be possible. And this has been proven over the years, since BGP has gained such consensus that it has become the most important protocol for IP networks – the true supporting structure of the "Internet ecosystem".

BGP is based on simple, yet effective concepts, which allow for an extremely flexible use of this protocol. Although it was born and designed as an inter-domain routing protocol, today BGP is broadly employed also in other fields, such as:

- In modern public Service Provider networks, where it plays a key role in the overall routing architecture, because – thanks to its proven scalability – it has turned out to be a very efficient tool also to distribute external routing information within the network.

- In MPLS services control plane;

- For "painless" IPv4 to IPv6 migration, without major impacts on the backbone of the Service Providers;

- As private network access protocol to Service Provider networks;

- As IGP in big Data Centers, where it acts as routing protocol on the underlay network, and as transfer for several kinds of information on the overlay network.

Rather than an actual routing protocol in the traditional sense, BGP is routing policy application protocol. Indeed, in its definition, the protocol designers did not focus on some of the typical aspects of standard routing protocols, such as convergence speed and security. Rather, they focused on making the exchange of large quantities of IP prefixes scalable – and they certainly succeed in doing so, if we consider that today, in the routers used by large IP networks, BGP can manage the exchange of routing information related to almost one million IP prefixes.

All this has driven us to follow BGP's evolution up close, and to spread its knowledge to a vast audience of insiders. This is how the idea of writing a second edition of the original book came about. Following the spirit of the first edition, this edition also pursued the goal of combining theory and practice, and tried not to be only a (debatable) presentation of the standard. This is why, apart from explaining in detail and with many examples how the protocol works and its role in IP networks and in the entire Internet ecosystem, the book also includes many practical application examples, resulting from many years of experience.

In the way it is conceived, the book requires solid notions on TCP/IP architecture, and on IP routing fundamentals in particular. Moreover, since it covers several configuration aspects, both in Cisco (IOS/IOS-XE/IOS-XR) and in Juniper (JUNOS) environments, it also requires a basic knowledge of these Operating Systems. Nevertheless, we firmly believe that being knowledgeable about a specific Operating System is not so important, once the basic concept behind the protocol and its services have been acquired. Jumping from one technology to another is just a question of learning the basic commands, and understanding how the protocol was implemented by that specific developer, with this last aspect being crucial in machine TCL scenarios.

In general, this is an upper-intermediate level book, while the notions on BGP can be read both by readers with basic knowledge who wish to deepen its concepts, and by those with no understanding of this standard. It is addressed to the wide audience of Internetworking experts, both on the Service Provider network and on the private network side (see all institutions such as Banks, Industries, Public Administrations, many of which have Corporate Networks based on the IP/MPLS backbone).

We hope that reading it will help, apart from understanding the standard's theoretical-practical fundamentals, also to grasp the importance of an intensive use of BGP in IP networks.

Flavio Luciani
Antonio Prado
Tiziano Tofoni

PRESENTATION

I was born in 1963 and I've always been attracted to technology; telecommunications have always fascinated me. I've always been curious about stories.

One of my favourite stories about telecommunications was about the Reiss Romoli Graduate School.

It talked about a graduated school founded in 1976, under the initiative of the STET Group, and then passed on to Telecom Italia, devoted to post-graduate education of young minds who would be sent for months to L'Aquila, in a campus equipped with all amenities (labs, swimming pool, gym, library), and there they were trained to become the new ranks of engineers and executives of the former monopoly.

I met many of these former young people, trained at the Reiss Romoli, who, over the years, went on to cover strategic positions in Tim and in other Italian ISP, and I've listened to their many stories. Stories of a top-level school.

Stories of young people who studied hard, and who were also young people trying to enjoy that experience in the best way possible, and so they held "harmless breakouts" at night from this barrack-school that sometimes did not agree with their age.

Nice stories.

It was rumoured they had very good, and very passionate professors.

To me, the school and its professors were sort of legends, because I never met them. L'Aquila is a city I'm familiar with. I lived there for a while, when I was working at the Physics Labs underneath the Gran Sasso mountains. For some reason, I never visited the campus of the Reiss Romoli School in L'Aquila.

Then, one day, Flavio Luciani, our CTO at Namex, talked to me about meeting one of these mythical professors, Tiziano Tofoni, and told me about the possibility of working with him.

During an ITNOG event in Bologna, I met Tiziano and *"BGP: From Theory to Practice"*, the book he wrote and published in 2011, and discovered it was a stable book in our community. Many of the technicians and engineers employed in Italian ISPs were formed by that book.

During the conference breaks, we came up with the idea that saw us collaborate all these years – train the employees of Namex-partner ISPs, through the great experience of the Reiss Romoli School.

The matter was that many ISPs connecting to Namex needed to train their newly hires and hold update courses for existing staff. Finding these courses on the market was certainly no easy task.

There weren't many companies offering training on such specific topics, like the one ISPs are interested in (BGP, MPLS, DNS, IPv6, etc.), on the market; and even less of them were able to offer a quality equalling that of the Reiss Romoli School. What's more, the cost was very high, especially for smaller ISPs.

There were other lunches after that event. I had the chance to see the old campus at the Reiss Romoli School, even if only from the outside, since it is no longer open.

We decided to found the Namex *School Of Advanced Networking*, with the motto "Training Course for ISPs made by ISPs".

It was 2019.

The first SOAN catalogue started with the classes that were part of the Reiss Romoli catalogue (3 days, and, in some cases, exam + final certification), which we decided to enrich with contributions/workshops by our CTO Flavio Luciani and by experts/friends from Namex-member ISPs, such as Antonio Prado – a benchmark of the Italian ISP and PA community, whom I met many years earlier, when he was working for one of Namex-member ISPs.

We decided to offer the classes free of charge, using part of the revenue from the services offered by Namex to the ISPs. Tiziano's book on BGP was the reference book of the most popular class – that on BGP.

It was a success. Since then, Namex has provided, in all editions, over 50 classes, training hundreds of people, and – more importantly – it fostered a moment of aggregation and debate between the people that "deal with the Internet" in Italy.

It's something I'm especially proud of, and I hope it will go down in Namex history (small in absolute terms, yet so big for us living it).

The cherry on top is this new edition of the BGP book, wanted by "Admiral" Tiziano, with his First Officers Antonio and Flavio. Namex has enthusiastically joined the sponsorship request, right from the start, counting on the fact that it can continue to be a reference for all those professionals dealing with interdomain interconnection, and with the Internet ecosystem in general, for many years to come.

A big thank you to Antonio, Flavio and Tiziano, who worked on this new edition.

A thank you to the Reiss Romoli School, editor of the book, which has trained Italian telecommunication professionals for decades, keeping the quality level very high.

And lastly, a thank you to Namex-member ISPs, which, with their feedback, prompted us to start the Namex *School Of Advanced Networking* and to improve it, year after year.

Maurizio Goretti
Namex CEO

ACKNOWLEDGEMENTS

This book is to me a moment of professional and – above all – personal growth. And it wouldn't be so, without my two travel companions and friends, Tiziano Tofoni and Antonio Prado, whom I want to thank from the bottom of my heart. To my family, for their love and patience. To my father, who would be proud of me.

Flavio Luciani

I would love to thank hundreds of people, because I've learned something from each and every one of them, during my career. The first people I want to thank are my friends Flavio and Tiziano, with whom I shared this experience (and, I hope, many more to come), and then Mauro Angiolillo, my inseparable sparring partner, and Professor Fabio Fioravanti, for his precious advice. Lastly, my parents, for listening to me, my children who always bring me down to earth, and Belinda, my wife, who has always supported me.

Antonio Prado

During the creation of this book, I benefited from the help of many people, who I'm proud to call my Friends (with a capital F), and to whom I want to offer my deepest gratitude.
I also wish to thank the many Friends of Italian ISPs with whom I had interesting debates on the role of BGP and of its actual applications in the networks of ISPs.
Last but not least, as in every book I ever wrote, I want to thank the two women of the house, Vicky and Fiammix (Maria Vittoria and Fiammetta). Without their evening tiredness (which allowed me to focus on my work), and without their patience in bearing my constant absent-mindedness, this book probably would have never seen the light of day. I dedicate this work to them.

Tiziano Tofoni

The authors wish to thank Reiss Romoli srl, editor of the book, Namex CEO Maurizio Goretti, for the enthusiasm with which he joined the project, and Belinda Menzietti, for her patient and professional editing.

Last but certainly not least, a big thank you to Simone Morandini for the immense contribution provided in the revision of this book.

Those who fall for practice without science are like the helmsman who enters
a ship without a rudder or compass who never has certainty where he is going.
Always practice must be built on top of good theory.

(Leonardo da Vinci)

1 – INTRODUCTION

BGP (Border Gateway Protocol) was created as a standard EGP (Exterior Gateway Protocol) protocol, that is, it was developed to exchange routing information between different Autonomous Systems (ASes). The version currently used is number 4, defined in RFC 1771 – *A Border Gateway Protocol* 4 (*BGP*-4), March 1995, rewritten with the same title in January 2006 as RFC 4271. Its main characteristics are the following:

- it is a Path Vector routing protocol, which means it is conceptually similar to a Distance Vector protocol, although with hops measured in terms of numbers of ASes, instead of number of routers;

- it supports CIDR (Classless Inter Domain Routing);

- it determines optimal paths through a very complex selection process, based on metrics of different kinds;

- due to the presence of different types of metrics, it allows the creation of routing policies both for outbound and inbound traffic in the AS;

- it allows a reliable exchange of routing information, achieved through TCP connections;

- updates are event-driven.

All those features make BGP a routing policy application protocol, rather than an actual routing protocol. In fact, protocol designers did not consider some of the typical aspects present in IGP routing protocols when defining it, such as, for instance, speed of convergence, load balancing, etc. Instead, they focused on making the management of large quantities of IP prefixes scalable – and succeeded in doing so, if we consider that today, in routers installed in big IP networks, BGP is capable of managing the exchange of routing information related to hundreds of thousands of IP prefixes. In this regard, there's an interesting statement by Yakov Rekhter, who, together with Kirk Lougheed, may be considered the father of BGP:

"Kirk Lougheed and myself's goal was to build a routing protocol able to convey 1000 routes and not fall into pieces. If you think the total routes being today in the Internet, we pushed the envelope a bit."

The purpose of this chapter is explaining some of the key definitions to understand BGP, and, above all, define an operating model that will be constantly referenced in the next chapters.

1.1 HISTORICAL NOTES

In the early days of the Internet, what is today known as the "network of networks" was actually a single network – ARPANET, developed at the end of the 1960s – and its satellite extension – SATNET, developed in the mid-1970s. Routers – which were called gateways back then – exchanged routing information through a single Distance Vector protocol known as GGP (Gateway-to-Gateway Protocol), then evolved into RIP (Routing Information Protocol), which remained for many years the only Internet routing protocol.

As the number of users and nodes grew, it became evident that adopting a model without any kind of hierarchy was not scalable. A single routing protocol was not enough to manage the network's complexity. Eric Rosen – who worked as Engineer at Bolt Beranek and Newman Inc. at the time – pointed out (in RFC 827 – *Exterior Gateway Protocol (EGP)*, October 1982) the flat model's scalability issues, and the need to adopt a hierarchical model, dividing the Internet into a set of ASes, i.e. networks managed by the same administration. One of the ASes – called Core AS – comprised ARPANET and SATNET, and worked as the Internet's Backbone. All the other ASes – called stub AS – were connected by one or more routers (Exterior Gateways) to the Core AS. Generally speaking, communication between stub ASes occurred through the Core AS. The exchange of routing information between ASes was delegated to a new protocol, standardized in RFC 827.

However, in a matter of years, due to the continuous growth of the Internet, EGP revealed many limitations, essentially linked to the fact that it had been designed based on the Internet Hub-and-Spoke model (all the stub ASes (Spoke) connected to a single Core AS (Hub)). Among them:

- the lack of loop avoidance mechanisms;

- the fact that only classful routing was supported (RFC 1817 – *CIDR and Classful routing*, August 1995);

- the fact that the routing information communication mechanism was based, as in Distance Vector protocols, on periodic transmission of the entire IP routing table to the nearest neighbors (the timeframe was set to 2 minutes);

- the impossibility to define inbound and/or outbound traffic management policies in an AS.

In January 1989, at the 12th IETF Meeting in Austin, Texas, Yakov Rekhter and Kirk Lougheed – Head Researcher at IBM's T.J. Watson Research Center the former, and Engineer at Cisco Systems the latter – sat down at a table (according to "The Packet" newsletter, Volume 1, Number 2, published in Winter of 1989 by Cisco Systems, Leonard Bosack, Cisco co-founder, was also with them) and laid the foundations for a new inter-AS routing protocol – Border Gateway Protocol (BGP) – jokingly called The Two-Napkin Protocol, because BGP's initial project was drawn on some restaurant napkins (which, some say, were even soiled with ketchup!).

Lougheed himself shed some light on this episode, by stating: *"After I wrote up the notes on two napkins, I made a second copy, also on napkins. I gave Yakov that first copy and took the second copy for myself. Apparently Yakov made photocopies of his napkins and these photocopies are the origin of the images you've seen. Having no sense of history, I discarded my napkins at some point."*

Photocopies of the drawings contained in those napkins are now displayed on the walls of the *Routing Protocol Development* department, in Cisco Systems headquarters in Santa Clara, CA. They are shown in Figure 1.1.

In a short while, the first practical implementation of BGP was created from this draft, and then the first standard, defined in RFC 1105 – *A Border Gateway Protocol (BGP)*, June 1989, written by Yakov Rekhter and Kirk Lougheed.

NOTE: In Lougheed's words: *"Once back home I started drafting what eventually became RFC 1105. Yakov and I passed that document back and forth while developing and refining our own implementations in a classic iterative process. By the time RFC 1105 was published there were two implementations, my Cisco router implementation and Yakov's IBM router implementation on the NSFnet backbone. We naturally tested for interoperability. I think the gated implementation came out after RFC 1105."*

The standardization process involved several stages, which led to the definition of a second and third version, published in RFC 1163 of June 1990 and in RFC 1267 of October 1991, respectively. Version 4 – the final one – was published in March 1995, in RFC 1771 – *A Border Gateway Protocol 4* (*BGP*-4), written by Y. Rekhter and T. Li, who worked for Cisco Systems. RFC 1771 was rewritten in January 2006 by the same authors, alongside S. Hares, in RFC 4271.

From Rekhter and Lougheed's napkins was born the most important protocol of today's Internet, the one that glues the "network of networks" together. BGP-4 is *de facto* the standard protocol, universally employed as inter-domain routing protocol. Over the years, it underwent continuous updates, which enhanced its functions, stability and scalability.

Despite being created as an inter-domain routing protocol, over time, BGP expanded its field of application, and today it is employed:

- in modern public networks of big ISPs (Internet Service Provider), where it plays a key role in the overall routing architecture, because – thanks to its proven scalability – it has turned out to be a very efficient tool also to distribute IP prefixes external to the AS inside an AS;

- in the control plane of VPN services based on the BGP/MPLS model;

- as an access protocol of private networks (Enterprise networks) to ISP networks.

Without fear of contradiction, we can say that BGP is the most important routing protocol for IP networks.

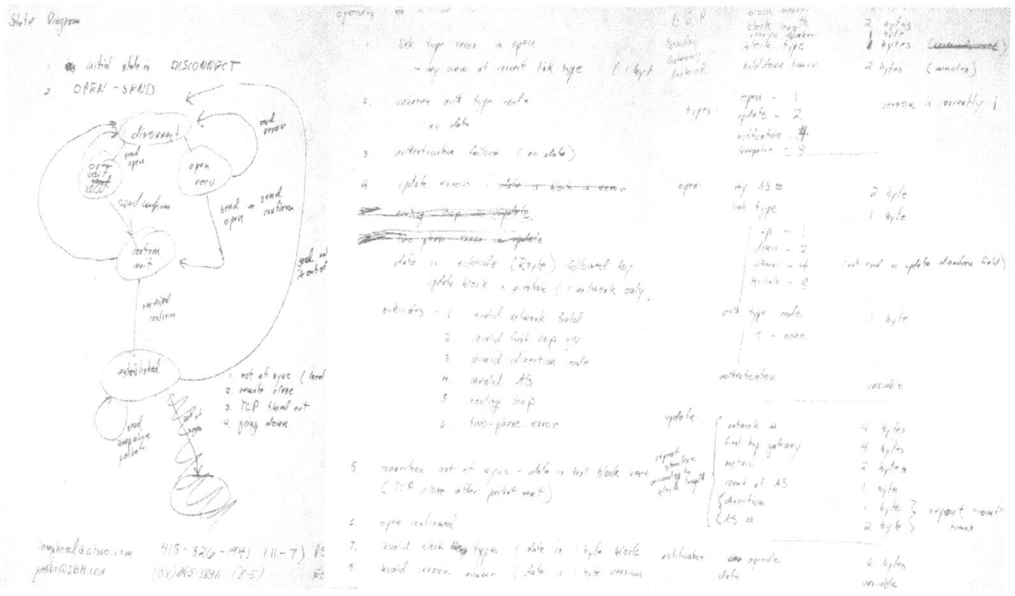

Figure 1.1 a – The *Two-Napkins Protocol*

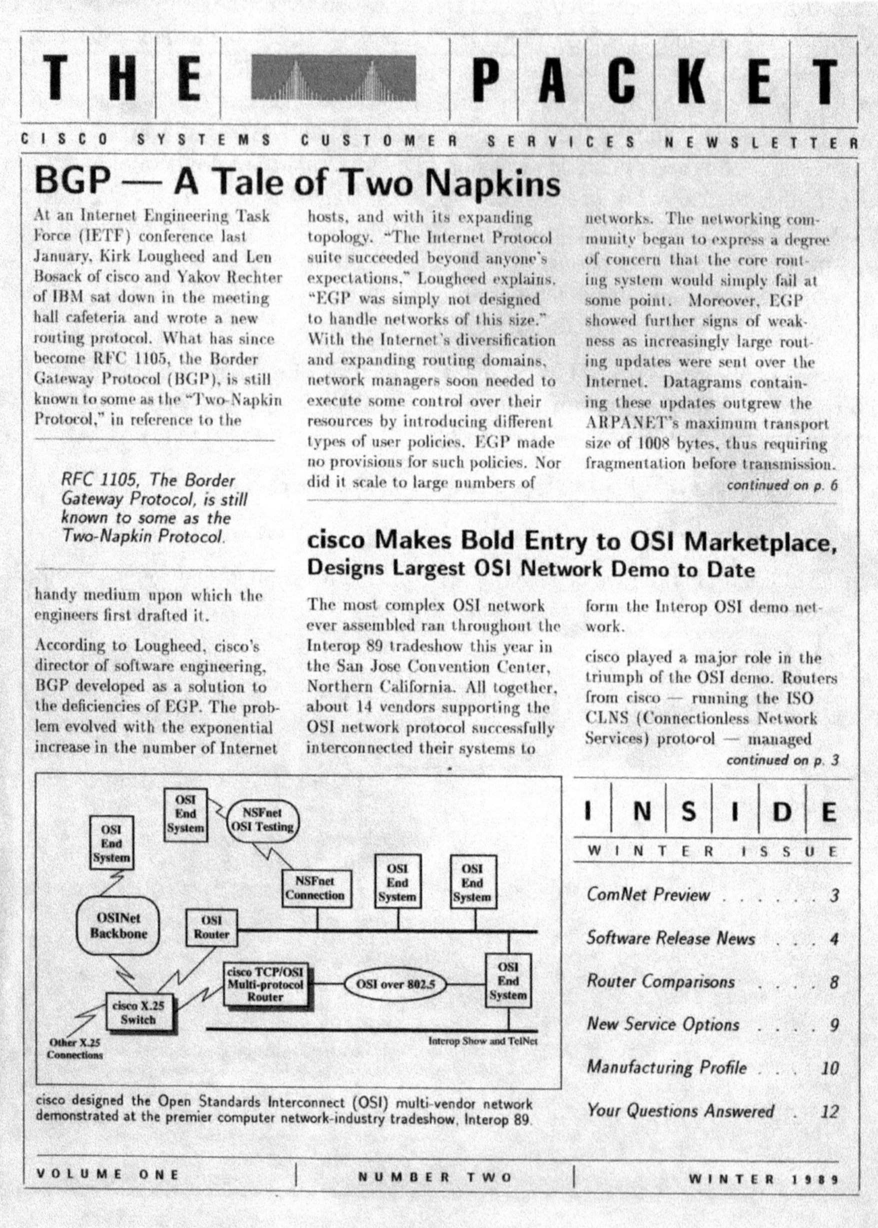

THE PACKET

CISCO SYSTEMS CUSTOMER SERVICES NEWSLETTER

BGP — A Tale of Two Napkins

At an Internet Engineering Task Force (IETF) conference last January, Kirk Lougheed and Len Bosack of cisco and Yakov Rechter of IBM sat down in the meeting hall cafeteria and wrote a new routing protocol. What has since become RFC 1105, the Border Gateway Protocol (BGP), is still known to some as the "Two-Napkin Protocol," in reference to the

RFC 1105, The Border Gateway Protocol, is still known to some as the Two-Napkin Protocol.

handy medium upon which the engineers first drafted it.

According to Lougheed, cisco's director of software engineering, BGP developed as a solution to the deficiencies of EGP. The problem evolved with the exponential increase in the number of Internet

hosts, and with its expanding topology. "The Internet Protocol suite succeeded beyond anyone's expectations," Lougheed explains. "EGP was simply not designed to handle networks of this size." With the Internet's diversification and expanding routing domains, network managers soon needed to execute some control over their resources by introducing different types of user policies. EGP made no provisions for such policies. Nor did it scale to large numbers of

networks. The networking community began to express a degree of concern that the core routing system would simply fail at some point. Moreover, EGP showed further signs of weakness as increasingly large routing updates were sent over the Internet. Datagrams containing these updates outgrew the ARPANET's maximum transport size of 1008 bytes, thus requiring fragmentation before transmission.

continued on p. 6

cisco Makes Bold Entry to OSI Marketplace,
Designs Largest OSI Network Demo to Date

The most complex OSI network ever assembled ran throughout the Interop 89 tradeshow this year in the San Jose Convention Center, Northern California. All together, about 14 vendors supporting the OSI network protocol successfully interconnected their systems to

form the Interop OSI demo network.

cisco played a major role in the triumph of the OSI demo. Routers from cisco — running the ISO CLNS (Connectionless Network Services) protocol — managed

continued on p. 3

cisco designed the Open Standards Interconnect (OSI) multi-vendor network demonstrated at the premier computer network-industry tradeshow, Interop 89.

INSIDE

WINTER ISSUE

VOLUME ONE | NUMBER TWO | WINTER 1989

Figure 1.1 b – *The Packet.*

Through the eyes of a modern provider, we must admit that BGP, despite its best intents, was born with an original sin: it assumes that all Internet networks are reliable secure.

The fact that it has been created before security (in a broad sense) became an issue, has marked its development since the 1990s. This aspect – which we will explore in depth in Chapter 10, when we talk about security – can be easily summarized in Internet expert Randy Bush's scathing yet spot-on line: *"You're in Hackerville here on the Internet. Period. All of this stuff lacks formal discipline. It's paint and spackle"*.

1.2 DEFINING AN AUTONOMOUS SYSTEM

An Autonomous System (AS) is a set of routers managed by a single entity which usually (but not necessarily!) employs a single, internal IGP (Interior Gateway Protocol).

From a technical standpoint, we can find its definition in RFC 1930 – *Guidelines for creation, selection, and registration of an Autonomous System (AS)*, March 1996, that reads:

"An autonomous system is a group of one or more IP prefixes, managed by one or more network providers, with a UNIQUE and WELL-DEFINED routing policy."

NOTE: IGP are routing protocols used within an AS. The most used protocols in today's enterprise and ISP networks are OSPF and IS-IS Link State protocols. IGPs now considered obsolete are RIP and EIGRP; the latter was a Cisco proprietary protocol, subsequently standardized (RFC 7868).

From the outside world, an AS is seen as a single entity identified by a number, coded at 16 or 32 bits, and assigned by five RIRs (Regional Internet Registries): RIPE (Europe, Western Asia and former URSS), APNIC (Asia-Pacific Area: Central Asia, South-east Asia, Indo-China, Oceania), ARIN (North America, Atlantic Islands), LACNIC (Central-South America, Caribbean), AfriNIC (Africa).

The exchange of routing information between ASes occurs through protocols from the EGP (Exterior Gateway Protocol) family, which today, in practice, consists only of BGP. Figure 1.2 below shows the relationship between IGP, EGP and ASes.

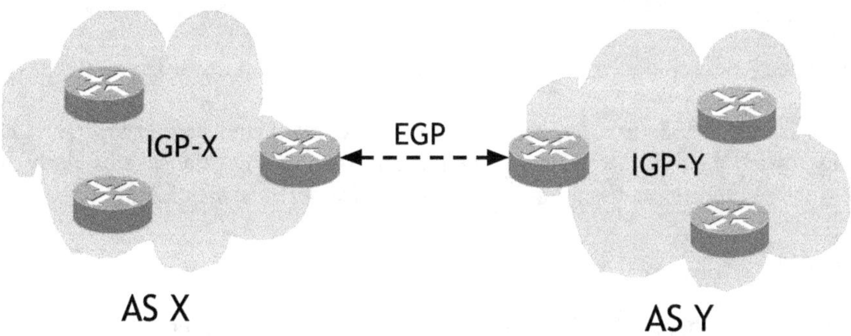

Figure 1.2 – Relationship between IGP and EGP and ASes.

Until 2007, the AS numbers available were only those taken from a 16-bit space that fell within the 0 - 65535 interval. However, only those between 1 and 64511 could be publicly assigned (and not every one of them, see the next note). Values between 64512 and 65534 cannot be assigned to public ASes (i.e. directly on the Internet), and are reserved for private use. The last value, 65535, is reserved (RFC 7300 – *Reservation of Last Autonomous System (AS) Numbers*, July 2014). Generally speaking, they are assigned by ISPs to customers that use BGP as an access protocol to their network. Value AS=0 is reserved to certain BGP security aspects (see RFC 7607 – *Codification of AS 0 Processing*, August 2015), covered in Chapter 10.

NOTE: Values between 64496 and 64511 cannot be assigned to a public AS; they are reserved to documentation (RFC 5398), and will be used extensively in this textbook. Number 112 is also unavailable (RFC 7534 – *AS112 Nameserver Operations*, May 2015), as it has been destined to the special purpose of hosting anycast instances for authoritative DNS servers for reverse resolutions of IPv4 and IPv6 address spaces that cannot be routed on the Internet (for instance, those described in RFC 1918 – *Address Allocation for Private Internets*, February 1996, but not only those). AS number 23456 (better known as AS_TRANS) cannot be freely assigned, because it is used to facilitate communications between a router that doesn't support the 32-bit AS notation, and one that uses a 32-bit AS (RFC 6793 – *BGP Support for Four-Octet Autonomous System (AS) Number Space*, December 2012). More details on this in Annex A.1.

The limited availability of public AS numbers led to a 32-bit expansion of the AS number, standardized in RFC 4893 – *BGP Support for Four-octet AS Number Space*, May 2007.

NOTE: AS representation was done through a 16-bit number, and then through a 32-bit number (e.g., the AS number 65551 can be represented as 65551 in the asplain format or as 1.15 in the asdot+ format), as regulated by RFC 5396 – *Textual Representation of Autonomous System (AS) Numbers*, December 2008. For further details, see Annex A.1.

Even in the 32-bit space, ASes have special use reserved numbers. Indeed, the 65536-65551 interval is reserved to documentation, see RFC 5398 – *Autonomous System (AS) Number Reservation for Documentation Use*, December 2008, the 4200000000-4294967294 interval (approx. 95 million ASes) is for private use, see RFC 6996 – *Autonomous System (AS) Reservation for Private Use*, July 2013, and the last, number 4294967295, is reserved to possible future uses, see RFC 7300 – *Reservation of Last Autonomous System (AS) Numbers*, July 2014.

Based on their outgoing connection and on how transit traffic is processed, ASes can be classified into:

- single-homed ASes: characterized by a single (stub AS) or redundant connection toward only one other AS;

- multi-homed ASes: characterized by more than one connection toward several ASes.

NOTE: In the literature, definitions are not always concordant. Indeed, very often, redundant connectivity toward a single AS is also defined as multi-homed. For the sake of clarity, in this textbook, we prefer to use the term home for an AS, hence our classification .

1.2.1 Single-homed AS

A single-homed AS is characterized by a single connection, or, as it generally occurs in practice, a redundant connection toward another AS. In case of single connection, we talk about stub AS.
A typical example of stub AS is a private network AS, or a small ISP connecting to the network of a larger ISP, through a single connection. A stub AS with a single connection toward the ISP does not need to know all the Internet prefixes. In fact, with a single connection pointing outside (see Figure 1.3), reachability of the prefixes outside the AS can be guaranteed through a simple default route on the access router connected to the ISP's network.
Therefore, in theory, a stub AS doesn't need to use BGP on its access router to exchange routing information with the ISP to which it is connected. Some stub ASes use BGP anyway as access protocol, even in similar situations, to compensate, for instance, for Level 2 network deficiencies (e.g. access via an Ethernet network, where convergence may be slow).

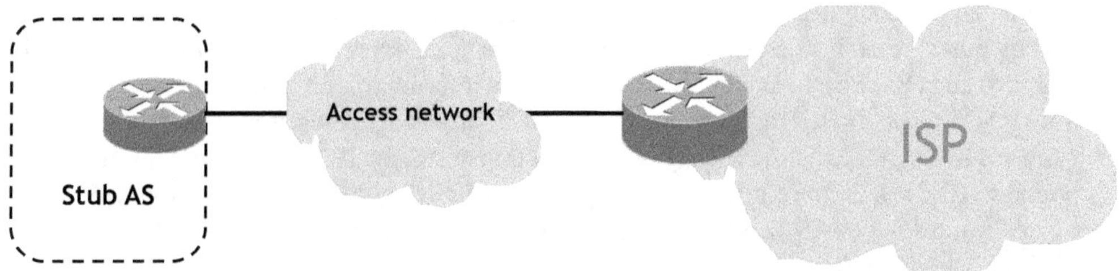

Figure 1.3 – Single-homed AS with single connection (stub AS).

In case of redundant connections (fault-tolerant), in order to optimize the stub AS inbound/outbound traffic, it is convenient to use BGP. We will go over those aspects in Chapter 7.

1.2.2 Multi-homed AS

As we were saying, typical examples of a multi-homed AS include private network ASes, or small ISPs, that connect to the network of two or more public ISPs for reliability reasons, or ISPs that exchange IP routing information with more than one AS (see Figure 1.4). The exchange of routing information between ASes occurs through BGP, or rather, as we will see in the next chapter, through BGP sessions.

We can identify two types of multi-homed AS:

- multi-homed Transit ASes: they allow exchange of traffic between different ASes, using their own resources as transit;

- multi-homed Non-Transit ASes: they do not allow external traffic to transit on the AS.

NOTE: For an AS, transit traffic is defined as the set of IP packets with both source and destination addresses that do not belong to any of the IP subnets used by the AS.

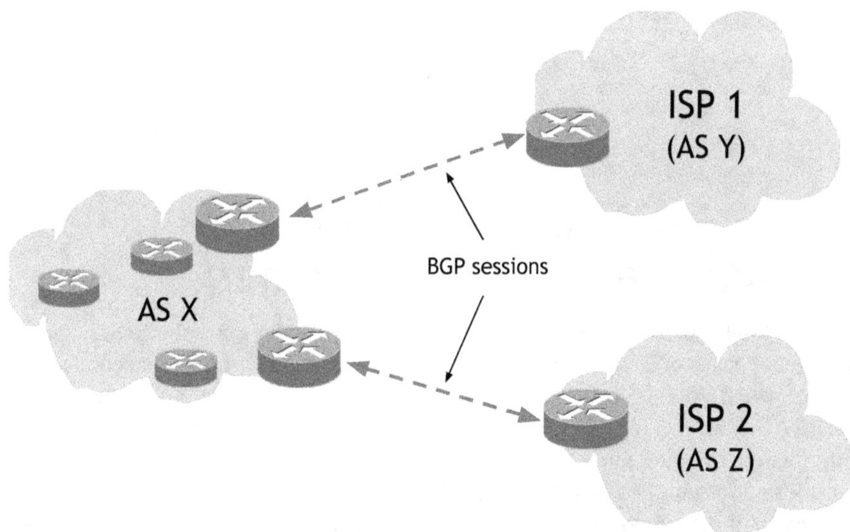

Figure 1.4 – Multi-homed AS.

A multi-homed AS becomes a transit AS when it propagates BGP advertisements of the prefixes received by other ASes. For instance, in Figure 1.5, the three ASes X, Y and Z have prefixes (P1, P2), (P3, P4) and (P5, P6), respectively. AS X receives information on how to reach prefixes (P3, P4) from AS Y, through BGP advertisements. If AS X propagates the information received from AS Y toward AS Z, AS X automatically becomes a transit AS for IP traffic from AS Z toward AS Y's prefixes (P3, P4). In the same way, if the prefixes (P5, P6) AS X receives from AS Z were propagated toward AS Y, AS X would automatically become a transit AS for IP traffic from AS Y toward AS Z's prefixes (P5, P6).

In order to prevent a multi-homed AS to become a transit AS, it is sufficient that it does not propagate the advertisement from other ASes. In particular, a multi-homed non-transit AS only announces its own prefixes outbound. For instance, in Figure 1.5, AS X, to prevent becoming a transit AS for traffic exchanged by AS Y and Z, should only announce its own prefixes, and avoid propagating (as in the example above) the prefixes received from AS Y and Z.

NOTE: It is worth mentioning that possible BGP configuration errors on the network of a multi-homed AS could cause unpleasant situations. Indeed, if an AS involuntarily acts as a transit AS for other units, it would mean that it is surrendering part of its Internet access bandwidth. On the other hand, if an AS voluntarily exploits the configuration error of another AS, it would engage in unethical behavior. We will go back to this in Chapter 10.

In multi-homed ASes, it is a good practice to use BGP for its loop prevention and routing policy definition properties. Those aspects will be treated further in Chapter 7.

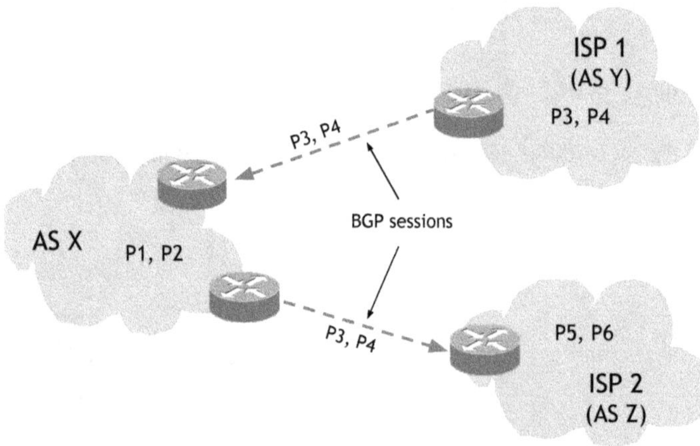

Figure 1.5 – Multi-homed Transit AS.

1.3 BGP AND THE INTERNET ECOSYSTEM

The entire Internet can be modeled as a flow graph, where nodes consist of ASes, and connections between nodes consist of BGP sessions (Figure 1.6). BGP sessions are logical connections between routers, on which routing information is exchanged. This information, suitably propagated between all ASes, allows reaching all system devices (hosts), and therefore the entire great ocean of information on the Internet.

Routing information comprises pairs of the following kind: <IP prefix, prefix length>. For the sake of simplicity, in this textbook we will refer to those pairs simply as IP prefixes, using the classic notation "IP prefix/IP prefix length" (e.g. 203.0.113/24). Every AS injects a set of IP prefixes – that is, IP address blocks generally assigned by a RIR to the AS administrator (or at least, that's how it should be) – into the system.

NOTE: Observing the hierarchy when managing numerical resources (hierarchy that from IANA proceeds to RIRs, and from those to NIR/LIR) is essential for Internet operation. In fact, it is worth remembering that, failing to observe the hierarchy can cause service interruptions in particular areas of the Internet, at best, and, in worst case scenarios, it can unleash illicit behavior that constitutes punishable crimes.

Logically announced prefixes within an AS are automatically propagated (unless routers are instructed to behave otherwise) on the different BGP sessions, following the rules described in Paragraph 2.1. Propagation can be seen as a selective flooding mechanism, through which IP prefixes are spread to all ASes of the Internet system.

In order for the system to work, it is not necessary to spread all IP prefixes to all the routers on the Internet. The type of prefixes to spread and their recipients basically depend on the AS topology and function. For instance, as mentioned earlier in Paragraph 1.2., it is not necessary to spread all the IP prefixes of the Internet world to the routers of a stub AS. Because of the way the stub AS is connected to the AS graph, it just requires a default route that allows it to reach one AS, which in turn is capable of reaching all the Internet prefixes, through a given path.

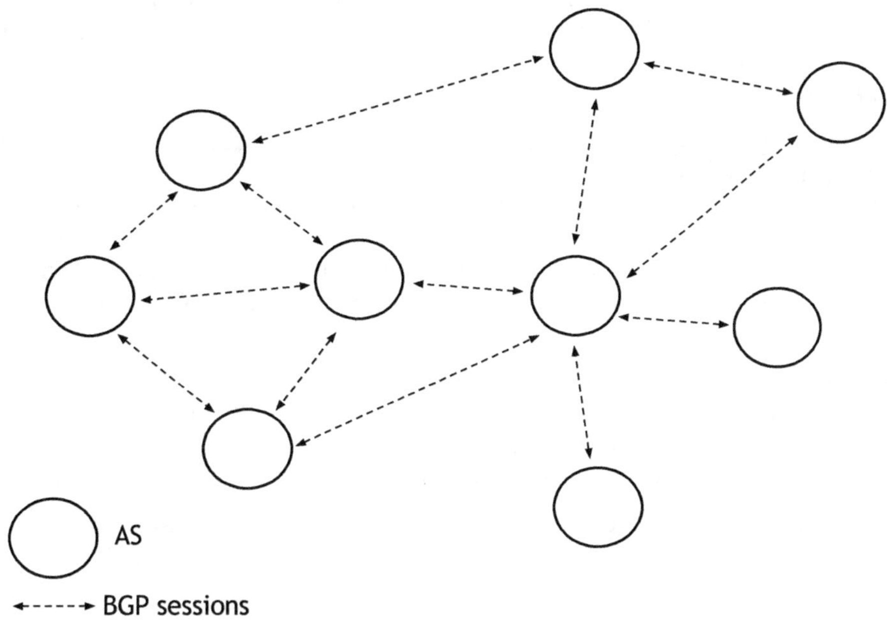

Figure 1.6 – Internet model.

1.3.1 Relationships between ISPs: peering and transit

One of the main issues of the Internet – already known in the days of the old telephone world – is how to connect all devices (PCs, smartphones, tablets, servers, etc.) that have a public IP address (i.e., directly connected on the Internet) scattered throughout cyberspace.

According to Martin Libicki – cybersecurity expert – cyberspace consists of three layers:

- physical: the physical components of cyberspace (underwater cables, antennas, satellites and optical fibers, etc.);

- syntactic: protocols, rules and natural properties governing the operation and interaction between the different physical components of cyberspace;

- semantic: the result of the interaction between the first two levels is what gives meaning to the processes of the underlying levels, ensuring their operation.

Obviously, it is inconceivable that each ISP, when reaching all the different devices connected to the networks of the other ISPs, is directly connected to all other ISPs worldwide. There must necessarily be an interconnecting mechanism, with different networks acting as transit for the other networks. Interconnection can be direct or indirect (transit), through one or more networks that accept to transport traffic.

There are two kinds of interconnection agreements between ISPs:

- **Peering**: two or more ISPs interconnect directly to one another, to exchange traffic between their clients. This is often done without interconnection or traffic charges (in the literature, these are called settlement-free agreements). Please note that peering is a non-transitive relationship, i.e., if ISP-A has a peering agreement with ISP-B, and ISP-B has a peering agreement with ISP-C, this does not imply that ISP-A has a peering agreement with ISP-C. Peering agreements are exclusively between two ISPs (bilateral). What's more, in such a situation, ISP-A cannot use ISP-B as transit to exchange traffic with ISP-C.

- **Transit**: an ISP accepts to transport the traffic originated by an ISP and directed to another ISP. Since no ISP directly connects to all the other ISPs, an ISP providing a transit service will deliver part of the traffic indirectly through one or more transit ISPs. The transit service provider usually receives economic compensation for the service.

Figure 1.7 below, shows the difference between peering and transit relationships.

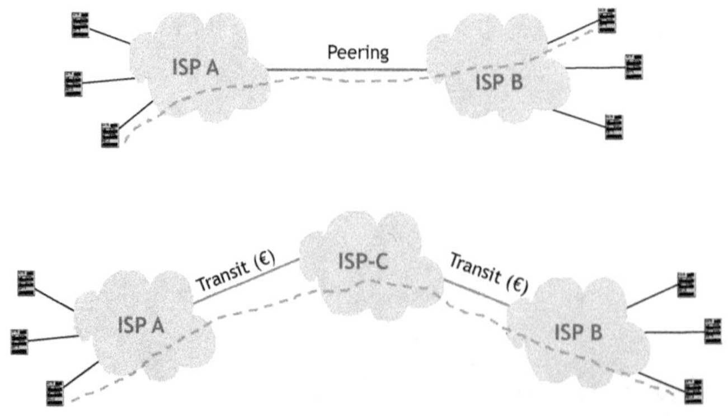

Figure 1.7 – Relationships between ISPs: peering and transit.

1.3.2 Internet eXchange Point (IXP)

An Internet Exchange Point (IXP), traditionally known as NAP (Network or Neutral Access Point), is a physical infrastructure that allows different ASes to exchange Internet traffic between one another.

NOTE: Whether they are commercial or not, in general, European IXPs are managed neutrally with respect to their participants. If a participating ISP or carrier or content network owned and managed the IXP, potential conflicts of interests could arise. Neutrality is the reason for the success of many big Northern European IXPs.

By promoting AS interconnection through peering agreements that are usually free of charge (at least until the power relations between the ASes involved are balanced), an IXP allows ASes to save part of the bandwidth they buy from their Upstream Providers, with efficiency and reliability gains.

NOTE: An Upstream Provider is generally a big transit ISP that provides access to the Internet to a local ISP or content network.

The main purpose of an IXP is allowing ISP networks to connect to one another directly, rather than making traffic pass through one or more external Upstream Providers. This offers the following advantages:

- **Speed**: a direct connection between two ASes, without intermediate passages, minimizes the latency of the packets crossing them, improving network performance, especially toward all real-time interactive or content applications.

- **Efficiency**: diversifying the connections of an Internet provider toward the rest of the ISPs, allows for greater routing control (by enhancing local Internet connectivity and security), increased network infrastructure redundancy, and therefore a higher number of possible paths toward a given destination.

- **Cost**: fixed costs related to being associated with an IXP (including interconnection costs toward the IXP data center and toward the Fabric) are generally lower (per exchange bandwidth unit) compared to Internet transit costs. Most of the times, peering agreements between participants to an IXP take place free of charge, which makes access to the Internet cheaper, and therefore available to a larger number of end users in a certain country or region (think about developing economies).

The typical infrastructure of an IXP – also called IXP Fabric – consists of one or more switches to which different participants connect their routers. In addition, it might include servers through which the IXP provider offers additional services to its participants (e.g. aggregate and target AS traffic statistics), as well as services that allow for correct Internet operation: e.g., anycast replicas of root name servers and analysis tools such as Routing Information Services (RIS), managed by Regional Internet Registries and hosted precisely inside the IXP infrastructures.

NOTE: The most used switching technology in IXPs has switched from ATM (very popular in the 1990s) to Ethernet. Some IXP migrated to more scalable solutions, such as the IP Fabric with VXLAN transport and EVPN control plane.

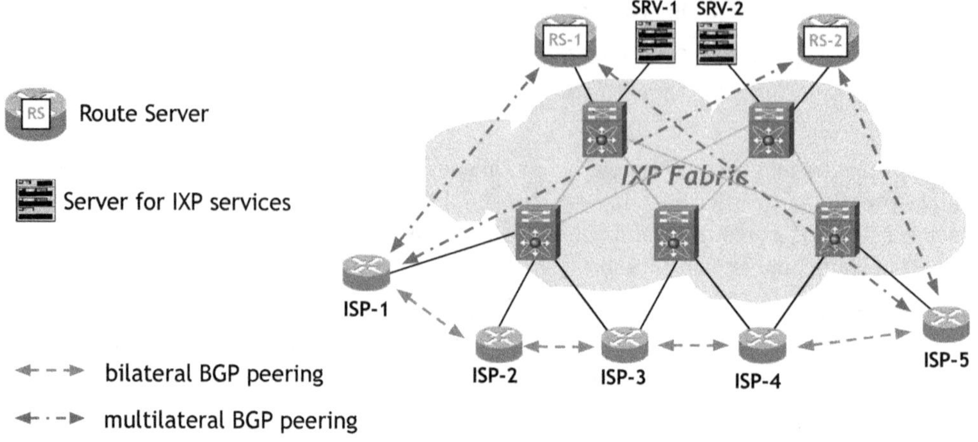

Figure 1.8 – IXP infrastructure.

Through BGP, routers establish peering agreements that allow ISPs to exchange Internet traffic. Peering agreements are called bilateral, when they are established directly between ISPs. There might be numerous bilateral agreements, therefore, in order to reduce them, IXPs make special devices called Route Servers available, which are used to reflect BGP advertisements from one ISP to all the other ISPs. So an ISP, instead of managing N-1 peerings, where N is the total quantity of ISPs within the IXP it wants to exchange routing information with, just needs a BGP peering toward a Route Server, or rather, by redundancy, two BGP peerings toward two Route Servers, to drastically reduce the number of BGP peerings. In this case, we talk about multilateral agreements. As mentioned earlier, the main purpose of an IXP is providing a physical infrastructure, through which network providers can interconnect and exchange traffic, gaining common advantages. Over the years, the role of IXPs has changed. Through an increasingly broader and diversified participation, they expanded their services from simple peering to facilitating a market where participants can purchase different services they need from other participants (e.g., DDoS mitigation services as well as access services). On one hand, this new nature is a strength for IXPs, which can attract more and more providers (which consider participation as a new business opportunity); on the other hand, participants can benefit from a broader service range.

1.3.3 ISP Classification

The ISP classification generally accepted among networking professionals was first drafted in *An analysis of internet inter-domain topology and route stability*, published in 1997 by Ramesh Govindan and Anoop Reddy. Then, a more structured definition can be found in Geoff Huston's article, *Interconnection, Peering, and Settlements* of 1999:

- **First level (Tier-1)**: An AS (usually, though not necessarily, an ISP) capable of connecting to the entire Internet, without purchasing transit services from other ISPs (transit free). Tier-1 ISPs generally have peering agreements between them, and do not use the default route. Therefore, this group of ASes (very few, less than 20 worldwide) is often called Default Free Zone (DFZ).

- **Second level (Tier-2)**: a network communicating with the other networks, by purchasing at least two IP transits to reach the entire Internet. Possible examples are big national ISP networks. Tier-2 ISPs too, generally have peering agreements between them. Usually, peering between Tier-2 ISPs occurs through direct private connections (PNI – Private Network Interconnection), often achieved using the passive interconnection infrastructure (MMR, Meet-Me-Room). In this case, we talk about private peering, as opposed to public peering, where ISPs connect using the IXP Fabric.

- **Third level (Tier-3)**: a network that must necessarily purchase a right to transit from other networks (at least two) to reach the Internet. Usually, Tier-3 ISPs work within a limited territory (usually a region), and are very aggressive in their pricing policies. Their clients generally include retail or small businesses. Usually, Tier-3 establish peering agreements with Content Providers; interconnection often occurs within the IXP, and prefixes are exchanged through Route Servers (Content Providers, with their PoP scattered throughout the world, try to limit the number of BGP sessions, by enabling bilateral sessions only above a certain traffic threshold).

NOTE: The need to have at least two transit relations with other independent systems is one of the requirements a RIR may request in order to assign an AS number. See document RIPE-679 – *Autonomous System (AS) Number Assignment Policies*, March 2017, that reads: *"A network must be multi-homed in order to qualify for an AS Number."*. The RIR established practice consists in deeming even the subscription of a transit agreement with two different independent systems sufficient, without necessarily requiring the interconnections to be operational.

There are many reasons why network professionals use level hierarchy to describe the network, the most important being a greater understanding of the political and economic reasons behind a network, based on how and with whom it communicates.

NOTE: We should specify that the classification suggested and used herein, only aims at showing what we observe every day in the Internet ecosystem. This means that, since the Network is perpetually changing, an independent system can shift from one category to the other, based on the expansion and growth policies it applies.

1.4 BASIC OPERATION

BGP's basic operation is very simple, and, in some ways, it resembles the old RIP. Each router, after establishing some sort of relationship with another router – belonging to the same AS or not – informs it of the IP prefixes it can reach, by linking to each prefix a distance measured in terms of number of ASes it needs to cross, to reach the AS originating the prefix.

The relationship that a router establishes with another router is called BGP session. Inside a BGP session, routing information is exchanged through special protocol messages, called BGP UPDATE, to which a set of BGP attributes may be associated. Some of these attributes are mandatory, while others are optional (see Chapter 2), and they have different functions, the most important being the definition of suitable traffic management policies.

UPDATE messages can also be used to notify the need to eliminate (withdraw) the advertisements of a previously sent prefix to the other routers, due to the impossibility of finding available paths toward those prefixes. This BGP behavior would lead to network instability, due to the route flapping phenomenon – close advertisements and withdrawals of the same IP prefix, due to close up/down transitions of a BGP session. Route flapping causes a significant engagement of the routers' CPU on the entire network, due to the propagation of UPDATE messages. If not properly regulated, this phenomenon could lead to serious operating issues on the entire Internet. In Chapter 8, we will see how the Route Flap Damping mechanism (although this topic generated much discussion among experts) helps to mitigate the instability caused by route flapping.

Even the aggregation of IP prefixes – which we'll see in Chapter 5 – can be a valid tool to ensure stability.

Figure 1.9 below summarizes the basic operation described herein. In the figure, the BGP table is a memory area where the router keeps the BGP advertisements received from each neighbor with whom it has established a BGP session.

1.4.1 BGP as Path Vector protocol

Generally, IP routing protocols fall within two categories: *Distance Vector* and *Link State*. In Distance Vector protocols, the routing process announces the "Distance Vector" to its neighbors, comprising a set of elements, where each element is a <IP prefix, distance> pair. The IP prefix is a reachable prefix (i.e., there is a path to reach it in the IP routing table), and the distance is the minimum cost to reach it, calculated by each type of routing protocol in the relevant manner. For instance, RIP – the first Distance Vector protocol ever developed – uses the Hop Count metrics to calculate the minimum distance, meaning it measures the distance in terms of number of routers to cross to reach the one where the IP prefix is located, by applying the Bellman-Ford algorithm, formulated in the mid-1950s. On the other hand, Link State protocols employ a more sophisticated criterion to determine the optimal paths. First, they determine the network topology, through a relevant message exchange, then the metric related to each connection, and lastly, based on the SPF (Shortest Path First) algorithm – created in 1959 by Dutch mathematician Edsger W. Dijkstra – they calculate the minimum cost path. The two most important examples of routing protocols based on the Link State algorithm are OSPF – Open Shortest Path First (version 2 in RFC 2328; and version 3 in RFC 5340, which supports IPv6) and IS-IS – Intermediate System to Intermediate System, in ISO/IEC 10589:2002.

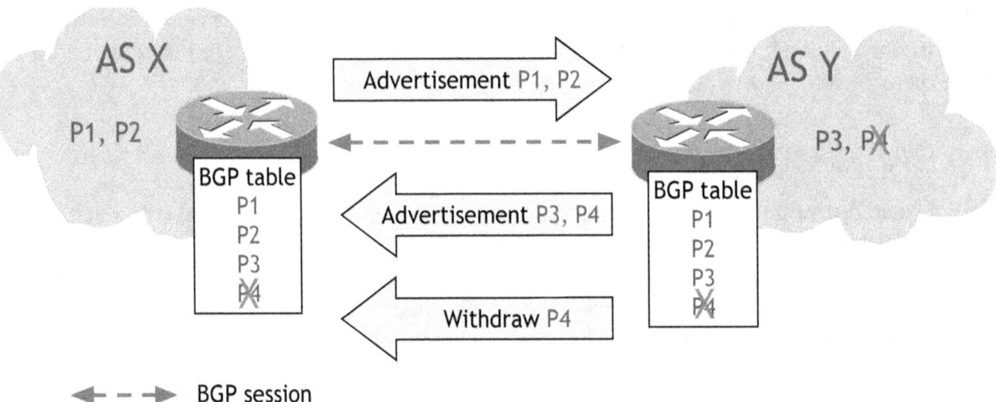

Figure 1.9 – Basic BGP operation.

Even though its operation resembles a Distance Vector protocol, BGP does not actually belong to the Distance Vector type, nor to the Link State type. It belongs to the Path Vector type. The reason behind this, is the presence of a special attribute – the Path Vector (which, as we will see, is actually called AS_PATH) – a sorted list (Vector) of the AS crossed by the BGP advertisements. Path Vector indicates the path to cross to reach a prefix, in terms of ASes. For instance, in Figure 1.10 below, prefix 192.0.2/24, belonging to AS 64503, will be announced to AS 64501 both by AS 64502 and by AS 64505. In the first advertisement, the Path Vector is [64502 64503], while in the second is [64505 64504 64503]. This is why BGP is referred to as a Path Vector protocol.

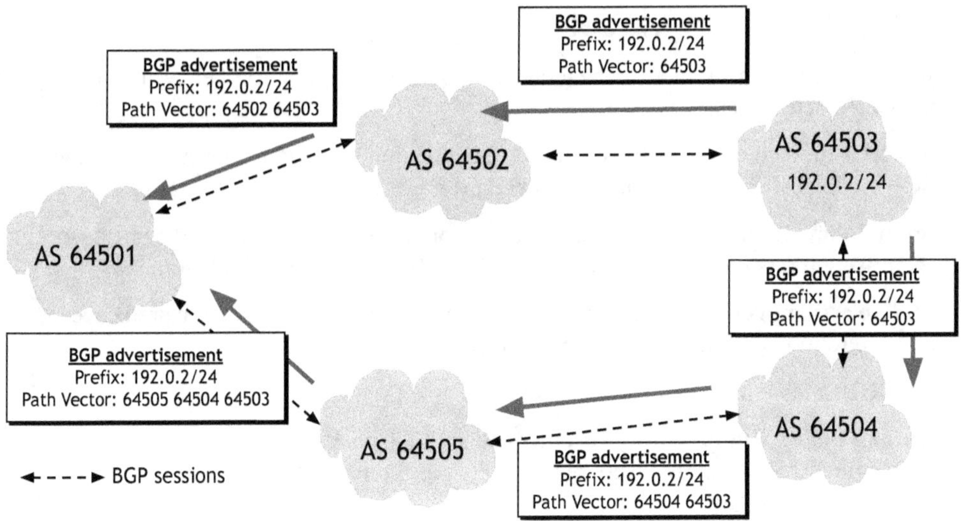

Figure 1.10 – The Path Vector attribute.

We will see later on how the Path Vector plays an essential role in BGP operation.

From the basic operation description above, we can notice once again how BGP is conceptually very simple, and maybe this explains also why it is so flexible. The complex part of BGP concerns one of the essential aspects it was designed for, that is its routing policy definition applications. And this is surely the most important and interesting aspect in this protocol.

1.4.2 Selecting the best path

Generally, as shown in the example in Figure 1.10, a router receives advertisements of the same prefix from different sessions. The advertisements of all prefixes exchanged are stored in certain memory areas, linked to each BGP session (see Section 1.4.3), and then subject to possible handling through BGP attributes and/or by applying filtering policies. The BGP process within each router chooses the best path among all the advertisements of the same prefix; the best path (and only that) is propagated on the BGP sessions, following specific rules that we will see in Paragraph 2.1.

The best path is selected according to a well-established and sorted sequence of choices, based on different metrics or advertisement properties. This sorted sequence of choices is called the selection process, and it generates a unique best path, in the end. For instance, referring to Figure 1.10, the routers of AS 64501 have two possible paths to reach prefix 192.0.2/24: they can transit through AS 64502 or through AS 64505 and AS 64504. Which path should they choose? Intuitively, we should choose the shortest path. Since BGP does not give us any information on the AS internal layout, we can define the shortest path as the one that crosses the fewest ASes. According to this criterion, the best path would be the one using AS 64502 as transit.

However, are we sure that it wouldn't be more convenient for AS 64501 to transit through AS 64505? Some of the reasons could be a higher bandwidth available, more advantageous business agreements, and so on. Through the selection process (more on this in Paragraph 2.5), BGP makes a series of metrics available, to manage the selection and choose the best path for the AS administrator's requirements.

1.4.3 BGP Process Model

The BGP process within a router can be modeled as shown in Figure 1.11 below, and it comprises the following macro-blocks:

- **Adj-RIB-in**: memory areas linked to each BGP session, where advertisements received from BGP sessions are stored (through UPDATE messages).

- **Input Policy Engine**: a set of inbound routing policies applied to the advertisements received, comprising filters on the advertisements and/or BGP attribute manipulation.

- **BGP selection process**: it chooses, among the advertisements of the same prefix accepted by inbound routing policies, the best path to reach the prefix.

- **Loc-RIB**: a table that contains the best paths.

- **Output Policy Engine**: a set of outbound routing policies applied to the best paths to propagate on the other BGP sessions, comprising filters on the advertisements and/or BGP attribute manipulation.

- **Adj-RIB-out**: memory areas linked to each BGP session, where the outbound advertisements to be propagated on BGP sessions are stored.

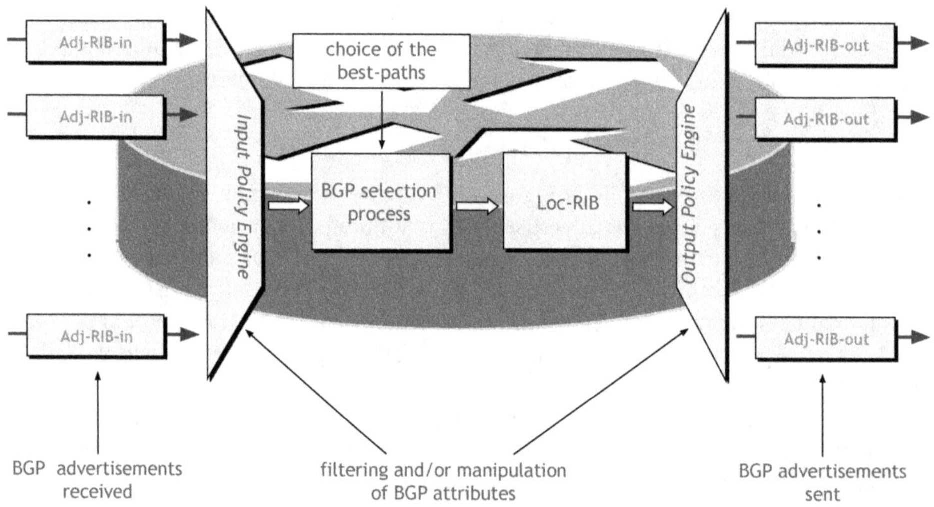

Figure 1.11 – BGP Process Model.

The partition of the memory used by the BGP process in Adj-RIB-in, Loc-RIB and Adj-RIB-out is purely logical, and it is the one described in standard BGP documents (RFC 1771 and RFC 4271). In practical implementations, each device manufacturer manages the memory areas to be assigned to the BGP process as they best see fit. Hereinafter, for the sake of simplicity, we will define the BGP table as the set of advertisements deemed valid for the selection process, i.e., the set of all BGP advertisements received that have been processed by inbound routing policies.

NOTE: The best paths determined by the BGP selection process are not necessarily installed in the IP routing table (RIB, Routing Information Base) and then transferred to the FIB (Forwarding Information Base) to be used in traffic forwarding. Indeed, if the same prefix is announced to the router via BGP and also in other ways (dynamic routing protocol, static routing, directly connected prefix), the router chooses which advertisement to install in the RIB, based on a level of preference assigned by the router to each routing protocol. Please be aware that the level of preference (known in Cisco documents as administrative distance, or in Juniper documents as preference value), is a number assigned locally by the router to each routing protocol, and expressing a level of preference for the protocol. For instance, let's assume that a prefix Pfx is announced to the router both by BGP and by OSPF. Which of the two protocols does the router consider more reliable? In other words, what information *<Pfx, Next-Hop>* will be installed in the RIB, the one announced by OSPF or the one announced by BGP? The rule used by all manufacturers is preferring the advertisement of the protocol with the lowest preference level. Note that preference level values are assigned by manufacturers according to different logics, and so it is common to see completely different numbers, which can be varied through a configuration, if needed.

The complex part in the practical implementation of BGP, consists of two routing policy blocks, which are the core of the protocol. In Section 1.4.4 below, we will see what routing policy means, and throughout the textbook we will go over the tools available to implement them, along with several practical applications.

1.4.4 Routing Policies

One of the main reasons behind BGP's success as a routing protocol of the networks based on the TCP/IP architecture, is the option of creating very flexible routing policies that meet (almost) all the network administrators' needs.
A routing policy defines the rules adopted by an AS to manage inbound and outbound traffic, and the BGP advertisement acceptance and sending rules.
There are basically two tools to define a routing policy:

- filtering of BGP advertisements;

- BGP attribute manipulation.

Filtering allows a router to choose what BGP advertisements to accept and/or propagate. Based on the application direction, filtering can be of two types:

- *Inbound*: Allows choosing the advertisements to accept and to reject, between all the BGP advertisements received on the different BGP sessions. The advertisements accepted take part in the selection process. Vice versa, the advertisements rejected are deemed invalid for the selection process.

- *Outbound*: Allows choosing, between all the best paths determined, which ones to propagate to the routers with active BGP sessions.

Filtering can also be used to choose which prefixes to redistribute from an IGP protocol to BGP. Examples of filters are:

- rejecting all advertisements from IP prefixes with too big a mask (e.g., longer than 24 bits);

- not propagating the advertisements of IP prefixes received from a specific AS to other ASes (e.g., to prevent an AS from becoming a transit AS);

- rejecting all advertisements from prefixes that cannot be routed on the Internet (e.g., private IP prefixes from RFC 1918, Martian List, etc.).

Manipulation of BGP attributes allows one to change the value of BGP attributes, according to one's needs. Having control over BGP attribute values allows conditioning the choices of the best path selection process, and therefore defining suitable AS inbound and/or outbound traffic management policies.

There are many different routing policies, with obvious applications in case of multi-homed ASes or stub ASes with redundant connections. For stub ASes with single connection, it makes little sense to speak about routing policies, except for aspects relating to advertisements filtering, since stub ASes have no alternative ways to manage inbound and/or outbound traffic. Some examples of routing policies are:

- sending/receiving traffic using a first-choice AS (primary AS), and, in case of loss of connectivity toward it, using a backup AS;

- balancing inbound and/or outbound traffic between two or more paths;

- choosing the most convenient paths, based on the prefix. For instance, in a primary/backup configuration, it may be convenient to make traffic toward local prefixes of backup ASes pass through a backup connection.

The practical implementation of routing policies requires complex configurations that use specific tools made available by the BGP implementations of the different manufacturers. We will go over the tools made available by Cisco and Juniper platform later in this book.

Figure 1.12 shows an example of a routing policy application to check the advertisements received/propagated, and affect the results of the selection process.

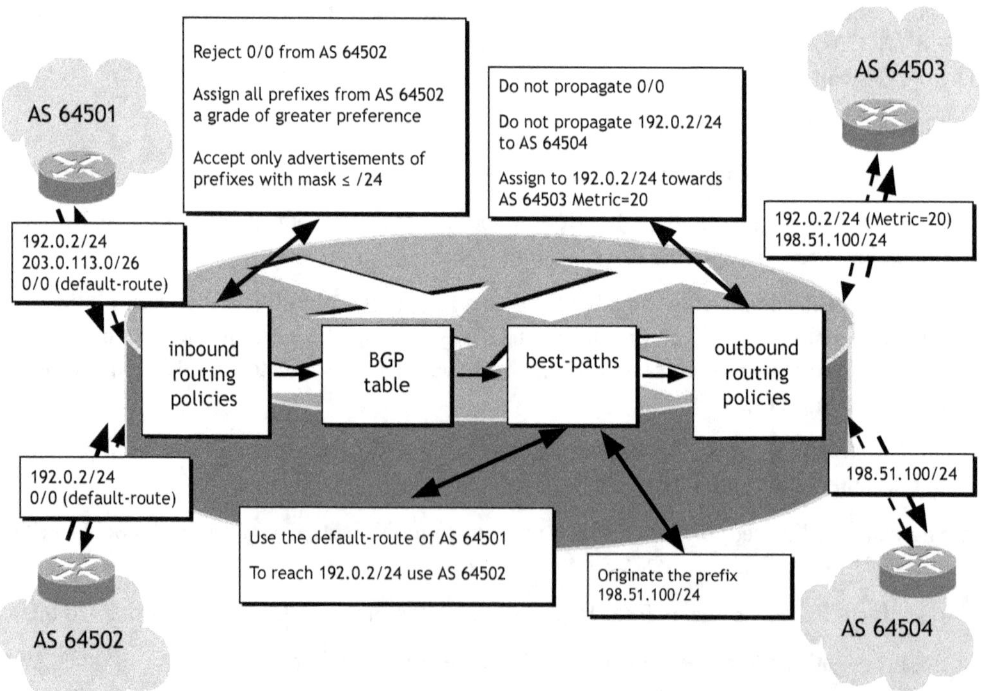

Figure 1.12 – Example of inbound/outbound routing policies.

By applying the inbound routing policies specified in the figure, we obtain the following results:

- the default route advertisement sent by AS 64502 is rejected, while the one sent by AS 64501 is accepted;

- the advertisement of prefix 203.0.113/26 sent by AS 64501 is rejected, because the prefix mask is too big (greater than /24);

- the advertisements of prefix 192.0.2/24 sent by AS 64501 and 64502 are both accepted, however, the advertisements coming from AS 64502 is assigned a greater preference value (through the special BGP attribute Local Preference, which we'll see in the next chapter).

The advertisements accepted are stored, along with their attributes, in the BGP table, and the selection process is applied to them, with the following results:

- best path for prefix 192.0.2/24: AS 64502;

- best path for default route: AS 64501.

NOTE: The BGP table is a set of BGP advertisements, with the purpose of providing information on how to reach the networks of the different autonomous systems. We should highlight that each BGP advertisement in the table is linked to the AS that originated it on the Internet.

The BGP table also includes advertisements of prefix 198.51.100/24, which becomes the best path, as it is the only one present.

Lastly, let's consider best path propagation only in BGP sessions toward AS 64503 and AS 64504. Before being propagated, prefixes undergo the outbound routing policies, with the following results:

- the best path of prefix 192.0.2/24 is propagated only to AS 64503 with metric 20 (through the special BGP attribute MED, which we will see in the next chapter);

- the best path of prefix 198.51.100/24 is propagated to both AS 64503 and 64504;

- the best path of the default route undergoes an output filtering process and is not propagated (although it remains in the BGP table).

This basic example shows that there can be many different routing policies, and, if they are defined well, they can meet (almost) all network administrators' needs.

SUMMARY

In this opening chapter, we described the role BGP plays in the Internet ecosystem, and its manifold applications in Service Provider networks; then, we paved the way for a conceptual model on which the BGP process operation depends. Everything we presented here will be explored further in the next chapters.

Worth remembering:

1. BGP's role in the Internet ecosystem and its applications in the services offered by Service Providers (e.g. BGP/MPLS services).
2. The concept of Autonomous System and its numbering method. In addition, you should remember the AS classification into single-homed (stub AS) and multi-homed, and the further division of the latter into transit AS and non-transit AS.
3. BGP's basic operation, BGP sessions and the Path Vector protocol. In particular, the BGP UPDATE message exchange, and the best path selection.
4. The operating model described in Figure 1.11, which will be the logic behind the entire textbook.
5. And last but not least, what is perhaps BGP's greatest value, the option of creating routing policies on AS inbound and outbound traffic.

2 - SESSIONS, MESSAGES, AND ATTRIBUTES

In Chapter 1, we went over BGP's general definitions, main macro-blocks and basic operation. In this chapter, we will begin to see some technical details, required to work with the protocol. Specifically, we will learn more about how BGP sessions are made, what rules they follow, what messages the protocol uses to exchange routing information, what BGP attributes are used in the selection process, and, lastly, how the selection process works. These last two aspects – BGP attributes and selection process – are highly interdependent, since the selection process is based on BGP attributes, which are the basis to correctly define and implement inbound and outbound routing policies.

2.1 BGP SESSIONS

A BGP session is a reliable communication channel between two routers, where BGP messages are exchanged. BGP uses a TCP connection established on well-known port 179, as reliable channel. BGP sessions may be established both between directly connected routers (layer 2), and between remote routers (provided they are connected at IP level).

NOTE: In IANA official registry, port 179 belongs to the System Ports range, and is assigned to the BGP service for TCP, UDP and SCTP. Formally, the assignee is Kirk Lougheed.

Routers at both endpoints of a BGP session are called BGP Neighbors, while routers with an active BGP process are called BGP Speakers. The terminology is summarized in Figure 2.1.
BGP sessions can be of two types:

1. external BGP (eBGP) sessions: established between routers belonging to different ASes;

2. internal BGP (iBGP) sessions: established between routers belonging to the same AS.

This distinction is paramount in the BGP process, since different session types have different operating rules (see Sections 2.1.2 and 2.1.3).

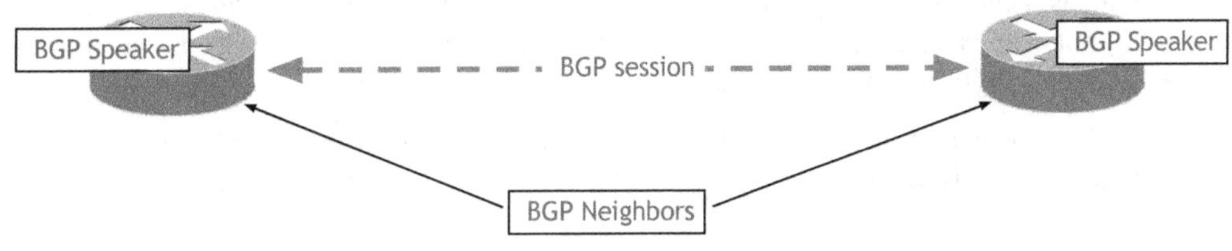

Figure 2.1 – BGP terminology.

2.1.1 Creating a BGP session

The creation of a BGP session entails two fundamental steps:

- establishing the TCP connection on well-known port 179;

- initializing the session.

TCP connection establishment operations can be initialized by both endpoint routers, and they generally start downstream of a manual configuration. One of the two routers plays an active role in establishing the connection, by starting the classic three-way-handshake (Figure 2.2).

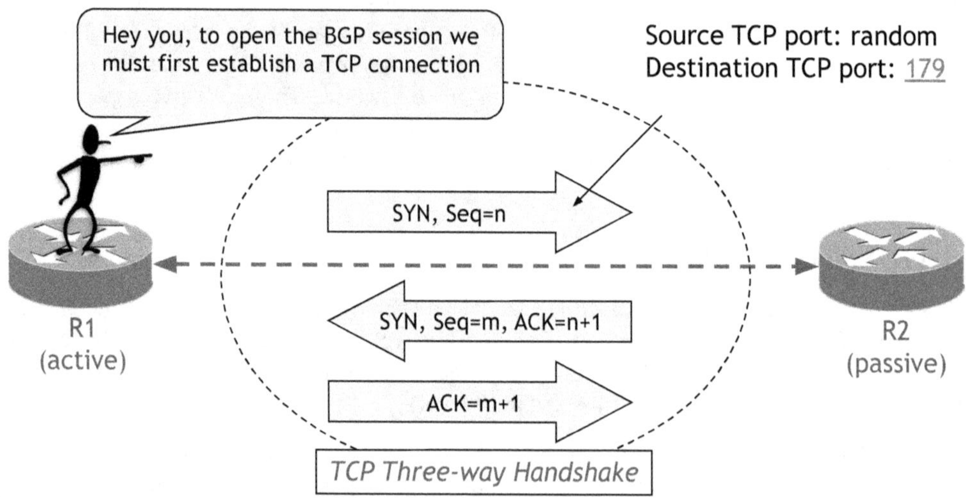

Figure 2.2 – Establishing a TCP connection between BGP Neighbors.

NOTE: If two routers attempt to establish a TCP connection at the same time, two connections are established (TCP connection collision); however, after the first BGP message (OPEN message) is exchanged, one of the two is automatically closed. Which of the two depends on the BGP process identifier, which is the 32-bit value associated with the process and conveyed through the OPEN message (see Section 2.3.1). The connection initialized by the router with the lower BGP identifier is closed. However, this does not entail that, when establishing a TCP connection, the active router is always the one with the higher BGP identifier. Actually, it might happen that the router with the lower BGP identifier starts the TCP connection establishing procedure first, and concludes it successfully. In this case, there is no TCP connection collision, since the other router did not even attempt to establish a connection. Moreover, the collision could be outright prevented, by configuring a BGP process as passive with respect to the TCP connection.

Once the TCP connection has been established, the next step is to initialize the BGP session, during which the two BGP Neighbors exchange the BGP OPEN message (Figure 2.3).

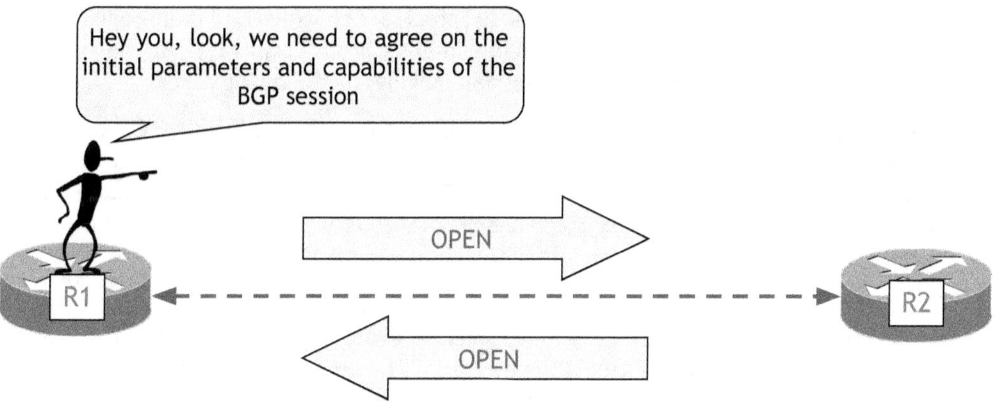

Figure 2.3 – Initializing a BGP session.

Certain parameters are negotiated through the OPEN message, such as the protocol version and a Hold Time. The protocol version must be the same for both BGP Neighbors, or the BGP session cannot be established.

NOTE: In theory, the protocol version can be negotiated, and possibly the two BGP Neighbors can agree on the highest version supported by both. However, nowadays, this is just an academic issue. All routers have been supporting version 4 for years.

The Hold Time parameter sets the period of time after which, without receiving any BGP message, the session is automatically closed. During the session initialization phase, the two BGP Neighbors can suggest two different Hold Time values; however, in the end, the common minimum value between the two is selected.

Lastly, OPEN messages are also used to negotiate certain functions (BGP Capabilities) used by the protocol to expand its field of action (e.g. supporting advertisements of prefixes other than IPv4) and improve its performance (e.g. Route Refresh, Outbound Route Filtering, etc.). We will come back to BGP Capabilities several times in this textbook, and describe their use.

Routers perform other checks on the OPEN message, such as, for instance, the AS number validity, that is, if the AS number contained in the message matches the number specified in the configuration, or the validity of a possible authentication, and so on. If there are no errors, the session is established. Generally, after the initial best path exchange of the prefixes included in the BGP table, no other messages are exchanged between the two routers, unless the BGP table is altered.

In order to keep the session open (which would otherwise be closed once the Hold Time expires), empty BGP messages – called KEEPALIVE (Figure 2.4) – are periodically exchanged.

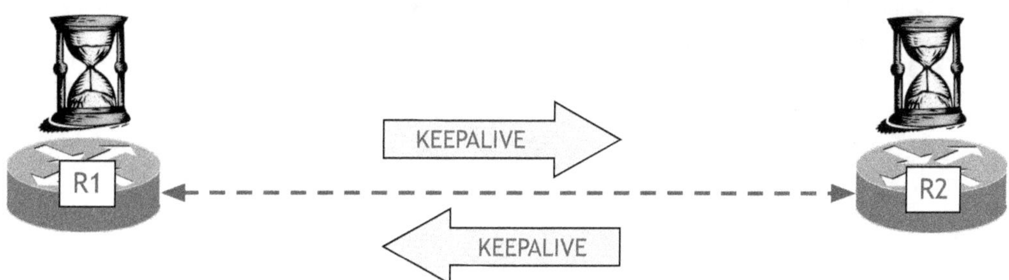

Figure 2.4 – Maintaining the BGP session through KEEPALIVE messages.

There are 5 steps to establish a BGP session, and the process is governed by a finite-state machine, which, for the sake of brevity, we will not include in this Chapter, whilst referring the reader to Appendix A.3, for more information on it. A session includes the following states:

- **Idle**: the starting state, in which a BGP Speaker attempts to establish a TCP connection toward a BGP Neighbor, starts a timer called ConnectRetry, and switches to the next state, Connect. Generally, the event that allows the TCP connection procedure to be initialized is determined by a configuration command. If the BGP Neighbor's IP address cannot be reached, the session remains in the Idle state.

- **Connect**: in this state, the BGP Speaker is waiting to receive the TCP segments to complete the TCP connection. If the three-way-handshake is successful, the BGP Speaker resets the ConnectRetry timer, sends a BGP OPEN message to the BGP Neighbor, and switches to the OpenSent state. If the TCP connection is not successful, the session switches to the Active state and the ConnectRetry timer is reset.

- **Active**: in this state, BGP tries again to establish the TCP connection with the BGP Neighbor. If the TCP connection is successful, the BGP Speaker resets the ConnectRetry timer, sends a BGP OPEN message to the BGP Neighbor, and switches to the OpenSent state. If the ConnectRetry timer expires when the session is in the Active state, the session switches back to the Connect state and the timer is reset. If the BGP Neighbor tries to establish the TCP connection through an invalid IP address (i.e. different than the address specified in the configuration), the BGP Speaker refuses the connection, resets the ConnectRetry timer, and remains in the Active state.

- **OpenSent**: when the session is in this state, the BGP Speaker has already sent the OPEN message, and is waiting for the reply OPEN message by the BGP Neighbor. Once the OPEN message is received, all its fields are checked and, in case of errors, a NOTIFICATION message is sent to the BGP Neighbor, and the session switches back to the Idle state. If, on the other hand, the OPEN message received does not contain any error, a KEEPALIVE message is sent to the BGP Neighbor, and the session switches to the OpenConfirm state.

- **OpenConfirm**: in this state, the BGP Speaker is waiting for a KEEPALIVE or NOTIFICATION message communicating any possible errors. If a KEEPALIVE message is received, the session switches to the Established state. If the Hold Time expires before a KEEPALIVE message is received, or if a TCP reset flag is received (in the TCP header), the session switches back to the Idle state.

- **Established**: when the session reaches this state, communication between the two BGP Neighbors is completely established, and they can exchange routing information and other BGP messages. If the Hold Time expires, or another error condition is notified by the BGP Neighbor through a NOTIFICATION message, the BGP Speaker closes the TCP connection, and the session switches back to the Idle state.

2.1.2 Rules in eBGP Sessions

eBGP sessions are established by default between directly connected routers (layer 2). This is because, on eBGP sessions, all BGP messages are encapsulated within IP packets with TTL=1 by default.

NOTE: why in eBGP sessions the TCP messages for opening the TCP connection and the BGP messages are encapsulated in IP packets with TTL=1 is a kind of mystery. In fact, in all the various RFCs of the BGP versions, from 1 to 4, there is no mention of it. Nor is there any mention of it in RFC 904 – *Exterior Gateway Protocol Formal Specification*, April 1984, which defined the specifications of the EGP protocol. It is probable that it all started with one manufacturer (Cisco?) and that all the others then followed.

In order to establish a session, one (convenient) option is to use IP addresses associated with physical or logical interfaces at both endpoints of the layer 2 connection (Figure 2.5). The reason for this being that, in any case, if one of the two interfaces at both endpoints of the connection is out of service, this would cause a loss of connectivity at layer 3, and therefore of the BGP session, which, after a certain time, is closed, since the Hold Time has expired. In reality, many manifacturers, in this situation have BGP implementations that allow closing the BGP session by default, as soon as the router detects that the interface is out of service at layer 2 or physically. We will circle back to these aspects in Chapter 12, on BGP convergence.

For instance, in Figure 2.5, the routers of AS 64501 and 64502 are directly connected at layer 2, and use the addresses of the physical interfaces at both endpoints of the connection, as IP addresses of the TCP connection. Assuming that the active router is that of AS 64501, the TCP connection is characterized by quadruple: <192.0.2.1:11004, 192.0.2.2:179>, where the source TCP port 11004 is chosen by router RA.

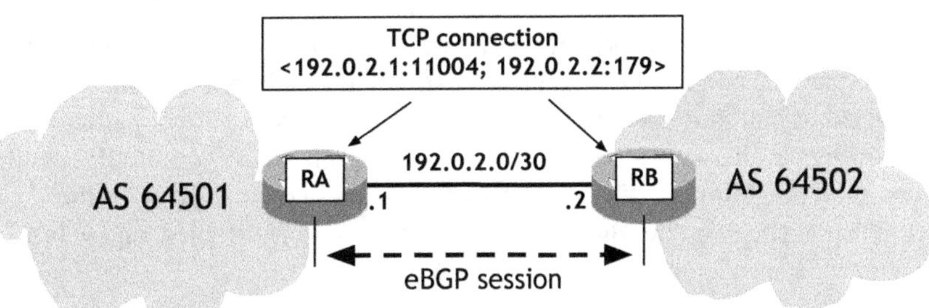

Figure 2.5 – eBGP session between directly connected routers (default).

BGP implementations from different manufacturers – such as Cisco and Juniper – include the option of establishing eBGP sessions even between routers not directly connected at layer 2 (multihop eBGP sessions), through a special configuration command. The configuration command only varies the default TTL of IP packets transporting BGP messages, bringing it to a sufficient value to establish the session. For instance, in Figure 2.6, in order to establish a multihop eBGP session between routers RA and RC, if the IP addresses of the physical interfaces are used, it will be sufficient to set up the two routers so that they send BGP messages encapsulated within IP packets with TTL=2, instead of the default value (TTL=1).

An interesting multihop eBGP session application occurs when two routers have a multi-link connection (Figure 2.7).

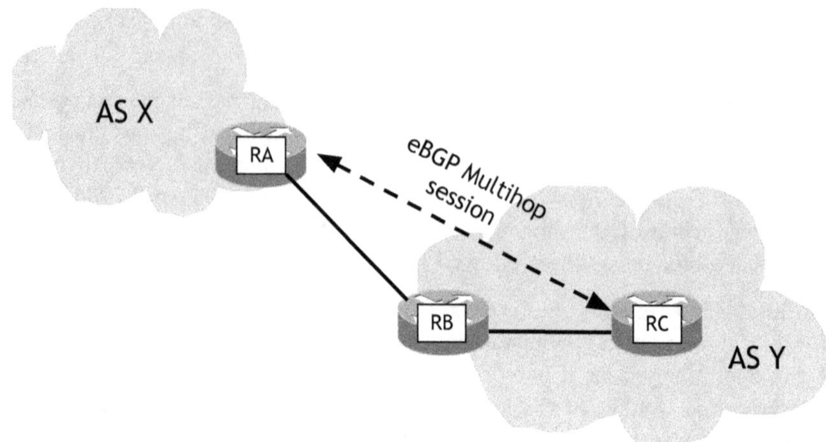

Figure 2.6 – Multihop eBGP session.

In this situation, it is convenient (and recommended) to use the IP addresses of two Loopback interfaces – connected to one another at layer 3 – as endpoints of the eBGP session. The advantage is that, if any of the physical connections are out of service, this does not interrupt the eBGP session, as the Loopback interfaces are still connected at layer 3. Only if all connections between two routers are out of service, the BGP session is closed.

In this particular case, using Loopback interfaces may require a multihop eBGP session. This is because the BGP process, before starting the eBGP session establishing procedure, checks if the IP address of the BGP Neighbor is part of the networks directly connected to the router (as in the case shown in Figure 2.5). Since the IP address of the BGP Neighbor's Loopback interface is not directly connected, a multihop eBGP session is required. Actually, in this particular case, some manufacturers provide alternative commands, in place of the multihop eBGP session (e.g., in Cisco routers, the "**neighbor ... disable-connected-check**" command). With these commands, the direct connection check on the BGP Neighbor's IP address is disabled, and value TTL=1 can be used.

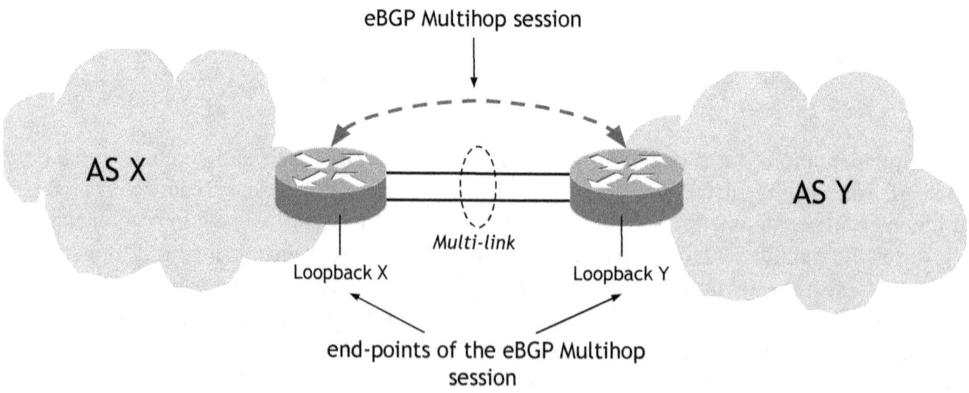

Figure 2.7 – Multihop eBGP session on a multi-link connection.

NOTE: In the multi-link connection example in Figure 2.7, it is sometimes possible to adopt alternative solutions. For instance, if the two connections – as it almost always happens in practical applications – were of the Ethernet type and had the same speed, it would be possible to create a LAG (Link Aggregation Group, also known as port-channel or ether-channel) including the two (or more) connections, and hence return to the case shown in Figure 2.5, by assigning two IP addresses belonging to the same subnet IP to the LAG endpoints. Another possible solution would be to configure the two connections as layer 3, and therefore create two BGP sessions, one on each connection. However, this solution is not ideal, and it should only be used in peculiar cases. The reasons for this are at least two: two advertisements are generated for each prefix, one per session, therefore increasing the memory used; moreover, the additional session and the greater BGP table size entail a higher CPU and memory use. On the other hand, it is a solution that also has advantages, such as no need for an additional routing process to connect the two Loopback interfaces and the ability to perform load balancing based on the bandwidth of the connections (see Section 9.2.6).

In order to propagate BGP advertisements, eBGP sessions adopt the following rule:

Every BGP advertisement received from a router on an eBGP session, if it becomes the best path, is <u>automatically</u> propagated to all active BGP sessions (eBGP and iBGP), except for the one from which the advertisement was received.

This rule is summarized in Figure 2.8. Router RA receives an advertisement from an eBGP session, which, just like any other BGP advertisement, undergoes a selection process. If it becomes the new best path, it is automatically propagated on all active BGP sessions (eBGP and iBGP). The only (eBGP) session excluded is the one from which the advertisement was received.

Actually, this rule is present in BGP's standard documents (RFC 1771 and RFC 4271). In recent years, however, it became clear that leaving eBGP communication propagation free to evolve – as provided for in standard documents – could lead to incidents such as to cause issues to entire portions of the Internet, or downright to the entire Internet, in the most severe cases.

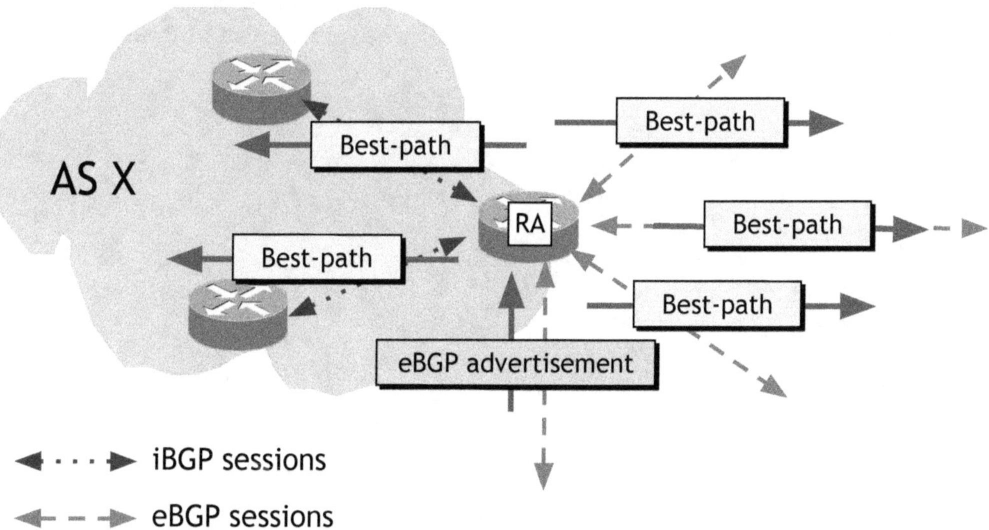

Figure 2.8 – Propagating BGP advertisements coming from an eBGP session.

Therefore, it would be best if automatic eBGP routing propagation is forbidden by default, thus forcing ISP administrators to always build appropriate routing policies (hopefully without errors, even though no RFC can remedy this!).

RFC 8212 – *Default External BGP (EBGP) Route Propagation Behavior without Policies*, July 2017, introduces two variations to BGP's default behavior, one concerning inbound advertisements, and the other outbound advertisements:

- routes contained in an Adj-RIB-In associated with an EBGP Neighbor SHALL NOT be considered eligible in the Decision Process if no explicit Import Policy has been applied;

- routes SHALL NOT be added to an Adj-RIB-Out associated with an EBGP Neighbor if no explicit Export Policy has been applied.

which, in short, means that no inbound and/or outbound advertisement can be accepted/ propagated, if an inbound and/or outbound policy has not been explicitly configured. In practice, this entails that basic configurations shouldn't allow the automatic acceptance or propagation of eBGP advertisements.

NOTE: Not all vendors support RFC 8212, therefore it is always best to check whether it is supported or not on the relevant documents. Also, within the same vendor, there might be situations where one OS supports this new rule, while others don't (see Section 3.1.3 for further details).

2.1.3 Rules in iBGP Sessions

Differently from eBGP sessions, iBGP sessions can be established by default also between routers not directly connected. The only requirement to keep in mind is a layer 3 connectivity between the IP addresses used to establish the session (which is rather obvious, considering that the BGP session is based on a TCP connection!).

In order to establish an iBGP session, it is advisable (but not mandatory!) to use Loopback addresses defined on the BGP Neighbors (Figure 2.9). This is because Loopback interfaces, being virtual, never go out of service, thus allowing the iBGP session to remain active as long as the network IGP routing protocol allows a layer 3 connection between the two BGP Neighbors.

Figure 2.9 – iBGP session.

The Loopback interfaces used should be mutually reachable at layer 3, that is, a bidirectional ping between the two interfaces must be possible. This implies that the Loopback interfaces should be announced in the AS' IGP routing process.

NOTE: Sometimes, based on special BGP implementations, the bidirectional ping between the IP addresses used is not sufficient to establish an iBGP session. Indeed, some BGP implementations (e.g. various Cisco implementations) require the explicit presence of /32 IP subnets, used as session endpoints, in the RIB. This is problematic especially with the IS-IS protocol, where the areas by default are equivalent to OSPF Totally NSSA. If two BGP Neighbors belong to different areas, they do not have the explicit presence of /32 IP subnets within their RIB, as the one outside the area would only be reachable through a default route. And this prevents the iBGP session from being established. In order to solve this issue, we need to inject the /32 IP subnets within the LSDB L1 of the BGP Neighbor relevant areas, through the Route Leaking mechanism, so that they are explicitly present in the RIBs of the BGP Neighbors. The same goes for Totally Stubby and Totally NSSA OSPF areas.

In order to propagate BGP advertisements, iBGP sessions adopt the following rule (also known as split horizon rule):

Every BGP advertisement received from a router on an iBGP session, if it becomes the best path, is automatically propagated to all active eBGP sessions, but not on iBGP sessions.

This rule is summarized in Figure 2.10. Router RA receives an advertisement from an iBGP session, which, just like any other BGP advertisement, undergoes a selection process. If it becomes the new best path, it is automatically propagated on all active eBGP sessions. It is not propagated on the other iBGP sessions. It should be noted that, in this case too, automatic propagation on eBGP sessions depends on the support of RFC 8212, mentioned earlier.

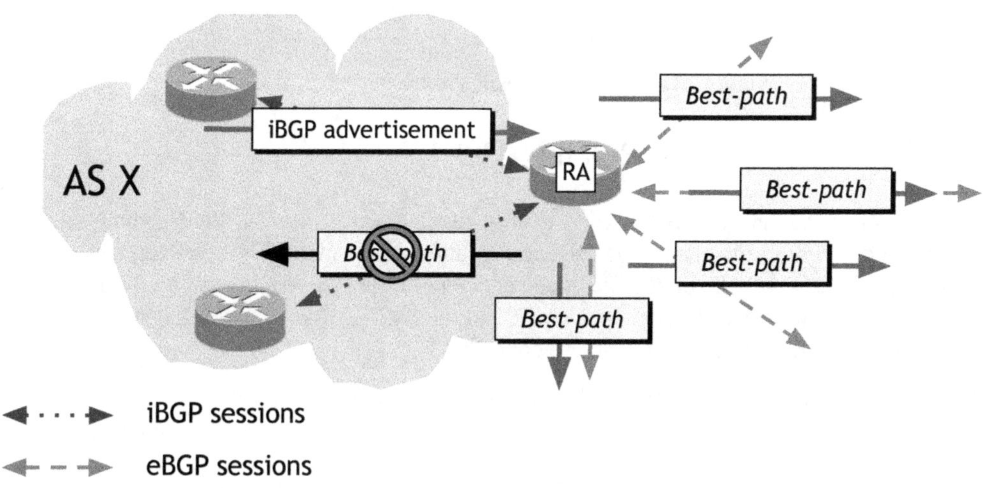

Figure 2.10 – Propagating BGP advertisements coming from an iBGP neighbor.

Figure 2.11 shows an example of BGP advertisement propagation, which uses the rules set out above for eBGP and iBGP sessions. Assuming that no filter is applied, or, for platforms supporting RFC 8212, that "all-pass" inbound/outbound filters have been applied, propagation occurs as follows: the advertisement of prefix 192.0.2/24, within AS 64503, is automatically propagated to AS 64502 on the eBGP session between the two ASes. Router RA, which receives the advertisement on an eBGP session – provided that it is the best path for prefix 192.0.2/24 – automatically propagates the advertisement on all active BGP sessions; the figure shows only the iBGP sessions toward RB, RC and RD. Routers RB and RC, as they receive the advertisement on an iBGP session, do not propagate it to the other iBGP sessions (split horizon rule). On the other hand, router RD propagates it only on the eBGP session toward AS 64501 (provided that it is the best path for prefix 192.0.2/24), and not on the iBGP sessions toward RB and RC.

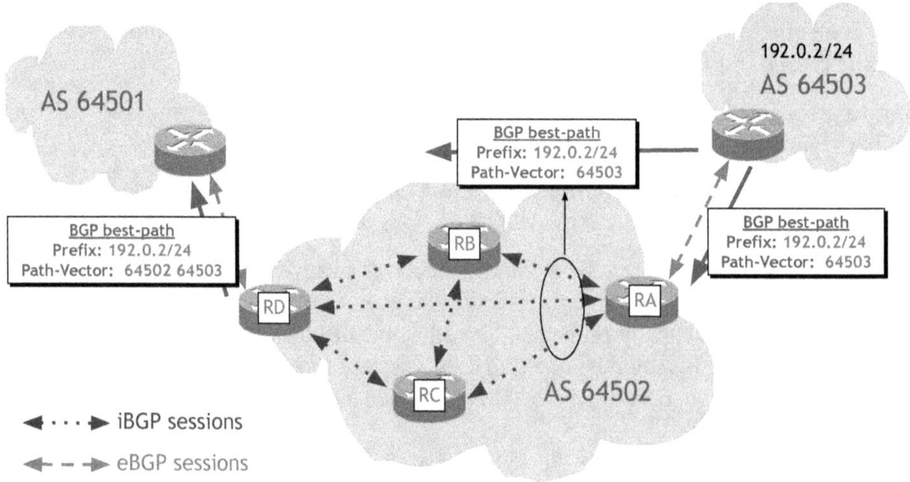

Figure 2.11 – Example of BGP advertisement propagation.

2.2 iBGP/IGP SYNCHRONIZATION

NOTE: This paragraph can be skipped in first reading since the iBGP/IGP synchronization concept is deemed obsolete, and it is currently disabled in the majority of platforms by default. It was included for the sake of completeness, and also to shed some light on how IP packets are routed toward IP prefixes advertised via iBGP, and the iBGP/IGP interaction. Therefore, we still recommend you to read it, to deepen these concepts.

In a transit AS, it is crucial that every AS router has a way to reach each external prefix within its RIB, to prevent traffic from falling into a "black hole". In order to grasp this concept, let's take into account the example in Figure 2.12, where we included, in part (a) the propagation of BGP advertisements of prefix 192.0.2/24 (control plane), local to AS 64503, and in part (b), the path of a packet (data plane) that, from AS 64501, is headed toward Host 192.0.2.1 in AS 64503.

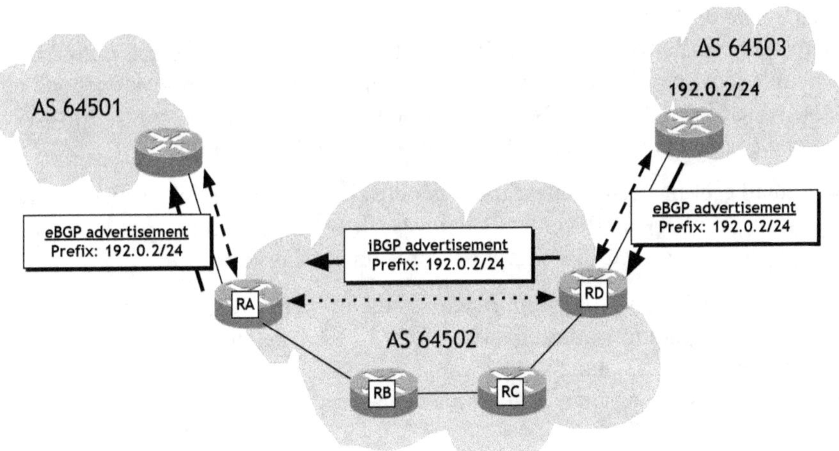

Figure 2.12 a – Example of "black hole": control plane.

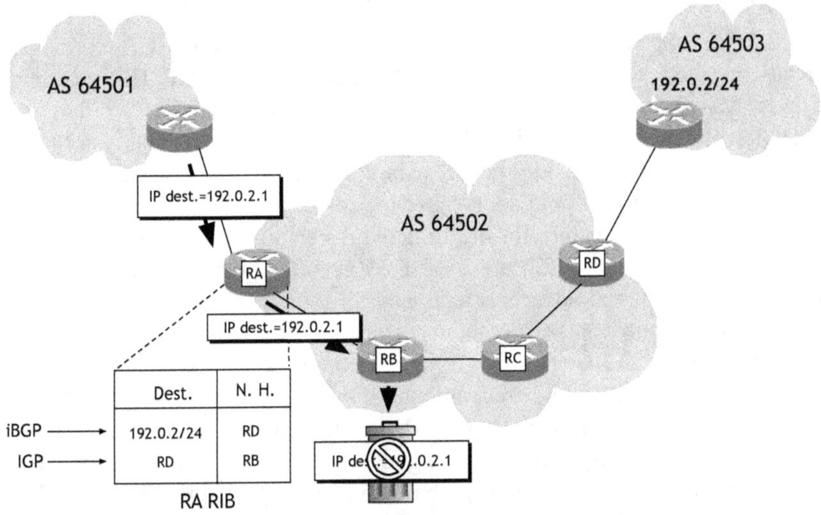

Figure 2.12 b – Example of "black hole": data plane.

The advertisement of prefix 192.0.2/24 is propagated by AS 64503 toward AS 64502 on an eBGP session. Router RD of AS 64502 automatically propagates the advertisement within it only on the iBGP session between RD and RA, and then this last router propagates it toward AS 64501, using an eBGP session. Notice that routers RB and RC of 64502 will not include a path toward prefix 192.0.2/24 within their RIB, since they have not received any BGP advertisement of the prefix, and the eBGP advertisement received by RD has not been redistributed within the network's IGP protocol (e.g. OSPF, IS-IS). Router RA will install prefix 192.0.2/24 within its RIB with, let's say, with one of RD interfaces as Next-Hop.

NOTE: In Paragraph 2.4, we will see that this is not BGP's default behavior; however, the default Next-Hop may be changed through a suitable configuration.

Lastly, let's assume that, in RA's RIB, there is a path toward RD with RB as the Next-Hop, determined by the IGP protocol of AS 64502.

Now, let's assume that RA receives an IP packet bound to Host 192.0.2.1 from AS 64501. RA makes a double lookup of its RIB (recursive lookup), the first on the row corresponding to prefix 192.0.2/24, which has RD as the Next-Hop – and it's not directly connected to RA – and the second to find a path toward RD, which has the Next-Hop RB as result.

NOTE: Actually, in modern routers, there is only one lookup, and is carried out on the FIB, which, starting from the RIB content, removes all recursions, thus speeding up the packet forwarding process (e.g., see Cisco Express Forwarding algorithm).

As final result of the recursive lookup, RA sends the packet to RB, which will reject it, because it does not have any path toward prefix 192.0.2/24 in its RIB. Therefore, the traffic toward Host 192.0.2.1 ends up in a "black hole".

In order to avoid this issue, some BGP implementations use the following synchronization rule between iBGP and IGP:

When a BGP Speaker receives an advertisement on an iBGP session, before considering it suitable to take part in the selection process – and therefore make it a possible candidate to be propagated toward the eBGP sessions – it must already have an IGP path within the RIB.

In other words, a BGP Speaker propagates an iBGP advertisement on eBGP sessions if and only if it has already received the advertisement from the same prefix via IGP. This guarantees that all the routers in its AS will include a path toward the prefix in their RIB, thus avoiding any possible traffic black holes. However, the trouble is that, in big networks, it is absolutely not recommended to redistribute all the prefixes outside the AS within the Internal IGP process, since this would determine overload issues that would soon cause the router to go out of service, due to the way IGPs work. The routing architecture for big IP networks entails that prefixes outside the AS are imported inside the AS through a full mesh of iBGP sessions (actually, iBGP sessions between edge routers receiving external advertisements and all the other AS routers are enough; iBGP sessions between transit-only routers are not necessary for this purpose).

The reason lies in the fact that BGP has been designed to manage a large amount of advertisements, and so it is well-suited to manage the great amount of them imported into an AS. The role of IGP – which is still present (except in special cases, where only static routing is used) – is to propagate information for layer 3 internal connectivity (e.g. connectivity between the Loopback interfaces used to establish iBGP sessions). We will go back to these aspects in Chapter 8, where we will specify the roles of BGP and IGPs (generally OSPF or IS-IS) in modern routing architectures of large ISP networks.

In the case of a full mesh of iBGP sessions between routers in the AS, the traffic black holes issue is solved automatically, without having to redistribute the external prefixes in the IGP process, while leaving the task of distributing this routing information to BGP, through iBGP sessions. By adopting this solution, the synchronization can be safely disabled.

2.3 BGP MESSAGES

BGP messages are transported by TCP/IP packets on a connection established on TCP port 179, as source or destination. Currently, there are 5 types of messages:

1. OPEN

2. UPDATE

3. NOTIFICATION

4. KEEPALIVE

5. ROUTE REFRESH

The length of BGP messages may vary between 19 and 4,096 byte (RFC 4271) for OPEN and KEEPALIVE, and 65,535 byte (RFC 8654 – *Extended Message Support for BGP*, October 2019) for the other messages.

All messages have a common header, whose format is shown in Figure 2.13. The fields have the following meaning:

- **Marker** (16 bytes): made up only of "1", is included only for compatibility reasons with older versions. RFC 1771 included its use also to transport a possible hash function for authenticating messages in connection with the Authentication Information optional parameter of the OPEN message (e.g., MD5, see Section 10.2.1). RFC 4271 took out this option (but not the option of authenticating BGP messages, see Section 10.2.1).

- **Length** (2 bytes): it refers to the message's total length, including the header.

- **Type** (1 byte): it refers to the message type; the codes used are those shown in Figure 2.13.

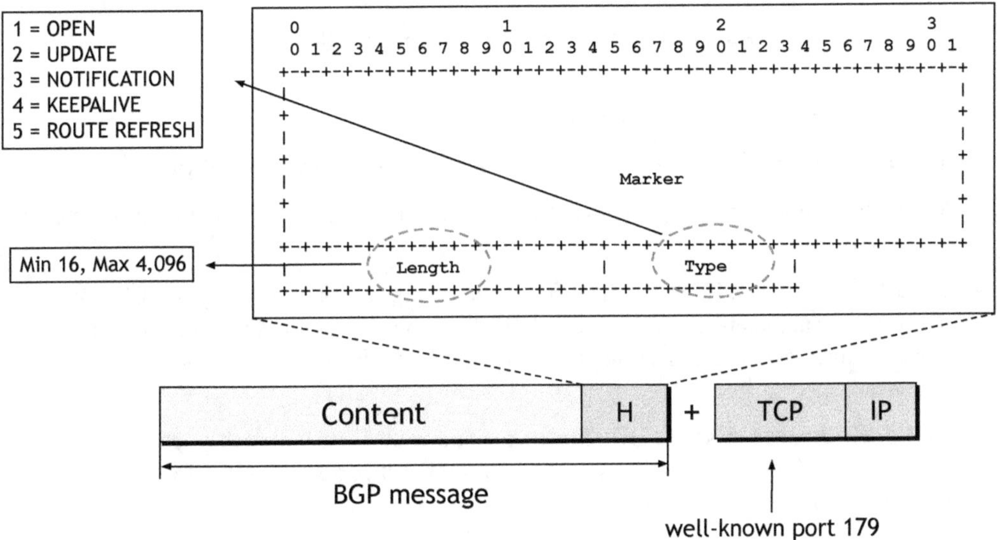

Figure 2.13 – Common BGP messages header.

2.3.1 OPEN message

The OPEN message (Type=1), as mentioned earlier in Paragraph 2.1, is the first BGP message exchanged between two BGP Neighbors, immediately after establishing the TCP connection. Its format is shown in Figure 2.14.

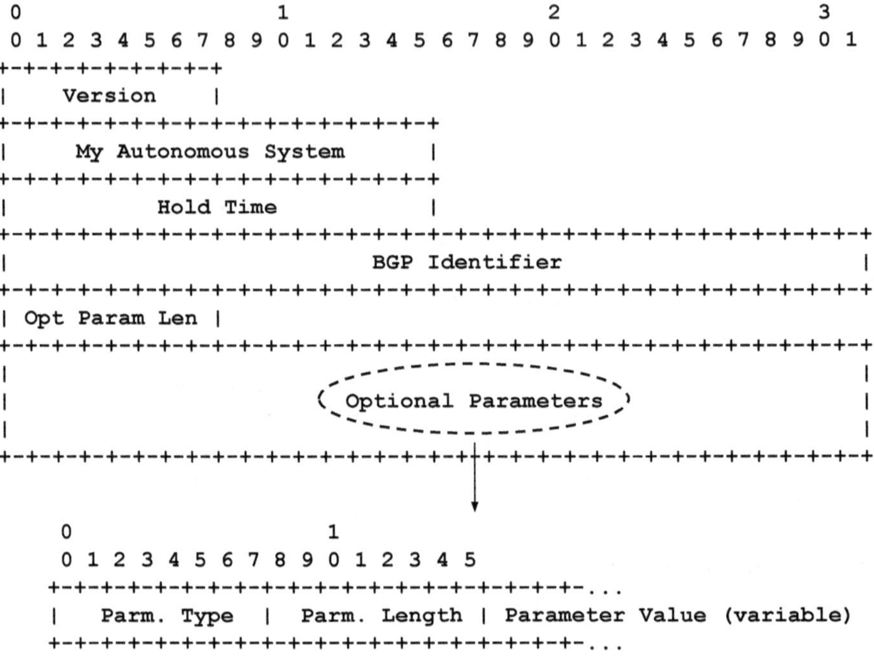

Figure 2.14 – Format of the OPEN message (RFC 4271).

The meaning of the different fields is the following:

- **Version** (1 byte): BGP version. In current implementation, its value is always 4.

- **My Autonomous System** (2 bytes): AS number which the router generating the message belongs to.

- **Hold Time** (2 bytes): it refers to the time after which, without receiving any BGP message, the session is automatically closed; two BGP Neighbors can submit two different Hold Time values in the session initialization phase, but in the end the minimum value between the two is selected.

- **BGP Identifier** (4 bytes): the BGP identifier of the router originating the message. Normally, the BGP Identifier is expressed as an IP address, but it is treated by the BGP process as an unsigned integer.

NOTE: Although RFC 6286 – *Autonomous-System-Wide Unique BGP Identifier for BGP-4, June 2011* – loosens the concept of uniqueness, by making it valid only within the AS perimeter, current implementations by several manufacturers use this rule in a different way. For instance, Cisco's IOS XE states that two BGP Neighbors cannot have the same BGP Identifier, both for iBGP and eBGP sessions. On the other hand, Cisco's IOS XR and JUNOS implementations, allow establishing e/iBGP sessions, even if the two BGP Identifiers match. To avoid any issues, in practical applications it is always best for the BGP Identifiers of two BGP Neighbors to be different.

- **Optional Parameter Length** (1 byte): referred to the total length of the following optional parameter field; a null value implies that no option is available.

- **Optional Parameters** (variable length): contains a list of optional parameters. Each parameter is identified by a TLV coding: <Type, Length, Value>. Currently, the only optional parameter defined is the Capabilities (Parameter Type=2) parameter, used to indicate the type of BGP Capability supported by the BGP Neighbor. Former RFC 1771 included also the Authentication Information (Parameter Type=1) parameter, which was used to specify the authentication method, but its use has been declared obsolete by RFC 4271.

A BGP Capability is a function supported by the BGP Speaker. The Parameter Value field contains a TLV triple, <Capability Code, Capability Length, Capability Value>.

NOTE: RFC 8810 – *Revision to Capability Codes Registration Procedures*, August 2020, revised the Capability Code values assignment criteria, which are allocated as follows: values within the 1-63 range, at IETF's disposal; values between 64 and 238, assigned to standard functions; values between 239 and 254, for experimental uses; and lastly value 255, reserved.

The standard values assigned can be checked at this link:
https://www.iana.org/assignments/capability-codes/capability-codes.xhtml
Some of the most important values include:

- Multiprotocol BGP (Capability Code=1): see Paragraph 2.6.

- Route Refresh (Capability Code=2): see Paragraph 6.5.

- Outbound Route Filtering (Capability Code=3): see Paragraph 6.6.

- Graceful Restart (Capability Code=64): see Appendix A.5

- 4 byte AS Support (Capability Code=65): see Appendix A.1

BGP Capabilities were introduced in RFC 3392 – *Capabilities Advertisement with BGP-4*, November 2002, rewritten and updated with the same title as RFC 5492 of February 2009.
Below is the analysis of an OPEN message obtained through wireshark, one of the most popular protocol analyzers (packet sniffer), mostly used to troubleshoot network issues, analyses and protocol development (its characteristics are similar to the well-known tcpdump). The message was sent during the establishment of an eBGP session between two routers belonging to AS 64510 and 64501, respectively. In particular, the message was generated by a router within AS 64501.

Border Gateway Protocol - OPEN Message
  Marker: ffffffffffffffffffffffffffffffff
  Length: 53
  Type: OPEN Message (1)
  Version: 4
  My AS: 64501
  Hold Time: 180
  BGP Identifier: 192.168.0.11
  Optional Parameters Length: 24
  Optional Parameters

```
Optional Parameter: Capability
Parameter Type: Capability (2)
Parameter Length: 6
Capability: Multiprotocol extensions capability
  Type: Multiprotocol extensions capability (1)
  Length: 4
  AFI: IPv4 (1)
  Reserved: 00
  SAFI: Unicast (1)
Optional Parameter: Capability
  Parameter Type: Capability (2)
  Parameter Length: 2
  Capability: Route refresh capability (Cisco)
    Type: Route refresh capability (Cisco) (128)
    Length: 0
Optional Parameter: Capability
  Parameter Type: Capability (2)
  Parameter Length: 2
  Capability: Route refresh capability
    Type: Route refresh capability (2)
    Length: 0
Optional Parameter: Capability
  Parameter Type: Capability (2)
  Parameter Length: 6
  Capability: Support for 4-octet AS number capability
    Type: Support for 4-octet AS number capability (65)
    Length: 4
    AS Number: 64501
```

Among the several parameters transported, we can easily recognize:

- The BGP-ID of the router that generated the message: 192.168.0.11.

- The Hold Time value suggested: 180 sec.

- The message transports 4 BGP Capabilities: Multiprotocol extensions (Capab. Code=1), Prestandard Route Refresh, Cisco proprietary (Capab. Code=128), Route refresh standard (Capab. Code=2), 4 byte AS number support (Capab. Code=65).

NOTE: Capability code=128, used by Cisco to negotiate the pre-standard Route Refresh function, was deemed obsolete by RFC 8810, mentioned earlier.

Some BGP Capabilities, such as those just described, are sent by default, while others are subject to suitable configuration commands. There are no general rules on default capabilities, every manufacturer has its own strategy.

2.3.2 UPDATE message

An UPDATE message (Type=2), whose format is shown in Figure 2.15, is BGP's most important message, and is used to announce – in its original version – IPv4 prefixes with the related BGP attributes, and/or withdraw any previously advertised IPv4 prefixes. The meaning of the different fields is the following:

- **Unfeasible Routes Length** (2 bytes): indicates the total length of the following Withdrawn Routes field; if set to 0, it implies that there are no prefixes to be withdrawn.

- **Withdrawn Routes** (variable length): contains the list of IPv4 prefixes to withdraw, because they can no longer be reached by the router originating the message. Each IPv4 prefix is represented by the pair <prefix length, prefix>, where the prefix length is expressed by a quantity of bits (from 0, i.e. all IP addresses, to 32), and the prefix is followed by the minimum quantity of bits necessary to make the field fall within an octet boundary. For instance, prefix IPv4 192.0.2/24 is represented by pair <24, 192.0.2> (in binary: <00011000, 11000000.00000000.00000010>).

- **Total Path Attribute Length** (2 bytes): indicates the total length of the following Path Attributes field; a null length implies the absence of BGP attributes, and consequently of prefixes to advertise. This is because, as we will see in Paragraph 2.4, some BGP attributes are mandatory, so the presence of at least one prefix to advertise implies a non-empty Path Attributes field.

- **Path Attributes** (variable length): contains the list of BGP attributes linked to the group of prefixes to announce. Each BGP attribute is expressed through triplet <Attribute Type, Attribute Length, Attribute Value>. The general format and that of the individual attributes will be seen in Paragraph 2.4.

- **Network Layer Reachability Information** (NLRI) (variable length): contains a list of the IPv4 prefixes to advertise, i.e. the best paths present in the BGP table of the router originating the message, which have all the same BGP attributes associated. This field has the same representation we've already seen for the Withdrawn Routes field.

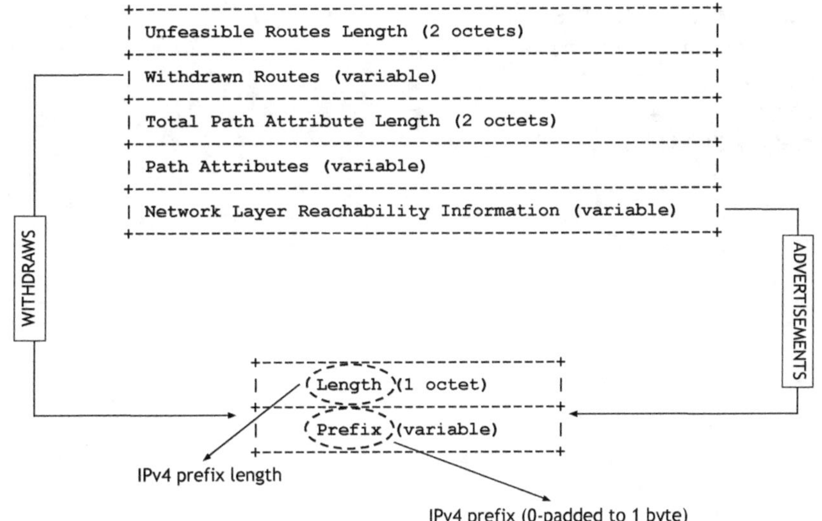

Figure 2.15 – Format of the UPDATE message (RFC 4271).

A BGP Speaker generates UPDATE messages immediately after establishing a BGP session with a BGP Neighbor, to communicate all the best paths present in its BGP table, and then to communicate any variations in the BGP table (triggered updates).

The quantity of messages generated to announce the prefixes depends on the attributes associated: an UPDATE is generated for each group of prefixes with the same associated attributes. For instance, if a BGP Speaker announces 5 new prefixes, 3 of which with attributes (A, B, C) associated to them, and 2 with attributes (X, Y, Z) instead, only two UPDATE messages would be generated. On the other hand, in order to withdraw a prefix, a cumulative UPDATE message is generated, since the associated attributes are not specified during withdrawal.

NOTE: The NLRI field just described is present in BGP's original version, and structured to advertise only IPv4 prefixes. Over the years, BGP – as we will see further on – has been expanded to transport various types of information (e.g. IPv6, VPN-IPv4/v6 prefixes, MAC addresses, etc.), and the NLRI field has a different structure for each type of information (see Paragraph 2.6).

Below is the analysis of an UPDATE message obtained with wireshark. The message was sent to a BGP Neighbor after establishing a BGP session, once the state machine reached the Established state, to announce the IPv4 prefix 203.0.113/24. A series of BGP attributes (indicated as Path Attributes) are associated with the advertisement, and we will go over their meaning in the next Paragraph 2.4.

Border Gateway Protocol - UPDATE Message
   Marker: ffffffffffffffffffffffffffffffff
   Length: 54
   Type: UPDATE Message (2)
   Withdrawn Routes Length: 0
   Total Path Attribute Length: 27
   Path attributes
     Path Attribute - ORIGIN: IGP
     Path Attribute - AS_PATH: 64502
     Path Attribute - NEXT_HOP: 10.1.3.2
     Path Attribute - MULTI_EXIT_DISC: 0
   Network Layer Reachability Information (NLRI)
     203.0.113.0/24
       NLRI prefix length: 24
       NLRI prefix: 203.0.113.0

2.3.3 NOTIFICATION message

A NOTIFICATION message (Type=3), whose format is shown in Figure 2.16, is used to notify any possible error conditions.

<pre>
 0   1   2   3
 0 1 2 3 4 5 6 7 8 9 0 1 2 3 4 5 6 7 8 9 0 1 2 3 4 5 6 7 8 9 0 1
+-+
| Error code | Error subcode | Data |
+-+-+-+-+-+-+-+-+-+-+-+-+-+-+-+-+   +
| |
+-+
</pre>

Figure 2.16 – Format of the NOTIFICATION message (RFC 1771).

The meaning of the different fields is the following:

- **Error Code** (1 byte): indicates the error type.

  - 1=Message Header Error.

  - 2=Open Message Error.

  - 3=Update Message Error.

  - 4=Hold Timer Expired.

  - 5=Finite State Machine Error.

  - 6=Cease.

  - 7=ROUTE-REFRESH Message Error.

- **Error Subcode** (1 byte): provides detailed info on the error. We will not include all codes here. For more information on them, see RFC 4271. For instance, for error code 2 (Open Message Error), some of the possible sub-codes are: 1=Unsupported version number, 2=Bad peer AS, etc.

- **Data** (variable length): used as error diagnostics. The content depends on the two previous values. For instance, if a BGP Speaker receives a message with an unsupported Type field value in the common header, it would send a NOTIFICATION message with Error Code=1 (Message Header Error), Error Subcode=3 (Bad Message Type) and the unsupported Type value received in the Data field.

2.3.4 KEEPALIVE message

KEEPALIVE messages (Type=4) are periodically exchanged to keep the session open, and prevent its teardown once the Hold Time expires. In this case, the format cannot be specified, since KEEPALIVE messages are empty. These messages only comprise the common 19-byte BGP header, with the Type field set to 4.

2.3.5 ROUTE REFRESH message

We will talk about this message in Chapter 6 (see Section 6.5.2).

2.4 BGP ATTRIBUTES

BGP attributes are the key tool for the entire protocol's operation, and to establish the routing policies, since they have an essential impact in the best path selection, within BGP's selection process.

According to a preliminary classification, BGP attributes are divided into two classes:

- **Well Known**: these attributes must be necessarily recognized by any BGP implementation.

- **Optional**: these attributes may go unrecognized by a BGP implementation.

NOTE: Today, the distinction between Well Known and Optional attributes is only of historical significance, rather than of real one. The main current BGP implementations support all attributes.

In turn, Well Known attributes are divided into:

- **Well Known Mandatory**: these are mandatory attributes that must be present in all UPDATE messages with a non-empty NLRI field. Well Known Mandatory attributes are:

  - ORIGIN

  - AS_PATH

  - NEXT_HOP

- **Well Known Discretionary**: these attributes do not need to be present in all BGP advertisements. Well Known Discretionary attributes are:

  - LOCAL_PREF (Local Preference)

  - ATOMIC_AGGREGATE

In turn, Optional attributes are divided into:

- **Optional Transitive**: if the attribute is not recognized by the BGP implementation, this must ignore it and still transfer it to its BGP Neighbors. Optional Transitive attributes are:

  - AGGREGATOR

  - COMMUNITY

  - EXTENDED_COMMUNITY

  - LARGE COMMUNITY

  - AS4_PATH

  - AS4_AGGREGATOR

The last two attributes were introduced in RFC 4893, for an easier transition between 2-byte AS numbers and 4-byte AS numbers (see Appendix A.1).

- **Optional Non-Transitive**: if the attribute is not recognized by the BGP implementation, this must ignore it and not transfer it to its BGP Neighbors. Optional Non-Transitive attributes are:

  - MULTI_EXIT_DISC (MED, Multiple Exit Discriminator)

  - AIGP (Accumulated IGP metric)

  - ORIGINATOR_ID

- o CLUSTER_LIST
- o MP_REACH_NLRI
- o MP_UNREACH_NLRI

For the reader's convenience, the classification is summarized in Figure 2.17.

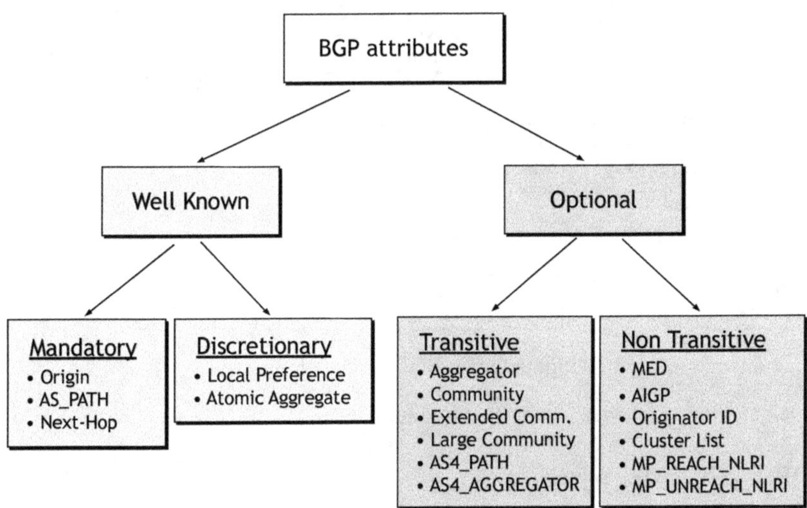

Figure 2.17 – BGP attributes classification.

The general attribute format (TLV type) is shown in Figure 2.18. The meaning of the different fields is the following:

- **Attribute Type** (2 bytes): is a field divided into two parts:
  - o **Attribute Flags** (1 byte): "bit 0" indicates whether an attribute is Well Known ("bit 0"=0) or Optional ("bit 0"=1); "bit 1" is always 1 for Well Known attributes, while for Optional attributes, it is 0 if the attribute is Optional Non Transitive, or 1 if it is Optional Transitive; "bit 2" (bit Partial) indicates whether the attribute has been recognized by all BGP Speakers ("bit 2"=0=Complete) or if there is at least one BGP Speaker that did not recognize it ("bit 2"=1=Partial). For Well Known and Optional Non-Transitive attributes, the bit Partial is always 0; "bit 3" (bit Extended) indicates the length of the Attribute Length field: if "bit 3"=0, the length is 1 byte, otherwise it is 2 bytes. All remaining bits are null and ignored upon reception.
  - o **Attribute Type** (1 byte): indicates the attribute type. The values for each attribute are described hereafter.
- **Attribute Length** (1 or 2 bytes, based on the "bit 3" value of the Attribute Flags field): indicates the length (in byte) of the Attribute Value field.
- **Attribute Value** (variable length): its content depends on the attribute, and we will go over each case later on.

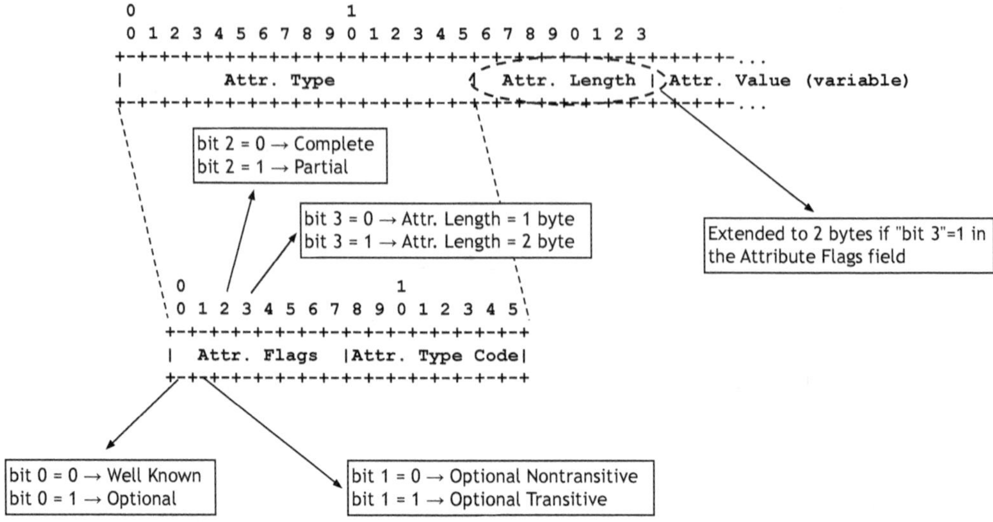

Figure 2.18 – BGP attribute format.

Let's see each attribute and their properties in detail.

2.4.1 ORIGIN attribute

It is a Well Known Mandatory attribute with Attribute Type Code=1. It specifies the origin of an IP prefix. It can take on three different values:

- IGP (numerical value 0): the IP prefix was originated directly by the router.

- EGP (numerical value 1): the IP prefix was learned through EGP (RFC 904, it hasn't been used for years, as it has been replaced by BGP).

- INCOMPLETE (numerical value 2): the IP prefix was learned in some other way (for instance, through a redistribution process from any routing protocol within BGP).

Once it has been defined by the BGP Speaker, it is propagated as is on all the ASes. Generally, BGP implementations allow its variation, based on the configuration. It is used in the BGP selection process according to the following order of preference: IGP→EGP→INCOMPLETE (see Paragraph 2.5). Its format is shown in Figure 2.19. The Attribute Value field has a length of 1 byte, and it can take on the values shown in the figure.

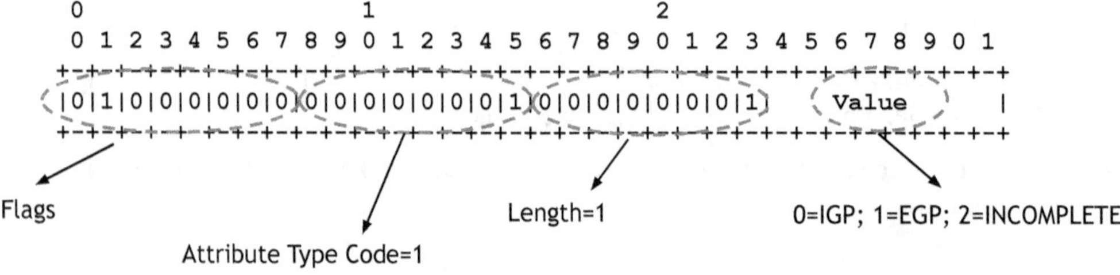

Figure 2.19 – ORIGIN attribute format.

2.4.2 AS_PATH attribute

It is a Well Known Mandatory attribute with Attribute Type Code=2. It specifies the (ordered or unordered) list of ASes (2-bytes long) crossed by a BGP advertisement. It comprises a series of segments, each one represented by the triple <Path Segment Type, Path Segment Length, Path Segment Value>. The Path Segment Length contains the number of ASes (and not the number of bytes) present in the Path Segment Type field. The Path Segment Type specifies the segment type. There are 4 types of segments:

- AS_SEQUENCE (Path Segment Type=2): is an ordered list of ASes. The number of ASes in the list is specified by the Path Segment Length field. AS_SEQUENCE segments are used by BGP Speakers to update the sorted list (Path Vector) of ASes crossed by a BGP advertisement.

- AS_SET (Path Segment Type=1): is an unordered list of ASes. The number of ASes in the list is specified by the Path Segment Length field. AS_SET segments are used by BGP Speakers that aggregate prefixes, in order to keep memory the ASes crossed by the prefixes being aggregated (obviously, if more specific prefixes were learned through BGP). In this case, the ASes order doesn't matter.

- AS_CONFED_SEQUENCE and AS_CONFED_SET: see Section 8.4.2.

The Path Segment Value field contains ASes coded through a 2-byte long number. The format is shown in Figure 2.20.

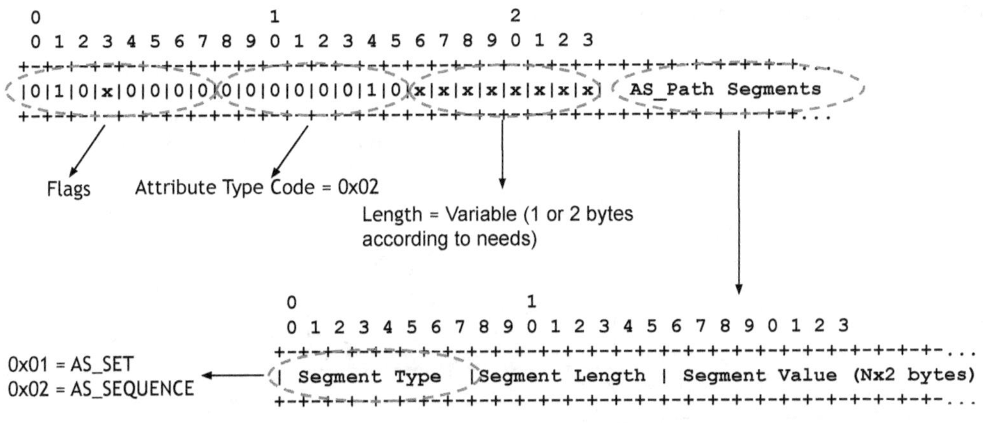

Figure 2.20 – AS_PATH attribute format.

NOTE: RFC 6472 – *Recommendation for Not Using AS_SET and AS_CONFED_SET in BGP*, December 2011, strongly advises against using AS_SET and AS_CONFED_SET segments.

The AS_PATH is processed according to the following rules:

- When a BGP Speaker sends an UPDATE message to an iBGP Neighbor, the AS_PATH attribute is not modified.

- When a BGP Speaker sends an UPDATE message to an eBGP Neighbor, the AS_PATH attribute is modified as follows:

  o If the first segment in the AS_PATH is an AS_SEQUENCE, the BGP Speaker adds its AS number at the top of the list contained in the segment (i.e., leftmost).

- o If the first segment in the AS_PATH is an AS_SET, the BGP Speaker adds a new AS_SEQUENCE segment containing only its AS number.

- o If the AS_PATH is empty, the BGP Speaker adds a new AS_SEQUENCE segment containing only its AS number.

When a BGP Speaker originates a prefix – i.e. it adds it to its own BGP table by some criterion – the AS_PATH attribute is processed as follows:

- If the prefix advertisement is sent to an eBGP Neighbor, the BGP Speaker includes its own AS number in an AS_SEQUENCE segment which is included in the AS_PATH attribute. In this case, the AS number of the BGP Speaker will be the only one present in the AS_SEQUENCE segment, and the segment will be the only one present in the AS_PATH.

- If the prefix advertisement is sent to an iBGP Neighbor, the BGP Speaker includes an empty AS_PATH in the advertisements. An empty AS_PATH only comprises the Attribute Type and Attribute Length fields, with the latter being equal to zero.

The AS_PATH attribute has two essential functions within BGP. The first is preventing routing information loops, and is based on the following rule:

A BGP Speaker does not send any advertisement containing the eBGP Neighbor's AS number in the AS_PATH attribute to an eBGP Neighbor.

Alternatively, some BGP implementations use the following equivalent rule:

A BGP Speaker rejects any advertisement containing its own AS number in the AS_PATH attribute.
This rule prevents the indefinite propagation of BGP messages (*routing information loop*). In order to understand this application, let's consider the example shown in Figure 2.21.

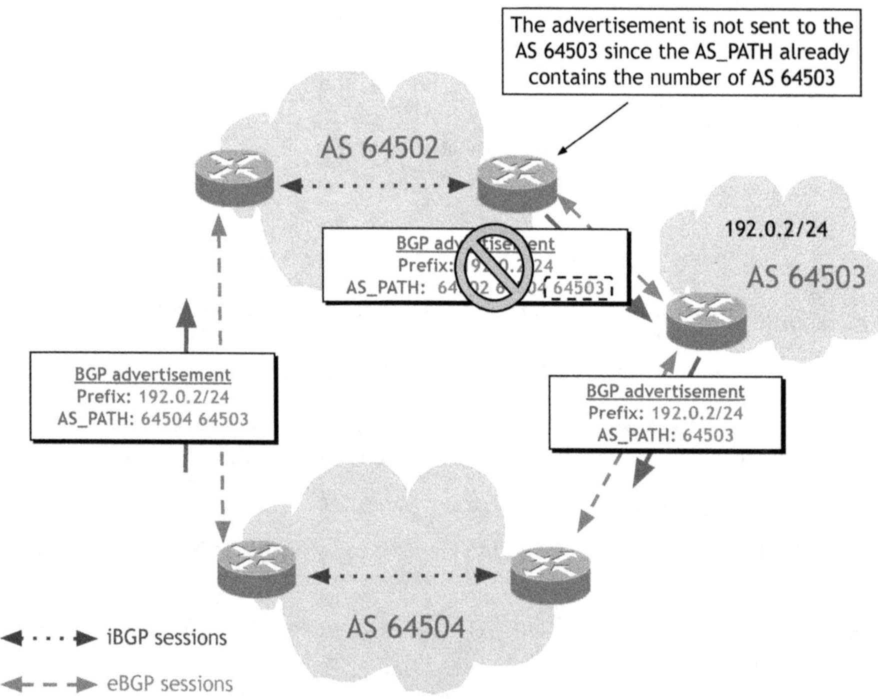

Figure 2.21 – Using the AS_PATH attribute to prevent routing information loop.

Prefix 192.0.2/24, within AS 64503, is added to the BGP table of a BGP Speaker in AS 64503 with empty AS_PATH, and then automatically propagated on eBGP sessions toward ASes 64502 and 64504 through UPDATE messages. For the sake of simplicity, we will only consider the UPDATE message propagated toward AS 64504. Upon exiting AS 64503, its AS_PATH will only comprise the AS_SEQUENCE=[64503] segment. Assuming that the advertisement is the prefix best path in every BGP Speaker, it will be automatically propagated on the iBGP session within AS 64504, where the AS_PATH does not change, then on the eBGP session toward AS 64502, where the AS_PATH will only comprise one AS_SEQUENCE=[64504 64503] segment, and lastly on the iBGP session within AS 64502, where the AS_PATH does not change. Now, if we did not adopt any rule, the advertisement would go back to AS 64503 and starts all over again, continuing this process indefinitely, and creating a routing information loop. On the other hand, the rule above stops the propagation from AS 64502 to AS 64503, since the number of AS 64503 is contained in the AS_PATH, thus stopping the routing information loop.

The second important function of the AS_PATH is being one of the possible metrics used by the BGP selection process to determine the best paths. The rule – which will be seen in detail in the next Paragraph 2.5 – is the following: *the path with the lowest number of ASes contained in the AS_PATH attribute is selected.*

NOTE: When determining the number of ASes contained in the AS_PATH, each AS_SET segment counts as one, regardless of the number of ASes contained in it.

A possible application of this rule occurs when managing the AS inbound traffic. The number of ASes contained in the AS_PATH attribute can be artificially increased (AS_PATH Prepending, see Section 7.3.2), to force an AS inbound traffic.

2.4.3 NEXT_HOP attribute

It is a Well Known Mandatory attribute with Attribute Type Code=3. It specifies the Next-Hop to be used to reach the prefixes contained in the NLRI field (BGP Next-Hop). The format is shown in Figure 2.22.

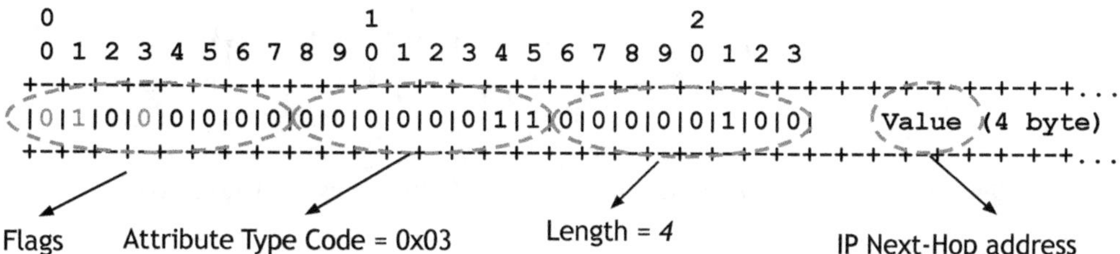

Figure 2.22 – NEXT_HOP attribute format.

The definition and processing of the NEXT_HOP attribute are among BGP's most important aspects. The following rules apply by default:

- *The NEXT_HOP attribute is modified only when BGP messages are forwarded on eBGP sessions; the IP address of the BGP Next-Hop is the one used by the BGP Speaker to open the TCP connection toward the BGP Neighbor. This rule is illustrated in Figure 2.23.*

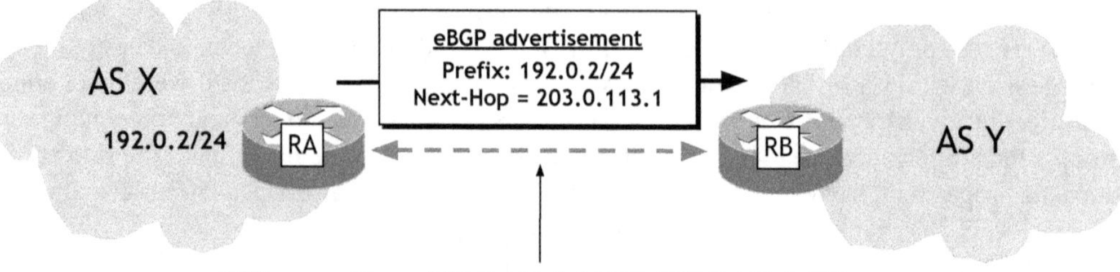

Figure 2.23 – NEXT_HOP attribute in eBGP sessions.

- *If a BGP advertisement of a prefix within an AS is propagated on an iBGP session between two routers within the same AS, the IP address entered in the NEXT_HOP attribute is the same used by the BGP Speaker propagating the advertisement to open the TCP connection toward the BGP Neighbor. This rule is illustrated in Figure 2.24.*

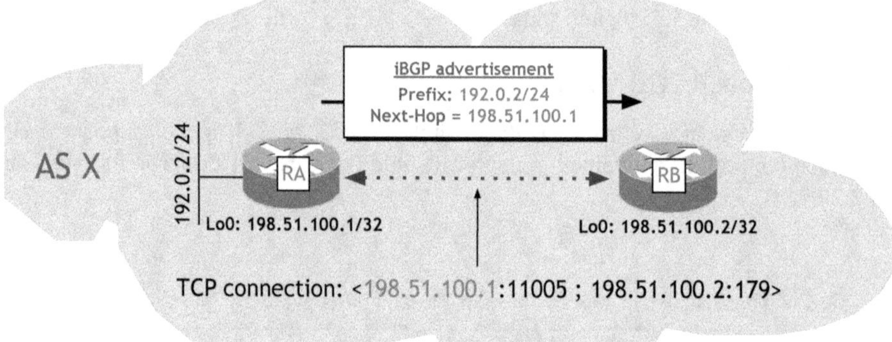

Figure 2.24 – NEXT_HOP attribute in local prefix advertisements on iBGP sessions.

- *If an advertisement of a prefix outside an AS, received on an eBGP session, is propagated on an iBGP session, the NEXT_HOP attribute doesn't change. This rule is illustrated in Figure 2.25.*

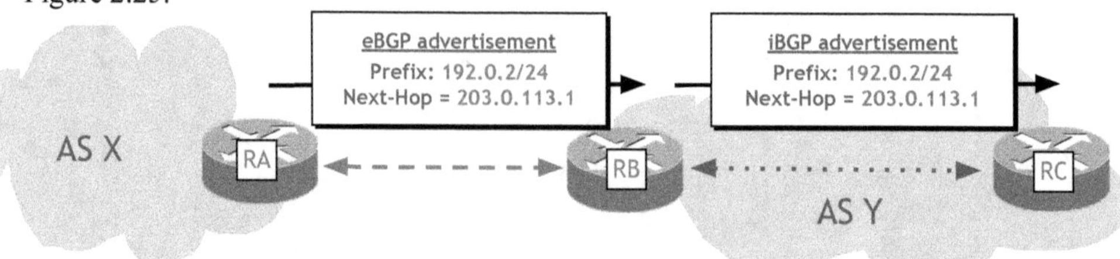

Figure 2.25 – NEXT_HOP attribute propagation.

This last rule has a very important practical implication. Indeed, as we will see in Paragraph 2.5 below, a BGP advertisement, in order to be deemed valid for the selection process, must have a reachable Next-Hop.

For instance, let's consider the propagation of BGP messages in Figure 2.26. The advertisement of prefix 192.0.2/24, local to AS 64503, is sent to the BGP Neighbor RD of AS 64502. According to the first rule above, the NEXT_HOP attribute – if we assume an eBGP session established by using the IP addresses of the physical interfaces as endpoints – will take on the value of 203.0.113.1. According to the third rule above, the advertisement is propagated on the iBGP session between RD and RA, keeping the NEXT_HOP attribute unchanged. When RA receives the advertisement, before considering it for the selection process, checks if it has in its RIB a path to the prefix 203.0.113.0/30 used to number the connection interfaces between the two BGP Neighbors of ASes 64503 and 64502. If the answer is yes, it considers the advertisement for the selection process, and if this becomes the new best path, it propagates that toward AS 64501, using – according to the first rule above – its own address 198.51.100.1, as IP address in the NEXT_HOP attribute. Vice versa, if the answer is negative, it deems the advertisement invalid, and does not admit it to the selection process (therefore, since it can never become the best path, it will never be propagated on eBGP sessions).

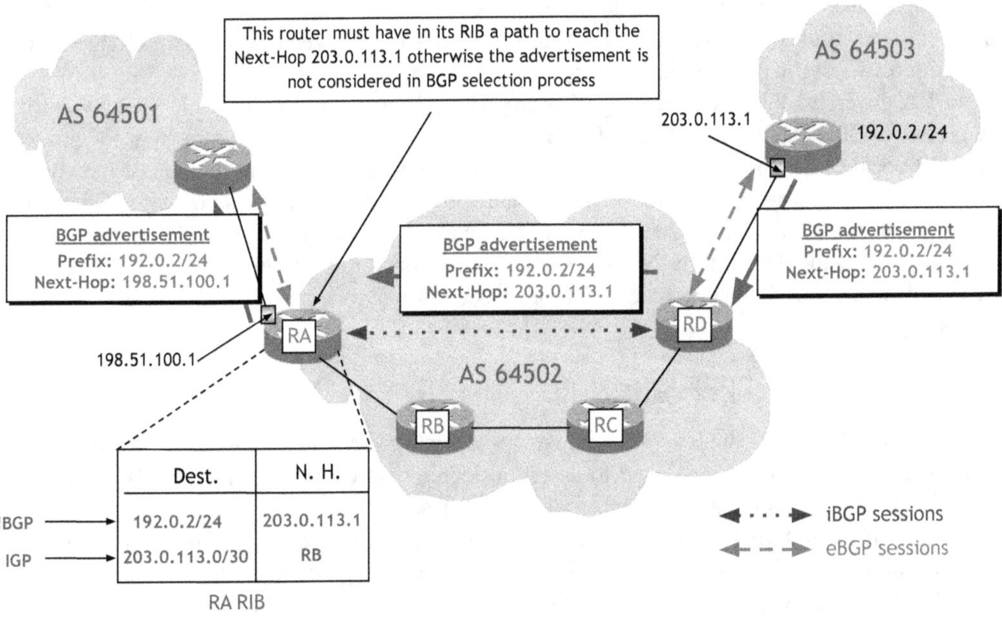

Figure 2.26 – Example of NEXT_HOP attribute processing.

NOTE: Since 2000, it is also possible to number point-to-point links using an IPv4 /31 network, where only two addresses are available, which can both be assigned to the only two devices within the network. The rationale behind this practice is explained in RFC 3021 – *Using 31-Bit Prefixes on IPv4 Point-to-Point Links*, December 2000. However, we would like to point out that, in some cases – perhaps in older implementations – this option is not available.

The presence in RD's RIB of the prefix containing the NEXT_HOP attribute, implies a redistribution of prefix 203.0.113.0/30 within AS 64502's IGP process. This is not a good practice, for at least two reasons:

- The prefixes containing addresses used in other ASes (for instance, in Figure 2.26, IP prefix 203.0.113.0/30) are included in the IGP routing protocol, thus exposing the routers of AS 64502 to possible security issues.

- The size of both the LSDBs and the RIBs are increased, thus slowing down the routers' performance.

In order to solve this issue, leading routers manufacturers provide a configuration command, which allows to vary the NEXT_HOP attribute default rules, by overriding external BGP Next-Hop value with TCP connection endpoint IP address when propagating the advertisement toward a specific iBGP Neighbor. This makes propagation of any external IP prefix within the AS useless. Going back to the example in Figure 2.26, the configuration command allows RD, while propagating the advertisement from RD to RA, to replace the current IP address in the NEXT_HOP attribute with its own IP address used to setup iBGP session with RA. We will go over these configuration details in Chapter 3 (see Section 3.1.4).

Lastly, we have a peculiar management of the NEXT_HOP attribute in broadcast networks. Let's consider the example in Figure 2.27, where the eBGP sessions between RA↔RB and RB↔RC, use the IP addresses of the physical interfaces.

When RA generates the advertisement of prefix 192.0.2/24, using the first rule we saw earlier, the NEXT_HOP attribute is set to 203.0.113.1. When propagating the advertisement toward RC, the BGP Speaker RB, by realizing that the BGP Neighbor is on the same broadcast network as the Next-Hop, does not change the attribute, and propagates the advertisement with the same NEXT_HOP attribute, equal to 203.0.113.1 (Third-party Next-Hop).

Please note that the Third-party Next-Hop mechanism does not apply when the BGP sessions are established using other interfaces than the Broadcast network physical ones (e.g., Loopback interfaces).

2.4.4 LOCAL_PREF attribute

The LOCAL_PREF attribute is a Well Known Discretionary attribute with Attribute Type Code=5. It specifies a metric that can be used to assign a degree of preference to an advertisement. The value length, known as Local Preference (LP), is 4 bytes.

It is mainly used in outbound routing policies to force the traffic exit point from an AS, and it is the first standard metric value considered in the BGP selection process.

The LP value is generally assigned (though not necessarily), by BGP Speakers that receive an eBGP advertisement. The assignment is based on the configuration or on a default value, which, although not specified in RFCs, in the main routing platforms (e.g. Cisco and Juniper routers) is equal to 100 (see also RFC 4277 – *Experience with the BGP-4 Protocol*, January 2006).

Once the LP value has been assigned, the LOCAL_PREF attribute is propagated only within the AS, and removed from AS outbound advertisements. This allows all the routers within an AS to choose a common exit point for traffic bound toward a certain prefix (or toward all of them, based on the configuration mode). The selection rule is the following: *the advertisement with the highest LP value is preferred.*

As an application example, let's consider Figure 2.28 below (Note: in the figure, b-p=best path). Prefix 192.0.2/24, within AS 64503, is propagated on the eBGP sessions toward ASes 64501 and 64502, and then from AS 64501 toward AS 64502. Therefore, AS 64502 receives two eBGP

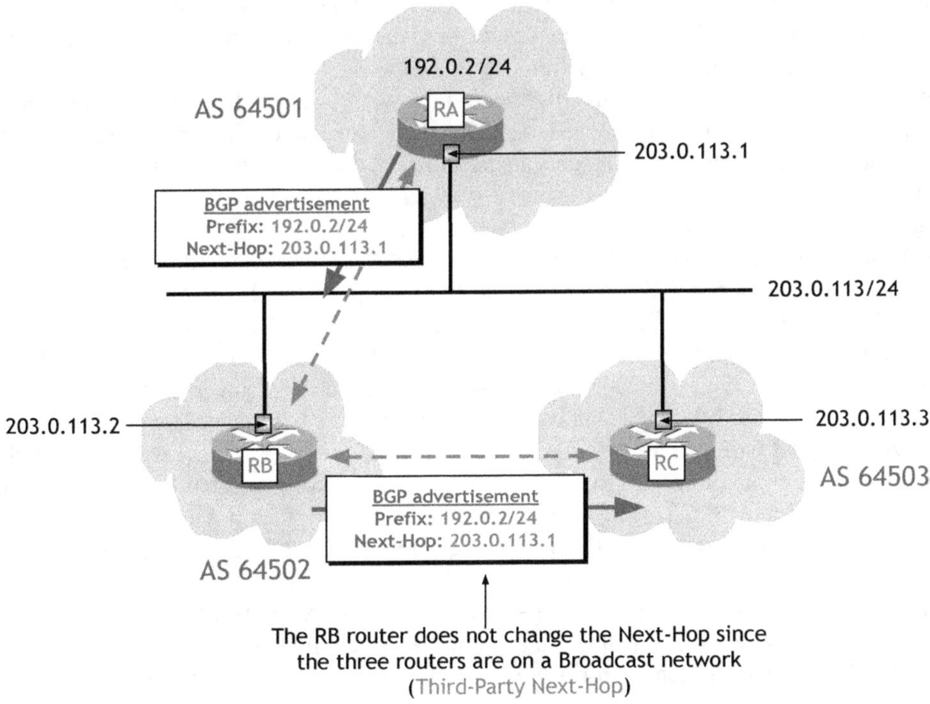

Figure 2.27 – Managing the NEXT_HOP attribute in Broadcast networks.

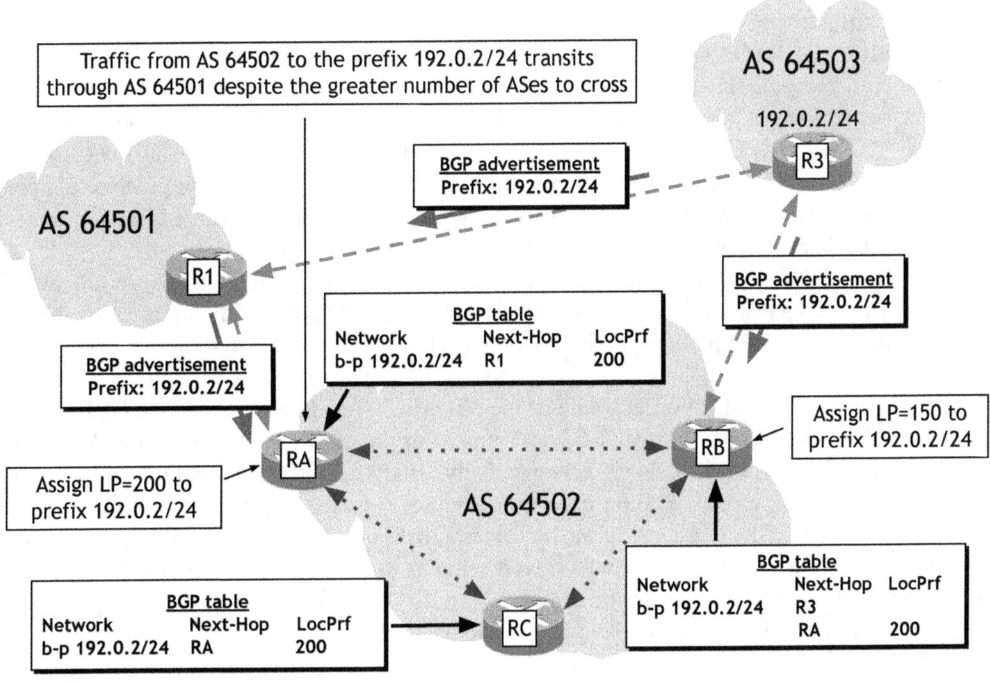

Figure 2.28 – Example of LOCAL_PREF attribute use.

advertisements of the prefix: the first enters router RA, while the second enters router RB. Let's suppose we assign a value of LP=200 by configuration to the advertisement entering from RA, and of LP=150 to the advertisement entering from RB.

According to the rule above, the advertisements propagate within AS 64502 through iBGP sessions, leaving the LP values unchanged. Actually, their propagation depends on the sequence through which the eBGP and iBGP sessions are established, even if the final result is (obviously) the same.

The Figure shows the BGP advertisements present in the routers of AS 64502, at the end of the UPDATE BGP message exchange. It is worth noting that, on router RC, contrarily to what one might think, there is only one iBGP advertisement, coming from router RA (Next-Hop=RA), with LP=200. There is no identical advertisement coming from RB. And the reason for this lies in BGP's operation. Besides the eBGP advertisement coming from R3, router RB receives an iBGP advertisement from RA with LP=200, and so it will choose the iBGP advertisement as the best path, since it has a higher LP. As you know, BGP only propagates best paths, however, due to the split horizon rule, RB will not propagate the advertisement of prefix 192.0.2/24 within AS 64502, since the best path comes from an iBGP advertisement. If it had propagated it earlier, it would withdraw it through an UPDATE message. Therefore, each router within AS 64502 – e.g. RC – will only have in the BGP table the advertisement of prefix 192.0.2/24 from RA, with LP value equal to 200.

It should be noted that the outbound traffic from AS 64502, toward prefix 192.0.2/24, in terms of crossed ASes, follows the longest path. This is proof that the administrator of AS 64502, through the LOCAL_PREF attribute, can choose according to her/his needs, how to manage the outbound traffic from his AS.

2.4.5 ATOMIC_AGGREGATE and AGGREGATOR attributes

Both these attributes are involved in IP prefix aggregation (see Paragraph 5.3).

The ATOMIC_AGGREGATE attribute is a Well Known Discretionary attribute (Attribute Type Code=6), with zero length. Its presence notifies the other BGP Speakers that the router sending the advertisement has aggregated the prefixes, with consequent BGP attribute memory loss. The ATOMIC_AGGREGATE attribute should not be added when, in the AS_PATH attribute, there is an AS_SET type AS_PATH segment, since this means that in the aggregation process, memory is kept of the ASes crossed by the more specific prefixes. We will go over this attribute more thoroughly in Chapter 5 (see also Figure 2.29).

The AGGREGATOR attribute is an Optional Transitive attribute, and is used to notify which router has executed a prefix aggregation operation to other BGP Speakers. It is formed by the pair of parameters <AS, BGP Identifier>, where the two parameters refer to the router that aggregated the prefixes.

Figure 2.29 shows an application example of the ATOMIC_AGGREGATE and AGGREGATOR attributes. AS 64503 receives two BGP advertisements of prefixes 192.0.2.0/25 (from AS 64501) and 192.0.2.128/25 (from AS 64502), respectively. BGP Speaker RA, with BGP Identifier 203.0.113.1, performs an aggregation operation, and advertises the aggregate prefix 192.0.2/24 toward an external BGP Neighbor. In the hypothesis that RA does not want to keep memory of the AS_PATH of the more specific prefix advertisements, the ATOMIC_AGGREGATE attribute is added to the UPDATE message. In addition, to notify the identity of the BGP Speaker that executed the aggregation to the BGP Neighbor, the AGGREGATOR attribute – consisting of the pair <AS=64503, BGP Identifier=203.0.113.1> – is added.

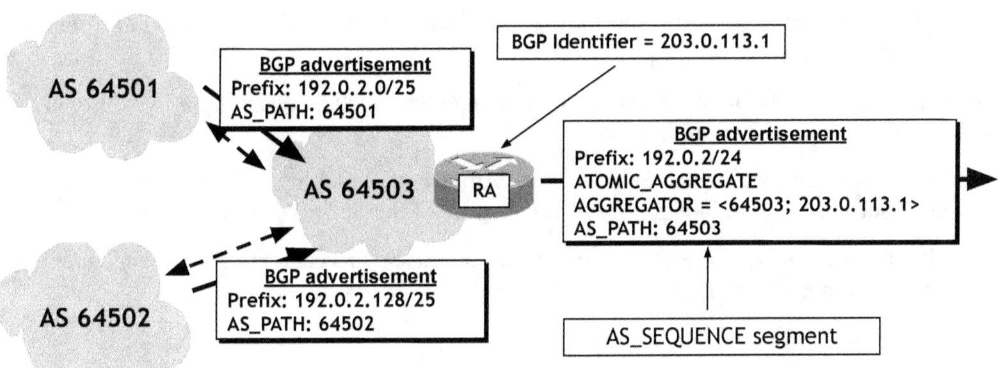

Figure 2.29 – Example of ATOMIC_AGGREGATE and AGGREGATOR attributes use.

If, through a suitable configuration, we want to retain memory of the AS_PATH of the more specific prefix advertisements that make up the aggregation, RA's BGP Speaker would issue the advertisement without the ATOMIC_AGGREGATE attribute, and with an identical AGGREGATOR attribute instead. In addition, the AS_PATH would include two segments: an AS_SET segment containing AS numbers AS 64501 and 64502, and an AS_SEQUENCE segment containing AS number 64503. More details on this in Chapter 5.

2.4.6 COMMUNITY attributes

One of the most useful BGP attributes in applications is the COMMUNITY attribute. Interestingly enough, this attribute is not included in the original BGP definition document, version 4 (RFC 1771, then rewritten in RFC 4271). The COMMUNITY attribute was actually introduced by RFC 1997 – *BGP Communities Attribute*, August 1996.

The COMMUNITY attribute is an "opaque" Optional Transitive attribute, used to classify BGP advertisements according to administration needs, and possibly perform actions based on the attribute's value. The fact that it is an "opaque" attribute means that, differently from other BGP attributes, such as AS_PATH, LOCAL_PREF, etc., it does not transport data used by BGP in a well-defined way (for instance, as we saw in Section 2.4.4, the LOCAL_PREF attribute is used as a metric in the BGP selection process); instead, it transports data that can be used by BGP in many different ways, based on the AS administrator's will.

NOTE: Henceforth, we will use 'COMMUNITY' to indicate the entire attribute, and 'Community' to indicate the single values contained in it.

Over the years, spurred by new necessities, the COMMUNITY attribute has undergone a progressive expansion of the space dedicated to the numerical value. There are three versions of it:

- Standard COMMUNITY (Attribute Type Code=8): characterized by an Attribute Value field containing one or more Community values, each one with a 4-byte size.

- Extended COMMUNITY (Attribute Type Code=16): characterized by an 8-byte Attribute Value field.

- Large COMMUNITY (Attribute Type Code=32): characterized by a 12-byte Attribute Value field.

The COMMUNITY attribute (any type) is used to classify BGP advertisements according to administration needs, and possibly perform actions based on the attribute's value. For instance, it can be used to define:

- routing policies for homogeneous groups of prefixes, such as assigning a Local Preference value based on a Community value;

- QoS policies, based on the Service Level Agreements established between customers and ISPs, such as differentiating the levels of Quality of Service offered to customers;

- filtering policies, such as not accepting BGP advertisements containing a certain Community value within the attribute;

- the traffic's origin;

- the nature of the relationship with another ISP (peering, transit);

- etc.

Moreover, the fact of having a bigger, more structured space than in the past, leaves room for imagination, as it happens in IPv6 numbering plans, where, with a large amount of bits available (perhaps too many!), it is possible to define more advanced numbering plans, compared to IPv4. If we want to draw up a general classification, COMMUNITY applications can be divided into two categories:

- Information applications, where community values are used as a sort of label to apply to the advertisements received. For instance, these are used to define the origin of an advertisement, the nature of the relationship with the ISP from which an advertisement is received, or the advertisement routing scope.

- Application followed by actions, where Community values are used as "match" conditions. An example of this could be the following: if a BGP Speaker receives an eBGP advertisement containing the Community value X in the COMMUNITY attribute, then it performs the action "assign Local Preference=Y".

The values of the COMMUNITY attribute (of any type) are assigned on a configuration basis, both to inbound and outbound BGP advertisements. The COMMUNITY attributes propagation strategy depends on the manufacturer's implementation. For instance, in Cisco implementations, a BGP Speaker receiving an advertisement with certain Community values, does not propagate these values on the other BGP (iBGP or eBGP) sessions, by default (with some subtle difference in IOS XR). However, this rule can be varied on a configuration basis. On the other hand, in Juniper implementations, COMMUNITY attributes are propagated automatically.
In the following chapters, we will see other useful applications of the COMMUNITY attribute.

Standard COMMUNITY attribute

The standard COMMUNITY attribute was originally defined by RFC 1997, cited above, and is characterized by a Nx4 byte Attribute Value field. This is because each Community value is 4-byte long, and each advertisement can be associated with any number of Community values.
Community values are generally represented in an AS:NN format, where AS is the AS number (2 byte) and NN an arbitrary value (2 byte). In standards, Community values are expressed in a hexadecimal format, while manufacturers prefer a decimal notation in routers. For instance, decimal value 64501:90 is expressed in the hexadecimal format as 0xFBF5005A (64501=0xFBF5, 90=0x005A).

RFC 1997 defines three Community values with a special meaning (well-known Community):

- NO_EXPORT (0xFFFFFF01=65535:65281): all BGP advertisements with this Community value associated with them, should not be propagated outside an AS, that is, they should not be propagated on an eBGP session. They can only be propagated within the AS.

- NO_ADVERTISE (0xFFFFFF02=65535:65282): all BGP advertisements with this Community value associated with them, should not be propagated on any BGP (iBGP or eBGP) session.

- NO_EXPORT_SUBCONFED (0xFFFFFF03=65535:65283): used in BGP Confederations (see Paragraph 8.4).

As indicated in the IANA registry, values within the [0x00000000, 0x0000FFFF] interval are reserved, while those within the [0x00010000-0xFFFEFFFF] interval are reserved for private use. Figure 2.30 shows an application example of well-known Community NO_EXPORT and NO_ADVERTISE values. Advertisements X and Y are sent by AS 64503 to AS 64502, and they have COMMUNITY attributes containing the NO_ADVERTISE and NO_EXPORT values, respectively, while advertisement Z has no COMMUNITY attribute associated with it. RD's BGP Speaker, after executing the selection process – assuming that the advertisements are best paths – only propagates advertisement Z toward AS 64501, and advertisements Y and Z on the iBGP session toward RA. Router RA will propagate only advertisement Z toward external AS 64501, but not advertisement Y, since the latter has the COMMUNITY attribute containing the NO_EXPORT value associated with it. Propagation occurs by default without associating any particular Community value with the advertisements, except for well-known ones.

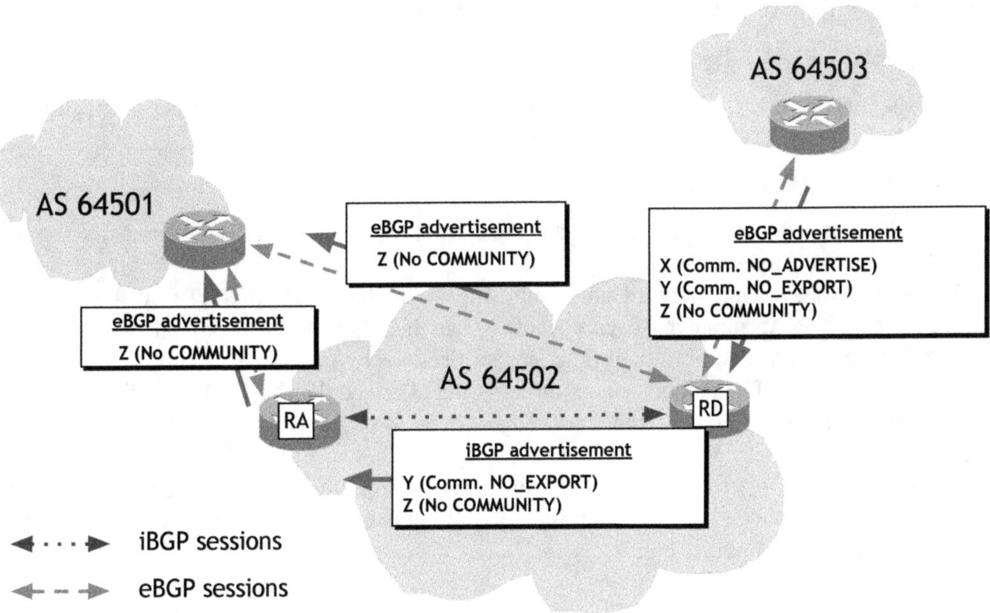

Figure 2.30 – Example of well-known Community NO_EXPORT and NO_ADVERTISE values use.

Extended COMMUNITY attribute

Soon enough, the space reserved to Community values in standard COMMUNITY attributes (equal to 4 bytes), turned out to be insufficient for new BGP applications, especially those within BGP/MPLS services. In order to solve this issue, the Extended COMMUNITY attribute was defined by RFC 4360 – *BGP Extended Communities Attribute*, February 2006. Apart from doubling the space for Extended Community values, RFC 4360 also defined its general structure, shown in the following Figure 2.31 (excerpt from RFC 4360):

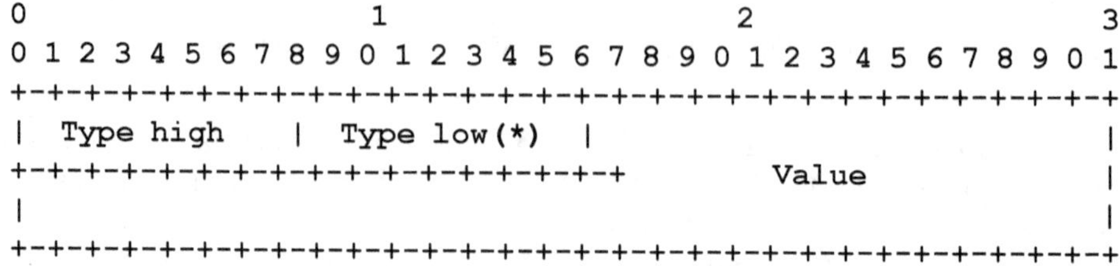

Figure 2.31 – General value format of an Extended Community.

For details about the format, see RFC 4360 directly; our only intent here is illustrating a particular Extended Community value used in many BGP/MPLS services, the Route Target. By referring to perhaps the most popular BGP/MPLS service (and surely the most widespread) – the L3VPN service – the Route Target (RT) is a value associated with each VPN-IPv4 prefix exported by a PE, which is transported within an Extended COMMUNITY attribute. RT values have the **Type low** field always equal to 0x02, while the **Type high** field can take on values 0x00, 0x01 and 0x02, based on the Value field format (which is 6 bytes). The Value field has three possible formats:

- **Type=0x00-02**: AS-2byte:NN format (e.g., 64501:1234).

- **Type=0x01-02**: IP-address:NN format (e.g., 192.0.2.1:1234).

- **Type=0x02-02**: AS-4byte:NN format (e.g., 65541:1234).

where NN is an arbitrary number available to the administrator. The last format is specified by RFC 5668 – 4-*Octet AS Specific BGP Extended Community*, October 2009.

Large COMMUNITY attribute

The introduction of 4-byte AS numbers has caused issues to the use of both standard and Extended COMMUNITY attributes.

Having a 4-byte space available for Community values, standard COMMUNITY attributes cannot be used with 4-byte AS numbers. If you decide to use them anyway (and obviously not with the AS:NN format), this would limit their practical applications by far.

Extended COMMUNITY attributes have similar issues. They could be used, but the field managed by the network administrator would be reduced to 2 bytes, a space deemed insufficient in practical applications.

Therefore, the need arose to solve (possibly for good) the amplitude issue for Community values, by introducing values with a greater amplitude, so as to give network administrators a long-lasting tool to base their BGP policies on.

The solution was introducing Large Community values, described in RFC 8092 – *BGP Large Communities Attribute*, February 2017, which expand the field available to network administrators from 6 to 12 bytes, while also removing the two "**Type high**" and "**Type low**" bytes. The format of a Large Community is shown in Figure 2.32 below (excerpt from RFC 8092).

```
 0                   1                   2                   3
 0 1 2 3 4 5 6 7 8 9 0 1 2 3 4 5 6 7 8 9 0 1 2 3 4 5 6 7 8 9 0 1
+-+-+-+-+-+-+-+-+-+-+-+-+-+-+-+-+-+-+-+-+-+-+-+-+-+-+-+-+-+-+-+-+
|                      Global Administrator                     |
+-+-+-+-+-+-+-+-+-+-+-+-+-+-+-+-+-+-+-+-+-+-+-+-+-+-+-+-+-+-+-+-+
|                      Local Data Part 1                        |
+-+-+-+-+-+-+-+-+-+-+-+-+-+-+-+-+-+-+-+-+-+-+-+-+-+-+-+-+-+-+-+-+
|                      Local Data Part 2                        |
+-+-+-+-+-+-+-+-+-+-+-+-+-+-+-+-+-+-+-+-+-+-+-+-+-+-+-+-+-+-+-+-+
```

Figure 2.32 – General value format of a Large Community.

The "**Global Administrator**" field is a 4-byte AS number (actually, RFC 8092 says it should be the number of a 4-byte AS), while the other two fields are left to the network administrator's discretion. Generally, the "**Global Administrator**" value matches the AS number that gives meaning to the Large Community.

Furthermore, RFC 8092 establishes a canonical representation of a Large Community value as:

Global Administrator:Local Data Part 1:Local Data Part 2

For instance, the administrator of AS 65536 (which is a 4-byte AS), can define and use the Large Community values 65536:1:2, 65536:0:1, 65536:0:0, etc., assigning a meaning to each of them.

RFC 8195 – *Use of BGP Large Communities*, June 2017, shows some examples of how Large Community values are assigned in information applications. In order to inform other ISPs about the geographic region from which an AS imports the BGP advertisements, an ISP can assign a Large Community value that contains information on the advertisements' geographical origins to each advertisement. For instance, AS 65536 could use the first field available (**Local part 1**) to define the format, and the second (**Local part 2**) to define a code related to the origin.

Two solutions described in RFC 8195 – which can be used at the same time – are based on standard ISO 3166-1 and UN M.49 codes. The first standard assigns a code to each nation worldwide. For instance, for Italy, the code is 380, for US 840, etc. By assigning value 1 to the "**Local part 1**" field, which, for instance, indicates the use of standard ISO 3166-1, AS 65536 could use the following diagram:

Large Community	Description
65536:1:380	Advertisements received from Italy
65536:1:036	Advertisements received from Australia
65536:1:840	Advertisements received from the United States
. . .	. . .

Standard UN M.49 defines the geographic regions. For example, Europe has code 150, which in turn is divided in 4 sub-areas: Eastern Europe-code 151, Northern Europe-code 154, Western Europe-code 155, Southern Europe-code 039. Here too, by assigning value 2 to the "**Local part 1**" field, which, for instance, indicates the use of standard UN M.49, AS 65536 could use the following diagram:

Large Community	Description
65536:2:2	Advertisements received from Africa
65536:2:9	Advertisements received from Oceania
65536:2:150	Advertisements received from Europe
. . .	. . .

As one last example of information application of a Large Community, AS 65536 could use the following diagram to define the relationship with the ISP that sends it the advertisements:

Large Community	Description
65536:3:1	Advertisements locally originated
65536:3:2	Advertisements received from a Customer
65536:3:3	Advertisements received from a peering ISP
65536:3:4	Advertisements received from a transit ISP

Obviously, those Large Community values can be combined with one another. For example, an advertisement can have the two Large Community values: 65536:1:380+65536:3:3 associated with it, to indicate that it has been received by an ISP located in Italy, with which a peering relationship has been established.

Just to clarify the importance of defining the geographical origin of an advertisement, let's consider the scenario in Figure 2.33 below.

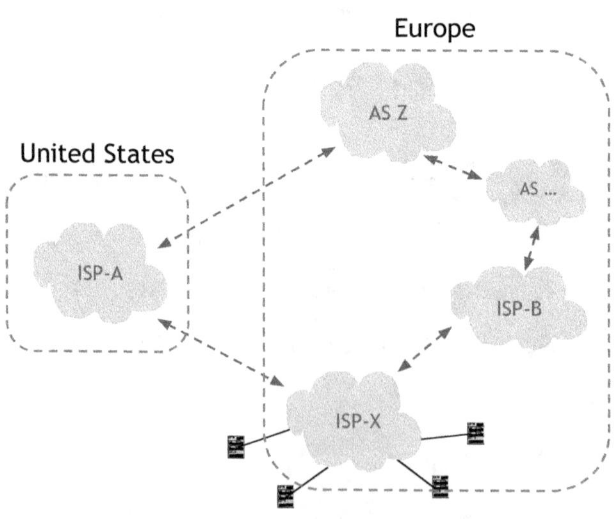

Figure 2.33 – Example of a Large Community use.

If ISP-X received an advertisement of the same IP prefix from ISP-A and ISP-B, then it would be best to make the traffic transit through the geographically closer AS (optimal routing). For instance, assuming that ISP-X and ISP-B are both in Europe and ISP-A is in the US, it could happen that the prefix of AS Z "closer" to ISP-A than to ISP-B, according to the AS_PATH, but located in Europe (as shown in the figure), is reached through ISP-A, which is geographically farthest, rather than through ISP-B, which is geographically closer, thus entailing a greater delay in IP packet delivery. Unfortunately, in BGP advertisements, the concept of geographical proximity does not exist; therefore, in order to solve the optimal routing issue, we need to adopt a few tricks. A very simple idea is for the Upstream Providers – ISP-A and ISP-B in the figure – to associate Large Community values to BGP advertisements, based on their geographical location.

For instance, let's assume that ISP-A and ISP-B associate Large Community values AS_ISP-A:2:150 and AS_ISP-B:2:150 with the prefix advertisements originating from ASes located in Europe, and that these values are propagated together with the advertisements toward ISP-X. In order for the traffic originated in ISP-X to reach the AS prefixes located in Europe through ISP-B, it is sufficient to apply the following policy to ISP-X's router:

- assign the Local Preference=200 value to all the advertisements coming from ISP-B and containing the Large Community value AS_ISP-B:2:150;

- assign the default Local Preference=100 value to all the advertisements coming from ISP-A and containing the Large Community value AS_ISP-B:2:150.

With this policy, every router of ISP-X will reach the local prefixes of European ASes through ISP-B, due to the highest Local Preference value.

NOTE: Actually, in this specific example, we could also use standard Community or Extended Community values, albeit with less flexibility.

2.4.7 MULTI_EXIT_DISC (MED) attribute

MED is an Optional Non Transitive attribute with Attribute Type Code=4. It specifies a metric that can be used in the selection process, which somehow resembles the IGP metrics, since, in choosing the best path, BGP uses the following rule: *among all advertisements of the same prefix coming from the same AS, the one with the lowest MED value associated with it is preferred.*
It is important to note that the MED can be compared if and only if the advertisements come from the same AS. Actually, this is the default rule, which can be varied on a configuration basis.
The MED value length is 4 bytes. It is typically used to define inbound routing policies, to force the traffic's entry point in an AS. This metric is weaker than LOCAL_PREF, and is considered later in the BGP selection process (see Paragraph 2.5).
Generally, the MED value is assigned on a configuration basis by BGP Speakers that send eBGP advertisements, even though it can also be assigned for advertisements received from the outside and propagated within the same AS. Once the MED value is assigned, it is propagated only within the AS receiving the advertisement, and is removed if the advertisement is propagated to other ASes. When an AS receives an advertisement without a MED attribute, according to RFC 4271, it automatically propagates that within its own AS, by assigning a value of MED=0.

Figure 2.34 below summarizes the MED attribute default treatment, and how it can be assigned. Considering the eBGP advertisement of network 192.0.2/24 sent by AS 64501 to AS 64502, this is propagated within AS 64502 with the MED value received (=200), assigned to the advertisement by router RA of AS 64501 through suitable configuration. When router RC of AS 64502 propagates the advertisement toward an eBGP session (toward AS 64503 in the Figure), it eliminates the MED attribute by default, unless there is a configuration that allows adding it with a certain value. When router RD of AS 64503 internally propagates the advertisement of prefix 192.0.2/24, the MED attribute is updated to the default value of 0.

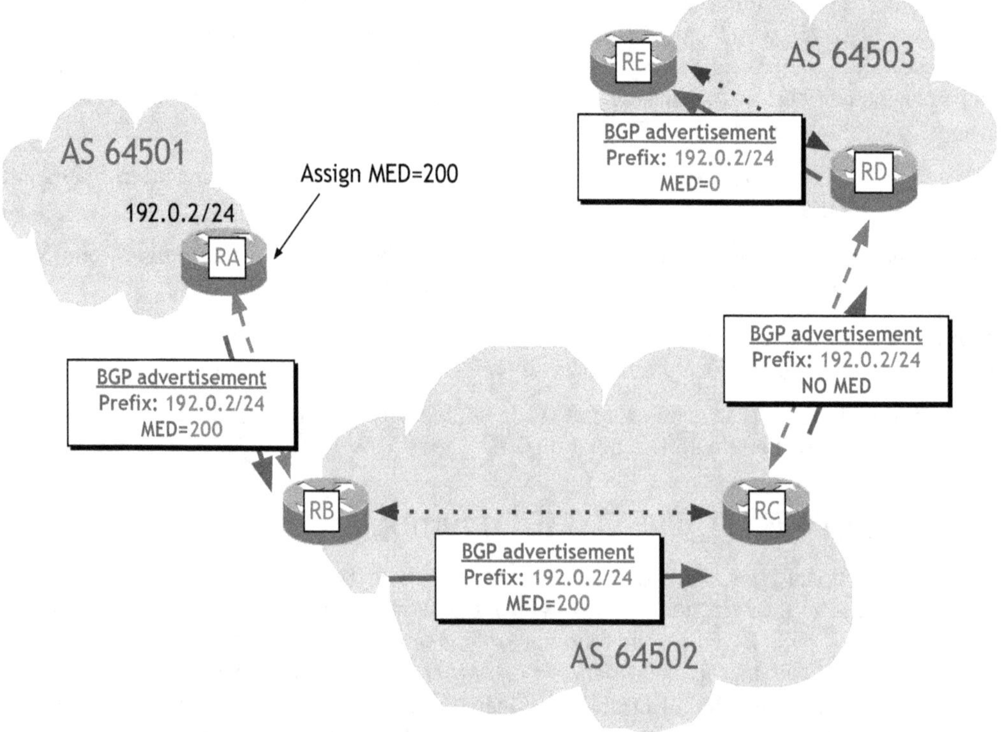

Figure 2.34 – Example of MED attribute propagation.

2.4.8 Other attributes

The missing attributes will be treated in the following paragraphs, or in the Appendix:

- MP_REACH_NLRI and MP_UNREACH_NLRI: used by Multiprotocol BGP (see Paragraph 2.6).

- CLUSTER_LIST and ORIGINATOR_ID: used by Route Reflectors (see Chapter 8).

- AS4_PATH and AS4_AGGREGATOR: used for compatibility purposes between 2-byte ASes and 4-byte ASes (see Appendix A.1).

- AIGP: used to create optimal inter-AS paths (see Section 7.4.2).

2.5 BGP SELECTION PROCESS

Every BGP Speaker has an internal selection process to determine the best path to reach each prefix within the BGP table. Remember that only the best paths are propagated to the other BGP Neighbors (downstream of any outbound filtering policies). In addition, the best paths are candidates (be careful, candidates only!) to be added to the RIB. Generally speaking, a best path may not be added to the RIB, due to other existing paths toward the prefix that the router might have learned from other (static/dynamic) routing protocols with a greater degree of preference.

The selection process is based on many factors (metrics, attributes, etc.), and in the end it generates only one best path, even though major manufacturers' implementation offer the option to install more than one best path in the RIB (BGP multipath), provided that the protocol's degree of preference allows it.

Despite this being the most important aspect of BGP, strangely enough the original standard version (RFC 1771) did not provide any accurate information on the selection process; it only supplied the tools to define it. On the other hand, RFC 4271 gave an accurate definition of it. Nevertheless, device manufacturers took "some freedom" and started implementing (or rather, expanding) the selection process in their own ways. In any case, all the processes we reviewed here comply with the sequence of decisions specified by RFC 4271.

Before presenting the sequence of decisions defined by RFC 4271, it is important to highlight that only valid advertisements can take part in the selection process. Usually, the different manufacturers' implementations define an advertisement invalid if:

- the IP address contained in the NEXT_HOP attribute cannot be reached;

- it has been rejected by filtering policies on inbound advertisements;

- it has been suppressed by the Route Flap Damping mechanism (see Paragraph 8.8).

In addition, there is a very important security aspect, defined in the Resource Public Key Infrastructure (RPKI) architecture, described in detail in Chapter 10. BGP advertisement validation through the RPKI modifies the BGP selection process: when it is enabled, all advertisements with an Invalid validation status are not used (or at least shouldn't be used) in the BGP selection process. Therefore, an Invalid advertisement can never get into the RIB, which, ultimately, is the main purpose of the RPKI architecture. In any case, even Invalid advertisements can participate in the BGP selection process, by using special configuration commands, that we will see later on.

2.5.1 Decision process

The selection process described by RFC 4271 is based on subsequent eliminations, starting from set **V** of valid advertisements of the same prefix, and continuing with a precise sequential logic. The (ordered) sequence of decisions is the following (Note: notation $V^{(x)}$ indicates the set of remaining advertisements, after step "**x**"):

1. Remove from set **V** the advertisements with the lowest Local Preference value, in other words, keep only those advertisements with Local Preference value identical to the highest value.

2. Remove from set $V^{(1)}$ the advertisements with the longest AS_PATH attribute value, in other words, choose those advertisements with the minimum number of elements in the AS_PATH attribute.

3. Remove from set $V^{(2)}$ the advertisements with the highest ORIGIN attribute value, in other words, choose those advertisements with the minimum ORIGIN attribute value (0=IGP; 1=EGP; 2=INCOMPLETE).

4. Remove from set $V^{(3)}$ the advertisements with the highest MED attribute value, in other words, choose those advertisements with the minimum MED value. MED can be compared if and only if the advertisements come from the same AS. Furthermore, any advertisement with no MED assigned is to be regarded as MED=0.

NOTE: Actually, current BGP implementations require the entire AS_PATH to match in order to compare the MED values, even though the main manufacturers provide commands to relax this restriction.

5. If at least one advertisement has been received by an eBGP Neighbor, remove from set $V^{(4)}$ any iBGP advertisements, in other words, choose advertisements coming from eBGP sessions, instead of those coming from iBGP ones. Otherwise, skip to the next step. The reason for this point is intuitively easy: if there is a path that can route traffic toward the outside, that path should be preferred, rather than using paths that would consume internal resources to reach a destination outside the AS. This routing mode is curiously known as hot potato routing. We will let the reader unfold this clear analogy.

NOTE: Sometimes, in practical applications, due to service quality reasons, it may be convenient to keep the traffic in one's network as much as possible, and then deliver it to another AS. This routing mode is called cold potato routing, because, in a way, it is the opposite of hot potato routing.

6. Remove from set $V^{(5)}$ the advertisements with the highest IGP cost value toward the BGP Next-Hop, in other words, choose those advertisements with the "closest" Next-Hop, according to the IGP cost resulting from the RIB IP. This too is fairly intuitive: try to consume as little internal resources as possible to route the traffic toward destinations outside the AS.

7. Remove from set $V^{(6)}$ the advertisements with the highest BGP Identifier value, in other words, choose those advertisements generated by the BGP Neighbor with the lowest BGP Identifier.

8. Remove from set $V^{(7)}$ the advertisements with the highest BGP Neighbor Address value, in other words, choose the advertisement coming from the BGP Neighbor with the lowest Neighbor Address.

NOTE 1: The BGP Neighbor Address is the IP address used by the BGP Neighbor for TCP connection.

NOTE 2: IP addresses are compared by considering the actual numerical value of the address, converted from a binary 32-bit number into a decimal number. For instance, IP address 192.0.2.1 corresponds to the 32-bit sequence "11000000 00000000 00000010 00000001", which, converted into a decimal number, is equal to 33,221,225,985.

The set $V^{(8)}$ obtained from this procedure contains one and only one element, while this is not necessarily true for set $V^{(7)}$ (see example 3 in Section 2.5.4).

Figure 2.35 summarizes the standard decision sequence we just described, which leads to choosing the final best path.

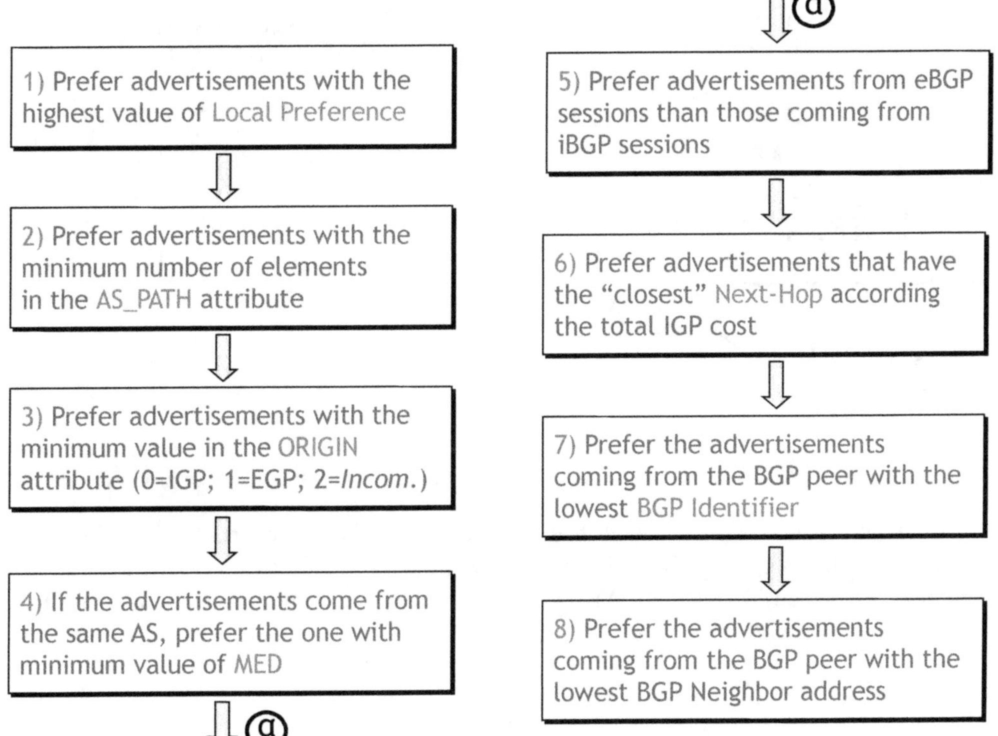

Figure 2.35 – The standard BGP best path selection process.

In Paragraph 7.1, we will see how the selection process is actually implemented by Cisco and Juniper routers. Both implementations follow the pattern above, and expand it with other steps and rules. Then, the selection process is modified if Route Reflectors are used. We will go over them when the time comes (see Paragraph 8.3).

2.5.2 Example 1

Let's consider the scenario described in Figure 2.36, where an ISP (AS 64510) (assumingly a Tier-2 ISP), has two eBGP sessions with two Tier-1 Upstream Providers, with AS 64501 and 64502 respectively.
AS 64510 receives two advertisements of IP prefix 192.0.2/24 from the two ASes 64501 and 64502. Let's assume that a Local Preference value of 200 is assigned to the advertisement received by AS 64501, while the Local Preference value of the advertisement received by AS 64502 is left as per default, which we'll assume to be 100.
With this definition of Local Preference value in mind, the BGP selection process chooses as best path, for both routers RA and RB, the path transiting on Upstream Provider 1 (Note: for router RB, the path goes through RA and then toward Upstream Provider 1). And this applies even if the length of the AS_PATH of the advertisement coming from Upstream Provider 1 is greater than that of the advertisement coming from Upstream Provider 2, because the BGP selection process analyzes the Local Preference value first, and then the AS_PATH length.

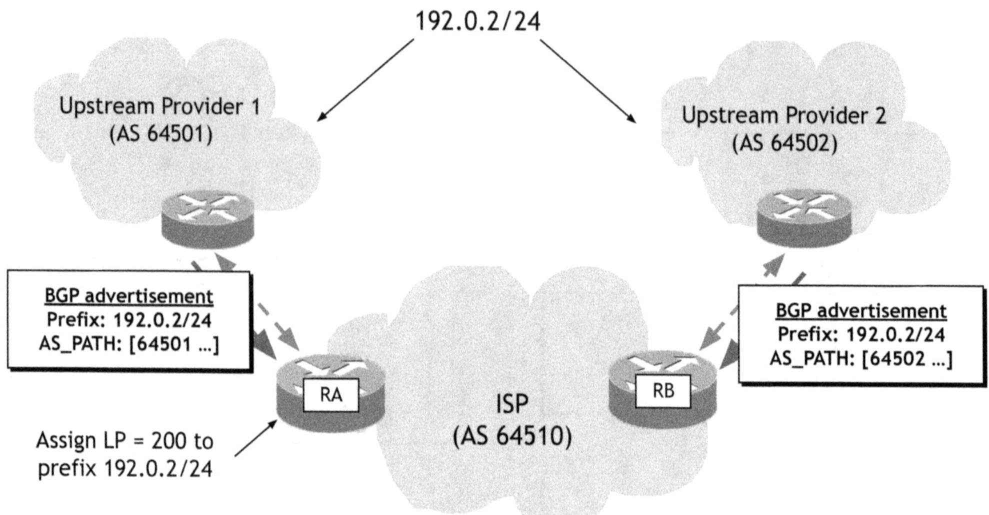

Figure 2.36 – Example of LOCAL_PREF attribute use in the BGP selection process.

If the default Local Preference value had been assigned to both advertisements of prefix IP 192.0.2/24, the first step of the selection process would not be sufficient to choose the best path, therefore it would consider the AS_PATH length, and subsequently all the other points, according to the sequence described in Section 2.5.1

2.5.3 Example 2

Let's consider the scenario described in Figure 2.37, where an ISP (AS 64502) (assumingly a Tier-3 ISP), has two eBGP sessions toward the same Tier-2 Upstream Provider, with AS 64501. The two sessions end on routers RC and RD.

AS 64502 advertises its prefix 192.0.2/24 on both eBGP sessions; the one ending on RC, associates a MED value of 100 with the advertisement, while the other a MED value of 200. Without loss of generality, let's assume that the advertisement on session RB↔RD is sent as first. The BGP selection process on RD chooses it as the best path, since it is the only advertisement. Then, it propagates that internally on the iBGP sessions, until the advertisement also reaches RC, which will also choose it as the best path, being the only advertisement in this case too. In this iBGP advertisement, the MED value remains the same, equal to 200.

Then, RC will also receive the advertisement of the same IP prefix from RA. Now, RC will apply the selection process, since it has two advertisements from the same IP prefix – the one coming from RD and the one coming from RA. Assuming that both RC and RD do not apply any configuration to associate a Local Preference value other than the default one, the first step of the selection process does not allow choosing the best path. And not even the second one, since the AS_PATHs of both advertisements match, and are equal to [64502]. The third step compares the ORIGIN attribute values; let's assume that they are both equal to 0 (=IGP). Therefore, we continue with the next step, which is based on MED values comparison. MED values can be compared because the AS_PATH of both advertisements is identical. So the best path is the advertisement with the lowest MED value, i.e. the one coming from RA. What happens now lies outside the scope of the selection process. We will include it for the sake of completion. Router RC propagates the new best path on its iBGP sessions. Router RD receives the advertisement of its new best path (with Next-Hop RC), installs it in its RIB (provided that the same prefix has not been advertised by another protocol with better degree of preference), and then sends an UPDATE message to withdraw the best path previously sent. Please note that RD will not propagate the advertisement received from RC within AS 64501, due to the Split Horizon rule.

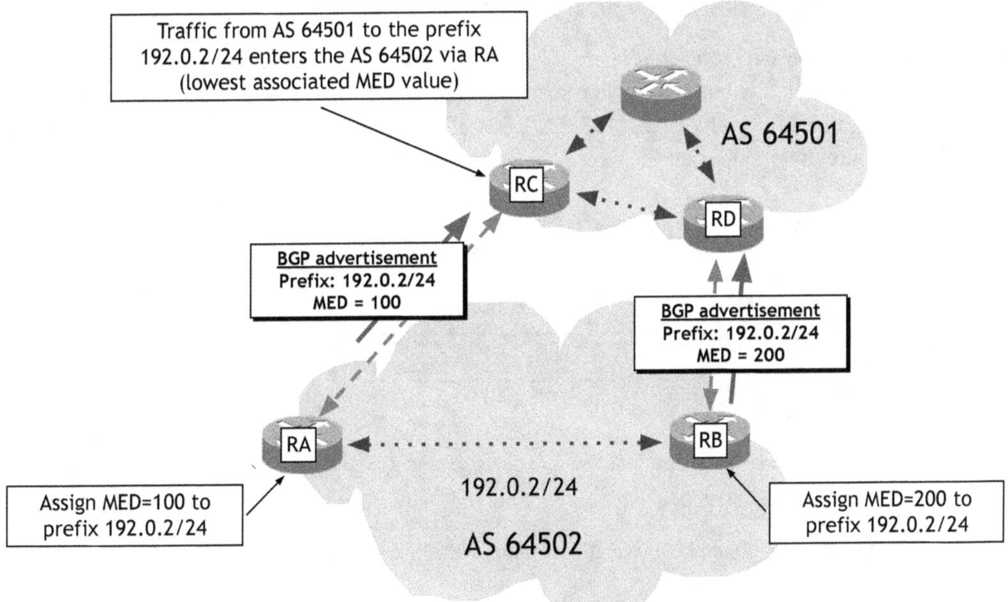

Figure 2.37 – Example of MED attribute use in the BGP selection process.

The example shown highlights an "unwritten" aspect of BGP: *an AS cannot affect the routing policies of another AS, unless the latter allows it.* On closer inspection, this is exactly what happens in the example in Figure 2.37, where AS 64502 imposes to AS64501 the traffic exit point from its own network (i.e. for the traffic to exit from router RC).

BGP provides a stronger metric to decide, regardless of the MED values linked to inbound advertisements, the traffic exit point from one's own AS: Local Preference. This explains why, in the BGP selection process, Local Preference is a stronger metric than the MED, meaning that it is assessed before the MED, along the decision-making sequence.

For instance, if router RD had assigned a Local Preference value of 200 to the advertisement coming from RB, while RC had left it as default (e.g.100), traffic would have exited from AS 64501 through router RD, rather than router RC. And this regardless of the MED value of the inbound advertisements.

2.5.4 Example 3

Let's consider the scenario described in Figure 2.38, where two ISPs (AS 64501 and AS 64502) have a simple peering relationship, and, for redundancy reason, there is a double physical connection between them. In order to use BGP's KEEPALIVE messages to detect if the connections are working, two eBGP sessions are established, one for each connection. The two sessions use as Neighbor Address:

- session 1: 192.0.2.1 (R1 side) – 192.0.2.0 (R2 side);

- session 2: 192.0.2.3 (R1 side) – 192.0.2.2 (R2 side).

Let's assume that the two routers R1 and R2 do not apply any policy allowing them to modify the values of the BGP attributes, and therefore that they use default values, and that router R2 of AS 64502 advertises its prefix 203.0.113/24. Let's also assume that the values contained in the ORIGIN attribute match and that they are equal to 0 (=IGP).

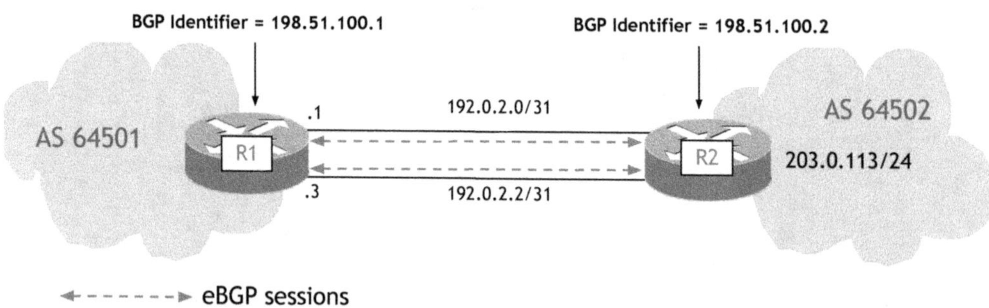

Figure 2.38 – Example of Neighbor Address attribute use in the selection process.

The BGP process active on R1 will receive two advertisements of the prefix 203.0.113/24, one for each BGP session. Therefore, it must then activate the selection process to determine the best path. Let's summarize the entire decision-making sequence to see which one between the two advertisements will be selected as the best path:

1. the Local Preference values are identical, and equal to the default value (generally 100);

2. the AS_PATH length is identical, equal to 1 (AS_PATH=[64502]);

3. The value contained in the ORIGIN attribute is identical, and equal to 0 (=IGP);

4. the MED value is not present in the advertisements, so it cannot be compared;

5. they are both eBGP advertisements;

6. step 6 cannot be applied, since both advertisements are eBGP.

Now, we can activate (through a suitable configuration) a multipath BGP, and therefore add prefix 203.0.113/24 with two Next-Hops in the RIB: 192.0.2.0 and 192.0.2.2. In any case, even by applying BGP multipath, the BGP process will continue the selection, until a single best path is elected.

7. the BGP Identifiers are identical, and equal to 198.51.100.2;

8. the Neighbor Addresses are (inevitably) different, and the lower one is 192.0.2.0.

In conclusion, since the advertisement with the lowest Neighbor Address is selected as the best path, the advertisement received on Session 1 becomes the best path.

2.6 MULTIPROTOCOL BGP

BGP (version 4) was standardized both in the initial version of RFC 1771, and in its revision, RFC 4271, to transport IPv4 routing information. The evolution of IP networks, and the introduction of new IPv6-based routing schemes, new layer 2 and layer 3 services – such as the L2VPN and L3VPN services, based on the BGP/MPLS model – stimulated the expansion of BGP for transporting routing information other than IPv4. This extension, known as Multiprotocol BGP (and hereinafter shortened as MP-BGP), was defined in RFC 4760 – *Multiprotocol Extensions for BGP-4*, January 2007, which updated the former RFC 2858.

The different types of routing data transmitted via BGP are called address-families, and each one is identified by a pair of numerical codes. Support of a specific address-family is negotiated when the BGP session is established.

An important aspect we should highlight is that, in the multiprotocol extension, BGP's structure (sessions, messages, attributes, selection process, etc.) remains the same, and only the type of routing information (NLRI) advertised changes. And also the fact that the BGP Identifier is a 32-bit value doesn't change.

NOTE: Current BGP implementations entail the possibility of transporting routing information (NLRI) related to different protocols on the same BGP session. For instance, two BGP Neighbors that use the same BGP session, can negotiate the option of exchanging routing information related to IPv4 and IPv6 prefixes, and also other kinds of NLRI, if needed. This is a pretty frequent scenario in practical applications.

2.6.1 Address-family support negotiation

MP-BGP operation is negotiated by two BGP Neighbors through the OPEN message, using the BGP Capability "Multiprotocol Extensions", with Capability Code=1, Capability Length=4 and Capability Value, comprising the three fields (total length: 4 bytes) shown in Figure 2.39 below.

```
0         7        15        23        31
+-------+-------+-------+-------+
|      AFI      | Res.  | SAFI  |
+-------+-------+-------+-------+
```

Figure 2.39 – Format of the Capability Value of the BGP Capability "Multiprotocol BGP" (RFC 4760).

The three fields have the following meaning:

- AFI (Address Family Identifier) (2 bytes): identifies the type of information (which isn't necessarily routing data!) that a BGP Speaker wants to propagate (NLRI). The most common AFI standard values, established by RFC 1700 – *ASSIGNED NUMBERS*, October 1994, are the following: IPv4→AFI=1, IPv6→AFI=2. Other values are used mainly in BGP/MPLS services, such as, for instance AFI=25, for L2VPN services.

- Reserved (1 byte): unspecified field. It is set to a value of 0x00.

- SAFI (Subsequent Address Family Identifier) (1 byte): provides more information on the address family specified in the AFI field. The most common SAFI standard values are the following: Unicast→SAFI=1 (RFC 4760), RPF Multicast→SAFI=2 (RFC 4760), MPLS

Labels →SAFI=4 (RFC 8277), BGP Flowspec→SAFI=133/134 (RFC 5575), VPN-IPv4/ VPN-IPv6 prefixes →SAFI=128 (RFC 4364 and 8277); the latter is used for unicast L3VPN services based on the BGP/MPLS model (see Chapter 11).

Among the most common examples, there are: AFI/SAFI=1/1 identifies unicast IPv4 prefixes, AFI/SAFI=2/1 identifies unicast IPv6 prefixes, AFI/SAFI=1/128 for VPN-IPv4 prefixes, AFI/SAFI=25/70 for L2VPN EVPN advertisements, etc. Below is the analysis obtained with wireshark of the portion of an OPEN message, which highlights the negotiation of the BGP Capability "Multiprotocol Extensions", related to the address-family identified by pair AFI/SAFI=2/1 (IPv6 unicast).

Border Gateway Protocol - OPEN Message
```
  Marker: ffffffffffffffffffffffffffffffff
  Length: 57
  Type: OPEN Message (1)
  Version: 4
  My AS: 64501
  Hold Time: 180
  BGP Identifier: 203.0.113.1
  Optional Parameters Length: 28
  Optional Parameters
    Optional Parameter: Capability
      Parameter Type: Capability (2)
      Parameter Length: 6
      Capability: Multiprotocol extensions capability
        Type: Multiprotocol extensions capability (1)
        Length: 4
        AFI: IPv6 (2)
        Reserved: 00
        SAFI: Unicast (1)
. . . < rest of the output omitted > . . .
```

2.6.2 MP_REACH_NLRI and MP_UNREACH_NLRI attributes

The MP-BGP extension is based on the observation that the only specific IPv4 data transported by BGP messages are the NEXT_HOP and AGGREGATOR attributes, which contain an IPv4 address, and the Withdrawn Routes and NLRI fields of UPDATE messages. Therefore, in order to expand BGP to transporting address families other than IPv4, the only two things to add are:

- the option of defining Withdrawn Routes and NLRI in the format specified by AFI/SAFI codes;

- the option of associating a Next-Hop with NLRI, in the format specified by AFI/SAFI codes.

RFC 4760 states that, in any case, every router needs to have a 32-bit BGP Identifier, which can be represented with an IPv4 address notation. The AGGREGATOR attribute can use this identifier, so it doesn't need any extension.

In order to ensure compatibility with standard BGP, and to streamline the introduction of multiprotocol functions in BGP, RFC 4760 introduced the two Optional Non Transitive MP_REACH_NLRI (Attribute Type=14) and MP_UNREACH_NLRI (Attribute Type=15) attributes, already mentioned in Section 2.4.8.

The MP_REACH_NLRI attribute is used to advertise a set of NLRI, with the Next-Hop information linked to it, while the MP_UNREACH_NLRI attribute is used to withdraw any previously advertised NLRI. Both attributes were classified as Optional Non Transitive, to allow BGP Speakers that don't support MP-BGP to ignore the two attributes and avoid transferring them to other BGP Neighbors. The MP_REACH_NLRI attribute format is shown in Figure 2.40 below. The meaning of the different fields is the following:

- **Address Family Identifier** (2 bytes): is the AFI code identifying the address family of which to propagate the routing information.

- **Subsequent AFI** (1 byte): is the SAFI code providing additional information on the address family of which to propagate the routing information.

- **Length of Next Hop Network Address** (1 byte): is the length of the following field, Network Address of Next Hop.

- **Network Address of Next Hop** (variable length): contains the BGP Next-Hop, generally an IPv4 or IPv6 address.

- **Network Layer Reachability Information** (NLRI): contains one or more NLRIs in the format specified by the AFI/SAFI codes.

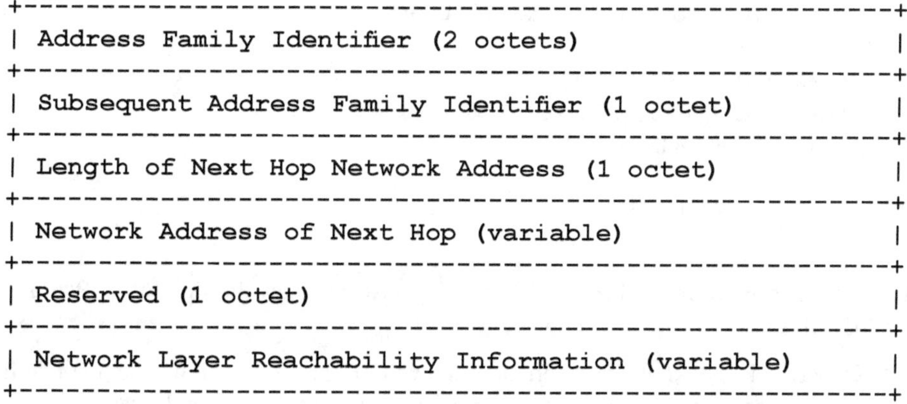

```
+-----------------------------------------------------------------+
| Address Family Identifier (2 octets)                            |
+-----------------------------------------------------------------+
| Subsequent Address Family Identifier (1 octet)                  |
+-----------------------------------------------------------------+
| Length of Next Hop Network Address (1 octet)                    |
+-----------------------------------------------------------------+
| Network Address of Next Hop (variable)                          |
+-----------------------------------------------------------------+
| Reserved (1 octet)                                              |
+-----------------------------------------------------------------+
| Network Layer Reachability Information (variable)               |
+-----------------------------------------------------------------+
```

Figure 2.40 – Format of the MP_REACH_NLRI attribute (RFC 4760).

An UPDATE message that includes the MP_REACH_NLRI attribute must also contain the ORIGIN and AS_PATH attributes, both on eBGP and iBGP sessions. Furthermore, RFC 4760 specifies that, if the message is sent on iBGP sessions, it must also include the LOCAL_PREF attribute. If the UPDATE message only contains NLRI in the MP_REACH_NLRI attribute, it shouldn't (for obvious reasons) include the NEXT_HOP attribute (see the wireshark analysis below); if it is included, the BGP Speakers receiving the UPDATE message will ignore it.

Below is the analysis, obtained with wireshark, of the portion of an UPDATE message containing the MP_REACH_NLRI attribute, used to advertise IPv6 prefix 2001:db8::4/128 on an eBGP session supporting the unicast IPv6 address-family (AFI/SAFI=2/1). Notice that the NEXT_HOP attribute is not included (although it is part of the well-known mandatory attributes), because the BGP Next-Hop to use is included in the field **Network Address of Next Hop** (=2001:db8:1:11::2).

Border Gateway Protocol - UPDATE Message

Marker: ffffffffffffffffffffffffffffffff
Length: 100
Type: UPDATE Message (2)
Withdrawn Routes Length: 0
Total Path Attribute Length: 77
Path attributes
Path Attribute - MP_REACH_NLRI
    Flags: 0x80, Optional, Non-transitive, Complete
    Type Code: MP_REACH_NLRI (14)
    Length: 54
    Address family identifier (AFI): IPv6 (2)
    Subsequent address family identifier (SAFI): Unicast (1)
  Next hop network address (32 bytes)
    Next Hop: 2001:db8:1:11::2
    Next Hop: fe80::5205:ff:fe13:2
  Number of Subnetwork points of attachment (SNPA): 0
  Network layer reachability information (17 bytes)
    2001:db8::4/128
      MP Reach NLRI prefix length: 128
      MP Reach NLRI IPv6 prefix: 2001:db8::4
Path Attribute - ORIGIN: IGP
. . .
Path Attribute - AS_PATH: 64503
. . .

NOTE: The field **Network Address of Next Hop** also includes the link-local IPv6 address fe80::5205:ff:fe13:2.

The MP_UNREACH_NLRI attribute format is shown in Figure 2.41 below. The first two fields, Address Family Identifier and Subsequent Address Family Identifier, have the same meaning we saw earlier for the MP_REACH_NLRI attribute, while the Withdrawn Routes field contains one or more NLRIs to be withdrawn, in the format specified by the AFI/SAFI codes.

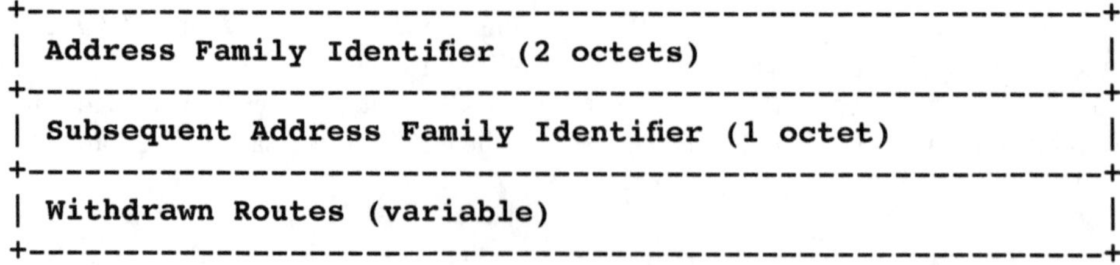

```
+-----------------------------------------------------------------+
| Address Family Identifier (2 octets)                            |
+-----------------------------------------------------------------+
| Subsequent Address Family Identifier (1 octet)                  |
+-----------------------------------------------------------------+
| Withdrawn Routes (variable)                                     |
+-----------------------------------------------------------------+
```

Figure 2.41 – Format of the MP_UNREACH_NLRI attribute (RFC 4760).

Below is the analysis, obtained with wireshark, of the portion of an UPDATE message containing the MP_UNREACH_NLRI attribute, for the unicast IPv6 address-family (AFI/SAFI=2/1).

Border Gateway Protocol - UPDATE Message

Marker: ffffffffffffffffffffffffffffffff
Length: 29
Type: UPDATE Message (2)
Withdrawn Routes Length: 0
Total Path Attribute Length: 6
Path attributes
  Path Attribute - MP_UNREACH_NLRI
    Flags: 0x80, Optional, Non-transitive, Complete
    Type Code: MP_UNREACH_NLRI (15)
    Length: 3
    Address family identifier (AFI): IPv6 (2)
    Subsequent address family identifier (SAFI): Unicast (1)
    Withdrawn routes (0 bytes)

NOTE: Actually, this particular UPDATE message, known as End-of-RIB marker, does not withdraw any NLRI previously advertised (**Withdrawn Routes Length: 0**), but rather it is used by a BGP Speaker to indicate to one of its BGP Neighbors that it is done sending its routing information (for further details, see Appendix A.5).

2.6.3 A MP-BGP application: BGP for IPv6

One of the most important MP-BGP applications is transporting IPv6 routing information. The AFI code characterizing IPv6 is AFI=2, while the SAFI code depends on the type of information transported (e.g., for unicast IPV6 prefixes, SAFI=1, for unicast IPv6 prefixes with an MPLS label associated to them, SAFI=4, for VPN-IPv6 prefixes used in the VPN IPv6 BGP/MPLS service, SAFI=128, etc.).

The peculiar MP-BGP aspects concerning IPv6 routing information transport are detailed in RFC 2545 – *Use of BGP-4 Multiprotocol Extensions for IPv6 Inter-Domain Routing*, March 1999. As you know, IPv6 uses three address types: link-local, unique local and global. BGP does not differentiate if an address is used for private purposes or globally, therefore in the IPv6 extension it only considers whether the address is link-local or non link-local.

Distinguishing between link-local and non link-local addresses is important, because some IPv6 routing protocols (e.g. RIPng, OSPFv3) use link-local addresses as Next-Hop. However, the use of link-local addresses in BGP should be avoided, because, while they might be legitimate in eBGP sessions between directly connected routers, they cannot be used to establish BGP sessions between remote routers, since link-local addresses are non-routable, and therefore a prefix with a link-local remote Next-Hop cannot be entered in the RIB. For these reasons, RFC 2545 recommends including, if the IPv6 addresses used for the BGP session are on the same subnet (e.g., eBGP sessions between directly connected routers), two Next-Hops, the non link-local address used to activate the BGP session, and the link-local address of the interface on the network segment.

Vice versa, when the IPv6 addresses used in the BGP session do not belong to the same subnet (e.g., multihop BGP sessions and iBGP sessions between remote routers), RFC 2545 recommends to advertise only one Next-Hop, according to standard BGP rules. Figure 2.42 summarizes the above in one example.

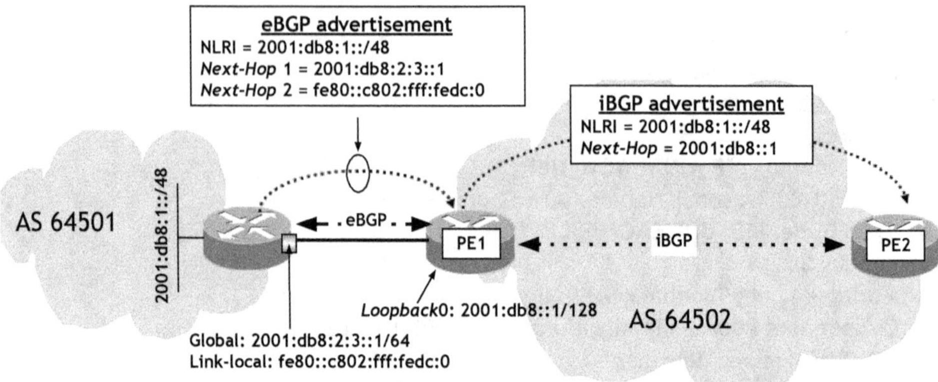

Figure 2.42 – Managing the Next-Hop in BGP for IPv6.

In the figure, the eBGP session is established using the global addresses of the physical interfaces, while the iBGP session is established by using the global addresses of two Loopback interfaces. The Next-Hop is managed according to standard BGP session rules, and so it remains unchanged on the iBGP session. As we saw earlier, in Section 2.4.3, it is always possible to change the Next-Hop default management, through a suitable configuration command, in order to redefine it according to the value of the address used for the iBGP session (see Section 3.1.4).

The Next-Hops are transported in the "Network Address of Next Hop" field of the MP_REACH_NLRI attribute. Generally, the NEXT_HOP attribute (Attribute Type Code=3) is not sent. One example is shown in the wireshark analysis of the portion of an UPDATE message containing the MP_REACH_NLRI, attribute, we saw earlier, in Section 2.6.2.

SUMMARY

In this chapter, we presented the basic BGP theory, and, in particular, BGP session concepts and the two session types – eBGP and iBGP – protocol messages, BGP attributes, and lastly the standard selection process logic. We also mentioned the iBGP/IGP synchronization issue, which is now an outdated topic. To make the discussion lighter, we chose not to elaborate on the protocol state machine (which is, in any case, described in Appendix A.3), and we only talked about the states crossed during BGP session establishment. Lastly, a very important topic we covered is the multiprotocol BGP extension, through which BGP's scope of use can be expanded to transport routing information other than IPv4, and sometimes also to transport non-routing information.

Worth remembering:

1. The BGP Session concept and its two types, eBGP and iBGP. In particular, you should keep in mind the best practices when using IP addresses as endpoints of BGP sessions: physical interface addresses, for sessions between directly connected routers (layer 2), and Loopback interfaces, for sessions between non-directly-connected routers.

2. Default rules to establish eBGP and iBGP sessions.

3. Advertisement propagation rules on eBGP and iBGP sessions, and the Split Horizon rule in particular.

4. BGP messages and their use.

5. BGP attributes, their classification and use. Moreover, you should remember the most important attributes that affect the best path selection (e.g. Local preference, AS_PATH, MED, etc.).

6. The sequence of decisions leading to the choice of a best path, that is, the standard selection process.

7. The multiprotocol BGP extension.

3 – FROM THEORY TO PRACTICE ...

After seeing the basic theory that regulates BGP's operation, in this chapter we will see how this can be implemented in practice in two of the most important technologies used in ISP networks: Cisco and Juniper.

The reasons why we chose to describe BGP's operation for those technologies are basically two:

1. Cisco and Juniper were the first to implement BGP. All the most recent BGP innovations were mostly guided by Cisco and Juniper engineers, who had a driving role in their development.

2. Cisco and Juniper are by far the leaders in the router market for ISP networks, where BGP finds its natural usage environment.

In any case, we firmly believe that, once you've understood the "theory", it will be very easy to switch from one technology to the other, at least when it comes to basic configurations (probably less so for advanced configurations, such as policy application).

This chapter does not try to cover the whole set of commands that Cisco and Juniper routers made available for BGP implementation purposes; apart from basic commands, we will only cover the most important ones for practical purposes (which, in any case, are those used in the majority of on-field implementations). For further commands and detail, we invite you to read the ample official documentation made available by the two manufacturers.

To make the discussion as easy as possible, from now on, we will refer to the test network shown in Figure 3.1 below, where we simulated a typical scenario in practical applications. A Tier-2 ISP, with AS number 64501, has, on one side, two customers it provides basic Internet access services to, and, on the other side, two eBGP sessions with two Upstream Providers, with (4-byte) AS numbers 65541 and 65542, respectively. The two customers, exchanging IPv4 routing information with the Tier-2 ISP through eBGP sessions, have AS number 65101 assigned to them, which, as you may remember, is part of the private (16-bit) AS numbers.

NOTE: The practice of assigning the same private AS number to the customers of an ISP is recommended by RFC 2270 – *Using a Dedicated AS for Sites Homed to a Single Provider*, January 1998.

Customer-side eBGP sessions are established through point-to-point links. On the Upstream Provider side, physical connections are always point-to-point, made on the passive infrastructure (Meet-Me-Room) of an IXP, using PNIs, while eBGP sessions are established between two Internet Gateways (GTW-1 and GTW-2) and the two routers UP-1 and UP-2 of the two Upstream Providers, using the IP addresses of the point-to-point physical links.

The Tier-2 ISP network comprises Cisco routers adopting the IOS XR operating system (typical of Cisco platforms for large networks) and Juniper routers adopting the JUNOS operating system. In Cisco's case, we will also specify the configuration for routers adopting the IOS XE operating system, generally used in lower-level platforms.

The network thus conceived also allows showing how Cisco and Juniper BGP implementations interact correctly – as it should be, since BGP is a standard protocol.

The interfaces of Cisco routers with IOS XR operating system (PE1 and GTW-1) belong to the GigabitEthernet0/0/0/X type, while the interfaces of Juniper routers belong to the ge-0/0/X type.

The interfaces of router CE1, adopting the IOS XE operating system, belong to the GigabitEthernetX type. Figure 3.1 shows the values of X.
The network numbering plan is the following:

Loopback0 interfaces:

- PE1=192.168.0.11/32.
- PE2=192.168.0.12/32.
- GTW-1=192.168.1.11/32.
- GTW-2=192.168.1.12/32.
- CE1=10.1.99.11/32.
- CE2=10.1.99.12/32.

CE-PE links:

- CE1↔PE1=10.1.11.0/30 (.1 PE side); CE1↔PE2=10.1.12.4/30 (.5 PE side).
- CE2↔PE1=10.1.11.4/30 (.5 PE side); CE2↔PE2=10.1.12.0/30 (.1 PE side).

GTW-UP links:

- GTW-1↔UP-1=172.20.1.0/31 (.0 GTW-1 side).
- GTW-2↔UP-2=172.20.2.0/31 (.0 GTW-2 side).

The IS-IS protocol was configured on the Tier-2 ISP network, on a single area (area 49.0001), and on a single Level 2, to keep things simple.

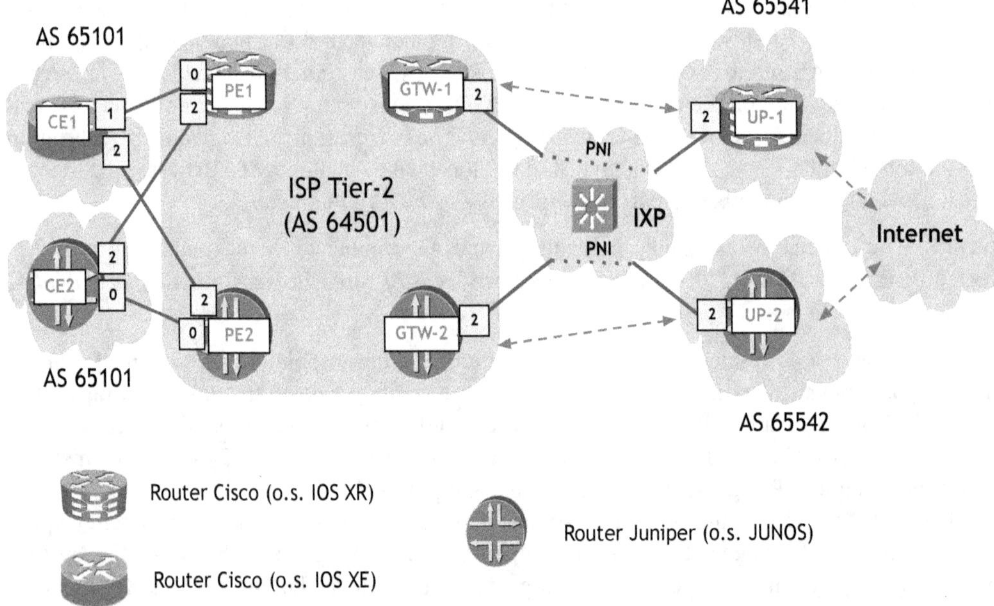

Figure 3.1 –Test network for the implementation of BGP.

In this chapter, we will focus on BGP's basic configurations, and on some of its functions useful in practical applications, such as configuration scalability.

NOTE 1: In order to understand it, this chapter requires a background knowledge of Cisco and Juniper router configurations, Cisco IOS XE/XR and Juniper JUNOS Operating Systems, and basic troubleshooting commands.

NOTE 2: Hereafter, we will sometimes be obliged to use IP prefixes other than those reserved to documentation, due to the shortage of prefixes specified by RFC 5737 – *IPv4 Address Blocks Reserved for Documentation*, January 2010.

3.1 ESTABLISHING A BGP SESSION

Establishing a BGP session is fairly easy, and requires three essential actions:

1. defining the AS the router belongs to;

2. defining the BGP Identifier (hereinafter shortened to BGP-ID);

3. defining the IP address and AS number of the BGP Neighbor.

Then, as always, there is a wealth of configuration commands for protocol tuning and function enabling (timers, filters, attribute handling, security policies, etc.), which we will see in detail later.

3.1.1 Basic configurations

When configuring a BGP session, whether iBGP or eBGP, we first need to specify the AS of the router we are configuring. On this matter, Cisco and Juniper strategies differ.
In Cisco platforms, the same command is adopted for all IOS versions (IOS XE, IOS XR and NX-OS). Here, we show the command for the IOS XE and IOS XR versions, but it is the same also for the other versions.

IOS XE:
router(config)# **router bgp** *AS-number*

IOS XR:
RP/0/RP0/CPU0:router(config)# **router bgp** *AS-number*

In JUNOS, the AS number is configured under the hierarchy **[routing-options]**:

[edit routing-options]
autonomous-system *AS-number*;

The AS-number value identifies the AS the router belongs to. Remember that the AS number is propagated with the OPEN message in the My Autonomous System field, and it must be the same for all the routers within an AS.
For 16-bit ASes, the value should be within the interval [1; 65,534], with numbers from 64,512 to 65,534 reserved for private use.

NOTE: RFC 7300 – *Reservation of Last Autonomous System (AS) Numbers*, July 2014, reserves the numbers at the end of the 16-bit and 32-bit AS blocks – 65535 and 4294967295 respectively – as being "Last Autonomous System Numbers". The reason that 65535 is reserved is because it is used by a bunch of reserved BGP communities (see for instance the well-known communities defined in Section 2.4.6).

For 32-bit ASes, there are two possible representations: the standard decimal representation, or the asdot+ representation (see Appendix A.1), both supported by Cisco and Juniper platforms.

NOTE: In a router engine, it is not possible to activate more than one BGP process with different ASes. For instance, when erroneously attempting to enter the "**router bgp ...**" command into a Cisco platform, with an AS number different than the one previously used in an active BGP process, the following error message is displayed: "**BGP is already running; AS is ...**". On the other hand, in Juniper platforms, it is impossible to add another AS number. Any attempt at this will overwrite the existing one.

In order for the BGP process to be activated, the router must be able to elect a BGP-ID, which, as mentioned earlier, is propagated through the OPEN message in the BGP Identifier field.

NOTE: Despite RFC 4271 stating that the identifier is an IP address assigned to one of the interfaces of the BGP Speaker, Cisco and Juniper routers (as well as other implementations) allow setting any other IP address. In any case, the BGP process interprets it as a 32-bit value. The only limit to observe, to avoid interaction issues between routers using different operating systems – as mentioned earlier, in Section 2.3.1 – is that the BGP-ID should not match the BGP Neighbors endpoint of a session.

Actually, this step might not entail any configuration command, since each platform usually has an automatic BGP-ID selection criterion. Generally, when it's not configured manually, the BGP-ID of a Loopback interface is selected. If a platform offers the option of configuring more than one Loopback interface (e.g. Cisco router), the one with the highest IP address is chosen as BGP-ID. If the Loopback interfaces are missing – although this is not a good configuration practice – the IP address of an up/up physical interface is selected.

NOTE: As best practice, we always recommend to specify the BGP-ID manually. This ensures an easier reading of "**show ...**" commands, where the Neighbors' BGP-ID is always present, and it also helps to immediately identify the BGP-ID, by simply viewing the configuration file. In order to avoid duplicates, it is best (although not necessary) for the BGP-ID to match the IP address of a Loopback interface.

In Cisco platforms, manual configuration of the BGP-ID is done through the following commands:

<u>IOS XE</u>:
router(config)# **router bgp** *AS-number*
router(config-router)# **bgp router-id** *BGP-ID*

<u>IOS XR</u>:
RP/0/RP0/CPU0:router(config)# **router bgp** *AS-number*
RP/0/RP0/CPU0:router(config-bgp)# **bgp router-id** *BGP-ID*

In JUNOS, the BGP-ID is configured under the hierarchy **[routing-options]**:

[edit routing-options]
router-id *BGP-ID***;**

NOTE: In JUNOS, the router-id thus defined is valid also for other protocols, such as OSPF, LDP, etc., while in Cisco platforms, different IDs can be manually defined for each protocol.

One last step of the basic procedure to establish a BGP session is defining the IP address and AS number of the BGP Neighbor. This process is completely manual, and it may require one simple command per session, or a few additional ones.
The configurations to execute in Cisco platforms are:

<u>IOS XE</u>:
router(config)# **router bgp** *AS-number*
router(config-router)# **neighbor** *IP-neighbor* **remote-as** *AS-neighbor*

<u>IOS XR</u>:
RP/0/RP0/CPU0:router(config)# **router bgp** *AS-number*
RP/0/RP0/CPU0:router(config-bgp)# **address-family** *afi safi*
RP/0/RP0/CPU0:router(config-bgp-af)# **exit**
RP/0/RP0/CPU0:router(config-bgp)# **neighbor** *IP-neighbor*
RP/0/RP0/CPU0:router(config-bgp-nbr)# **remote-as** *AS-neighbor*
RP/0/RP0/CPU0:router(config-bgp-nbr)# **address-family** *afi safi*

where the pair "*afi safi*" indicates the type of routing information transported by the BGP session. For instance, the "**address-family ipv4 unicast**" command enables transport of IPv4 unicast information (AFI/SAFI=1/1), "**address-family ipv6 unicast**" enables transport of IPv6 unicast information (AFI/SAFI=2/1), "**address-family l2vpn evpn**" enables transport of EVPN protocol information (AFI/SAFI=25/70), and so on.

NOTE: The IOS XR configuration also requires the explicit declaration of the type of routing information exchanged between BGP Neighbors, through the "**address-family** *afi safi*" command, both at global BGP process level, and at Neighbor level. This is because, in IOS XR – differently from IOS/IOS XE, where the address family ipv4 unicast is enabled by default – no address families are enabled by default.

In JUNOS, the configuration style is slightly different. All BGP-relevant commands are executed at "BGP routing process" level, reached through the **[edit protocols bgp]** command. Commands can be configured at three levels:

- Global: general BGP process commands.

- Group: specific commands of a group of BGP sessions.

- Session: specific commands of a session toward a specific BGP Neighbor.

The general BGP configuration diagram is the following:

[edit protocols bgp]
global-level commands;
group *group-name* {
  < **type** *session-type* >; # *Optional*
  group-level commands;
  neighbor *IP-neighbor* {
  session-level commands;
  }
}

where commands executed at global level are general BGP process commands that apply to all BGP sessions; those executed at group level, are specific for a group of BGP sessions; and those executed at session level, are specific for a session toward a specific BGP Neighbor.

Many of the three-level commands are identical to one another. The general rule is that a command executed at a more specific level trumps a command executed at a less specific level; that is, a command executed at group level trumps the same command executed at global level, while a command executed at session level trumps the same command executed at group level.

NOTE: The use of session groups is a more elegant configuration style, since it allows grouping similar BGP sessions (e.g. a group for iBGP sessions, a group for eBGP sessions toward Upstream Providers, a group for eBGP sessions toward customers, etc.). Moreover, it has positive implications on how BGP advertisements are created and sent (see Paragraph 3.2)

The basic configurations to execute to establish a BGP session are the following:

[edit protocols bgp]
group *group-name*
< type external | internal >; # *Optional*
neighbor *IP-neighbor* **<peer-as** *AS-neighbor***>**;
}

The AS-number and AS-neighbor values allow the router to establish whether the session is eBGP or iBGP. Indeed, if AS-number ≠ AS-neighbor, the session is eBGP, or vice versa, the session is iBGP.

The optional "**type external | internal**" command is used to specify the type of group sessions, whether eBGP or iBGP. Theoretically, eBGP and iBGP sessions can be included in the same group, although this is usually not recommended, because having a cleaner configuration is always preferable. If the "**type external**" command is specified for a group, then all the group sessions must necessarily be eBGP. If, on the other hand, the "**type internal**" command is specified for a group, then all the group sessions must necessarily be iBGP. In this case, specifying the AS number is pointless (even if allowed), because, once the session type is identified as iBGP, the group inherits the router AS number as the BGP Neighbors' AS number.

Once the session establishing commands are executed on both BGP Neighbors, the two BGP Neighbors exchange messages to open the TCP connection, and then the OPEN message. Appendix A.2 includes a wireshark analysis of all the messages exchanged, both those related to the TCP three-way-handshake and the BGP messages.

The two BGP Neighbors carry out some checks on these packets and on the OPEN message, and their outcome affects the BGP session completion. For the session to be established, the following conditions must be met:

1. The source IP address of the TCP/IP packets transporting the segments to open the TCP connection must match the address specified in the BGP Neighbor's "**neighbor** ..." command. By default, the source IP address is that of the interface forwarding the packet.

2. The AS number contained in the "**My Autonomous System**" field of the OPEN message must match the AS number specified in the "**neighbor ... remote-as/peer-as ...**" command of the BGP Neighbor.

3. If configured, the message authentication (see Section 10.2.1) must pass the MD5 hash function check (or any other security mechanism used).

In addition, for eBGP sessions, the two eBGP Neighbors check that the two routers are directly connected. This check is carried out through the source IP address of the TCP/IP packets transporting the BGP messages. If this belongs to the same IP subnet as the packet reception interface, then the check is passed, otherwise a multihop eBGP session should be used (see

Section 3.1.5). Concerning the first condition, it should be noted that the source IP address of the packets transporting the TCP segments matches the IP address of the interface sending the packets by default, while the target IP address matches the one configured in the "**neighbor ...**" command. This poses an issue, when Loopback interfaces are used to establish the BGP session (a typical example of this are iBGP sessions, see Section 2.1.3). Indeed, without changing the default source IP address, the IP packets transporting TCP segments would have a source IP address that doesn't match the one used in the BGP Neighbor's "**neighbor ...**" command. In order to solve this issue, we need to instruct the BGP process via the configuration commands specified below, and use, as source IP address, the IP address of the interface used to establish the BGP session (which, theoretically, could be any interface, not necessarily a Loopback interface, even if this is the most common case).

IOS XE:
router(config)# **router bgp** *AS-number*
router(config-router)# **neighbor** *IP-neighbor* **update-source** *interface*

IOS XR:
RP/0/RP0/CPU0:router(config)# **router bgp** *AS-number*
RP/0/RP0/CPU0:router(config-bgp)# **neighbor** *IP-neighbor*
RP/0/RP0/CPU0:router(config-bgp-nbr)# **update-source** *interface*

JUNOS
[edit protocols bgp]
local-address *local-IP-address*;
group *group-name* {
  local-address *local-IP-address*;
  neighbor *IP-neighbor* **<peer-as** *AS-neighbor*> {
    local-address *local-IP-address*;
  }
}

NOTE: Do not be mistaken by the fact that the "**local-address**..." command appears three times. This does not mean that the command should be repeated three times, but only that it can be executed at three different configuration levels: global, group and session.

Even though it is a good practice (for greater configuration symmetry) to add "**neighbor** *IP-neighbor* **update-source** ..." and "**local-address** ..." commands to both endpoints of a BGP session, it would actually be enough to add them to one side only. For instance, let's say we want to establish an eBGP session between routers CE1 and PE1 of our lab network, using the IP addresses of the Loopback0 interfaces as the session's endpoints (=10.1.99.11 for CE1 and 192.168.0.11 for PE1). The configurations executed are:

PE1 (Cisco IOS XR)
```
router bgp 64501
bgp router-id 192.168.0.11
address-family ipv4 unicast
!
  neighbor 10.1.99.11
    remote-as 65101
    update-source Loopback0
    ignore-connected-check
    address-family ipv4 unicast
```

<u>CE1</u> (Cisco IOS XE)
```
router bgp 65101
  bgp router-id 10.1.99.11
  neighbor 192.168.0.11 remote-as 64501
  neighbor 192.168.0.11 disable-connected-check
```

The "**neighbor … disable-connected-check**" command (IOS XE) and the equivalent "**neighbor … ignore-connected-check**" (IOS XR), already mentioned in Section 2.1.2, allow disabling the check on the direct connection of the BGP Neighbor's IP address. Alternatively, as stated earlier, we would have to configure a multihop eBGP session.

This is the sequence of events that occurs when the configuration is executed:

1. PE1 starts a connection attempt toward 10.1.99.11 with source IP 192.168.0.11, i.e., it sends a "TCP SYN" encapsulated in an IP packet with source and destination IP addresses 192.168.0.11 and 10.1.99.11, respectively.

2. CE1 starts a connection attempt toward 192.168.0.11 with source IP 10.1.11.2 (= IP address of CE1's Gi1 interface toward PE1).

3. PE1 receives the connection attempt from CE1, but rejects it, because it is configured to accept connections from 10.1.99.11 and not from 10.1.11.2. In other words, there is no coincidence between the source IP address of the connection request received, and the address in the "**neighbor …**" command.

4. CE1 receives the connection attempt from PE1, accepts it, because it is configured to accept connections from 192.168.0.11, and replies with a "TCP SYN" encapsulated in an IP packet with the source and target IP addresses 10.1.99.11 and 192.168.0.11, respectively.

5. PE1 receives this IP packet and replies with a "TCP ACK" thus completing the three-way-handshake.

The TCP connection is established. PE1 is the TCP client and CE1 is the server. Please note in the sequence that PE1 starts the three-way-handshake, via the "**neighbor 10.1.99.11 update-source Loopback0**" command, with the source IP address that CE1 expects (=192.168.0.11, Loopback0 of PE1) and the destination IP address of the "**neighbor 10.1.99.11 …**" command. CE1 receives "TCP SYN" and since target address 10.1.99.11 is one of its own addresses, replies to the connection request with "TCP SYN ACK" with source and destination IP addresses reversed, with respect to the IP packet received that transports "TCP SYN". Remember, this is TCP/IP's normal behavior, and it occurs regardless of the presence of the "**neighbor … update-source …**" command on CE1. The main point is that the "**neighbor … update-source …**" command only affects how the TCP connection is initialized by the BGP process, and not how the BGP process replies to the connection attempt. As long as the BGP process receives connection requests from allowed IP addresses – i.e., those configured in the "**neighbor … remote-as …**" commands – the BGP process will reply to the connection attempt.

As proof, we can see, with the "**show bgp ipv4 neighbors …**" display command, that the TCP connection has actually been established, and that PE1 is the client (we'll leave the other details to the reader):

```
CE1#show bgp ipv4 unicast neighbors | begin Connection
Connection state is ESTAB, I/O status: 1, unread input bytes: 0
Connection is ECN Disabled, Minimum incoming TTL 0, Outgoing TTL 1
Local host: 10.1.99.11, Local port: 179
```

```
Foreign host: 192.168.0.11, Foreign port: 33154
. . . < rest of the output omitted > . . .
```

Everything we mentioned so far also applies to JUNOS platforms. Only those platforms using IOS XR require the "**neighbor** ... **update-source** ..." command on both sides of the session. Indeed, the BGP implementation of the Cisco IOS XR, in the absence of the command, is designed to always reply with a "TCP RST" (reset) to any connection attempt. Again, it is always a good practice to execute the command on both sides of the BGP session.

Lastly, many of the current BGP implementations avoid the TCP connection collisions issue, making a BGP neighbor "passive", i.e. the BGP neighbor can only listen on the well-known port 179. As a consequence, the router never starts the three-way-handshake procedure to open the TCP connection, thus saving processing time. The commands available, to be executed only on one side of the session, are:

IOS XE:
router(config)# **router bgp** *AS-number*
router(config-router)# **neighbor** *IP-neighbor* **transport connection-mode passive**

IOS XR:
RP/0/RP0/CPU0:router(config)# **router bgp** *AS-number*
RP/0/RP0/CPU0:router(config-bgp)# **neighbor** *IP-neighbor*
RP/0/RP0/CPU0:router(config-bgp-nbr)# **session-open-mode passive-only**

JUNOS
[edit protocols bgp group *group-name*]
neighbor *IP-neighbor* {
  < **peer-as** *AS-neighbor* >;
  passive;
}

This completes the set of basic configurations. Before presenting other aspects, let's see an example of application of the above-mentioned commands.

3.1.2 Example

To put what we've seen so far into practice, using the example network in Figure 3.1, let's first establish the CE-PE eBGP sessions. Starting from the network numbering plan, described in this chapter's introduction, the basic configurations to execute are:

CE1 (IOS XE)
```
router bgp 65101
  bgp router-id 10.1.99.11
  neighbor 10.1.11.1 remote-as 64501
  neighbor 10.1.11.1 description *** EBGP SESSION WITH PE1 ***
  neighbor 10.1.12.5 remote-as 64501
  neighbor 10.1.12.5 description *** EBGP SESSION WITH PE2 ***
```

CE2 (JUNOS)
```
[edit routing-options]
router-id 10.1.99.12;
autonomous-system 65101;
[edit protocols bgp]
```

```
group PE {
  peer-as 64501;
  neighbor 10.1.12.1 {
    description "*** EBGP SESSION WITH PE2 ***";
  }
  neighbor 10.1.11.5 {
    description "*** EBGP SESSION WITH PE1 ***";
  }
}
```

<u>PE1</u> (IOS XR)

```
router bgp 64501
  bgp router-id 192.168.0.11
  address-family ipv4 unicast
  !
  neighbor-group CE
    remote-as 65101
    address-family ipv4 unicast
  !
  neighbor 10.1.11.2
    use neighbor-group CE
    description *** EBGP SESSION WITH CE1 ***
  !
  neighbor 10.1.11.6
    use neighbor-group CE
    description *** EBGP SESSION WITH CE2 ***
```

<u>PE2</u> (JUNOS)

```
[edit routing-options]
router-id 192.168.0.12;
autonomous-system 64501;

[edit protocols bgp]
group CE {
  peer-as 65101;
  neighbor 10.1.12.6 {
    description "*** EBGP SESSION WITH CE1 ***";
  }
  neighbor 10.1.12.2 {
    description "*** EBGP SESSION WITH CE2 ***";
  }
}
```

NOTE: In configuring router PE1 (Cisco IOS XR), we used the "**neighbor-group**" configuration style, which we'll see in detail in Paragraph 3.2. Nonetheless, the configuration is sufficiently self-explanatory.

To check that the sessions are in the Established state, we can give the following commands to CE1 and CE2:

```
CE1#show bgp ipv4 unicast summary
BGP router identifier 10.1.99.11, local AS number 65101

. . . < output omitted > . . .

Neighbor   V    AS MsgRcvd MsgSent TblVer InQ OutQ  Up/Down State/PfxRcd
10.1.11.1  4 64501     817     892     17   0    0 13:26:50          16
10.1.12.5  4 64501    1782    1766     17   0    0 13:26:46          16

aft@CE2> show bgp summary

. . . < output omitted > . . .

Peer                 AS    InPkt   OutPkt   OutQ    Flaps   Last Up/Dwn
State|#Active/Received/Accepted/Damped...
10.1.11.5         64501       19       11      0        0         4:44
Establ inet.0: 16/16/16/0
10.1.12.1         64501       18        9      0        0         3:13
Establ inet.0: 0/16/16/0
```

We will go over the views obtained with these commands in detail in Paragraph 3.3. All you need to know now is that the four sessions created are properly in the Established state. In the view on CE1 (Cisco IOS XE), this can be seen from the fact that, in the "**Up/down**" column, there is a timer, while in the "**State**" column there is nothing. The timer indicates for how long a session has been in the Established state. In the view on CE2 (JUNOS), the state is explicitly shown ("**Establ**"). Let's move on to creating the PE-GTW iBGP sessions. In this example, we will create a full mesh of iBGP sessions between the two PEs and the two GTWs, for a total of 6 sessions. The additional configurations to execute on PE1 and PE2 are the following:

NOTE: The configurations on the two GTWs are practically the same, apart (obviously) from the IP addresses, and we will not include them here.

<u>PE1</u> (IOS XR)
```
router bgp 64501
!
neighbor-group IBGP
  remote-as 64501
  update-source Loopback0
  address-family ipv4 unicast
!
neighbor 192.168.0.12
  use neighbor-group IBGP
  description *** IBGP SESSION WITH PE2 ***
!
neighbor 192.168.1.11
  use neighbor-group IBGP
  description *** IBGP SESSION WITH GTW-1 ***
!
neighbor 192.168.1.12
  use neighbor-group IBGP
```

```
  description *** IBGP SESSION WITH GTW-2 ***
!
```

<u>PE2</u> (JUNOS)

```
[edit protocols bgp]
group IBGP {
  type internal;
  local-address 192.168.0.12;
  neighbor 192.168.0.11 {
    description "*** IBGP SESSION WITH PE1 ***";
  }
  neighbor 192.168.1.11 {
    description "*** IBGP SESSION WITH GTW-1 ***";
  }
  neighbor 192.168.1.12 {
    description "*** IBGP SESSION WITH GTW-2 ***";
  }
}
```

Now, we just have to create the two eBGP sessions between the two routers GTW of AS 64501 and the two Upstream Providers. The configurations are the same as those we already saw for the CE-PE eBGP sessions, so we will leave them to you, to practice.

To conclude this example, let's check that all sessions are in the Established state, with the same commands we saw earlier. We will do it on the two routers PE1 and GTW-2:

```
RP/0/0/CPU0:PE1#show bgp summary

. . .

BGP router identifier 192.168.0.11, local AS number 64501

. . . < output omitted > . . .
```

Neighbor	Spk	AS	MsgRcvd	MsgSent	TblVer	InQ	OutQ	Up/Down	St/PfxRcd
10.1.11.2	0	65101	203	182	18	0	0	02:52:12	0
10.1.11.6	0	65101	383	354	18	0	0	02:52:10	0
192.168.0.12	0	64501	380	346	18	0	0	02:52:11	0
192.168.1.11	0	64501	179	174	18	0	0	02:52:11	0
192.168.1.12	0	64501	384	346	18	0	0	02:52:11	16

```
aft@GTW-2>show bgp summary

. . . < output omitted > . . .
```

Peer	AS	InPkt	OutPkt	OutQ	Flaps	Last Up/Dwn
State|#Active/Received/Accepted/Damped...						
172.20.2.1	65542	4950	5440	0	0	3:16
Establ inet.0: 16/16/16/0						
192.168.0.11	64501	375	415	0	1	3:06:37
Establ inet.0: 0/0/0/0						
192.168.0.12	64501	5430	5421	0	0	3:03:00
Establ inet.0: 0/0/0/0						
192.168.1.11	64501	4945	5443	0	0	3:04:22
Establ inet.0: 0/0/0/0						

All sessions created are in the *Established* state.

NOTE: The creation of a full mesh of iBGP sessions – which is essential for IP networks adopting the BGP/MPLS routing architecture – or merely importing the IP prefixes outside the AS within the AS via BGP, is not a very scalable procedure. Indeed, in a network with N routers, the number of iBGP sessions is N*(N-1)/2, and it increases quadratically as the number of routers within the network increases. In Chapter 8, we will go over some techniques to overcome this issue, the most popular being, in practical applications, the one using the Route Reflection function.

3.1.3 Supporting RFC 8212

In our example network, in order to simulate a portion of the FIRT (Full Internet Routing Table), we made ASes 65541 and 65542 generate a set of 15 IP prefixes and the default route. Actually, as you can see from the view obtained with the "**show bgp summary**" command, shown at the end of the previous section, GTW-2 receives from BGP Neighbor 172.20.2.1 – which is the router of Upstream Provider 2 (AS 65542) – 16 BGP advertisements (as inferred by the second number of the quadruple "**inet.0: 16/16/16/0**", further details in Paragraph 3.3).

Let's see what happens on GTW-1, Cisco router with IOS XR operating system, which has an eBGP session with Upstream Provider 1 (AS 65541).

```
RP/0/0/CPU0:GTW-1#show bgp summary

. . .

BGP router identifier 192.168.1.11, local AS number 64501

. . . < output omitted > . . .

Some configured eBGP neighbors (under default or non-default vrfs) do
not have both inbound and outbound policies configured for IPv4 Unicast
address family. These neighbors will default to sending and/or receiving
no routes and are marked with '!' in the output below. Use the 'show bgp
neighbor <nbr_address>' command for details.

Neighbor        Spk      AS MsgRcvd MsgSent TblVer InQ OutQ  Up/Down St/PfxRcd
172.20.1.1        0   65541    3181    3147     99   0    0 00:06:39       0!
192.168.0.11      0   64501    2852    2864     99   0    0 00:30:11        0
192.168.0.12      0   64501    6271    5699     99   0    0 00:30:11        0
192.168.1.12      0   64501    6310    5726     99   0    0 00:30:11       16
```

As you can see, the number of prefixes received on the eBGP session with BGP Neighbor 172.20.1.1 – which is the router of Upstream Provider 1 (AS 65541) – is 0. The reason behind this is that IOS XR is compliant with RFC 8212, already mentioned in Section 2.1.2.

NOTE: The view also shows that GTW-1 receives 16 prefixes from BGP Neighbor 192.168.1.12 (=GTW-2). Those derive from the automatic propagation of eBGP advertisements that GTW-2 received from Upstream Provider 2 and that are propagated on the iBGP session between the two GTWs.

We remind you that RFC 8212 states that, on an eBGP session, no inbound and/or outbound advertisement can be accepted/propagated, unless an explicit inbound and/or outbound routing policy has been configured. In practice, this entails that basic configurations shouldn't allow the automatic acceptance or propagation of eBGP advertisements.

NOTE: RFC 8212 does not concern advertisement propagation on iBGP sessions, which follow the rules already described in Section 2.1.3.

And this is exactly what happens with IOS XR, which behaves differently than IOS/IOS XE and JUNOS, when it comes to eBGP sessions. Because, in those platforms that use IOS XR, a BGP Speaker doesn't accept and doesn't send advertisements on eBGP sessions, by default. The eBGP session reaches the Established state in any case, but it is basically useless.

In order for BGP advertisements to be sent and received on eBGP sessions, it is necessary to define filters through routing policies, and enable them both inbound and outbound. We will go over the routing policies for IOS XR in the next chapter (see Paragraph 4.2). For the sake of completeness, let's see a minimal example of "all-pass" routing policy configuration (which allows accepting/sending all BGP advertisements).

NOTE: In the following configuration, "ALL" is the routing policy's name.

RP/0/RP0/CPU0:router(config)# **route-policy ALL**
RP/0/RP0/CPU0:router(config-rpl)# **pass**
RP/0/RP0/CPU0:router(config-rpl)# **end-policy**

Routing policies are applied within the hierarchy **"neighbor→address-family"**, by specifying the application direction (**in** for inbound, **out** for outbound). For instance, to apply the ALL routing policy in both direction, the following additional configurations must be executed on router GTW-1:

```
router bgp 64501
 neighbor 172.20.1.1
  address-family ipv4 unicast
    route-policy ALL in
    route-policy ALL out
```

IOS XR signals that the routing policies are missing with a message in the "**show bgp summary**" command shown above, "**Some configured eBGP neighbors . . .**". Please note that "0!" is shown in the last view column, under "**St/PfxRcd**". Zero indicates that no prefix has been received, and "!" that no routing policy has been enabled for that eBGP Neighbor.

NOTE: The same message also appears by omitting one of the two filters. For instance, if we omit the outbound filter, the same message appears; however, in the last column, besides "!", there could be a non-zero number, to indicate that some prefix has been received.

Let's repeat the "**show bgp summary**" command on router GTW-1, to see what changes in the routing policy application.

```
RP/0/0/CPU0:GTW-1#show bgp summary

. . .

BGP router identifier 192.168.1.11, local AS number 64501

. . . < output omitted > . . .
```

Neighbor	Spk	AS	MsgRcvd	MsgSent	TblVer	InQ	OutQ	Up/Down	St/PfxRcd
172.20.1.1	0	65541	3470	3440	109	0	0	04:47:56	16
192.168.0.11	0	64501	3133	3148	109	0	0	14:11:28	0
192.168.0.12	0	64501	6887	6265	109	0	0	2d04h	0
192.168.1.12	0	64501	6929	6292	109	0	0	2d04h	7

As you can notice from the view, now the number of prefixes received by Upstream Provider 1 is 16.

NOTE: The reason why GTW-1 receives only 7 prefixes from GTW-2 is that GTW-2 receives, for 9 out of the 16 IP prefixes advertised by the two Upstream Providers, two BGP advertisements, one from Upstream Provider 2 and the other from GTW-1, which propagates its own best paths on the iBGP session. Now, if the iBGP advertisement received from GTW-1 becomes the best path, according to the Split Horizon rule, the advertisement is not propagated again to GTW-1. So, out of the 16 advertisements received by Upstream Provider 2, only 16-9=7 (the best paths) will be propagated to GTW-1 on the iBGP session.

In conclusion, of the three operating systems considered in this book, only IOS XR supports RFC 8212 by default, while IOS XE and JUNOS do not support it, by default. Actually, IOS XR adopted the strategy suggested by RFC 8212 long before the RFC was published. In IOS XE, support for RFC 8212 – even if not by default – can be set via the **"bgp safe-ebgp-policy"** command, within the BGP process configuration.

In the same way, in JUNOS, since version 20.3R1, support to RFC 8212 can be set with the command:

[edit protocols bgp defaults ebgp]
no-policy {
   advertise (accept | reject | reject-always);
   receive (accept | reject | reject-always);
}

which allows specifying the BGP default behavior, for those advertisements sent and/or received on eBGP sessions, without explicitly configured routing policies. The difference between the **"reject"** and **"reject-always"** options, is that, with the first, the (inbound and/or outbound) advertisements of the IPv4/IPv6 unicast address families are rejected both on the primary routing instance (RIB) and on VRF routing instances (virtual-router and no-forwarding), while, with the second option, all eBGP advertisements are rejected.

NOTE: Apart from Cisco IOS XR, there are other implementations that support RFC 8212 by default, such as, for instance, Nokia SR OS (from version 19.5.R1), and certain BGP open implementations, such as: BIRD, from version 2.0.1, OpenBGPD, from version OpenBSD 6.4, FRRouting, from version 7.4. For an updated list, see the link "https://github.com/bgp/RFC8212".

3.1.4 Managing the BGP Next-Hop

Circling back to our example network, after adding the routing policies on GTW-1 – as we did in the previous section – there is still an issue. Indeed, according to eBGP/iBGP advertisement propagation rules described in Sections 2.1.2 and 2.1.3, and taking into account the routing policies applied on GTW-1, we would expect to see the best paths propagated by the two GTWs on PE1 and PE2. And that's what happens, the best paths arrive; however, they don't translate into RIB entries, even though they are the only prefix advertisements.

For instance, both Upstream Providers advertise prefix 203.0.113/24, which is present as the best path in GTW-1's BGP advertisement table, as shown in the following view:

```
RP/0/0/CPU0:GTW-1#show bgp

. . .

Network              Next Hop      Metric    LocPrf    Weight       Path
. . .

*> 203.0.113.0/24    172.20.1.1       0          0       65541      64496 i
. . .
```

NOTE: In the view, the fact that the advertisement is the best path is indicated by the symbol ">" on the left. Further details in Paragraph 3.3.

Now, this best path is surely propagated on the iBGP sessions toward PE1 and PE2 (and even GTW-2, but we are not interested in this, right now). Being the only advertisement of prefix 203.0.113/24, it should become a best path and thus end up in the RIBs of PE1 and PE2. But this doesn't happen, as shown in the following views:

```
RP/0/0/CPU0:PE1#show route 203.0.113.0/24

. . .

% Network not in table
aft@PE2> show route 203.0.113.0/24
. . . < output empty > . . .
```

We already mentioned this issue in Section 2.4.3; it is caused by the way the BGP Next-Hop contained in the NEXT_HOP attribute is managed, and is one of BGP's most intriguing aspects. In particular, it stems from BGP's default rule, described in Figure 2.25, which is to leave the BGP Next-Hop unchanged when propagating eBGP advertisements on iBGP sessions. Transposed to our example, this means that the advertisements of prefix 203.0.113/24 propagated by GTW-1, will have as BGP Next-Hop 172.20.1.1, as shown by the view above. However, this address cannot be reached by the RIBs of PE1 and PE2, as shown in the following views:

```
RP/0/0/CPU0:PE1#show route 172.20.1.0/31

. . .

% Network not in table
aft@PE2> show route 172.20.1.0/31

. . . < output empty > . . .
```

Now, in Paragraph 2.5, we've seen that a BGP advertisement, in order to be deemed valid for the selection process, must have a reachable Next-Hop. This does not apply to our case, therefore the advertisements of prefix 203.0.113/24 received by GTW-1 cannot take part in the selection process, so they cannot be elected as best paths and, lastly, they cannot be included in the RIB.

In order to check that the advertisements do not become best paths, let's consider the two following views:

```
RP/0/0/CPU0:PE1#show bgp

. . .

Network            Next Hop      Metric     LocPrf     Weight      Path
. . .

* i203.0.113.0/24   172.20.1.1      0         100         0     65541 64496 i

. . .

aft@PE2> show route protocol bgp 203.0.113.0/24
inet.0: 28 destinations, 29 routes (12 active, 0 holddown, 17 hidden)
```

In PE1 view (Cisco with IOS XR), notice the absence of symbol ">" on the left, and in PE2 view (JUNOS) there is nothing. Actually, in PE2, the advertisement is there, but it is "hidden". Indeed, JUNOS adds all invalid advertisements to a hidden section of the RIB, which can be viewed via the "**show route hidden**" command. The following view shows the hidden advertisement of prefix 203.0.113/24:

```
aft@PE2> show route hidden 203.0.113.0/24
inet.0: 28 destinations, 29 routes (12 active, 0 holddown, 17 hidden) +
= Active Route, - = Last Active, * = Both
203.0.113.0/24 [BGP/170] 12:58:41, MED 0, localpref 100, from 192.168.1.11
  AS path: 65541 64496 I, validation-state: unverified
    Unusable
```

In this last view, there are also two useful pieces of information. The first is that the hidden section of the RIB contains 17 entries, which are the advertisements of the 16 IP prefixes, with the default route having two advertisements (we'll leave the explanation to you). The second useful information is that the Next-Hop cannot be used ("**Unusable**").

The solution to this problem has been described in Section 2.4.3, where we said that the classiest solution is to vary the default management of the NEXT_HOP attribute, by allowing the insertion of an actual IP address in the advertisement propagation toward a specific BGP Neighbor.

NOTE: Changing the BGP Next-Hop is useful only in iBGP sessions; for eBGP sessions, it is automatic (see Section 2.4.3).

Cisco and Juniper platforms permit this, through suitable routing policy commands or applications. These are the configurations to be executed:

IOS XE:
router(config)# **router bgp** *AS-number*
router(config-router)# **neighbor** *IP-neighbor* **next-hop-self**

IOS XR:
RP/0/RP0/CPU0:router(config)# **router bgp** *AS-number*
RP/0/RP0/CPU0:router(config-bgp)# **neighbor** *IP-neighbor*
RP/0/RP0/CPU0:router(config-bgp-nbr)# **address-family** *afi safi*
RP/0/RP0/CPU0:router(config-bgp-nbr-af)# **next-hop-self**

JUNOS
[edit policy-options policy-statement *policy-name*]
then {
  next-hop self;
}

[edit protocols bgp]
export *policy-name*;
group *group-name* {
  export *policy-name*;
  neighbor *IP-neighbor* **<peer-as** *remote-AS*> {
  export *policy-name*;
  }
}

NOTE: Even in Cisco platforms, it is possible to use a JUNOS-like solution, through suitable routing policies, by executing a "**set next-hop ...**" command. However, the solution described above is the easiest and most widespread in practical applications.

With these commands, the BGP process uses its own BGP session endpoint IP address as IP address to add to the NEXT_HOP attribute.

These configurations must be executed on all the network's edge routers, and applied to internal iBGP sessions. For instance, in our network in Figure 3.1, they should be executed both on GTWs and on PEs. And for the two GTWs, the additional configurations to be executed are the following:

GTW-1 (Cisco IOS XR)
```
router bgp 64501
  neighbor-group IBGP
    address-family ipv4 unicast
    next-hop-self
```

GTW-2 (JUNOS)
```
[edit policy-options policy-statement NHS]
then {
  next-hop self;
}
[edit protocols bgp]
group IBGP {
  export NHS;
}
```

To verify the effect of these configurations, let's see what happens on PE routers, concerning prefix 203.0.113/24.

```
RP/0/0/CPU0:PE1#show bgp
. . .
Network                 Next Hop    Metric    LocPrf    Weight      Path
. . .
*> i203.0.113.0/24   192.168.1.11      0        100         0     65541 64496 i
. . .

aft@PE2> show route protocol bgp 203.0.113.0/24

inet.0: 28 destinations, 29 routes (28 active, 0 holddown, 0 hidden)   +
= Active Route, - = Last Active, * = Both

203.0.113.0/24    *[BGP/170] 04:20:58, MED 0, localpref 100, from
  192.168.1.11 AS path: 65541 64496 I, validation-state: unverified
    > to 172.16.1.11 via ge-0/0/1.0
```

As you can see, this time the two PEs include the advertisements of prefix 203.0.113/24 in the selection process, and, being the only ones, they become the best paths. So, in the RIBs of PE1 and PE2, we will find the related entries:

```
RP/0/0/CPU0:PE1#show route 203.0.113.0/24
. . .
Routing entry for 203.0.113.0/24
  Known via "bgp 64501", distance 200, metric 0
  Tag 65541, type internal
```

```
  Installed Nov 21 11:23:02.513 for 04:29:39
  Routing Descriptor Blocks
    192.168.1.11, from 192.168.1.11
    Route metric is 0
  No advertising protos.

aft@PE2> show route 203.0.113.0/24

inet.0: 28 destinations, 29 routes (28 active, 0 holddown, 0 hidden)  +
= Active Route, - = Last Active, * = Both
203.0.113.0/24     *[BGP/170] 04:20:58, MED 0, localpref 100,
                                             from 192.168.1.11
                  AS path: 65541 64496 I, validation-state: unverified
                  >  to 172.16.1.11 via ge-0/0/1.0
```


As you can see, there are now two entries in the RIBs of PE1 and PE2, which are then downloaded in the forwarding tables (FIB) for traffic switching.

NOTE: There is a major difference between Cisco and Juniper's RIB views. While Cisco's view shows the BGP Next-Hop (=192.168.1.11), Juniper's view shows the IGP Next-Hop (=172.16.1.11) to reach the BGP Next-Hop. In order to see the BGP Next-Hop, the "**extensive**" clause must be added. Further details in Paragraph 3.3.

3.1.5 Multihop eBGP sessions

In Section 2.1.2, when we introduced the rules for eBGP sessions, we saw that they can be established by default only between directly connected routers. Indeed, all BGP messages are issued by eBGP Neighbors, encapsulated in TCP/IP packets with IP TTL=1.

If an eBGP session between non-directly connected routers (multihop eBGP sessions) must be established, we need to change the default IP TTL, by bringing it to a sufficient value to establish the session. The following configurations allow this:

IOS XE:
router(config)# **router bgp** *AS-number*
router(config-router)# **neighbor** *IP-neighbor* **ebgp-multihop** [*TTL*]

IOS XR:
RP/0/RP0/CPU0:router(config)# **router bgp** *AS-number*
RP/0/RP0/CPU0:router(config-bgp)# **neighbor** *IP-neighbor*
RP/0/RP0/CPU0:router(config-bgp-nbr)# **ebgp-multihop** [*TTL*]

JUNOS
[edit protocols bgp]
multihop <ttl *value-TTL*>;
group *group-name* {
  multihop <ttl *value-TTL*>;
  neighbor *IP-neighbor* **<peer-as** *remote-AS*> {
    multihop <ttl *value-TTL*>;
  }
}

If omitted, TTL values take on a value of TTL=255 in Cisco platforms, and of TTL=64 in Juniper platforms using JUNOS.

Let's see two practical examples of application of these commands. In the first example, we are going to assume that a customer of our Tier-2 ISP of the network shown in Figure 3.1 – with its own multi-homed AS to several Upstream Providers – requests sending of the FIRT. The customer could be a big company, or another operator – generally called OLO (Other Licensed Operator) – to which the Tier-2 ISP provides wholesale services.

In order not to overload its own routers, the Tier-2 ISP adopts the following strategy: it adds a server (even a commercial one) – which we'll refer to as FIRT server (even if it is sometimes improperly called Route Server) – to the network; the FIRT server features an operating system that supports BGP implementation. In this example, it is irrelevant how the FIRT is served to the FIRT server. The FIRT server behaves for all intents and purposes as a router, except that it is outside any forwarding path. Its only purpose is providing the FIRT to all external customers that request it. Keeping the FIRT server outside the forwarding paths is very easy: it is sufficient to set the IGP metrics of its interfaces to very high values. The complete scenario is displayed in Figure 3.2 below, where the affected IP addresses and the customer (public) AS number (AS 64999) are shown.

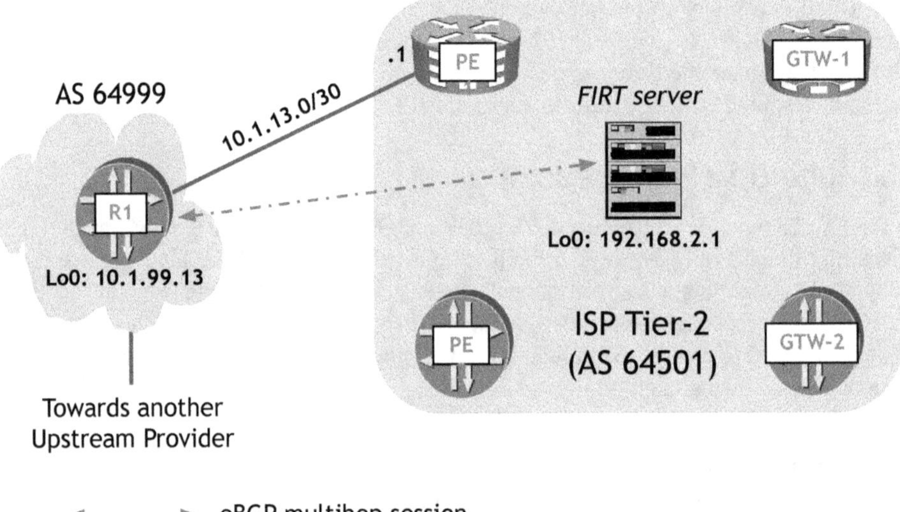

Figure 3.2 – Example of application of an eBGP multihop session.

In order to send the entire FIRT to the customer, a multihop eBGP session is established between the customer's router R1 and the FIRT server. Let's assume that Cisco IOS XE is installed on the FIRT server, and that it has a Loopback0 interface with IP address 192.168.2.1/32, advertised in IGP. Moreover, let's imagine that a layer-3 connection has been established between the IP addresses of the two Loopback0 interfaces of the FIRT server and R1 (192.168.2.1 and 10.1.99.13, respectively). How this connection has been established is beyond the scope of this example. You can "come up" with your own solution.

The configurations to be executed to establish the multihop eBGP session are shown below.

<u>FIRT server</u> (Cisco IOS XE)
```
router bgp 64501
  neighbor 10.1.99.13 remote-as 64999
  neighbor 10.1.99.13 ebgp-multihop
  neighbor 10.1.99.13 update-source Loopback0
```

<u>R1</u> (JUNOS)
```
[edit protocols bgp]
group FIRT-SERVER {
  local-address 10.1.99.13;
  neighbor 192.168.2.1 {
    multihop;
    peer-as 64501;
  }
}
```

An important detail is missing to close this example. All the advertisements that the FIRT server sends to R1 will have, by default, according to BGP's standard rules, BGP Next-Hop 192.168.2.1 (see Section 2.4.3). This implies that traffic sent by R1 toward the Hosts of the FIRT prefixes will transit through the FIRT server. However, we mentioned earlier that it is a good practice to keep the FIRT server outside the forwarding path. To solve this issue, we need to change the BGP Next-Hop of the advertisements sent by the FIRT server to R1. This can be done with the tools we will see in Chapter 4. For the sake of completion, the following minimal configuration on the FIRT server allows setting the BGP Next-Hop to IP address 10.1.13.1, that is, the IP address of the PE1 interface to which R1 is connected.

```
route-map SET-NH permit 10
  set ip next-hop 10.1.13.1
!
router bgp 64501
    neighbor 10.1.99.13 route-map SET-NH out
```

As a check, let's verify on R1 the BGP Next-Hop for the advertisement of prefix 203.0.113/24, which is part of the FIRT.

```
aft@R1> show route 203.0.113.0/24 extensive | match "Protocol | Source"
                    Source: 192.168.2.1
                    Protocol next hop: 10.1.13.1
```

As you may notice, the advertisement comes from BGP Neighbor 192.168.2.1 (FIRT server) and has, as BGP Next-Hop, indicated in the view as "**Protocol next hop**", IP address 10.1.13.1, specified in the configuration.

Now, as a second example, let's see how an eBGP session is established between two routers with a multi-link connection. We've dealt extensively with this scenario in Section 2.1.2, where we said that the optimal solution is to establish an eBGP session using two Loopback interfaces. The scenario in the example and the IP addresses used are summarized in Figure 3.3, below.

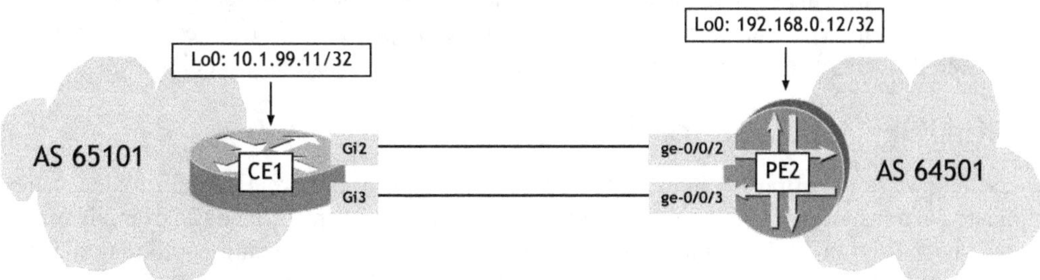

Figure 3.3 – EBGP (multihop) session between two routers with multi-link connection.

For the test, we will use routers CE1 and PE2, belonging to the network shown in Figure 3.1, to which we added a connection that has the GigabitEthernet3 interface on CE1 and the ge-0/0/3 interface on PE2 as endpoints.

The first step is to connect the IP addresses of the two preset Loopback interfaces of CE1 and PE2 (10.1.99.11 and 192.168.0.12) at layer 3. Just like in the previous example, how this connection has been established is beyond the scope of this example. You can "come up" with your own solution.

The configurations to be executed to establish the multihop eBGP session are shown below.

CE1 (Cisco IOS XE)

```
router bgp 65101
  neighbor 192.168.0.12 remote-as 64501
  neighbor 192.168.0.12 ebgp-multihop
  neighbor 192.168.0.12 update-source Loopback0
```

PE2 (JUNOS)

```
[edit protocols bgp]
group CE {
  neighbor 10.1.99.11 {
    peer-as 65101;
    multihop;
    local-address 192.168.0.12;
  }
}
```

With these configurations, the multihop eBGP session reaches switches to the Established state:

```
aft@PE2> show bgp summary
. . .
Peer                AS    InPkt      OutPkt      OutQ      Flaps      Last Up/Dwn
State|#Active/Received/Accepted/Damped...
10.1.99.11          65101      21         19         0          0          4:37:00
Establ inet.0: 0/0/0/0
```

This example finds some interesting applications in the live networks. For instance, think about a CE connected to a PE of a different AS, through a single point-to-point connection. Generally, in those cases, in order to establish the eBGP session, the IP addresses assigned to the connection endpoint interfaces are used. And, usually, this is a good rule to follow, since it streamlines the configuration procedure, as the layer-3 connection of IP addresses is automatic, and it only requires a standard (non-multihop) eBGP session. However, think about a scenario where, at some point, you need to increase the connection's bandwidth, and therefore decide to add a second link, then a third, and so on. With such configurations as in our example, there is no need to do anything, except add the connections and assign the IP addresses to the connection endpoints.

3.1.6 BGP Sessions for IPv6

Everything we saw for BGP sessions, concerning the transport of IPv4 routing information, can be replicated to transport IPv6 routing information, therefore we will only include an example of this. As we saw in Section 2.6.3, the main difference when transporting IPv6 routing information is that here we use BGP's multiprotocol extension (MP-BGP), described in Paragraph 2.6.

In this example, we will use the test network in Figure 3.1, and we'll see how we can establish eBGP and iBGP sessions. In particular, we will establish two eBGP sessions from router CE1 (Cisco IOS XE) to the two routers PE1 (Cisco IOS XR) and PE2 (Juniper JUNOS), and a complete mesh of iBGP sessions between routers PE and GTW.

NOTE: In our example, we'll assume that all routers are dual stack, that is, capable of supporting both IPv4 and IPv6 control plane and data plane, at the same time. Cisco platforms with IOS XR and Juniper platforms with JUNOS are dual stack by default, while Cisco platforms with IOS and IOS XE become dual stack after executing the global "**ipv6 unicast-routing**" command.

The IPv6 numbering plan adopted is the following (only the relevant addresses):

Loopback0 interfaces:

- PE1=2001:db8::11/128 - PE2=2001:db8::12/128.

- GTW-1=2001:db8:1::11/128 - GTW-2=2001:db8:1::12/128.

CE-PE links:

- CE1↔PE1=2001:db8:1:11::/126   (:1 PE side; :2 CE side).

- CE1↔PE2=2001:db8:1:12::4/126   (:5 PE side; :6 CE side).

BGP session configuration for IPv6 in a Cisco environment is very similar to those of BGP sessions for IPv4. Since a single session can be used to transport routing information both for IPv4 and IPv6 prefixes, and also other types (e.g., VPN-IPv4, VPN-IPv6 prefixes, etc.), an elegant configuration style first disables the default transport type (i.e. transport of IPv4 routing data only), and then enables the family of prefixes it wants to transport the routing data of, on a case by case basis. In order to do so, in IOS/IOS XE, the "**no bgp default ipv4-unicast**" command is used, while in IOS XR no command is required, because no address-family is enabled by default in IOS XR.

In IOS and IOS XE, transport of IPv6 routing information is enabled through the "**address-family ipv6 unicast**" configuration mode, via the "**neighbor** *IPv6-neighbor* **activate**" command. Otherwise, the steps to follow are the same as in BGP for IPv4. In IOS XR, the configuration of BGP sessions for IPv6 is identical to the one we saw for IPv4, except for the different address-family.

Concerning the "**neighbor** *IPv6-neighbor* **...**" command, we should highlight that the address of the BGP Neighbor must be an IPv6 address (usually Global Unicast or Unique Local). Theoretically, the session could be established even with IPv4 addresses, however this raises an issue related to the BGP Next-Hop. For instance, in IOS XE (and also in JUNOS) a specific IPv6 address – obtained from the IPv4 address used as endpoint of the BGP session – would be advertised as BGP Next-Hop. The structure of this address is "**::ffff:x.y.w.z**", where "**x.y.w.z**" is the IPv4 address (IPv4-mapped IPv6 address). For instance, IPv4 address 192.0.2.1 corresponds to IPv6 address "**::ffff:192.0.2.1**". Since the router that receives the advertisement does not have any path toward this address in the IPv6 RIB, it does not accept the advertisement. For instance, by activating the "**debug bgp ipv6 unicast updates**" debug command, upon receiving the UPDATE messages, the following error message is received:

```
*Apr  1 15:26:47.495: BGP(1): 203.0.113.1 rcv UPDATE about 2001:db8::1/128
 -- DENIED due to: non-connected MP_REACH NEXTHOP;
```

IOS XR follows RFC 2545's advice instead, and adds both global and link-local addresses to the advertisements.

As best practice, in order to avoid situations that prevent connectivity, it is advisable to avoid transporting IPv6 routing information on sessions using IPv4 addresses as endpoints of the BGP session.

NOTE: Theoretically, when defining directly-connected BGP Neighbors, it would be possible to use link-local addresses. In this case, however, we need to indicate, with the "**neighbor** *IPv6-neighbor-link-local* **update-source** *interface*" command, which link-Local IPv6 address is used to open the TCP connection. Nevertheless, not all IOS versions support the use of link-local addresses to define BGP peers, so it is best to avoid using them altogether. The impossibility of using link-local addresses is notified by the message "**% BGP(v6): Invalid scope. Unable to configure link-local peer.**". Considering the virtually endless availability of Global Unicast addresses, in order to prevent any possible issues, it is preferable not to use any link-local addresses.

Another aspect we should highlight is the BGP-ID definition, which – as mentioned in Paragraph 2.6 for MP-BGP – is 32-bit long, and is represented with the same notation as IPv4 addresses (however, it is not an IPv4 address, but rather a simple mnemonic representation of a 32-bit number!)

NOTE: The BGP-ID selection procedure for IPv6 is the same as for IPv4 (see Section 3.1.1). This implies that in IPv6-only routers (that is, with no interface assigned an IPv4 address), manual configuration is required. In any case, it is a good practice to manually configure the BGP-ID. As it is essential for BGP's operation, its definition is mandatory, otherwise the BGP process simply won't work.

Let's see now the configuration for Cisco CE1 (IOS XE) and PE1 (IOS XR) routers; we will omit the configuration for GTW-1 (IOS XR), because it is similar to PE1's. In doing so, we will assume that the BGP sessions for IPv4 are active.

CE1
```
router bgp 65101
  bgp router-id 10.1.99.11
  no bgp default ipv4-unicast
  neighbor 10.1.11.1 remote-as 64501
  neighbor 10.1.12.5 remote-as 64501
  neighbor 2001:db8:1:11::1 remote-as 64501
  neighbor 2001:db8:1:12::5 remote-as 64501
  !
  address-family ipv4
    neighbor 10.1.11.1 activate
    neighbor 10.1.12.5 activate
  exit-address-family
  !
  address-family ipv6
    neighbor 2001:db8:1:11::1 activate
    neighbor 2001:db8:1:12::5 activate
  exit-address-family
```

PE1 (only additional configurations for IPv6)
```
router bgp 64501
  bgp router-id 192.168.0.11
  address-family ipv6 unicast
  !
```

```
neighbor-group IBGP-v6
  remote-as 64501
  update-source Loopback0
  address-family ipv6 unicast
    next-hop-self
!
neighbor-group INTERNET-CUSTOMERS-v6
  remote-as 65101
  address-family ipv6 unicast
    route-policy ALL in
    route-policy ALL out
!
neighbor 2001:db8::12
  use neighbor-group IBGP-v6
  description *** IBGP SESSION-v6 WITH PE2 ***
!
neighbor 2001:db8:1::11
  use neighbor-group IBGP-v6
  description *** IBGP SESSION-v6 WITH GTW-1 ***
!
neighbor 2001:db8:1::12
  use neighbor-group IBGP-v6
  description *** IBGP SESSION-v6 WITH GTW-2 ***
!
neighbor 2001:db8:1:11::2
  use neighbor-group INTERNET-CUSTOMERS-v6
  description *** eBGP SESSION-v6 WITH CE1 ***
```

NOTE: You've probably noticed that, when configuring iBGP sessions, we used the IPv6 addresses of Loopback interfaces as iBGP session endpoints, as per best practice. Those addresses must be connected at layer 3 via an IGP protocol for IPv6. In our example, since we'd already used IS-IS to advertise the IPv4 subnets linked to the Loopback interfaces, we used the multi-topology IS-IS extension, to advertise both the IPv4 and the IPv6 subnets linked to the Loopback0 interfaces, with the same IS-IS routing process.

Configuring BGP sessions for IPv6 in a Juniper environment is much easier. Indeed, it is sufficient to specify the family or families of prefixes you want to transport the routing information of, at global, group or session level. In particular, transport of routing information of IPv6 prefixes is enabled via the command:

family inet6 {
  unicast;
}

Referring to our example, the configuration for router PE2 is the following:

PE2
```
[edit protocols bgp]
group CE-v6 {
  family inet6 {
    unicast;
  }
  peer-as 65101;
  neighbor 2001:db8:1:12::6;
}
group IBGP-v6 {
  family inet6 {
    unicast;
  }
  type internal;
  local-address 2001:db8::12;
  export NHS;
  neighbor 2001:db8:1::11;
  neighbor 2001:db8::11;
  neighbor 2001:db8:1::12;
}
```

NOTE: JUNOS too allows using link-local addresses to establish BGP sessions for IPv6. For JUNOS too – as we saw for Cisco IOS – an additional configuration is required, to specify which link-local IPv6 address is used to open the connection. This specification is done via the "**local-interface** interface" command in the hierarchy "[**edit protocols bgp group** *group-name* **neighbor** *link-local-ipv6-address*]"

Verification commands on completed configurations are the same as those we saw for BGP sessions for IPv4. In Cisco platforms, in "**show** …" commands, it is sufficient to use *<afi, safi>* "**ipv6 unicast**" as a pair. For instance, on router PE1, the session state is checked as follows:

PE1
```
RP/0/0/CPU0:PE1#show bgp ipv6 unicast summary

. . .
BGP router identifier 192.168.0.11, local AS number 64501
. . . < output omitted > . . .
Neighbor        Spk     AS MsgRcvd MsgSent TblVer InQ OutQ  Up/Down St/PfxRcd
2001:db8::12     0 64501     590     546     14   0    0 00:22:16         1
2001:db8:1::11 0 64501       280     285     14   0    0 00:18:36         0
2001:db8:1::12 0 64501       593     546     14   0    0 00:22:16         0
2001:db8:1:11::2
                 0 65101     312     282     14   0    0 04:40:15         1
2001:db8:1:11::6
                 0 65101     619     563     14   0    0 04:40:20         0
```

In JUNOS, the session state check command is exactly the same as the one we saw for IPv4. The example below refers to router PE2.

<u>PE2</u>

```
aft@PE2> show bgp summary
. . . < output omitted > . . .
Peer                     AS    InPkt   OutPkt   OutQ   Flaps   Last Up/Dwn
State|#Active/Received/Accepted/Damped...
. . . < BGP session state for IPv4 omitted > . . .

2001:db8::11            64501      62       65      0       2        29:31
Establ inet6.0: 0/1/1/0
2001:db8:1::11         64501      53       57      0       2        25:46
Establ inet6.0: 0/0/0/0
2001:db8:1::12         64501      70       69      0       1        30:54
Establ inet6.0: 0/0/0/0
2001:db8:1:12::2       65101     817      808      0       0        35:09
Establ inet6.0: 0/0/0/0
2001:db8:1:12::6       65101     810      806      0       0        35:06
Establ inet6.0: 1/1/1/0
```

Try to analyze these views by yourself, as a useful exercise.

3.2 CONFIGURATION SCALABILITY

In practical applications, especially in medium-large ISP networks, the sessions to be configured on a router may be in the tens, if not in the hundreds. As we saw in the previous paragraph, establishing a BGP session requires each one of them to be configured, and also additional configurations (that we'll explore later on) on other aspects, such as policies, timer tuning, and the application of new functionalities.

For this reason, and in order to streamline the work for network administrators, several techniques were developed to make configurations more scalable. For the most part, these techniques are related to the creation of configuration templates, which can be reused for different BGP Neighbors. This is the visible part of these techniques. Then, there is a hidden part that allows improving the overall protocol scalability, since it reduces the quantity of UPDATE messages that BGP Neighbors exchange. Moving on to the technologies covered in this book, JUNOS uses only the Peer Group concept, shown in Section 3.2.1. Instead, Cisco platforms use different techniques and configuration styles, based on the platform.

3.2.1 BGP peer-group

In its standard operation, when a router needs to create a BGP UPDATE message to send to a BGP Neighbor, it analyses any possible outbound routing policies, configured at BGP Neighbor level (outbound filters, attribute modification and/or addition, etc.), and then it creates the consequent BGP UPDATE message.

Let's assume that a BGP Speaker has a high number of BGP sessions, and that the outbound routing policies are identical, for most BGP sessions (or even all of them): in this case, the creation of BGP UPDATE messages results in identical messages. In such a situation, logic dictates that the router creates only one BGP UPDATE message, and replicates its transmission to all the sessions sharing the same outbound routing policies. And this is exactly the idea behind the definition of a BGP peer-group:

A BGP peer-group is a set of BGP Neighbors sharing an identical outbound routing policy.

The adoption of a BGP peer-group generates considerable CPU savings, since, instead of constantly engaging it to create an identical BGP UPDATE message, every single time, it is engaged just once, and then the message created is replicated on all sessions, toward all the BGP Neighbors belonging to the BGP peer-group. In order to create the common BGP UPDATE message, the BGP process elects, among the BGP Neighbors belonging to the BGP peer group, a peer group leader (the one with the lowest BGP-ID) and creates the BGP UPDATE message as if it were addressed to the peer group leader.

Apart from saving benefits in the CPU (and this is the true, most important reason why they were introduced), using BGP peer-groups also generates more compact, elegant, and easier-to-update-and-manage configurations, especially in scenarios in which a BGP Speaker has many BGP Neighbors toward which it applies the same outbound routing policies.

There are two possible types of BGP peer-groups:

- Static: BGP Neighbors belonging to the BGP peer-group are defined on a configuration basis. This is the approach adopted by Juniper and Cisco IOS XE platforms. And it is also the approach that makes configurations more compact and elegant.

- Dynamic: BGP Neighbors belonging to the BGP peer-group are automatically defined by the router, with no manual configuration required. This approach is adopted by Cisco platforms, which create BGP peer-groups to internally optimize the generation of UPDATE messages, even if no explicit configuration has been executed.

In Cisco routers, static BGP peer-groups need to be configured, while dynamic ones are automatically defined. Later on, we will see the implementation details both for static and dynamic BGP peer-groups. From a configuration standpoint, (static) BGP peer-groups are based on the configuration template concept, that is, the set of commands that can be associated in block to each BGP Neighbor. In Juniper platforms, the set of these commands (as we saw earlier) is defined within a BGP Neighbor group, and so it applies to all the group's BGP Neighbors. On the other hand, Cisco's platforms require the explicit definition of a configuration template. There are many possible scenarios where using a BGP peer-group is advantageous, such as when employing Route Reflectors (see Chapter 13), in IXPs, etc. Many examples could be named. We will limit ourselves to one, and we will leave the others for later. The example is summarized in Figure 3.4 below, which shows the scenario of router PE within the network of an ISP with many customers connected. The ISP, following the advice of RFC 2270 – *Using a Dedicated AS for Sites Homed to a Single Provider*, January 1998, assigns a single AS number to all the customers accessing via BGP.

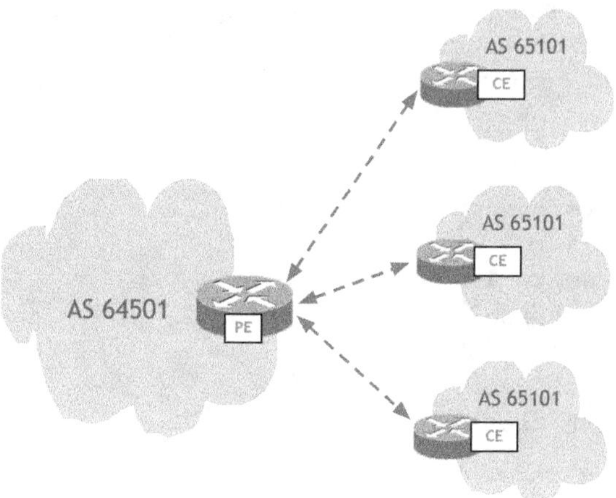

Figure 3.4 – Scenario of a possible BGP peer-group application.

Generally, ISPs tend to standardize their routing policies toward their customers, and this entails the application of identical inbound/outbound policies. For instance, among the policies applied, there could be:

- common traffic management policies, both inbound and outbound;

- filters of various kinds (based on prefixes, on the AS_PATH, etc.), both inbound and outbound;

- maximum number of prefixes accepted;

- messages authentication;

- etc.

In such a situation, the application of BGP peer-groups brings many advantages, in terms of configuration scalability, since, for each additional customer, only one configuration command needs to be entered, which is the one defining if the new BGP Neighbor belongs to the BGP peer-group.

Concerning configurations, we already saw and used JUNOS', because – as mentioned in Paragraph 3.1 – the use of BGP peer-groups is mandatory in JUNOS. Even if only one BGP session is established, it is still necessary to define a group. In Cisco platforms with IOS XE (or standard IOS), they are optional.

Configuring a BGP peer-group in IOS and IOS XE requires the following steps:

- Assigning a name to the BGP peer-group.
  router(config)# **router bgp** *AS-number*
  router(router-config)# **neighbor** *peer-group-name* **peer-group**

- Defining the configuration template (parameters, filters, policies, etc.).
  router(router-config)# **neighbor** *peer-group-name* <parameter/filter/*policy*>
  ...
  router(router-config)# **neighbor** *peer-group-name* <parameter/filter/*policy*>

- Defining the BGP Neighbors belonging to the BGP peer-group.
  router(router-config)# **neighbor** *peer IP* - **peer-group** *peer-group-name*
  ...
  router(router-config)# **neighbor** *IP peer* - **peer-group** *peer-group-name*

If we want to apply these configurations to the example in Figure 3.4, and assuming that, for each customer, the ISP applies common filters for both inbound and outbound advertisements, and common routing policies for inbound and outbound traffic, the configurations to be executed are the following:

```
router bgp 64501
  neighbor CUSTOMERS peer-group
!
  neighbor CUSTOMERS remote-as 65101
  neighbor CUSTOMERS outbound-filter
  neighbor CUSTOMERS inbound-filter
  neighbor CUSTOMERS outbound-policy
  neighbor CUSTOMERS inbound-policy
!
  neighbor neighbor-customer-1-IP CUSTOMER peer-group
  . . .
  neighbor neighbor-customer-N-IP CUSTOMER peer-group
```

For each additional customer, it is sufficient to repeat the last command, with the IP address of the new BGP Neighbor.

The same configuration for JUNOS is the following:

```
[edit protocols bgp]
group CUSTOMERS {
  peer-as 65101;
  import policy-name-imp;
  export policy-name-exp ;
  neighbor customer-neighbor-1-IP ;
  . . .
  neighbor customer-neighbor-N-IP ;
}
```

Cisco platforms also have an internal function to automatically identify BGP peer-groups without any configuration commands. The dynamic BGP peer-group function – which in Cisco's literature is indicated as BGP Update Group – automatically identifies the BGP Neighbors sharing the same outbound routing policies, and optimizes the generation of BGP UPDATE messages and their replications on different BGP sessions.

Differently from static peer-groups, the identification of BGP peer-groups is done automatically, without any configuration. Dynamic BGP peer-groups introduce a decoupling between the optimization of the BGP UPDATE message generation and a compact configuration style. This makes it possible, in Cisco platforms, to use styles that allow the creation of much more flexible and powerful configuration templates, which we'll see in the next two sections (BGP Peer Templates, available in IOS and IOS XE, and BGP Configuration Templates, available only in IOS XR).

3.2.2 BGP peer templates

There are two versions of BGP peer templates, one available in IOS and IOS XE, and the other available only in IOS XR, called BGP configuration templates. We will go over the latter in Section 3.2.3. In both cases, BGP peer templates should be seen as a configuration optimization tool, rather than (differently from classic BGP peer-groups) a tool to optimize the generation of BGP UPDATE messages (which is what dynamic BGP peer-groups are for).

BGP peer templates are based on two types of templates:

- Peer session templates: used to create configuration templates that group all commands at session level, such as: **description**, **ebgp-multihop**, **remote-as**, **version**, **update-source**, and others.

- Peer policy templates: used to create configuration templates that group all policy commands, such as: **filter-list**, **prefix-list**, **route-map**, **default-originate**, **next-hop-self**, **route-reflector-client**, **unsuppress-map**, and others.

NOTE: Apart from "**next-hop-self**" – that we've already covered in Section 3.1.4 – we will see these commands over the next chapters.

In order to maximize their reusability, peer templates adopt the inheritance concept, that is, the option of creating general peer templates to be included in more specific peer templates and create nested (hierarchical) peer templates.

The general inheritance rules are:

- a peer session template can inherit the configuration of another peer session template;

- a peer policy template can inherit the configuration of another peer policy template;

- a BGP Neighbor can inherit the configuration of a peer policy template and/or of a peer session template.

NOTE: There are small differences in the inheritance of peer session templates and peer policy templates. A peer session template can inherit at best the commands of only another peer session template. On the other hand, peer policy templates can inherit up to 8 peer policy templates.

Peer template configuration is done directly within the BGP process, through the following commands:

```
router(config)# router bgp AS-number
router(config-router)# peer-session template peer-session-template-name
router(config-router-stmp)# session commands
router(config-router-stmp)# [inherit peer-session peer-session-template-name]
router(config-router-stmp)# exit-peer-session
router(config-router)# peer-policy template peer-policy-template-name
router(config-router-ptmp)# routing policies commands
router(config-router-ptmp)# [inherit peer-policy peer-policy-template-name seq-num]
...
router(config-router-ptmp)# exit-peer-policy
router(config-router)# neighbor IP-neighbor inherit peer-session peer-session-template-name
router(config-router)# neighbor IP-neighbor inherit peer-policy peer-policy-template-name
```

Notice that inheritance is defined by the **"inherit peer-session ..."** and **"inherit peer-policy ..."** commands. The latter has, as a mandatory parameter, the sequence number, which establishes the order with which inherited peer policy templates are applied. The same inheritance commands, applied to BGP Neighbors, allow applying the peer templates to the BGP Neighbors. Only one peer session template and one peer policy template can be applied.

Now, let's see an example of configuration that shows the flexibility and elegance of BGP peer templates. Let's assume that a router of AS 64500, providing a transit service to its customers, has 5 customers connected via BGP. The 5 customers have AS numbers $6450x$, $x=1,\dots,5$. The parameters and policies applied are summarized in the following table.

			AS 64501	AS 64502	AS 64503	AS 64504	AS 64505
Session	BGP version				X		
	eBGP standard session				X		X
	eBGP Multi-hop session		X	X		X	
Policy	Outbound	default-route only	X	X			
		Default-route + local prefixes AS 64500			X	X	
		Full Internet Routing Table					X
	Inbound	Accepting max 5 prefixes from customers			X		

Let's see the corresponding complete configuration, using the peer templates:

NOTE: The configuration includes some commands that will be described in the following chapters; for now, just focus on the peer template construct.

```
router bgp 64500
! PEER SESSION TEMPLATE DEFINITION
  template peer-session COMMON-PARAM
    version 4
    timers 30 90
  exit-peer-session
!
  template peer-session MULTIHOP-EBGP
    multihop-ebgp
    update-source Loopback0
    inherit peer-session COMMON-PARAM
  exit-peer-session
! CONTINUES
```

The first part of the configuration consists in the definition of the peer session templates. In particular, two peer session templates were defined, called "COMMON-PARAM" and "MULTIHOP-EBGP", respectively. The first defines the BGP version to be used (**"version 4"**) and the two timers related to the KEEPALIVE messages (period=30 sec; Holdtime=90 sec). The second defines TTL's value for multihop eBGP sessions (TTL=255) and the IP address to use in the TCP connection (Loopback0 interface address). Moreover, it inherits the two previous parameters, defining the BGP version and the two timers related to the KEEPALIVE messages. Theoretically, the two peer session templates could have been aggregated in the single peer session template:

```
template peer-session SINGLE
  version 4
  timers 30 90
  multihop-ebgp
  update-source Loopback0
exit-peer-session
```

The reason why they are sometimes written separately, is their greater reusability. For instance, *peer session template* "COMMON-PARAM" can be used independently from *peer session template* "MULTIHOP-EBGP", and this would not be possible, if the two peer session templates were aggregated.

```
! PEER POLICY TEMPLATE DEFINITION
template peer-policy INBOUND-POLICIES
    maximum-prefix 5
 exit-peer-policy
!
 template peer-policy DEFAULT-ONLY
   default-originate
   prefix-list DEFAULTONLY out
   inherit peer-policy INBOUND-POLICIES 10
 exit-peer-policy
!
 template peer-policy DEFAULT-AND-LOC
   filter-list 20 out
   default-originate
   inherit peer-policy INBOUND-POLICIES 10
 exit-peer-policy
!
 template peer-policy FIRT
   prefix-list ANY out
   inherit peer-policy INBOUND-POLICIES 10
 exit-peer-policy
! CONTINUES
```

The second part of the configuration consists in the definition of peer policy templates. In particular, the following peer policy templates were defined:

- INBOUND-POLICIES: it allows limiting the maximum number of prefixes accepted by the relevant BGP Neighbor to 5.

- DEFAULT-ONLY: it allows generating only the default route via BGP. In addition, it inherits the peer policy template INBOUND-POLICIES.

- DEFAULT-AND-LOC: it allows generating the default route via BGP, and applies an outbound filter to propagate only the prefixes within AS 64500 (including the default route) to the BGP Neighbors. In addition, it inherits the peer policy template INBOUND-POLICIES.

- FIRT: it allows sending all prefixes and it also inherits the peer policy template INBOUND-POLICIES.

The last part of the configuration consists in applying the peer session template and peer policy template to the different BGP Neighbors.

```
! APPLICATION TO BGP NEIGHBORS
  neighbor IP-neighbor-AS64501 remote-as 64501
  neighbor IP-neighbor-AS64501 inherit peer-session MULTIHOP-EBGP
  neighbor IP-neighbor-AS64501 inherit peer-session DEFAULT-ONLY
 !
  neighbor IP-neighbor-AS64502 remote-as 64502
  neighbor IP-neighbor-AS64502 inherit peer-session MULTIHOP-EBGP
  neighbor IP-neighbor-AS64502 inherit peer-session DEFAULT-ONLY
 !
  neighbor IP-neighbor-AS64503 remote-as 64503
  neighbor IP-neighbor-AS64503 inherit peer-session COMMON-PARAM
  neighbor IP-neighbor-AS64503 inherit peer-session DEFAULT-AND-LOC
 !
  neighbor IP-neighbor-AS64504 remote-as 64504
  neighbor IP-neighbor-AS64504 inherit peer-session MULTIHOP-EBGP
  neighbor IP-neighbor-AS64504 inherit peer-session DEFAULT-AND-LOC
 !
  neighbor IP-neighbor-AS64505 remote-as 64505
  neighbor IP-neighbor-AS64505 inherit peer-session COMMON-PARAM
  neighbor IP-neighbor-AS64505 inherit peer-session FIRT
```

Peer template application to the different BGP Neighbors follows the policy scheme defined in the table at the beginning of this example. We are going to leave verification of consistency with the policies defined by the administrator of AS 64500 to you.

Cisco IOS XE provides several commands to control the configuration and collect statistics on peer templates. We will not include them here, to make the discussion lighter. If you are interested, see the copious documentation available on the official website, www.cisco.com.

3.2.3 BGP configuration templates

The BGP peer template version available in Cisco platforms using IOS XR – called BGP configuration template – is based on three types of templates:

- Address-family group: it groups the specific commands of a certain address-family.

- Session group: it groups commands that do not depend on the address-family.

- Neighbor group: it groups commands shared by one or more BGP Neighbors.

As with BGP peer templates, in order to maximize their reusability, BGP configuration templates adopt the inheritance concept, that is, the option of creating general templates to include in more specific templates and create nested (hierarchical) templates.

The general inheritance rules for configuration not dependent on a specific address-family are the following:

- a session group can inherit the configuration of another session group;

- a neighbor group can inherit the configuration of the session group and/or of other neighbor groups;

- a neighbor can inherit the configuration of the session group and/or of a neighbor group.

On the other hand, the general inheritance rules for configurations dependent on a specific address-family are the following:

- an address-family group can inherit the configuration of another address-family group;

- a neighbor group can inherit the configuration of an address-family group and/or of other neighbor groups;

- a neighbor can inherit the configuration of an address-family group and/or of a neighbor group.

Moreover, as general rule, a BGP Neighbor configured only to use any "*group" never inherits commands explicitly configured for the BGP Neighbor. In other words, the same previous rule valid for BGP peer templates applies, that is, commands given at a more specific level always trump the same commands given at a more general level. For instance, let's consider the following configuration:

```
router bgp 64500
  neighbor-group AS-64501
    timers 30 90
  exit
  neighbor 192.0.2.1
    remote-as 64501
    use neighbor-group AS-64501
    timers 10 30
```

For BGP Neighbor 192.0.2.1 the value of the two KEEPALIVE and Holdtime timers is 10 sec and 30 sec, respectively.

Now, let's take a look at the configuration commands required to define the different groups (address-family/session/neighbor) and their application method to BGP Neighbors.

Configuring an *address-family group*
RP/0/RP0/CPU0:router(config)# **router bgp** *AS-number*
RP/0/RP0/CPU0:router(config-bgp)# **af-group** *af-group-name* **address-family** *afi safi*
RP/0/RP0/CPU0:router(config-bgp-afgrp)# . . .

Configuring a *session group*
RP/0/RP0/CPU0:router(config)# **router bgp** *AS-number*
RP/0/RP0/CPU0:router(config-bgp)# **session-group** *session-group-name*
RP/0/RP0/CPU0:router(config-bgp-sngrp)# . . .

Configuring a *neighbor group*
RP/0/RP0/CPU0:router(config)# **router bgp** *AS-number*
RP/0/RP0/CPU0:router(config-bgp)# **neighbor-group** *neighbor-group-name*
RP/0/RP0/CPU0:router(config-bgp-nbrgrp)# . . .

Application to *BGP neighbors*
RP/0/RP0/CPU0:router(config)# **router bgp** *AS-number*
RP/0/RP0/CPU0:router(config-bgp)# **neighbor** *IP-neighbor*
RP/0/RP0/CPU0:router(config-bgp-nbr)# **use {session-group | neighbor-group}** *name*
RP/0/RP0/CPU0:router(config-bgp-nbr)# **address-family** *afi safi*
RP/0/RP0/CPU0:router(config-bgp-nbr-af)# **use af-group** *af-group-name*

In the following example, we will see how to apply these configuration techniques to our example network, in Figure 3.1. Let's assume that router PE1, apart from the two CEs shown in the figure, also has a third CE router connected, as shown in Figure 3.5 below. The new router CE3 is connected to PE1 through a point-to-point connection, with IP addresses taken from subnet 10.1.13.0/30 (.1 PE1 side).

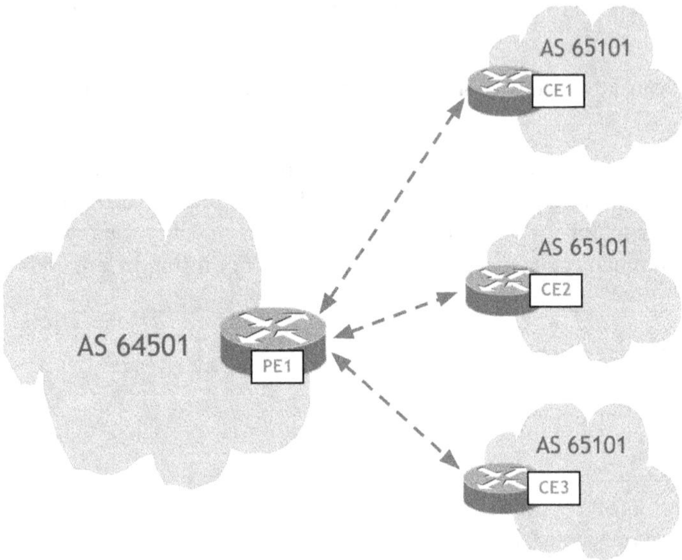

Figure 3.5 – Example of application of the BGP configuration template.

The following policies and parameters apply to each customer:

- common route-policies, both inbound (CUSTOMERS-IN) and outbound (CUSTOMERS-OUT);

- maximum number of prefixes accepted: 5;

- use of BFD with parameters: period of BFD Hello=50 msec, BFD Holdtime=250 msec (=5x50);

- period of KEEPALIVE=30 sec and Holdtime=90 sec;

- same remote AS (=65101).

The configurations executed are:

```
router bgp 64501
 bgp router-id 192.168.0.11
 !
 af-group CUSTOMERS address-family ipv4 unicast
  route-policy CUSTOMERS-IN in
  route-policy CUSTOMERS-OUT out
  maximum-prefix 5
 !
 session-group CUSTOMERS
  remote-as 65101
```

```
  bfd fast-detect
  bfd multiplier 5
  bfd minimum-interval 50
  timers 30 90
 !
 neighbor-group INTERNET-CUSTOMERS
  use session-group CUSTOMERS
  address-family ipv4 unicast
   use af-group CUSTOMERS
 !
 neighbor 10.1.11.2
  use neighbor-group INTERNET-CUSTOMERS
 !
 neighbor 10.1.11.6
  use neighbor-group INTERNET-CUSTOMERS
 !
 neighbor 10.1.13.2
  use neighbor-group INTERNET-CUSTOMERS
```

Here too, an interesting fact to notice is that we can add a new customer simply by adding two commands. For instance, assuming we add CE4, with BGP Neighbor 10.1.14.2, the two configuration lines to execute are:

```
neighbor 10.1.14.2
  use neighbor-group INTERNET-CUSTOMERS
```

Below are some useful views to check the validity of the configurations executed.
The first two views show the parameters and policies of address-family group "CUSTOMERS" and of session group "CUSTOMERS". Notation "[]" indicates that the commands specified are not inherited from any group.

```
RP/0/0/CPU0:PE1#show bgp af-group CUSTOMERS configuration
. . .
af-group CUSTOMERS address-family IPv4 Unicast
  maximum-prefix 5 75                     []
  policy CUSTOMERS-IN in                  []
  policy CUSTOMERS-OUT out                []

RP/0/0/CPU0:PE1#show bgp session-group CUSTOMERS configuration
. . .
session-group CUSTOMERS
 remote-as 65101        []
 timers 30 90 3         []
 bfd fast-detect        []
 bfd mininterval 50     []
 bfd multiplier 5       []
```

The two following views allow checking who inherits address-family group "CUSTOMERS" and session group "CUSTOMERS". In particular, the views show that both groups are used within neighbor group "INTERNET-CUSTOMERS" (notation "**n:INTERNET-CUSTOMERS**", where "**n**" stands for neighbor group) and that the final users are three CEs.

```
RP/0/0/CPU0:PE1#show bgp af-group CUSTOMERS users

. . .

IPv4 Unicast: 10.1.13.2    10.1.11.6    10.1.11.2    n:INTERNET-CUSTOMERS


RP/0/0/CPU0:PE1#show bgp session-group CUSTOMERS users

. . .

Session: 10.1.13.2         10.1.11.6    10.1.11.2    n:INTERNET-CUSTOMERS
```

The next view shows the configuration of the neighbor group "INTERNET-CUSTOMERS". Notation [**s:CUSTOMERS**] indicates that the commands specified have been inherited from session group "CUSTOMERS", while notation [**a:CUSTOMERS**] indicates that the commands specified are inherited from address-family group "CUSTOMERS".

```
RP/0/0/CPU0:PE1#show bgp neighbor-group INTERNET-CUSTOMERS configuration

. . .

neighbor-group INTERNET-CUSTOMERS
 remote-as 65101                          [s:CUSTOMERS]
 timers 30 90 3                           [s:CUSTOMERS]
 bfd fast-detect                          [s:CUSTOMERS]
 bfd mininterval 50                       [s:CUSTOMERS]
 bfd multiplier 5                         [s:CUSTOMERS]
 address-family IPv4 Unicast              []
  maximum-prefix 5 75                     [a:CUSTOMERS]
  policy CUSTOMERS-IN in                  [a:CUSTOMERS]
  policy CUSTOMERS-OUT out                [a:CUSTOMERS]
```

To conclude the check, let's see the configuration view of "**neighbor 10.1.11.2**" (CE1), including the groups from which the commands were inherited. For instance, the "**remote-as 65101**" command was inherited from neighbor group "INTERNET-CUSTOMERS", which, in turn, inherited it from session group "CUSTOMERS", (notation [**n:INTERNET-CUSTOMERS s:CUSTOMERS**]), while the "**maximum-prefix 5 75**" command was inherited from neighbor group "INTERNET-CUSTOMERS", which in turn inherited it from address-family group "CUSTOMERS", (notation [**n:INTERNET-CUSTOMERS a:CUSTOMERS**]).

```
RP/0/0/CPU0:PE1#show bgp neighbors 10.1.11.2 configuration

. . .

neighbor 10.1.11.2
  remote-as 65101                [n:INTERNET-CUSTOMERS  s:CUSTOMERS]
  timers 30 90 3                 [n:INTERNET-CUSTOMERS  s:CUSTOMERS]
  bfd fast-detect                [n:INTERNET-CUSTOMERS  s:CUSTOMERS]
  bfd mininterval 50             [n:INTERNET-CUSTOMERS  s:CUSTOMERS]
  bfd multiplier 5               [n:INTERNET-CUSTOMERS  s:CUSTOMERS]
  address-family IPv4 Unicast    [n:INTERNET-CUSTOMERS]
    maximum-prefix 5 75          [n:INTERNET-CUSTOMERS  s:CUSTOMERS]
    policy CUSTOMERS-IN in       [n:INTERNET-CUSTOMERS  s:CUSTOMERS]
    policy CUSTOMERS-OUT out     [n:INTERNET-CUSTOMERS  s:CUSTOMERS]
```

3.2.4 Dynamic BGP peer definition

In some platforms (e.g. Cisco, Juniper), BGP Neighbors can be defined, other than in a static manner (i.e. by manually setting the IP address and AS number of the BGP Neighbors, as we saw until now), also dynamically. A dynamic definition can be used when there is a possibility that the BGP Neighbors can change dynamically over time, or even with very high numbers of BGP Neighbors, and possibly the need to add more.

In such situations, in order to make the configuration scalable, we can use the mechanism known as BGP Dynamic Neighbor, available in Cisco IOS XE/XR and in JUNOS, which makes the BGP process "listen" for any BGP Neighbors with an IP address falling within a predefined set of addresses. It is important to notice that, through this mechanism, the BGP process does not take any initiative, i.e., it does not initiate the three-way-handshake for any BGP Neighbor whose address falls within the predefined address set. This saves a lot of configuration lines and – more interestingly – allows introducing new BGP Neighbors, without any new configuration, and also saving up CPU, as it avoids TCP connection collisions.

A use case in practical applications occurs in Hub-and-spoke topologies, such as the L3VPN service based on Cisco's proprietary implementation DMVPN (Dynamic Multipoint VPN), where the need arises – if BGP is used as internal routing protocol – to establish hundreds if not thousands of Hub↔Spoke BGP sessions, since Hubs are limited (generally a few units) and Spokes even thousands. In this scenario, the BGP Dynamic Neighbor technique is very useful, as it allows to introduce new Spokes without any new configuration on the Hubs, thus making the system a lot more scalable from a configuration standpoint.

The dynamic definition specifies the predefined set of addresses the BGP Neighbor's IP address must belong to, through the pair prefix/netmask. The commands used for the BGP Neighbor's dynamic definition are the following:

<u>IOS XE</u>:
router(config)# **router bgp** *AS-number*
router(config-router)# **bgp listen range** *prefix/netmask* **peer-group** *peer-group-name*
! OPTIONAL: allows limiting the maximum number of BGP sessions
router(config-router)# **bgp listen limit** *session-limit-number*

NOTE: In IOS XE, the BGP Dynamic Neighbor mechanism requires the use of BGP peer-groups.

<u>IOS XR</u>:
RP/0/RP0/CPU0:router(config)# **router bgp** *AS-number*
RP/0/RP0/CPU0:router(config-bgp)# **neighbor** *prefix/netmask*

<u>JUNOS</u>
[edit protocols bgp]
group *group-name* {
  allow *prefix/netmask*;
}

For example, let's consider router PE2 (Juniper) from the example network in Figure 3.1. The configuration toward CEs can be shortened as follows:

```
[edit protocols bgp]
group CE {
    peer-as 65101;
    allow 10.1.0.0/16;
}
```

This configuration allows PE2 to receive requests for eBGP sessions initialized by any CE with AS number 65101 and IP address within IP subnet 10.1/16.

3.3 CHECKING BGP OPERATION

BGP implementations – both open and those from traditional manufacturers, such as Cisco, Juniper, etc. – provide a sufficiently rich set of commands to check the protocol's actual operation. There are "**show…**" type commands, and then commands to view certain BGP dynamic processes ("**debug …**" commands in Cisco platforms, "**traceoptions …**" commands in Juniper platforms), which are the essential tools to troubleshoot any possible fault.

In particular, "**show**…" commands display:

- the characteristics and state of BGP sessions;

- the advertisement's structure (BGP Next-Hop, BGP Neighbor, metrics, etc.);

- the advertisements received/announced via BGP from/to a specific BGP Neighbor.

While "**debug/traceoptions** ..." commands – which should be used with caution, due to their heavy CPU usage – display the dynamic process relating to:

- session creation;

- events (state transitions, UPDATE sending/receiving, etc.);

- BGP message structure and exchange;

- . . .

Before going over the set of configuration check commands, we want to highlight a very important difference between Cisco and Juniper routers.

In Cisco routers, all the advertisements received from the different BGP Neighbors, not rejected by any possible inbound filters, are stored in a special memory area (BGP table), whose content can be viewed. The best path is selected among them, for each prefix, and displayed in the BGP table with the symbol ">". Even advertisements not valid for the selection process are added to the same table, however they will obviously never become best paths. On the other hand, in Juniper routers, all advertisements received (even those rejected by inbound filters) are added to the RIB. Of those, the advertisements not valid for the selection process are added to a hidden part of the RIB.

NOTE: Even if all the following examples refer to IPv4 BGP sessions and advertisements, the same check commands – with due variations – apply also to IPv6 BGP sessions and advertisements.

3.3.1 Session characteristics and state

The characteristics and state of BGP sessions can be displayed with the following commands – all very similar to one another:

<u>IOS XE</u>:
router(config)# **show bgp** *afi safi* **summary**

<u>IOS XR</u>:
RP/0/RP0/CPU0:router(config)# **show bgp** *afi safi* **summary**

<u>JUNOS</u>:
user@router> **show bgp summary**

NOTE: In older versions of Cisco IOS and IOS XE, it was possible to use the "**show ip bgp summary**" command, only for address-family ipv4 unicast BGP sessions.

Those commands are some of the most useful ones, and usually the first to be executed, to check the state of a BGP session. Let's see a few examples of their application on the routers in our network (Figure 3.1), with the related comments.

<u>CE1</u> (IOS XE)
```
CE1#show bgp ipv4 unicast summary
BGP router identifier 10.1.99.11, local AS number 65101
BGP table version is 17, main routing table version 17
16 network entries using 3968 bytes of memory
32 path entries using 4352 bytes of memory
8/8 BGP path/bestpath attribute entries using 2304 bytes of memory
8 BGP AS-PATH entries using 320 bytes of memory
0 BGP route-map cache entries using 0 bytes of memory
0 BGP filter-list cache entries using 0 bytes of memory
BGP using 10944 total bytes of memory
BGP activity 34/18 prefixes, 67/35 paths, scan interval 60 secs
18 networks peaked at 10:51:36 Nov 25 2020 UTC (00:04:25.687 ago)

Neighbor  V    AS MsgRcvd MsgSent TblVer InQ OutQ  Up/Down State/PfxRcd
10.1.11.1 4 64501      12       4     17   0    0 00:00:41           16
10.1.12.5 4 64501      11      12     17   0    0 00:00:43           16
```

For each BGP session, the command provides:

- IP address used by the BGP Neighbor for the BGP session (**Neighbor** column);

- protocol version (**V** column);

- AS number the BGP Neighbor belongs to (**AS** column);

- number of BGP messages sent and received (**MsgRcvd** and **MsgSent** columns);

- BGP table version, increased by 1 at every variation (**TblVer** column);

- BGP messages in inbound (**InQ** column) and outbound (**OutQ** column) queues;

- session uptime (**Up/Down** column): if down => "**never**", if up, how long ago it was established;

- session state (**State** column): if empty, the state is Established, otherwise, it is the reached state (usually Idle or Active);

- number of prefixes received (**PfxRcd** column).

In the general section, the command also provides general info, such as: BGP-ID, router AS number, and memory used.

<u>PE1</u> (IOS XR)
```
RP/0/0/CPU0#show bgp ipv4 unicast summary
BGP router identifier 192.168.0.11, local AS number 64501
BGP generic scan interval 60 secs
Non-stop routing is enabled
BGP table state: Active
Table ID: 0xe0000000   RD version: 22
```

```
BGP main routing table version 22
BGP NSR Initial initsync version 2 (Reached)
BGP NSR/ISSU Sync-Group versions 0/0
BGP scan interval 60 secs

BGP is operating in STANDALONE mode.

Process     RcvTblVer   bRIB/RIB    LabelVer   ImportVer  SendTblVer  StandbyVer
Speaker        22          22          22         22         22          0

Neighbor        Spk     AS MsgRcvd MsgSent TblVer InQ OutQ  Up/Down St/PfxRcd
10.1.11.2        0  65101    2492    2886     22   0    0 00:21:59         0
10.1.11.6        0  65101    3112    2822     22   0    0 23:24:59         0
10.1.13.2        0  65101    3070    2822     22   0    0 23:25:00         0
192.168.0.12 0  64501    3083    2813     22   0    0 23:24:59         0
192.168.1.11 0  64501    1411    1409     22   0    0 23:24:58        10
192.168.1.12 0  64501    3100    2813     22   0    0 23:24:58         7
```

The view is very similar to the one we saw for IOS XE. Except that, instead of the BGP version (which is still 4), there is the number of the BGP Speaker in charge of the Neighbor (**Spk** column). When BGP operates in standalone mode (as in this case: **BGP is operating in STANDALONE mode**), the BGP Speaker process number is always 0. For the sake of brevity, we won't go into detail on the BGP Speaker concept, also because it is not widely used in practical applications.

<u>PE2</u> (JUNOS)

```
aft@PE2>show bgp summary
Groups: 2 Peers: 5 Down peers: 0
Table    Tot Paths  Act Paths  Suppressed   History  Damp State  Pending
inet.0         17        16           0         0          0        0
Peer               AS    InPkt    OutPkt     OutQ     Flaps   Last Up/Dwn
State|#Active/Received/Accepted/Damped...
10.1.12.2        65101    4917      4880        0         0        59:15
Establ inet.0: 0/0/0/0
10.1.12.6        65101      86        84        0         2        34:46
Establ inet.0: 0/0/0/0
192.168.0.11     64501    2838      3109        0         2        37:41
Establ inet.0: 0/0/0/0
192.168.1.11     64501    8515      9338        0         0        57:07
Establ inet.0: 9/10/10/0
192.168.1.12     64501    9360      9339        0         0        57:00
Establ inet.0: 7/7/7/0
```

In the first part, the command provides some general pieces of information, such as: BGP peer group number (**Groups: 2**), BGP Neighbor number (**Peers: 5**) and number of sessions in the down state (**Down peers: 0**), type of RIB used (**inet.0**), total quantity of active (**Act Paths 16**) and received (**Tot Paths 17**) prefixes. And therefore, for each BGP session:

- IP address used by the BGP Neighbor for the BGP session (**Peer** column);

- AS number the BGP Neighbor belongs to (**AS** column);

- number of BGP messages received and sent (**InPkt** and **OutPkt** columns);

- BGP messages in the outbound queue, ready to be sent (**OutQ** column);

- number of times the session has been closed and re-established (**Flaps** column);

- time elapsed since the last state change from Established to any other state, or from any other state to Established (**Last Up/Down** column);

- session state (**State** column): if Established, information on the advertisement is displayed, such as active/received/accepted/damped; otherwise, the state reached is displayed. For instance, 10 prefixes (all accepted) were received from BGP Neighbor 192.168.1.11 (GTW-1), 9 of which were elected best paths and are therefore active in the RIB (i.e., used to route traffic); none of them was subject to Route Flap Damping.

NOTE: To know more on the meaning of damped advertisement, see the Route Flap Damping mechanism in Paragraph 8.8.

To gain more information on a single BGP session, you can use the following commands:

IOS XE:
router(config)# **show bgp** *afi safi* **neighbors** [*IP-neighbor*]

IOS XR:
RP/0/RP0/CPU0:router(config)# **show bgp** *afi safi* **neighbors** [*IP-neighbor*]

JUNOS:
user@router> **show bgp neighbors** [*IP-neighbor*]

Since the views generated by these commands are very long, we will not include them here, for the sake of brevity. Let's just say that they allow obtaining information such as: IP addresses and TCP ports used; type of BGP session (eBGP/iBGP); session state; KEEPALIVE message timers (period and holdtime); negotiated BGP capabilities, and address-families supported, and so on.

3.3.2 Display of BGP advertisements

One essential aspect to assess whether a configuration is working or not, is viewing the BGP advertisements generated locally by a BGP Speaker, and exchanged with other BGP Neighbors. For this purpose, Cisco and Juniper adopt different strategies, but the final result is (obviously) the same. As mentioned earlier, Cisco includes all advertisements in a table called BGP table, or BGP RIB. While Juniper includes all advertisements in the RIB, in separate sub-tables, if necessary. In Cisco platforms, the commands to execute are basically the same, except for the default command, and they are:

IOS XE:
router(config)# **show bgp** *afi safi* ...

IOS XR:
RP/0/RP0/CPU0:router(config)# **show bgp** [*afi safi*]...

The only difference is that in IOS XE it is always necessary to specify the type of address-family, while in IOS XR this is only necessary for address-families other than IPv4 unicast.

NOTE: Commands have many options, and we will go over some of them later on. Those options are especially important in large network routers – where the BGP RIB can contain hundreds of thousands of advertisements – in order to display only the advertisements that match certain characteristics (e.g. all the advertisements of a particular prefix; all the advertisements generated by a specific AS, or coming from a specific AS; etc.).

Let's see an application of the basic commands to router CE1 (IOS XE). The view for routers with IOS XR is basically the same, and we will omit it. For the sake of brevity, we will shorten the view only to three advertisements, plus the default route:

CE1 (IOS XE)
```
CE1#show bgp ipv4 unicast
BGP table version is 17, local router ID is 10.1.99.11
Status codes: s suppressed, d damped, h history, * valid, > best, i -
internal, r RIB-failure, S Stale, m multipath, b backup-path, f RT-Filter,
x best-external, a additional-path, c RIB-compressed, t secondary path,
L long-lived-stale,
Origin codes: i - IGP, e - EGP, ? - incomplete
RPKI validation codes: V valid, I invalid, N Not found
   Network          Next Hop       Metric LocPrf Weight Path
 *  0.0.0.0         10.1.12.5                      0 64501 65542 i
 *>                 10.1.11.1                      0 64501 65542 i

 . . .

 *  192.0.2.0       10.1.12.5                      0 64501 65542 64497i
 *>                 10.1.11.1                      0 64501 65542 64497i
 *  198.51.100.0    10.1.12.5                      0 64501 65541 64508i
 *>                 10.1.11.1                      0 64501 65541 64508i
 *  203.0.113.0     10.1.12.5                      0 64501 65541 64496 i
 *>                 10.1.11.1                      0 64501 65541 64496 i
```

Notice that, for each prefix, there are two BGP advertisements, coming from PE1 (Next-Hop 10.1.11.1) and PE2 (Next-Hop 10.1.12.5). The advertisements are shown in order of arrival, with the most recent one being first. In the first column (**Network**), before the prefix, symbol "*" indicates that the advertisement is valid, symbol ">" indicates the best path, and "i" (where present) indicates that the advertisement was received from an iBGP session. The **Next-Hop**, **Metric** and **LocPrf** columns indicate the BGP Next-Hop, the MED value and the Local Preference value, respectively. In this specific case, the values are not shown, since the advertisements received from CE1 do not contain these attributes. The **Weight** column indicates Cisco's proprietary weight parameter, whose meaning and use will be explained later in this book. Lastly, the **Path** column contains the AS_PATH and ORIGIN attributes. Concerning the latter, symbol "i" indicates ORIGIN=IGP, while symbol "?" indicates ORIGIN=INCOMPLETE. Actually (although very rarely), it is (theoretically) possible to see also the symbol "e", which indicates ORIGIN=EGP.

NOTE: Symbol "*" in the first column – which, according to the legend, indicates that the advertisement is valid – is a little misleading. Indeed, even those advertisements with an unreachable BGP Next-Hop – which, therefore, do not take part in the selection process – are indicated as valid, when in practice they aren't, for the selection process.

Greater detail is obtained by specifying the prefix. Let's see an example of the result obtained for prefix 192.0.2/24.

```
CE1#show bgp ipv4 unicast 192.0.2.0/24
BGP routing table entry for 192.0.2.0/24, version 12
Paths: (2 available, best #2, table default)
  Advertised to update-groups:
     3
  64501 65542 64497
```

```
      10.1.12.5 from 10.1.12.5 (192.168.0.12)
        Origin IGP, localpref 100, valid, external
        rx pathid: 0, tx pathid: 0
    64501 65542 64497
      10.1.11.1 from 10.1.11.1 (192.168.0.11)
        Origin IGP, localpref 100, valid, external, best
        rx pathid: 0, tx pathid: 0x0
```

The view shows that, for prefix 192.0.2/24, there are two paths (advertisements) available, and the best path is the second one (**Paths: (2 available, best #2, table default)**). For each path, the following data are shown: AS_PATH, BGP Next-hop, IP address used by the BGP Neighbor to establish the BGP session (indicated after **from**), BGP-ID of the BGP Neighbor that sent the advertisement (indicated in round brackets), and Origin (**Origin**) and Local Preference (**localpref**) values. Lastly, it indicates whether the advertisement is valid (**valid**), eBGP (**external**) or iBGP (**internal**), and if it is the best path (**best**). For instance, for the advertisement elected as the best path: AS_PATH=[64501 65542 64497], BGP Next-Hop=10.1.11.1, address of BGP peer=10.1.11.1, BGP-ID of BGP peer=192.168.0.11, Origin=0 (IGP), Local Preference=100 (default).

Another useful information contained in the view is the set of BGP Neighbors to which the advertisement was propagated. Even though we did not configure any BGP peer-group, IOS XE uses dynamic BGP peer-groups all the same. In this example, it created one, internally numbered as 3 (**Advertised to update-groups: 3**). To know which BGP Neighbors the advertisement has been propagated to, we just need to check what are the BGP Neighbors belonging to this dynamic BGP peer-group. This can be done with the following command (which we shortened, for the sake of brevity):

```
CE1#show bgp ipv4 uni update-group 3 | begin member
  Has 1 member:
    10.1.12.5
```

from which we infer that CE1 propagates the advertisement toward BGP Neighbor 10.1.12.5 (PE2).

In Juniper platforms, the command to execute is the following:

user@router> **show route protocol bgp [table** *table*]

where the option "**table**" can be used to narrow down the advertisements to a certain address-family type. JUNOS adds BGP advertisements to different tables, based on the relevant address-family (e.g., inet.0 for the advertisements belonging to the IPv4 unicast address-family, inet6.0 for those belonging to the IPv6 unicast address-family, bgp.l3vpn.0 for the advertisements belonging to the VPN-IPv4 address-family, etc.).

Let's see an example of how this command is applied to router PE2, for the same prefix 192.0.2/24 (belonging to the IPv4 unicast address-family).

```
aft@PE2> show route protocol bgp table inet.0 192.0.2/24
inet.0: 31 destinations, 32 routes (31 active, 0 holddown, 0 hidden)     +
= Active Route, - = Last Active, * = Both
192.0.2.0/24  *[BGP/170] 09:43:46, MED 0, localpref 100, from 192.168.1.12
                  AS path: 65542 64497 I, validation-state: unverified
                > to 172.16.1.12 via ge-0/0/1.0
```

The view shows that the advertisement was received by BGP Neighbor 192.168.1.12 (GTW-2), and then the usual metrics: MED (=0), Local Preference (=100) and AS_PATH (=[65542 64497]).

Concerning the BGP Next-Hop, it is not included in this view. Indeed, differently from Cisco's views, the Next-Hop present is the IGP Next-Hop to reach the BGP Next-Hop. In order to see the BGP Next-Hop, we need to view the advertisement in detail.

```
aft@PE2> show route protocol bgp table inet.0 192.0.2/24 detail
inet.0: 31 destinations, 32 routes (31 active, 0 holddown, 0 hidden)
192.0.2.0/24 (1 entry, 1 announced)
  *BGP   Preference: 170/-101
         Next hop type: Indirect, Next hop index: 0
         Address: 0xce33610
         Next-hop reference count: 14
         Source: 192.168.1.12
         Next hop type: Router, Next hop index: 610
         Next hop: 172.16.1.12 via ge-0/0/1.0, selected
         Session Id: 0x142
         Protocol next hop: 192.168.1.12
         Indirect next hop: 0xccbefb0 1048576 INH Session ID: 0x147
         State: <Active Int Ext>
         Local AS: 64501 Peer AS: 64501
         Age: 3d 9:56:19       Metric: 0       Metric2: 10
         Validation State: unverified
         ORR Generation-ID: 0
         Task: BGP_64501.192.168.1.12
         Announcement bits (3): 0-KRT 3-BGP_RT_Background 4-Resolve tree 4
         AS path: 65542 64497 I
         Accepted
         Localpref: 100
         Router ID: 192.168.1.12
```

The BGP Next-Hop is displayed as "**Protocol next hop: 192.168.1.12**", and it is therefore 192.168.1.12.

A more compact view can be obtained through the "**terse**" option:

```
aft@PE2> show route protocol bgp table inet.0 192.0.2/24 terse

. . .
A V Destination        P Prf   Metric 1   Metric 2   Next hop      AS path
* ? 192.0.2.0/24       B 170       100          0                  65542 64497 I
    unverified                                            >172.16.1.12
```

The information shown is basically the same as above. In column "**A**", symbol "*" indicates that the route is active, that is, used for traffic forwarding; we will see the meaning of column "**V**" in Chapter 10. Column "**P**" indicates the protocol (**B**=BGP), column "**Prf**" indicates the Degree of Preference that JUNOS assigns to BGP (by default=170), column "**Metric 1**" indicates the Local Preference value, while column "**Metric 2**" indicates the MED value. The last two columns contain the IGP Next-Hop (and not the BGP Next-Hop), the AS_PATH and the Origin value.

NOTE: JUNOS's Degree of Preference is equivalent to Cisco platforms' Administrative Distance. JUNOS always assigns a value of 170 to BGP advertisements. On the other hand, Cisco platforms assign different values based on the type of advertisement: 20 for eBGP advertisements and 200 for iBGP and for locally-generated advertisements.

Below we see the same prefix detail on PE1 (IOS XR):


```
RP/0/0/CPU0:PE1#show bgp 192.0.2.0/24
. . .
BGP routing table entry for 192.0.2.0/24
. . .
Paths: (1 available, best #1)
  . . .
  Advertised to update-groups (with more than one peer):
    0.3
  65542 64497
    192.168.1.12 (metric 10) from 192.168.1.12 (192.168.1.12)
      Origin IGP, metric 0, localpref 100, valid, internal, best, group-best
      Received Path ID 0, Local Path ID 0, version 14
```

An interesting aspect of this view is the "**metric 10**" after the BGP Next-Hop (=192.168.1.12), which indicates the total IGP cost to reach the BGP Next-Hop. This can also be seen in PE1's RIB:

```
RP/0/0/CPU0:PE1#show route 192.168.1.12/32
. . .
Routing entry for 192.168.1.12/32
  Known via "isis TT", distance 115, metric 10, type level-2
  Routing Descriptor Blocks
    172.16.1.12, from 192.168.1.12, via GigabitEthernet0/0/0/1
      Route metric is 10
  No advertising protos.
```

Please note that this metric value is only included in iBGP advertisements (and the reason is pretty obvious).

To conclude this section, let's go over a few useful commands to verify the advertisements sent and received on a certain BGP session.

The following commands can be used to verify the advertisements sent:

<u>IOS XE/XR</u>:
*(config)# **show bgp** *afi safi* **neighbors** *IP-neighbor* **advertised-routes**

<u>JUNOS</u>:
user@router> **show route advertising-protocol bgp** *IP-neighbor*

As an example, let's see the advertisements sent by GTW-1 to BGP Neighbor 192.168.0.12 (PE2) and those sent by GTW-2 to PE1 .


```
RP/0/0/CPU0:ASBR-1#show bgp ipv4 unicast neighbors 192.168.0.12
                                             advertised-routes
. . .
Network              Next Hop          From              AS Path
0.0.0.0/0            192.168.1.11      172.20.1.1        65541i
. . .
198.51.100.0/24      192.168.1.11      172.20.1.1        65541 64508i
```

```
203.0.113.0/24      192.168.1.11    172.20.1.1          65541 64496i
. . .

aft@GTW-2> show route advertising-protocol bgp 192.168.0.11
inet.0: 26 destinations, 36 routes (26 active, 0 holddown, 0 hidden)
Prefix              Nexthop      MED      Lclpref     AS path
* 0.0.0.0/0           Self         0        100          65542 I

. . .
* 192.0.2.0/24        Self         0        100          65542 64497 I
. . .
```

"**Self**" below column "**Nexthop**" indicates that the advertisements have been sent with the NEXT_HOP attribute, containing its own IP address; in particular, the IP address used by PE2 to establish the iBGP session with PE1 (=192.168.1.12).

In order to verify the advertisements received, in Cisco platforms, we need to enable the soft-reconfiguration inbound function first, while no other additional command is required in JUNOS. We will talk about how to enable the soft-reconfiguration inbound function in Chapter 6, along with the commands to view the advertisements received. For JUNOS, the command to execute is the following:

user@router> **show route receive-protocol bgp** *IP-neighbor*

As an example of this last command, let's see the advertisements that router CE2 receives from PE1.

```
aft@CE2> show route receive-protocol bgp 10.1.11.5
inet.0: 21 destinations, 37 routes (21 active, 0 holddown, 0 hidden)
Prefix              Nexthop      MED    Lclpref    AS path
0.0.0.0/0           10.1.11.5                      64501 65542 I

. . .
192.0.2.0/24        10.1.11.5                      64501 65542 64497 I
198.51.100.0/24     10.1.11.5                      64501 65541 64508 I
203.0.113.0/24      10.1.11.5                      64501 65541 64496 I
. . .
inet6.0: 7 destinations, 7 routes (7 active, 0 holddown, 0 hidden)
```

We leave it to you to find out why there is no value below the **MED** and **Lclpref** columns.

3.4 TROUBLESHOOTING A BGP SESSION

As you may have noticed, establishing a BGP session is a process that requires a very "manual" configuration, therefore subject to more errors. And an incorrect configuration may cause several issues, including:

- one or more BGP sessions do not reach the Established state;

- the routing policy configured does not work as planned;

- the filtering policies remove advertisements that shouldn't be rejected and, vice versa, accept prefixes that should be rejected.

In this paragraph, we will only delve into point one – the reasons why a BGP session does not reach the Established state.

Some of the most frequent reasons are:

- the IP address used to open the session cannot be reached;

- the "AS-neighbor" value configured does not match with the BGP Neighbor's AS number;

- an eBGP session uses an address of a network not directly connected as IP address to open the session (Note: remember that, in eBGP sessions, TCP/IP packets transporting BGP messages start with TTL=1 by default);

- the source IP address used by the TCP/IP packets transporting the BGP messages does not match the one configured in the "**neighbor** ..." command of the BGP Neighbor.

In all those cases, the session reaches the Active state, at best, or it fluctuates between the Idle, Connect and Active states.

Now, let's see how we can find out why a BGP session does not reach the Established state, through a few examples. As a basic reference, we are going to take the example of the multihop eBGP session achieved in Figure 3.2.

3.4.1 Unreachable IP-neighbor address: symptoms

First, let's consider the case in which the IP address used to open the BGP session with a BGP Neighbor is not reachable, that is, there is no prefix that contains it in the RIB.

For instance, let's assume that the FIRT server in Figure 3.2 does not have a path to reach the BGP Neighbor 10.1.99.13 in its RIB:

```
FIRT-SERV#show ip route 10.1.99.13
% Network not in table
```

while router R1 has a path toward the BGP Neighbor 192.168.2.1:

```
aft@R1> show route 192.168.2.1
inet.0: 22 destinations, 38 routes (22 active, 0 holddown, 0 hidden)     +
= Active Route, - = Last Active, * = Both
192.168.2.1/32      *[Static/5] 00:00:18
                    > to 10.1.13.1 via ge-0/0/0.0
```

By using "**show bgp ... summary**" commands on both routers, we can verify the session state (Note: we could also use "**show bgp ... neighbors**" commands).

```
FIRT-SERV#show bgp ipv4 unicast summary
BGP router identifier 192.168.2.1, local AS number 64501
BGP table version is 1, main routing table version 1
Neighbor    V    AS MsgRcvd MsgSent TblVer InQ OutQ Up/Down State/PfxRcd
10.1.99.13 4 64999       0       0      1   0    0   never        Idle

aft@R1> show bgp summary
. . .
Peer             AS    InPkt     OutPkt    OutQ     Flaps    Last Up/Dwn
State|#Active/Received/Accepted/Damped...
192.68.2.1     64501       0          0        0        0       11:48:00

Connect
```

The session state on router FIRT-SERV is fixed at Idle, because, since it doesn't have any information to reach address 10.1.99.13 in its RIB, it cannot even send the first TCP segment of the Three-Way-Handshake (TCP SYN) to the BGP Neighbor. The session state on router R1 fluctuates between Idle, Connect and Active, since it regularly sends the first TCP segment of the Three-Way-Handshake to the BGP Neighbor 172.16.1.12, and then it listens for a reply. The sequence is Idle→Connect→Active→Idle, where the shift to the Idle state is very quick, while the time spent in the Connect and Active states is much longer. The fact that, in the view we just saw, R1's BGP process is in the Connect state is completely random, because it may have been in the Active state as well.

To avoid this kind of issues, a practical tip is to verify the layer-3 connectivity between the two IP addresses used for the session, for instance, by executing an extended ping beforehand, and specifying the source IP address:

```
aft@R1> ping 192.168.2.1 source 10.1.99.13 rapid
PING 192.168.2.1 (192.168.2.1): 56 data bytes
!!!!!
--- 192.168.2.1 ping statistics ---
5 packets transmitted, 5 packets received, 0% packet loss
round-trip min/avg/max/stddev = 2.864/4.774/9.238/2.375 ms
```

3.4.2 Incorrect AS number: symptoms

Another common error occurs when the AS is not correctly configured. For instance, let's consider the configurations of the multihop eBGP session in Section 3.1.5, where an incorrect AS number (65102 instead of 64999) has been configured by mistake on router R1. The screen of the FIRT-SERVER console, if the "**bgp log-neighbor-changes**" command is enabled in the BGP process configuration, will constantly display messages such as:

```
%BGP-3-NOTIFICATION: sent to neighbor 10.1.99.13 active 2/2 (peer in
wrong AS) 2 bytes FE4E
```

which indicate that R1 receives BGP NOTIFICATION messages signaling an incorrect AS configuration (**(peer in wrong AS) 2 bytes FE4E**) (Note: FE4E is the value 65102 (incorrect AS number) represented in hexadecimal format).

The same occurs by activating the message tracking function on router CE2 (JUNOS), with the following additional configurations:

```
[edit protocols bgp]
traceoptions {
  file bgp.log;
  flag state;
}
```

By viewing the "**bgp.log**" file, the following additional messages are obtained:

```
aft@CE2> show log bgp.log
. . .
... bgp_handle_notify:4274: NOTIFICATION received from 192.168.2.1 (External
AS 64501): code 2 (Open Message Error) subcode 2 (bad peer AS number)
value 65102
... bgp_peer_close_and_restart: closing peer 192.168.2.1 (External AS 64501),
state is 5 (OpenConfirm) event RecvNotify
```

What happens is that the BGP Neighbors establish the TCP connection, switching to the OpenSent state, but the OPEN messages exchanged afterward highlight the AS configuration error, therefore the session does not switch to the next OpenConfirm state, goes back to the initial Idle state and the TCP connection is aborted. Then, it switches back to the Connect state and to the Active state. Once the TCP connection is reactivated, it switches back to the OpenConfirm state, and starts all over.

The following wireshark analysis shows the OPEN message sent by R1 to FIRT-SERVER, which contains an incorrect AS number (=65102), and the following BGP NOTIFICATION message through which the AS number error is notified

No.	Time	Source	Destination	Protocol	Length	Info
12	4.281589	10.1.99.13	192.168.2.1	BGP	117	**OPEN Message**

Frame 12: 117 bytes on wire (936 bits), 117 bytes captured (936 bits) on interface 0
Ethernet II, Src: 50:26:00:0c:00:03 (50:26:00:0c:00:03), Dst: 50:26:00:0d:00:00 (50:26:00:0d:00:00)
Internet Protocol Version 4, Src: 10.1.99.13, Dst: 192.168.2.1
Transmission Control Protocol, Src Port: 179, Dst Port: 21480, Seq: 1, Ack: 58, Len: 63

Border Gateway Protocol – OPEN Message
    Marker: ffffffffffffffffffffffffffffffff
    Length: 63
    Type: OPEN Message (1)
    Version: 4
    My AS: 65102   # incorrect AS
    Hold Time: 90
    BGP Identifier: 10.1.99.13
    Optional Parameters Length: 34
    Optional Parameters

No.	Time	Source	Destination	Protocol	Length	Info
13	4.283430	192.168.2.1	10.1.99.13	BGP	77	**NOTIFICATION Message**

Frame 13: 77 bytes on wire (616 bits), 77 bytes captured (616 bits) on interface 0
Ethernet II, Src: 50:26:00:0d:00:00 (50:26:00:0d:00:00), Dst: 50:26:00:0c:00:03 (50:26:00:0c:00:03)
Internet Protocol Version 4, Src: 192.168.2.1, Dst: 10.1.99.13
Transmission Control Protocol, Src Port: 21480, Dst Port: 179, Seq: 58, Ack: 64, Len: 23

Border Gateway Protocol - NOTIFICATION Message
    Marker: ffffffffffffffffffffffffffffffff
    Length: 23
    Type: NOTIFICATION Message (3)
    Major error Code: OPEN Message Error (2)
    Minor error Code (Open Message): Bad Peer AS (2)
    Bad Peer AS: 65102

When receiving the BGP NOTIFICATION message, R1 sends a "TCP FIN ACK" to close the TCP connection.

No.	Time	Source	Destination	Protocol	Length	Info
14	4.289560	10.1.99.13	192.168.2.1	TCP	60	**179→21480 [FIN, ACK]**

Seq=64 Ack=81 Win=16384 Len=0

3.4.3 Insufficient IP TTL: symptoms

In the FIRT-SERVER configuration, let's assume to omit the "**neighbor 10.1.99.13 ebgp-multihop**" command, required to increase the IP TTL of the IP packets transporting the BGP messages sent, or to configure an insufficient TTL value. As a consequence, the session state (for the sake of brevity, we will omit the execution of the "**show bgp ... summary**" command):

- on FIRT-SERVER remains Idle, because the IP packets transporting the TCP segments for the Three-Way-Handshake do not reach their destination due to the IP TTL expiry, which is equal to 1 by default;

- on R1, it remains Active, because it regularly sends the first TCP segment of the Three-Way-Handshake to BGP Neighbor 192.168.1.1, and then it listens for a reply. The session switches from the Idle state to the Active state, after a quick passage in the Connect state.

What really happens, as shown by the following wireshark analysis, is that R1 sends the "TCP SYN" and the FIRT-SERVER replies directly with "TCP RST ACK", that is, by rejecting (reset) the TCP connection.

```
No.    Time        Source          Destination      Protocol Length Info
52 84.436570    10.1.99.13       192.168.2.1         TCP     78    63579→179 [SYN] Seq=0
Win=16384 Len=0 MSS=1460 WS=1 TSval=3220490543 TSecr=0 SACK_PERM=1
```

```
No.    Time        Source          Destination      Protocol Length Info
53 84.447132    192.168.2.1      10.1.99.13          TCP     54    179→63579 [RST, ACK] Seq=1
Ack=1 Win=0 Len=0
```

We have a slightly different outcome by omitting the "**multihop ...**" command on R1 (JUNOS), although, in the end, the final result is the same: the session does not reach the Established state. The sequence of events is shown in the following wireshark analysis:

```
No.    Time        Source         Destination     Protocol  Length Info
5 4.435905      192.168.2.1      10.1.99.13         TCP        58    50191→179 [SYN] Seq=0
Win=16384 Len=0 MSS=1460
```

```
No.    Time        Source         Destination     Protocol  Length Info
6 4.448823      10.1.99.13       192.168.2.1      TCP        58    179→50191 [SYN, ACK] Seq=0
Ack=1 Win=16384 Len=0 MSS=1460
```

```
No.    Time        Source         Destination      Protocol  Length Info
7 4.451511      192.168.2.1      10.1.99.13        TCP       54    50191→179 [ACK] Seq=1 Ack=1
Win=16384 Len=0
```

This initial section completes the three-way-handshake. For the sake of brevity, we omitted the details of the single patterns; however, the difference with the previous case is clear. Indeed, while Cisco platforms, without the "**neighbor ... ebgp-multihop**" command, sent "TCP RST ACK" directly, rejecting the connection, JUNOS platforms complete the three-way-handshake, sending the TCP/IP packets with TTL=255 (not shown), even without the "**multihop ...**" command. The result is that the two BGP Neighbors exchange OPEN messages, and R1, apart from the OPEN message, also sends a BGP NOTIFICATION message to FIRT-SERVER, with main code 6 (cease) and subcode 5 (connection rejected). In this phase too, JUNOS platforms send TCP/IP packets containing OPEN NOTIFICATION messages with TTL=255 (not shown).

No.	Time	Source	Destination	Protocol	Length	Info
8	4.454450	192.168.2.1	10.1.99.13	BGP	111	**OPEN Message**

No.	Time	Source	Destination	Protocol	Length	Info
9	4.460806	10.1.99.13	192.168.2.1	BGP	104	**OPEN Message, NOTIFICATION Message**

Now, the two BGP peers exchange TCP messages to close the connection.

No.	Time	Source	Destination	Protocol	Length	Info
10	4.460832	10.1.99.13	192.168.2.1	TCP	54	**179→50191 [FIN, ACK]** Seq=51 Ack=58 Win=16384 Len=0

No.	Time	Source	Destination	Protocol	Length	Info
11	**4.462770**	**192.168.2.1**	**10.1.99.13**	**TCP**	**54**	**50191 → 179 [ACK]** Seq=58 Ack=52 Win=16334 Len=0

No.	Time	Source	Destination	Protocol	Length	Info
12	4.467492	192.168.2.1	10.1.99.13	TCP	54	**50191→179 [FIN, PSH, ACK]** Seq=58 Ack=52 Win=16334 Len=0

No.	Time	Source	Destination	Protocol	Length	Info
13	4.472002	10.1.99.13	192.168.2.1	TCP	54	**179→50191 [ACK]** Seq=52 Ack=59 Win=16383 Len=0

In this case, the execution of "**show bgp ... summary**" commands would show an *Idle* state for both BGP Neighbors.

3.4.4 Incorrect TCP/IP packets' source IP address

Sometimes, it may occur that, due to a configuration error, either the TCP/IP packet source IP address is incorrect, or the command to define a value other than the default one (the address of the physical/logical interface transmitting the packet) is omitted on both sides of the session. To define it in another way, remember that the "**neighbor** *IP-neighbor* **update-source ...**" (IOS XE/XR) and "**local-address ...**" commands are used (JUNOS).

> **NOTE**: Concerning what we said earlier, in Section 3.1.1, the "**neighbor** *IP-neighbor* **update-source ...**" (IOS XE/XR and "**local-address ...**" commands (JUNOS), can be executed even on only one of the two BGP Neighbors, without any resulting issues. In any case, it is best to execute them on both sides of the session (which is in any case mandatory in Cisco platforms that use IOS XR).

By way of example, let's assume to execute the following configurations on R1 and on FIRT-SERVER:

<u>R1</u> (JUNOS)

```
[edit protocols bgp]
group FIRT-SERVER {
    local-address 10.1.99.1;  # INCORRECT IP ADDRESS
    neighbor 192.168.2.1 {
        multihop;
        peer-as 64501;
    }
}
```

<u>FIRT server</u> (Cisco IOS XE)
```
router bgp 64501
  neighbor 10.1.99.13 remote-as 64999
  neighbor 10.1.99.13 ebgp-multihop
  neighbor 10.1.99.13 update-source Loopback0
```

What happens is the same exchange sequence of TCP and BGP messages we saw in Section 3.4.3. Here too, just like in the previous section, executing the "**show bgp ... summary**" commands would show an Idle state for both BGP Neighbors.

SUMMARY

BGP implementations in Cisco IOS/IOS XE/IOS XR and in JUNOS for Juniper platforms, are among the most popular and widespread in practical applications.

In this chapter, we described the basic commands to establish BGP (eBGP, eBGP multihop and iBGP) sessions and the best practices to employ when choosing the session's endpoint IP addresses. Another important aspect introduced in this chapter were the configuration scalability techniques, very useful in those scenarios with many BGP sessions, to achieve more compact, scalable and elegant configurations. These techniques mainly affect Cisco platforms, which defined quite a few of them, through the IOS development, while Juniper platforms with JUNOS have always resorted just to the Peer Group concept.

Lastly, we introduced the most important troubleshooting commands for BGP sessions, including a few examples of configuration errors, and the tools to identify them.

Worth remembering:

1. Basic commands to establish BGP sessions and usage rules.

2. Checks carried out by BGP Neighbors to establish the session correctly.

3. How to change the default management of the Next-Hop attribute.

4. Configuration scalability techniques: BGP peer-group (IOS/IOS XE/JUNOS) BGP peer template (IOS/IOS XE), BGP configuration template (IOS XR).

5. Main commands to check BGP's operation and troubleshooting techniques. In particular, knowing how to "read" the commands is key, to view the details of all the advertisements of a given IP prefix.

4 – ADVERTISEMENT MANIPULATION TOOLS

BGP is first and foremost a policy application protocol. Indeed, in almost all practical applications, there is the need to manipulate BGP advertisements in some way or another, and also to carry out advertisement filtering operations, to accept or reject some of them.

Typical filtering objectives include:

- during a redistribution process from any routing protocol to BGP, checking redistributed prefixes;

- not accepting advertisements from specific prefixes, such as (typical in BGP), all the advertisements of prefixes with a mask length greater than 24 bits, or of so-called Bogon prefixes, etc;

- advertising only local prefixes to an AS (to prevent the AS from becoming a transit AS);

NOTE: Bogon prefixes are networks that should never be visible within the Internet. A Bogon network is a fake or invalid network. Sometimes, these networks are called Martian, as they could come from Mars (where obviously there are no valid networks!), however, they are not exactly the same thing, as explained by RFC 3871 – *Operational Security Requirements for Large Internet Service Provider (ISP) IP Network Infrastructure*, September 2004. Indeed, Martian networks group private and reserved networks, as defined by RFC 1918, RFC 5735 and RFC 6598. While Bogon networks include, asides from Martians, also those routing spaces that have not yet been allocated to a Regional Internet Registry by IANA (Internet Assigned Numbers Authority). Therefore, to summarise, we can say that Bogon = Martian + Unallocated (RIR + IANA). They are often found as DDoS attack source addresses. For the updated list, you can see several websites, such as https:// team-cymru.com/community-services/bogon-reference/.

Attribute manipulation mainly concerns the creation of appropriate routing policies, both for the AS inbound and outbound traffic. The objectives include:

- assigning a preset Local Preference value to a BGP advertisement;

- manipulating the AS_PATH of a BGP advertisement;

- associating a MED value to an outbound advertisement.

All BGP implementations provide more or less sophisticated configuration tools for advertisement filtering and manipulation. Even if logically equal to one another, these tools differ from manufacturer to manufacturer, and sometimes – as in the case of Cisco platforms – even within the same manufacturer. In this chapter, we will go over the tools available in Cisco platforms with IOS XE/XR and in Juniper platforms with JUNOS. And in the next chapters, we will see how these tools are applied within BGP sessions.

4.1 CISCO IOS XE TOOLS

In Cisco platforms with IOS XE (and even in those with standard IOS), there are many tools available, the most important being:

- prefix-list: available in all IOS versions, this tool is used to filter advertisements based on IPv4/IPv6 prefixes. Despite being available also in IOS XR, they are only applied in the standard IOS and in IOS XE;

- filter-list: available in IOS and IOS XE versions, this tool is used to filter advertisements based on the AS_PATH attribute;

- community-list: available in IOS and IOS XE, this tool is used to identify a defined set of (standard or extended) Community values;

- route-map: available in IOS and IOS XE, this tool is used both for advertisement filtering and manipulation. This is the only tool in IOS and IOS XE to manipulate the fields of routing protocol advertisements.

In this Paragraph, we will see prefix-lists, community-lists and route-maps. We will treat filter-lists in Paragraph 4.4, talking about AS_PATH attribute manipulation.

4.1.1 Prefix-list

Filter definition based on IP prefixes resorts to special expressions called prefix-lists, designed especially to define sets of IP prefixes. Actually, in BGP's first implementations, Cisco used standard access-lists (ACL) to this end, also and especially used for IP packet filtering in the data plane. However, using an IP ACL as filter has the following downsides:

- subnet masks cannot be controlled;

- entering a new line could mean having to completely rewrite the ACL (even though this issue was subsequently solved by adopting named ACLs);

- extended IP ACLs may be difficult to write.

The only advantage is the knowledge that many network administrators have of ACLs, due to their broad use in several contexts (e.g. traffic classification and filtering, "interesting" traffic definition in Dial on-Demand Routing (DDR), etc.). On the other hand, prefix-lists may significantly improve performance, compared to standard ACLs:

- a prefix-list is a tree structure, rather than a sequential one;

- they support incremental updates: single lines are identified by a sequence number, so they can be added or removed without having to rewrite the entire prefix-list;

- they bring greater flexibility, since they can control subnet masks (e.g., representing all prefixes with subnet mask $\leq$ /24, representing all subnets of network 172.16.0.0/12 with subnet mask $\leq$ /20, etc.).

A prefix-list can be configured with the following commands:

router(config)# {**ip** | **ipv6**} **prefix-list** *name* [**seq** *sequence-number*] **permit**|**deny** *prefix/mask*
[**ge** *minimum-mask-length*] [**le** *maximum-mask-length*]

where with the "**ge**" (greater or equal) and "**le**" (less or equal) options, we can set an interval for the subnet mask value. Prefix-lists have a name and a sequence number. Processing is done line by line, based on the sequence number. Omitting "**le**" and "**ge**" identifies only the exact prefix. Conversely, lines with optional keywords "**le**" and "**ge**" allow identifying all prefixes with a mask length between the two values (included). Obviously, the "**ge**" value should be lower or – at best – equal to the "**le**" value, and it should be specified in advance, in the configuration line. Moreover, the "**ge**" value should be strictly higher than the "mask" value.

Permit and **deny** clauses allow, when applying a prefix-list, accepting or rejecting BGP advertisements. Another important aspect to consider, which often leads to unwanted operations, is that, just like standard ACLs, a prefix-list has a final implicit deny all.

The rules to assess whether a prefix belongs to a prefix-list are very easy. Let's consider the general form of a prefix-list:

{ip | ipv6} prefix-list *name* **permit|deny** *P/M* **ge** *Mmin* **le** *Mmax*

and let's assume that we want to assess whether the *Px/Mx* prefix belongs to the prefix-list. Without the "**le**" and "**ge**" options, the *Px/Mx* prefix should match the one specified in the prefix-list, that is, it should be *Px=P* e *Mx=M*. Otherwise, the prefix should be a subnet of the *P/M* prefix specified in the prefix-list, with a mask comprised between the interval [*Mmin; Mmax*], endpoints included. If the "**ge**" option is missing, the mask should be comprised within the interval [*M; Mmax*], while if the "**le**" option is missing, the mask should be comprised between the interval [*Mmin*; 32].

In order to better understand how prefix-lists work, let's see a few practical examples.

Example 1

Consider the following prefix-list:

```
ip prefix-list NO-RFC1918 5 deny 10.0.0.0/8 le 32
ip prefix-list NO-RFC1918 10 deny 172.16.0.0/12 le 32
ip prefix-list NO-RFC1918 15 deny 192.168.0.0/16 le 32
ip prefix-list NO-RFC1918 20 permit 0.0.0.0/0 le 32
```

It allows all prefixes except for private prefixes as per RFC 1918 and their subnets. In this example, it is important to notice the last line. It allows all possible IP prefixes (a sort of permit all). Indeed, each IP prefix is a subnet of prefix 0.0.0.0/0 with mask lower or equal to 32 bit. By omitting this line, a possible application of this prefix-list would cause to reject all BGP advertisements, due to the final implicit deny all.

Example 2

Consider the following prefix-lists:

```
ip prefix-list A permit 203.0.113.0/24
!
ip prefix-list B permit 203.0.113.0/24 le 28
!
ip prefix-list C permit 203.0.113.0/24 ge 26
!
ip prefix-list D permit 0.0.0.0/0
!
ip prefix-list E permit 0.0.0.0/0 ge 8 le 24
```

These prefix-lists allow:

- prefix-list **A**: only prefix 203.0.113.0/24;

- prefix-list **B**: all prefixes that are subnets of prefix 203.0.113/24 with mask length in the interval [24; 28] (endpoints included);

- prefix-list **C**: all prefixes that are subnets of prefix 203.0.113/24 with mask length greater than or equal to /26;

- prefix-list **D**: only the default route;

- prefix-list **E**: all prefixes with mask length between /8 and /24 (endpoints included).

Below are IOS / IOS XE commands that allow viewing the structure of a prefix-list, or part of it.

router# **show {ip | ipv6} prefix-list [detail | summary]** *prefix-list-name* **[seq** *seq-number*]

Also, in IOS/IOS XE, it is possible to use a prefix-list as check, in the BGP table viewing command:

router# **show bgp {ipv4 | ipv6} unicast prefix-list** *prefix-list-name*

This command is very useful in practical applications, to view the advertisements in the BGP table related to a set of prefixes allowed by the prefix-list. It is useful especially in those routers with all or part of the FIRT, which usually contains hundreds of thousands of advertisements in the BGP table.

For instance, let's assume we want to highlight in CE1's BGP table of our sample network (see Figure 3.1) all the prefixes with a mask equal to /24. The prefix-list that identifies them is:

```
ip prefix-list ONLY-/24 seq 5 permit 0.0.0.0/0 ge 24 le 24
```

that, applied to the BGP table view, generates the following result:

```
CE1#show bgp ipv4 unicast prefix-list ONLY-/24
 .  .  .
    Network          Next Hop        Metric LocPrf   Weight  Path
*   192.0.2.0        10.1.12.5                            0   64501 65542 64497 i
*>                   10.1.11.1                            0   64501 65542 64497 i
*>  198.51.100.0     10.1.11.1                            0   64501 65541 64508 i
*                    10.1.12.5                            0   64501 65541 64508 i
*   203.0.113.0      10.1.12.5                            0   64501 65541 64496 i
*>                   10.1.11.1                            0   64501 65541 64496 i
```

4.1.2 Community-list

Very often, in practical applications, we have to apply constructs such as:

if {advertisement contains a certain Community set} **then** {perform certain actions}

In order to implement such constructs, different tools are employed to analyse the relevant conditions. IOS and IOS XE use community-lists, tools similar to standard ACLs, which share some properties with them, such as:

- they are assessed sequentially, line by line;

- they can be standard or extended;

- they have an implicit deny all at the end.

Standard community-lists are used to establish a well-defined Community set, while extended community-lists are used to define a Community set through Regular Expressions. We will go over extended community-lists in Appendix A.4. Here, we will only describe standard community-lists, which, in any case, are the most widespread in practical applications.

NOTE: We will treat Regular Expressions in the following Paragraph 4.4, when talking about AS_PATH attribute manipulation. Although the context is entirely different, Regular Expressions used in extended community-lists are absolutely identical.

The configuration command to define, in IOS and IOS XE, a community-list is the following:

router(config)# **ip community-list** {1-99 | **standard** *name*} **permit** | **deny** *value-1 value-2...*

Standard community-lists have numbers between 1 and 99. If more than one value is specified, they should be intended in that the consequent match condition, referring to the community-list, is met if the advertisement contains all the Community values specified. The "**internet**" keyword can be used to define any Community value, while the "**no-export**", "**no-advertise**" and "**local-as**" keywords can be used for well-known Communities NO_EXPORT, NO_ADVERTISE and NO_EXPORT_SUBCONFED.

By way of example, let's consider the following community-list:

```
ip community-list standard TEST permit 64501:150 64501:200
```

It identifies all the advertisements with both Community values specified.

NOTE: IOS XE supports also the community-lists that identify Extended Community value sets, which – as you may remember – are 8-byte long (see Section 2.4.6) and Large Community value sets, which are 12-byte long. The configuration is the same as the one that identifies standard Community sets, with the only difference of replacing keyword "**community-list**" with "**extcommunity-list**" or "**large-community-list**". Moreover, in the case of Extended Communities, we also need to specify, before the value, the type of Extended Community (e.g. "**rt**" for Route Target, "**soo**" for Site of Origin, etc.).

4.1.3 Route-map

Route-maps are an essential tool in Cisco IOS and IOS XE, and, apart from BGP, they are also applied in policy-based routing, for traffic classification and in several other configuration aspects. In BGP – as we will cover extensively later on – they are particularly widespread, such as for advertisement filtering, to define attribute-related values as LOCAL_PREF, MED, COMMUNITY, etc. They are the only tools made available by Cisco IOS and IOS XE to change the fields of UPDATE messages.

Route-maps are groups of commands used to carry out "**if** {*conditions*} – **then** {*perform actions*}" operations. When applied to BGP, route-maps allow assessing several conditions that can be based on ACL, prefix-list, AS_PATH, BGP-ID of the router originating an advertisement, address of the BGP Next-Hop, BGP Communities associated to the BGP advertisement, etc. The complete list varies, based on the IOS version, and should be checked on a case by case basis. Actions can affect Cisco's proprietary Weight parameter and the values associated to the different BGP attributes, such as Origin, BGP Next-Hop, BGP Community, Local Preference, MED, etc.

A route-map comprises one or more "**if** {*conditions*} – **then** {*perform actions*}" blocks associated with a sequence number, just like in prefix-lists. Similarly to prefix-lists, route-maps can be "**permit**" or "**deny**".

The processing logic, described as a pseudo-code, is the following:

if {*conditions met*}
then {
  if {*route-map belongs to the "**permit**" type*}
  then {*perform "**set**" actions*}
  else {*do not perform "**set**" actions*}
  exit route-map
}
else {*process the following instruction group with higher sequence number*}

In BGP, route-maps also filter (inbound or outbound) advertisements: "**permit**" type command groups indicate the acceptance/sending of advertisements that meet the conditions, while "**deny**" type command groups indicate their rejection.

A route-map is configured through command groups belonging to the type indicated here, processed according to the sequence number (*sn*).

router(config)# **route-map** *name* [**permit** | **deny** *sn*]
router(config-route-map)# **match** *condition*-1

. . .

router(config-route-map)# **match** *condition*-N
router(config-route-map)# **set** *value*-1

. . .

router(config-route-map)# **set** *value*-N
router(config-route-map)# [**continue** [*sn*]]

The name is a mnemonic that identifies the route-map. "**Match**" type commands specify the conditions, while "**set**" type commands specify the actions. The essential rules characterising route-map processing are:

- if no "**permit**" or "**deny**" keyword is specified, the default is "**permit**";

- there is a final implicit deny all, that is, a final last hidden line of the "**route-map** *name* **deny** *sn*" type;

- the permit all condition is defined by a group of "**permit**" commands without "**match**" conditions;

- more than one "**match**" condition of the same type is treated with OR, and more than one "**match**" condition of different types are treated with AND.

NOTE: The "**continue** …" option is used to alter the normal processing flow of a route-map. Without specifying a sequence number, it allows processing the following instruction group with a higher sequence number. By specifying a sequence number, it allows skipping to the next instruction group with that sequence number.

Here are some useful "**match**" conditions in practical applications:

- **match {ip | ipv6} address** *ACL*: match referring to an ACL. "*ACL*" can be either the number or the name of an ACL;

- **match {ip | ipv6} address prefix-list** *p-l*: match referring to a prefix-list. "*p-l*" is the name of the prefix-list;

- **match community** *c-l*: match referring to a community-list. "*c-l*" can be either the number or the name of a community-list;

- **match {ip | ipv6} next-hop {***ACL* **| prefix-list** *p-l***}** : match referring to the BGP Next-Hop of an advertisement. "*ACL*" and "*p-l*" have the same meaning we saw for the first two conditions;

- **match {ip | ipv6} route-source {***ACL* **| prefix-list** *p-l***}**: match referring to advertisements received from a specific BGP Neighbor. "*ACL*" and "*p-l*" have the same meaning we saw for the first two conditions;

- . . . (*see the manufacturer's official documents*).

The most common "**set**" actions are:

- **set origin {igp | egp | incomplete}**: used to define a value of the ORIGIN attribute;

- **set local-preference** *LP*: used to define a Local Preference value;

- **set metric** *MED*: used to define a MED value;

- **set as-path prepend [***string* **| last-as** *number***]**: used to manipulate the AS_PATH attribute (for further details, see Chapter 7);

- **set {ip | ipv6} next-hop** *IP-NH*: used to manipulate the NEXT_HOP attribute. "*IP-NH*" is the IPv4/v6 address of the new BGP Next-Hop;

- **set community (***value-1* **[***value-2***]** ...) **[additive]**: used to add/overwrite one or more Community values;

- **set extcommunity {rt | soo ...} (***value***-1 [***value***-2] ...) [additive]**: used to add or overwrite one or more Extended Community values of various types (**rt**=Route Target, **soo**=Site Of Origin, etc.);

- . . . (*see the manufacturer's official documents*).

Given the fact that the route-map processing logic often generates confusion, let's see its operation more closely, with the general example shown in Figure 4.1. below. The intriguing – and often confusing – part is the relationship between the route-map "permit" or "deny" clauses, and the "permit" or "deny" present in an ACL or in a prefix-list used in the "match" condition.

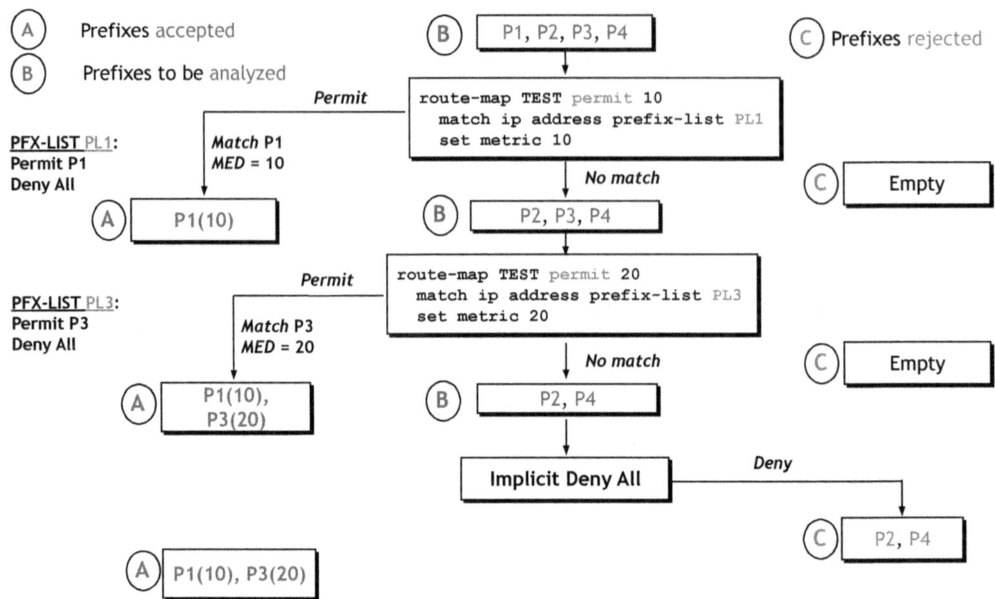

Figure 4.1 – Example of route-map processing.

In the figure, we indicated **A**={*set of accepted prefixes*}, **B**={*set of prefixes to be analysed*} and **C**={*set of rejected prefixes*}. The prefix-lists on which the "**match**" conditions are based are described summarily, by specifying the prefixes subject to "**permit**" or "**deny**" conditions. The TEST route-map analyzes prefixes P1, …, P4 one by one. Let's see how the analysis is carried out, for each prefix.

Prefix P1 analysis

P1 meets the "**match**" condition of the first group of commands (sn=10), as it is permitted by prefix-list PL1, therefore, due to the route-map "**permit**" clause, the prefix is accepted and the MED value is set to 10 (**set metric**=10). P1 is not analysed by the following groups of commands, because it met the first group's "**match**" condition. The route-map processing ends.

Prefix P2 analysis

Prefix P2 does not meet the "**match**" condition of the first group of commands, since it is not allowed by prefix-list PL1, therefore it is analysed by the second group with sn=20. P2 does not meet even the second group's "**match**" condition, since it is not allowed by prefix-list PL3, therefore it is analysed by the last group – which does not actually exist – and the Implicit Deny All applies. As final result, prefix P2 is rejected.

Prefix P3 analysis

P3 does not meet the "**match**" condition of the first group of commands, therefore it is analysed by the second group with sn=20. P3 meets the "**match**" condition of the second group of commands, as it is permitted by prefix-list PL3, therefore, due to the route-map "**permit**" clause, the prefix is accepted and the MED value is set to 20 (**set metric**=20).

Prefixe P4 analysis

Prefix P4 does not meet the "**match**" conditions of the first two groups of commands, and is analysed by the last hidden group (Implicit Deny All). As a final result, the prefix is rejected.

Let's see some examples:

Example 1
```
route-map SET-METRIC permit 10
  match ip address prefix-list ABC
  set metric 5
route-map SET-METRIC permit 20
!
ip prefix-list ABC permit 198.51.100.0/24
```

According to this route-map, if the advertisement contains to prefix 198.51.100/24, then the value of the MED attribute is set to 5, otherwise nothing happens (Note: the absence of line "**route-map SET-METRIC permit 20**" would entail the rejection of all the advertisements of prefixes other than 198.51.100/24).

Example 2
```
route-map SET-METRIC permit 10
  match community 1 2
  set metric 5
route-map SET-METRIC permit 20
!
ip community-list 1 permit 64501:1 64501:2
ip community-list 2 permit 64501:3
```

According to this route-map, if the advertisement contains the pair of Community values [64501:1. 64501:2] or Community value 64501:3, or both, then the value of the MED attribute is set to 5, otherwise nothing happens (Note: the absence of line "**route-map SET-METRIC permit 20**" would entail the rejection of all BGP advertisements without the pair of Community values [64501:1. 64501:2] or value 64501:3).

Example 3

```
route-map SET-METRIC permit 10
  match ip address prefix-list ABC
  match community 3
  set metric 5
route-map SET-METRIC permit 20
!
ip prefix-list ABC permit 198.51.100.0/24
ip community-list 3 permit 64501:3
```

According to this route-map, if the advertisement contains to prefix 198.51.100/24 and contains Community value 64501:3, then the value of the MED attribute is set to 5, otherwise nothing happens (Note: the absence of line "**route-map SET-METRIC permit 20**" would entail the rejection of all BGP advertisements of prefixes other than 198.51.100/24 and of the same prefix without the Community value specified. For instance, the advertisement of prefix 198.51.100/24 with Community 64501:1 would be rejected).

Example 4

```
route-map SET-LP permit 10
  set local-preference 150
  set origin igp
```

According to this route-map, all advertisements are assigned a Local Preference value of 150 and an Origin value of IGP (=0). Don't forget that the absence of "match" conditions is equivalent to a permit all.

4.2 CISCO IOS XR TOOLS: ROUTING POLICIES

Differently from IOS XE, IOS XR does not have all the tools we saw in Paragraph 4.1. There is only one tool available, and it includes all the single tools we saw in the previous section (such as prefix-list, community-list, etc.). We will see later on that JUNOS adopts the same philosophy. This entails more compact – yet surely more complex – configurations. The key elements are routing policies, written in a special language, the Route Policy Language (RPL).

NOTE: We have no intention of illustrating all the operating details of routing policies, which, by the way, are not used only in BGP, but also in other routing protocols. We will just focus on those aspects deemed more useful in BGP practical applications. As for the rest – as usual – you can refer to Cisco's official documents on IOS XR.

4.2.1 Basic aspects

In IOS XR, routing policies have the same role as route-maps: they filter and manipulate advertisements. Even though the basic concepts are similar, the configuration method is completely different, and it closely resembles that of common programming languages.
Modularity and re-usability have been significantly improved, compared to route-maps; also, they can be parametrized (similarly to standard subroutines in programming languages).
Other advantages over route-maps include:

- the option of nesting both routing policies (i.e. apply routing policies within other routing policies), and conditions;

- the set of conditions has been significantly extended;

- there is the option of defining a set of values (e.g. sets of prefixes, Communities, Extended Communities, ASes) that can be reused within several routing policies.

A routing policy is configured through sets of commands, grouped between "**route-policy** . . . " and "**end-policy**" commands:

route-policy *RP-name*
commands
end-policy

Rp-name is a mnemonic that identifies the routing policy. It includes two types of commands:

- conditions: akin to "**match**" type commands in route-maps;

- actions: akin to "**set**" type commands in route-maps.

The main acceptance/rejection functions are carried out through "**pass**" or "**drop**" commands for filtering, and "**set**" commands for attribute manipulation.
A routing policy must contain at least one action to execute. Conditions, on the other hand, are optional. Actions are executed if and only if the conditions are met. The absence of conditions implies that all advertisements are allowed, and therefore the actions present are executed (equivalent to the absence of "match" conditions in route-maps).

There are three types of actions:

- **pass**: used to accept an advertisement. The explicit use of the "**pass**" action implies the continuation of the routing policy processing;

- **drop**: used to reject an advertisement. The explicit use of the "**drop**" action implies the termination of the routing policy processing;

- **set**: used to edit the parameters and/or attributes (in case of BGP advertisements) of routing protocols' advertisements.

Notice that any modification action corresponds to an implicit acceptance ("**pass**"). By way of example, let's consider the following routing policy:

```
route-policy SET-LP
  set local-preference 150
end-policy
```

Every BGP advertisement processed by this routing policy is always accepted, and the Local Preference value is set to 150.

Similarly to route-maps, routing policies have a final implicit deny all. This is because the default action is "**drop**". For instance, the following routing policy:

```
route-policy DROP-ALL
end-policy
```

can be used to reject any advertisement. By contrast, the following routing policy is used to accept all advertisements:

```
route-policy ACCEPT-ALL
  pass
end-policy
```

Lastly, in the case of more than one "**pass**" or "**drop**" action, processing stops when the "**drop**" action is reached. For instance, the following routing policy (whose value is merely indicative):

```
route-policy TEST-PASS-DROP
  pass
  drop
  pass
end-policy
```

implies the rejection of all advertisements. Indeed, the first "**pass**" action allows accepting the advertisement, but also to continue the routing policy processing. Since the following term is the "**drop**" action, the advertisement is rejected and the routing policy processing ends. Therefore, the last "**pass**" action is never assessed. The final result is that any advertisement processed by the TEST-PASS-DROP routing policy is rejected.

4.2.2 Conditions definition and Operators

Conditions are the equivalent of match conditions in route-maps, and are used to identify routing protocol advertisements, based on several fields, depending on the protocol type.

NOTE: Hereinafter, we will only deal with BGP-related conditions. Routing policies can also be applied to other protocols (e.g. OSPF, IS-IS), for which there are specific conditions. However, we will not go over them, as they exceed the bounds of this context.

The conditions' configuration style follows standard programming language logic. The general configuration syntax is the following:

route-policy *RP-name*
  if *condition-*1 **then**
    *action-*1
    [elseif *condition-*2 **then**
      *action-*2 **]**
  else
    *action-*3
  endif
end-policy

In the case of more than one "**if-endif**" blocks, they are processed in sequence, as they appear in the configuration file. Every condition is expressed in the form "attribute operator value", where attribute is a possible attribute (e.g. MED, Local Preference, etc.), operator is a term for comparison, and value an attribute value. There are two types of operators: comparison operators and Boolean operators. Comparison operators are used to compare numerical and non-numerical attributes. In order to compare numerical attributes with a value, the following operators are available:

- **eq** (*equal*): compares a numerical attribute with one single value. The condition is met if the attribute has exactly the value specified. For instance, the condition "**if med eq 10 then** …" is met by BGP advertisements with MED=10;

- **le** (*less or equal*): used to verify if a numerical attribute belongs to the interval [0, *value*]. In other words, the condition is met if the attribute's value is lower or (at best) equal to the value specified. For instance, condition "**if med le 10 then**…" is met by BGP advertisements with MED$\leq$10;

- **ge** (*greater or equal*): used to verify if a numerical attribute's value is higher than or (at worst) equal to a preset value. In other words, the condition is met if the attribute's value is higher than or (at worst) equal to the value specified.

Then, there are two operators used to compare non-numerical operators:

- **is**: compares a non-numerical attribute with one single value. For instance, the condition "**if destination is (192.0.2.0/24) then** …" is met by BGP advertisements of the prefix 192.0.2/24;

- **in**: compares a non-numerical attribute with a set of values. For instance, the condition "**if destination in (0.0.0.0/0 le 24) then** …" is met by BGP advertisements of prefixes with mask length ≤ 24.

Then, there are the three standard Boolean operators AND, OR, NOT:

- **and**: the outcome of the comparison between two conditions is positive if and only if they are both met;

- **or**: the outcome of the comparison between two conditions is positive if at least one is met;

- **not**: used to negate a condition.

For instance, the condition "**med eq 20 and not local-preference eq 100**" is met by BGP advertisements with MED=20 and, at the same time, a Local Preference value other than 100. Notice that the correct interpretation implies the knowledge of the operator's precedence. In a complex operators combination, it is essential to keep in mind that the routing policy applies the operators according to the NOT→AND→OR order. If in doubt, or if you want to change the default precedence, you can use round brackets. The routing policy evaluates the content between brackets first, and then the rest.

The figure shows an example where a complex operators combination is rewritten with round brackets. The two versions are perfectly equivalent.

if med eq 20 and not local-preference eq 100 or origin is igp then ...

is equivalent to:

if ((med eq 20) and (not (local-preference eq 100))) or (origin is igp) then ...

The use of round brackets allows changing the normal precedence flow. For instance, let's consider the three cases below:

- **if med eq 20 and not local-preference eq 100 or origin is igp then** ...

- **if med eq 20 and (not local-preference eq 100 or origin is igp) then** ...

- **if med eq 20 and not (local-preference eq 100 or origin is igp) then** ...

In the first case, the condition is met by BGP advertisements with Origin=IGP or MED=20 and Local Preference other than 100. In the second case, the condition is met by BGP advertisements with MED=20 and Local Preference other than 100 or Origin=IGP. In the third case, the condition is met by BGP advertisements with MED=20, Local Preference other than 100 and Origin other than IGP.

By way of example of how operators are used, consider the following routing policy:

```
route-policy TEST
  if destination in (10.0.0.0/8 ge 16 le 24) then
    set local-preference 150
  endif
end-policy
```

This allows accepting only those advertisements of prefixes that are subnets of prefix 10/8, with a mask comprised within the interval [16, 24]. The reason for this is that an action (in this case, "**set local-preference 150**") is equivalent to an implicit "**pass**". All advertisements that do not meet the condition "**if destination** ..." are rejected, due to the implicit "**drop**". If we rewrite the routing policy as follows:

```
route-policy IMPLICIT-DROP-TEST
  if destination in (10.0.0.0/8 ge 16 le 24) then
    set local-preference 150
  else
    pass
  endif
end-policy
```

then all advertisements would be accepted, and only the advertisements of subnets of prefix 10/8 with mask included within interval [16, 24] would be assigned a Local Preference value of 150. All the others would be assigned the default value (=100).

4.2.3 Nested routing policies

The writing of complex routing policies should be optimised by exploiting reusability and modularity, as much as possible. To this end, the option of nesting a routing policy within another routing policy can be of help. The application is done through the "**apply** *RP-name*" command. Here is an example of configuration where the CHILD routing policy is used within the FATHER routing policy.

```
route-policy CHILD
  if local-preference 150 then
    set community (64501:12) additive
  endif
end-policy
!
route-policy FATHER
  if med eq 20 then
    apply CHILD
  endif
end-policy
```

Notice that the configuration in the figure could be rewritten differently, without resorting to nesting, as follows:

```
route-policy FATHER
  if med eq 20 then
    if local-preference 150 then
      set community (64501:12) additive
    endif
  endif
end-policy
```

However, this style goes against of modularity, since the CHILD routing policy could be reused in some other configuration section.

4.2.4 Defining actions

Just like for route-maps, actions can be used to modify the attributes and/or parameters contained in advertisements. They are defined by the "**set …**" command. A routing policy affects the advertisement's attributes, possibly changing them based on the construct.

NOTE: "**set …**" commands for BGP attribute's value definition are similar to those we saw for route-maps, and they will not be treated here. This excludes AS_PATH manipulation and Community value definition commands, shown in the following examples. Actually, there are other "**set …**" commands that concern BGP, but they are less used in practical applications. For reference, see Cisco's official documents.

Let's consider the following routing policy, applied to an advertisement with Origin=IGP, MED=20, Local preference=100.

```
route-policy TEST
  if med eq 20 then
    set local-preference 150
  endif
  if local-preference eq 100 then
    set origin incomplete
  endif
  if origin is igp then
    set local-preference 200
  endif
end-policy
```

After applying the routing policy, the advertisement will have the attributes values as follows: Origin=INCOMPLETE, MED=20, Local Preference=200. We will now analyse the operation sequence in depth.

The first condition "**if med eq 20**" is met, therefore the Local Preference value is set to 150. Since the action is an implicit pass, the second condition "**if local-preference eq 100**" is analysed. Be mindful that the Local Preference value considered is not the one from the previous action, but rather the value of the original advertisement (i.e. equal to 100). Therefore, the second condition is met and the Origin value is set to INCOMPLETE. Lastly, even the last condition is met, so the Local Preference value is set to 200, and this is the final value, instead of value 150 defined with the first condition.

The main point of the previous example is that, when more than one "**set**" action concerns the same attribute/parameter, the last action configured applies. For instance, with the following configuration:

```
route-policy TEST
  set med 10
  set med 20
  set med 30
end-policy
```

an advertisement analysed by this routing policy will have a MED value=30, that is, the last one configured.

NOTE: This configuration makes little sense, and its only purpose is to show what happens when more than one "**set**" action concerns the same attribute/parameter.

There are "**set**" type commands related to attributes concerning a set of values, rather than a single value. Examples of this are AS_PATH and COMMUNITY attributes. In similar situations, it is possible that all actions apply. For instance, let's consider the following configuration:

```
route-policy AS-PATH-PREPEND
  prepend as-path 64501 2
  prepend as-path 64502 2
end-policy
```

where command "**prepend as-path** *AS N*" allows adding the AS number N times before the AS_PATH. The two "**prepend as-path** *AS N*" commands are applied in sequence. Let's assume to apply this routing policy to an advertisement with AS_PATH=[64999]. At the end of processing, the AS_PATH will be [64502 64502 64501 64501 64999].

> **NOTE**: in the "**prepend as-path** ..." command, the N value is optional. Without it, it is assumed that N=1. By way of example, if we execute the same configuration without value "**2**", at the end of processing the AS_PATH would become [64502 64501 64999].

Let's consider the following configuration as an additional example:

```
route-policy ADD-COMMUNITY
  set community (64501:20) additive
  set community (64501:30) additive
end-policy
```

Let's assume to apply this routing policy to an advertisement that already contains Community value 64501:10. At the end of processing, the advertisement will have the three Community values 64501:10, 64501:20 and 64501:30 associated with it.

> **NOTE**: the "**additive**" clause in the "**set community** ..." command, indicates that the Community value should be added to any value already present in the advertisement; without it, the Community value overwrites all present values. If we'd omitted the "**additive**" clause in the first "**set community** ..." command of our example, at the end of processing, the advertisement would have had the two Community values 64501:20 and 64501:30 associated with it. If, on the other hand, we'd omitted it on the second command, and left it on the first, at the end of processing, the advertisement would have had only Community value 64501:30 associated to it.

4.2.5 Parametrization

An interesting aspect of the Route Policy Language, which – as we mentioned earlier – increases modularity and reusability, is the parameterization option. This includes two types:

- global parameters: parameters that can be reused in any routing policy;

- parameterized routing policies: routing policies that can be reused within another routing policy.

By defining global parameters, we can parameterize certain variables. Global parameters are recalled and used within routing policies. Global parameters are defined in the "**policy-global ... end-global**" section; they have a name, must be enclosed in quotes and separated by a comma. Reference to global parameters within the route-policy is done by placing the symbol "**$**" before the parameter's name. Notice that the same set of parameters can be used by more than one routing policy.

For instance, let's consider the following configuration:

```
policy-global
  # GLOBAL PARAMETERS
  AS '65201',
  Lo0 '192.0.2.1',
  DefaultWeight '0',
  DefaultLP '150',
  DefaultMED '0'
end-global
!
route-policy SETLP
  if as-path originates-from '$AS' then
    set local-preference $DefaultLP
  endif
end-policy
```

The "**policy-global ... end-global**" section defines the global parameters. Two of them are used in the SETLP routing policy.

The second parametrization type is used to create parameterized routing policies that can be reused within another routing policy, thus allowing a modular approach to routing policy creation. The concept is similar to that of subroutines in standard programming languages: a parametrized routing policy is created, and it can be recalled within other routing policies with the "**apply ...**" command, as shown in the following example. A parameterized routing policy can be recalled several times within the same routing policy or by other routing policies, every time with different parameters. For instance, let's consider the following configuration:

```
route-policy SETLP($LP)
  set local-preference $LP
end-policy
!
route-policy TEST
  if as-path neighbor-is '64501' then
    apply SETLP(150)
  elseif as-path neighbor-is '64502' then
    apply SETLP(200)
  endif
end-policy
```

The SETLP routing policy has the Local Preference value as variable. It is recalled twice within the TEST routing policy, the first time with value 150, and the second time with value 200.

4.2.6 Sets of values

Conditions within a routing policy may refer to a set of values. Sets of values can be defined directly inside the routing policy (inline set), or grouped – for greater reusability – in a separate set identified by a name (named set). Regardless of how values are defined – whether by an inline set or a named set – their processing is of the logical OR type: the condition is met if and only if the advertisement to be processed contains at least one value present in the set.

The general configuration of a routing policy referring to an inline set is the following:

route-policy *RP-name*
    if *operator attribute* (*value*-1, *value*-2, ...) **then**
      action
    endif
end-policy

An example of condition defined by a set of inline set type values is the following:

```
route-policy SETLP
  if community matches-any (64501:10,64501:20) then
    set local-preference 150
  endif
end-policy
```

In this routing policy, the attribute used by the condition is a Community value and the set is that of the two Community values 64501:10 and 64501:20.

Named sets concern AS values, standard or extended Communities, or prefixes. Values are defined in the "*Type*-set **... end-set**» section, separated by a comma. The possible "*Type*-**sets**" are:

- **as-path-set**: a set of AS numbers;

- **community-set**: a set of standard Community values;

- **extcommunity-set**: a set of Extended Community values;

- **prefix-set**: a set of prefixes. When defining prefix sets, you can use the "**ge**", "**le**" and "**eq**" operators.

The general configuration of a routing policy referring to a named set is divided into two parts; the first defines the named set, while the second applies it to the routing policy:

Type-**set** *value-set-name*
    value-1,
    value-2,
    ...
    value-N
end-set
!
route-policy *RP-name*
    if *attribute* **in** *value-set-name* **then**
      action
    endif
end-policy

Let's see an example of named sets for prefixes. The following prefix-set identifies all the prefixes that can be used in private networks, specified by RFC 1918.

```
prefix-set RFC1918
  10.0.0.0/8 le 32,
  172.16.0.0/12 le 32,
  192.168.0.0/16 le 32
end-set
```

The following is a community-set.

```
community-set COMM-64501
  64501:10,
  64501:20,
  64501:30
end-set
```

We'll see other examples in the next chapters.

4.2.7 Prefix-based conditions

The conditions based on IP prefixes use the keyword "**if destination in** ...":

route-policy *RP-name*
    if destination in *inline-set* | *prefix-set* **then**
        action
    endif
end-policy

Let's see two configuration examples. We will see many others later on. Let's assume we want to define a routing policy that accepts only the default route, rejecting all the other advertisements. The configuration to execute is the following:

```
route-policy DEFAULT-ONLY
  if destination in (0.0.0.0/0) then
    pass
  endif
end-policy
```

Let's assume we want to create a set to define all the private prefixes of RFC 1918, and apply this set to a routing policy that rejects the advertisements of these prefixes. The configurations to execute are:

```
prefix-set RFC1918
  10.0.0.0/8 le 32,
  172.16.0.0/12 le 32,
  192.168.0.0/16 le 32
end-set
!
route-policy NO-RFC1918
  if destination in RFC1918 then
    drop
  else
```

```
      pass
   endif
end-policy
```

4.2.8 Community value-based conditions

Community management in IOS XR is done through Community sets that can be both inline and named. In both types, we can specify the Community values by using numerical or mnemonic values, or Regular Expressions.

When using numerical values, possible representations include:

- *AS*:*number*: e.g. "**64501:10**";

- *AS*:[*min..max*]: e.g. "**64501:[10..20]**" that represents all the Community values belonging to the "64501:x" type, with x comprised between 10 and 20;

- *AS*:*: e.g. "**64501:***", that represents all the Community values belonging to the "**64501:x**" type, with any x value.

Possible mnemonic values are those we already saw for community-lists: "**internet**" to indicate any Community value, and "**no-export**", "**no-advertise**" and "**local-as**", for well-known Community values. When applying a community-set to define the routing policy conditions, we can use three different operators:

- **is-empty**: condition met if an advertisement does not contain any Community attribute;

- **matches-any**: condition met if an advertisement contains at least one Community value specified inline or present in the community-set;

- **matches-every**: condition met if an advertisement contains all the Community values specified inline or present in the community-set.

The following example will help you understand the difference between "**matches-any**" and "**matches-every**" operators. Let's say we want to analyse a BGP advertisement with the three Community values 64501:10, 64501:20 and 64501:30 associated with it, through the following routing policies:

```
community-set TEST
  64501:10,
  64501:50
end-set
!
route-policy COMM-1
  if community matches-any TEST then
    pass
  endif
end-policy
!
route-policy COMM-2
  if community matches-every TEST then
    pass
  endif
end-policy
```

When it is analysed by the COMM-1 routing policy, the advertisement is accepted, because the operator used is "**matches-any**", which, in this case, indicates that the advertisement is accepted if and only if at least one Community value is equal to at least one between those present in the TEST community-set. On the other hand, when it is analysed by the COMM-2 routing policy, the advertisement is rejected (due to the implicit drop), because the operator used is "**matches-every**", which, in this case, indicates that the advertisement is accepted if and only if it contains all Community values present in the TEST community-set.

NOTE: If the advertisement, aside from the three Community values specified earlier, had also value 64501:50, it would have been accepted.

4.3 JUNOS TOOLS

JUNOS, just like IOS XR, uses only the routing policy tool. The structure is similar to what we saw for IOS XR routing policies, even though the syntax is completely different. Even their use is similar: when applied to BGP, these tools allow both filtering the advertisements and manipulating the attributes.

In JUNOS, a routing policy comprises zero or more "**if** {*conditions*} - **then** {*actions*}" terms, processed in sequence. Actually, the processing logic is more similar to IOS XE's route-maps than routing policies.

if {*conditions met*}
then {*perform actions*
    continue/end processing
    }
else {*processes following term*}

JUNOS routing policies work on the terms within the RIB, and may be applied both to the import and export direction. When applied to the import direction, they control which advertisements can be accepted and added to the RIB; when applied to the export direction, they control the routing data to be propagated.

NOTE: Even though all the following examples refer to advertisements of IPv4 prefixes, the same tools can be used also for advertisements of IPv6 prefixes.

4.3.1 How do routing policies work

A routing policy comprises several terms. Switching from one term to the next is done according to specific rules, and it depends on the presence of termination actions and on the "**next term**" clause, which indicates that the following term is being processed.

In order to describe their operation, let's assume to have a routing policy with N configured terms. Processing is done by analysing the different terms in sequence, in the order they appear in the configuration file. Initially, the first term's conditions are verified. If they are not met, then the second term is verified, otherwise:

1. the actions are performed;

2. it is verified if a termination action and the "**next term**" clause are present. If there is a termination action, but the "**next term**" clause is not present, the routing policy processing ends. Otherwise, the following term is analysed.

These two points are identical for all the terms configured. If the conditions were not met, there is an implicit term. Figure 4.2 below summarises what we have just said.

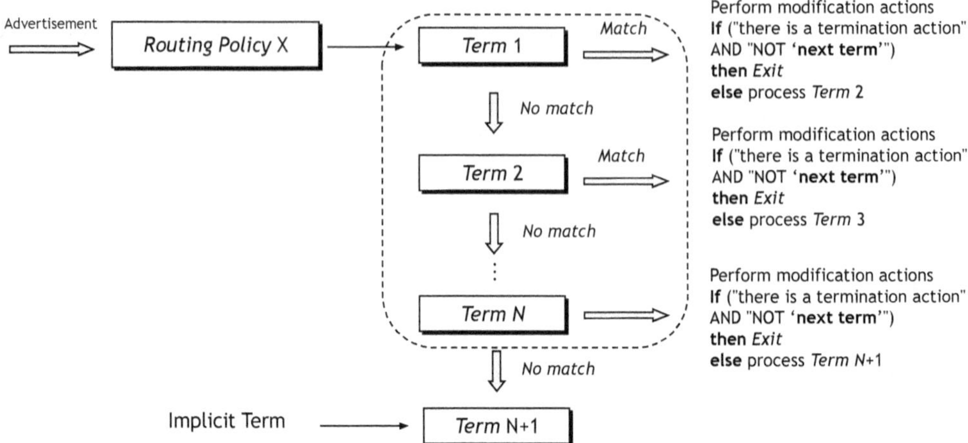

Figure 4.2 – Routing policy processing logic.

An important aspect that sets JUNOS routing policies apart from similar tools in IOS XE/XR, is that the implicit term is not "**deny all**" or "**drop**", but rather BGP's default behaviour. In a sense, the implicit term processes the advertisements in the same way as without applying the routing policy.

The same processing logic applies in the case of more than one routing policy applied in sequence (policy-chain). The only difference is that, if the first routing policy explicitly configured conditions are not met, the second policy is analysed, and so on, until the last one. The implicit term applies only to the last one. Moreover, in order to process the following routing policy in any case, the "**next policy**" clause is used. The policy-chain processing logic is summarised in Figure 4.3 below.

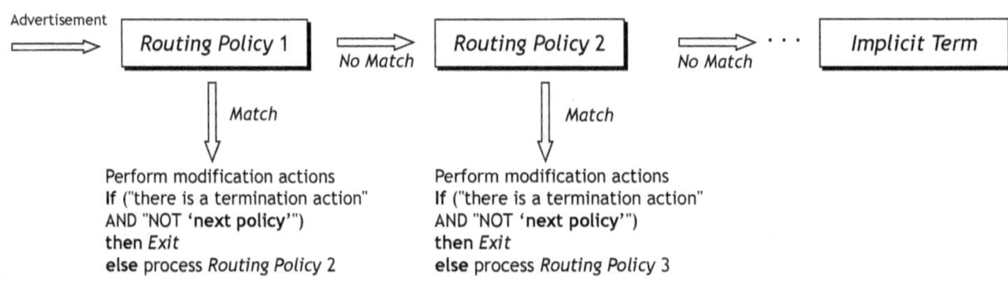

Figure 4.3 – Policy-chain processing logic.

NOTE: A policy-chain can always be rewritten as a single routing policy with several terms. In complex configurations, using a policy-chain can be useful to reuse the single routing policies that make up the policy-chain.

Similarly to what happens in Cisco route-maps, in the case of more than one condition, those that refer to the same parameter/attribute are processed according to a logical OR, while conditions of different nature are processed according to a logical AND.

Conditions refer to different BGP parameters/attributes, such as: IP prefixes, AS_PATH, Local Preference, Origin, Community, BGP Next-hop values, etc.

Moreover, there are three types of actions:

- termination: used to terminate the processing of a routing policy;

- flow control: used to alter the default processing logic;

- parameter/attribute modification: used to modify the parameters and/or attributes of BGP advertisements (and, in general, of a routing protocol).

There are two termination actions:

- **accept**: if applied to the inbound direction, it allows adding the advertisement that meets the conditions to the RIB. If applied to the outbound direction, it allows the advertisement of the best paths (active paths in JUNOS language) that meet the conditions;

- **reject**: if applied to the inbound direction, it prevents adding the advertisement that meets the conditions to the RIB. If applied to the outbound direction, it prevents the advertisement of the best paths that meet the conditions.

Flow control actions are the afore-mentioned "**next term**" and "**next policy**". Modification actions are "**set …**" type actions, and we will treat them extensively throughout the book.

NOTE: A routing policy must contain at least one action to execute. Conditions, on the other hand, are optional. The absence of conditions implies that all advertisements are allowed, and therefore the actions present are executed.

4.3.2 Configuration

Routing policies are configured within the "**policy-options**" configuration hierarchy, and have their own name, assigned through the "**policy-statement**" command. The general configuration is the following:

[edit policy-options]
policy-statement *RP-name* {
  term *term-1-name* {
    from {
      conditions;
    }
    then {
      actions;
    }
  }
  ...
  term *term-N-name* {
    from {
      conditions;
    }
    then {
      actions;
    }
  }
}

NOTE: If the routing policy only comprises one term, the term name can be omitted.

How to switch from one term to the next has been described in the previous section. Actually, this is the part of the configuration that creates more errors in practical applications, so it should be understood carefully. Especially the seemingly innocuous presence of termination actions can lead to unwanted processes. Let's see an easy example to highlight this issue.

Consider the following routing policy comprising three terms:

NOTE: In the second term, we used a condition based on a "route-filter", which will be discussed in the next Section 4.3.3; in any case, it is fairly intuitive, as it only defines prefix 203.0.113/24.

```
[edit policy-options policy-statement TEST]
term NHS {
  then {
    next-hop self;
  }
}
term ACCEPT-203.0.113/24 {
  from {
    route-filter 203.0.113.0/24 exact;
  }
  then accept;
}
term DROP {
  then reject;
}
```

Let's consider the processing of a BGP advertisement of prefix 203.0.113/24. Processing starts from the first term (NHS). No condition is defined in this term, only the "**then next-hop self**" action.

NOTE: We already saw a routing policy with this only action in Section 3.1.4 on "Managing the BGP Next-Hop".

Since we did not explicitly define any termination action, according to the processing rules we saw in Section 4.3.1 above, whatever the prefix or other content of the advertisement, the action is executed, and then the following term is processed (**ACCEPT-203.0.113/24**). In this term, the "**route-filter ...**" condition is met, so the action (**accept**) is executed; since this is a termination action and there is no "next term" clause, the routing policy processing ends here.

Let's now consider the processing of a BGP advertisement of any prefix other than 203.0.113/24. Concerning the first term, processing is identical. On the other hand, the condition is not met for the second term, so we move to the third term, which rejects all BGP advertisements. In this last term there is only the "**reject**" action, which is a termination action, so the routing policy processing ends here.

In summary, the TEST routing policy lets only the advertisements of prefix 203.0.113/24 pass, and performs the "**next-hop self**" action on it.

Let's assume we want to add the "**accept**" action only to the first term, leaving the other two unchanged:

```
[edit policy-options policy-statement TEST]
term NHS {
  then {
    next-hop self;
    accept;
  }
}
   . .  < other two terms unchanged > . . .
```

The result is quite surprising: all BGP advertisements pass, and the "**next-hop self**" action is applied to all of them. The reason is simple: the explicit presence of the "**accept**" action causes the routing policy processing to end immediately, without processing the following terms. This shows how important the explicit (or implicit) presence of termination actions is.

We have a similar situation in the policy-chains. Let's consider the following configuration, where RP2 is the name of any routing policy:

```
[edit policy-options policy-statement NHS]
then {
  next-hop self;
}


[edit protocols bgp]
export [NHS RP2];
```

In this case, since in the first routing policy (NHS) there is no explicit termination action, also the second routing policy RP2 is processed in sequence. If, in the NHS routing policy, apart from the "**next-hop self**" action, we'd added the "**accept**" action, the second routing policy RP2 would not have been processed.

These two examples show that we need to pay special care to how termination conditions are used. Their improper use could lead to unwanted processing.

4.3.3 Prefix-based conditions: route-filter and prefix-list

JUNOS provides two tools to identify the sets of prefixes and their use in routing policy conditions: route-filters and prefix-lists.

NOTE: To avoid language mix-ups with the terms used in Cisco platforms, you should keep in mind that JUNOS route-filters are the same as prefix-lists in Cisco platforms with IOS / IOS XE (see Section 4.1.1), while JUNOS prefix-lists are the same as prefix-sets in Cisco platforms with IOS XR.

A route-filter is configured through the command:

route-filter *prefix/mask* [*match-type*][*action*]

The (optional) action specifies the type of action to be executed. When added to a route-filter, any action after the "**then**" clause is not executed.

The match-type specifies a possible mask value interval. The following keywords can be added:

- **exact**: allows only the exact match of the prefix/mask pair. For instance, filter "**route-filter 192.0.2.0/24 exact**" allows only prefix 192.0.2/24.

- **orlonger**: allows the match of the prefix/mask pair and of all its more specific prefixes. For instance, filter "**route-filter 192.0.2.0/24 orlonger**" allows prefix 192.0.2/24 and all its subnets.

- **longer**: allows the match of all the prefix/mask pair's more specific prefixes. For instance, filter "**route-filter 192.0.2.0/24 longer**" allows all the subnets of prefix 192.0.2/24, but not prefix 192.0.2/24.

- **upto** */mask_max*: allows the match of the prefix/mask pair and all its more specific prefixes with a mask equal to *mask_max*, at best. For instance, filter "**route-filter 192.0.2.0/24 upto /28**" allows prefix 192.0.2/24 and all its subnets with mask length of up to 28.

- **prefix-length-range** */mask_min-/mask_max*: allows the match of all the more specific prefixes of the *prefix/mask* pair with a mask comprised within the interval [*mask_min; mask_max*], including the end values. For instance, filter "**route-filter 192.0.2.0/24 prefix-length-range /26-/30**" allows all the subnets of prefix 192.0.2/24 with mask length comprised between 26 and 30.

- *prefix* **through** *more-specific-prefix*: allows the match of all prefixes within the subnet tree, comprised between the prefix (included) and the more specific prefix. For instance, filter "**route- filter 192.0.2.0/24 through 192.0.2.224/27**" allows, apart from prefix 192.0.2/24, all the following subnets: 192.0.2.128/25, 192.0.2.192/26 and 192.0.2.224/27. Figure 4.4 below shows the subnet tree of prefix 192.0.2/24 up to subnets /27, highlighting the subnets that belong to the filter.

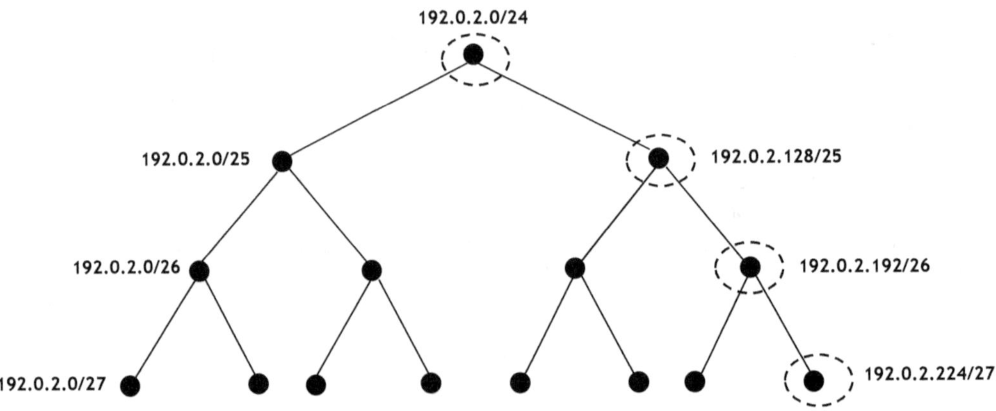

Figure 4.4 – Subnet tree of prefix 192.0.2/24 (up to /27), highlighting the subnets that belong to the match-type "*prefix* **through** *more-specific-prefix*".

Let's see some examples. Let's consider the following route-filters:

```
route-filter 192.0.2/24 orlonger  # ROUTE-FILTER A
route-filter 192.0.2/24 longer  # ROUTE-FILTER B
route-filter 0.0.0.0/0 exact  # ROUTE-FILTER C
route-filter 0.0.0.0/0 prefix-length-range /16-/24  # ROUTE-FILTER D
route-filter 0.0.0.0/0 upto /24  # ROUTE-FILTER E
```

These route-filters allow:

- route-filter **A**: prefix 192.0.2/24 and all its subnets;

- route-filter **B**: all the subnets of prefix 192.0.2/24, except for the prefix itself;

- route-filter **C**: only the default route;

- route-filter **D**: all IP prefixes with mask length comprised between /16 and /24 (included);

- route-filter **E**: all IP prefixes with mask length lower or equal to /24.

A somewhat atypical aspect is multiple route-filter management. According to Section 4.3.1, in the case of more than one condition belonging to the same type, they are processed according to a logical OR. However, this does not apply to route-filters. Indeed, several route-filter conditions are treated according to a longest-match prefix logic: only the route-filter of the prefix that meets the longest-match prefix algorithm is considered. To clarify this concept, let's take a look at the following configuration:

```
[edit policy-options policy-statement MULTIPLES-RF]
from {
  route-filter 10.0.0.0/16 longer reject;
  route-filter 10.0.1.0/24 longer;
  route-filter 10.0.0.0/8 orlonger accept;
}
then {
  metric 10;
}
```

and analyse the processing of prefix 10.0.1/24. Out of the three prefixes listed in the route-filters, the longest-match prefix is the second one. Therefore, this prefix will be processed by the second route-filter, while the other two will not be considered. Since the match-type of the second route-filter is "**longer**", this means that prefix 10.0.1/24 does not meet the condition, and therefore, since there are no other explicitly configured terms, it will be processed according to the implicit term, which – as we saw earlier – corresponds to BGP's standard behaviour, that is, as if the routing policy had not been applied.

Another tool provided by JUNOS for IP prefix-based conditions is the prefix-list. In JUNOS, prefix-lists are simple IP prefix lists. Just like for route-filters, we can link a prefix-list both to match and action type. The only match types allowed are "**exact**", "**longer**" and "**orlonger**". The actions are the same we saw for routing policies (termination, flow control and parameter/attribute modification).

A prefix-list must be configured under the "**policy-options**" configuration hierarchy, while the application to a routing policy must be done under the "**from**" clause.

[edit policy-options]
prefix-list *PL-name* {
  prefix-1;
  ...
  prefix-N;
}
policy-statement *RP-name* {
  from prefix-list *PL-name;*
  ...
}

The condition is met if and only if the BGP advertisement contains a prefix contained exactly in the prefix-list. When applying a routing policy, you can specify, using the "**prefix-list-filter**" clause in the "**from**" condition, the match and action type.

[edit policy-options]
policy-statement *RP-name* {
  from prefix-list-filter *PL-name action match-type;*
  ...
}

For instance, considering the following configuration of a prefix-list and two routing policies using it:

```
[edit policy-options]
prefix-list RFC-1918 {
  10.0.0.0/8;
  172.16.0.0/12;
  192.168.0.0/16;
}
policy-statement RP1 {
  from {
    prefix-list RFC-1918;
  }
  then accept;
}
policy-statement RP2 {
  from {
    prefix-list-filter RFC-1918 orlonger;
  }
  then accept;
}
```

The prefix-list lists the three "root" prefixes of the IP subnets that can be used for private use, as specified by RFC 1918. The condition of the first routing policy RP1 is met if and only if the advertisement contains exactly one of the prefixes present in prefix-list RFC-1918 (and not its possible subnets!). On the other hand, the condition of the second routing policy RP2 is met if and only if the advertisement contains one of the prefixes included in prefix-list RFC-1918 or, thanks to the "**orlonger**" match-type, one of its subnets.

4.3.4 Community value-based conditions

JUNOS too has its own tools to assess the conditions based on Community values, and also to base possible actions on them, which could also include a manipulation of the Communities. Operating logics are similar to those we already saw for Cisco IOS XE's community-lists, and for Community-based conditions we saw for IOS XR. The configuration process always entails the definition of a set of Community values first (similarly to Cisco IOS XR community-sets). The configuration is executed within the "**policy-options**" configuration hierarchy (if there is only one value, brackets can be omitted):

[edit policy-options]
community *name* **members** [*value*-1 *value*-2 ... *value*-N]

> **NOTE**: In order to define the set of Community values, Regular Expressions can be used. We will mention this aspect in Appendix A.4.

Conditions are used through the following configuration:

[edit policy-options]
policy-statement *RP-name* {
  term *term*-1-*name* {
    from community [*name*-1 ... *name*-N];
    then {
      actions;
    }
  }
}

where, as you may notice, there is the option of applying more Community sets. The general rule when considering more than one value within a set, is that they should be processed according to a logical AND, that is, the condition is met if and only if the advertisement contains all the Community values specified. The rule when processing more than one set within the "**from community** ..." command, is that they should be processed according to a logical OR.
Let's consider the following configuration as an example:

```
[edit policy-options]
policy-statement CHECK-COMM {
  from community [ COMM-1 COMM-2 ];
  then accept;
}
community COMM-1 members 64501:10
community COMM-2 members [ 64501:20 64501:30 ]
```

The condition is met by all those advertisements that have at least the Community value 64501:10, or both Community values 64501:20 and 64501:30. Besides conditions, Communities can also be manipulated through actions. There are three types of actions:

- **add**: allows adding one or more Community values to any value already present in the advertisement;

- **delete**: allows deleting one or more Community values from any value already present in the advertisement;

- **set**: allows overwriting all Community values present in the advertisement.

For instance, let's assume we want to add the two Community values 64501:20 and 64501:30 to those already present in an advertisement of prefix 203.0.113/24. The configuration to execute is the following:

```
[edit policy-options]
policy-statement ADD-COMM {
  from {
    route-filter 203.0.113.0/24 exact;
  }
  then community add COMM-2;
}
community COMM-2 members [ 64501:20 64501:30 ]
```

Everything we said so far concerns standard Communities. Configurations are the same also for Extended Communities and Large Communities. The only difference is how Extended/Large Community values are defined. For Extended Communities, we need to specify the type, while for Large Communities, we need to place the "**large**" keyword before them, and define the value with three digits, separated by "::". Here is an example of configuration:

```
[edit policy-options]
community EXT-COMM members [ target:64501:10 origin:64501:20 ]
community LARGE-COMM members large:64501:20:30
```

NOTE: In the Extended Community definition, **"target"** indicates Route Target Extended Communities, widely used in L2VPN/L3VPN BGP/MPLS services; **"origin"** indicates Route Origin Extended Communities, which identify a router that sends the advertisement.

4.4 AS_PATH-BASED CONDITIONS

Filters based on the AS_PATH attribute are very useful in practical applications, since they allow selective filtering actions, based on the ASes present within the attribute. For instance, let's assume that, in order to avoid turning it into a transit AS, we do not want to propagate the advertisements received from other ASes toward the outside, but only those that originated in our own AS.

Since – as we will see in Chapter 5 – the advertisements originated locally within an AS are characterised by an empty AS_PATH, in order to reach the desired purpose, we just need to create an outbound filter that only allows forwarding those advertisements with an empty AS_PATH.

Creating AS_PATH attribute-based filters requires tools to identify certain AS values within the AS_PATH. Current Cisco and Juniper's (and also other manufacturers) BGP implementations use Regular Expressions (hereinafter abbreviated as RegExp), which are expressions resulting from the UNIX Operating System, capable of identifying the desired portions of the AS_PATH. The RegExp's use logic is summarised in Figure 4.5 below.

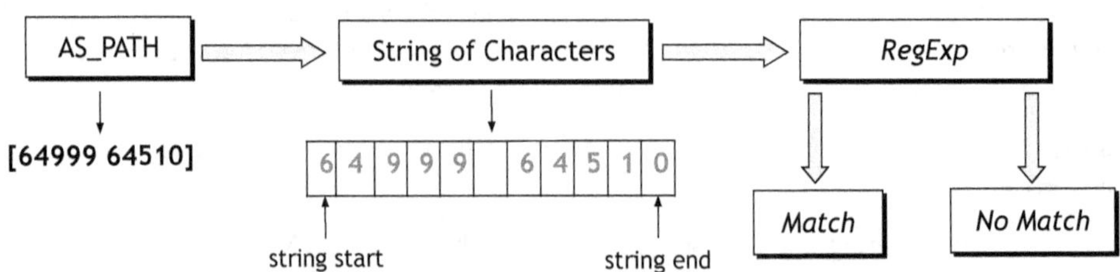

Figure 4.5 – RegExp operating logic.

In general, a RegExp can be seen as an expression that, applied to a string of characters, generates a positive (match) or negative (no match) result. In our case, the string of characters derives directly from the AS_PATH.

Cisco and Juniper's implementation define RegExps differently; however, they both use them according to the figure's description.

4.4.1 Regular Expressions in Cisco platforms

In all Cisco IOS types, the AS_PATH is seen as a string of characters, including spaces and special characters. Special characters include curly brackets – used for the AS_SET segments (see Paragraph 5.3) – and round brackets – used in BGP Confederations (see Paragraph 8.4). RegExps have two types of characters:

- regular: characters to be verified (generally numbers);

- control (metacharacters): characters with a special meaning.

A group of regular characters between round brackets is considered by a metacharacter as a single regular character. Metacharacters can be grouped into three types:

- Atoms: independent metacharacters used to define or expand the regular characters before or after the atom. Atoms and their meaning are summarised in Table 4.1 below.

Atom	Definition
.	(dot) It represents any character, spaces included.
^	It represents the beginning of a string.
$	It represents the end of a string.
_	(underscore) It represents the following characters: comma; left curly bracket; right curly bracket; beginning of a string; end of a string; space.
|	It represents an OR between two strings.
\	It represents an *escape* character that allows considering the following metacharacter as a regular character.

Table 4.1 – Atom list.

- Multipliers: they follow atoms or regular characters, and are used to describe repetitions of the previous characters. Multipliers and their meaning are summarised in Table 4.2 below.

Multiplier	Definition
*	It represents zero or more repetitions of the previous character.
+	It represents one or more repetitions of the previous character.
?	It represents zero or one repetition of the previous character.
\n	It represents a single repetition of the n-th group of characters between round brackets.

Table 4.2 – Multiplier list.

NOTE: In order to prevent multiplier "**?**" from being interpreted as an Help request, in RegExp it should be preceded by "Ctrl-V" (acting as escape character in the command line interface).

- Intervals: used to specify an interval of characters. A set of regular characters between square brackets represents any one of the characters between the brackets. The endpoints of the interval are used to indicate an interval of regular characters, separated by "-" (dash). For instance, [1-4] represents characters 1,2,3,4 (alternative representation [1234]), [a-d] represents characters a,b,c,d (alternative representation [abcd]).

Table 4.3 below shows some examples of RegExps that use the atom metacharacters described earlier.

RegExp	Definition
^1.$	It represents a two-character string starting with regular character 1 and ending with any character (e.g. "1 ", "12", "1A").
^1234_	It represents a string starting with 1234 followed by one of the characters represented by "_" (e.g. "1234", "1234 100", "1234 100 200").
^1234$	It represents string "1234" only.
_1234_	It represents a string starting with 1234 preceded and followed by one of the characters represented by "_" (e.g. "100 1234 200", "1234 123", "123 1234").
10$\|20$	It represents a string ending with 10 or 20 (e.g. "10", "20", "123 110", "123 20").
^\(65500\)$	It represents string "(65500)" only.

Table 4.3 – Examples of RegExps that use the atom metacharacters described earlier.

While Table 4.4 below shows some examples of RegExps that use the multiplier metacharacters described earlier.

RegExp	Definition
123*4	It represents "124", "1234", "12334", "123334", etc.
123+4	It represents "1234", "12334", "123334", etc.
123?4	It represents "124", "1234", "12345", etc.
1(23)?4	It represents "14", "1234", "71234", etc.
1(.)23(.)\1\2	It represents "1x23yxy" where x and y are any regular character.

Table 4.4 – Examples of RegExps that use multipliers.

Now, let's see some significant examples of RegExps applied to the AS_PATH attribute, and their meaning in terms of AS:

- **_64501_**: represents an AS_PATH that contains AS number 64501 (e.g.: AS_PATH of advertisements that crossed AS 64501);

- **^64501$**: represents an AS_PATH that contains only AS number 64501 (e.g.: AS_ PATH of advertisements of local prefixes originated within AS 64501, communicated to eBGP Neighbors);

- **_64501$**: represents an AS_PATH that has AS number 64501 as the last AS in the list (e.g.: AS_PATH of advertisements of local prefixes originated by AS 64501);

- **^64501_**: represents an AS_PATH that has AS number 64501 as the first AS in the list (e.g.: AS_PATH of advertisements of prefixes received by an eBGP Neighbor of AS 64501);

- **^[0-9]+$**: represents an AS_PATH containing any single AS number (e.g.: AS_PATH of advertisements of local prefixes originated by any AS and received by an eBGP Neighbor);

- **^([0-9]+)(_\1)*$**: represents an AS_PATH that contains more copies of the same AS, such as "1 1 1", "2 2", etc. (e.g.: AS_PATH of advertisements received by an eBGP Neighbor that applies the AS_PATH prepending mechanism);

- **_([0-9]+)_\1_\1_\1_\1_**: represents an AS_PATH containing 5 or more consecutive copies of the same AS, in any position of the AS_PATH (e.g.: [1 2 2 2 2 2 3 4], [1 1 1 1 1 1 2 3]). The number of consecutive copies can be varied, by adding or removing the terms "\1_";

- **^(64501_)+([0-9]+)?$**: represents an AS_PATH that contains one or more copies of AS number 64501 and possibly also a single AS number (e.g.: AS_PATH of advertisements coming from AS 65401 or from an AS adjacent to AS 64501);

- **^$**: represents an empty AS_PATH (e.g.: AS_PATH of advertisements of local prefixes generated by an AS);

- **.***: represents any AS_PATH.

In IOS and IOS XE, AS_PATH-based conditions use special ACLs called filter- lists, which, in turn, use RegExps. A filter-list is configured through one or more lines of the following command:

router(config)# **ip as-path access-list** *filter-list-number* **permit** | **deny** *RegExp*

When you write a filter-list, keep in mind that, similarly to traditional ACLs, prefix-lists, community-lists, etc., a filter-list has an implicit deny all at the end.

A filter-list can be applied directly through the "**neighbor ... filter-list ...**" command, or by using a route-map:

router(config)# **route-map** *name* **permit | deny**
router(config-route-map)# **match as-path** *filter-list-number*

In IOS XR, RegExps can be used inline or in a named-set, such as "**as-path-set**". For inline use, the general configuration is the following:

route-policy *RP-name*
  if as-path in (ios-regex '*RegExp***') then**
    actions

  . . .

  endif
end-policy

For use with a named-set such as "**as-path-set**", the configurations to execute are:

as-path-set *name-as-path-set*
  ios-regex '*RegExp-1***',**
  ...
  ios-regex '*RegExp-N***',**
end-set
!
route-policy *RP-name*
if as-path in *name-as-path-set* **then**
  actions

  . . .

  endif
end-policy

By way of example, let's assume we want to assign a Local Preference value of 200 to all the advertisements originated by ASes 64500 and 64501. The configurations to execute using a named-set are:

```
as-path-set PRIMARY
  ios-regex '_64500$',
  ios-regex '_64501$'
end-set

route-policy SET-LP
  if as-path in PRIMARY then
    set local-preference 200
  endif
end-policy
```

To simplify configuration, IOS XR also provides some mnemonics, summarised in Table 4.5 below:

Match criteria	Description
is-local	Match on any prefix with an empty AS_PATH (equivalent to RegExp ' ^$ ').
neighbor-is *AS*	Match on the first value of the AS_PATH (equivalent to RegExp ' ^AS_').
originates-from *AS*	Match on the last value of the AS_PATH (equivalent to RegExp '_AS$ ').
passes-through *AS*	Match on an AS in any part of the AS_PATH (equivalent to RegExp '_AS_').
length *length*	Match on an AS_PATH with a certain length.

Table 4.5 – IOS XR mnemonics for elementary RegExps.

For instance, the following routing policy:

```
route-policy TEST-REGEXP
  if as-path in (ios-regex '^$') then
    set local-preference 200
  endif
  if as-path in (ios-regex '^64501_') then
    set local-preference 180
  endif
  if as-path in (ios-regex '_64502$') then
    set local-preference 160
  endif
  if as-path in (ios-regex '_64503_') then
    set local-preference 140
  endif
end-policy
```

is equivalent to:

```
route-policy TEST-REGEXP
  if as-path is-local then
    set local-preference 200
  endif
  if as-path neighbor-is '64501' then
    set local-preference 180
  endif
  if as-path originates-from '64502' then
    set local-preference 160
  endif
  if as-path passes-through '64503' then
    set local-preference 140
  endif
end-policy
```

Since RegExp are sometimes difficult to write, we always recommend checking that they work as expected before applying them. In Cisco routers, this can be done by applying the RegExp to the "**show bgp** *afi safi* **regexp** *RegExp*" command, which allows you to view the prefixes that meet the RegExp in the BGP table.

NOTE: In IOS XR, the RegExp must be included between double quotation marks ("RegExp").

For instance, let's assume we want to check, on router GTW-1 of the sample network of Figure 3.1, RegExp "^(65541_)+([0-9]+)?$", which identifies all the advertisements coming from AS 65541 or from an AS near AS 65541. The result is the following:

```
RP/0/0/CPU0:GTW-1#show bgp ipv4 unicast regexp "^(65541_)+([0-9]+)?$"
. . .

Network              Next Hop      Metric LocPrf   Weight   Path
*> 0.0.0.0/0         172.20.1.1                 0        0   65541 i
*> 111.111.0.0/16    172.20.1.1                 0        0   65541 i
*> 142.1.0.0/16      172.20.1.1                 0        0   65541 64508 i
*> 142.2.0.0/16      172.20.1.1                 0        0   65541 64508 i
*> 190.1.0.0/16      172.20.1.1                 0        0   65541 64496 i
*> 198.51.100.0/24   172.20.1.1                 0        0   65541 64508 i
*> 203.0.113.0/24    172.20.1.1                 0        0   65541 64496 i
```

An alternative way is to create a routing policy that uses a RegExp as a condition, and then apply it to the "**show bgp** *afi safi* **route-policy** *RP-name*" command.

4.4.2 Regular Expressions in Juniper platforms

JUNOS adopts a different approach from Cisco IOS, since it considers the AS_PATH as a set of AS numbers, rather than a string of single characters. This means that JUNOS treats AS numbers as single entities, and not as a sequence of single characters. For instance, in Cisco IOS, AS 64501 is considered a 5-character sequence: 6, 4, 5, 0 and 1; in JUNOS, on the other hand, it is considered as a single string. In a way, it is as if, in JUNOS, single characters were made up of single AS numbers. Another difference between Cisco IOS and JUNOS is that, in Cisco IOS, the atoms at the beginning of the string " ^ " and at the end of the string " $ ", when necessary, must be explicitly present. While in JUNOS their presence is implicit, therefore their use is optional.

In JUNOS, a RegExp is comprised by two entities:

- Term: it can be a single AS, a group of AS or a wildcard, made up by character "." (period). If there is a space in the term, the RegExp should be between quotes: "...".

- Operator (optional): specifies the structure of the match condition. The majority of Operators specify the number of Term repetitions. Operators are placed immediately after the Term, except for the vertical bar (|) and the dash (-), which are placed between the two Terms, and round and square brackets that include the Terms. Table 4.6 below shows a list of the most useful Operators in practical applications, and their meaning.

Operator	Definition
{m,n}	Number of repetitions between *m* and *n* of a Term. *m* and *n* are positive integers with *m<n*.
{m}	Exactly *m* repetitions of *Term*. *m* must be a positive integer.
{m,}	*m* or more repetitions of *Term*. *m* must be a positive integer.
*	Zero or more repetitions of *Term*. It is equivalent to {0,}.
+	One or more repetitions of *Term*. It is equivalent to {1,}.
?	Zero or one repetition of *Term*. It is equivalent to {0,1}.
|	OR operation.
-	Placed between an initial value and a final one, it indicates a value interval.
^	Beginning of a string. It is added implicitly, therefore its use is optional.
$	End of a string. It is added implicitly, therefore its use is optional.
(...)	A group of *terms* considered as a single set. Any space is ignored.

Table 4.6 – List of Operators and their use.

Now, let's see some significant examples of RegExps applied to the AS_PATH attribute, and their meaning in terms of AS.

- **64501**: represents an AS_PATH that contains only AS number 64501 (e.g.: AS_ PATH of advertisements of local prefixes originated within AS 64501, communicated to eBGP Neighbors);

- **.*64501.***: represents an AS_PATH that contains AS number 64501 (e.g.: AS_PATH of advertisements that crossed AS 64501). It can also be written as ".* **64501** .*";

- **.*64501**: represents an AS_PATH that has AS number 64501 as the last AS in the list (e.g.: AS_PATH of advertisements of local prefixes originated by AS 64501). It can also be written as ".* **64501**";

- **64501.***: represents an AS_PATH that has AS number 64501 as the first AS in the list (e.g.: AS_PATH of advertisements received by an eBGP Neighbor of AS 64501). It can also be written as "**64501** .*";

- **.*(64512-65535).***: represents an AS_PATH that contains at least one private AS. Useful in edge routers, to reject advertisements with at least one private AS number. It can also be written as ".* **(64512-65535)** .*";

- **.**: represents an AS_PATH containing any single AS number (e.g.: AS_PATH of advertisements of local prefixes originated by any AS and received by an eBGP Neighbor);

- **"..?"**: represents an AS_PATH that contains any AS number, possibly followed also by another single AS number (e.g.: AS_PATH of advertisements originited from one or two ASes away);

- **"( )"**: represents an empty AS_PATH (e.g.: AS_PATH of advertisements of local prefixes originated within an AS. It can also be written as "()";

- **.***: represents any AS_PATH.

In JUNOS, AS_PATH-based conditions use a configuration procedure similar to the one we saw earlier, for Community value-based conditions (see Section 4.3.4). First, a set of AS values is defined through a RegExp. The configuration is executed within the "**policy-options**" configuration hierarchy:

[edit policy-options]
as-path *name RegExp*;

Conditions are used through the following configuration:

[edit policy-options]
policy-statement *RP-name* {
  term *term-1-name* {
    from as-path [*name-1 ... name-N*];
    then {
      actions;
    }
  }
}

where, as you may notice, there is the option of applying more AS sets. The rule when processing more than one set within the "**from as-path** ..." command, is that they should be processed according to a logical OR.

Let's consider the following configuration as example:

```
[edit policy-options]
policy-statement REJ-AS-64497-64508 {
  from as-path [ FROM-64497 FROM-64508 ];
  then reject;
}
as-path FROM-64497 ".* 64497"
as-path FROM-64508 ".* 64508"
```

This allows rejecting advertisements originated by AS 64497 or 64508. Now, let's assume we also want to reject the advertisements originated by another AS, AS 64505. We just need to add the "**as-path FROM-64505 ".* 64505"**" line to the configuration, under the **[edit policy-options]** hierarchy, and add "**FROM-64505**" to the condition. However, if we continue to add AS sets to the "**from as-path** ..." condition, we could have readability issues. In order to make the configuration more scalable, JUNOS uses the AS path groups:

[edit policy-options]
as-path-group *name-as-path-group* {
  as-path *name-1 RegExp-1*;
  ...
  as-path *name-N RegExp-N*;
}

which, in the condition, are recalled by the "**from as-path-group** *name-as-path-group*" command.

By applying to the above configuration an AS path group and adding AS 64505 to the ASes whose advertisements we want to reject, the configuration becomes:

```
[edit policy-options]
policy-statement REJ-AS {
  from as-path-group FROM-AS;
  then reject;
}
as-path-group FROM-AS {
  as-path FROM-64497 ".* 64497"
  as-path FROM-64508 ".* 64508"
  as-path FROM-64505 ".* 64505"
}
```

Here, you can immediately notice the advantage of using the AS path groups: to add a new configuration, you just need to write a new line of the AS path group, without touching the "**from as-path-group ...**" condition.

Lastly, in JUNOS too you can check if a RegExp works, by applying it to the advertisements in the RIB, through the "**show route protocol bgp aspath-regex** *RegExp*" command. For instance, let's assume we want to check, on router GTW-2 of Figure 3.1, the advertisements originated by AS 64497 or by AS 64508. The RegExp to use is the following: "**.* 64497 | * 64508**", that identifies all advertisements originated in ASes 64497 and 64508. The result is the following (for the sake of simplicity, we used also the "**terse**" option, for a shorter view):

```
aft@GTW-2> show route aspath-regex ".* 64497 | .* 64508" terse
. . . < output omitted > . . .

A V Destination        P Prf   Metric 1  Metric 2  Next hop  AS path
. . . < output omitted > . . .

* ? 192.0.2/24          B 170      100       0         65542 64497 I
  unverified                                           >172.20.2.1
* ? 198.51.100.0/24     B 170      100       0         65541 64508 I
  unverified                                           >172.16.1.11
    ?                   B 170      100       0         65542 64498 64508 I
  unverified                                           >172.20.2.1
```

SUMMARY

An essential aspect of BGP is the application of policies, the need to manipulate BGP advertisements in some way or another, and also to carry out advertisement filtering operations, to accept or reject some of them.

In this chapter, we introduced the main tools that the different types of Cisco IOS and JUNOS make available to create a policy.

Even if logically equal to one another, all the tools differ from manufacturer to manufacturer, and sometimes – as in the case of Cisco platforms – even within the same manufacturer. In this chapter, we described the tools available in Cisco platforms with IOS/ IOS XE, IOS XR and in Juniper platforms with JUNOS. In the next chapters, we will use these tools very often, as they are essential in BGP applications.

Worth remembering:

1. Tools available in Cisco IOS XE (and also in IOS): prefix-lists, community-lists, filter-lists, route-maps.

2. Routing policies in IOS XR.

3. Routing policies in JUNOS.

4. Regular Expressions in Cisco's different IOS types and in JUNOS, and their use.

5 – GENERATING BGP ADVERTISEMENTS

Until now, we've seen the theoretical and practical aspects of BGP sessions, their implementation in Cisco and Juniper platforms, and how to troubleshoot incorrect configurations. But in hindsight, BGP sessions alone would not be very useful, if there wasn't a router that commanded the BGP process to advertise certain prefixes.

For instance, let's suppose that an ISP needs to advertise its own IP prefix to the Internet, whose subnets are used for its own customers. In order to do this, the ISP must generate a BGP advertisement of the prefix locally, and then propagate this advertisement toward the other ASes. The locally-generated advertisement will be advertised by the BGP Speaker on all BGP sessions, or part of them, based on the type of platform and configurations executed. Thanks to this initial propagation, the advertisement will be propagated according to the rules of e/iBGP sessions – which we covered extensively in Paragraph 2.1 – in a sort of advertisement flooding.

There are many ways to generate an advertisement: through manual commands, by creating advertisements of aggregate prefixes, or through redistribution processes in BGP from a routing protocol other than BGP.

Every BGP implementation has its own technique. Cisco implementations use different commands for each kind of generation, while JUNOS implementation uses routing policies as the only tool. Obviously, the final result – aside from certain details on BGP attributes associated with locally-generated advertisements by default – is always the same: generating and propagating BGP advertisements.

5.1 MANUAL GENERATION

The manual generation of an advertisement depends on the platform adopted. Cisco platforms use a specific command, while JUNOS-based Juniper platforms use routing policies.

The operating logic in Cisco platforms – common to the other methods we will see (aggregation and redistribution) – entails the addition of an advertisement with certain attributes to the BGP table. After this addition, the BGP process propagates the advertisement.

In Juniper platforms, the operating logic is similar, but it is achieved through different tools.

5.1.1 Manual generation in Cisco platforms

The manual addition of an IPv4/IPv6 prefix in the BGP table is done through the following commands:

<u>IOS XE</u> (and also classic IOS)

For <u>IPv4</u> prefixes:

router(config)# **router bgp** *AS-number*
router(config-router)# **address-family ipv4 unicast**
router(config-router-af)# **network** *IPv4-prefix* **mask** *mask* [**route-map** *name*]

NOTE: If the mask specification is omitted, this implies that it is assumed as the natural mask.

For <u>IPv6</u> prefixes:

router(config)# **router bgp** *AS-number*
router(config-router)# **address-family ipv6 unicast**
router(config-router-af)# **network** *IPv6-prefix/mask-length* [**route-map** *name*]

<u>IOS XR</u>
RP/0/RP0/CPU0:router(config)# **router bgp** *AS-number*
RP/0/RP0/CPU0:router(config-bgp)# **address-family {ipv4 | ipv6} unicast**
RP/0/RP0/CPU0:router(config-bgp-af)# **network** *IPv4/v6-prefix/mask-length* [**route-policy** *name*]

Through the route-maps/routing policies, we can specify the values of BGP attributes, such as LOCAL_PREF, MED, ORIGIN, COMMUNITY, AS_PATH etc.
The effect of the "**network** …" command is the prefix propagation on all internal and external BGP sessions. If you don't want to propagate the prefix on certain BGP sessions, you need to configure filters that prevent the advertisement.
Every local prefix manually added to the BGP table is displayed as a new prefix with the following well-known mandatory attributes:

- AS_PATH: empty;

- ORIGIN: IGP;

- NEXT_HOP: identical to the one in the IP routing table. If the Next-Hop is directly connected, then Next-Hop=0.0.0.0 (=:: in case of IPv6 prefixes), indicating that the Next-Hop is the router itself.

When an IP prefix is added to the BGP table through the "**network** …" command, the process is subject to the following rule:
For the IP prefix to be added to the BGP table, its exact presence (prefix and mask) is required in the IP routing table (RIB).

NOTE: Actually, this rule applies only if the automatic summarization is disabled (via the "**no auto-summary**" command), which is included by default in Cisco IOS most recent versions. The automatic summarization aspect is related to the first versions of BGP (and other routing protocols, such as RIP and EIGRP), and it is now obsolete, if not inconvenient, therefore we will not cover it.

Once you add the prefix to the BGP table, if it becomes unreachable (i.e. it disappears from the IP routing table), it is removed from the BGP table, and an UPDATE message to withdraw the prefix is sent to the BGP Neighbors.
Now, let's see with an example how the "network …" command works. Let's assume that router CE1 (Cisco with IOS XE) wants to advertise to its ISP AS 64501 the two IP prefixes 195.31.0/24 and 128.0.1/24, the second of which is directly connected (and therefore present in the RIB), and the first of which is reachable through a static route with Next-Hop=1.0.0.2. Figure 5.1 below shows the relevant portion of the test network of Figure 3.1.

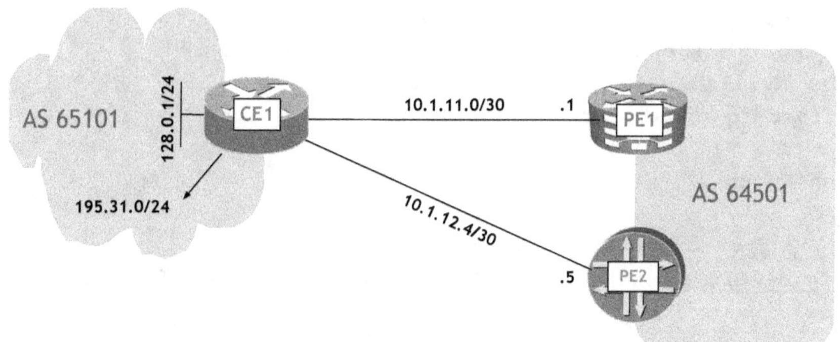

Figure 5.1 – Connection of router CE1 to AS 64501.

The two prefixes are both present in CE1's RIB. Checking the (exact) presence of the two prefixes in CE1's RIB is essential, because the "**network** …" command has no effect without it.

```
CE1#show ip route
. . .
  128.0.0.0/16 is variably subnetted, 2 subnets, 2 masks
C       128.0.1.0/24 is directly connected, GigabitEthernet3
L       128.0.1.1/32 is directly connected, GigabitEthernet3
. . .
S       195.31.0.0/24 [1/0] via 1.0.0.2
. . .
```

Within CE1's BGP process, let's execute the following configurations:

```
router bgp 65101
  network 128.0.1.0 mask 255.255.255.0 route-map SET-MED
  network 195.31.0.0
!
route-map SET-MED
  set metric 10
```

In the first "**network** …" command, the SET-MED route-map was associated, to vary the default MED value (=0) for prefix 128.0.1/24, and setting it to MED=10. The second "**network** …" command is used to add prefix 195.31.0/24 to the BGP table.
Prefix 128.0.1/24 is added to the BGP table with Next-Hop = 0.0.0.0 (since the prefix is present in the RIB as directly connected), while the second with Next-Hop =1.0.0.2 (that is, the Next-Hop present in the RIB):

```
CE1#show bgp ipv4 unicast 128.0.1.0
BGP routing table entry for 128.0.1.0/24, version 21
Paths: (1 available, best #1, table default)
  Advertised to update-groups:
     1        2
  Refresh Epoch 1
  Local
    0.0.0.0 from 0.0.0.0 (10.1.99.11)
      Origin IGP, metric 10, localpref 100, weight 32768, valid, sourced,
      local, best
```

```
CE1#show bgp ipv4 unicast 195.31.0.0
BGP routing table entry for 195.31.0.0/24, version 18
Paths: (1 available, best #1, table default)
  Advertised to update-groups:
     1         2
  Refresh Epoch 1
  Local
    1.0.0.2 from 0.0.0.0 (10.1.99.11)
      Origin IGP, metric 0, localpref 100, weight 32768, valid, sourced,
      local, best
```

Once added to the BGP table, the two prefixes are propagated both toward PE1 and toward PE2, following standard rules. For instance, the BGP Next-hop becomes 10.1.11.2 for the advertisements sent to PE1 and 10.1.12.6 for the advertisements sent to PE2. This can be easily checked via the following "**show ...**" commands:

```
RP/0/0/CPU0:PE1#show bgp ipv4 unicast neighbors 10.1.11.2 received routes
. . .
BGP router identifier 192.168.0.11, local AS number 64501
. . .

      Network            Next Hop       Metric    LocPrf     Weight       Path
*> 128.0.1.0/24        10.1.11.2          10                      0      65101 i
*> 195.31.0.0/24       10.1.11.2           0                      0      65101 i

aft@PE2> show route receive-protocol bgp 10.1.12.6

inet.0: 35 destinations, 40 routes (35 active, 0 holddown, 1 hidden)
   Prefix                 Nexthop          MED        Lclpref        AS path
*  128.0.1.0/24          10.1.12.6          10                       65101 I
*  195.31.0.0/24         10.1.12.6           0                       65101 I
```

5.1.2 Manual generation in Juniper platforms

As we already mentioned in the introduction of this chapter, JUNOS adopts a single method to generate advertisements, through routing policies. In order to generate the advertisement of a specific IP prefix, you can use route-filters or prefix-lists in the routing policy conditions (see Section 4.3.3). The use of route-filters has the advantage of allowing the selective application of actions, on a prefix by prefix basis. For instance, if we want to assign to prefix Pfx-1 different BGP attributes than those of prefix Pfx-2, we would need to use route-filters, instead of prefix-lists. We will clarify this in the next example.

The configuration procedure includes two steps:

1. creating the routing policy;

2. applying the routing policy in the export direction, at global, group or single session level.

Let's see an example of configuration that allows generating the same advertisements of prefixes as in the previous section, with the same property, but on router CE2 of the sample network of Figure 3.1. The routing-policy to be configured is the following:

```
[edit policy-options policy-statement GEN-PFX]
term GEN-195 {
  from {
```

```
      route-filter 195.31.0.0/24 exact;
  }
  then accept;
}
term GEN-128 {
  from {
    route-filter 128.0.1.0/24 exact;
  }
  then {
    metric 10;
    accept;
  }
}

[edit protocols bgp]
group PE {
  export GEN-PFX;
  peer-as 64501;
  neighbor 10.1.12.1;
  neighbor 10.1.11.5;
}
```

A more compact but less flexible configuration than the routing policy, which can be applied when there is no need to change the default values of BGP attributes, can be obtained by using a prefix-list, as shown below:

```
[edit policy-options]
prefix-list GEN-128-195 {
  128.0.1.0/24;
  195.31.0.0/24;
}
policy-statement GEN-PFX {
  from {
    prefix-list GEN-128-195;
  }
  then accept;
}
```

NOTE: If you wanted to propagate the advertisements on one session only, it would be sufficient to apply the routing policy at session level. For instance, if you want to propagate the advertisements only to PE2, the configuration to execute is the following:

```
[edit protocols bgp]
group PE {
  peer-as 64501;
  neighbor 10.1.12.1 {
    export GEN-PFX;
  }
  neighbor 10.1.11.5;
}
```

5.2 DEFAULT ROUTE GENERATION

In practical applications, it is very common to generate and advertise a default route via BGP. One example could be a stub AS connected to an ISP through a single or redundant connection. Another example is an AS multi-homed to several ISPs, whose routers do not have sufficient resources to contain the entire FIRT. In both cases, the customers could ask the ISP to send it a simple default route, to be used to route the outbound traffic. In case of ASes multi-homed to several ISPs, this leads to a sub-optimal routing process – this is the price to pay to preserve its own routing and forwarding resources.

As usual, every BGP implementation has its own techniques to generate and propagate a default route. We will see how it works for Cisco (IOS XE/XR) and Juniper (JUNOS) implementations.

5.2.1 Default route generation in Cisco platforms

The generation and subsequent propagation via BGP of a default route can be done either within a single session or for all BGP sessions.

If you want to propagate a default route on all active BGP sessions (both eBGP and iBGP), the recommended configuration method is the "**network . . .**" command, which requires – as you may remember – the existence of a default route in the IP routing table.

As an alternative, you can use the "**default-information originate**" command, alongside the "**redistribute** *protocol*" command, where *protocol* is the protocol through which the default route is present in the RIB (e.g., if the default route is present in the RIB as static route, you need to execute the "**redistribute static**" command).

Below are the configurations to be executed for the two default route generation methods, both in IOS / IOS XE and in IOS XR. Both methods specified are equivalent.

<u>IOS XE</u>
router(config)# **router bgp** *AS-number*

! Method 1
! *Default route* IPv4
router(config-router)# **address-family ipv4 unicast**
router(config-router-af)# **network 0.0.0.0**
! *Default route* IPv6
router(config-router)# **address-family ipv6 unicast**
router(config-router-af)# **network ::/0**

! Method 2
router(config-router)# **address-family {ipv4 | ipv6} unicast**
router(config-router-af)# **redistribute** *protocol*
router(config-router-af)# **default-information originate**

<u>IOS XR</u>
RP/0/RP0/CPU0:router(config)# **router bgp** *AS-number*

! Method 1
! *Default route* IPv4
RP/0/RP0/CPU0:router(config-bgp)# **address-family ipv4 unicast**
RP/0/RP0/CPU0:router(config-bgp-af)# **network 0.0.0.0/0**
! *Default route* IPv6
RP/0/RP0/CPU0:router(config-bgp)# **address-family ipv6 unicast**
RP/0/RP0/CPU0:router(config-bgp-af)# **network ::/0**

! Method 2
RP/0/RP0/CPU0:router(config-bgp)# **default-information originate**
RP/0/RP0/CPU0:router(config-bgp)# **address-family {ipv4 | ipv6} unicast**
RP/0/RP0/CPU0:router(config-bgp-af)# **redistribute** *protocol*

There is also the option of selectively generating the default route for each BGP Neighbor. In this case, the configuration is easier.

<u>IOS XE</u>
router(config)# **router bgp** *AS-number*
router(config-router)# **address-family {ipv4 | ipv6} unicast**
router(config-router-af)# **neighbor** *IPv4/v6-neighbor* **default-originate**

<u>IOS XR</u>
RP/0/RP0/CPU0:router(config)# **router bgp** *AS-number*
RP/0/RP0/CPU0:router(config-bgp)# **neighbor** *IPv4/v6-neighbor*
RP/0/RP0/CPU0:router(config-bgp-nbr)# **address-family {ipv4 | ipv6} unicast**
RP/0/RP0/CPU0:router(config-bgp-nbr-af)# **default-originate**

This generation method does not entail the addition of a default route in the BGP table, nor the presence of a default route in the RIB; it simply triggers the advertisement of a default route through an UPDATE message to a specific BGP Neighbor.

NOTE: The default route generated in this way is never subject to outbound filtering. Even by activating an outbound filter that blocks any advertisement, the default route is still forwarded.

For example, let's suppose that we want to propagate a default route from router PE1 (Cisco IOS XR) toward the two CEs. Using the configuration-group tool described in Section 3.2.3, starting from the configuration of the example in Figure 3.5, we just need to add an instruction to the address-family group CUSTOMERS:

```
router bgp 64501
 bgp router-id 192.168.0.11
 !
 af-group CUSTOMERS address-family ipv4 unicast
  default-originate
```

We will see how to check that the two CEs receive the default route from PE1 in the next Section 5.2.2.

5.2.2 Default route generation in Juniper platforms

Generating a default route is a particular case of what we saw in Section 5.1.2, since a default route can be seen as a prefix to be added to the BGP process and propagated to other BGP Neighbors. The steps to follow are: adding a default route to the RIB and then exporting it through a routing policy. Addition to the RIB can occur with any criteria, such as for instance through a static route with a "**reject**" or "**discard**" Next-Hop.

By way of example, let's suppose that we want to propagate a default route from router PE2 toward the two CEs. First, we add a default route to the RIB through a static route with Next-Hop=discard. The configuration is the following:

```
[edit routing-options]
static {
  route 0.0.0.0/0 discard;
}
```

The second step is defining the routing policy:

```
[edit policy-options policy-statement DEF-ROUTE]
from {
  route-filter 0.0.0.0/0 exact;
}
then accept;
```

And the last step is applying the routing policy to export the default route on all desired BGP sessions:

```
[edit protocols bgp]
group CE {
  export DEF-ROUTE;
  peer-as 64501;
  neighbor 10.1.12.1;
  neighbor 10.1.11.5;
}
```

In order to check if the procedure is correct, we must verify if the default route is present in the BGP table of CE1 and in the RIB of CE2:

```
CE1# show bgp ipv4 unicast
. . .
      Network          Next Hop           Metric  LocPrf  Weight Path
*>    0.0.0.0          10.1.11.1                            0 64501 i
*                      10.1.12.5                            0 64501 i

aft@CE2> show route protocol bgp 0.0.0.0/0 exact terse
. . .
A V Destination      P  Prf  Metric 1  Metric 2  Next hop      AS path
* ? 0.0.0.0/0        B  170       100            64501 I
  unverified                               >10.1.11.5
  ?                  B  170       100            64501 I
  unverified                               >10.1.12.1
```

5.2.3 Conditional generation

The conditional generation of a default route is useful in practical applications, to prevent possible traffic losses. For instance, let's assume that in our test network of Figure 3.1 the two Upstream Providers do not advertise the default route to AS 64501, but only the FIRT. In order to save internal resources, AS 64501, instead of propagating the entire table to the other routers within its backbone, advertises a default route from router gateways GTW-1 and GTW-2 toward the internal routers.

NOTE: This strategy entails a non-optimal routing process, since routers PE cannot see the distance of the destination from the two router gateways. The problem is that the PEs choose the router closer to them according to a selection process metric, without taking into account the actual traffic destination. In doing so, they could choose as exit point the router gateway farther from the destination (e.g., in terms of number of ASes to cross). This is the same issue that occurs in routing Link State routing protocols such as OSPF and IS-IS, partitioned into Stub/Not-so-Stubby o Totally Stubby/Not-so-Stubby areas (the last ones are the default areas for IS-IS). In any case, this might be the right compromise between routing optimality and the quantity of resources required for traffic forwarding.

In order to avoid possible traffic black-holing, the default route is advertised if and only if the connection of the router gateways toward the two Upstream Providers is working.

The general configurations to be executed in the IOS XE/XR are those we already saw in Section 5.2.1, plus a route-map for IOS XE and a routing policy in IOS XR.

<u>IOS XE</u>
router(config)# **router bgp** *AS-number*
router(config-router)# **address-family {ipv4 | ipv6} unicast**
router(config-router-af)# **neighbor** *IPv4/v6-neighbor* **default-originate route-map** *name*

<u>IOS XR</u>
RP/0/RP0/CPU0:router(config)# **router bgp** *AS-number*
RP/0/RP0/CPU0:router(config-bgp)# **neighbor** *IPv4/v6-neighbor*
RP/0/RP0/CPU0:router(config-bgp-nbr)# **address-family {ipv4 | ipv6} unicast**
RP/0/RP0/CPU0:router(config-bgp-nbr-af)# **default-originate route-policy** *name*

The route-map in IOS XE and the routing policy in IOS XR are used to "condition" the advertisement of the default route, that is, the default route is generated/withdrawn if and only if the prefixes permitted by the route-map or routing policy are present/absent in the RIB.

In JUNOS, the configuration is a little bit more articulated. First, the condition needs to be defined:

```
[edit policy-options]
condition condition-name {
  if-route-exists {
    mask/prefix;
    table {inet.0 | inet6.0};
  }
}
```

The condition is used through the following routing policy:

```
[edit policy-options]
policy-statement RP-name {
  from {
    protocol protocol;
    route-filter {0.0.0.0/0 | ::/0} exact;
    condition condition-name;
  }
  then accept;
}
```

Then, the routing policy must be applied in the export direction on the affected sessions.
By way of example, let's see the configurations to be executed on routers GTW-1 (IOS XR) and GTW-2 (JUNOS) to advertise the IPv4 default route within the AS, conditioned to the up/down status of the links toward the Upstream Providers, numbered 172.20.1.0/31 and 172.20.2.0/31.

NOTE: We omitted the filters that prevent FIRT propagation within the backbone from the configurations. We will go over the filtering aspects in Chapter 6.

<u>GTW-1</u> (IOS XR)
```
route-policy COND
  if rib-has-route in (172.20.1.0/31) then
    pass
  endif
end-policy
!
router bgp 64501
  bgp router-id 192.168.1.11
  address-family ipv4 unicast
  !
  neighbor-group IBGP
    remote-as 64501
    update-source Loopback0
    address-family ipv4 unicast
      default-originate route-policy COND
      next-hop-self
!
  neighbor 192.168.0.11
    description "*** iBGP SESSION WITH PE1 ***";
    use neighbor-group IBGP
!
  neighbor 192.168.0.12
    description "*** iBGP SESSION WITH PE2 ***";
    use neighbor-group IBGP
!
  neighbor 192.168.1.12
    description "*** iBGP SESSION WITH GTW-2 ***";
    use neighbor-group IBGP
!
```

The "**rib-has-route in (172.20.1.0/31)**" condition of the routing policy is pretty much self-explanatory: it is met if and only if prefix 172.20.1.0/31 (point-to-point connection to UP-2) is present in the RIB.

<u>GTW-2</u> (JUNOS)
```
[edit policy-options]
policy-statement COND-DEF-ROUTE {
  from {
    protocol static;
    route-filter 0.0.0.0/0 exact;
    condition COND;
  }
  then accept;
}

condition COND {
  if-route-exists {
    172.20.2.0/31;
    table inet.0;
  }
}

[edit protocols bgp]
group IBGP {
type internal;
  local-address 192.168.1.12;
  export [ NHS COND-DEF-ROUTE ];
  neighbor 192.168.1.11;
  neighbor 192.168.0.11;
  neighbor 192.168.0.12;
}
```

Notice that, in GTW-2's RIB, there is the static route configured in Section 5.2.2 above, which allows installing the default route in the RIB with Next-Hop=discard. This is an essential step for JUNOS.

With these configurations, in standard operating conditions, the default route is regularly propagated by the two router gateways to the two PE routers. For the sake of simplicity, let's see its presence on PE1:

```
RP/0/0/CPU0:PE1#show bgp
. . .
     Network            Next Hop          Metric     LocPrf      Weight      Path
*    i0.0.0.0/0         192.168.1.11                   100            0      i
*>   i                  192.168.1.12                   100            0      i
```

NOTE: The way the two routers PE choose the best path depends on the choices of the administrator of AS 64501. As we will see, it is possible, using certain BGP metrics, to choose the desired router gateway, or to enable the multipath BGP and thus balance the outbound traffic toward the Upstream Providers. We will see these aspects in detail in Chapter 7.

Now, let's assume that the connection of router gateway GTW-1 to UP-1 is out of service. The out-of-service situation is confirmed by the absence of prefix 172.20.1.0/31 in GTW-1's RIB:

```
RP/0/0/CPU0:GTW-1#show route 172.20.1.0/31

. . .

% Network not in table
```

Due to the out-of-service situation, the default route is withdrawn by GTW-1, and therefore it will no longer be present in PE1's BGP table:

```
RP/0/0/CPU0:PE1#show bgp

. . .

      Network        Next Hop         Metric     LocPrf     Weight       Path
*>i 0.0.0.0/0       192.168.1.12                 100          0          i
```

The following is a wireshark analysis of one of the three UPDATE messages (one for each PE and one toward GTW-2) sent by GTW-1 to withdraw the default route.

```
Internet Protocol Version 4, Src: 192.168.1.11, Dst: 192.168.0.11
Transmission Control Protocol, Src Port: 179, Dst Port: 44874, Seq: 1, Ack: 20, Len: 24
Border Gateway Protocol - UPDATE Message
  Marker: ffffffffffffffffffffffffffffffff
  Length: 24
  Type: UPDATE Message (2)
  Withdrawn Routes Length: 1
  Withdrawn Routes
     0.0.0.0/0
  Total Path Attribute Length: 0
```

The same occurs if the connection between GTW-2 and UP-2 is out of service. For the sake of brevity, we will omit the result.

5.3 IP PREFIX AGGREGATION

Prefix aggregation is a very important aspect for each IP routing protocol, as it has strong implications both on network scalability and stability. This is especially true for BGP, which is the protocol that uses prefix aggregation the most.

The idea behind prefix aggregation in BGP is very simple: through a special configuration command, an aggregate prefix is created and added to the BGP table or to the IP routing table, depending on the implementation. The BGP process treats the aggregate prefix as a new prefix present in one of these tables, and propagates it on the different BGP sessions, following standard propagation rules. The IP prefix aggregation process generates major issues that need to be taken into account, in order to prevent incorrect configurations with consequent network malfunctioning. In particular, the issues concern:

- the relationship between the BGP attributes of the more specific components of the aggregate prefix and those inherited from the aggregate prefix;

- the possibility that a forwarding loop is generated.

At first, we will go over the tools and techniques available to manage these two important issues. Then, we will see some aggregation scenarios, and lastly we will see the implementation in Cisco and Juniper platforms.

5.3.1 Aggregation and BGP Attributes

The aggregation process causes a major issue: what BGP attributes should be associated with the aggregate prefix? There are two possible solutions available:

- ignoring the attributes associated with the more specific prefixes completely. In this case, we lose memory of the attributes;

- using a combination of the attributes of the more specific prefixes. In this case, the memory of the attributes of the prefixes within the aggregates is retained, although with a few limitations. For instance, for the AS_PATH attribute, the order of the elements is important. Using the set of AS_PATHs of the more specific prefixes for the aggregate, the order is lost.

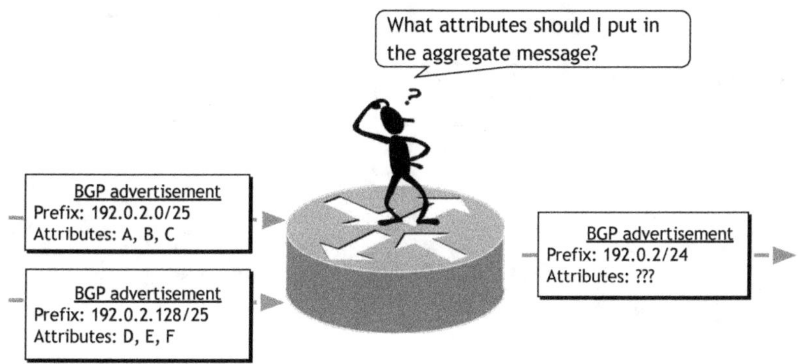

Figure 5.2 – Aggregation and BGP Attributes.

Further on, we will see how Cisco and Juniper's BGP implementations deal with this issue. RFC 4271 specifies two important attributes for the aggregation process, which we already saw in Section 2.4.5: ATOMIC_AGGREGATE and AGGREGATOR.
Another important attribute involved in the aggregation process is the AS_PATH attribute. Indeed, as mentioned above, in the aggregation without any memory loss, the AS_PATH order makes no sense. The AS_PATH of the more specific prefixes are added to the AS_PATH of the aggregate prefix through an AS_SET type segment.

Figure 5.3 shows the use of the three attributes ATOMIC_AGGREGATE, AGGREGATOR and AS_PATH in the two aggregation cases, with and without memory loss. The differences lie in the presence of the ATOMIC_AGGREGATE attribute in the case of aggregation with memory loss, and the presence of an AS_SET type AS_PATH segment, in the case of memory retention.

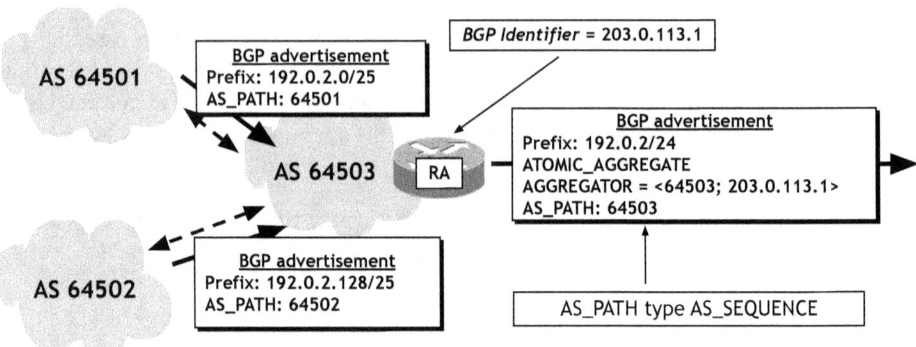

Figure 5.3 a – Aggregation with memory loss.

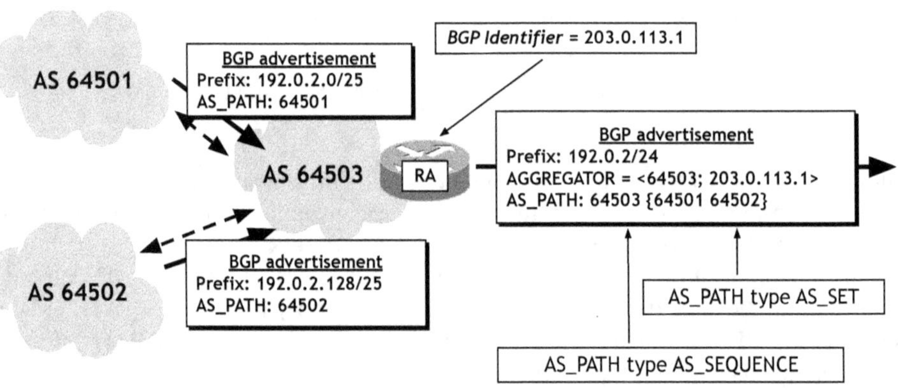

Figure 5.3 b – Aggregation without memory loss.

5.3.2 Loop prevention

One of the typical issues of aggregation processes is the possible creation of loops at data plane level (forwarding loops). In order to understand where the issue may arise, let's consider the example in Figure 5.4.

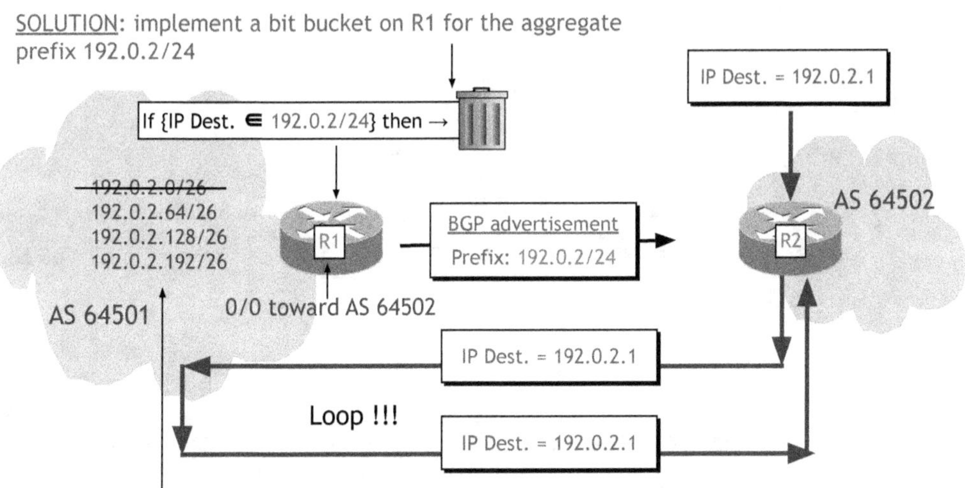

Figure 5.4 – Possible forwarding loop in an aggregation process.

Let's assume that router R1 has, in its own IP routing table, the 4 prefixes 192.0.2.0/26, 192.0.2.64/26, 192.0.2.128/26 and 192.0.2.192/26, and a default route with Next-Hop R2. Moreover, let's assume that there is an active eBGP session between R1 and R2, and that, on it, R1 advertises aggregate prefix 192.0.2/24 to R2. Let's consider the case of an IP packet that reaches R2, with target address 192.0.2.1. In normal operating conditions, it is routed toward R1, through aggregate prefix 192.0.2/24 advertised by R1 and present in R2's IP routing table, and then forwarded by R1 toward the final destination. Let's assume that, at a certain point, due to an out of service, prefix 192.0.2.0/26 disappears from R1's RIB. As earlier, the IP packet with destination 192.0.2.1 is regularly forwarded by R2 toward R1, where it cannot be routed toward the final destination, because prefix 192.0.2.0/26 is missing from the RIB of R1. However, since there is a default route with Next-Hop R2, the packet is sent back to R2, thus creating a forwarding loop.

The solution to prevent the forwarding loop is very simple: it is sufficient to add the aggregate prefix with a bit bucket as virtual Next Hop to the RIB of the BGP Speaker where the aggregation takes place. This way, every packet directed toward a more specific prefix of the aggregate and not included in the RIB is rejected.

Going back to our example, when the packet with destination 192.0.2.1 reaches R1, since, in its IP routing table, there is aggregate prefix 192.0.2/24 with the bit bucket as Next-Hop, the packet is rejected and no longer sent to R2, thus removing the forwarding loop.

5.3.3 Aggregation scenarios

IP prefix aggregation within BGP can be applied to several scenarios. Let's see a few typical examples and possible issues, resulting from unwise aggregation design.

The simplest, most common scenario in practical applications is the one described in Figure 5.5 below.

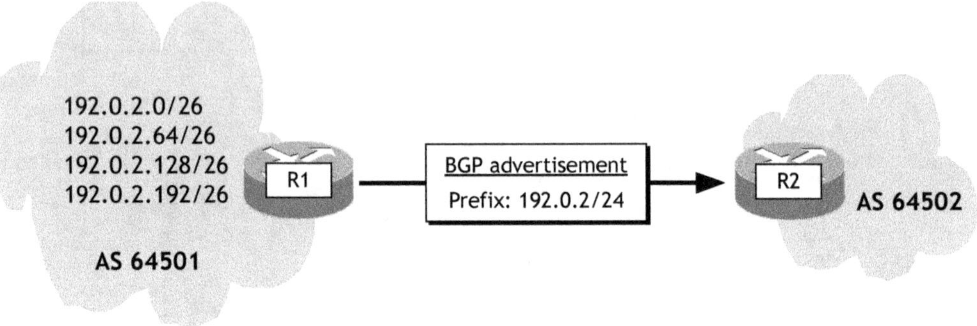

Figure 5.5 – Aggregation with suppression of the subnets of the aggregate prefix.

Router R1 aggregates the 4 prefixes from 192.0.2.0/26 to 192.0.2.192/26, in a single prefix 192.0.2/24 and advertises this prefix, by suppressing the subnets of the aggregate prefix, that is, the more specific prefixes. This means that R1 will send an UPDATE message through which it will advertise prefix 192.0.2/24 and, at the same time, will withdraw the 4 more specific prefixes, by adding them to the "Withdrawn routes" list.

A second simple scenario is the one shown in Figure 5.6, where an enterprise network has a multi-homed connection to two ISPs, and uses blocks of addresses taken from both. An hypothetical customer X has two eBGP sessions toward two ISPs, ISP-1 and ISP-2, which use the two blocks of addresses 203.0.113/24 and 198.51.100/24 respectively, and provide to customer X with subnets 203.0.113.0/26 and 198.51.100.0/26, respectively. The two ISPs advertise toward other ASes whole blocks comprising also the subnets assigned to customer X. Aggregation is done at ISP-1 and ISP-2 router level, respectively.

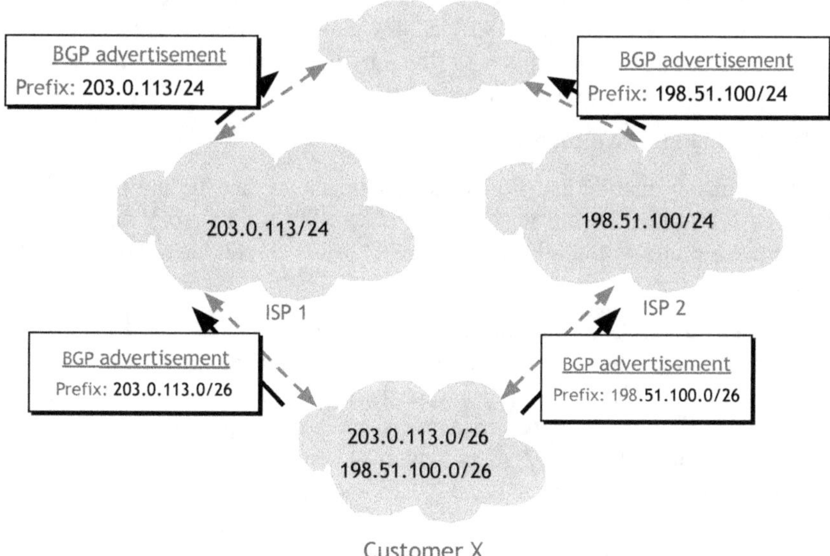

Figure 5.6 – Aggregation scenario for a multi-homed customer to two different ISPs with address blocks provided by both ISPs.

The issue in this aggregation scenario is that a possible out of service of the ISP-1 network will block traffic toward subnet 203.0.113.0/26 of customer X. The same goes for an out of service of ISP-2: traffic toward subnet 198.1.51.100.0/26 of customer X would be blocked. In order to prevent this issue, ISP-2 must also advertise subnet 203.0.113.0/26 and ISP-1 subnet 198.1.51.100.0/26. However, this entails an increase of the prefixes circulating in the Internet, and does not go down well with the ISPs, which, to avoid too-big RIBs, typically block the advertisements of prefixes with a length mask greater than 24 bit.

Always with reference to Figure 5.6, if customer X adopts its own address block (called PI, Provider Independent block), that does not intersect the two blocks of the ISPs, the two ISPs, in order to allow customer X to be reached, must advertise also the customer's PI block, beside their own block. If, on the other hand, customer X would use a subnet provided by a specific ISP – for instance 203.0.113.0/26 provided by ISP-1 – it would be necessary to distinguish the two cases in which ISP-1 would advertise or not the subnet assigned to customer X. If ISP-1 advertised only aggregate block 203.0.113/24 and ISP-2 its own block 1981.51.100/24 and subnet 203.0.113.0/26 of customer X, then all traffic toward customer X would flow through ISP-2. Only in case of out of service of the ISP-2 network, the traffic would reach customer X through ISP-1. For customer X, ISP-2 would be the primary ISP, while ISP-1 would be the backup one. If ISP-1 would also advertise the subnet of customer X, other ASes would have the option of defining routing policies to (possibly) use ISP-1 as primary ISP for traffic toward customer X.

A third interesting aggregation example occurs when a hypothetical customer X, with the 4 local prefixes shown in Figure 5.7, has a redundant connection to a single ISP. Out of the 4 prefixes, two are advertised by R11 (192.0.2.0/26 and 192.0.2.64/26) and two by R12 (192.0.2.128/26 and 192.0.2.192/26).

In this case, more than one aggregation scenario is possible. The first scenario entails that the customer advertises only aggregate prefix 192.0.2/24, without its more specific components. This causes all traffic toward the 4 local prefixes to flow on one of the two connections, leaving the other as backup. There could be two negative effects:

- an unbalanced use of the two connections;

- a non-optimal traffic distribution. For instance, supposing that the primary connection is only between R11 and R21 and that prefix 192.0.2.192/26 is directly connected to R12, traffic toward this prefix would follow the path R21→R11→R12, instead of the shortest path R22→R12.

A solution to this issue could be the one shown in Figure 5.7.
The aggregate prefix and a subset of specific prefixes are advertised on each eBGP session. In Figure 5.7, by way of example, the aggregate and the more specific prefixes 192.0.2.0/26 and 192.0.2.64/26 are advertised on the upper connection, while the aggregate and the more specific prefixes 192.0.2.128/26 and 192.0.2.192/26 are advertised on the lower connection. This implies that traffic from the ISP toward prefixes 192.0.2.0/26 and 192.0.2.64/26 will flow on the upper connection, while traffic toward the other two prefixes will flow on the lower connection. If a connection is out of service, due to the presence of the aggregate prefix in the RIBs of R21 and R22 (and also in the other ISP routers), traffic toward all more specific prefixes will flow on the other connection. Figure 5.7 also highlights an important practical aspect: in order to prevent specific prefixes from being propagated outside the ISP's AS, they are advertised with a COMMUNITY attribute containing the NO_EXPORT well-known Community value. Therefore, the ISP will advertise toward the outside only the aggregate prefix, possibly aggregating it to a bigger block.

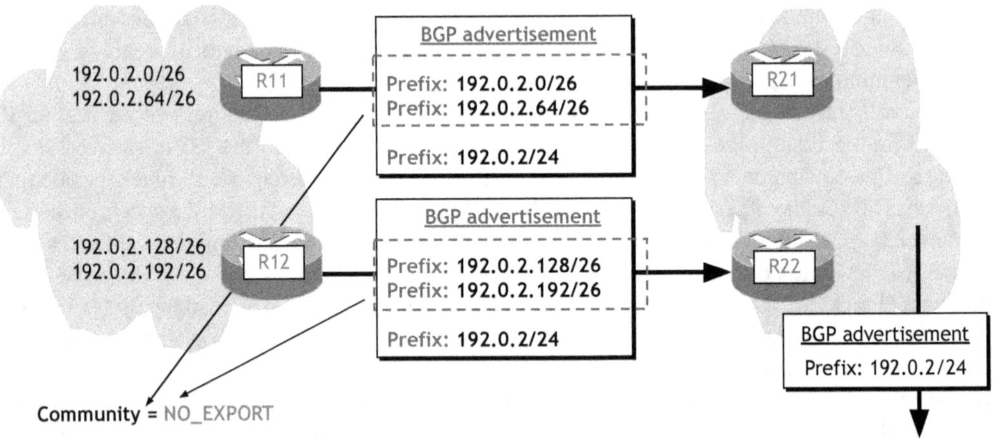

Figure 5.7 – Aggregation scenario of a Customer with redundant connectivity to a single ISP.

5.3.4 Configuration in Cisco platforms

In Cisco IOS, propagating an aggregate prefix requires first the addition of the aggregate prefix to the BGP table, through a special configuration command. The BGP process treats the aggregate prefix as a new prefix added to the BGP table, and propagates it on the different BGP sessions, following standard propagation rules.

There are two methods to inject an aggregate prefix into the BGP table: using the "**network ...**" command, as we saw in Section 5.1.1, or using the "**aggregate-address ...**" command.

Remember that the "**network ...**" command requires that the prefix to be added to the BGP table is present in the RIB. For this purpose, the trick of adding the aggregate prefix to the IP routing table, through a static route with virtual interface Null 0 as the Next-Hop is often used. However, the "**network ...**" command is not very flexible, as it doesn't allow operations such as "suppress all the more specific prefixes", or "keep memory of the BGP attributes", etc. For this reason, its use is not recommended.

The second method, using the "**aggregate-address ...**" command, offers many options for a flexible use of aggregation. The complete command is the following:

<u>IOS XE</u>
router(config)# **router bgp** *AS-number*

! Aggregation of <u>IPv4</u> prefixes:

router(config-router)# **address-family ipv4 unicas**t
router(config-router-af)# **aggregate-address** *IPv4-prefix mask-length* [**summary-only**]
[*other options*]

! Aggregation of <u>IPv6</u> prefixes:

router(config-router)# **address-family ipv6 unicast**
router(config-router-af)# **aggregate-address** *IPv6-prefix/mask-length* [**summary-only**]
[*other options*]

<u>IOS XR</u>
RP/0/RP0/CPU0:router(config)# **router bgp** *AS-number*
RP/0/RP0/CPU0:router(config-bgp)# **address-family {ipv4 | ipv6} unicast**
RP/0/RP0/CPU0:router(config-bgp-af)# **aggregate-address** *IP-prefix/mask*
[**summary-only**] [*other options*]

When an IP prefix is added to the BGP table through the "**aggregate-address ...**" command, the process is subject to the following essential rule:

For the aggregate prefix to be added to the BGP table, there must be at least one specific prefix in the BGP table which is best-path.

The "**summary-only**" option is one of the most useful, and allows suppressing the advertisement of all the more specific prefixes. Notice that, by default, the BGP process – apart from advertising the aggregate prefix – also advertises the more specific prefixes. On the other hand, this is quite obvious, if you think that the effect of the "**aggregate-address...**" command is only that of adding the aggregate prefix to the BGP table.

Other options include:

- **as-set**: used to keep memory of BGP attributes. As already mentioned in the Note of Section 2.4.2, RFC 6472 – *Recommendation for Not Using AS_SET and AS_CONFED_SET in BGP*, December 2011, strongly advices against the use of AS_SET and AS_CONFED_SET segments, as they prevent the correct identification of the advertisement origin, and this causes issues when safety architectures are applied (e.g., see RPKI architecture in Chapter 10);

- **advertise-map** (IOS XE only): used to create the aggregate using only the prefixes allowed by a route-map;

- **suppress-map** (IOS XE only): used to suppress the advertisement of the more specific prefixes allowed by a route-map;

- **attribute-map** (IOS XE only): used to change the BGP attributes associated by default with the aggregate prefix. Attributes are defined through a route-map;

- **route-policy** … (IOS XR only): with the "**suppress-route**" action, it allows suppressing the sending of certain specific components (see Example 2 below). With the other actions, it allows changing the default BGP attributes.

Once the aggregate has been created without specifying the "**as-set**" option, the related well-known mandatory BGP attributes are the following by default (similar to those associated to the prefixes added to the BGP table through the "**network** …" command):

- NEXT_HOP: 0.0.0.0 (::/0 for IPv6); indicates that the Next-Hop is the router;

- AS_PATH: empty;

- ORIGIN: IGP.

Using the "**as-set**" option changes the well-known mandatory attributes as follows:

- NEXT_HOP: 0.0.0.0 (::/0 for IPv6); indicates that the Next-Hop is the router;

- AS_PATH: AS_SET type segment containing the union of all the ASes crossed by more specific prefixes;

- ORIGIN: INCOMPLETE if at least one of the more specific prefixes has ORIGIN=INCOMPLETE, otherwise IGP.

And also:

- the LOCAL_PREF attribute takes on a value equal to the highest Local Preference value of more specific prefixes;

- the COMMUNITY attribute contains the union of all Community values of more specific prefixes.

Let's see some examples of application of this command. All the following examples refer to router GTW-1 of our sample network in Figure 3.1. Let's assume that the following IP address block has been assigned to AS 64501: 195.31/16. Several subnets of this prefix have been assigned to customers by AS 64501. In particular, the customer with router CE1 was assigned IP subnets 195.31.0.0/26 and 195.31.0.64/26, while the customer with router CE2 was assigned IP subnets 195.31.0.128/26 and 195.31.0.192/26.

NOTE: In none of these examples we will use the "**as-set**" options, because, as we mentioned earlier, it is strongly discouraged.

Example 1

In this example, router GTW-1 advertises only the aggregate prefix, while suppressing the sending of the more specific components. The configurations to execute are:

```
router bgp 64501
  address-family ipv4 unicast
    aggregate-address 195.31.0.0/16 summary-only
```

As a result of this configuration, the aggregated prefix is inserted into the GTW-1 BGP Table:

```
RP/0/0/CPU0:GTW-1#show bgp 195.31.0.0/16

. . .
Paths: (1 available, best #1)
  Advertised to peers (in unique update groups):
    172.20.1.1
  Path #1: Received by speaker 0
  Advertised to peers (in unique update groups):
    172.20.1.1
  Local, (aggregated by 64501 192.168.1.11)
    0.0.0.0 from 0.0.0.0 (192.168.1.11)
      Origin IGP, localpref 100, weight 32768, valid, aggregated,
                                  atomic-aggregate, best, group-best
        Received Path ID 0, Local Path ID 0, version 225
```

This view shows that IOS XR adds the aggregate prefix to the BGP table by default, with the AGGREGATOR attribute (**aggregated by 64501 192.168.1.11**) and the ATOMIC_AGGREGATE attribute – which indicates that there is no AS_SET type AS_PATH segment in the AS_PATH – associated with it.

The result of the "**summary-only**" option is the suppression of all the more specific prefixes, highlighted by an "**s**" ("suppressed") in place of "*****" in the "Network" column of the "**show bgp**" command. This means that the more specific prefixes will not be propagated on e/iBGP sessions.

```
RP/0/0/CPU0:GTW-1#show bgp | i 195.31

. . .
*> 195.31.0.0/16      0.0.0.0                                  32768 i
s>i195.31.0.0/26      192.168.0.11          0     100     0    65101 i
s>i195.31.0.64/26     192.168.0.11          0     100     0    65101 i
s>i195.31.0.128/26    192.168.0.11                100     0    65101 i
s>i195.31.0.192/26    192.168.0.11                100     0    65101 i
```

NOTE: As we've seen earlier in Section 5.3.2, the solution to avoid forwarding loops is to add, in the RIB of the BGP Speaker that carries out the aggregation, the aggregate prefix with a bit bucket as virtual Next-Hop (=Null0 in Cisco platforms). All types of Cisco IOS do this automatically. By way of example, for the case we just described, we have:

```
RP/0/0/CPU0:GTW-1#show route | i 195.31.0.0/16

...
B   195.31.0.0/16 [200/10] via 0.0.0.0, 00:45:04, Null0
```

<u>Example 2</u>

Let's suppose that router GTW-1, to optimise the routing process and balance the inbound traffic, decides to advertise, besides the aggregate prefix, also the two subnets assigned to the customer with router CE1: 195.31.0.0/26 and 195.31.0.64/26. In order to do this, it is sufficient to create a routing policy with the "**suppress-route**" action to suppress only the advertisement of the subnets of the customer with router CE2.

```
route-policy SUPPRESS
  if destination in (195.31.0.128/26, 195.31.0.192/26) then
    suppress-route
  endif
end-policy
!
router bgp 64501
  address-family ipv4 unicast
    aggregate-address 195.31.0.0/16 route-policy SUPPRESS
```

The result of the application of the SUPPRESS routing policy is the suppression only of the two subnets assigned to the customer with router CE2. This means that the two subnets will not be propagated on e/iBGP sessions.

```
RP/0/0/CPU0:GTW-1#show bgp | i 195.31

. . .
*> 195.31.0.0/16        0.0.0.0                                    32768 i
*>i195.31.0.0/26        192.168.0.11        0      100      0      65101 i
*>i195.31.0.64/26       192.168.0.11        0      100      0      65101 i
s>i195.31.0.128/26      192.168.0.11               100      0      65101 i
s>i195.31.0.192/26      192.168.0.11               100      0      65101 i
```

NOTE: Cisco IOS XE also offers the option, on single BGP sessions, to not suppress the advertisements of certain prefixes, specified by a route-map. The command is the following:

```
router(config)# router bgp AS-number
router(router-config)# neighbor IP-neighbor unsuppress-map route-map-name
```

5.3.5 Configuration in Juniper platforms

In Juniper routers, prefix aggregation is done with the routing policies. This configuration method is very flexible, but is also more complex. Configuration requires three essential steps:

1 Creating the aggregate and adding it to the RIB. The essential rule to follow is that, for the addition to be effective, at least one "active" more specific prefix of the aggregate must be present in the RIB. The aggregate can be assimilated to a static route, which has the bit bucket as Next Hop (the same, in Cisco routers, of a static route pointing to the virtual interface Null0). In order to create the aggregate and add it to the RIB, the following configuration is used:

[edit routing-options]
aggregate {
  < defaults {
    options;
  } >

```
    route IP-prefix/mask {
    options;
    }
}
```

NOTE: To add an IPv6 aggregate prefix to the IPv6 RIB, the configuration is the same, but it must be done within the configuration hierarchy **[edit routing-options rib inet6.0]**.

The options can be used to define the BGP attributes such as ORIGIN, AS_PATH, ATOMIC_AGGREGATE, etc. (see the following examples). If the options are defined under the "**defaults**" clause, they apply to all aggregate prefixes defined; otherwise, if they are defined under the "**route**" clause, they are specific for the aggregate prefix.

2   Defining a routing policy that allows the aggregate defined in 1. Note that unless otherwise specified within the routing policy, due to BGP's default policies, also the specific prefixes that form the aggregate are exported.

```
[edit policy-options policy-statement RP-name]
from {
    protocol aggregate;
    other conditions;
}
then {
    actions
}
```

3   Applying the routing policy to the BGP process, in the export direction.

Once the aggregate has been created, it is added to the RIB by default, with the following well-known mandatory BGP attributes:

- NEXT_HOP: "reject" (indicates the bit bucket). You can choose a "discard" option instead of "reject" through configuration;

- AS_PATH: union of the AS_PATHS of the more specific prefixes. When the advertisement is propagated, the AS_PATH will include the union of the AS_PATHS of the more specific prefixes, in an AS_SET type segment;

- ORIGIN: IGP, or INCOMPLETE if at least one of the more specific prefixes has ORIGIN= INCOMPLETE.

Notice that, by default, JUNOS – if applicable – always adds an AS_SET type segment to the AS_PATH, to keep track of the ASes crossed by the more specific aggregate components. This goes against the rules of repeatedly mentioned RFC 6472, which advises against its use. The AS_SET segment can be eliminated with the following option, within the definition of the aggregate route, by adding the ATOMIC_AGGREGATE attribute (for the sake of completion, in the configuration, we also added the option to add the AGGREGATOR attribute, not required to remove the AS_SET segment):

```
[edit routing-options <rib inet6.0>]
aggregate {
  route IP-prefix/mask {
  as-path {
    atomic-aggregate;
```

```
    < aggregator AS BGP-ID >;
  }
}
```

Let's see the same two examples of the previous section, this time considering router GTW-2. Let's suppose to aggregate prefixes 195.31.0.X/26 of the CEs (X=0,64,128,192) on GTW-2 in prefix 195.31/16, without any configuration option, and export the prefix toward router UP-2. The configurations to execute are:

```
[edit routing-options]
aggregate {
  route 195.31.0.0/16;
}

[edit policy-options policy-statement SET-AGGR]
from protocol aggregate;
then accept;

[edit protocols bgp]
group UP {
  export SET-AGGR;
}
```

Let's check the presence of aggregate prefix 195.31/16 in GTW-2's RIB, and the detailed info:

```
aft@GTW-2>show route protocol aggregate 195.31/16 detail
inet.0: 36 destinations, 41 routes (36 active, 0 holddown, 0 hidden)
195.31.0.0/16 (1 entry, 1 announced)
    *Aggregate Preference: 130
        Next hop type: Reject, Next hop index: 0
        Address: 0xce30610
        Next-hop reference count: 2
        State: <Active Int Ext>
        Local AS: 64501
        . . . < output omitted > . . .
        AS path: 65101 I   (LocalAgg)
        Flags:                    Depth: 0        Active
        AS path list:
        AS path: 65101 I Refcount: 4
        Contributing Routes (4):
            195.31.0.0/26 proto BGP
            195.31.0.64/26 proto BGP
            195.31.0.128/26 proto BGP
            195.31.0.192/26 proto BGP
```

As you can see from the view, prefix 195.31/16 was added to GTW-2's RIB and is active. The prefix was assigned with the following default values:

- NEXT_HOP = Reject;

- AS_PATH = 65101;

- ORIGIN = IGP.

Moreover, in the final part, under the "**Contributing Routes**" lines, there are the 4 more specific prefixes that form the aggregate, and the protocol they were advertised with.

Now, let's see what prefixes are propagated toward router UP-2:

```
aft@GTW-2> show route advertising-protocol bgp 172.20.2.1
inet.0: 36 destinations, 41 routes (36 active, 0 holddown, 0 hidden)
  Prefix               Nexthop           MED          Lclpref         AS path
* 195.31.0.0/16        Self                                           65101 I
* 195.31.0.0/26        Self                                           65101 I
* 195.31.0.64/26       Self                                           65101 I
* 195.31.0.128/26      Self                                           65101 I
* 195.31.0.192/26      Self                                           65101 I
```

As evidenced by the view, apart from the aggregate prefix, GTW-2 also propagates the more specific prefixes toward UP-2.

If you want to filter all or part of the more specific prefixes, it would be sufficient to act on the routing policy. For instance, the following routing policy allows suppressing the propagation of all the more specific prefixes (equivalent to the "**summary-only**" option in Cisco routers):

```
[edit policy-options policy-statement SUMMARY-ONLY]
term AGGREGATE {
  from {
    route-filter 195.31.0.0/16 exact;
  }
  then accept;
}
term SUPPRESS {
  from {
    route-filter 195.31.0.0/16 longer;
  }
  then reject;
}

[edit protocols bgp]
group UP {
  export SUMMARY-ONLY;
}
```

For verification purposes, let's see the prefixes that GTW-2 sends to BGP Neighbor UP-2 (Neighbor Address=172.20.2.1):

```
aft@GTW-2> show route advertising-protocol bgp 172.20.2.1
inet.0: 36 destinations, 41 routes (36 active, 0 holddown, 0 hidden)
  Prefix               Nexthop      MED       Lclpref            AS path
* 195.31.0.0/16        Self                                      65101 I
```

As you can see, the more specific prefixes are not propagated.

In the same way, you can suppress part of the more specific prefixes (equivalent to the "**suppress-map**" or "**suppress-route**" option in Cisco routers). For instance, let's assume we want to repeat what we've done in Example 2 of Section 5.3.4 above, for router GTW-2, which, in this case, must advertise aggregate 195.31/16 and the two specific components of the customer with router CE2: 195.31.0.128/26 and 195.31.0.192/26.

The routing policy to be applied is the following:

```
[edit policy-options policy-statement SUPPRESS-CE1]
term AGGREGATE {
  from {
    route-filter 195.31.0.0/16 exact;
  }
  then accept;
}
term SUPPRESS-CE1 {
  from {
    route-filter 195.31.0.0/26;
    route-filter 195.31.64.0/26;}
  then reject;
}

[edit protocols bgp]
group UP {
  export SUPPRESS-CE1;
}
```

For verification purposes, let's see again the prefixes that GTW-2 sends to BGP Neighbor UP-2:

```
aft@GTW-2> show route advertising-protocol bgp 172.20.2.1
inet.0: 36 destinations, 41 routes (36 active, 0 holddown, 0 hidden)
  Prefix                 Nexthop         MED            Lclpref            AS path
* 195.31.0.0/16          Self                                             65101 I
* 195.31.0.128/26        Self                                             65101 I
* 195.31.0.192/26        Self                                             65101 I
```

As you can see, apart from the aggregate prefix, only the more specific prefixes of the customer with router CE2 were propagated. Lastly, there is the option to change the default attributes associated with the aggregate prefix. Particularly important is the association of the ATOMIC_AGGREGATE attribute, which automatically implies the loss of memory of the ASes crossed by the more specific prefixes. For example, let's assume that we want to set MED=10 (default: not specified), ORIGIN=INCOMPLETE (default: IGP) and that we want to add the ATOMIC_AGGREGATE and AGGREGATOR attributes. The configuration to execute is the following:

```
[edit routing-options]
aggregate {
  route 195.31.0.0/16 {
    metric 10;
    as-path {
      origin incomplete;
      atomic-aggregate;
      aggregator 64501 192.168.1.12;
    }
  }
}
```

For verification purposes, let's see how the detail of aggregate prefix 195.31/16 changes in GTW-2's RIB:

```
aft@GTW-2> show route protocol aggregate 195.31/16 detail
inet.0: 36 destinations, 41 routes (36 active, 0 holddown, 0 hidden)
195.31.0.0/16 (1 entry, 1 announced)
    *Aggregate Preference: 130
        Next hop type: Reject, Next hop index: 0
        Address: 0xce30610
        Next-hop reference count: 2
        State: <Active Int Ext>
        Local AS: 64501
        Age: 8:09          Metric: 10
        . . . < output omitted > . . .
        AS path: ?   (Atomic)
        Aggregator: 64501 192.168.1.12
        Flags:                    Depth: 0         Active
        Contributing Routes (4):
            195.31.0.0/26 proto BGP
            195.31.0.64/26 proto BGP
            195.31.0.128/26 proto BGP
            195.31.0.192/26 proto BGP
```

The view highlights that the MED value has been set to 10 (`Metric: 10`), the AS_PATH has become empty, and the ORIGIN attribute has become INCOMPLETE (`AS path: ?`), plus the ATOMIC_AGGREGATE (`(Atomic)`) and AGGREGATOR (`Aggregator: 64501 192.168.1.12`) attributes were added.

Assuming we want to send only the aggregate to router UP-2, that is, we want to apply the SUMMARY-ONLY routing policy we saw earlier, the result of this additional configuration is the following:

```
aft@GTW-2> show route advertising-protocol bgp 172.20.2.1
inet.0: 36 destinations, 41 routes (36 active, 0 holddown, 0 hidden)
  Prefix                   Nexthop              MED     Lclpref      AS path
* 195.31.0.0/16            Self                 10                   ?
```

5.4 REDISTRIBUTION IN BGP

The use of more than one protocol is fairly common in practical applications, and it can be necessary in many contexts, such as:

- during migration from an old IGP protocol toward a new IGP one; in these cases, more than one protocol must coexist for a certain period of time, until the new protocol replaces the old one;

- when use of another routing protocol is necessary, but the old protocol needs to be maintained to meet the needs of the entire routing domain;

- when different structures cannot update their routers or cannot implement a sufficiently stringent routing policy; in these cases, a policy allowing the use of more than one protocol is required, and consequently a border point management that allows connecting the different structures that implement different routing protocols.

Redistribution is defined as the capacity of a router (border router) of connecting different routing domains, each one with a different routing protocol, by allowing the mutual exchange of routing information.

Within a routing domain, each router has full knowledge of the native networks originated in it, but it is not capable of exchanging routing information with routers belonging to different domains, since the parts use different routing protocols.

A typical example could be a customer with routers that do not support BGP (highly improbable) or who is familiar with the use of a specific IGP protocol – such as OSPF – and does not want to migrate toward BGP, typically used by ISPs to import routing information within their backbones. In this case the border router uses two routing protocols and has the ability (since it has the information within its RIB) to add the prefixes learned from the OSPF protocol within the BGP routing process.

In BGP, the redistribution process follows the classic logic of importing the prefixes in the RIB learned through a certain routing protocol (not necessarily dynamic) into the BGP advertisement table. In BGP, the following prefixes can be redistributed:

- directly connected;

- acquired through static routes;

- acquired through dynamic routing protocols (RIP, OSPF, etc.).

The default well-known mandatory BGP attributes through which redistributed prefixes are added to the BGP advertisement table are similar to those we saw for those prefixes entered manually or through aggregation:

- AS_PATH: empty;

- ORIGIN: INCOMPLETE in Cisco platforms, IGP in Juniper platforms;

- NEXT_HOP: identical to the one in the IP routing table.

We have no intention of describing all the details of redistribution of IGP protocols in BGP, also because this is a topic that has become less and less important, over time. We will only mention the two most common cases in practical applications: the redistribution of static routes and the redistribution of routing information learned via OSPF.

5.4.1 Static route redistribution

Static route redistribution is done in Cisco platforms through the "**redistribute static**" command, and in Juniper platform through a routing policy.
For Cisco platforms, the configurations to execute are:

<u>IOS XE</u>:
router(config)# **router bgp** *AS-number*
router(config-router)# **address-family {ipv4| ipv6 } unicast**
router(config-router-af)# **redistribute static** [**metric** *metric*] [**route-map** *name*]

<u>IOS XR</u>:
RP/0/RP0/CPU0:router(config)# **router bgp** *AS-number*
RP/0/RP0/CPU0:router(config-bgp)# **address-family {ipv4 | ipv6} unicast**
RP/0/RP0/CPU0:router(config-bgp-af)# **redistribute static** [**metric** *metric*] [**route-policy** *name*]

Through the "**route-map**..." and "**route-policy**..." options, we can both filter the prefixes to be redistributed, and specify the Local Preference, MED, Origin, Community, etc. values. The "**metric**" option can be used to specify a value of the MED attribute other than the default one (=0).

NOTE: If the MED attribute value is defined both in the "**metric**" option and in the route-map/routing policy, the value configured by the latter will apply.

In JUNOS, a routing policy is used for any kind of redistribution, which is then applied to the BGP process in the export direction. In particular, when it comes to redistributing static routes, the configurations to execute are:

[edit policy-options policy-statement *RP-name***]**
from {
  protocol static;
  other conditions;
}
then {
  actions
  accept;
}
[edit protocols bgp]
export *RP-name***;**

Among the other conditions, you can specify route-filters to filter the advertisements redistributed, and not redistribute all the static routes present in the RIB.

NOTE: The "**accept**" action is the one that allows the redistribution of the prefixes identified by the conditions. By default, all prefixes that do not meet the conditions are not redistributed. Indeed, in JUNOS, the default policy is to not redistribute prefixes automatically from one protocol to the next.

Let's see an application of these configurations through an example. Let's assume, in our sample network in Figure 3.1, that the following static routes have been defined on routers PE1 and PE2:

- on PE1: Target networks 195.31.0.0/26 and 195.31.0.64/26, Next-Hop=10.1.11.2;

- on PE2: Target networks 195.31.0.128/26 and 195.31.0.192/26, Next-Hop=10.1.12.2.

Suppose that we want to redistribute in the BGP process only the first prefix, both for PE1 and for PE2, and to associate a MED attribute value equal to 10 and a value Origin=IGP to BGP advertisements. The configurations to execute are (Note: The Origin value should be redefined only for PE1, since it is IGP by default for PE2).

PE1 (IOS XR)
```
route-policy SET-ATTR
  if destination in (195.31.0.0/26) then
    set med 10
    set origin igp
  endif
end-policy
!
router bgp 64501
  address-family ipv4 unicast
    redistribute static route-policy SET-ATTR
```

PE2 (JUNOS)
```
[edit policy-options policy-statement RED-STA]
from {
  protocol static;
  route-filter 195.31.0.128/26 exact;
}
then {
  metric 10;
  accept;
}

[edit protocols bgp]
group IBGP {
  export RED-STA;
```

To verify that the configurations had the desired effect, on router PE1, we just need to check that only prefix 195.31.0.0/26 was added to the BGP table:

```
RP/0/0/CPU0:PE1#show bgp
. . .
```

Network	Next Hop	Metric	LocPrf	Weight	Path
*> 195.31.0.0/26	10.1.11.2	10		32768	i
*>i195.31.0.128/26	192.168.0.12	10	100	0	i

As you can notice, prefix 195.31.0.0/26 has been regularly added to the BGP table with the Next-Hop inherited from the RIB (=10.1.11.2), the AS_PATH attribute empty, value Origin=IGP and the value of the MED attribute equal to 10. The second prefix has not been added, since it is not allowed by the SET-ATTR routing policy. We'll leave the explanation of why prefix 195.31.0.128/26 is present to you.

On router PE2, since JUNOS does not have a BGP table, but uses only the RIB instead, the only way of checking if the configurations executed are correct is to check the BGP advertisements sent to the other internal BGP Neighbors.

For instance, the following view shows the advertisements sent to BGP Neighbor GTW-1:

```
aft@PE2>show route advertising-protocol bgp 192.168.1.11
inet.0: 19 destinations, 21 routes (19 active, 0 holddown, 0 hidden)
  Prefix                    Nexthop              MED      Lclpref      AS path
* 195.31.0.128/26           Self                 10       100          I
```

As you may notice, PE2 only sends the advertisement of prefix 195.31.0.128/26, with the values of the desired attributes. We will leave the remaining details to you, as a useful exercise.

5.4.2 OSPF→BGP redistribution

Redistribution of routing information learned through OSPF - or OSPv3 in case of IPv6 - in BGP, follows the same logic we saw for static route redistribution. The configurations are similar, the only thing that varies a little are the options available, but the rest of the commands are identical: you just need to replace the type of protocol to be redistributed: "**ospf/ospfv3/ospf3**" (based on the platform) instead of "**static**". For Cisco platforms, the general configurations to execute are:

IOS XE:
router(config)# **router bgp** *AS-number*
router(config-router)# **address-family {ipv4| ipv6 } unicast**
router(config-router-af)# **redistribute ospf** *process-ID* [**metric** *metric*] [**match {internal | external {1 | 2}]** [**route-map** *name*]

IOS XR:
RP/0/RP0/CPU0:router(config)# **router bgp** *AS-number*
RP/0/RP0/CPU0:router(config-bgp)# **address-family {ipv4 | ipv6} unicast**
RP/0/RP0/CPU0:router(config-bgp-af)# **redistribute {ospf | ospfv3}** *process-ID* [**metric** *metric*] [**match {internal| external 1| external 2}]** [**route-policy** *name*]

The "**route-map**…" and "**route-policy**…" options allow the same operations we saw in the previous section for static route redistribution. "**match** …" type options allow to narrow down the type of OSPF route to be redistributed (within the domain, external E1/E2, in some versions also external NSSA N1/N2).
The general configurations to execute in JUNOS are:

[edit policy-options policy-statement *RP-name*]
from {
  protocol {ospf | ospf3};
  other conditions;
}
then {
  actions
  accept;
}
[edit protocols bgp]
export *RP-name*;

Now, let's go over the same example of the previous section, assuming that the prefixes were advertised via OSPF. For this purpose, we created an OSPF adjacency with PE-CE connection in area 0 and advertised the same networks. We will not show the OSPF configurations, as they are not relevant with what we want to describe here.

<u>PE1</u> (IOS XR)

```
route-policy SET-ATTR
  if destination in (195.31.0.0/26) then
    set med 10
    set origin igp
  endif
end-policy
!
router bgp 64501
  address-family ipv4 unicast
    redistribute ospf route-policy SET-ATTR
```

<u>PE2</u> (JUNOS)

```
[edit policy-options policy-statement RED-STA]
from {
  protocol ospf;
  route-filter 195.31.0.128/26 exact;
}
then {
  metric 10;
  accept;
}

[edit protocols bgp]
group IBGP {
  export RED-STA;
```

As you may notice, the routing policy configuration both in IOS XR and in JUNOS are identical to the ones in the example in the previous section. Even the rest of the configurations is identical: it is sufficient to replace "**static**" with "**ospf**".

SUMMARY

After seeing the theoretical and practical aspects of BGP sessions, their implementation in Cisco and Juniper platforms, and troubleshooting aspects, in this chapter we talked about a crucial topic: how to generate the BGP advertisements to propagate on the sessions; without this, the entire castle of BGP sessions wouldn't make much sense.

We saw that, in broad terms, it is possible to identify three ways to generate an advertisement: through manual commands, by creating advertisements of aggregate prefixes, or through redistribution processes in BGP from a different routing protocol.

We saw how different BGP implementations treat this issue. Cisco implementations use different commands for each kind of generation, while JUNOS implementation uses routing policies as the only tool. The final result – aside from certain details on BGP attributes associated with locally-generated advertisements by default – is always the same advertisements.

Another useful aspect in practical applications that we saw in this chapter is how to generate a default route and advertise it to the different BGP Neighbors. In particular, we also explained the conditional generation of the default route, useful also in practical applications to prevent traffic black-holes.

Worth remembering:

1. BGP advertisement generation methods: manual, aggregation and redistribution.

2. Prefix aggregation and how to use it for scalability and stability purposes over the entire Internet.

3. How to generate a default route and how to condition the generation to the presence/absence of one or more IP prefixes in the RIB.

4. Redistribution of routing information learned from other protocols in BGP.

5. Cisco and Juniper configurations to generate BGP advertisements and implementation differences.

The route filtering concept is very simple: it allows the BGP process of a router to choose what advertisements it should accept and/or propagate on active BGP sessions.
Examples of filters are:

- not accepting advertisements from IP prefixes with too big a mask (e.g., higher than 24 bits);

- not propagating the advertisements of IP prefixes received from a specific AS to other AS (e.g., to prevent an AS from becoming a transit AS);

- filtering all advertisements of prefixes that cannot be propagated on the Internet (e.g., private IP prefixes from RFC 1918, Martian List, etc.).

It should be noted that filtering policies are essential for the correct operation of the Internet's ecosystem, and they help to limit damage to one's own and other networks. Without suitable filtering, incidents such as route leaks and prefix hijacking (see Chapters 8 and 10) would be very frequent, and they would have greater impact within the entire ecosystem.
Practical route filtering applications entail two basic steps:

- advertisement identification: it can be done based on the different fields within the BGP advertisements, such as: NLRI, AS_PATH, COMMUNITY attributes, etc.;

- deciding which advertisements should be accepted or rejected.

Each one of these steps has related configuration operations.

6.1 FILTERING TYPES

Based on the application direction, filtering can be of two types:

- inbound: allows choosing the advertisements to accept or to reject, between all the advertisements received on the different BGP sessions. Only the advertisements of accepted prefixes take part in the selection process;

- outbound: allows choosing, among all the best paths of each IP prefix, which ones should be propagated on e/iBGP sessions.

Filtering can also be used to choose which prefixes to redistribute from IGP to BGP.

6.1.1 Inbound filtering

The logical scheme of an inbound filter is shown in Figure 6.1 below.

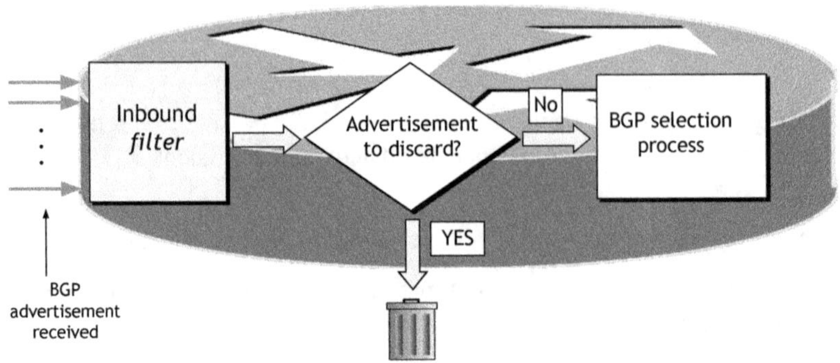

Figure 6.1 – Logical scheme of an inbound filter.

If the advertisements received from different BGP sessions need to be rejected according to the filter logic, they do not take part in the best path selection process. Based on their implementation or configuration, these advertisements may be kept in a memory area, to remain available for future operations (e.g. application of a new filter), or completely rejected. Further along we will see how Cisco and Juniper routers behave on this matter.

Vice versa, if they are not to be rejected, they can take part in the selection process. Figure 6.2 below shows one of the most useful inbound filtering application in practice: rejecting BGP advertisements of certain types of prefixes – such as the default route, privately used prefixes (RFC 1918), Martian Lists (reserved prefixes that shouldn't circulate within the Internet), prefixes whose mask is too long, etc.

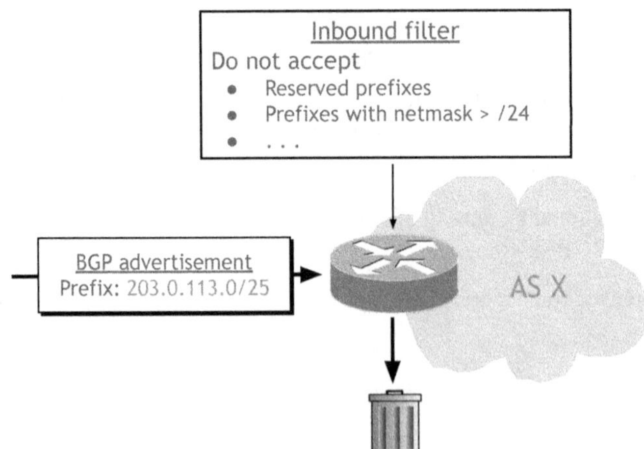

Figure 6.2 – Example of an inbound filter.

In order to implement this kind of filters, we can use the tools we extensively covered in Chapter 4, such as prefix-lists, route-maps and routing policies. In the coming sections, we will go over some practical applications and configuration examples.

6.1.2 Outbound filtering

The logical scheme of an outbound filter is shown in Figure 6.3 below. When the BGP process propagates a best path toward the different BGP sessions, if it needs to be rejected according to the filter logic, the advertisement remains in the Loc-RIB for local use. Vice versa, if it is not to be rejected, it is added to the Adj-RIB-out table and then regularly propagated toward the different BGP sessions, according to the propagation rules described in Sections 2.1.2 and 2.1.3.

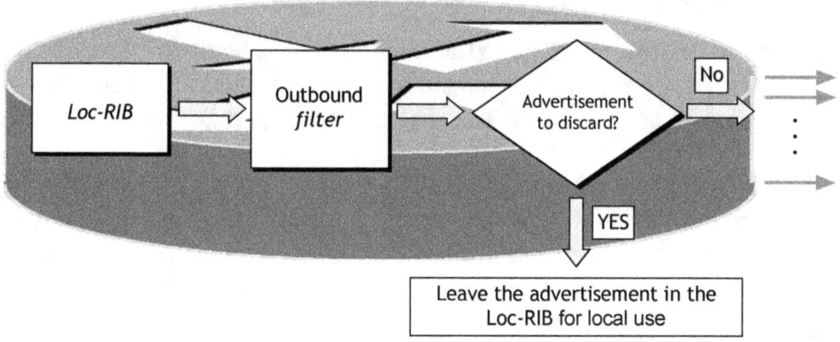

Figure 6.3 – Logical scheme of an outbound filter.

Figure 6.4 below shows an example of outbound filtering application, very useful in practice. Let's assume that, in order to avoid turning it into a transit AS, we do not want to propagate the advertisements received from other ASes toward the outside, but only those originated in our own AS. Since the advertisements originated locally within an AS are characterized by an empty AS_PATH (see Chapter 5), in order to reach the desired purpose, we just need to create an outbound filter that only allows forwarding those advertisements with an empty AS_PATH, and reject all the others.

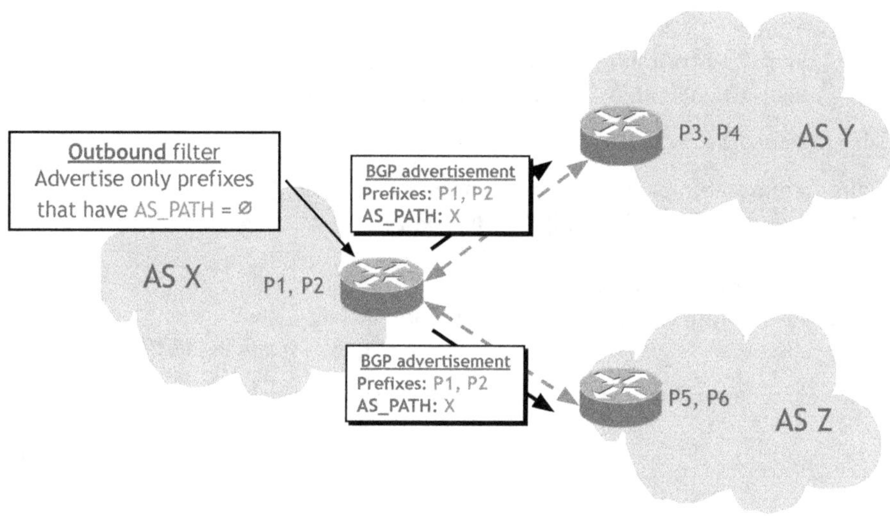

Figure 6.4 – Example of an outbound filter.

In order to implement this kind of filters, we need mechanisms that act on the AS_PATH attribute of the UPDATE messages. Filters based on the AS_PATH attribute are very useful in practical applications, since they allow selective filtering actions, based on the ASes present within the AS_PATH attribute.

Creating AS_PATH attribute-based filters requires tools that allow identifying certain AS values within the AS_PATH. To this end, current Cisco and Juniper's BGP implementations use Regular Expressions, as we saw in Chapter 4 (see Paragraph 4.4).

6.2 PREFIX FILTERING

Prefix filtering affect the content of the NLRI field in BGP advertisements directly. There are multiple application scenarios, such as inbound and outbound filtering of special prefixes such as those specified in RFC 1918, Martian lists, default routes, prefixes whose mask is greater (or lower) than a preset value, etc.

Creating prefix-based filters requires a tool that allows identifying certain sets of prefixes within the NLRI field. Current BGP implementations use very powerful tools, all essentially based on the same concept. We introduced these tools in Chapter 4, and now we will go over their application. In general, the configuration of filters based on the NLRI field comprises two steps:

1. defining the filter;

2. applying the filter to the inbound/outbound advertisements of a specific BGP Neighbor.

The more conceptually complex phase is the first one, which requires having a very clear idea on what you want to filter and why. The second phase, as you'll see, is very simple.

6.2.1 Prefix filtering in Cisco IOS XE

As we saw extensively in Chapter 4, the main tool that Cisco IOS XE provides to identify a set of prefixes is the prefix-list. Actually, it is also possible to filter them using a route-map, and including a prefix-list in the conditions. However, if our only goal is filtering, the easiest procedure is to create a prefix-list and apply it at BGP Neighbor level.

In IOS XE, the filter can be applied directly with the commands:

router(config)# **router bgp** *AS-number*
router(config-router)# **address-family {ipv4 | ipv6} unicast**
router(config-router-af)# **neighbor** *IP-neighbor* **prefix-list** *PL-name* **in | out**

or through a route-map:

router(config)# **route-map** *RM-name* **permit | deny** *seq-number*
router(config-route-map)# **match {ip | ipv6} address prefix-list** *PL-name*
!
router(config)# **router bgp** *AS-number*
router(config-router)# **address-family {ipv4 | ipv6} unicast**
router(config-router-af)# **neighbor** *IP-neighbor* **route-map** *RM-name* **in | out**

Let's see two examples of filter application that can be useful in practice.

<u>Example 1</u>

Let's consider the issue of wanting to block the reserved prefixes that shouldn't "circulate" in the Big Internet (Martian List) both inbound and outbound in the edge routers of a public IP network. They include:

1. Prefixes used for private addressing plans (defined by RFC 1918):

   - 10/8 and all its subnets;

   - 172.16/12 and all its subnets;

   - 192.168/16 and all its subnets.

2. Prefixes reserved for various purposes (defined by RFC 5735):

   - space 0/8: used to indicate a host on a certain subnet locally;

   - space 127/8: reserved for internal router uses (e.g.127.0.0.1 simulates an internal Loopback and is used as test of the TCP/IP protocol stack);

   - space 169.254/16: reserved for "IPv4 Link Local" type addresses, i.e. addresses that are valid only to communicate within a network segment (link) or for the broadcast domain to which a host is connected. Similar addresses in IPv6 belong to subnet fe80::/10;

   - prefix 192.0.0/24: reserved for use in protocols defined by IETF;

   - prefixes 192.0.2/24, 198.51.100/24 and 203.0.113/24: reserved for documentations;

   - prefix 192.88.99/24: reserved for use in the 6to4 IPv4→IPv6 transition mechanism (currently discouraged by RFC 7526);

   - prefix 198.18.0.0/15: reserved for use in interconnection tests between devices made by different manufacturers;

   - multicast addresses: 224.0.0.0/4 (RFC 5771 – *IANA Guidelines for IPv4 Multicast Address Assignments*, March 2010);

   - addresses reserved for future use and experimentation: 240.0.0.0/4 (RFC 1112 – *Host Extensions for IP Multicasting*, August 1989).

3. Shared Address Space 100.64.0.0/10 (defined by RFC 6598): reserved for ISPs for the Carrier Grade NAT (CGNAT) functionality.

Apart from these prefixes, let's suppose that we also want to block the default route and all prefixes with mask length greater than 24 (i.e., all prefixes with mask length from /25 to /32).

The prefix-list that prevents accepting/sending all these prefixes, and lets all the others through, is the following:

```
! RFC 1918
ip prefix-list NET-NOT-ALLOWED seq 5 deny 10.0.0.0/8 le 32
ip prefix-list NET-NOT-ALLOWED seq 10 deny 172.16.0.0/12 le 32
ip prefix-list NET-NOT-ALLOWED seq 15 deny 192.168.0.0/16 le 32
! RFC 5735
ip prefix-list NET-NOT-ALLOWED seq 20 deny 0.0.0.0/8 le 32
ip prefix-list NET-NOT-ALLOWED seq 25 deny 127.0.0.0/8 le 32
ip prefix-list NET-NOT-ALLOWED seq 30 deny 169.254.0.0/16 le 32
```

```
ip prefix-list NET-NOT-ALLOWED seq 35 deny 192.0.0.0/24 le 32
ip prefix-list NET-NOT-ALLOWED seq 40 deny 192.0.2.0/24 le 32
ip prefix-list NET-NOT-ALLOWED seq 45 deny 192.88.99.0/24 le 32
ip prefix-list NET-NOT-ALLOWED seq 50 deny 198.18.0.0/15 le 32
ip prefix-list NET-NOT-ALLOWED seq 55 deny 198.51.100.0/24 le 32
ip prefix-list NET-NOT-ALLOWED seq 60 deny 203.0.113.0/24 le 32
! RFC 6598
ip prefix-list NET-NOT-ALLOWED seq 65 deny 100.64.0.0/10 le 32
! D-E CLASSES
ip prefix-list NET-NOT-ALLOWED seq 70 deny 224.0.0.0/3 le 32
! DEFAULT ROUTE
ip prefix-list NET-NOT-ALLOWED seq 80 deny 0.0.0.0/0
! ALLOW MASK LE 24
ip prefix-list NET-NOT-ALLOWED seq 85 permit 0.0.0.0/0 le 24
```

Notice the last line, which allows all prefixes with mask lower than or equal to /24: without it, due to the final implicit deny all of prefix-lists, all BGP advertisements would be blocked!

In order to apply two filters – an inbound and an outbound one – that would block both inbound and outbound Martian prefixes toward a certain BGP Neighbor, we need to execute the following configurations:

```
router bgp AS-number
  neighbor IP-neighbor prefix-list NET-NOT-ALLOWED in
  neighbor IP-neighbor prefix-list NET-NOT-ALLOWED out
```

Example 2

As a second example, let's consider our test network in Figure 3.1, and assume that AS 64501 has the public address block 195.31/16 available and assigns the customer with router CE1 the subnet 195.31.0.0/25. In addition, the edge routers of AS 64501 send only the default route to CE1 via BGP. In order to prevent the ISP from inadvertently advertising prefixes other than the default route, or even the entire full routing table, thus saturating CE1's resources, on router CE1 it would be best to configure an inbound filter that allows accepting only the default route. In addition, to prevent the propagation toward the ISP of prefixes other than the one assigned, it would be best to configure an outbound filter allowing only the advertisement of the prefix assigned by the ISP to the customer.

The configurations to execute on CE1 are:

```
ip prefix-list ONLY-DEFAULT seq 5 permit 0.0.0.0/0
ip prefix-list PFX-65101 seq 5 permit 195.31.0.0/25
!
router bgp 65101
network 195.31.0.0 mask 255.255.255.128
neighbor 10.1.11.1 remote-as 64501
neighbor 10.1.11.1 prefix-list ONLY-DEFAULT in
neighbor 10.1.11.1 prefix-list PFX-65101 out
```

6.2.2 Prefix filtering in Cisco IOS XR

The only tool that Cisco IOS XR provides for filter creation is the routing policy. Within a routing policy, for configuration compactness, elegance and scalability reasons, it is best to add the prefixes to be filtered within a "**prefix-set**".

Basically, we already went over filtering configurations in Chapter 4, so we will only show them by repeating the examples of the previous section.

Example 1

Below are the configurations equivalent to the same example of the previous section.

```
prefix-set DENY-NET
  10.0.0.0/8 le 32,
  172.16.0.0/12 le 32,
  192.168.0.0/16 le 32,
  0.0.0.0/8 le 32,
  127.0.0.0/8 le 32,
  169.254.0.0/16 le 32,
  192.0.0.0/24 le 32,
  192.0.2.0/24 le 32,
  192.88.99.0/24 le 32,
  198.18.0.0/15 le 32,
  198.51.100.0/24 le 32,
  203.0.113.0/24 le 32,
  100.64.0.0/10 le 32,
  0.0.0.0/0 ge 25,
  0.0.0.0/0,
  224.0.0.0/3 le 32
end-set
!
route-policy NET-NOT-ALLOWED
  if destination in DENY-NET then
    drop
  else
    pass
  endif
end-policy
!
router bgp AS-number
  neighbor IP-neighbor
    address-family ipv4 unicast
      route-policy NET-NOT-ALLOWED in
      route-policy NET-NOT-ALLOWED out
```

The above configurations also show the flexibility of a "**prefix-set**". For instance, if we wanted to remove the default route from the list of prefixes to reject, we would only need to cancel line "**0.0.0.0/0**" from the "**prefix-set**".

Example 2

Let's assume the same scenario as in Example 2 in the previous section, but with the parts reversed, that is, we want to create filters on router PE1 (IOS XR) that accept only prefix 195.31.0.0/25 assigned to the customer, and send only the default route.

The configurations to execute are:

```
route-policy ONLY-DEFAULT
  if destination in (0.0.0.0/0) then
    pass
  endif
end-policy
!
route-policy CE1
  if destination in (195.31.0.0/25) then
    pass
  endif
end-policy
!
router bgp 64501
  neighbor 10.1.11.2
    remote-as 65101
    address-family ipv4 unicast
      route-policy CE1 in
      route-policy ONLY-DEFAULT out
```

As you can see, besides command syntax, the ideas are the same as the ones we saw in Example 2 of the previous section.

6.2.3 Prefix filtering in JUNOS

As per IOS XR, the only tool that JUNOS provides to create filters is the routing policy. Basically, we already went over filtering configurations in Chapter 4, so we will only show them by repeating the examples of the previous section. Here too, within a routing policy, for configuration compactness, elegance and scalability reasons, it is best to add the prefixes to be filtered within a **"prefix-list"**.

Example 1

Below are the configurations equivalent to the same example of the previous section.

```
[edit policy-options]
prefix-list MARTIAN {
10.0.0.0/8;
172.16.0.0/12;
192.168.0.0/16;
0.0.0.0/8;
127.0.0.0/8;
169.254.0.0/16;
192.0.0.0/24;
192.0.2.0/24;
192.88.99.0/24;
```

```
198.18.0.0/15;
198.51.100.0/24;
203.0.113.0/24;
100.64.0.0/10;
224.0.0.0/3;
}

policy-statement NET-NOT-ALLOWED {
  term MARTIAN {
    from {
      prefix-list-filter MARTIAN orlonger;
    }
    then reject;
  }
  term NO-GE-25 {
    from {
      route-filter 0.0.0.0/0 prefix-length-range /25-/32;
    }
    then reject;
  }
  term NO-DEFAULT-ROUTE {
    from {
      route-filter 0.0.0.0/0 exact;
    }
    then reject;
  }
  term ACCEPT {
    then accept;
  }
}

[edit protocol bgp]
export NET-NOT-ALLOWED;
import NET-NOT-ALLOWED;
```

NOTE: JUNOS has default Martian lists (that do not include the prefixes of RFC 1918). The router ignores all routing information associated to these prefixes, which are therefore never installed in the RIB. The list of Martian prefixes could change, based on the JUNOS version and on the indications of the IANA – the institution that governs the assignment of IP addresses at global level. JUNOS provides the "**show route martians [table** *table*]" command, which allows to view all preset Martian prefixes or those belonging to a specific table. For instance, the "**show route martians table inet.0**" command allows viewing the IPv4 Martian prefixes. Moreover, JUNOS has some commands to add and remove Martian prefixes from the default list.

<u>Example 2</u>

Let's suppose we want to create the same scenario of Example 2 in the previous sections, between routers CE2 and PE2, both Juniper with JUNOS.

Let's assume that AS 64501 assigns subnet 195.31.0.128/25 to the customer with router CE2. In addition, the edge routers of AS 64501 send only the default route to CE2 via BGP.

The filters that allow limiting the exchange of prefixes to the default route and to prefix 195.31.0.128/25 only are the following (identical on CE2 and PE2):

```
[edit policy-options policy-statement ADV-195.31.0.128/25]
term ADVERTISE {
  from {
    route-filter 195.31.0.128/25 exact;
  }
  then accept;
}
term REJECT {
  then reject;
}

[edit policy-options policy-statement ONLY-DEFAULT]
term DEFAULT {
  from {
    route-filter 0.0.0.0/0 exact;
  }
  then accept;
}
term REJECT {
  then reject;
}
```

Lastly, these filters should be applied to the BGP process in a specular way on CE2 and PE2, as follows:

On CE2:
```
[edit protocols bgp]
group PE {
  import ONLY-DEFAULT;
  export ADV-195.31.0.128/25;
}
```

On PE2:
```
[edit protocols bgp]
group CE {
  export ONLY-DEFAULT;
  import ADV-195.31.0.128/25;
}
```

6.3 AS_PATH-BASED FILTERS

The filters based on the AS_PATH attribute work directly on the AS values contained in the attribute. There are multiple application scenarios, including: outbound filtering of prefixes to avoid becoming a transit AS, selective filtering of the prefixes received from an Upstream Provider to accept only those prefixes toward which the majority of traffic is directed, etc.

Creating AS_PATH attribute-based filters requires a tool that allows identifying certain sets of ASes within the attribute. Current BGP implementations use very powerful tools, all essentially based on the same concept: Regular Expressions (RegExp). We introduced these tools in Chapter 4 (see Paragraph 4.4, in particular), and now we will go over their application. The processing logic is summarized in Figure 6.5 below:

Here too, the configuration of filters based on the AS_PATH attribute comprises two steps:

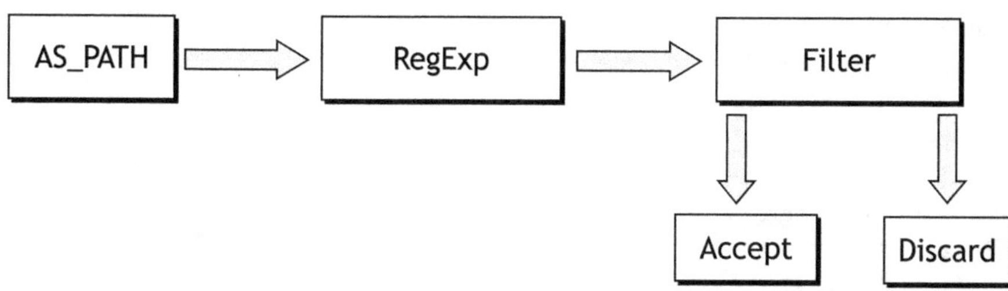

Figure 6.5 – Logic scheme of filters based on the AS_PATH attribute.

1. defining the filter;

2. applying the filter to the inbound/outbound advertisements of a specific BGP Neighbor.

The most complex phase from a conceptual standpoint is the first one, which requires the definition of appropriate RegExps, which are sometimes very hard to write.

6.3.1 How to avoid becoming a transit AS

In Figure 6.2, we saw that, in order to avoid becoming a transit AS, an AS should only advertise its own local prefixes. Whether they are generated manually or through the aggregation of prefixes or through a redistribution process from any kind of routing process within BGP (including also static routes and directly connected networks), they are characterized by the fact of having an empty AS_PATH. Therefore, in order to achieve this purpose, it is sufficient to create an outbound filter that allows only to forward advertisements with an empty AS_PATH, and filters out all the others.

By way of example, let's assume that, in our sample network in Figure 3.1, AS 64501 wants to apply an outbound filter to avoid becoming a transit AS for its two Upstream Providers AS 65541 and AS 65542, by advertising only its own aggregate prefix 195.31/16.

The configurations to execute are:

<u>GTW-1</u> (IOS XR)

```
route-policy LOCALONLY
  if as-path is-local then
    pass
```

```
  endif
end-policy
!
router bgp 64501
  address-family ipv4 unicast
    aggregate-address 195.31.0.0/16 summary-only
!
neighbor 172.20.1.1
  remote-as 65541
  address-family ipv4 unicast
    route-policy LOCALONLY out
```

NOTE: The "**if** ..." condition is equivalent to the following extended version "**if as-path in (ios-regex '^\$') then** ..." (see Section 4.4.1).

<u>GTW-2</u> (JUNOS)

```
[edit policy-options]
policy-statement LOCALONLY {
  term LOCAL {
    from {
      protocol aggregate;
      as-path EMPTY;
    }
    then accept;
  }
  term REJECT {
    then reject;
  }
}
as-path EMPTY "()";

[edit protocols bgp]
group EXT {
  export LOCALONLY;
}
```

With these configurations, as you can see in the following views, GTW-1 and GTW-2 only advertise aggregate prefix 195.31/16.

```
RP/0/0/CPU0:GTW-1#show bgp neighbors 172.20.1.1 advertised-routes
. . .
Network                 Next Hop            From              AS Path
195.31.0.0/16           172.20.1.0          Local Aggregate   64501i

aft@GTW-2> show route advertising-protocol bgp 172.20.2.1
inet.0: 30 destinations, 32 routes (30 active, 0 holddown, 0 hidden)
Prefix                  Nexthop        MED      Lclpref        AS path
* 195.31.0.0/16         Self                                   I
```

6.3.2 Selective filtering of prefixes received from an Upstream Provider

Within the same sample network of Figure 3.1, let's suppose that AS 64501 does not want to import the FIRT from the two Upstream Providers, but only the prefixes originated locally by the two Upstream Providers and by the ASes adjacent to them. Basically, AS 64501 is interested in advertisements of prefixes within a maximum distance of two ASes.

The purpose is creating two routing policies – one for GTW-1 (IOS XR) and the other for GTW-2 (JUNOS) – with appropriate RegExps (which we already saw in Paragraph 4.4). The configurations to execute are:

<u>GTW-1</u> (IOS XR)

```
route-policy FROM-AS65541
  if as-path in (ios-regex '^(65541_)+([0-9]+)?$') then
    pass
  endif
end-policy
!
router bgp 64501
  neighbor 172.20.1.1
    remote-as 65541
    address-family ipv4 unicast
      route-policy FROM-AS65541 in
```

<u>GTW-2</u> (JUNOS)

```
[edit policy-options]
policy-statement FROM-AS65542 {
  term ACCEPT {
    from as-path AS-65542;
    then accept;
  }
  term REJECT {
    then reject;
  }
}
as-path AS-65542 "65542+ .?";

[edit protocols bgp]
group EXT {
  import FROM-AS65542;
}
```

NOTE: For an alternative configuration, see Section 10.3.2, where there are commands that allow filtering the advertisements based on the length of the AS_PATH attribute.

For verification purposes, we can check the BGP advertisements that GTW-1 and GTW-2 receive from their respective BGP Neighbors:

```
RP/0/0/CPU0:GTW-1#show bgp neighbors 172.20.1.1 routes
. . .
    Network              Next Hop       Metric   LocPrf   Weight   Path
*> 111.111.0.0/16       172.20.1.1        0                  0     65541 i
*> 142.1.0.0/16         172.20.1.1        0                  0     65541 64508 i
*> 142.2.0.0/16         172.20.1.1        0                  0     65541 64508 i
*> 190.1.0.0/16         172.20.1.1        0                  0     65541 64496 i
*> 198.51.100.0/24      172.20.1.1        0                  0     65541 64508 i
*> 203.0.113.0/24       172.20.1.1        0                  0     65541 64496 i
Processed 6 prefixes, 6 paths
```

NOTE: The "**show bgp neighbors 172.20.1.1 routes**" command allows viewing the advertisements received from BGP Neighbor 172.20.1.1 downstream of the filter application. In order to view all the advertisements received from the same BGP Neighbor before the filter is applied, the "**show bgp neighbors 172.20.1.1 received routes**" command is used, which, however, requires the activation of the Soft Reconfiguration Inbound (see Section 6.5.1).

```
aft@GTW-2> show route table inet.0 receive-protocol bgp 172.20.2.1
inet.0: 30 destinations, 32 routes (19 active, 0 holddown, 11 hidden)
    Prefix               Nexthop        MED      Lclpref     AS path
*  126.0.0.0/8          172.20.2.1      0                    65542 64498 I
*  190.10.0.0/16        172.20.2.1      0                    65542 64497 I
*  192.0.2/24           172.20.2.1      0                    65542 64497 I
*  222.222.0.0/16       172.20.2.1      0                    65542 I
```

NOTE: The command we just executed is used to view the advertisements received from BGP Neighbor 172.20.2.1 downstream of the filter application. JUNOS automatically adds the advertisements rejected by the filter to the hidden part of the RIB, and they can be viewed with the "**show route table inet.0 hidden**" command. In our example, the advertisements rejected by the filter are 11.

6.3.3 Filtering advertisements within an IXP

Let's assume we want to add to our sample network of Figure 3.1 a new router of a Tier-2 ISP (AS 65543) interconnected to the peering LAN of the IXP via Cisco router GTW-3 with IOS XE. The peering LAN has subnet IP 172.30.1/24 associated to it, and the IP addresses of the connected devices we are interested in are:

- GTW-1 (AS 64501): 172.30.1.11;

- GTW-2 (AS 64501): 172.30.1.12;

- GTW-3 (AS 65543): 172.30.1.13.

AS 65543 also has two point-to-point links toward the two Upstream Providers, derived from the IXP passive infrastructure using PNIs. The numbering plans adopted are:

- GTW-3↔UP-1=172.23.1.0/31 (.0 GTW-3 side);

- GTW-3↔UP-2=172.23.2.0/31 (.0 GTW-3 side).

Moreover, AS 65543 in turn has two Tier-3 ISPs (AS 65536 and 65537), to which it provides transit service. The diagram is summarized in Figure 6.6 below.

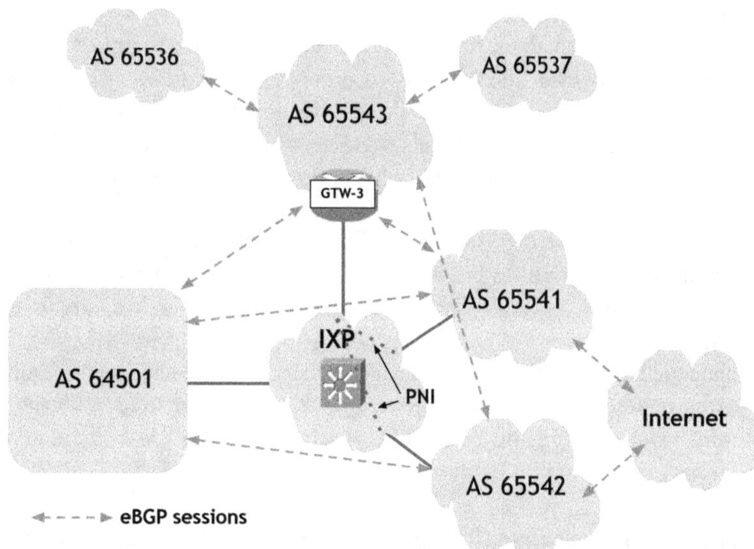

Figure 6.6 – Sample network with the addition of AS 65543.

Now, as per good interconnection practices, AS 65543 advertises its own local prefixes and those of its customers (ISP, in this case) to the other ASes connected to the peering LAN and to any possible Upstream Providers to which it is interconnected. In order to have a scalable configuration, AS 65543 uses an outbound filter based on the AS_PATH attribute that allows advertising these prefixes and that can be used in the future without varying the configuration, even for new customers.

Since the router of AS 65543 connected to the peering LAN uses Cisco IOS XE, in order to define the filter, we have to adopt the filter-list tool we saw in Section 4.4.1 and apply it at BGP Neighbor level. As usual, the key aspect is defining the RegExp. The configurations to execute are:

```
ip as-path access-list 1 permit ^([0-9]+)?$
!
router bgp 65543
  neighbor IP-neighbor filter-list 1 out
```

We will leave the assessment of the RegExp used to you. What we would like to point out is that the RegExp is very generic, and it selects null AS_PATHs or an AS_PATH containing only one generic AS number, and it is also highly scalable, since the addition of a new customer does not require its variation.

NOTE: The BGP Neighbors to which the filter-list is applied depend on the bi/multi-lateral sessions that AS 65543 wants to establish.

6.4 COMMUNITY-BASED FILTERS

In Section 2.4.6, we saw that the COMMUNITY attribute can be used to define homogeneous classes of prefixes for filtering, routing policy definition and/or Service Quality purposes, etc.

Some Community values are preset (well-known Community) and are basically used to filter the advertisements in the outbound direction. For instance, as we've seen in Section 2.4.6, if the NO_EXPORT Community (0xFFFFFF01) has been assigned to an advertisement, then it shouldn't be propagated on eBGP sessions.

Theoretically, filtering based on the COMMUNITY attribute can be applied to both inbound and outbound directions; however, the majority of practical applications occur in the outbound direction. A typical application can be found in advertisement filtering toward other ISPs: the typical policy of an ISP is not to propagate advertisements coming from other ISPs, with whom the ISP has a peering agreement, to other ISPs, whilst allowing the propagation of advertisements of prefixes of its own customers.

The creation of filters based on the COMMUNITY attribute requires two tools: on one hand, a tool to write the Community values in the advertisements, and on the other hand, a tool to identify the presence of certain Community values within the UPDATE messages. We explained both these tools in Chapter 4.

In order to associate the Community values to the advertisements, we can use route-maps in Cisco IOS XE and routing policies in Cisco IOS XR and JUNOS. In order to identify the presence of certain Community values within the UPDATE messages, we can use community-lists in the route-map conditions of Cisco IOS XE, and routing policies in Cisco IOS XR and JUNOS.

6.4.1 A preliminary step: COMMUNITY attribute propagation

One important aspect that we haven't yet considered is how COMMUNITY attributes associated to BGP advertisements are propagated. The various BGP implementations differ on this matter, and behave differently, based on the operating system adopted by the routers.

In the different Cisco IOS types, COMMUNITY attributes are never automatically propagated on eBGP sessions, by default. In IOS and IOS XE, they are never automatically propagated, not even on iBGP sessions, while for IOS XR, propagation on iBGP sessions is automatic.

In IOS/IOS XE, propagation can be activated, on each session, through the following command:

router(config)# **router bgp** *AS-number*
router(router-config)# **neighbor** *IP-neighbor* **send-community [standard | extended | both]**

which must be executed on all e/iBGP sessions where you want to transport the COMMUNITY attribute. The "**standard**" and "**extended**" options narrow down the propagation to just the standard or extended COMMUNITY attributes (see Section 2.4.6), while the "**both**" option allows the propagation of both types of COMMUNITY.

In IOS XR, the activation is only required on eBGP sessions, and the command to execute is the following:

RP/0/RP0/CPU0:router(config)# **router bgp** *AS-number*
RP/0/RP0/CPU0:router(config-bgp)# **neighbor** *IP-neighbor*
RP/0/RP0/CPU0:router(config-bgp-nbr)# **address-family ipv4 unicast**
RP/0/RP0/CPU0:router(config-bgp-nbr-af)# **send-community-ebgp**

Notice that, if you want to add (via route-map or route-policy) a Community value to an outbound BGP advertisement, you need to configure the propagation manually, or the advertisement would be sent without the COMMUNITY attribute. Omitting the command that allows propagating COMMUNITY attributes is one of the most frequent configuration errors.

In JUNOS, there are no propagation issues, since all types of COMMUNITY are propagated automatically by default.

6.4.2 Case study

Generally an AS – such as our AS 64501 from the sample network expanded with the new AS 65543 shown in Figure 6.6 – has three types of eBGP sessions: those toward the Upstream Providers, those toward ISPs with which it shares peering relations (see Section 1.3.1), and lastly those toward customers.

In our sample network, they are the sessions between AS 64501 and ASes 65541 and 65542 – the two Upstream Providers – the session with AS 65543 with which it shares a peering relation – and the sessions toward the two customers belonging to AS 65101 (even if they have the same AS number, they are still two different ASes), respectively. The session type diagram is summarized in Figure 6.7 below.

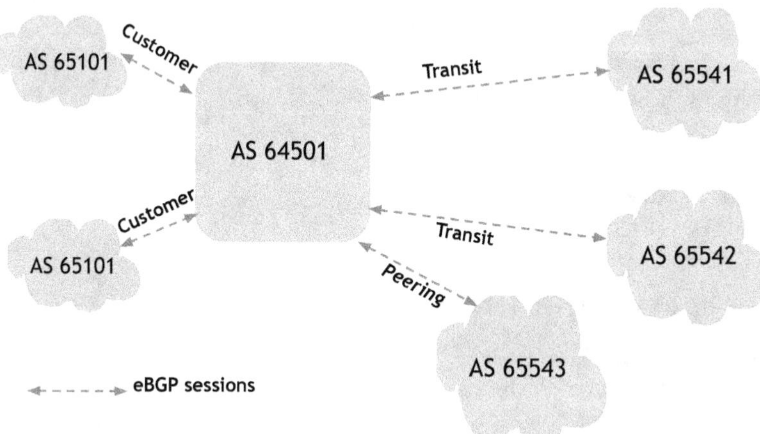

Figure 6.7 – Types of eBGP sessions of AS 64501 from the sample network.

Now, according to the routing information exchange rules, partially mentioned in Section 1.3.1:

- BGP advertisements exchanged between two ISPs with a peering relation (in our example, ASes 64501 and 65543) can be propagated to their respective customers, but not to other ISPs;

- BGP advertisements received by an ISP from its Upstream Providers can be propagated to the respective customers, but not to other ISPs. For instance, the advertisements that AS 64501 receives from AS 65541 and 65542 can be propagated toward the customers of AS 64501, but not toward ISP 65543;

- the advertisements received by ISP from customers and those originated locally can be propagated to all the other ISPs (perhaps by aggregating the prefixes).

In order to achieve this strategy, AS 64501 decided to associate different Community values, based on the provenance, to the advertisements received, and thus filter them accordingly. In particular, AS 64501 associates the following Community values:

- **64501:100** to the advertisements coming from the two Upstream Providers (and, in general, from all the other Upstream Providers);

- **64501:200** to the advertisements coming from AS 65543 (and in general from all the other ISPs with which it holds a peering relation);

- **64501:300** to the advertisements coming from its customers and to locally originated prefixes.

The general configurations to be applied can be divided in two parts. The first defines the routing policies to assign the Community values and then applies them to the inbound direction. The second defines the filters based on Community values and then applies them to the outbound direction.

On Cisco routers that use IOS XR (PE1 and GTW-1), for configuring the first part, three routing policies are created, one for each type of eBGP session, through which the desired Community values are assigned.

```
route-policy SETCOMM-CUST
  set community (64501:300) additive
end-policy
!
route-policy SETCOMM-PEER
  set community (64501:200) additive
end-policy
!
route-policy SETCOMM-TRANSIT
  set community (64501:100) additive
end-policy
```

On routers with JUNOS (PE2 and GTW-2), the equivalent configurations are:

```
[edit policy-options]
policy-statement SETCOMM-CUSTOMER {
  then {
    community add CUSTOMER;
    accept;
  }
}
policy-statement SETCOMM-PEER {
  then {
    community add PEER;
    accept;
  }
}

policy-statement SETCOMM-TRANSIT {
  then {
    community add TRANSIT;
    accept;
  }
}
community CUSTOMER members 64501:300;
community PEER members 64501:200;
community TRANSIT members 64501:100;
```

These routing policies must be applied to the inbound direction, based on the session type. For instance, on the sessions between two PEs and the two CEs, "**SETCOMM-CUSTOMER**" routing policies should be applied on PE1 and PE2. And so on for the other session types.

NOTE: In the configuration, there is the "**additive**" option for IOS XR and the "**add**" option for JUNOS, which, as you may remember, are used to preserve any Community values already present in the advertisements and that can be used for other purposes.

Now, let's see the second part of the configuration, i.e. the filters to be applied to the outbound direction, in order to comply with the aforementioned rules on routing information exchange. Actually, out of the three Community values defined in this example, only one is used. Upon closer examination, it is sufficient to allow only the propagation of the customers' prefixes (also aggregate), and prevent the propagation of the others. In our example, it is sufficient to allow the propagation of the prefixes of the two customers toward AS 65543 with which AS 64501 has a peering relation, and toward the two Upstream Providers with which it has a transit relation. At the same time, the prefixes advertised by AS 65543 to AS 64501, as per the rules above, should not be propagated to other ISPs with which AS 64501 has a peering relationship, nor toward the Upstream Providers.

The additional configurations to be executed on the two router gateways to achieve this objective are the following:

<u>GTW-1</u> (IOS XR)

```
route-policy ONLY-CUSTOMER
  if community matches-any (64501:300) then
    pass
  endif
end-policy
!
router bgp 64501
  neighbor 172.20.1.1
    description *** EBGP SESSION WITH AS 65541 (TRANSIT) ***
    remote-as 65541
    address-family ipv4 unicast
      route-policy ONLY-CUSTOMER out
!
neighbor 172.30.1.13
  remote-as 65543
  description *** EBGP SESSION WITH AS 65543 (PEERING) ***
  address-family ipv4 unicast
    route-policy ONLY-CUSTOMER out
```

<u>GTW-2</u> (JUNOS)

```
[edit policy-options policy-statement ONLY-CUSTOMER]
term ACCEPT {
  from community CUSTOMER;
  then accept;
}
term REJECT {
  then reject;
}

[edit protocols bgp]
group EXT {
  export ONLY-CUSTOMER;
```

```
}
group PEER {
  export ONLY-CUSTOMER;
}
```

Now, you may wonder why we assigned Community values to the advertisements coming from ISPs with which they have peering and transit relations, when only the Community value associated to the customers' advertisements is used. We did this for flexibility and other possible application reasons.

For instance, let's suppose that the customers ask their Upstream Provider AS 64501 not to receive the FIRT, but only a default route and the prefixes advertised by the ASes with which AS 64501 has a peering relation. For this purpose, it is sufficient to apply the following filters to the two routers where the customers are attested:

<u>PE1</u> (IOS XR)

```
route-policy NO-FIRT-OUT
  if community matches-any SETCOMM-TRANSIT then
    drop
  else
    pass
  endif
end-policy
!
router bgp 64501
  neighbor-group INTERNET-CUSTOMERS
    remote-as 65101
    address-family ipv4 unicast
      route-policy NO-FIRT-OUT out
  !
  neighbor 10.1.11.2
    use neighbor-group INTERNET-CUSTOMERS
!
neighbor 10.1.11.6
  use neighbor-group INTERNET-CUSTOMERS
!
```

<u>PE2</u> (JUNOS)

```
[edit policy-options policy-statement NO-FIRT-OUT]
term REJECT {
  from {
    community TRANSIT;
  }
  then reject;
}
term ACCEPT {
  then accept;
}

[edit protocols bgp group CE]
export NO-FIRT-OUT;
```

These simple examples show how a wise use of the COMMUNITY attribute allows for great flexibility in filter definition. As we will see in Chapter 7, among the other applications of the COMMUNITY attribute, there is the option of creating routing policies in a flexible and elegant way.

6.5 FILTER APPLICATION

Once defined (based on its implementation), a filter does not necessarily enter into effect.

The first method to apply a filter is simply resetting the BGP sessions (hard reset), by administratively shutting the session down and then restoring it. However, this method is not recommended, because:

- It causes the loss of all prefixes received from the BGP Neighbor(s) and thus an interruption of traffic forwarding;

- the new session is established (based on the implementation) after about ten seconds, after which the BGP advertisements are exchanged again, applying the new inbound/outbound filters;

- It can lead to very long FIB convergence times, when the number of BGP advertisements received by the BGP Neighbor is very high (e.g. full routing table).

Better filter application methods are based on soft reset techniques, which allow applying a filter without interrupting the traffic and without shutting down/restoring the BGP session. Soft reset techniques are based on an elementary observation: in general, in order to apply a new filter, you need to:

- for outbound filters, resend the best paths contained in the Loc-RIB table to the BGP Neighbors toward which a new filter has been configured;

- for inbound filters, process all the best paths received from the BGP Neighbors for which a new filter has been configured.

In the first case, the operation is quite simple, since the best paths are always available. However, it is a little more complex for inbound filters, since all the advertisements received from the BGP Neighbors for which a new filter has been configured may not be available, because they could have been previously rejected by an existing filter. Current BGP implementations for inbound filter application support two soft reset functions:

- soft reconfiguration inbound: it is based on complete availability of the Adj-RIB-in table, containing all the advertisements received from a certain BGP Neighbor;

- route refresh: it is based on the idea of requesting the BGP Neighbors to resend the content of their Adj-RIB-out table. The request is done through the ROUTE REFRESH (Type=5) message.

In the next two sections, we will see these functions better and their support in Cisco and Juniper implementations treated in this book.

6.5.1 The soft reconfiguration function

In general, the soft reconfiguration function consists in making the new inbound or outbound filter process all the best paths.

As we mentioned earlier, in case of outbound filters, this is especially simple, because all the best paths are available in the Loc-RIB table. So it is sufficient, through a suitable configuration command, to order the BGP process to resend the best paths toward those BGP Neighbors where the new outbound filters were applied. In this case, we talk about soft reconfiguration outbound. However, concerning the soft reconfiguration inbound, the best paths previously sent by the BGP Neighbors (based on the implementation) are not always available. For instance, in Cisco platforms, the advertisements rejected by previous filters are not stored in the BGP advertisement table, and therefore are not available for the possible application of a new inbound filter. On the other hand, Juniper platforms store all advertisements rejected by previous filters in a hidden memory area of the RIB, making them locally available.

NOTE: Through the following configuration command, it is possible to make the default behaviour of Juniper platforms the same of the Cisco ones:

[edit protocols bgp group *group-name*]
keep none;

With this command, Juniper routers do not store the advertisements rejected by inbound filters in any memory area.

The idea behind a soft reconfiguration inbound is keeping a copy of all BGP advertisements received, even those rejected by possible inbound filters. When a new filter is applied, it is sufficient to order the BGP process to request the new filter to process all the advertisements received. This method is very simple, however it entails greater memory consumption.

NOTE: The greater memory consumption should not be underestimated, especially in older devices in which, especially given the current size of the full routing table, it might be necessary to give up the soft reconfiguration function.

While this occurs by default in Juniper platforms, in Cisco platforms it needs to be configured through a specific configuration command. The commands to be executed for IOS XE/XR are:

IOS XE
router(config)# **router bgp** *AS-number*
router(config-router)# **address-family {ipv4 | ipv6} unicast**
router(config-router-af)# **neighbor** *IP-neighbor* **soft-reconfiguration inbound**

IOS XR
RP/0/RP0/CPU0:router(config)# **router bgp** *AS-number*
RP/0/RP0/CPU0:router(config-bgp)# **neighbor** *IP-neighbor*
RP/0/RP0/CPU0:router(config-bgp-nbr)# **address-family {ipv4 | ipv6} unicast**
RP/0/RP0/CPU0:router(config-bgp-nbr-af)# **soft-reconfiguration inbound [always]**

NOTE: The "**always**" option should always be used when the BGP Neighbor supports the route refresh.

Enabling the soft reconfiguration inbound allows the BGP process to create a memory area where all the advertisements received on a certain BGP session before the application of a filter can be copied to. This is also useful to view the advertisements before applying any inbound filter. The following commands can be used:

IOS XE
router# **show bgp** *afi safi* **neighbors** *IP-neighbor* **received-routes**

IOS XR
RP/0/RP0/CPU0:router# **show bgp** *afi safi* **neighbors** *IP-neighbor* **received routes**

It should be noted that these two commands don't give any result, if the soft reconfiguration inbound is not enabled.

The only consequence of enabling the soft reconfiguration inbound is the creation of the memory area (Adj-RIB-in table) where the advertisements received by a specific BGP Neighbor will be stored. The command does not apply any new filter: in order to apply them, commands such as "**clear bgp** …" are required.

IOS XE

router# **clear bgp** *afi safi* {* | *IP-neighbor* | *peer-group-name*} [**soft**] [**in** | **out**]

IOS XR

RP/0/RP0/CPU0:router# **clear bgp** *afi safi* {* | *IP-neighbor*} **soft** [**in** | **out**]

NOTE: In IOS XE, the presence of the "**soft**" word is not necessary. It produces the same results, whether it is present or not.

With the soft reconfiguration inbound function enabled, "**clear bgp** …" commands for filter application use the advertisements contained in the Adj-RIB-in associated to a certain BGP session directly.

Actually, "**clear bgp** ..." commands are necessary only in IOS/IOS XE, because, both in IOS XR and in JUNOS, soft reconfiguration mechanisms (if enabled) are automatically applied at every "**commit**" for each new filter configured.

NOTE: In IOS XR, this behavior can be disabled via the "**bgp auto-policy-soft-reset disable**" command.

6.5.2 The route refresh function

The route refresh is defined by RFC 2918 – *Route Refresh Capability for BGP-4*, September 2000, which is used to request a BGP Neighbor to retransmit the best paths in the Adj-RIB-out table.

Its support is negotiated through the OPEN message, with the optional Route Refresh BGP Capability (Capability Code=2; CapabilityLength=0). Both in the different IOS types and in JUNOS, the Route Refresh BGP Capability is automatically negotiated. In any case, the negotiation can be assessed through "**show bgp neighbors** …" commands. Below is the command applied to router CE1 of our sample network for the session with PE1.

```
CE1#show bgp ipv4 unicast neighbors 10.1.11.1 | i refresh
Route refresh: advertised and received(new)
```

NOTE: The "**new**" in the view indicates that the standard version of the Route Refresh BGP Capability is negotiated. In older IOS and IOS XE versions, a Cisco proprietary version was negotiated.

The same command executed on CE2 (JUNOS), for the session toward PE1, shows the same result:

```
aft@CE2> show bgp neighbor 10.1.12.1 | match "Refresh capability"
  Peer supports Refresh capability (2)
```

The best path request to the BGP Neighbor is done through the ROUTE REFRESH (Type=5) message, whose format is shown in Figure 6.8 below.

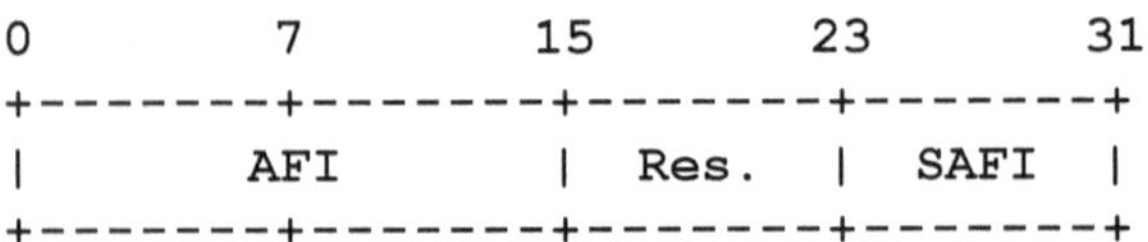

Figure 6.8 – Format of the ROUTE REFRESH message (RFC 2918).

The total length of the ROUTE REFRESH message is equal to 23 bytes (19 bytes of common header + 4 bytes of content). The AFI (Address Family Identifier) and SAFI (Subsequent Address Family Identifier) fields contained in the message represent the address family for which the retransmission of the best paths in the Adj-RIB-out table is requested to the BGP Neighbor. We already saw the most important AFI/SAFI codes in Sections 2.6.1 and 3.1.1.

NOTE: There is an updated version of the route refresh function, specified in RFC 7313 – *Enhanced Route Refresh Capability for BGP-4*, July 2014, which uses the reserved field (Res) of the ROUTE REFRESH message to define two additional types: BoRR (Beginning of a Route Refresh) (Res=1) and EoRR (End of a Route Refresh) (Res=2). Value Res=0 indicates the standard ROUTE REFRESH message (and, as we will see in the next Paragraph 6.6, also its extension for the Outbound Route Filtering function). These two new messages facilitate route refresh operations by marking the start and the end of the complete best path readvertisement by the BGP Neighbor. The advanced function is negotiated through a BGP Capability with Capability Code=70 and Capability Length=0. However, it is not supported by all BGP implementations (e.g., concerning the implementations covered in this book, at least until its publication, it is supported only by Cisco IOS XE).

Sending of the ROUTE REFRESH message, in Cisco routers, is triggered by the same "**clear bgp**..." commands we saw in the previous Section 6.5.1 for the soft reconfiguration inbound function. In Juniper routers, the same commands are:

- for outbound filters: user@router> **clear bgp neighbor** [*IP-neighbor*] **soft**;

- for inbound filters: user@router> **clear bgp neighbor** [*IP-neighbor*] **soft-inbound**.

Downstream of the execution of these commands, if the soft reconfiguration inbound is not enabled, the BGP process sends a ROUTE REFRESH message to the BGP Neighbor. In JUNOS, it is sent only if the "**keep none**" command described earlier is configured (see first Note of Section 6.5.1). Upon receiving the message, the BGP Neighbor resends the set of best paths, which are then processed by the new filter.

To conclude, here is the wireshark analysis of a ROUTE REFRESH message.

Border Gateway Protocol - ROUTE-REFRESH Message
  Marker: ffffffffffffffffffffffffffffffff
  Length: 23
  Type: ROUTE-REFRESH Message (5)
  Address family identifier (AFI): IPv4 (1)
  Subtype: **Normal route refresh request [RFC2918] with/without ORF [RFC5291] (0)**
  Subsequent address family identifier (SAFI): Unicast (1)

The message analysed is of the standard type (i.e., all the bits of the Reserved field are null).

6.6 OUTBOUND ROUTE FILTERING

In order to apply an inbound filter, as we saw in Paragraph 6.4, the most effective mechanism is using the ROUTE REFRESH message, which allows requesting a BGP Neighbor to retransmit the best paths present in its Adj-RIB-out table. However, this mechanism, as the number of best paths within the Adj-RIB-out grows, entails the transmission of a large number of UPDATE messages, by the BGP Neighbor that receives the ROUTE REFRESH message. The consequence is a significant and useless CPU engagement to create UPDATE messages, many of which will be rejected once they reach their destination, due to the filter.

A simple idea to reduce the number of UPDATE messages generated (and transmitted) is to communicate to the BGP Neighbor the structure of the inbound filter to be adopted locally as outbound filter, thus eliminating the transmission of all the advertisements that the filter would reject, with consequent reduction in the number of UPDATE messages. This function, known as Outbound Route Filtering (ORF), is negotiated between BGP Neighbors when a session is opened, by adding a BGP Capability in the OPEN message (see below for further details).

Figure 6.9 summarizes the benefits resulting from using the ORF. Let's assume that router RB needs to apply the new inbound filter FILT-in and that the Adj-RIB-out table of BGP Neighbor RA contains 250,000 best paths. Let's also assume that the application of the FILT-in filter causes the rejection of 240,000 advertisements. Without applying the ORF, BGP Neighbor RA, after the ROUTE REFRESH message received from RB, creates thousands of UPDATE messages containing the 250,000 best paths and sends them to RB, which, applying the FILT-in filter, eliminates 240,000 of them which therefore were sent uselessly. With the ORF, RB communicates to RA the structure of the FILT-in filter, which is then applied by RA as outbound filter (hence the name ORF). The result is that RA sends to RB only 10,000 best paths, thus significantly reducing the number of UPDATE messages transmitted. As we will see later on, the filter is sent through a suitably extended ROUTE REFRESH message.

The ORF is a standard mechanism defined by RFC 5291 – *"Outbound Route Filtering Capability for BGP-4"*, August 2008.

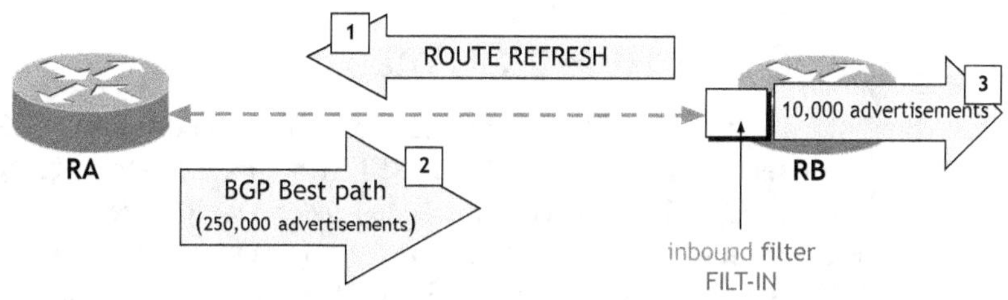

Figure 6.9a – Inbound filtering without ORF.

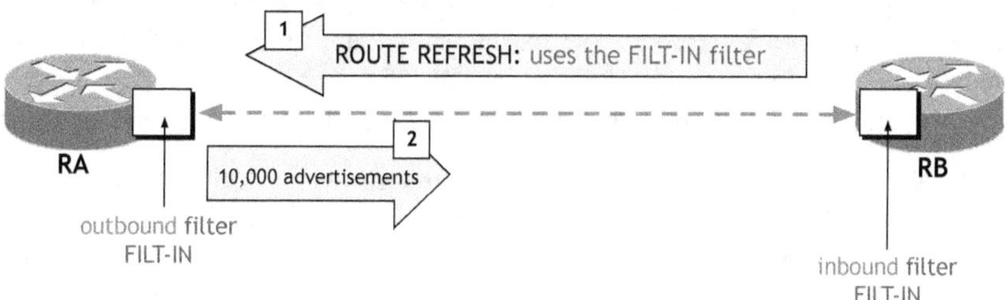

Figure 6.9b – Inbound filtering with ORF.

6.6.1 Filter description

The crucial aspect of the ORF is the filter description, that is, how filters are communicated to a BGP Neighbor. A filter is described by a set of homogeneous ORF elements (ORF entry). An ORF entry is made up of a quintuple such as:

<AFI/SAFI, ORF-Type, Action, Match, ORF-value>

Homogeneous ORF entries are characterized by identical ORF-type and AFI/SAFI. The AFI/SAFI pair, as we saw in Section 6.5.2, represents the family of addresses for which the best path sending is requested. The ORF-Type value indicates the type of BGP attribute on which the filter is based (NLRI, AS_PATH, COMMUNITY) and determines the content of the ORF-value field. The Action component controls the variation requests of an ORF filter. It can take on the three following values:

- ADD: allows requesting a BGP Neighbor to add an ORF entry to the ORF filter previously sent;

- REMOVE: allows requesting a BGP Neighbor to remove an ORF entry to the ORF filter previously sent;

- REMOVE-ALL: allows requesting a BGP Neighbor to remove all ORF entries previously sent.

The Match component defines the type of clause (permit/deny) the ORF entry is subjected to, and it is meaningful only if the Action component is of the ADD or REMOVE type. It can take on two values:

- PERMIT: allows requesting the BGP Neighbor that processes the ORF entry to propagate the best paths that meet the ORF entry;

- DENY: allows requesting the BGP Neighbor that processes the ORF entry not to propagate the best paths that meet the ORF.

6.6.2 Extended ROUTE REFRESH message

ORF entries are communicated to a BGP Neighbor through suitably extended ROUTE REFRESH messages. A BGP Speaker separates a normal ROUTE REFRESH message from one containing ORF entries based on the Length field of the BGP message header. Don't forget that the length of a normal ROUTE REFRESH message is equal to 23 bytes (19 bytes of common header + 4 bytes of content). A ROUTE REFRESH message that contains ORF entries can be identified by a total length ≥ 24 bytes.

Every extended ROUTE REFRESH message can transport more than one ORF entry, as long as they all share the same AFI/SAFI code. The format, shown in Figure 6.10, consists of a common part, formed by the same fields present in a simple ROUTE message (2 bytes AFI, 1 byte reserved, 1 byte SAFI) and by the When-to-refresh field (1 byte long), which can take on two values:

- IMMEDIATE (0x01): indicates that, after processing all the ORF entries received in the extended ROUTE REFRESH message, the BGP Speaker immediately readvertises to the BGP Neighbor that sent the message all the best paths in its Adj-RIB-Out table with the same AFI/SAFI as the message, filtering all the best paths according to the content of the ORF entries received.

- DEFER (0x02): as above, with the difference that the best paths in the Adj-RIB-Out table, filtered based on the ORF entries received, are readvertised only after receiving a new ROUTE REFRESH message, which can be simple or extended, with the When-to-refresh field set to IMMEDIATE.

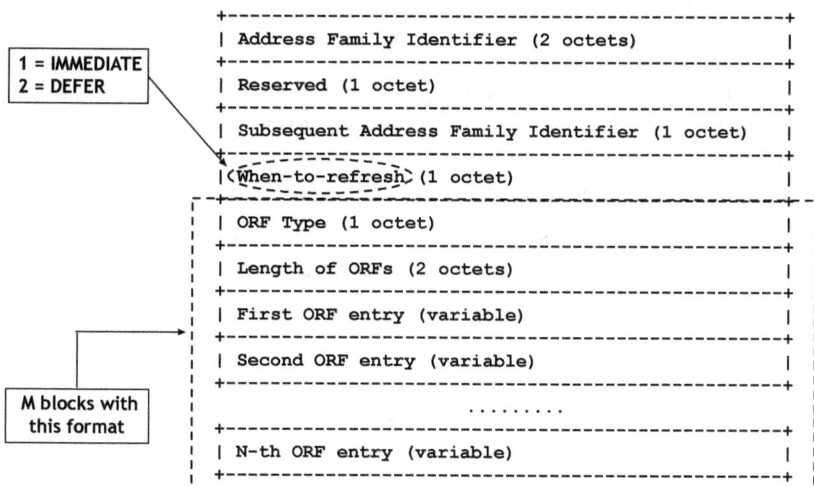

Figure 6.10 – Format of the extended ROUTE REFRESH messages.

After the When-to-refresh field, extended ROUTE REFRESH messages contain a set of ORF entry blocks, grouped by ORF-Type. Every block comprises:

- ORF-Type (1 byte): indicates the type of ORF entry. Value zero is reserved, values 1-27 are assigned by the IANA, while the remaining values can be used as desired by the different device manufacturers.

- Length of ORFs (2 bytes): indicates the overall length of the ORF entries contained in the block.

- One or more ORF entries.

The format of each ORF entry is shown in Figure 6.11.

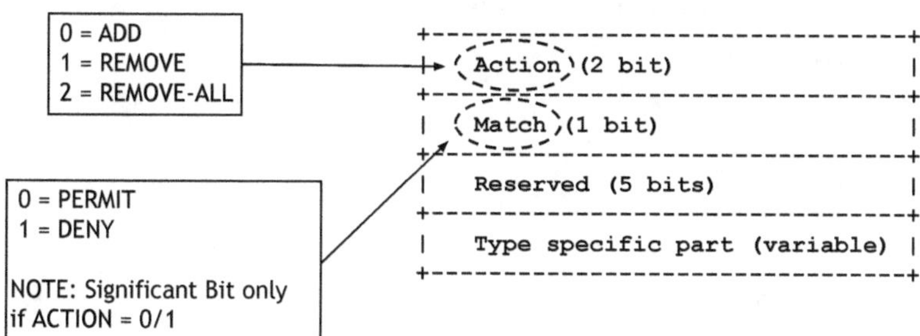

Figure 6.11 – ORF entry format.

The Type specific part field depends on the ORF type. The most common standard ORF-Type is the Address Prefix ORF, specified by RFC 5292 – *Address-Prefix-Based Outbound Route Filter for BGP-4*, August 2008 and characterized by ORF-Type=64. The Type specific part field is shown in Figure 6.12 with the different fields taking on the following meaning:

- Sequence: specifies a value that allows defining the processing order between all the Address Prefix ORF entries.

- Minlen: indicates the minimum mask value required for the match. A null value indicates an unspecified Minlen.

- Maxlen: indicates the maximum mask value required for the match. It cannot exceed the length of an address of the AFI/SAFI family. For instance, for IPv4 unicast prefixes characterized by AFI/SAFI=1/1, it cannot exceed 32 bit; for IPv6 unicast prefixes characterized by AFI/SAFI=2/1, it cannot exceed 128 bit.

- <Length; Prefix>: represents the coding of a prefix belonging to the family defined by the AFI/SAFI values. For instance, in the case of IPv4 unicast prefixes, the coding matches the one we saw for the UPDATE message (see Section 2.3.2).

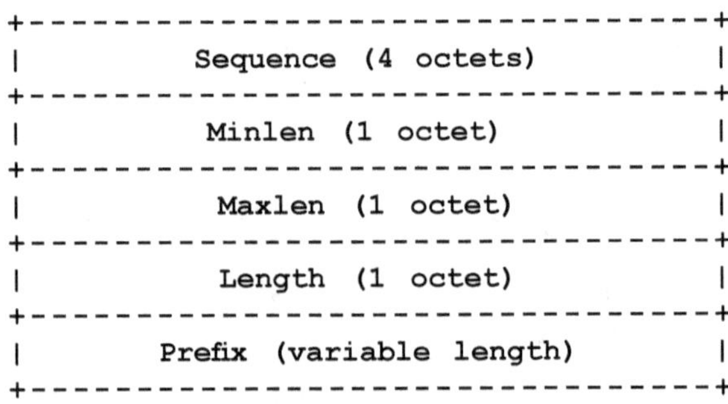

```
+-----------------------------------------+
|          Sequence  (4  octets)          |
+-----------------------------------------+
|           Minlen  (1  octet)            |
+-----------------------------------------+
|           Maxlen  (1  octet)            |
+-----------------------------------------+
|           Length  (1  octet)            |
+-----------------------------------------+
|         Prefix  (variable  length)      |
+-----------------------------------------+
```

Figure 6.12 – Specific component of the Address Prefix ORF-Type.

It should be noted that, by definition, it should always be $0 \leq$ Length $<$ Minlen $\leq$ Maxlen.
For instance, let's assume that a BGP Speaker wants to add to a prefix-list filter for IPv4 unicast prefixes (previously sent to one of its BGP Neighbors) the following line (for the sake of simplicity, we will adopt the notation of prefix-lists in IOS / IOS XE Cisco):

```
ip prefix-list ABC seq 15 permit 192.0.2.0/24 ge 26 le 30
```

The fields specified above take on the following values:

- *AFI/SAFI* = 1/1;

- *ORF-Type* = 64;

- *Action* = 0 (*ADD*);

- *Match* = 0 (*PERMIT*);

- *Sequence* = 15;

- *Minlen* = 26;

- *Maxlen* = 30;

- *Length* = 24;

- *Prefix* = 192.0.2 (*3 byte*);

NOTE: RFC 7543 – *Covering Prefixes Outbound Route Filter for BGP-4*, May 2015, defined another ORF-Type called Covering Prefixes ORF (CP-ORF), which we will not cover here, since it can be applied only to peculiar contexts, such as the L3VPN Virtual Hub-and-Spoke, and in the Ethernet VPN (EVPN) model to establish L2VPN-type BGP/MPLS services.

6.6.3 Negotiating the ORF function

As mentioned earlier, the ORF function is negotiated through a BGP Capability characterized by Capability Code=3 and variable Capability Length. The Capability Value format is shown in Figure 6.13 below.

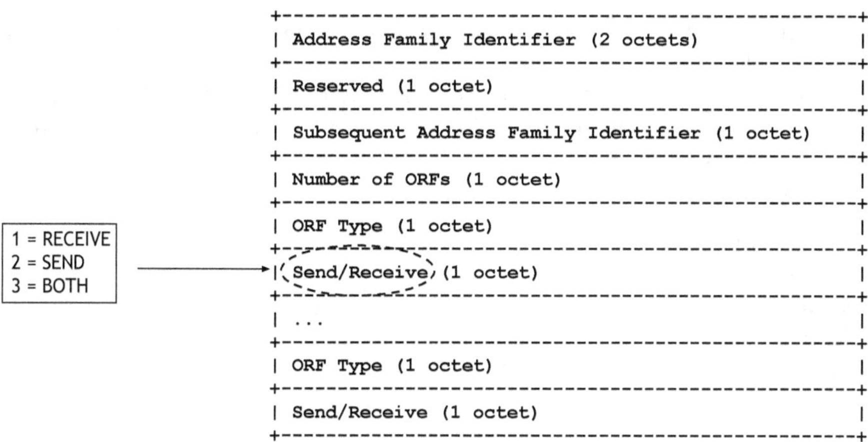

Figure 6.13 – ORF Capability format.

In the OPEN message, a BGP Capability should be added for each address family you want to enable the ORF function for.

The meaning of all fields – except for Send/Receive – is identical to that specified earlier for the extended ROUTE REFRESH message. While the Send/Receive field indicates whether the sender of the OPEN message has the option of accepting (Send/Receive=1), sending (Send/Receive=2) and accepting/sending (Send/Receive=3) extended ROUTE REFRESH messages.

Now let's see how to implement the ORF function in the two technologies covered by this book.

6.6.4 Configuration aspects

The different types of Cisco IOS support the Address Prefix ORF (ORF-Type=64). The implementation is done through two configuration steps:

- Negotiation of the ORF Capability through the command:

    <u>IOS XE</u>
    router(config)# **router bgp** *AS-number*
    router(config-router)# **address-family {ipv4 | ipv6} unicast**
    router(config-router-af)# **neighbor** *IP-neighbor* **capability orf prefix-list**
    {send | receive | both}

IOS XR
RP/0/RP0/CPU0:router(config)# **router bgp** *AS-number*
RP/0/RP0/CPU0:router(config-bgp)# **neighbor** *IP-neighbor*
RP/0/RP0/CPU0:router(config-bgp-nbr)# **address-family {ipv4 | ipv6} unicast**
RP/0/RP0/CPU0:router(config-bgp-nbr-af)# **capability orf prefix {send | receive | both}**

where the "**send | receive | both**" options enable the BGP Speaker to accept (Send/Receive = 1), send (Send/Receive = 2), and accept/send (Send/Receive = 3) extended ROUTE REFRESH messages, respectively.

- Sending of the new filter and consequent reception from the BGP Neighbor of the best paths filtered, through the "**clear bgp** *afi safi* * | *IP-neighbor* **in [prefix-filter]** command.

The "**prefix-filter**" option, if used, allows communicating to the BGP Neighbor a possible new prefix-list filter or the variation of an existing filter, with consequent use by the BGP Neighbor as outbound filter; its absence entails the sending of a normal ROUTE REFRESH message.

In JUNOS, it is only possible to configure the BGP process to accept filters based on prefixes using the Address Prefix ORF (ORF-Type=64). The implementation is done through the following group of commands:

```
[edit protocols bgp]
outbound-route-filter {
  <bgp-orf-cisco-mode>;
  prefix-based {
    accept {
    (inet | inet6);
    }
  }
}
```

which can be applied directly at global, group or single BGP Neighbor level.

The optional "**bgp-orf-cisco-mode**" command is useful for interoperability purpose with Cisco routers, which, in the old IOS versions, used the proprietary value 130 instead of the standard value 3 to negotiate the BGP Capability (or, as Cisco called it, Cooperative route filtering capability) and ORF-Type 128 instead of standard value 64. The "**inet**" and "**inet6**" options specify the AFI code (**inet**=IPv4=1, **inet6**=IPv6=2), while the SAFI code is fixed and equal to 1 (unicast addresses).

Both keywords can be specified. In this way, the router is enabled to accept the filters both for IPv4 and IPv6 prefixes.

Let's see two examples of application, using pairs of routers from our sample network, extended by adding AS 65543 (see Figure 6.6).

Example 1

Let's consider the eBGP session between the router of AS 65543 (Cisco IOS XE) and the router of Upstream Provider AS 65541 (Cisco IOS XR).

The router of Upstream Provider AS 65541 advertises to the router of AS 65543 a total of 16 IP prefixes (one of which is the default route). The router of AS 65543, through the prefix-list ORF-TEST, filters the advertisements and accepts only three of them, containing the following prefixes: the default route, 198.51.100/24 and 203.0.113/24.

The initial configurations are:

<u>AS 65543</u> (IOS XE)
```
router bgp 65543
  neighbor 172.23.1.1 remote-as 65541
  neighbor 172.23.1.1 prefix-list ORF-TEST in
!
ip prefix-list ORF-TEST seq 5 permit 198.51.100.0/24
ip prefix-list ORF-TEST seq 10 permit 203.0.113.0/24
ip prefix-list ORF-TEST seq 15 permit 0.0.0.0/0
```

<u>AS 65541</u> (IOS XR)
```
router bgp 65541
  address-family ipv4 unicast
  neighbor 172.23.1.0
    remote-as 65543
    address-family ipv4 unicast
      route-policy ALL out
      route-policy ALL in
```

where the routing policy **ALL** permits all prefixes. Before the ORF is applied, as you can easily notice from the "**debug...**" below, the Upstream Provider AS 65541 sends the best paths of all the 16 prefixes present in its BGP table. Therefore router AS 65543 is tasked with rejecting all unwanted prefixes, by applying the prefix-list ORF-TEST filter in the inbound direction.
The prefix rejection is marked by notation "**DENIED due to: distribute/prefix-list**".

```
AS-65543# debug bgp ipv4 unicast update
AS-65543# clear bgp ipv4 unicast 172.23.1.1 in
AS-65543#

*Jan 8 17:23:31.945: BGP(0): 172.23.1.1 rcvd UPDATE w/ attr: nexthop
172.30.1.1, origin i, metric 0, merged path 65541 64508 64505, AS_PATH
*Jan 8 17:23:31.947: BGP(0): 172.23.1.1 rcvd 220.42.1.0/24 -- DENIED due
to: distribute/prefix-list;
*Jan 8 17:23:31.949: BGP(0): 172.23.1.1 rcvd 137.2.0.0/16 -- DENIED due
to: distribute/prefix-list;
*Jan 8 17:23:31.950: BGP(0): 172.23.1.1 rcvd 137.1.0.0/16 -- DENIED due
to: distribute/prefix-list;

*Jan 8 17:23:31.952: BGP(0): 172.23.1.1 rcvd UPDATE w/ attr: nexthop
172.30.1.1, origin i, metric 0, merged path 65541 64496, AS_PATH
*Jan 8 17:23:31.954: BGP(0): 172.23.1.1 rcvd 203.0.113.0/24
*Jan 8 17:23:31.955: BGP(0): 172.23.1.1 rcvd 190.1.0.0/16 -- DENIED due
to: distribute/prefix-list;
*Jan 8 17:23:31.956: BGP(0): 172.23.1.1 rcvd UPDATE w/ attr: nexthop
172.30.1.1, origin i, metric 0, merged path 65541 64508, AS_PATH
*Jan 8 17:23:31.958: BGP(0): 172.23.1.1 rcvd 198.51.100.0/24
*Jan 8 17:23:31.959: BGP(0): 172.23.1.1 rcvd 142.2.0.0/16 -- DENIED due
to: distribute/prefix-list;
```

```
*Jan 8 17:23:31.960: BGP(0): 172.23.1.1 rcvd 142.1.0.0/16 -- DENIED due
to: distribute/prefix-list;
```

. . . < *output omitted* > . . .

By activating the ORF, the router of AS 65543 can communicate to the router of AS 65541 the prefix-list structure, and therefore allow it to apply the prefix-list ORF-TEST filter to all the advertisements sent to the router of AS 65543. Consequently, the router of AS 65541 instead of sending the advertisements of all the 16 prefixes in its Adj-RIB-out table, only sends three of them. The ORF is activated through the following additional commands:

AS 65543 (IOS XE)
```
router bgp 65543
  neighbor 172.23.1.1 capability orf prefix-list send
```

AS 65541 (IOS XR)
```
router bgp 65541
  neighbor 172.23.1.0
    address-family ipv4 unicast
      capability orf prefix receive
```

The negotiation of the ORF Capability can be checked by activating the "**debug**" below:

```
AS-65543# debug bgp ipv4 unicast
AS-65543#

*Jan 8 17:25:37.522: BGP: 172.23.1.1 active rcvd OPEN w/ optional parameter
type 2 (Capability) len 9

*Jan 8 17:25:37.522: BGP: 172.23.1.1 active OPEN has CAPABILITY code: 3,
length 7

*Jan 8 17:25:37.523: BGP: 172.23.1.1 active OPEN has ORF CAP for afi/safi: 1/1

*Jan 8 17:25:37.523: BGP: 172.23.1.1 active OPEN has Prefixlist ORF
capability as RECEIVE for afi/safi: 1/1
```

The following views show: the BGP table of the router of AS 65543 and the check that the prefix-list filter has been actually communicated to the router of AS 65541.

```
AS-65543#show bgp ipv4 unicast
. . .
     Network          Next Hop        Metric   bLocPrf   Weight    Path
*>   0.0.0.0          172.23.1.1                            0      65541 i
*>   198.51.100.0     172.23.1.1        0                   0      65541 64508 i
*>   203.0.113.0      172.23.1.1        0                   0      65541 64496 i

RP/0/0/CPU0:AS-65541# show bgp ipv4 unicast neighbors 172.23.1.0
received prefix-filter
. . .
Number of entries: 3
ipv4 prefix ORF 172.30.1.13
  5 permit 198.51.100.0/24 ge 24 le 24
  10 permit 203.0.113.0/24 ge 24 le 24
  15 permit 0.0.0.0/0
```

Notice that the content of AS-65543's BGP table does not depend on the application of the ORF, but only on the prefix-list ORF-TEST filter applied to the inbound direction. The ORF helps to save on the CPU workload, and the final result is the same.

After applying the ORF – as you can easily notice in the "**debug**" executed and shown below – the router of AS 65541 does not send the best paths of all the 16 prefixes present in its BGP table; instead, it applies the prefix-list ORF-TEST filter directly to the outbound and sends only the best paths allowed by the filter.

As you may notice, on the router of AS 65543, there is no rejected prefix this time.

```
AS-65543#debug bgp ipv4 unicast update
AS-65543#clear bgp ipv4 unicast 172.23.1.1 in
AS-65543#

*Jan 8 17:25:53.474: BGP(0): 172.23.1.1 rcvd UPDATE w/ attr: nexthop
172.30.1.1, origin i, merged path 65541, AS_PATH

*Jan 8 17:25:53.475: BGP(0): 172.23.1.1 rcvd 0.0.0.0/0...

*Jan 8 17:25:55.699: BGP(0): 172.23.1.1 rcvd UPDATE w/ attr: nexthop
172.30.1.1, origin i, metric 0, merged path 65541 64496, AS_PATH

*Jan 8 17:25:55.699: BGP(0): 172.23.1.1 rcvd 203.0.113.0/24...

*Jan 8 17:25:55.700: BGP(0): 172.23.1.1 rcvd UPDATE w/ attr: nexthop
172.30.1.1, origin i, metric 0, merged path 65541 64508, AS_PATH

*Jan 8 17:25:55.702: BGP(0): 172.23.1.1 rcvd 198.51.100.0/24...
```

Example 2

Let's consider the eBGP session between router CE1 of AS 65101 (Cisco IOS XE) and router PE2 of AS 64501 (Juniper JUNOS).

Here too, router CE1, through the prefix-list ORF-TEST, filters the advertisements and accepts only three of them, containing the same prefixes of Example 1: the default-route, 198.51.100/24 and 203.0.113/24.

The configuration of router CE1 is basically the same we already saw for the router of AS 65543 in Example 1:

```
router bgp 65101
  neighbor 10.1.12.5 remote-as 64501
  neighbor 10.1.12.5 capability orf prefix-list send
  neighbor 10.1.12.5 prefix-list ORF-TEST in
!
ip prefix-list ORF-TEST seq 5 permit 198.51.100.0/24
ip prefix-list ORF-TEST seq 10 permit 203.0.113.0/24
ip prefix-list ORF-TEST seq 15 permit 0.0.0.0/0
```

The configuration to execute on PE2 is the following:

```
[edit protocols bgp group CE]
peer-as 65101;
outbound-route-filter {
  bgp-orf-cisco-mode;
  prefix-based {
    accept {
      inet;
```

```
    }
  }
}
neighbor 10.1.12.6 {
  description "*** EBGP SESSION WITH CE1 ***";
}
```

With this configuration, PE2 can accept the filters based on the prefixes that use the Address Prefix ORF (ORF-Type=64). We can verify with the following command that PE2 actually receives the ORF-TEST filter from CE1:

```
aft@PE2> show bgp neighbor orf 10.1.12.6 detail
Peer: 10.1.12.6+11851 Type: External
  Group: CE

  inet-unicast
    Filter updates recv: 3 Immediate: 1
    Filter: prefix-based receive
      Updates recv: 3
    Received filter entries:
      seq 5 198.51.100.0/24 permit minlen 0 maxlen 0
      seq 10 203.0.113.0/24 permit minlen 0 maxlen 0
      seq 15 /0 permit minlen 0 maxlen 0
```

NOTE: The null value of "**minlen**" and "**maxlen**", according to RFC 5292, indicates that these values are not specified in the filter.

To conclude, below is the wireshark analysis of the extended ROUTE REFRESH message sent by CE1 to PE2 to communicate the structure of the prefix-list ORF-TEST filter.

Border Gateway Protocol - ROUTE-REFRESH Message
  Marker: ffffffffffffffffffffffffffffffff
  Length: 57
  Type: ROUTE-REFRESH Message (5)
  Address family identifier (AFI): IPv4 (1)
  Subtype: Normal route refresh request [RFC2918] with/without ORF [RFC5291] (0)
  Subsequent address family identifier (SAFI): Unicast (1)
  ORF information
    ORF flag: Immediate (1)
    ORF type: Cisco PrefixList ORF-Type (128) ! 128 = Cisco proprietary value (standard = 64)
    ORF length: 30
    ORFEntry PrefixList
      00.. .... = ORFEntry Action: Add (0)
      ..0. .... = ORFEntry Match: Permit (0)
      ORFEntry Sequence: 5
      ORFEntry PrefixMask length lower bound: 0
      ORFEntry PrefixMask length upper bound: 0
      198.51.100.0/24
        ORF prefix length: 24
        ORFEntry IP address: 198.51.100.0
    ORFEntry PrefixList

00.. .... = ORFEntry Action: Add (0)
..0. .... = ORFEntry Match: Permit (0)
ORFEntry Sequence: 10
ORFEntry PrefixMask length lower bound: 0
ORFEntry PrefixMask length upper bound: 0
203.0.113.0/24
  ORF prefix length: 24
  ORFEntry IP address: 203.0.113.0
ORFEntry PrefixList
00.. .... = ORFEntry Action: Add (0)
..0. .... = ORFEntry Match: Permit (0)
ORFEntry Sequence: 15
ORFEntry PrefixMask length lower bound: 0
ORFEntry PrefixMask length upper bound: 0
0.0.0.0/0
  ORF prefix length: 0
  ORFEntry IP address: 0.0.0.0

We'll leave the detailed analysis of the outcome to you.

SUMMARY

Filtering policies are essential for the correct operation of the Internet ecosystem, and are one of the most important application aspects to make it secure.

Filtering can act both on inbound advertisements (inbound filtering) and on outbound ones (outbound filtering).

Current BGP implementations provide a series of tools that allow creating filters based on the different fields contained in the BGP advertisements, such as the NLRI field, which contains the routing information advertised, the AS_PATH attribute and the COMMUNITY attribute.

In this chapter, we saw how to create filters based on these fields, the tools made available by Cisco IOS XE/XR and Juniper JUNOS implementations, and several application examples of practical interest. We will see more further along.

Lastly, in the last two paragraphs, we saw how to apply new filters, focusing the attention on the two soft reset techniques: soft reconfiguration inbound and route refresh, much less invasive with respect to traditional hard reset techniques. Then, we also saw an optimized use of the route refresh, the ORF, used to communicate a filter to the BGP Neighbor and apply it by saving on processing times and UPDATE message sending.

Worth remembering:

1. Filtering types: inbound and outbound.

2. Filtering applications and the two basic filter creation steps: advertisement identification and advertisement acceptance/reject logic.

3. The tools to create filters based on IP prefixes, on the AS_PATH and on the COMMUNITY attribute, and their implementation in Cisco platforms with IOS XE/XR and Juniper with JUNOS.

4. The application of new filters through soft reset techniques: soft reconfiguration inbound and route refresh.

5. The Outbound Route Filtering (ORF) function and its practical applications.

7 – TRAFFIC MANAGEMENT POLICIES

As we saw in Section 1.4.4, traffic management policies are one of the most interesting and complex aspects of the BGP protocol.

Through the attributes provided by BGP (e.g. LOCAL_PREF, MED, etc.), we can define how the AS' inbound and/or outbound traffic can be best managed, according to the AS' administrator needs. Examples of traffic management policies include:

- Primary/Backup configuration: inbound and/or outbound traffic uses a certain connection as primary connection, and only if this one is out of service, it uses an alternative connection (toward the same AS of the primary connection or a different AS).

- Load Balancing: inbound and/or outbound traffic is more or less equally divided on one or more connections to one or other ASes.

When specifying traffic management policies, the role of the selection process is crucial. As you know, it uses a decision-making sequence and rules to select the best path, based on the different BGP attributes (see Paragraph 2.5). Manipulating BGP attributes allows conditioning the choices of the best path selection process, and therefore defining suitable AS inbound and/or outbound traffic management policies.

Therefore, before seeing how traffic management policies can be implemented in practice, it is useful to see how the selection process works more closely.

7.1 SELECTION PROCESS IN CISCO AND JUNIPER ROUTERS

In Paragraph 2.5, we covered some of the rules followed by the selection process, and common to all BGP implementations. Now, let's see how Cisco and Juniper implementations actually define the decision-making sequence.

In both implementations, the selection process is applied only to the advertisements deemed valid, according to what we specified in Paragraph 2.5. Remember, an advertisement is considered invalid if at least one of the following conditions (already specified in Paragraph 2.5) is true:

- the IP address contained in the NEXT_HOP attribute cannot be reached;

- the advertisement has been filtered by inbound filtering policies;

- the advertisement has been suppressed by the Route Flap Damping mechanism (see Paragraph 8.8).

These conditions should be complemented by a further one, linked to the advertisement validation state determined by the RPKI architecture, which we will cover more in detail later on, in Section 10.6.1.

NOTE: In Chapter 8, we will see how the introduction of Route Reflectors and/or BGP Confederations mechanism entails some variations of the selection process. We will discuss them when we treat these aspects. Furthermore, also the introduction of the RPKI architecture entails some variations of the selection process, which we will cover in Chapter 10.

7.1.1 Selection process in Cisco routers

In Cisco implementations, if we assume that the advertisement is valid, the selection process develops as follows:

1 Prefer the advertisements with the highest weight parameter (Cisco proprietary metric) value.

2 Prefer the advertisements with the highest Local Preference value.

3 Prefer the advertisements originated locally by the router.

   NOTE: Locally originated advertisements include those learned by the BGP process through the **"network ..."** command, or the redistribution or aggregation process (via the **"aggregate-address ..."** command). The order of preference is: **"network ..."** → **"redistribute ..."** → **"aggregate-address ..."**.

4 Prefer the advertisements with the minimum number of elements in the AS_PATH attribute.

   NOTE: An AS_SET type AS_PATH segment contains 1 element (e.g.: AS_PATH [64501 64502 {64505 64506}] has length=3). AS_CONFED_SEQUENCE and AS_CONFED_SET type AS_PATH segments are ignored. For the meaning and use of these types of segments, see Paragraph 8.4.

   Step 4 can be skipped during configuration, through the BGP process **"bgp bestpath as-path ignore"** command (valid for all IOS types).

5 Prefer the advertisements with minimum ORIGIN attribute value (0=IGP; 1=EGP; 2=INCOMPLETE).

6 If the advertisements come from the same AS, prefer those with the minimum MED value. The MED values from different ASes can be compared by enabling the BGP process **"bgp always-compare-med"** (IOS/IOS XE) or **"bgp bestpath med always"** commands (IOS XR) (see Section 7.3.3).

7 Prefer the advertisements coming from eBGP sessions over those coming from iBGP sessions.

8 Prefer the advertisements with the "closest" Next-Hop, according to the IGP metric.

If the selection process can't find a best path until this point, you can add further paths to the RIB using the multipath BGP (described below). In any case, regardless of the multipath BGP application, the selection process always continues with the two following points:

9 Prefer the advertisements received from the BGP Neighbor with the lowest BGP-ID.
   One exception to this is, if the current best path comes from an eBGP advertisement, not changing the best path even if the BGP-ID of the new best path is lower (i.e., prefer "older" advertisements).
   In any case, you can always use the lowest BGP-ID, by configuring the BGP process **"bgp bestpath compare-routerid"** command (valid for all IOS types).

10 Prefer the advertisement coming from the BGP Neighbor with the lowest Neighbor Address.

The practical application of the selection process entails that, if there is more than one valid advertisement of one specific prefix, Cisco IOS creates an ordered list with sorting in reverse order to the moment of receipt, that is, the first advertisement in the list is the last one received (the most recent one), while the last advertisement in the list is the first one received (the oldest one).

So, the BGP process applies every point of the selection process by sequentially comparing the advertisements in the list. The first advertisement in the list is initially selected as best path, then the current best path is compared with the following advertisement in the list, and so on, until the list is completed. The best path resulting from the last comparison becomes the final one.

The paths chosen as best paths by the selection process are candidates to be added to the RIB. Their actual insertion depends on the Administrative Distance value (or Degree of Preference, see final note in Section 1.4.3), and, as we mentioned earlier, several paths can be added by using the multipath BGP.

Multipath BGP enabling is not automatic; it is done through the following configuration commands:

<u>IOS XE</u>
router(config)# **router bgp** *AS-number*
router(config-router)# **address-family ipv4 unicast**
router(config-router-af)# **maximum-paths [ibgp]** *path-number*

<u>IOS XR</u>
RP/0/RP0/CPU0:router(config)# **router bgp** *AS-number*
RP/0/RP0/CPU0:router(config-bgp)# **address-family ipv4 unicast**
RP/0/RP0/CPU0:router(config-bgp-af)# **maximum-paths {ebgp | ibgp}** *path-number*

where the maximum value of path-number allowed depends on the Cisco platform used (generally 8 or 16, default=1) and the "**ibgp**" option narrows down the selection to only the iBGP paths. Without the "**ibgp**" option, the selection is narrowed down to only the eBGP paths.

There are some important rules to consider, when applying the multipath BGP:

- Only those advertisements with the same Cisco-proprietary weight parameter and identical BGP LOCAL_PREF, AS_PATH (whole attribute, not just the length), ORIGIN, MED attributes are selected.

- eBGP advertisements: only the advertisements coming from the same AS as the best path are selected.

- iBGP advertisements: only the advertisements with different NEXT_HOP attributes and the same IGP cost toward the BGP Next-Hop are selected.

If the paths selected exceed the maximum number configured, the choice of those to be added to the RIB is done through points 9 and 10 of the selection process.

Let's see an application of these rules through two examples. First, let's consider the example of Figure 7.1, where router RA receives the eBGP advertisements of prefix 203.0.113/24 from BGP Neighbors R1, R2 and R3.

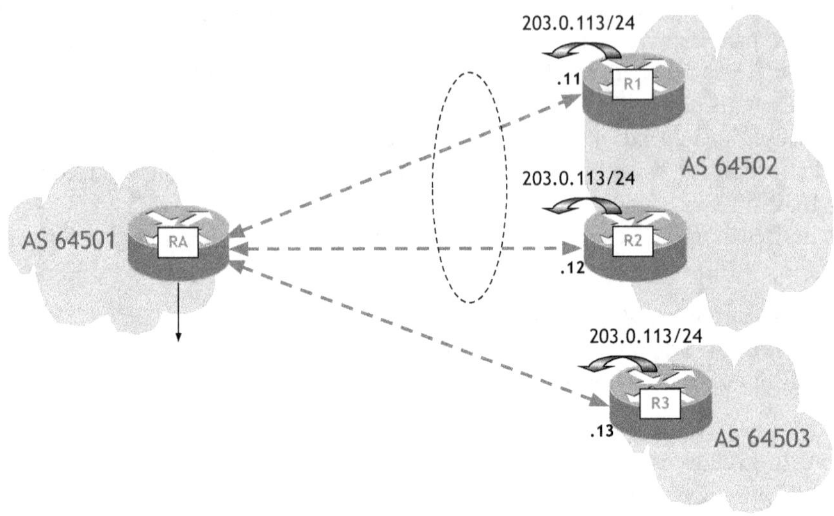

Figure 7.1 – Example of multipath BGP application to eBGP advertisements

RA's configuration is the following:

```
router bgp 64501
  neighbor 172.16.1.11 remote-as 64502
  neighbor 172.16.1.12 remote-as 64502
  neighbor 172.16.1.13 remote-as 64503
  maximum-paths 4
```

RA's BGP table highlights the three different advertisements:

```
RA# show bgp ipv4 unicast
 . . . < output omitted > . . .
     Network          Next Hop        Metric    LocPrf    Weight    Path
*    203.0.113.0      172.16.1.13       0                      0    64503 i
*                     172.16.1.12       0                      0    64502 i
*>                    172.16.1.11       0                      0    64502 i
```

The best path comes from AS 64502, from which also another advertisement arrives. Therefore, only the two paths deriving from the eBGP advertisements received from AS 64502 are installed in RA's RIB.

```
RA# show ip route bgp
B     203.0.113.0/24  [20/0] via 172.16.1.12, 00:01:04
                      [20/0] via 172.16.1.11, 00:01:04
```

On the other hand, Figure 7.2 below shows an example of multipath BGP application to iBGP advertisements. The example is taken from the sample network in Figure 3.1. Router CE1 advertises prefix 195.31.0.0/25 to AS 64501. The advertisement is propagated within AS 64501 by the two routers PE1 and PE2. Router GTW-1, as shown in the following view, receives two iBGP advertisements from the two BGP Neighbors PE1 and PE2:

```
RP/0/0/CPU0:GTW-1#show bgp 195.31.0.0/25
. . . < output omitted > . . .
Paths: (2 available, best #1)
. . . < output omitted > . . .
  65101
    192.168.0.11 (metric 20) from 192.168.0.11 (192.168.0.11)
      Origin IGP, metric 0, localpref 100, valid, internal, best,
                                                        group-best
      Received Path ID 0, Local Path ID 0, version 36
  Path #2: Received by speaker 0
  Not advertised to any peer
  65101
    192.168.0.12 (metric 20) from 192.168.0.12 (192.168.0.12)
      Origin IGP, metric 0, localpref 100, valid, internal
      Received Path ID 0, Local Path ID 0, version 0
```

All the values of the BGP attributes are identical, and the total IGP cost to reach the two BGP Next-Hop (192.168.0.11 for PE1 and 192.168.0.12 for PE2) is identical and equal to 20. The best path chosen by the BGP selection process is the one with BGP Next-Hop 192.168.0.11 (we will leave the reason for it to you, as a useful exercise).
Without enabling the multipath BGP, GTW-1 installs only the best path in its RIB.

```
RP/0/0/CPU0:GTW-1#sh route | i 195.31.0.0/25
B    195.31.0.0/25 [200/0] via 192.168.0.11, 00:29:15
```

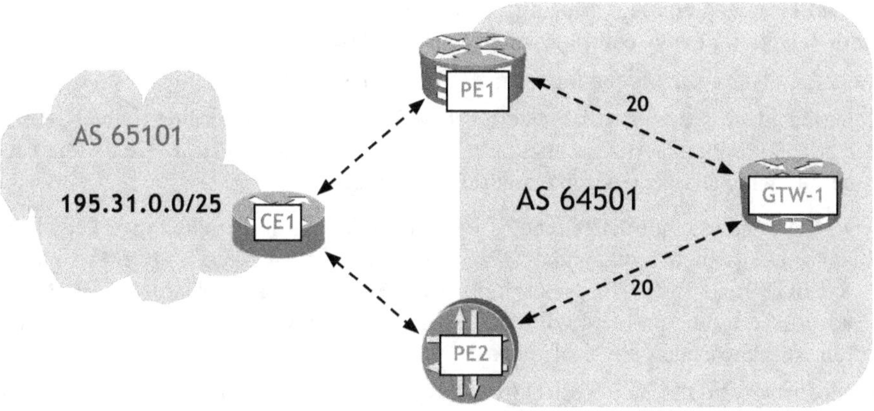

Figure 7.2 – Example of multipath BGP application to iBGP advertisements.

Now, let's suppose to enable the multipath BGP on GTW-1.

```
router bgp 64501
address-family ipv4 unicast
  maximum-paths ibgp 4
```

Consequently, both paths deriving from the iBGP advertisements will be installed in GTW-1's RIB:

```
RP/0/0/CPU0:GTW-1#show route 195.31.0.0/25
. . .
Routing entry for 195.31.0.0/25
  Known via "bgp 64501", distance 200, metric 0
  Tag 65101, type internal
. . .

  Routing Descriptor Blocks
    192.168.0.11, from 192.168.0.11, BGP multi path
      Route metric is 0
    192.168.0.12, from 192.168.0.12, BGP multi path
      Route metric is 0
```

7.1.2 Selection process in Juniper routers

In Juniper implementations, if we assume that the advertisement is valid, the selection process develops as follows:

1. Prefer the advertisements with the highest Local Preference value.
2. Prefer the advertisements with the minimum number of elements in the AS_PATH attribute.

   NOTE: For JUNOS too, the rule that an AS_SET type AS_PATH is equal to 1 (as seen for Cisco selection process) applies.

3. Prefer the advertisements with minimum ORIGIN attribute value (0=IGP; 1=EGP; 2=INCOMPLETE).
4. If the advertisements come from the same AS, prefer those with the minimum MED value. The MED values coming from different ASes can be compared by enabling the global **"path-selection always-compare-med"** command (see Section 7.3.3).
5. Prefer the advertisements coming from eBGP sessions over those coming from iBGP sessions:
6. Prefer the advertisements with the "closest" BGP Next-Hop, according to the IGP metric. In case of iBGP-only advertisements, the router also selects a "physical" Next-Hop, according to the following BGP Next-Hop resolution procedure:

   ➤ JUNOS analyses the RIBs inet.0 (which contains the IGP paths toward IPv4 prefixes) and inet.3 (which contains the MPLS path toward IPv4 prefixes) to find a path toward the BGP Next-Hop. The Next-Hop associated to the path toward the BGP Next-Hop advertised by the protocol with the best Degree of Preference (the lowest, in numerical terms) is chosen as "physical" Next-Hop.

   ➤ If paths toward the BGP Next-Hop with the same Degree of Preference are present in both RIBs inet.0 and inet.3, Next-Hop associated to the path toward the BGP Next-Hop in the inet.3 table is chosen as "physical" Next-Hop.

   ➤ If the Degree of Preference is the same and the best paths are present in the same RIB, the router evaluates the number of equal-cost paths for each protocol. The protocol ensuring the highest number of minimum-cost paths toward the BGP Next-Hop is selected.

To better understand this mechanism, let's consider the case of router R2 that receives more iBGP advertisements than prefix 203.0.113/24. Let's assume that the advertisement with the lowest IGP cost toward the BGP Next-Hop comes from the iBGP session with router R1 and that the latter advertises the prefix with BGP Next-Hop 192.168.0.1. Figure 7.3 below shows the advertisement and the available paths between R2 and the BGP Next-Hop 192.168.0.1, which are three: two MPLS paths, one belonging to the Hop-by-Hop type (established by IGP and by LDP), and one belonging to the Explicitly Routed type (established via RSVP-TE, through MPLS Traffic Engineering techniques). Both these paths are included in router R2's inet.3 table:

```
aft@R2> show route table inet.3 192.168.0.12/32

...

192.168.0.1/32 *[RSVP/7] 03:45:11, metric 3
                 > to 172.16.3.2 via ge-0/0/0.0,
                 label-switched-path R2-TO-R1
                 [LDP/9] 03:57:23, metric 1
                 > to 172.16.3.6 via ge-0/0/1.0,
                 Push 100416
```

Moreover, in R2's routing inet.0 table, there is a third minimum-cost IGP path (via IS-IS) toward the BGP Next-Hop 192.168.0.1/32:

```
tt@R-2> show route table inet.0 192.168.0.1/32

...

192.168.0.1/32 *[IS-IS/18] 00:04:35, metric 30
                 > to 172.16.3.6 via ge-0/0/1.0
```

Following the decision-making sequence above, the Next-Hop chosen as "physical" Next-Hop is the one associated to the protocol with the best Degree of Preference (i.e. lower in numerical terms), among all the paths present in the RIBs inet.0 and inet.3. Since, between the three paths available, the one with the best DoP is the one established via RSVP (DoP=7, vs DoP=9 of LDP and DoP=18 di IS-IS), the "physical" Next-Hop selected is 172.16.3.2, which can be reached through interface "**ge-0/0/0.0**" of R2.

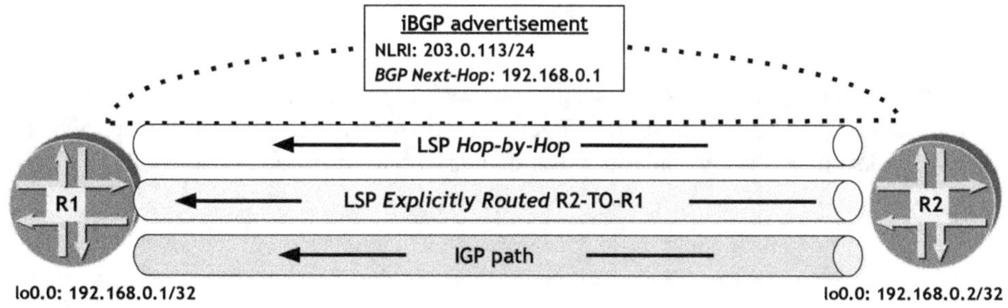

Figure 7.3 – Example of BGP Next-Hop resolution.

If the selection process can't find a best path until this point, you can add further paths to the RIB using the multipath BGP, in the same way we saw for the Cisco implementation. In any case, regardless of the multipath BGP application, the selection process always continues with the two following points:

7. Prefer the advertisements received from the BGP Neighbor with the lowest BGP-ID, with the same exception we saw in the Cisco implementation: if the current best path comes from an

eBGP advertisement, do not change the best path, even if the BGP-ID of the new best path is lower (i.e. prioritize "older" advertisements). In any case, you can always use the lowest BGP-ID by configuring the BGP process "**path-selection external-router-id**" command.

8. Prefer the advertisement coming from the BGP Neighbor with the lowest Neighbor Address.

If the selection process cannot find a single best path after the first 6 points, through the multipath BGP mechanism, you can install more than one active path in the RIB (while taking into account that adding active paths to the RIB is in any case regulated by the protocol's Degree of Preference). The multipath BGP application rules are the same we saw in previous Section 7.1.1 for Cisco routers. Enabling is not automatic; it is done through the following configuration command:

```
[edit protocols bgp]
group group-name {
  multipath {
    < multiple-as >;
  }
}
```

where the "**multiple-as**" option allows including advertisements coming from different ASes in the path selection. Without the "**multiple-as**" option, the selection is narrowed down to only the advertisement from the same AS.

It is important to notice that, even if the multipath BGP is enabled, the selection process still chooses a best path, which is propagated to the BGP Neighbors using points 7 and 8.

NOTE: In JUNOS, enabling the multipath BGP alone is not sufficient for traffic balancing purposes. The load balancing at FIB-level needs to be enabled too, because in JUNOS it is not set by default for any routing process. To do this, the following additional configurations are required:

```
[edit policy-options policy-statement RP-name]
then {
load-balance per-packet;
}
[edit routing-options forwarding-table]
export RP-name;
```

Although the command is "**load-balance per-packet**", traffic balancing takes place "per session", based on parameters such as the source/target IP addresses, type of protocol transported, TCP or UCP source/destination ports, and more. For details, see Juniper documents.

As an easy example of multipath BGP application in a Juniper environment, let's consider router CE2 of our sample network in Figure 3.1 and prefix 203.0.113/24, advertised to AS 64501 by the two Upstream Providers and then propagated to router CE2 by the two PEs. Without enabling the multipath BGP, assuming that all BGP attributes are the default ones, and that the AS_PATH length is identical, CE2 chooses as best path the less recent advertisement, or, if the **"path-selection external-router-id"** command is enabled, based on the lowest BGP-ID. In our case, as shown in the following view, CE2 chooses as best path the advertisement received from PE1 (Next-Hop=10.1.11.5), which is input in the FIB.

```
aft@CE2> show route forwarding-table matching 203.0.113.0/24
. . .
Destination         Type  RtRef   Next hop   Type   Index   NhRef  Netif
203.0.113.0/24      user      0   10.1.11.5  ucst   604     19     ge-0/0/2.0
```

Let's now assume that the load balancing at FIB-level and the multipath BGP are enabled:

```
[edit policy-options policy-statement LB]
then {
  load-balance per-packet;
}

[edit routing-options forwarding-table]
export LB;

[edit protocols bgp group PE]
multipath;
```

Let's see the effect of this configuration on the FIB:

```
aft@CE2> show route forwarding-table matching 203.0.113.0/24
. . .
Destination        Type RtRef Next hop   Type    Index  NhRef Netif
203.0.113.0/24     user     0            ulst 1048575      17
                               10.1.12.1  ucst     603      4  ge-0/0/0.0
                               10.1.11.5  ucst     604      4  ge-0/0/2.0
```

The view shows that this time two Next-Hops are installed in the FIB, and then used in load balancing (how the load balancing is achieved lies outside the scope of this discussion).

7.2 OUTBOUND TRAFFIC MANAGEMENT

Outbound traffic management consists in determining the rules for an AS' outbound traffic. As we mentioned several times, BGP is a very flexible protocol for routing policy application, and, to this end, it provides the LOCAL_PREF (Local Preference) value, which we covered extensively in Section 2.4.4. Actually, in Cisco routers, another proprietary parameter (weight) can also be used, as we will see shortly. For the sake of completeness, let's summarize the main properties of the (standard) LOCAL_PREF attribute:

- The LOCAL_PREF (LP) value is assigned (based on the configuration or a default value) by the BGP Speakers that receive an eBGP advertisement. Both in Cisco and Juniper routers, the default value is 100. One important rule to follow is that, once the LP value has been assigned, it shouldn't be changed within the AS.

- This is the most powerful metric provided by BGP, meaning that it ranks first (except for proprietary parameters) in BGP's selection process.

- Once the value has been assigned, the LP is propagated only within the AS, and removed from AS outbound advertisements.

- The selection rule is the following: the advertisement with the highest LP bound value is favored.

By way of example, let's consider the usual sample network of Figure 3.1 and assume that AS 64501 wants to implement the following outbound traffic management policy:

- Forwarding traffic toward the local prefixes of the Upstream Providers (AS 65541 and 65542) via a direct link; if the direct link is out of order, using the other AS as transit.

- Forwarding traffic toward the prefixes of other ASes using AS 65542 as transit. If the link toward AS 65542 is out of service, using AS 65541 as transit.

To achieve this purpose, it is sufficient to assign the LP values as follows:

- On router GTW-1: for prefixes originated by AS 65541, assign LP=200, and LP=50 to all the others.

- On router GTW-2: for all prefixes, assign the default value LP=100.

NOTE: The values chosen are purely indicative. The important thing is observing the orders of magnitude.

Shortly, we will see how we can configure these attributions, on Cisco and Juniper routers, and how to assess the results obtained through an example.

7.2.1 Outbound traffic management in Cisco routers

In Cisco routers, outbound traffic can be managed, apart from the standard LOCAL_PREF attribute, also through the proprietary weight parameter. However, this parameter has the disadvantage of being local to the router, therefore it is not propagated within an AS, and its use is less flexible than the LOCAL_PREF attribute. For this reason, and due to the fact that it is proprietary, we do not recommend its use (therefore we will not cover it herein). Remember that in Cisco routers the BGP selection process ranks the weight parameter first, and only then the LOCAL_PREF attribute.

The LP can be assigned to an advertisement in two ways:

- via manual configuration: allows assigning a certain LP value to all the advertisements learned by all BGP Neighbors;

- selectively: through the use of route-maps (IOS XE) or routing policies (IOS XR).

As mentioned earlier, the default value is 100. This means that a router assigns an LP value (=100) in any case, both to the advertisements received on eBGP sessions and to the advertisements originated locally.

The attribution via manual configuration is done with the "**bgp default local-preference** *LP-value*" command within the BGP process, and is valid for all IOS types. Basically, it redefines the default value from 100 to an arbitrary value (min 1; max 2^{32}-1).

The selective attribution of the Local Preference via route-map or route-policy is a lot more flexible, since it allows acting selectively based on several kinds of conditions.

> **NOTE**: When using the route-maps or route-policies to assign the parameters, you should remember that they also work as filters, therefore all the advertisements that do not meet any condition are rejected.

On the other hand, attribution via route-map or routing policy is done through the following commands:

<u>IOS XE</u>
router(config)# **route-map** *name* **permit** [*sequence-number*]
router(config-route-map)# *conditions*
router(config-route-map)# **<u>set local-preference</u>** *LP-value*

<u>IOS XR</u>
RP/0/RP0/CPU0:router(config)# **route-policy** *RP-name*
RP/0/RP0/CPU0:router(config-rpl)# *conditions*
RP/0/RP0/CPU0:router(config-rpl)# **<u>set local-preference</u>** *LP-value*

Let's see the application of these commands through an example. Let's assume we want to achieve the outbound routing policy specified at the beginning of this paragraph. In order to do this, only the following configuration on router GTW-1 is necessary.

```
route-policy BACKUP
  if as-path in (ios-regex '^65541$') then
    set local-preference 200
  else
    set local-preference 50
  endif
end-policy
!
router bgp 64501
  address-family ipv4 unicast
  neighbor 172.20.1.1
    remote-as 65541
    address-family ipv4 unicast
      route-policy BACKUP in
```

No configuration needs to be done on router GTW-2, since the attribution of the default value LP=100 is sufficient.

In order to check if the configuration is correct, let's consider three prefixes: one local to AS 65541 (111.111/16), one local to AS 65542 (222.222/16) and the other taken from the Internet (192.0.2/24). Through the routing policy configured, router GTW-1 assigns value LP=200 to prefix 111.111/16, since it is local to AS 65541 (and so its AS_PATH is [65541]). Router GTW-2 assigns the default value LP=100 to the same prefix. As a consequence, all the outbound traffic from AS 64501 directed toward prefix 111.111/16 will transit on the link between GTW-1 and UP-1.

Prefixes 222.222/16 and 192.0.2/24 have the same LP attribution. GTW-1 will assign value 50 to both, since they are not local to AS 65541. While GTW-2 will assign the default value LP=100 to both. In this instance, all the outbound traffic from AS 64501 directed toward these two prefixes will transit on the link between GTW-2 and UP-2.

For all prefixes, if a link is out of service, the other one can be used, since routers GTW-1 and GTW-2 have two advertisements for each prefix.

As verification on our sample network, let's see which are the best paths for these three prefixes on router PE1.

```
RP/0/RP0/CPU0:PE1# show bgp

. . .

    Network            Next Hop        Metric   LocPrf   Weight   Path
*>i111.111.0.0/16     192.168.1.11         0      200        0   65541 i
*>i222.222.0.0/16     192.168.1.12         0      100        0   65542 i
*>i192.0.2.0/24       192.168.1.12         0      100        0   65542 64497 i
```

We will leave checking that the LP values match the configuration executed and whether the best paths have been determined correctly to you.

7.2.2 Outbound traffic management in Juniper routers

In Juniper routers, outbound traffic is managed only through the standard LOCAL_PREF attribute. The LP can be assigned to an advertisement in two ways:

- through the "**local-preference** *value*" command, directly at global, group or BGP Neighbor level;
- selectively, through the use of routing policies.

In the first case, since the LOCAL_PREF attribute is never propagated on the eBGP sessions, the command is effective only toward the iBGP Neighbor. Also, this does not affect the LP value of the advertisements already present in the RIB, but only that of the advertisements sent on iBGP sessions. To clarify this point, let's go over the simple example of Figure 7.4 below.

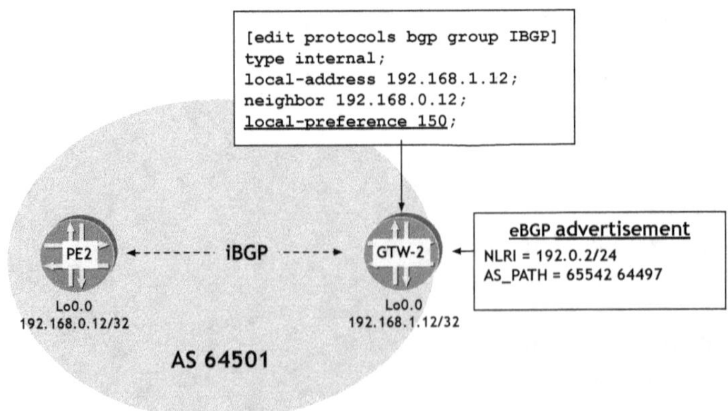

Figure 7.4 – LP attribution through the "**local-preference** *value*" command.

Router GTW-2 receives an eBGP advertisement of prefix 192.0.2/24 and it propagates it automatically on the iBGP session toward PE2. Due to the presence of the "**local-preference 150**" command within the iBGP group, the advertisement is propagated toward PE2 with LP=150:

```
aft@PE2> show route protocol bgp 192.0.2.0/24
. . .
192.0.2.0/24 *[BGP/170] 00:14:25, localpref 150,
                from 192.168.1.12 AS path: 65542 64497 I
                > to 172.16.1.12 via ge-0/0/1.0
```

In GTW-2's RIB, the advertisement remains with the default value LP (=100):

```
aft@GTW-2> show route protocol bgp 192.0.2.0/24
. . .
192.0.2.0/24 *[BGP/170] 00:29:38, localpref 100
                from 172.20.2.1 AS path: 65542 64497 I
                > to 172.20.2.1 via ge-0/0/0.0
```

Attribution through routing policies entails first the definition of a routing policy that assigns the LP value:

[edit policy-options policy-statement *RP-name*]
from {
  conditions;
}
then {
  local-preference *LP-value*;
}

and then its application as "**import/export**", at global, group or BGP Neighbor level directly.

As an application example, let's assume that we want to establish the same outbound routing policy as in the previous section, although on router GTW-2. In particular, the routing policy is the following:

- forwarding traffic toward the local prefixes of Upstream Provider AS 65542 through a direct link; if the direct link is out of order, using the other AS as transit;

- forwarding traffic toward the prefixes of other ASes using AS 65541 as transit. If the link toward AS 65541 is out of service, using AS 65542 as transit.

The required configuration on router GTW-2 is JUNOS' counterpart of the one we saw in the implementation example on Cisco routers.

```
[edit policy-options]
policy-statement SETLP-GTW2 {
term SETLP200 {
  from {
    protocol bgp;
    as-path LOC-AS65542;
  }
  then {
    local-preference 200;
  }
```

```
}
term SETLP50 {
  then {
    local-preference 50;
  }
}
as-path LOC-AS65542 65542;

[edit protocols bgp group EXT]
neighbor 172.20.2.1 {
  import SETLP-GTW2;
  peer-as 65542;
}
```

No configuration needs to be done on router GTW-1, since the attribution of the default value LP=100 is sufficient.

With this configuration, router GTW-2 assigns to all the BGP advertisements coming from AS 65542 the value LP=50, except for those originated locally in AS 65542, which are assigned value LP=200.

In order to assess if the configuration is correct, let's consider the same three prefixes of the previous section. Through the routing policy configured, router GTW-2 assigns value LP=200 to prefix 222.222/16, since it is local to AS 65542 (and so its AS_PATH is [65542]). Router GTW-1 assigns the default value LP=100 to the same prefix. As a consequence, all the outbound traffic from AS 64501 directed toward prefix 222.222/16 will transit on the link between GTW-2 and UP-2.

Prefixes 111.111/16 and 192.0.2/24 have the same LP attribution. GTW-2 will assign value 50 to both, since they are not local to AS 65542. While GTW-1 will assign the default value LP=100 to both. In this instance, all the outbound traffic from AS 64501 directed toward these two prefixes will transit on the link between GTW-1 and UP-1.

For all prefixes, if a link is out of service, the other one can be used, since routers GTW-1 and GTW-2 have two advertisements for each prefix.

7.3 INBOUND TRAFFIC MANAGEMENT

Inbound traffic management consists in determining the rules for an AS' inbound traffic. For this purpose, BGP provides the standard AS_PATH and MULTI_EXIT_DISC (MED) attributes. As we will see shortly, another elegant method is based on the COMMUNITY attribute.

The AS_PATH attribute allows managing the inbound traffic through the AS_PATH Prepending mechanisms, which we already mentioned at the end of Section 2.4.2.

The MED attribute, whose main properties were already covered in Section 2.4.7, can be considered within BGP as the equivalent of the IGP metric, although its use differs, since the MED does not have the same level of detail. For the sake of completeness, let's summarize its main features:

- The MED value is assigned based on the configuration, generally by BGP Speakers issuing an advertisement (and usually on eBGP sessions).

- A BGP Speaker that receives an advertisement with a certain MED value does not propagate the value outside the AS, but only within its own AS. If the advertisement is propagated to other ASes, the MED is removed by default.

- A BGP Speaker that receives an advertisement without the MED attribute, still assigns a value MED=0 (rule specified by RFC 4271 and followed both by Cisco and Juniper routers).

- By default, a router compares the MED values only in the advertisements coming from the same AS (this behavior can be varied, based on the configuration).

- It is one of BGP's "weak" metrics, meaning that, in the selection process, it comes after LOCAL_PREF, AS_PATH and ORIGIN, importance-wise.

- The selection rule is the following: the advertisement with the lowest MED value is favoured.

A very important aspect to notice is that an inbound traffic management policy affects the outbound traffic management policies of other ASes. Since an essential rule of BGP is that an AS cannot affect the traffic management policies of another AS, each AS must have stronger metrics available to determine its own traffic management policies. This explains why the LOCAL_PREF attribute ranks first in the standard selection process. Indeed, through this attribute, an AS can manage its outbound policies, regardless of any forcing that any other AS can impose through inbound policies.

7.3.1 Management criteria

As an example of inbound traffic management policy, let's consider Figure 7.5 below and let's assume that AS 65500 wants to implement the following traffic management policy (which allows a load balancing by destination):

- All traffic toward prefix 192.0.2.0/25 should enter the AS 65500 through router CE1.

- All traffic toward prefix 192.0.2.128/25 should enter the AS 65500 through router CE2.

There are two methods to reach this purpose:

- Increasing in a fictitious way the length of the AS_PATH attribute of the advertisements sent by AS 65500 to AS 64499 (prepending AS_PATH).

- Associating suitable values of the MED attribute sent by AS 65500 to AS 64499.

For instance, with the first method, you just have to make sure that:

- Prefix 192.0.2.0/25 is advertised with a standard AS_PATH (with length 1) on the BGP session between CE1 and RA, while on the eBGP session between CE2 and RB, it is advertised with AS_PATH with length 2, for instance, by adding a fictitious AS value beyond value 65500 (generally, the value of its own AS is repeated, even though this is not mandatory).

- Vice versa, prefix 192.0.2.128/25 is advertised with standard AS_PATH on the eBGP session between CE2 and RB, while on the eBGP session between CE1 and RA, it is advertised with an AS_PATH with length 2.

With the second method, you just have to make sure that:

- Prefix 192.0.2.0/25 is advertised with a lower MED (e.g. MED=10) on the eBGP session between CE1 and RA, with respect to the advertisement on the eBGP session between CE2 and RB (e.g. MED=20).

- Vice versa, prefix 192.0.2.128/25 is advertised with a lower MED (e.g. MED=10) on the eBGP session between CE2 and RB, with respect to the advertisement on the eBGP session between CE1 and RA (e.g. MED=20).

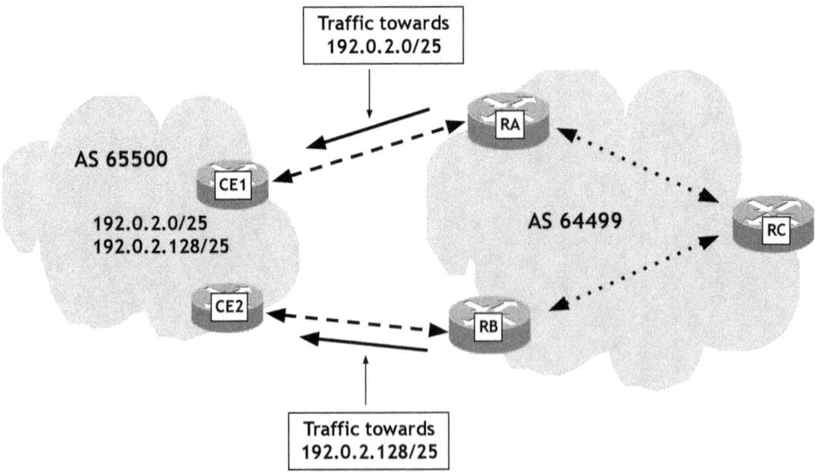

Figure 7.5 – Example of inbound routing policy.

Actually, there is a third method that requires a close agreement between ASes. Indeed, by prior agreement with the provider of another AS, it is also possible to use the COMMUNITY and LOCAL_PREF attributes jointly. That's because the traffic entry point in an AS depends on the traffic exit point of another AS, which, in turn, as we covered in the previous paragraph, can be manipulated through the LOCAL_PREF attribute. This method, shown in RFC 1998 – *An Application of the BGP Community Attribute in Multi-home Routing*, August 1996, represents one of the most interesting applications of the COMMUNITY attribute (see Section 7.3.4).

Shortly, we will see how we can configure these options, on Cisco and Juniper routers, and how to assess the results obtained through some examples.

7.3.2 Inbound traffic management via AS_PATH prepending

The basic idea of AS_PATH prepending exploits the rule of the BGP selection process, according to which, with the same LOCAL_PREF attribute (and the weight parameter in Cisco platforms), is selected as (possible) best path the advertisement with an AS_PATH with lower length.

When an advertisement is sent toward an eBGP Neighbor, it is possible to extend the AS_PATH length, via configuration, in a fictitious way, to show a longer AS_PATH to the routers of the other ASes. The AS_PATH can be extended both by the router sending the BGP advertisement (most frequent case), and by the router receiving it.

The rule followed by both manufacturers considered in this book is described in Figure 7.6 below. AS Y receives on router R1 an eBGP advertisement with AS_PATH=[X]. If router R1 was configured to add the string "X X" to the AS_PATH (AS_PATH prepending applied on entry), the resulting AS_PATH of the advertisement propagated on iBGP session toward R2 would become AS_PATH=[X X X]. The resulting AS_PATH consists of the (ordered) chain of the original AS_PATH (=[X]) and the string added by R1 (="X X"). If router R2 was configured to add the string "Y Y" to the AS_PATH (AS_PATH prepending applied on exit), the resulting AS_PATH of the advertisement propagated on the eBGP session toward an external AS would become AS_PATH=[Y Y Y X X X]. The resulting AS_PATH consisted of the (ordered) chain of the original AS_PATH (=[X X X]), of the string added by R2 (="Y Y") and of the AS to which the router that propagates the advertisement (="Y") belongs to.

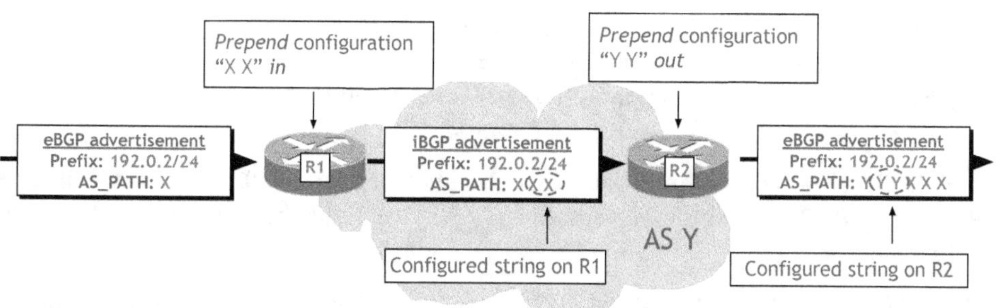

Figure 7.6 – Application of the AS_PATH prepending mechanism.

Usually, the AS_PATH prepending applies at the AS entry or exit point, it hardly applies to both cases at the same time. In Figure 7.6, it has been applied both at entry and at exit point, for the only educational purpose of showing how the AS_PATH changes in both cases. If, for instance, how is frequent in practical applications, only router R2 would have executed the AS_PATH prepending, the resulting AS_PATH would have been [Y Y Y X] with length 4 with respect to an AS_PATH=[Y X] without configuration of the AS_PATH prepending with length 2. Therefore, in this example, the

configuration of the AS_PATH prepending increases by two units the length of the AS_PATH.
As general rule, in AS_PATH prepending, it is possible to add any AS value, but we recommend using more copies of your own AS number, in order to prevent any possible issues due to the AS_PATH anti-loop properties.

NOTE: If, with the AS_PATH prepending, also filters based on the AS_PATH attribute are used (see Section 6.3), it would be best to remember that the string added to the AS_PATH is not considered by the filters, whether inbound or outbound. The Regular Expressions on which the filters are based, act on the AS_PATH of the advertisement received when the filter is applied to the inbound direction, or on the AS_PATH of the advertisement contained in the BGP table (for Cisco routers) or in the RIB (for Juniper routers), when the filter is applied to the outbound direction. In both cases, always before the application of the AS_PATH prepending mechanism.

In Cisco routers, the implementation of the AS_PATH prepending occurs via route-map in IOS XE and via routing policy in IOS XR and in JUNOS.

<u>IOS XE</u>
router(config)# **route-map** *name* **permit** *sequence-number*
router(config-route-map)# *conditions*
router(config-route-map)# <u>**set as-path prepend**</u> [*string* | **last-as** *number-of-times*]

The "**last-as** *number-of-times*" option allows repeating the first value in the AS_PATH list a certain number of times. It can be applied both to the AS_PATH prepending at entry and at exit, even if it finds its natural application at entry. For instance, let's take a BGP Speaker of AS 64503 which has three BGP sessions: two eBGPs, with AS 64502 and 64504 respectively, and an iBGP. Let's assume to apply the following configuration:

```
route-map SET-AS-PREP permit 10
  set as-path prepend last-as 2
!
router bgp 64503
  neighbor <IP-neighbor> remote-as 64502
  neighbor <IP-neighbor> route-map SET-AS-PREP in
  neighbor <IP-neighbor> remote-as 64503
  neighbor <IP-neighbor> update-source Loopback0
  neighbor <IP-neighbor> remote-as 64504
```

If the BGP Speaker receives from the eBGP Neighbor of AS 64502 an advertisement with AS_PATH = [64502 64501], the advertisement's AS_PATH of the propagated advertisement would become:

- AS_PATH=[**64502 64502** 64502 64501] in the case of advertisement propagated on the iBGP session, that is, a string (highlighted in bold) resulting from the repetition of two times the first value in the list of the AS_PATH received (="64502") would be added before the AS_PATH.

- AS_PATH=[64503 **64502 64502** 64502 64501] in the case of an advertisement propagated on the session toward the eBGP Neighbor of AS 64504, that is, as above, a string (highlighted in bold) resulting from the double repetition of the first value in the list of the AS_PATH received (="64502") would be added before the AS_PATH, and so, as per the classic propagation rule of the AS_PATH on the eBGP sessions, the AS number of the BGP Speaker (="64503") would be added.

<u>IOS XR</u>

RP/0/RP0/CPU0:router(config)# **route-policy** *RP-name*
RP/0/RP0/CPU0:router(config-rpl)# *conditions*
RP/0/RP0/CPU0:router(config-rpl)# <u>**prepend as-path**</u> {*AS* | **most-recent** } [*number-of-times*]

The "*AS number-of-times*" option allows repeating the AS number specified a certain number of times. For instance, the "**prepend as-path 64501 2**" option allows repeating the AS number 64501 twice. It is equivalent to the IOS XE "**set as-path prepend 64501 64501**" action. The "**most-recent** *number-of-times*" option allows repeating the first value in the AS_PATH list a certain number of times.

<u>JUNOS</u>
[edit policy-options policy-statement *RP-name*]
from {
  conditions;
}
then {
  as-path-prepend *string*;
}

Let's see the application of these commands through an example in our sample network. Let's assume that CE1 and CE2 advertise the following prefixes received internally on an iBGP session:

- CE1: 195.31.0.0/26 and 195.31.0.64/26;

- CE2: 195.31.0.128/26 and 195.31.0.192/26;

and that we want to implement a load balancing inbound routing policy, where:

- Inbound traffic on CE1 toward prefix 195.31.0.0/26 must first use the connection CE1↔PE1 and then the connection CE1↔PE2 as backup. Vice versa, traffic toward prefix 195.31.0.64/26 must first use the connection CE1↔PE2 and then the connection CE1↔PE1 as backup.

- Inbound traffic on CE2 toward prefix 195.31.0.128/26 must first use the connection CE2↔PE2 and then the connection CE2↔PE1 as backup. Vice versa, traffic toward prefix 195.31.0.192/26 must first use the connection CE2↔PE1 and then the connection CE2↔PE2 as backup.

Achieving such policy through the AS_PATH prepending is fairly easy: you just need to increase the length of the AS_PATH of the advertisements sent on the eBGP session established on the backup connection. The relevant configurations to execute are:

<u>CE1</u>
```
ip prefix-list CE1-0/26 permit 195.31.0.0/26
ip prefix-list CE1-64/26 permit 195.31.0.64/26
!
route-map SET-AS-PREP-CE1-0/26 permit 10
  match ip address prefix-list CE1-0/26
  set as-path prepend 65101
route-map SET-AS-PREP-CE1-0/26 permit 20
!
route-map SET-AS-PREP-CE1-64/26 permit 10
  match ip address prefix-list CE1-64/26
```

```
   set as-path prepend 65101
route-map SET-AS-PREP-CE1-64/26 permit 20
!
router bgp 65101
  neighbor 10.1.11.1 remote-as  64501
  neighbor 10.1.11.1 route-map  SET-AS-PREP-CE1-64/26 out
  neighbor 10.1.12.5 remote-as  64501
  neighbor 10.1.12.5 route-map  SET-AS-PREP-CE1-0/26 out
```

NOTE: The second empty line on the route-maps is essential. Without it, every prefix would be advertised on one session only, and so a possible session drop would lead to a traffic loss, since the BGP process of routers PE would have only one advertisement of each prefix, instead of two.

<u>CE2</u>
```
[edit policy-options]
policy-options{
  policy-statement ADV-195.31.0.128/26 {
    from {
      route-filter 195.31.0.128/26 exact;
    }
    then {
      as-path-prepend 65101;
      accept;
    }
  }
  policy-statement ADV-195.31.0.192/26 {
    from {
      route-filter 195.31.0.192/26 exact;
    }
    then {
      as-path-prepend 65101;
      accept;
    }
  }
}

[edit protocols bgp group PE]
peer-as 64501;
neighbor 10.1.12.1 {
    export ADV-195.31.0.192/26;
}
neighbor 10.1.11.5 {
    export ADV-195.31.0.128/26;
}
```

To check if our configurations are correct, let's see the paths toward the 4 prefixes advertised on the RIB of router GTW-1.

```
RP/0/0/CPU0:GTW-1#show route | i 195.31

. . .

B    195.31.0.0/26 [200/0] via 192.168.0.11, 00:06:16
B    195.31.0.64/26 [200/0] via 192.168.0.12, 00:06:16
B    195.31.0.128/26 [200/0] via 192.168.0.12, 01:07:04
B    195.31.0.192/26 [200/0] via 192.168.0.11, 01:26:41
```

We will leave checking if what we did corresponds exactly to our original objective to you.

7.3.3 Inbound traffic management via MED

The typical MED use scenario is the redundant connection between two ASes, described in Figure 7.5, to affect the choice of the traffic entry point in an AS.
A less trivial scenario is the one with more than one AS involved. For instance, let's consider the three ASes in Figure 7.7. Both ASes AS 64502 and 64503 advertise prefix 192.0.2/24 with the MED values specified in the figure.

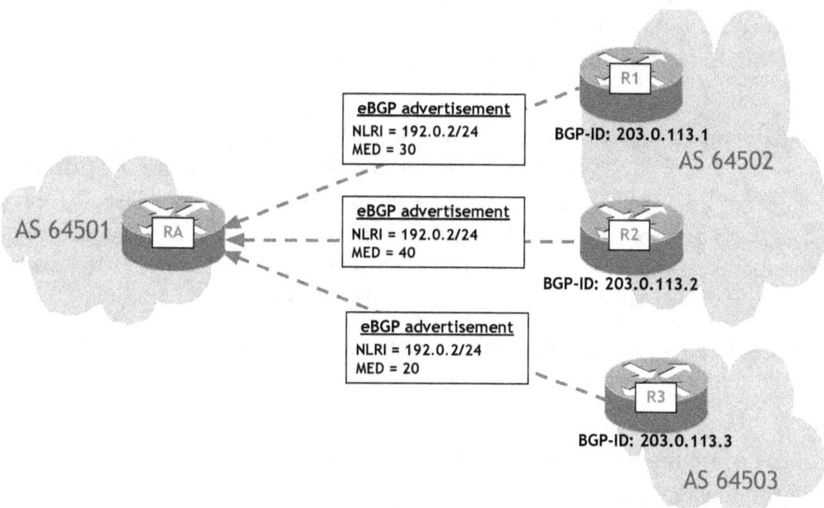

Figure 7.7 – MED use scenario with advertisements coming from different ASes.

If these two ASes, using the MED, wanted to influence AS 64501 to choose AS 64503 as transit for traffic toward prefix 192.0.2/24, they couldn't, because the MED is not taken into consideration by default, since the advertisements do not come from the same AS.
Following the standard selection process rules, with all BGP metrics being the same (Local Preference, AS_PATH length, etc.), the advertisement selected as best path is the one sent by R1 with the lowest BGP-ID.

In practice, there is a way to get around the obstacle, and that is, through a suitable configuration command, to make router RA of AS 64501 compare the MED even when the advertisements come from different ASes. The commands to execute in the platforms considered in this book are the following:

IOS XE
router(config)# **router bgp** *AS-number*
router(config-router)# **bgp always-compare-med**

IOS XR
RP/0/RP0/CPU0:router(config)# **router bgp** *AS-number*
RP/0/RP0/CPU0:router(config-bgp)# **bgp bestpath med always**

JUNOS
[edit protocols bgp]
path-selection always-compare-med

In any case, this requires coordination between the two ASes 64502 and 64503 in defining the MED values – very unlikely in production networks.

One possible practical application is in case of a multisite customer connected to the network of an ISP. For instance, in Figure 7.7, let's assume that ASes 64502 and 64503 are two sites of a same customer connected to the ISP with AS 64501; by allowing the routers of AS 64501 to always compare the MED, the customer is allowed to divide the inbound traffic as desired between its own sites.

NOTE: In Cisco platforms with IOS XE, the choice of the best path in the case of comparison of MED coming from different ASes (such as the example in Figure 7.7) depends on the advertisement arrival order. Since this could generate a bit of confusion, Cisco has provided the BGP process "**bgp deterministic-med**" command, allowing choosing the best path regardless of the advertisements' arrival order. This command is included by default in Cisco platforms with IOS XR and in JUNOS. More details on this in Appendix A.6.

In Cisco routers, MED values are defined via route-map in the IOS XE, and via routing policies in IOS XR, while Juniper platforms with JUNOS use routing policies.

IOS XE
router(config)# **route-map** *name* **permit** *sequence-number*
router(config-route-map)# *conditions*
router(config-route-map)# **set metric** *MED-value*

IOS XR
RP/0/RP0/CPU0:router(config)# **route-policy** *RP-name*
RP/0/RP0/CPU0:router(config-rpl)# *conditions*
RP/0/RP0/CPU0:router(config-rpl)# **set med** {[+ | -] *MED-value* | **igp-cost** | **max-reachable**}

In IOS XR, apart from the option of specifying a MED value directly via the "**set med** *MED-value*" command, there are also some possible actions available:

- The "+ *MED-value*" and "- *MED-value*" options allow to increase or decrease the MED in the BGP table by the "*MED-value*", respectively. When it is decreased, if the final MED value is negative, then MED=0.

- The "**igp-cost**" option is used to copy the total IGP cost value toward the BGP Next-Hop in the MED field of the outbound advertisement. Every time the latter varies, a new

BGP UPDATE message with MED value equal to the new total IGP cost is sent. The logic behind this option is to let traffic enter into the AS in the "closest" point to the destination (according to the IGP cost).

- The "**max-reachable**" option allows assigning to the MED the maximum value possible, equal to $2^{32}-1$ (=4,294,967,295).

NOTE: Some of these options are present also in the most recent versions of IOS and IOS XE.

<u>JUNOS</u>
[edit policy-options policy-statement *RP-name*]
from {
  conditions;
}
then {
  metric {*value* | **add** *MED-value* | **subtract** *MED-value* | **igp** [*offset*] | **minimum-igp** [*offset*]};
}

The "**add** *MED-value*" ("**subtract** *MED-value*") option allows adding (or removing) a quantity equal to the configuration value to/from the current MED (the MED present in the RIB). The "**igp** [*offset*]" and "**minimum-igp** [*offset*]" options allow correlating the IGP metric with the MED value. The "**igp**" option is used to copy the total IGP cost value toward the BGP Next-Hop in the MED field of the outbound advertisement. Every time the latter varies, a new BGP UPDATE message with MED field equal to the new total IGP cost is sent. Adding the optional "offset" value allows increasing (positive offset) or decreasing (negative offset) the offset value MED. The "**minimum-igp**" option has a similar logic, with the difference that the BGP UPDATE message is sent again only in case of a total IGP cost decrease The logic behind these options is to let traffic into the AS in the closest point to the destination (according to the IGP cost).

NOTE: JUNOS provides also the option of assigning the MED on a session-base, through the "**metric-out** {*MED-value* | **igp** [*offset*] | **minimum-igp** [*offset*]}" command, which can be executed directly at global, group or BGP Neighbor level.

Now, let's see how to apply these commands to implement this inbound routing policy of Section 7.3.2 above, using the MED instead of the AS_PATH prepending. Here too, creating a similar policy using the MED is fairly easy: by using the fact that the default value assigned to the MED on inbound eBGP advertisements is MED=0, it is sufficient to define a value MED>0 (e.g. MED=10) for the advertisements sent on the eBGP session established on the backup connection. The relevant configurations to execute are:

<u>CE1</u>
```
ip prefix-list CE1-0/26 permit 195.31.0.0/26
ip prefix-list CE1-64/26 permit 195.31.0.64/26
!
route-map SET-MED-CE1-0/26 permit 10
  match ip address prefix-list CE1-0/26
  set metric 10
route-map SET-MED-CE1-0/26 permit 20
!
route-map SET-MED-CE1-64/26 permit 10
  match ip address prefix-list CE1-64/26
```

```
    set metric 10
route-map SET-MED-CE1-64/26 permit 20
!
router bgp 65101
  neighbor 10.1.11.1 remote-as 64501
  neighbor 10.1.11.1 route-map SET-MED-CE1-64/26 out
  neighbor 10.1.12.5 remote-as 64501
  neighbor 10.1.12.5 route-map SET-MED-CE1-0/26 out
```

<u>CE2</u>

```
[edit policy-options]
policy-statement ADV-195.31.0.128/26 {
  from {
    route-filter 195.31.0.128/26 exact;
  }
  then {
    metric 10;
    accept;
  }
}
policy-statement ADV-195.31.0.192/26 {
  from {
    route-filter 195.31.0.192/26 exact;
  }
  then {
    metric 10;
    accept;
  }
}

[edit protocols bgp group PE]
peer-as 64501;
neighbor 10.1.12.1 {
  export ADV-195.31.0.192/26;
}
neighbor 10.1.11.5 {
  export ADV-195.31.0.128/26;
}
```

NOTE: JUNOS does not add the MED attribute to UPDATE messages, unless explicitly configured to do so. For instance, the advertisement of prefix 195.31.0.128/26 on the session between CE2 and PE2 does not contain the MED attribute, since it is not explicitly configured. In any case, JUNOS assumes MED=0 when it receives an advertisement without the MED attribute. In Cisco platforms, the MED attribute is always added, even when not explicitly configured. For instance, when CE1 advertises prefix 195.31.0.0/26 to PE1, even if route-map "SET-MED-CE1-64/26" does not explicitly assign any MED value, a MED attribute with MED=0 value is added in any case.

To check if our configurations are correct, let's see the paths toward the 4 prefixes advertised on the RIB of router GTW-1.

```
RP/0/0/CPU0:GTW-1#show bgp | i 195.31
. . .
B    195.31.0.0/26 [200/0] via 192.168.0.11, 01:21:02
B    195.31.0.64/26 [200/0] via 192.168.0.12, 01:21:02
B    195.31.0.128/26 [200/0] via 192.168.0.12, 00:28:54
B    195.31.0.192/26 [200/0] via 192.168.0.11, 00:48:32
```

As you can see, the result is exactly the same as the one obtained using the AS_PATH prepending.

7.3.4 Use of the COMMUNITY attribute

In Paragraph 6.4, we saw how the COMMUNITY attribute can be used to classify the advertisements and filter them accordingly.

Apart from filtering purposes, the COMMUNITY attribute can also be used to define the routing policies. The idea is simple, and it has been suggested for the first time in the aforementioned RFC 1998: an ISP defines the actions to be executed based on a Community value contained in the advertisements received. For instance, if an advertisement received contains the Community value 64501:150, the router would execute the action "Assign a Local Preference=150" and so on. Obviously, the customer must know the "Community value ↔ action performed by the ISP" correspondences in advance.

Now, let's see an interesting application of this method to manage inbound traffic. Starting from the obvious observation that the entry point in an AS can be determined by choosing the suitable exit point in another AS (subject to agreement between the ASes), it is possible, through an eBGP advertisement, communicating to another AS to assign a suitable Local Preference value to the advertisement. In this way, an AS has the option of choosing the entry point in its own AS, and asking the other AS to let the traffic out of its own AS through a suitable point. The tools to communicate the relevant LP attribution to an AS is the COMMUNITY attribute.

To better understand the entire mechanism, let's suppose we want to implement the same routing policy as in the two previous sections. Let's also suppose that the ISP adopts the following LP attribution policy:

- if an eBGP advertisement received contains the value of Community=64501:150, then it assigns the value LP = 150 to the advertisement;

- otherwise, it assigns the default value.

To implement the desired routing policy, it is sufficient to:

- On the eBGP session between CE1 and PE1, prefix 195.31.0.0/26 is advertised with Community=64501:150 and prefix 195.31.0.64/26 does not have Community=64501:150. Vice versa, on the eBGP session between CE1 and PE2, prefix 195.31.0.64/26 is advertised with Community=64501:150 and prefix 195.31.0.0/26 does not have Community=64501:150.

- On the eBGP session between CE2 and PE2, prefix 195.31.0.128/26 is advertised with Community=64501:150 and prefix 195.31.0.192/26 does not have Community=64501:150. Vice versa, on the eBGP session between CE2 and PE1, prefix 195.31.0.192/26 is advertised with Community=64501:150 and prefix 195.31.0.128/26 does not have Community=64501:150.

The relevant configurations that implement the desired inbound routing policy on the CEs are very similar to those we saw for the methods using the AS_PATH prepending and the MED. In addition, a routing policy must be added to the PE, which, when receiving advertisements containing Community value 64501:150, defines the Local Preference=150 value.

<u>CE1</u>
```
ip prefix-list CE1-0/26 permit 195.31.0.0/26
ip prefix-list CE1-64/26 permit 195.31.0.64/26
!
route-map SET-MED-CE1-0/26 permit 10
  match ip address prefix-list CE1-0/26
  set community 64501:150
route-map SET-MED-CE1-0/26 permit 20
!
route-map SET-MED-CE1-64/26 permit 10
  match ip address prefix-list CE1-64/26
  set community 64501:150
route-map SET-MED-CE1-64/26 permit 20
!
router bgp 65101
  neighbor 10.1.11.1 remote-as 64501
  neighbor 10.1.11.1 send-community
  neighbor 10.1.11.1 route-map SET-COMM-CE1-0/26 out
  neighbor 10.1.12.5 remote-as 64501
  neighbor 10.1.12.5 send-community
  neighbor 10.1.12.5 route-map SET-COMM-CE1-64/26 out
```

<u>CE2</u>
```
[edit policy-options]
policy-statement ADV-195.31.0.128/26 {
  from {
    route-filter 195.31.0.128/26 exact;
  }
  then {
    community add LP-150;
    accept;
  }
}
policy-statement ADV-195.31.0.192/26 {
  from {
    route-filter 195.31.0.192/26 exact;
  }
  then {
    community add LP-150;
    accept;
  }
}
community LP-150 members 64501:150;

[edit protocols bgp group PE]
peer-as 64501;
neighbor 10.1.12.1 {
  export ADV-195.31.0.128/26;
}
neighbor 10.1.11.5 {
  export ADV-195.31.0.192/26;
}
```

<u>PE1</u>
```
route-policy SETLP-150
  if community matches-any (64501:150) then
    set local-preference 150
  else
    pass
  endif
end-policy
!
router bgp 64501
  neighbor-group INTERNET-CUSTOMERS
    remote-as 65101
    address-family ipv4 unicast
    route-policy SETLP-150 in
  !
  neighbor 10.1.11.2
    use neighbor-group INTERNET-CUSTOMERS
  !
  neighbor 10.1.11.6
    use neighbor-group INTERNET-CUSTOMERS
```

<u>PE2</u>
```
[edit policy-options]
policy-statement SETLP-150 {
  from community LP-150;
  then {
    local-preference 150;
  }
}
community LP-150 members 64501:150;

[edit protocols bgp group CE]
peer-as 65101;
import SETLP-150;
neighbor 10.1.12.2;
neighbor 10.1.12.6;
```

Here too, to check if our configurations are correct, let's see the paths toward the 4 prefixes advertised on the RIB of router GTW-1.

```
RP/0/0/CPU0:GTW-1#show bgp | i 195.31
. . .
B    195.31.0.0/26 [200/0] via 192.168.0.11, 01:07:12
B    195.31.0.64/26 [200/0] via 192.168.0.12, 01:30:11
B    195.31.0.128/26 [200/0] via 192.168.0.12, 01:20:11
B    195.31.0.192/26 [200/0] via 192.168.0.11, 01:07:12
```

As you can see, the result is exactly the same as the one obtained using the AS_PATH prepending and the MED.

7.4 INTER-AS OPTIMAL ROUTING: THE AIGP ATTRIBUTE

Routing protocol rules do not always lead to optimal paths. We could mention several examples, both with OSPF and with IS-IS, where end-to-end paths are not optimal, bearing in mind the rules they use to determine optimal paths. The main reason behind this phenomenon may be the partition into areas, or the protocol redistribution mechanisms from external routing domains.

Even if it doesn't entail the partition into areas, BGP has its own partition concept, which is the AS. And, according to the rules that BGP follows to choose the optimal path, the phenomenon of non-optimal end-to-end paths can occur even with BGP.

In this paragraph, we want to describe how, by introducing a new BGP attribute, it is possible to solve the issue, when traffic source and destination belong to two different ASes, under a single administration.

7.4.1 The issue

There are many network situations that, despite being divided into different ASes, fall within the same administrative domain. This may occur because, by way of example:

- IGP does not scale, so there is the need of dividing the routing domain into separate and independent subdomains (an increasingly rare case, since single-area OSPF or IS-IS networks with hundreds if not thousands of routers are now in use).

- For historical reasons, an ISP manages two or more different ASes, whether because it has acquired another ISP and its network has not yet been merged into its own backbone IP, or perhaps because it has two networks on which it provides the same services to its customers (such as multiprovider L3VPN services).

- Different corporate units have an internal network, logically separated from the networks of other units.

- In L3VPN services based on the BGP/MPLS paradigm, BGP is used as CE-PE routing protocol, with CE belonging (as best practice) to a different AS than the provider's.

In such situations, it may be useful to allow BGP to make its own decisions, based on the IGP metric, so that it chooses the shortest end-to-end path between two routers, even if the routers are in two different ASes.

The example of Figure 7.8 below shows this basic issue.

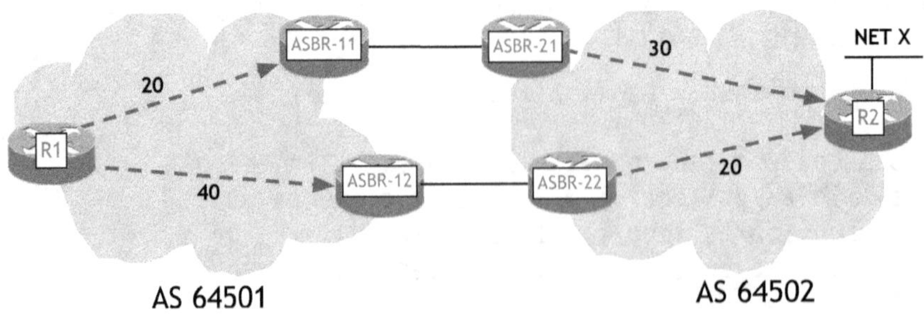

Figure 7.8 – Example of inter-AS optimal path.

The figure shows two ASes interconnected to one another via two pairs of ASBRs (Autonomous System Boundary Router). Two eBGP sessions are established between these two pairs. On both eBGP sessions, the two ASBRs of AS 64502 advertise IP prefix "NET X" to the two ASBRs of AS 64501. Internal reachability between the routers of an AS and the ASBRs of the same AS, is guaranteed by an IGP (OSPF or IS-IS, indifferently).

The figure also shows the optimal IGP costs (i.e. lowest ones) between the generic router of an AS and the ASBRs. For instance, the lowest IGP costs between router R1 of AS 64501 and the ASBRs of the same AS 64501 (ASBR-11 and ASBR-12) are 20 and 40, respectively. In the same way, the lowest IGP costs between the ASBRs of AS 64502 (ASBR-21 and ASBR-22) and router R2 of AS 64502 are 30 and 20, respectively.

The goal is making traffic originating from router R1 and directed toward a host of IP prefix "NET X" follow the lowest-cost path, that is:

R1→ASBR-11→ASBR-21→R2→NET X.

The first solution that comes to mind is using the MED attribute, whose operation resembles an IGP metric. However, the MED does not solve the issue. Let's see why. In order to represent to AS 64501 the "IGP distance" between the ASBRs and router R2, let's assume that ASBR-21 advertises prefix "NET X" with MED=30, that is, equal to the IGP distance between ASBR-21 and R2. And that ASBR-22 does the same, as shown in Figure 7.9 below.

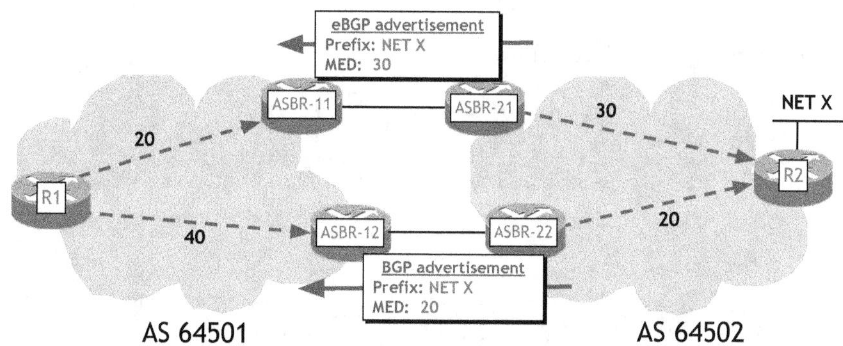

Figure 7.9 – Using the MED to determine an optimal inter-AS path.

Now, as we know, the MED does not vary within AS 64501, so R1 will receive one or two advertisements of prefix "NET X" based on the presence/absence of an iBGP session between ASBR-11 and ASBR-12. In any case, following the MED-based optimal path selection rule, with the same "stronger" metrics within the BGP selection process, R1 will choose as optimal BGP Next-Hop ASBR-12, that is, the wrong ASBR!

It is clear right away that the issue stems from the fact that the MED is not updated with IGP metrics by AS 64501, therefore the only way for R1 to determine the optimal path is to rely on the lowest MED value.

The issue is well known, and it has been brilliantly solved in other routing protocols. To solve this issue, BGP has introduced the new AIGP attribute.

7.4.2 The AIGP attribute

To solve the issue described in the previous section, RFC 7311 – *The Accumulated IGP Metric Attribute for BGP*, August 2014, introduced a new BGP attribute called Accumulated IGP (AIGP), whose purpose is to save the IGP metrics when advertisements are propagated within an AS.

Equally as the MED attribute, the AIGP is an Optional Non Transitive attribute, and it specifies a "cumulated" metric. We better explain what this means through our example. The idea behind it is simple: at every passage, the attribute takes into account the total cost from the BGP Speaker receiving the advertisement to the BGP Next-Hop.

For instance, let's assume to have enabled the use of AIGP in all BGP Speakers of the network in Figure 7.8. Moreover, let's assume that there are iBGP sessions between routers R1 and R2 and the respective ASBRs, supposing for both ASes the use of MPLS (which makes BGP's presence in internal routers useless). R2 advertises prefix "NET X" to its own ASBR-21 and ASBR-22 with attribute AIGP=0, since "NET X" is directly connected to R2 (notice that if prefix "NET X" had been learned from an IGP routing protocol and redistributed in BGP, it would have had AIGP=MED=total IGP cost present in the RIB).

The two ASBRs that receive this advertisement (ASBR-21 and ASBR-22) will propagate automatically (or with the help of routing policies, as in Cisco IOS XR) to respective ASBRs of AS 64501 the advertisement with attribute AIGP=30 (=IGP cost between ASBR-21 and BGP Next Hop R2) and AIGP=20 (=IGP cost between ASBR-22 and BGP Next Hop R2). Router R1, which receives the two advertisements, will add to the cost value contained in the AIGP attribute, its own IGP cost toward the respective BGP Next Hop (=20 for ASBR-11 and =40 for ASBR-12). The total AIGP value determined by R1 is:

- 30+20=50 for BGP Next Hop ASBR-11;

- 20+40=60 for BGP Next Hop ASBR-12.

This is summarized in Figure 7.10 below.

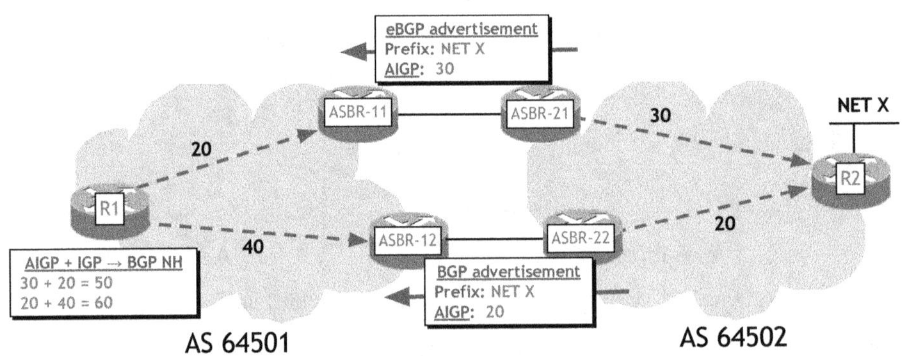

Figure 7.10 – Determination of the AIGP attribute value.

The deed is done: if router R1 chooses based on the AIGP attribute value, with all the "stronger" metrics of the BGP selection process being the same, it would choose as optimal path the lowest-cost path, namely R1→ASBR-11→ASBR-21→R2, which is the desired optimal path.

There is just one tiny, non-negligible detail missing: in BGP standard selection process, the AIGP attribute is not included. What now? Now it's time to go over some theory, and then we will switch to the practical implementations.

NOTE: If you are familiar with the OSPF protocol, you may have noticed an analogy between the way prefixes external to the domain are redistributed in OSPF and the use of the AIGP attribute. The analogy is the following:

- the use of MED only is equivalent to a type E2 redistribution;

- the use of the AIGP attribute is equivalent to a type E1 redistribution.

In conclusion, the introduction of the AIGP attribute allows expanding OSPF's concepts of E1/E2 type redistribution to BGP.

7.4.3 A bit of theory

After seeing how the AIGP attribute works and how it is updated, we will now see three theoretical aspects:

- the attribute's format;

- its role in BGP selection process;

- the AIGP attribute's creation and modification.

Remember that every BGP attribute is identified by the Attribute Type field (see the introduction in Paragraph 2.4), which is 26 for the AIGP attribute. For the AIGP attribute, the Attribute Value field comprises a series of TLV (Type-Length-Value) modules. RFC 7311 defined only one TLV module with Type=1, Length=11 (byte), Value=value of the AIGP attribute (8 byte). The 8 byte length is due to the fact that many IGP metrics are 4 byte long, and, with 8 byte, you can add a sufficient number of them for practical purposes.

The AIGP attribute complete format is shown in Figure 7.11 below.

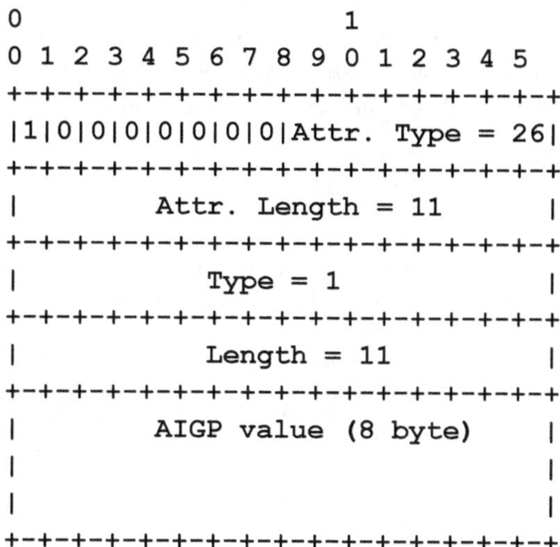

Figure 7.11 – AIGP attribute format.

Let's now switch to the second aspect: how is AIGP's value evaluated in the BGP selection process? In order for it to be useful, it should be a sufficiently strong metric, and not weak as the MED. RFC 7311 establishes that the AIGP value should be evaluated immediately after the Local Preference (which remains the strongest metric), and before the AS_PATH length. And, just like for the MED, the lowest value wins. In conclusion, the standard selection process is adjusted as follows:

1. choose the advertisement with the highest Local Preference value;

2. choose the advertisement with the lowest AIGP value;

3. choose the advertisement with the lowest AS_PATH length.

... < rest of the process remains the same > ...

Lastly, who creates and updates the AIGP attribute? According to RFC 7311, the AIGP attribute can only be added to those advertisements that meet at least one of the following conditions:

- the advertisements is the result of the redistribution in BGP of static routes with a Next Hop not pointing outside the set of ASes belonging to the same administrative domain;

- the advertisement is the result of the redistribution in BGP of any IGP (including directly connected networks);

- the advertisement has been learned from an iBGP session and has the AS_PATH attribute empty;

- the advertisement has been learned from an eBGP session and it has the AS_PATH attribute containing only ASes belonging to the same administrative domain as the BGP Speaker that receives the advertisement.

Moreover, a BGP Speaker shouldn't add the AIGP attribute if it doesn't use the BGP Next-Hop-Self (see Section 2.4.3).

The initial value of the AIGP attribute is usually defined through a routing policy, and is set according to the IGP cost value already present in the RIB (as is the case for MED). The AIGP attribute can be updated only by routers that support it. This implies that the AIGP attribute support configuration should be done on all BGP Speakers, otherwise, being a Non Transitive attribute, a BGP Speaker not enabled to support it, would remove the attribute when propagating the advertisements received.

7.4.4 Case Study

In order to understand how the AIGP attribute works up-close, we will refer to the network in Figure 7.12 below, comprising Cisco routers that support IOS XR.

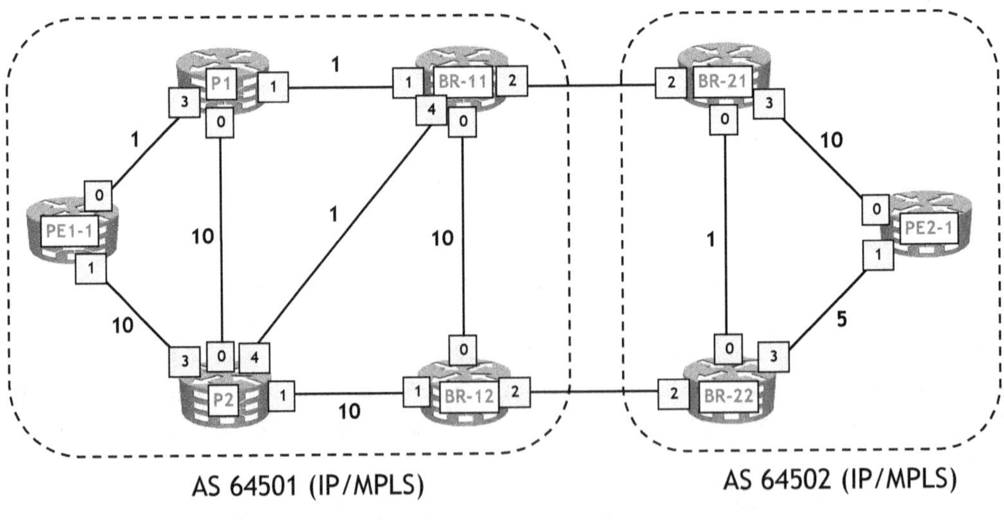

Figure 7.12 – Test network to verify the functioning of the AIGP attribute.

The network comprises the two ASes 64501 and 64502, belonging to the same administrative domain. The numbers associated to the different links are the (symmetrical) IGP metrics of the end interfaces. Router PE2-1, apart from the Loopback0 interface whose IP address is used for iBGP sessions, has a Loopback10 interface with IP address 203.0.113.1/32 configured, which is used as test network. LDP is enabled on all routers, except (obviously!) for the two links connecting the ASBRs (indicated with BR-xy in the figure, for the sake of brevity). On routers P1 and P2, BGP is not enabled.

The IP addresses of the Loopback0 interfaces are:

- Loopback0 BR-xy: 192.168.1.xy/32

- Loopback0 PEx-y: 192.168.0.xy/32

As you can notice in the figure, the optimal path from PE1-1 toward prefix 203.0.113.1/32 is:

PE1-1→P1→BR-11→BR-21→BR-22→PE2-1

(notice that the interconnection link metrics between ASBRs are not taken into account).

First, let's see the configuration that allows originating the AIGP attribute on router PE2-1 (only relevant configurations are shown):

PE2-1
```
route-policy SET-AIGP
  set aigp-metric igp-cost
end-policy
!
router bgp 64502
  address-family ipv4 unicast
    network 203.0.113.1/32 route-policy SET-AIGP
  !
  neighbor-group ASBR
    remote-as 64502
    update-source Loopback0
    address-family ipv4 unicast
      aigp
!
  neighbor 192.168.1.21
    use neighbor-group ASBR
    description "SESSION TOWARD BR-21"
  !
  neighbor 192.168.1.22
    use neighbor-group ASBR
    description "SESSION TOWARD BR-22"
```

NOTE: In the routing policy, you can manually define a different AIGP value, just by entering the desired value instead of "**igp-cost**".

With this configuration, router PE2-1 sends to the two BGP peers BR-21 and BR-22 the advertisement of prefix 203.0.113.1/32 with the value of the AIGP attribute equal to the cost value of prefix 203.0.113.1/32 in the RIB.

Since 203.0.113.1/32 is a directly connected network, this value is 0:

```
RP/0/0/CPU0:PE2-1# show bgp ipv4 unicast 203.0.113.1/32
. . .
BGP routing table entry for 203.0.113.1/32
Versions:
  Process               bRIB/RIB   SendTblVer
  Speaker                  7           7
. . .
Paths: (1 available, best #1)
  Advertised to update-groups (with more than one peer):
    0.2
  Path #1: Received by speaker 0
  Advertised to update-groups (with more than one peer):
    0.2
  Local
    0.0.0.0 from 0.0.0.0 (192.168.0.21)
      Origin IGP, metric 0, localpref 100, weight 32768, aigp metric 0,
      valid, local, best, group-best
      Received Path ID 0, Local Path ID 0, version 7
      Total AIGP metric 0
```

On all other BGP Speakers within the network (all the routers except for P1 and P2), it is sufficient to enable support to the AIGP attribute through the following commands:

```
router bgp AS-number
  neighbor IP-neighbor
    address-family ipv4 unicast
      aigp
```

Let's see the value taken on by the AIGP attribute on router BR-21:

```
RP/0/0/CPU0:BR-21# show bgp ipv4 unicast 203.0.113.1/32
. . .
BGP routing table entry for 203.0.113.1/32
Versions:
  Process               bRIB/RIB   SendTblVer
  Speaker                  8           8
. . .
Paths: (1 available, best #1)
  Advertised to peers (in unique update groups):
    172.16.35.3
  Path #1: Received by speaker 0
  Advertised to peers (in unique update groups):
    172.16.35.3
  Local
    192.168.0.21 (metric 7) from 192.168.0.21 (192.168.0.21)
      Origin IGP, metric 0, localpref 100, aigp metric 0, valid, internal,
      best, group-best
      Received Path ID 0, Local Path ID 0, version 8
      Total AIGP metric 7
```

The value marked as "**aigp metric 0**" indicates the value of the AIGP attribute received, while the value marked as "**Total AIGP metric 7**" indicates the cumulative value of the AIGP attribute resulting from the sum: Value of the AIGP attribute received (=0) + total IGP cost toward the BGP Next-Hop (=7).

Lastly, let's see the value taken by the AIGP attribute on router PE1-1:

```
RP/0/0/CPU0:PE1-1# show bgp ipv4 unicast 203.0.113.1/32

. . .

BGP routing table entry for 203.0.113.1/32
Versions:
  Process           bRIB/RIB   SendTblVer
  Speaker               8          8
. . .
Paths: (2 available, best #1)
  Not advertised to any peer
  Path #1: Received by speaker 0
  Not advertised to any peer
  65002
    192.168.1.11 (metric 3) from 192.168.1.11 (192.168.1.11)
      Origin IGP, metric 7, localpref 100, aigp metric 7, valid, internal,
      best, group-best
      Received Path ID 0, Local Path ID 0, version 8
      Total AIGP metric 10
  Path #2: Received by speaker 0
  Not advertised to any peer
  65002
    192.168.1.12 (metric 13) from 192.168.1.12 (192.168.1.12)
      Origin IGP, metric 6, localpref 100, aigp metric 6, valid, internal
      Received Path ID 0, Local Path ID 0, version 0
      Total AIGP metric 19
```

Now, the AIGP attribute update mechanism should be clear, so we'll leave checking if the AIGP values are correct to you. We only want to point out that PE1-1 chooses the advertisement with BGP Next-Hop 192.168.1.11 – i.e. the IP address of the Loopback0 interface of BR-11 used as endpoint of the iBGP session with PE1-1 – as best path. In conclusion, IP traffic from router PE1-1 toward IP prefix 203.0.113.1/32 follows the desired path. As further test, we executed the following traceroute:

```
RP/0/0/CPU0:PE1-1# traceroute 203.0.113.1

. . .

Type escape sequence to abort.
Tracing the route to 203.0.113.1
  1  10.1.11.1 [MPLS: Label 24001 Exp 0] 19 msec  59 msec  0 msec
  2  172.16.13.3 0 msec  0 msec  19 msec
  3  172.16.35.5 9 msec  0 msec  0 msec
  4  172.16.56.6 [MPLS: Label 24000 Exp 0] 19 msec  19 msec  9 msec
  5  10.2.22.2 19 msec  *  9 msec
```

The IP addresses in the traceroute result are those of the following interfaces:

- 10.1.11.1→interface Gi0/0/0/3 of P1;

- 172.16.13.3→interface Gi0/0/0/1 of BR-11;

- 172.16.35.5→interface Gi0/0/0/2 of BR-21;

- 172.16.56.6→interface Gi0/0/0/0 of BR-22;

- 10.2.22.2→interface Gi0/0/0/1 of PE2-1.

NOTE: The configurations in Juniper platforms follow the same logic. At the time this book was released, JUNOS supports the AIGP attribute only for address family IPv4 labelled-unicast (AFI/SAFI=1/4) and IPv6 labelled-unicast (AFI/SAFI=2/4). If you are interested in exploring JUNOS commands to implement the AIGP support, you can consult the official documents on Juniper website.

To wrap up this section, here is the wireshark analysis of the UPDATE message sent by BR-11 to PE1-1, to advertise test prefix 203.0.113.1/32. Among all the attributes associated to the message, there is also the AIGP attribute (for the sake of brevity, the others will not be shown).

Border Gateway Protocol - UPDATE Message
  Marker: ffffffffffffffffffffffffffffffff
  Length: 76
  Type: UPDATE Message (2)
  Withdrawn Routes Length: 0
  Total Path Attribute Length: 48
  Path attributes
    Path Attribute - ORIGIN: IGP
    Path Attribute - AS_PATH: 64502
    Path Attribute - NEXT_HOP: 192.168.1.11
    Path Attribute - MULTI_EXIT_DISC: 7
    Path Attribute - LOCAL_PREF: 100
    Path Attribute - AIGP: 7
      Flags: 0x80, Optional, Non-transitive, Complete
      Type Code: AIGP (26)
      Length: 11
      AIGP Attribute: 7
        AIGP attribute type: Type AIGP TLV (1)
        AIGP TLV length: 11
        AIGP Accumulated IGP Metric: 7
  Network Layer Reachability Information (NLRI)
    203.0.113.1/32

We'll leave the detailed analysis of the outcome to you.

7.5 FINAL CASE STUDY

To conclude this chapter, we want to illustrate a Case Study based on our test network in Figure 3.1. Differently from all the other examples we've seen up to here, our Case Study will be entirely in IPv6 environment, so that you can realize that configuration differences are minimal, with a practical example. In the Case Study, we will also use the filtering techniques we explained in Chapter 6.

The IPv6 numbering plan is the following:

Loopback0 interfaces of routers PE and GTW:

- PE1=2001:db8:f100::11/128 - PE2=2001:db8:f100::12/128;

- GTW-1=2001:db8:f100:1::11/128 - GTW-2=2001:db8:f100:1::12/128

CE-PE links:

- CE1PE1=2001:db8:f001:1::2/127 (:2 PE side - :3 CE side);

- CE1PE2=2001:db8:f001:1::4/127 (:4 PE side - :5 CE side);

- CE2PE1=2001:db8:f002:2::4/127 (:4 PE side - :5 CE side);

- CE2PE2=2001:db8:f002:2::2/127 (:2 PE side - :3 CE side).

GTW-UP links:

- GTW-1UP-1=2001:db8:f200:1::2/127 (:2 GTW side; :3 UP side);

- GTW-2UP-2=2001:db8:f200:1::4/127 (:4 GTW side; :5 UP side).

Let's assume that AS 64501 has IPv6 prefix 2001:db8:f000::/36 available, assigned by a Regional Internet Registry, with which it provides IPv6 address blocks to its customers. AS 64501 assigns the following portion of the addressing space available to its two customers (Provider Aggregatable prefixes):

- CE1 (AS 65101): 2001:db8:f004::/48 and 2001:db8:f005::/48;

- CE2 (AS 65101): 2001:db8:f006::/48 and 2001:db8:f007::/48.

In addition, AS 64501 advertises only one IPv6 default route to its two customers, and the upstream providers both advertise an IPv6 default route to AS 64501.

7.5.1 Customer-side routing policies

As preliminary step, let's configure eBGP sessions PE↔CE and a complete mesh of iBGP sessions between PEs and GTWs. For the sake of brevity, we will only show the configurations of routers CE and PE.

CE1 (IOS XE)
```
router bgp 65101
  bgp router-id 10.1.99.11
  no bgp default ipv4-unicast
  neighbor 2001:db8:f001:1::2 remote-as 64501   ! EBGP-v6 SESSION WITH PE1
  neighbor 2001:db8:f001:1::4 remote-as 64501   ! EBGP-v6 SESSION WITH PE2
  !
  address-family ipv6
   neighbor 2001:db8:f001:1::2 activate
   neighbor 2001:db8:f001:1::4 activate
  exit-address-family
```

CE2 (JUNOS)
```
[edit routing-options]
router-id 10.1.99.12;
autonomous-system 65101;

[edit protocols bgp group PE-v6]
peer-as 64501;
neighbor 2001:db8:f002:2::4;   ! EBGP-v6 SESSION WITH PE1
neighbor 2001:db8:f002:2::2;   ! EBGP-v6 SESSION WITH PE2
```

PE1 (IOS XR)
```
router bgp 64501
  bgp router-id 192.168.0.11
  address-family ipv6 unicast
  !
  neighbor-group IBGP-v6
    remote-as 64501
    update-source Loopback0
    address-family ipv6 unicast
      next-hop-self
  !
  neighbor-group INTERNET-CUSTOMERS-v6
    remote-as 65101
    address-family ipv6 unicast
      route-policy ALL out
  !
  neighbor 2001:db8:f001:1::3   ! EBGP-v6 SESSION WITH CE1
    use neighbor-group INTERNET-CUSTOMERS-v6
    address-family ipv6 unicast
      route-policy FILTER-CE1 in
  !
  neighbor 2001:db8:f002:2::5   ! EBGP-v6 SESSION WITH CE2
```

```
    use neighbor-group INTERNET-CUSTOMERS-v6
    address-family ipv6 unicast
      route-policy FILTER-CE2 in
 !
  neighbor 2001:db8:f100:1::11 ! IBGP-v6 SESSION WITH GTW-1
    use neighbor-group IBGP-v6
  neighbor 2001:db8:f100:1::12 ! IBGP-v6 SESSION WITH GTW-2
    use neighbor-group IBGP-v6
  neighbor 2001:db8:f100::12   ! IBGP-v6 SESSION WITH PE2
    use neighbor-group IBGP-v6
```

<u>PE2</u> (JUNOS)

```
[edit protocols bgp]
group CE-v6 {
    family inet6 {
        unicast;
    }
    export ONLY-DR;
    peer-as 65101;
    neighbor 2001:db8:f002:2::3; # *** EBGP SESSION WITH CE2 ***
    neighbor 2001:db8:f001:1::5; # *** EBGP SESSION WITH CE1 ***
}
group IBGP-v6 {
    family inet6 {
      unicast;
}

    type internal;
    local-address 2001:db8:f100::12;
    export NHS;
    neighbor 2001:db8:f100::11;   # *** EBGP SESSION WITH PE2 ***
    neighbor 2001:db8:f100:1::11; # *** EBGP SESSION WITH GTW-1 ***
    neighbor 2001:db8:f100:1::12; # *** EBGP SESSION WITH GTW-2 ***
}
```

First, we will check that all BGP sessions are in the Established state. The check is done on routers PE1 and PE2.

<u>PE1</u> (IOS XR)

```
RP/0/0/CPU0:PE1#show bgp ipv6 unicast summary
. . . < output omitted > . . .
Neighbor  Spk      AS MsgRcvd  MsgSent TblVer  InQ OutQ  Up/Down St/PfxRcd
2001:db8:f001:1::3
            0   65101    1279     1171     21    0    0 00:14:43         0
2001:db8:f002:2::5
            0   65101    2537     2324     21    0    0 00:14:15         0
2001:db8:f100::12
            0   64501    2514     2310     21    0    0 00:13:24         0
2001:db8:f100:1::11
            0   64501    1157     1157     21    0    0 00:12:34         0
2001:db8:f100:1::12
            0   64501    2518     2310     21    0    0 00:13:25         0
```

<u>PE2</u> (JUNOS)
```
aft@PE2> show bgp summary
 . . . < output omitted > . . .
Peer                      AS    InPkt   OutPkt   OutQ  Flaps     Last Up/Dwn
State|#Active/Received/Accepted/Damped...
2001:db8:f001:1::5      65101    2535     2530      0      0  00:19:19 Establ
  inet6.0: 0/0/0/0
2001:db8:f002:2::3      65101    2549     2530      0      0  00:19:10 Establ
  inet6.0: 0/0/0/0
2001:db8:f100::11       64501    2319     2522      0      0  00:18:20 Establ
  inet6.0: 0/0/0/0
2001:db8:f100:1::11     64501    2319     2518      0      0  00:17:29 Establ
  inet6.0: 0/0/0/0
2001:db8:f100:1::12     64501    2530     2524      0      0  00:18:23 Establ
```

Let's assume to apply the following traffic filtering and management policies:

1. On CE1 and CE2, accepting from AS 64501 only the IPv6 default route and allowing only the advertisement of the two Provider Aggregatable prefixes assigned by AS 64501. On PE1 and PE2, allowing only the IPv6 default route to be sent to ASes 65101 and only the advertisements of the Provider Aggregatable prefixes to be received from ASes 65101.
2. Choosing as IPv6 default route for outbound traffic from CE1 the one sent by PE1 and for outbound traffic from CE2 the one sent by PE2.
3. Suppose that routers PE of AS 64501, when they receive advertisements from a CE with standard Community "64501:150", assigns Local Preference 150 to the advertisement. Use this information to ensure that:

    a. On CE1, traffic toward prefix 2001:db8:f004::/48 enters from PE1 and traffic toward prefix 2001:db8:f005::/48 from PE-2.

    b. On CE2, traffic toward prefix 2001:db8:f006::/48 enters from PE2 and traffic toward prefix 2001:db8:f007::/48 from PE1.

Below, the additional configurations executed on routers CE and PE, whose analysis we'll leave to you, as useful exercise.

<u>CE1</u> (IOS XE)
```
ipv6 prefix-list ONLY-DR seq 5 permit ::/0
ipv6 prefix-list IPv6-PA4 seq 5 permit 2001:db8:f004::/48
ipv6 prefix-list IPv6-PA5 seq 5 permit 2001:db8:f005::/48
!
route-map SET-COMM-CE1-PE1 permit 10
  match ipv6 address prefix-list IPv6-PA4
  set community 64501:150
route-map SET-COMM-CE1-PE1 permit 20
  match ipv6 address prefix-list IPv6-PA5
!
route-map SET-COMM-CE1-PE2 permit 10
  match ipv6 address prefix-list IPv6-PA5
  set community 64501:150
route-map SET-COMM-CE1-PE2 permit 20
  match ipv6 address prefix-list IPv6-PA4
```

```
!
route-map SET-LP permit 10
  match ipv6 address prefix-list ONLY-DR
  set local-preference 150
!
router bgp 65101
  address-family ipv6
    network 2001:db8:f004::/48
    network 2001:db8:f005::/48
    neighbor 2001:db8:f001:1::2 send-community
    neighbor 2001:db8:f001:1::2 route-map SET-LP in
    neighbor 2001:db8:f001:1::2 route-map SET-COMM-CE1-PE1 out
    neighbor 2001:db8:f001:1::4 send-community
    neighbor 2001:db8:f001:1::4 prefix-list ONLY-DR in
    neighbor 2001:db8:f001:1::4 route-map SET-COMM-CE1-PE2 out
  exit-address-family
```

<u>CE2</u> (JUNOS)

```
[edit policy-options]
policy-statement ONLY-DR-v6 {
  term DEFAULT-1 {
    from {
      neighbor 2001:db8:f002:2::2;
      route-filter ::/0 exact;
    }
    then {
      local-preference 150;
      accept;
    }
  }
  term DEFAULT-2 {
    from {
      neighbor 2001:db8:f002:2::4;
      route-filter ::/0 exact;
    }
    then accept;
  }
  term REJECT {
    then reject;
  }
}
policy-statement SET-COMM-CE2-PE1 {
  term SETCOMM-PA2 {
    from {
      rib inet6.0;
      route-filter 2001:db8:f007::/48 exact;
    }
    then {
      community set LP-150;
```

Chapter 7

```
      accept;
    }
  }
  term SETCOMM-PA1 {
    from {
      route-filter 2001:db8:f006::/48 exact;
    }
    then accept;
  }
  term REJECT {
    then reject;
  }
}
policy-statement SET-COMM-CE2-PE2 {
  term SETCOMM-PA1 {
    from {
      rib inet6.0;
      route-filter 2001:db8:f006::/48 exact;
    }
    then {
      community set LP-150;
      accept;
    }
  }
  term SETCOMM-PA2 {
    from {
      route-filter 2001:db8:f007::/48 exact;
    }
    then accept;
  }
  term REJECT {
    then reject;
  }
}
community LP-150 members 64501:150;

[edit protocols bgp]
group PE-v6 {
  import ONLY-DR-v6;
  peer-as 64501;
  neighbor 2001:db8:f002:2::4 {
    export SET-COMM-CE2-PE1;
  }
  neighbor 2001:db8:f002:2::2 {
    export SET-COMM-CE2-PE2;
  }
}
```

<u>PE1</u> (IOS XR)
```
prefix-set ONLY-PA-CE1
  2001:db8:f004::/48,
  2001:db8:f005::/48
end-set
!
prefix-set ONLY-PA-CE2
  2001:db8:f006::/48,
  2001:db8:f007::/48
end-set
!
route-policy ONLY-DR
  if destination in (::/0) then
    pass
  endif
end-policy
!
route-policy SETLP-150
  if community matches-any (64501:150) then
    set local-preference 150
  else
    pass
  endif
end-policy
!
route-policy FILTER-CE1
  if destination in ONLY-PA-CE1 then
    apply SETLP-150
  else
    drop
  endif
end-policy
!
route-policy FILTER-CE2
  if destination in ONLY-PA-CE2 then
    apply SETLP-150
  else
    drop
  endif
end-policy
!
router bgp 64501
  neighbor-group INTERNET-CUSTOMERS-v6
    remote-as 65101
    address-family ipv6 unicast
      route-policy ONLY-DR out
  !
```

```
 neighbor 2001:db8:f001:1::3
 use neighbor-group INTERNET-CUSTOMERS-v6
 address-family ipv6 unicast
   route-policy FILTER-CE1 in
 !
 neighbor 2001:db8:f002:2::5
   use neighbor-group INTERNET-CUSTOMERS-v6
   address-family ipv6 unicast
     route-policy FILTER-CE2 in
```

<u>PE2</u> (JUNOS)

```
[edit policy-options]
policy-statement ONLY-DR {
  term DR {
    from {
      rib inet6.0;
      route-filter ::/0 exact;
    }
    then accept;
  }
  term REJECT {
    then reject;
  }
}
policy-statement SETLP-150 {
  from community LP-150;
  then {
    local-preference 150;
  }
}
community LP-150 members 64501:150;

[edit protocols bgp]
group CE-v6 {
  import SETLP-150;
  export ONLY-DR;
}
```

In nominal conditions, without applying any filter, both CE1 and CE2 would receive, on the eBGP sessions with routers PE, apart from the advertisement of IPv6 default route, also all the IPv6 prefixes sent by the two Upstream Providers to routers GTW, and propagated from them through iBGP sessions to routers PE. Thanks to the filters applied, CE1 and CE2 receive – as planned – only the advertisements of the IPv6 default route, as shown by the following views:

```
CE1#show bgp ipv6 unicast
 . . . < output omitted > . . .
     Network              Next Hop           Metric  LocPrf  Weight  Path
 *>  ::/0                 2001:DB8:F001:1::1            150       0  64501 i
 *                        2001:DB8:F001:1::5                      0  64501 i
 *>  2001:DB8:F004::/48 ::                    0             32768  i
 *>  2001:DB8:F005::/48 ::                    0             32768  i
```

NOTE: The two IPv6 prefixes, apart the IPv6 default route, are those generated locally by CE1.

```
aft@CE2> show route table inet6.0 protocol bgp
. . . < output omitted > . . .
::/0               *[BGP/170] 1d 01:35:42, localpref 150
                      AS path: 64501 I, validation-state: unverified
                   >  to 2001:db8:f002:2::2 via ge-0/0/0.0
                    [BGP/170] 1d 01:34:11, localpref 100
                      AS path: 64501 I, validation-state: unverified
                   >  to 2001:db8:f002:2::4 via ge-0/0/2.0
```

Let's check on the RIBs of routers GTW if the BGP Next-Hop are the desired ones.

```
RP/0/0/CPU0:GTW-1#show bgp ipv6 unicast
. . . < output omitted > . . .
B    2001:db8:f004::/48 [200/0] via 2001:db8:f100::11, 2d17h
B    2001:db8:f005::/48 [200/0] via 2001:db8:f100::12, 2d17h
B    2001:db8:f006::/48 [200/0] via 2001:db8:f100::12, 2d17h
B    2001:db8:f007::/48 [200/0] via 2001:db8:f100::11, 2d17h
aft@GTW-2> show route table inet6.0 protocol bgp
. . . < output omitted > . . .
2001:db8:f004::/48 *[BGP/170] 1d 01:44:05, MED 0, localpref 150, from
2001:db8:f100::11
                        AS path: 65101 I, validation-state: unverified
                     >  to fe80::5226:ff:fe01:2 via ge-0/0/1.0
2001:db8:f005::/48 *[BGP/170] 1d 01:44:48, MED 0, localpref 150, from
2001:db8:f100::12
                        AS path: 65101 I, validation-state: unverified
                     >  to fe80::5226:ff:fe0c:3 via ge-0/0/1.0
2001:db8:f006::/48  *[BGP/170]   1d   01:44:48,   localpref   150,   from
2001:db8:f100::12
                        AS path: 65101 I, validation-state: unverified
                     >  to fe80::5226:ff:fe0c:3 via ge-0/0/1.0
2001:db8:f007::/48  *[BGP/170]   1d   01:44:05,   localpref   150,   from
2001:db8:f100::11
                        AS path: 65101 I, validation-state: unverified
                     >  to fe80::5226:ff:fe01:2 via ge-0/0/1.0
```

We will leave checking if the BGP Next-Hop are correct to you.

NOTE: While Cisco's RIB view shows the BGP Next-Hop, JUNOS' view shows the actual Next-Hop, downstream of the recursive lookup in the RIB. As per the IPv6 routing rule, the actual Next-Hop is the IPv6 link-local address of the Next-Hop interface (recognizable from the fact that it belongs to reserved IPv6 prefix fe80::/10).

To end this section, let's check the correct BGP Next-Hop choice for the IPv6 default route, for both CE1 and CE2.

```
CE1#show bgp ipv6 unicast ::/0
BGP routing table entry for ::/0, version 7
Paths: (2 available, best #1, table default)
  Flag: 0x100
  Not advertised to any peer
  Refresh Epoch 1
  64501
    2001:DB8:F001:1::2 (FE80::5226:FF:FE01:1) from 2001:DB8:F001:1::2
(192.168.0.11)
      Origin IGP, localpref 150, valid, external, best
      rx pathid: 0, tx pathid: 0x0

  . . .

  64501
    2001:DB8:F001:1::4 (FE80::5226:FF:FE0C:4) from 2001:DB8:F001:1::4
(192.168.0.12)
      Origin IGP, localpref 100, valid, external
      rx pathid: 0, tx pathid: 0

  . . .

aft@CE2> show route table inet6.0 ::/0 exact

. . .
::/0                *[BGP/170] 17:22:47, localpref 150
                      AS path: 64501 I, validation-state: unverified
                    >  to 2001:db8:f002:2::2 via ge-0/0/0.0
                     [BGP/170] 17:21:44, localpref 100
                      AS path: 64501 I, validation-state: unverified
                    >  to 2001:db8:f002:2::4 via ge-0/0/2.0
```

If CE1↔PE1 and CE2↔PE2 connections are out of service, as shown in the following views, thanks to the presence of the second advertisement, the BGP Next-Hop of the default route changes and becomes the backup route.

```
CE1#sh bgp ipv6 uni ::/0
BGP routing table entry for ::/0, version 8
Paths: (1 available, best #1, table default)
  Not advertised to any peer
  Refresh Epoch 1
  64501
    2001:DB8:F001:1::4 (FE80::5226:FF:FE0C:4) from 2001:DB8:F001:1::5
(192.168.0.12)
      Origin IGP, localpref 100, valid, external, best
      rx pathid: 0, tx pathid: 0x0

aft@CE2> show route table inet6.0 ::/0 exact

. . .
::/0                *[BGP/170] 17:33:10, localpref 100
                      AS path: 64501 I, validation-state: unverified
                    >  to 2001:db8:f002:2::4 via ge-0/0/2.0
```

7.5.2 Upstream Provider side aggregation and routing policies

Let's assume to apply the following Upstream Provider side traffic filtering and management policies:

1. On GTW-1 and GTW-2, advertising to ASes 65541 and 65542 only aggregate prefix 2001:db8:f000::/36, making sure that all the most specific components are suppressed.

2. Implementing the following routing policies for AS 64501:

   a. Only the local prefixes of AS 65541 and of its adjacent ASes are accepted by GTW-1. In the same way, only the local prefixes of AS 65542 and of its adjacent ASes are accepted by GTW-2.

   b. All IPv6 prefixes with mask length > 48 are rejected by both GTW routers.

   c. AS 64501 does not carry out transit traffic exchanged between ASes 65541 and 65542.

   d. Using GTW-1 to reach all local prefixes of AS 65541 and of its adjacent ASes. In the same way, using GTW-2 to reach all local prefixes of AS 65542 and of its adjacent ASes. For prefixes originated by ASes adjacent to both Upstream Providers, using transit on AS 65541 as first choice. For all other prefixes, choose the IPv6 default route advertised by AS 65542 as first choice.

The additional configurations for point 1 are the following:

<u>GTW-1</u> (IOS XR)
```
router bgp 64501
  address-family ipv6 unicast
    aggregate-address 2001:db8:f000::/36 summary-only
```

<u>GTW-2</u> (JUNOS)
```
[edit routing-options rib inet6.0 aggregate]
route 2001:db8:f000::/36 {
  as-path {
    atomic-aggregate;
  }
}

policy-statement IPv6-SUMMARY-ONLY {
  term AGGREGATE {
    from {
      protocol aggregate;
      rib inet6.0;
    }
    then accept;
  }
  term SUPPRESS {
    then reject;
  }
}

[edit protocols bgp group EXT-v6]
export IPv6-SUMMARY-ONLY;
```

Configurations for point 2 are a little bit more complex. As always, the key is defining inbound and outbound routing policies.

<u>GTW-1</u> (IOS XR)

```
route-policy FROM-AS65541
  if as-path in (ios-regex '^(65541_)+([0-9]+)?$') and destination in
  (::/0 le 48) and not destination in (::/0) then
    set local-preference 150
  elseif destination in (::/0) then
    set local-preference 50
  endif
end-policy
!
route-policy NO-TRANSIT
  if as-path is-local then
    pass
  endif
end-policy
!
router bgp 65541
  neighbor 2001:db8:f200:1::3  ! *** eBGP SESSION-v6 WITH UP-1 ***
    address-family ipv6 unicast
      route-policy FROM-AS65541 in
      route-policy NO-TRANSIT out
```

The NO-TRANSIT routing policy is necessary to avoid that the best paths that GTW-1 receives from GTW-2 are then propagated to AS 65541. Without this routing policy, AS 64501 could become transit for ASes 65541 and 65542.

<u>GTW-2</u> (JUNOS)

```
[edit policy-options]
policy-statement FROM-65542 {
  term ACCEPT {
    from {
      as-path AS-65542;
      route-filter ::/0 upto /48;
    }
    then accept;
  }
  term REJECT {
    then reject;
  }
}
as-path AS-65542 "65542+ .?";

[edit protocols bgp group EXT-v6]
import FROM-65542;
```

Let's now check that the operation of these routing policies is correct. First, let's check point 1, that is, if the two GTW routers only advertise aggregate prefix 200:db8:f000::/36.

```
RP/0/0/CPU0:GTW-1#show bgp ipv6 unicast neighbors
                                2001:db8:f200:1::3 advertised-routes
. . .

Network               Next Hop            From             AS Path
2001:db8:f000::/36    2001:db8:f200:1::2  Local Aggregate  64501 i


aft@GTW-2> show route table inet6.0 advertising-protocol bgp
                                            2001:db8:f200:1::5


inet6.0: 24 destinations, 26 routes (22 active, 0 holddown, 2 hidden)
  Prefix                  Nexthop           MED    Lclpref      AS path
* 2001:db8:f000::/36      Self                                  I
```

The check of point 1 also includes the check of point 2.c. Indeed, from these two views, we see that AS 64501 does not propagate the advertisements received from an Upstream Provider to the other Upstream Provider. And this is sufficient for AS 64501 not to become a transit for the traffic exchanged between the two Upstream Providers.

For points 2.a and 2.b, we should first check the characteristics of the advertisements received from the two Upstream Providers, before applying the inbound filters. To keep the discussion lighter, we won't do it here. We will just say that the two Upstream Providers advertise several IPv6 prefixes, some with a mask greater than /48 and others with a smaller mask, with variable AS_PATH length between 1 and 4.

Points 2.a and 2.b can be checked by verifying the advertisements received from the two Upstream Providers, downstream of the application of inbound filters.

```
RP/0/0/CPU0:GTW-1#show  bgp  ipv6  unicast  neighbors  2001:db8:f200:1::2
routes

. . .

   Network               Next Hop            Metric LocPrf Weight Path
*  ::/0                   2001:db8:f200:1::3            50      0 65541 i
*> 2001:db8:111::/48      2001:db8:f200:1::3      0   150      0 65541 i
*> 2001:db8:aa00::/40 2001:db8:f200:1::3         0   150      0 65541 64498 i


aft@GTW-2> show route table inet6.0 receive-protocol bgp
                                            2001:db8:f200:1::5

. . .

   Prefix                Nexthop             MED    Lclpref  AS path
*  ::/0                  2001:db8:f200:1::5                   65542 I
*  2001:db8:222::/48     2001:db8:f200:1::5   0               65542 I
   2001:db8:aa00::/40    2001:db8:f200:1::5   0               65542 64498 I
```

Lastly, for point 2.d, it is sufficient to check the RIB content.

```
RP/0/0/CPU0:GTW-1#show route ipv6 bgp
. . .
B*  ::/0 [200/0] via 2001:db8:f100:1::12, 02:11:11
B   2001:db8:111::/48 [20/0] via fe80::5226:ff:fe1c:3, 03:46:22,
                                               GigabitEthernet0/0/0/2
B   2001:db8:222::/48 [200/0] via 2001:db8:f100:1::12, 22:46:49
B   2001:db8:aa00::/40 [20/0] via fe80::5226:ff:fe1c:3, 03:46:22,
                                               GigabitEthernet0/0/0/2
. . . < local prefixes omitted > . .


aft@GTW-2> show route table inet6.0 protocol bgp
. . .
::/0                    *[BGP/170] 03:17:23, localpref 100
                          AS path: 65542 I, validation-state: unverified
                        > to 2001:db8:f200:1::5 via ge-0/0/2.0
2001:db8:111::/48  *[BGP/170] 03:50:32, MED 0, localpref 150, from
                                                   2001:db8:f100:1::11
                          AS path: 65541 I, validation-state: unverified
                        > to fe80::5226:ff:fe03:2 via ge-0/0/1.0
2001:db8:222::/48  *[BGP/170] 22:54:11, MED 0, localpref 100
                          AS path: 65542 I, validation-state: unverified
                        > to 2001:db8:f200:1::5 via ge-0/0/2.0
2001:db8:aa00::/40 *[BGP/170] 03:50:32, MED 0, localpref 150, from
                                                   2001:db8:f100:1::11
                          AS path: 65541 64498 I, validation-state: unverified
                        > to fe80::5226:ff:fe03:2 via ge-0/0/1.0
                         [BGP/170] 22:54:11, MED 0, localpref 100
                          AS path: 65542 64498 I, validation-state: unverified
                        > to 2001:db8:f200:1::5 via ge-0/0/2.0

. . . < local prefixes omitted > . .
```

From the views, we see that, as desired:

- The IPv6 default route used is the one advertised by AS 65542.

- The two prefixes 2001:db8:111::/48 and 2001:db8:222::/48, local to ASes 65541 and 65542 respectively, are reached through router GTW-1 first, and through router GTW-2 second (Note: addresses fe80::5226:ff:fe1c:3 and fe80::5226:ff:fe03:2 are the link-local addresses of the GigabitEthernet0/0/0/2 interfaces of router UP-1 and GigabitEthernet0/0/0/1 of router GTW-1).

- Prefix 2001:db8:aa00::/40, originated in AS 64498 adjacent to both ASes AS 65541 and 65542, is reached through router GTW-1.

This concludes our Case Study. For the sake of brevity, we omitted several details, which you can see yourself as useful exercise.

SUMMARY

This chapter is the most important one of the entire book. From a practical standpoint, routing policies are the most useful aspect of BGP. The chapter explains both the techniques used to manage outbound traffic (through the use of the standard BGP Local Preference attribute), and inbound traffic (through the MED attribute or the AS_PATH prepending mechanism). Furthermore, it showed how to use the BGP COMMUNITY attribute to define "standardized" routing policies. Just like for any technique and mechanism described herein, we also saw how these routing policies can be implemented and applied in Cisco platforms with IOS XE/XR and in Juniper platforms that adopt JUNOS. Lastly, we've introduced the AIGP attribute that can be used in specific cases, especially when different ASes fall within the same administrative domain. It shouldn't be used in an inter-provider environment.

Worth remembering:

1. How the standard selection process changes in Cisco IOS XE/XR and Juniper JUNOS implementations.

2. How to implement multipath BGP.

3. Use of the Local Preference attribute in managing outbound traffic and its configuration both in Cisco IOS XE/XR and in Juniper JUNOS.

4. Use of the AS_PATH prepending mechanism in managing inbound traffic and its configuration both in Cisco IOS XE/XR and in Juniper JUNOS.

5. Use of the MED attribute in managing inbound traffic and its configuration both in Cisco IOS XE/XR and in Juniper JUNOS.

6. Use of the COMMUNITY attribute to define standardized routing policies.

7. Use of the AIGP attribute to achieve optimal end-to-end inter-AS paths when ASes are managed within a single administration.

8 – BGP IN SERVICE PROVIDER NETWORKS

In the past, medium-big ISP networks based their internal routing architecture only on IGPs, and used BGP just for the interdomain routing protocol. The considerable growth of the number of customers that use IP services, and the consequent quantity of routing information, has highlighted the scalability limits of this model. The great quantity of routing information required for customer connectivity has increased so much that it can no longer be managed only via IGP.

Since the end of the 1990s, ISPs have begun to implement more scalable internal routing architectures on their IP networks, by using BGP alongside IGP, both with well-defined roles. Therefore, today BGP is used in the networks of big ISPs in three ways:

- as inter-domain routing protocol – BGP's "historical" use;

- as routing protocol for customer access – we will cover this extensively in the next Chapter 9;

- alongside an IGP protocol (usually OSPF or IS-IS), as an internal routing protocol to make the routing architecture more scalable.

However, despite the value of solving the scalability issue due to the large quantity of routing information to be processed, adding BGP to the internal routing architecture has also a downside, because of the additional complexity in managing the protocol by routers, and a few minor issues related to the different IGP protocols and BGP convergence speed. The experience gained on the field and the collaboration between the main device manufacturers and large ISPs have gradually helped to solve all scalability issues, insomuch so that the 'optimal' internal routing architecture for large public IP networks combines IGP and BGP, alongside scalability tools, such as Route Reflectors or BGP Confederations, and also the MPLS (Multi-Protocol Label Switching) standard. In this chapter, after a brief introduction of the main project issues of a large public IP network, we will go over the main aspects of the routing architecture pervasively adopted by large ISPs. We will also see some of the issues linked to the interconnection of ISP networks to their Upstream Providers, that is, ISPs that provide IP transit services that allow reaching all the hosts of the entire Internet.

8.1 PROLOGUE: ISP NETWORK ARCHITECTURE

The networks of ISPs or of large enterprise companies, just like all IP networks, are characterized by three essential elements:

- topology;

- numbering plan;

- routing architecture.

These are also the three aspects that guide design choices to create stable, scalable networks that can be easily expanded based on traffic needs. In this paragraph, we will focus on the first two topics, while the third one will be covered in Paragraph 8.2.

8.1.1 Topology: Access, Aggregation, Backbone

Creating a scalable, stable and easily expandable network topology follows the project guidelines that can be summarized in the next points:

- *Hierarchy*: this is the easiest way to create scalable networks. Hierarchy means the possibility of dividing the network into access and local switching areas, generally defined based on the geography and presence of an upper hierarchical tier, that "bonds" the different areas.

- *Modularity*: the project of a network needs to take into account any future development, so it should adopt an easily expandable network architecture. A modular topology minimizes expansion costs, makes traffic predictions easier, and increases the efficiency of troubleshooting.

- *Redundancy*: since (transmission or switching) network devices are subject to go out of service, it is best to design a network topology that takes into account multiple out of service occurrences. Therefore, a network should be sufficiently meshed so as to ensure physical connectivity between communication devices (routers), even in the case of a similar scenario. On the other hand, it should be noted that if the meshing is too thin, it is not convenient and it could cause slowdowns on the routing protocol convergence times (the greater the meshing, the greater the number of routes available, and thus the greater the time to determine the optimal paths).

- *Simplicity*: a simple project creates simpler and more standardized device configurations, a lower quantity of human errors in the network configuration phase, greater automation capacity and greater troubleshooting speed.

Medium-large IP networks often have hierarchical architectures based on three tiers:

- *Access level*: the level responsible for connectivity toward external customers. The access level can be on fixed or mobile networks, and is executed by specific nodes (e.g. Radio Base Stations, DSLAM, OLT for optic fiber access, etc.), which are often indicated as AN, Access Nodes.

- *Aggregation level (backhauling)*: an intermediate level used in large networks to reduce the complexity of interaction between the different access areas. Sometimes, in medium-sized networks, it corresponds to the transit level, leading in practice to a two-tier topology, rather than to a three-level one. In current networks, aggregation–level functions – except for legacy functions based on Frame Relay or ATM – are carried out by Ethernet multilayers switches that, based on the strategies adopted, can be used either as simple *Ethernet switches* or as layer-3 routers (IP), possibly with the addition of MPLS functions, bearing in mind that, in this case, the connection between routers is done through Ethernet technology, adopted as a simple layer-1 and 2 transport technology according to the OSI stack. This last solution is to be preferred, as it allows preventing all the issues related to the use of the Spanning Tree protocol – required in switched Ethernet networks to prevent dangerous forwarding loop issues (waste of bandwidth, non-optimal paths, etc.). Aggregation level nodes are often indicated as *Transport Nodes* (TN), basically because they carry out transport functions between the access network and the upper level (Core network). Aggregation level routers have two kinds of connection: uplink, toward the routers of the Core network, downlink toward the access level nodes. In the most common architectures, aggregation level routers/ switches have one or two uplink connections toward one or two routers of the transit level, and several downlink connections toward the access level nodes.

- *Core network*: a level with a dual function: activating the services requested by the customer (e.g. Virtual Private Networks, access to the IPv4/IPv6 Internet, circuit emulation. etc.), and interconnection between the aggregation levels. Customer services are activated in edge nodes with the aggregation network, and for this reason, the nodes are often indicated as Provider Edges (PE) or, in general, as Service Nodes (SN). Since the primary role of edge nodes is activating services, from a design standpoint, these nodes should be suitable to the quantity of services offered, and they should have a sufficient level of control plane scalability. The Core network includes pure transit nodes, often indicated as Providers (P) router or, in general, as TN. Since the primary role of transit nodes is to handle off large traffic volumes, from a design standpoint, they shouldn't execute any complex functions. Their configuration should be kept as simple as possible, by assigning only indispensable functions to the control plane, such as managing routing information and, only if the MPLS standard is implemented, managing MPLS labels and activating any explicit MPLS paths. The most complex functions are applied to this level, such as traffic routing policies to and from the customer, traffic control, Quality Service policies (e.g. traffic classification and/or coloring, scheduling, policing/shaping, etc.). The Core network has a primary role, therefore it should comprise suitable routers, with high-capacity and reliability transmission connections and a topology with a sufficient meshing to prevent network partitions, even in the case of multiple out of service occurrences.

Apart from those routers belonging to the three hierarchical levels described, ISP networks – and big ones in particular – can also have routers with specific functions, such as Route Reflection (see Paragraph 8.3), BGP neighborship toward Upstream Providers and other ISPs with simple peering agreements, shadow routers, that is, routers that detect the network performance measurements, etc. Based on their role, they should have suitable processing power. For instance, the Route Reflectors we covered in Paragraph 8.3 are often used only for BGP advertisement management work, and they do not handle traffic (or anyway they shouldn't, if the network has been correctly designed!), therefore even routers with a modest forwarding capacity are sufficient. On the other hand, these routers should have a lot of memory, since all BGP advertisements to and from the AS transit through them.

Figure 8.1 below summarizes the architecture based on the three hierarchical levels we've just described.

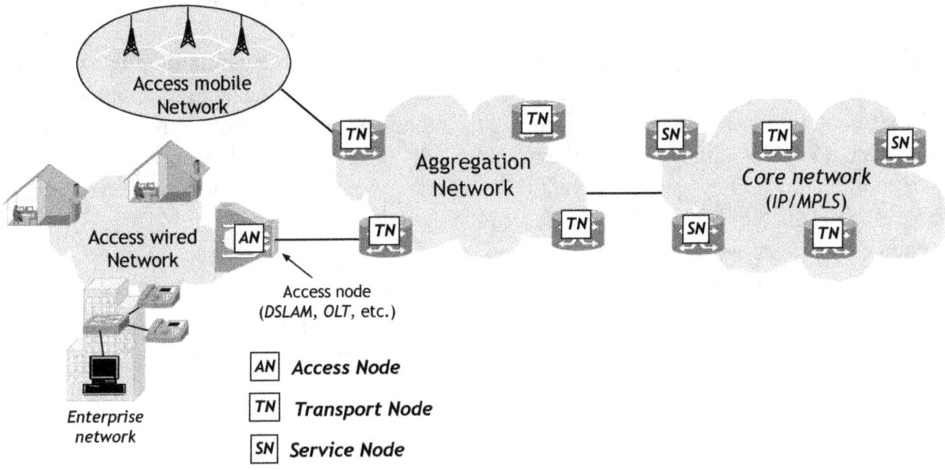

Figure 8.1 - Example of network architecture of a big ISP.

8.1.2 Numbering plan

Even if simple in appearance, the numbering plan project must be executed with care, by taking into account factors such as security, troubleshooting simplicity, and extendibility in case of significant network size growth.

The numbering plan of an ISP network should mainly deal with assigning IP (v4 or v6) addresses:

- To the Loopback interfaces of each router. Even if they are not indispensable from a theoretical standpoint, Loopback interfaces are very important in an "elegant" network project. They are mostly used as iBGP session ends, and possibly – based on the configuration choices – as identifiers in certain MPLS label distribution protocols.

- To the physical interfaces of the internal network infrastructures (e.g. LAN interfaces, point-to-point connections).

- For management purposes (e.g. *Telnet* applications, SSH).

For Loopback interfaces, /32 should be used in case of IPv4 routing, and /128 in case of IPv6 routing, while for physical interfaces we can use:

- For point-to-point connections, in case of IPv4 routing, /30 or /31 prefixes (if supported). In case of IPv6 routing, /127 prefixes (recommended) or /64 prefixes, for greater simplicity.

- For broadcast network segments (LAN), in the case of IPv4 routing, a prefix with subnet mask length based on the number of nodes, keeping into account any possible extensions. In case of IPv6 routing, /64 prefixes are generally used, for several reasons, which go beyond the scope of this text.

The first choice to be made, when defining a numbering plan on the backbone, is whether to allocate private or public addresses (prefixes of RFC 1918 for IPv4, unique-local prefixes, RFC 4193 – *Unique Local IPv6 Unicast Addresses*, October 2005, for IPv6). On this aspect there are several standpoints among the different ISPs, however many agree on the option of using private addresses, and there have been cases of migration from public to private numbering plans. The main reason behind the choice of using private addresses is the greater level of security, due to the fact that public routers are configured to not accept IP packets with private destination addresses (in IP Networking jargon, private addresses are non-routable on the Internet). This makes it virtually impossible for any hackers to take over a router and compromise the functions of the entire network. Actually, even by using public addresses, this possibility could be made virtually impossible: it would be sufficient not to propagate the block of addresses used for the numbering plan outside the AS, and add perimetral security mechanisms to prevent any packets destined to an address within the block to enter the network. However, this entails a higher configuration complexity; while, by using private addresses, many aspects are automatically solved by standard filters applied by the ISPs to public routers. They usually prevent BGP advertisements of non-routable prefixes, and filter all the traffic destined to private IP addresses on the data plane.

The choice of private addresses does not entail any operating issues, since, in a well-designed network, the routing inside the ISP network is kept completely isolated from the outside world. In other words, the routing process that regulates the determination of internal paths (usually OSPF or IS-IS, see Paragraph 8.2 below), doesn't need to have any adjacency to the routers outside the AS.

8.2 ROUTING ARCHITECTURE IN ISP NETWORKS

The basic idea for building a scalable network is to keep the IGP routing protocol to the lowest possible level of complexity. For instance, one thing that should be avoided is to inject a high number of prefixes into the IGP routing process, since this could easily lead to the saturation of internal resources, even in large routers. BGP is better for this purpose, since it has been designed to manage large volumes of IP prefixes.

Modern networks use Link State IGP protocols, and OSPF or IS-IS in particular. OSPF and IS-IS are protocols with similar characteristics, even if IS-IS is simpler and it has a few advantages in terms of scalability. However, this is not what drives the choice by an ISP; rather, what interests the most is usually the level of personal experience in configuring and troubleshooting the protocol.

The internal routing architecture of a large ISP network is based on a model that can be summarized as follows:

- IGP transports only internal network routing information (Loopback interface prefixes and IP prefixes used to number the internal infrastructure).

- A mesh of iBGP sessions between each PE router and all the other routers of the network (P and PE).

- A set of eBGP sessions to exchange routing information with customers or with other ISPs. On the customer side, other routing protocols can be used (e.g. OSPF, IS-IS, EIGRP, RIP), although today, the favorite protocol – especially in fault-tolerant settings – is BGP.

The iBGP session mesh is what makes this model weak. In large networks, the number of iBGP sessions could be too high and therefore difficult to manage. Calculating the right number of iBGP sessions required is easy to do. By indicating with N the total number of network routers, and with NP the number of P routers, the number of iBGP sessions is equal to:

$$\textit{Number of iBGP sessions} = [N \cdot (N\text{-}1) - NP \cdot (NP - 1)] / 2$$

where the subtracted item takes into account that iBGP sessions between P routers are not needed. For instance, a network with 200 PE routers and 72 P routers, requires $0.5*[272*(272–1) – 72*(72–1)] = 34{,}300$ iBGP sessions. In particular, for each PE router, 271 BGP Neighbors are configured. There are several solutions to drastically reduce the number of iBGP sessions. The most popular and used in production networks are the Route Reflection function (see Paragraph 8.3) and MPLS. The two solutions are not alternative, but rather they are used together to create an optimal routing architecture, on which all the most important network services are based.

8.2.1 Role of IGP and BGP

The routing model based on the use of IGP and BGP relies on a very simple rule:
Propagating external AS prefixes inside the network through BGP, rather than through a redistribution within IGP.

This simple rule clearly defines the role of the two protocols:

- BGP is used to propagate all the prefixes learned outside the AS within the network, including customer prefixes (both private and from small ISPs) and those communicated by other ISPs.

- IGP is used to create optimal paths within the network, and in particular between the interfaces whose IP address is used for iBGP sessions, which – as we mentioned often – should preferably be Loopback interfaces.

Now, let's see with an example the interaction between IGP and BGP within the network of an ISP, and how a packet is routed. Figure 8.2 below shows the propagation scheme for BGP advertisements and the optimal path determined by IGP.

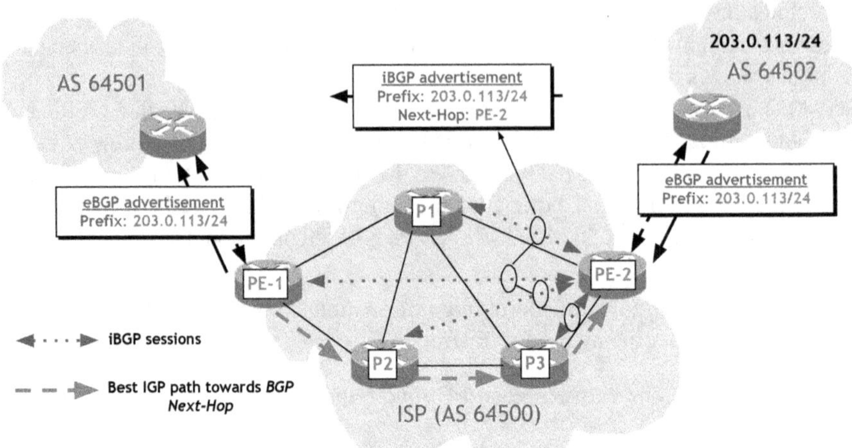

Figure 8.2 - BGP advertisement propagation and path toward the BGP Next-Hop.

The ISP (AS 64500) has two eBGP sessions toward a private customer (AS 64502) and toward another ISP (AS 64501). It receives from AS 64502, on router PE-2, an eBGP advertisement of prefix 203.0.113/24 that propagates to P routers P1, P2, P3 and PE-1 through the iBGP sessions between PE-2 and these routers. When propagating on iBGP sessions, as mentioned in Section 2.4.3, it is best to change the default management of the BGP NEXT_HOP attribute in the configuration, replacing the external BGP Next-Hop with the IP address used for the iBGP session (in the figure, it is used the router name, however, in practice, it should be the IP address of a Loopback interface).

In view of this propagation, PE-1 will install prefix 203.0.113/24 with Next-Hop PE-2 in its RIB.

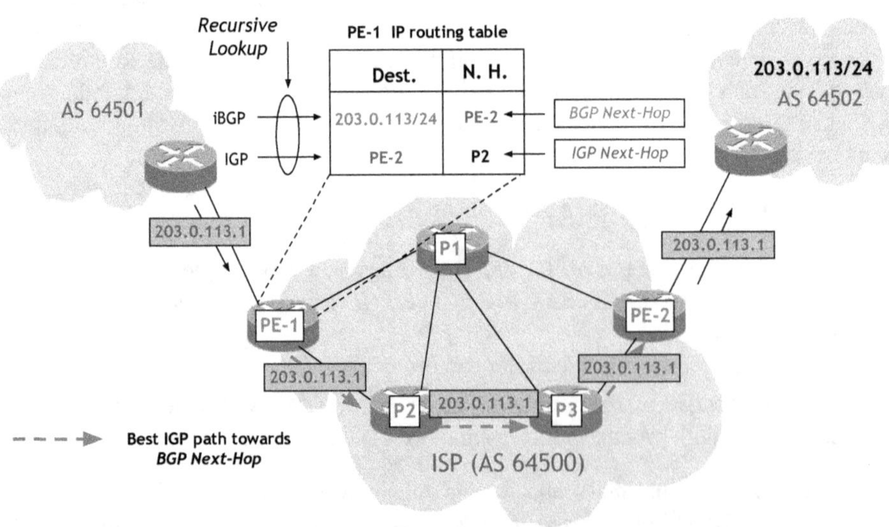

Figure 8.3 - Packet routing in the IGP+BGP routing architecture.

Since the Next-Hop PE-2 is contained within the iBGP advertisement, we will call this the BGP Next-Hop. Furthermore, IGP will allow installing the Next-Hop toward the BGP Next-Hop in the RIB of PE-1. We will call this the IGP Next-Hop. The advertisement is then propagated toward the ISP with AS=64501 through the eBGP session between ASes 64500 and 64501 (see Figure 8.3). Now let's assume that PE-1 receives from AS 64501 a packet directed toward the host 203.0.113.1, part of prefix 203.0.113/24. PE-1 carries out a first lookup on its RIB, from which it deduces that, in order to reach prefix 203.0.113/24 the Next-Hop is PE-2 (=BGP Next-Hop). Since the BGP Next-Hop is not directly connected, PE-1 must execute a second lookup on its RIB to find an (optimal) path toward the BGP Next-Hop PE-2. IGP has the task of finding the best path and route to reach PE-2; in this case, it consists in crossing P2 (IGP Next-Hop).

The IP packet is then sent to P2. P2 repeats exactly the same steps, by sending the packet to its IGP Next-Hop toward PE-2 (PE=3) and so on, until the packet reaches PE-2 When PE-2 receives the packet, it forwards it toward AS 64502, since it received the advertisement of prefix 203.0.113/24 from it, via eBGP.

NOTE: The double lookup executed on the RIB is indicated as a recursive lookup. Actually, the routers, to prevent the recursive lookup of each packet to be routed, determine the actual Next-Hop beforehand (=IGP Next-Hop). This information is then transferred through an internal (usually proprietary) protocol, to the Forwarding table (FIB). Then the routers use the information contained in the FIB to route the packets.

This routing architecture, although it requires two protocols instead of only IGP as in the past, has the advantage of keeping IGP's complexity down to a minimum. Indeed, its only purpose is propagating internally only the IP prefixes used for the numbering plan inside the network (Loopback interfaces, point-to-point connections and broadcast), with evident benefits in terms of memory consumption and, above all, greater convergence speed. An important rule to remember when designing the IGP implementation, is that, for security reasons, it should be completely isolated from the outside, that is, it shouldn't have any interaction with the routing protocols outside the AS. For this reason, default management of the NEXT_HOP attribute by BGP should be changed.

8.2.2 Reducing the number of iBGP sessions

As we mentioned earlier, one weakness of the routing model based on IGP and on BGP is the high number of iBGP sessions required. At BGP protocol level, there are two techniques that help to solve this issue:

- using the Route Reflection technique (see Paragraph 8.3);

- using a BGP Confederation (see Paragraph 8.4).

Big ISPs prefer to adopt the first solution, even if it entails adding further routers to the network (or even dedicated servers): the Route Reflectors (RR). Actually, the Route Reflection functions could be carried out also by some of the network routers, however, to prevent CPU overloads, it is best to use dedicated routers or servers.

Using the RR, the reduction of iBGP sessions is very high. If we resume the example we saw in the introduction to this section, and assume two iBGP sessions toward two different RRs for each P or PE router, the iBGP sessions required become 2x272 = 544, plus a few dozen sessions between the RRs (the exact number depends on the number of RRs installed), vs the 34,300 sessions required without the RRs. Although consistent, the reduction of sessions with the BGP Confederation technique is lower.

Apart from this, there is another advantage in using the RRs in the network. Let's assume we add a new PE to the network. Without RRs, we should edit both the new PE, by configuring a high number of iBGP sessions (e.g. 272, with the numbers above), and on all the other P and PE to configure the counterpart of the iBGP session toward the new PE. With the RRs, it is all solved by configuring a couple of iBGP sessions toward a couple of RRs on the new PE (in theory, one would be enough, we are going to add two for greater reliability purposes), and the counterpart of the iBGP session toward the new PE on the RRs. The others do not need any configuration.

8.2.3 BGP/MPLS routing architecture

A further reduction in the number of iBGP sessions can be obtained by introducing MPLS into the network. For readers not familiar with MPLS concepts, we will describe one of its basic features, for you to understand the context. MPLS is a data plane technology that uses the well-known label switching concept, meaning that, comparable with the old and obsolete Frame Relay and ATM standards, switching is done through a label (i.e. a simple number) present somewhere in the packet header. The router executing the switching will have an "MPLS forwarding table" that matches each inbound label to an outbound label and an IP Next-Hop. The resulting routing architecture is called BGP/MPLS.

The basic idea is that the only role of P routers is to act as transits for traffic between two PEs, one for inbound traffic and one for outbound traffic. By analyzing the situation described in Figures 8.2 and 8.3, we infer that the work actually done by P routers is transferring packets from an inbound PE router to an outbound PE router. Then why should all prefixes outside the AS be propagated also in the RIBs of P router? Is there a way to remove this superfluous knowledge, and thus reduce the work done by these routers (which should basically dedicate the majority of their processing power to handle traffic)?

Indeed, the issue could be solved by setting up tunnels to connect the inbound/outbound PE routers to one another, and masking the IP packet destination IP addresses to P routers. These tunnels could be made by MPLS paths, that is, paths where traffic is switched based on a label, rather than on the target IP address.

NOTE: In MPLS jargon, the paths are called Label Switched Paths (LSP) and can be considered the equivalent of virtual connections in old ATM and Frame Relay standards.

Figure 8.4 describes the basic idea. External prefixes, learned by a PE through any (static or dynamic) routing protocol and redistributed in the internal backbone BGP process, are propagated only to the other PE routers and not to P routers. So, in the end, only PE routers will have all the external prefixes in their RIB; the connection between PE routers is ensured by a complete mesh of MPLS paths, whose purpose is logically "connecting" PE routers .

The BGP/MPLS routing architecture further reduces the number of iBGP sessions to be configured; indeed, the iBGP sessions between PE routers and P routers are no longer necessary (and their quantity is NPE*NP, where NPE is the number of PE routers and NP is the number of P routers). Moreover, apart from the advantage of further reducing the iBGP sessions, it has undeniable advantages in terms of scalability, since, in P routers:

- It is no longer necessary to propagate the external prefixes via BGP. Actually, in P routers, it is no longer necessary to activate a BGP process. For this reason, the BGP/MPLS routing architecture is also indicated in literature as BGP core-free architecture.

- Search for the Next-Hop is sped up, since packet forwarding is based on MPLS labels, and their quantity is limited (one for each PE, in an optimal design!).

- Memory is saved, since it is no longer necessary to store large quantities of BGP advertisements.

The main point that allows the BGP/MPLS architecture to forward traffic, without having to propagate the advertisements of the prefixes outside P routers, is that P routers switch the packet not based on the target IP address, but rather based on an MPLS label, corresponding to the MPLS path connecting PE router receiving the packet from the outside (inbound PE, in the figure PE[i]), to PE router forwarding the packet outside the ISP network (outbound PE, in the figure PE[u]).

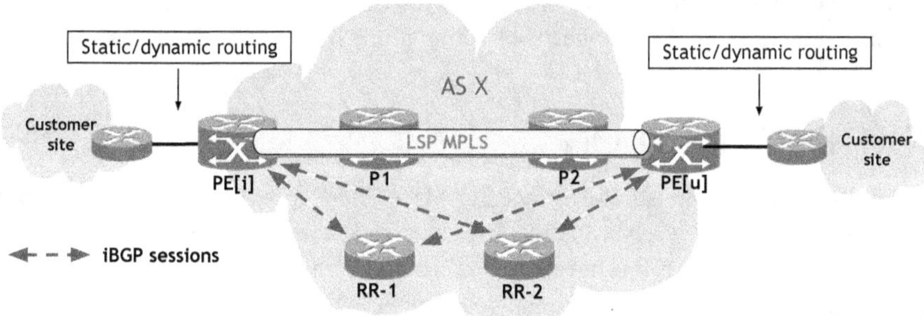

Figure 8.4 - Logic BGP/MPLS routing architecture diagram.

8.2.4 Configuration best practices

The configuration of a network that wants to use the BGP/MPLS routing architecture requires the activation of three essential components:

- An IGP routing protocol. In practical applications, Link State (OSPF or IS-IS) protocols are used.

- BGP. In particular, a complete mesh of iBGP sessions between all PE routers is required. For greater scalability purposes, the complete mesh can be done via Route Reflector or BGP Confederation.

- The MPLS forwarding mechanism. In particular, a complete mesh of MPLS paths between all PE routers is required.

To obtain an elegant and efficient practical implementation of a BGP/MPLS routing architecture, you should follow the guidelines below:

- Configure Loopback interfaces – shortened with Lo0 – on each router: P, PE and possible RR.

- Activate an internal IGP (OSPF or IS-IS) to mutually reach all Lo0 interfaces. In particular, if, for greater scalability reasons, we are using the Router Reflectors, there should be IP connectivity between the Lo0 interfaces of each PE router, and the Lo0 interfaces of the Router Reflectors.

- On each PE router, configure at least one iBGP session toward a RR; in practice, for reliability reasons, there should be at least two iBGP sessions toward two different RRs. Based on the services offered, it is possible to activate multiprotocol iBGP sessions (MP-iBGP), necessary to certain services based on the BGP/MPLS routing architecture, such as L2VPN and L3VPN.

- Create a complete mesh of MPLS paths between all PE routers.

NOTE: There are two ways to create the complete mesh of MPLS paths. The first, is to use LDP (Label Distribution Protocol) on all P and PE routers (generally recommended solution). The second, is to manually configure explicit MPLS paths between each pair of PE. Since the MPLS paths are unidirectional, this would entail the configuration of *NPE*(NPE-*1) explicit MPLS paths. This second alternative, aside from entailing a very long configuration, has the downside that adding a new PE entails the configuration of NPE-1 new explicit paths.

A network configured as such can be used, with minor additions, for important services, such as, for instance, BGP/MPLS IP Virtual Private Networks, Internet access, Layer-2 frame transport (such as PPP frames, Ethernet, etc.), Ethernet LAN emulation, IPv6 packet transport on IPv4/MPLS networks, etc.

8.3 ROUTE REFLECTION

The Route Reflection function is defined by RFC 4456 – *BGP Route Reflection: An Alternative to Full Mesh Internal BGP (IBGP)*, April 2006. The basic idea is very simple: in order to propagate an eBGP advertisement to all the relevant routers within an AS, instead of using an (almost) complete mesh of iBGP sessions, routers with special functions are used, which reflect the advertisement to all relevant routers. These routers are called Route Reflector (RR) and their special function is the Route Reflection. In order to understand this mechanism, let's consider a network with only 5 PE routers. When one of the PE receives an eBGP advertisement, in order to propagate it to the other 4 PEs, it requires 4 iBGP sessions toward them. In total, considering that BGP sessions are bidirectional, we would need 5*(5-1)/2 = 10 iBGP sessions. Let's take a look at Figure 8.5, and suppose that there is a router defined as RR (which can be one of the 5 PEs, or a sixth router, as in the figure). To propagate the eBGP advertisement, the PE that receives it (PE1 in the figure) sends it to RR, which in turn propagates it to the other PE routers through iBGP sessions. Therefore, the number of iBGP sessions required becomes 5, that is, all sessions between RR and the 5 PEs (actually, by integrating the Route Reflection function on one of the 5 PEs, the sessions required could be reduced to 4).

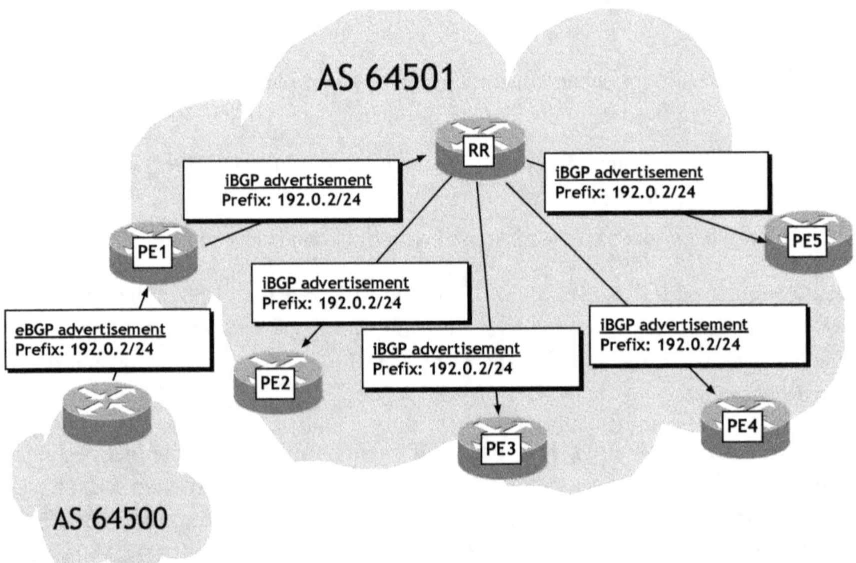

Figure 8.5 – The basic idea behind the Route Reflection.

As you may have noticed, the Route Reflection concept entails the violation of one of the basic principles of iBGP sessions, namely the split-horizon rule, which prevents the propagation of advertisements received from iBGP Neighbors on iBGP sessions. RRs break this rule, because the advertisements received on iBGP sessions can be "reflected" (propagated) on a selected number of iBGP sessions.

The iBGP Neighbors of an RR can be divided into two classes:

- *Client (RR-Client)*: iBGP Neighbors on which the RR reflects the BGP advertisements received. We will go over the propagation rules shortly.

- *Non-Client*: standard iBGP Neighbors of the RR.

A RR reflects the advertisements between these two groups, but it can also reflect advertisements between RR-Clients. One (or more) RR with its own RR-Clients forms a cluster, identified by a *Cluster ID* (4 byte long, usually expressed with the same decimal notation as IP addresses). As a design rule, in order for all the routers to receive all the advertisements, Non-Clients must have a complete mesh of iBGP sessions between one another. Figure 8.6 summarizes the terms we've just introduced.

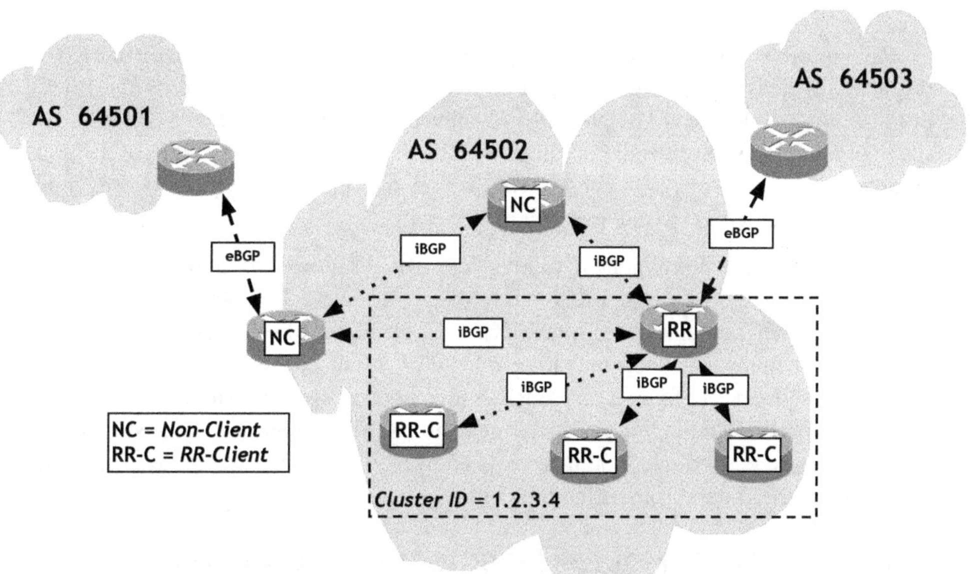

Figure 8.6 – Route Reflection terms.

8.3.1 Advertisement propagation rules

In order to understand the Route Reflection mechanism, we must be familiar with the rules to propagate the advertisements received from a RR and from its RR-Clients. Some of them are classic BGP rules, and we will include them for the sake of completeness:

- a RR only reflects the best path;

- a RR always reflect the advertisements to eBGP Neighbors;

- a RR propagates the advertisements received on eBGP sessions on all BGP sessions;

- a RR-Client follows the standard iBGP split-horizon rule.

The propagation of advertisements received from a RR on iBGP sessions – provided that they are best paths – follows the rules based on the advertisement origins (Note: these are the rules that violate the iBGP split-horizon):

- if the iBGP advertisement is received by a Non-Client, it is propagated to all RR-clients;

- if the iBGP advertisement is received by a RR-Client, it is propagated to all the other RR-clients and to all the Non-Clients.

NOTE: RFC 4456 has slightly modified this rule, by allowing the propagation also to the RR-client that originated the advertisement. In any case, this advertisement is rejected by the RR-Client that originated it, due to the ORIGINATOR_ID attribute that we will see in Section 8.3.3. The advantage of this modification is that it allows the RR to send a copy of a single BGP UPDATE message to all its RR-Clients, with consequent savings in terms of CPU space. However, not all manufacturers implement it (Cisco does, Juniper doesn't).

Moreover, to prevent the formation of routing loops, a RR does not modify (by default) the NEXT_HOP, AS_PATH, LOCAL_PREF and MED attributes. Actually, on this last point, despite having the same default (i.e. not modifying the attributes of reflected advertisements) the manufacturers can follow different operating rules. For instance, in Cisco routers, any "**set...**" commands in route-maps configured on the RR, and applied at the exit to modify these attributes, are ignored. Similarly, also the "**neighbor ... next-hop-self**" command is ignored. On the other hand, in Juniper routers, attribute modification is allowed. This is important to remember in case of interwork between routers from different brands.

8.3.2 Fault-tolerant Route Reflector configurations

In a cluster, a single RR constitutes a single point of failure, that is, if the RR is out of service, it would prevent the correct propagation of BGP advertisements to the RR-Clients. In real networks, fault-tolerant RR configurations are implemented, that is, clusters with several RRs. The correct design of a cluster should follow two basic rules (see Figure 8.7 that shows an AS with two clusters):

- each RR-Client of a cluster must have iBGP sessions with all the RRs within the cluster;

- within an AS, all the RRs and Non-Client routers should always have a complete mesh of iBGP sessions between them.

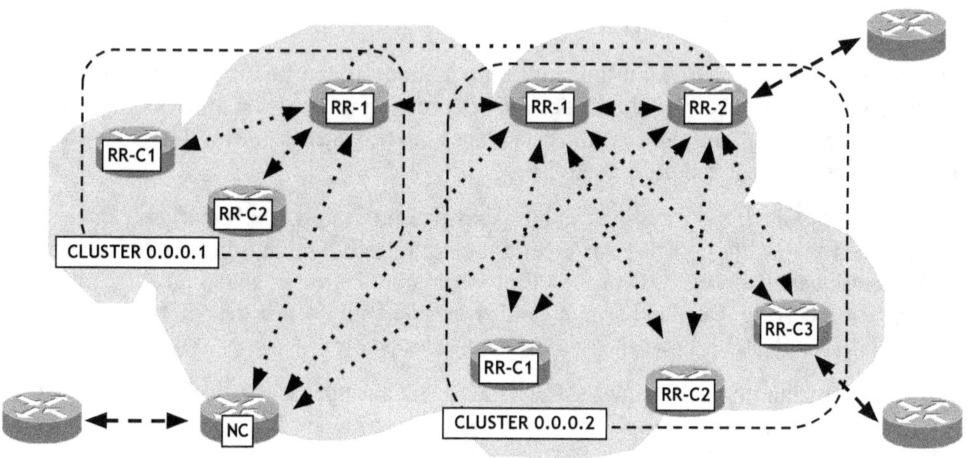

Figure 8.7 – Cluster design within an AS.

To prevent a complete mesh of iBGP sessions between RRs and Non-Clients to grow up to the network's scalability limits, using the feature that a RR can in turn be a RR-Client of another RR, it is possible to build cluster hierarchies.

One example is shown in Figure 8.8, where the complete mesh between the three RRs of the two clusters 0.0.0.1 and 0.0.0.2 is prevented, by creating a third cluster (0.0.0.12). In turn, the two RRs (Tier-2 RRs) RR-12.1 and RR-12.2 have as RR-Clients the three RRs (Tier-1 RR) RR-1.1, RR-2.1 and RR-2.2. From a practical standpoint, the need to implement hierarchical RR architectures is not very frequent.

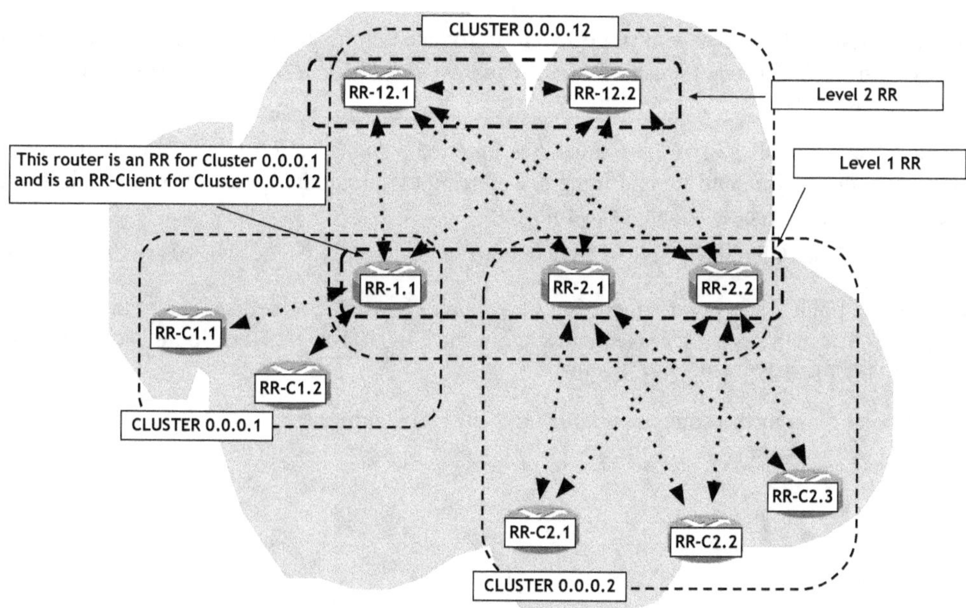

Figure 8.8 – RR hierarchy.

8.3.3 Loop prevention

A very important aspect of fault-tolerant configurations is the possibility that, due to wrong configurations and/or incorrect cluster design, both routing information loop (loop on the control plane) and forwarding loop (loop on the data plane) can be generated. RFC 4456 defines two new BGP attributes to detect and prevent any loop:

- ORIGINATOR_ID: an Optional Non Transitive attribute (*Attribute Type Code* = 9) that specifies the BGP-ID of the router originating a prefix within a cluster (in case of eBGP advertisements, the BGP-ID of the PE propagating them). It is automatically created by the first RR receiving the advertisement, and propagated only within the AS. Management of the ORIGINATOR_ID follows the two essential rules below:

  - ➤ a RR cannot create a new ORIGINATOR_ID attribute if it is already contained in the advertisement;

  - ➤ a BGP Speaker recognizing the ORIGINATOR_ID attribute must ignore the advertisement, if the ORIGINATOR_ID value matches its own BGP-ID.

- CLUSTER_LIST: an Optional Non Transitive attribute (*Attribute Type Code* = 10) that specifies the list of clusters crossed within an AS. Every time a RR reflects an advertisement, it adds its own *Cluster ID* on top of the list, unless the advertisement comes from an eBGP Neighbor, in which case the CLUSTER_LIST attribute is not created. The attribute is only propagated within the AS. Management of the CLUSTER_LIST follows the two essential rules below:

  - ➤ it is used as loop detection mechanism only by RRs;

  - ➤ a RR receiving an advertisement containing its own *Cluster ID* in the CLUSTER_LIST attribute must ignore the advertisement.

NOTE: Actually, the two new attributes were introduced in the initial standard version, defined by RFC 1966 – *BGP Route Reflection: An Alternative to Full Mesh IBGP*, June 1996, and further updated by RFC 4456.

The introduction of these two new attributes entailed a modification of the selection process, picked up both by Cisco and Juniper routers. Referring to the standard selection process described in Section 2.5.1, the process changes as follows:

- in point 7, the ORIGINATOR_ID attribute, if present, replaces the BGP-ID in the selection;

- between point 7 and point 8 there is a new point: choose the advertisement with the shortest CLUSTER_LIST (an advertisement without the CLUSTER_LIST attribute is considered as a CLUSTER_LIST with zero length).

The last point remains the comparison of BGP Neighbor Addresses.

8.3.4 Route Reflector and forwarding path

From a traffic forwarding standpoint, there are two ways to implement the RRs:

- RRs included in the paths followed by traffic (forwarding paths);

- RRs excluded from the paths followed by traffic (Out-of-Band RR).

When a RR is part of the forwarding path, not only does it have to execute the additional Route Reflection functions (managing several iBGP sessions, reflecting the advertisements, etc.), it also takes part in packet routing decisions. If it is excluded from it, it only executes the Route Reflection functions, and, in this case, the entire packet forwarding hardware is not used. This second solution should be preferred in practical applications, as it allows to decouple the RR's control plane from the forwarding path, allowing the use of much less costly and energy-consuming devices.

There are two ways to implement Out-of-Band RR:

- employing virtual Route Reflectors (vRR);

- using routers with modestly-sized FIB, and therefore inexpensive, with suitable CPU and memory power.

If you use vRRs, you can instantiate the Route Reflection function on commercial servers in bare metal mode, or instantiate it as VNF (Virtual Network Function) in an NFV (Network Function Virtualization) system. Obviously, in both cases, you need to have a software that implements all BGP functions, including the Route Reflection function, and all the BGP address-families that the ISPs use for their services. For this purpose, there are software from traditional vendors such as Cisco and Juniper on the market, or several open source ones (Bird, FRRouting, OpenBGPD, just to mention a few).

If you have routers with modestly-sized FIBs, with a simple configuration, you can prevent the download of all or part of the BGP best paths in the RIB and therefore in the FIB. In a certain way, it's as if, in this case, the routers behaved like simple servers, since their forwarding capacity is only partially or not exploited at all.

This technique is known as BGP Selective Route Download and can be activated through some simple commands, which we will see in Section 8.3.6.

8.3.5 Optimal Route Reflector allocation

The presence of one or more Route Reflectors (RR) creates issues with possible non-optimal paths. The problem stems from the fact that a RR, just like any BGP Speaker, performs the selection process, which, at some point, could use the point concerning the minimum IGP cost.

To explain this issue, let's see what happens with the reference scenario shown in Figure 8.9 below, where we assumed that the BGP Next-Hop-Self is active on PE routers.

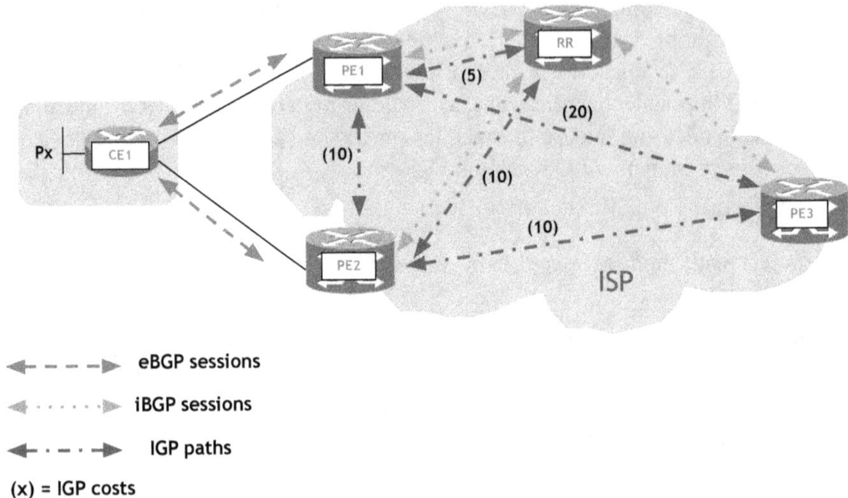

Figure 8.9 – Non-optimal routing with Route Reflector.

Router CE1 advertises prefix Px to PE routers PE1 and PE2, via eBGP. PE routers PE1 and PE2 propagate the advertisement to the RR, which executes the selection process on the two advertisements. Should all classic bgp attributes be equal, the selection process chooses as best path the advertisement received by PE1, because the IGP cost toward BGP Next-Hop PE1 – equal to 5 – is lower than the IGP cost toward BGP Next-Hop PE2 – equal to 10. RR propagates the best path to PE3, and, in PE3's BGP table, there will be only one advertisement of prefix Px, with BGP Next-Hop PE1. However, as you can see in the figure, the closest BGP Next-Hop to PE3 is not PE1 – with a distance of 20 (IGP cost from PE3 to PE1), but PE2, with a distance of 10. Basically, the RR chooses as best path its closest exit point, rather than the one closest to the traffic entry point. Even with two or more RR, sub-optimal routing is always lurking.

In networks where the RRs are not in the forwarding path, and their location is arbitrary, the issue becomes even more widespread. Apart from this, there are also scenarios in which an ISP wants complete control over the choice of traffic exit points of its customers, based, for instance, on other factors (e.g. traffic type, traffic volume, etc.).

One solution to this issue is using the BGP Add-Path function, which we will see in Chapter 12. This function allows advertising one or more alternative best paths, in addition to the best path. The critical aspect of the BGP Add-Path is that it significantly increases the number of BGP advertisements present in the RR-Clients. In scenarios where the network receives the Full Internet Routing Table (FIRT) in many points, this entails that the different RR-Clients could receive many advertisements of the same prefix (which, multiplied by the number of prefixes in the FIRT, could lead to significant memory footprint).

However, the non-optimal routing issue may still be present. Indeed, usually with the BGP Add-Path, not all possible alternative paths are sent (or memory issues could occur, as mentioned above), but rather only one subset of them. However, who is to say that this subset will also include the best exit point according to the IGP cost?

We could come up with some other fanciful workaround, but in reality what we need is a general solution that allows us to allocate the RRs at any point in the network, while maintaining the optimal routing principle.

A more general solution to this issue, already implemented by the main vendors, is contained in RFC 9107 – *BGP Optimal Route Reflection (BGP ORR)*, August 2021. The idea is very simple and ingenious, virtualizing the RR's position, or, in other words, making the RR's position independent from the best path selection process.

Let's see how it works in practice. As you know, the RR participates in the IGP process, which, as is the case in practical applications, is of the Link-State type (OSPF or IS-IS). The RR knows the network's total or partial topology.

For now, let's assume to have a single area (usually area 0) in the case of OSPF, and a single level (usually level 2) in the case of IS-IS. With this hypothesis, the RR, by taking part in the IGP process, has the entire LSDB (Link-State DataBase) available, thus it can determine the total IGP cost between each pair of RR-Client. In particular, it can determine a cost matrix, where the general matrix item <X, Y> is the overall IGP cost from RR-Client X to RR-Client Y (Note: the matrix diagonal is not used. Moreover, as it often occurs in practice, we will assume that the matrix is symmetrical, that is, that item <X, Y> matches item <Y, X>; even though, in reality, this is not indispensable).

In order to determine matrix item <X, Y>, the RR, having the entire LSDB available, just needs to determine the SPF tree with root in X, to obtain optimal costs toward all the other network routers, including RR-Client Y. Figure 8.10 below summarizes this concept.

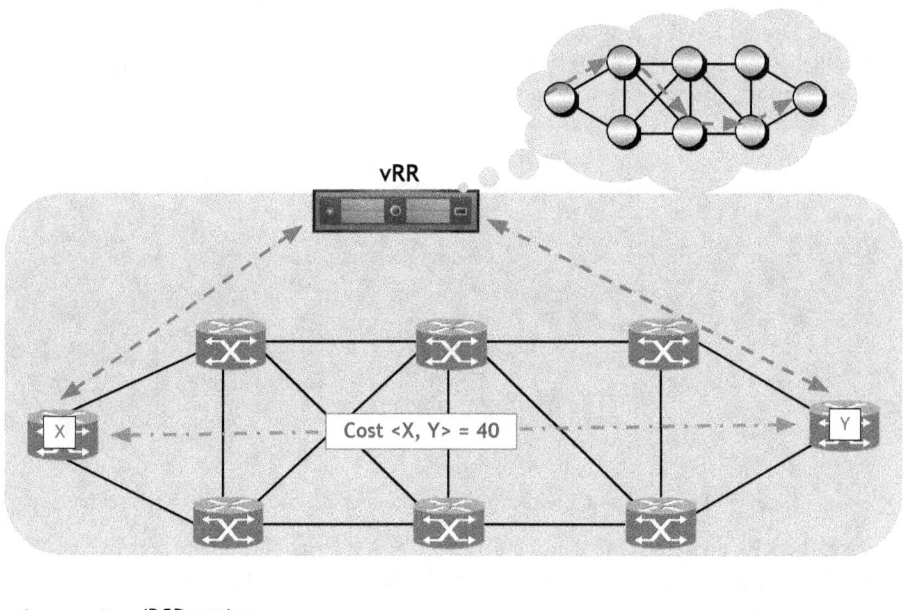

Figure 8.10 – The idea of BGP ORR

And we are good to go. To explain how, we will refer to the example in Figure 8.9 above. The RR determines three additional SPF trees, each one with a RR-Client as root (in the figure, PE1, PE2 and PE3). Downstream of these calculations, the RR keeps memory of the following cost matrix:

	PE1	PE2	PE3
PE1	-	10	20
PE2	10	-	10
PE3	20	10	-

When RR receives from PE1 and PE2 the advertisements of prefix Px, it executes the BGP selection process. Provided that it needs to base its decision only on the IGP cost toward the BGP Next-Hop, that is, with all the other BGP metrics specified in the previous points of the selection process being the same, the RR, when choosing the best path does not consider the cost between itself and the two BGP Next-Hop PE1 and PE2 as the cost to be compared, but rather the cost between the RR-Client to which it reflects the advertisement (PE-3, in this example) and the two RR-Clients that sent the advertisement (PE1 and PE2, in this example). Since the minimum IGP cost is the one between PE3 and PE2, the RR elects as best path the advertisement with BGP Next-Hop PE2, rather than the one with BGP Next-Hop PE1, as it would do by default. Therefore, the best path is propagated to PE3 with BGP Next-Hop PE2, allowing PE3 to follow the optimal routing logic.

Notice that, with this logic, the best-path is not unique, as it depends on the RR-Client to which the advertisement is reflected. Two different RR-Clients could receive two different best paths, based on their proximity to where the advertisement originated.

If the IGP domain is partitioned into different areas, it may occur that RR and RR-Client are located in different parts, and therefore RR does not recognize the entire network topology. However, this doesn't change anything, if the right precautions are adopted. For instance, let's assume that IGP is OSPF and that RR is in area 0 and RR-Clients X are Y in peripheral areas 10 and 20, respectively (see Figure 8.11 below).

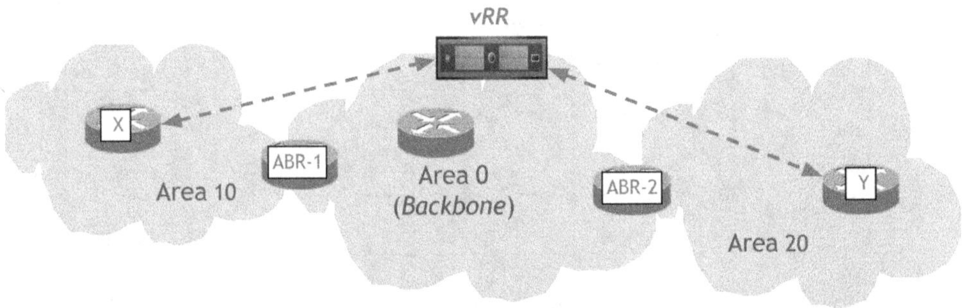

Figure 8.11 – BGP ORR with a routing domain partition into different areas.

In any case, the RR can determine the overall cost <X, Y> by adding the cost between ABR-1 and Y, specified in the Summary Link LSA that ABR-1 sends in area 10 to advertise the (inter-area) prefixes of Y, and the cost between X and ABR-1, specified in the Summary Link LSA that ABR-1 generates in area 0 to advertise the (inter-area) prefixes of X.

It should be noted that this idea, called BGP-ORR (BGP – Optimal Route Reflection) in the aforementioned RFC 9107, is not an alternative to the BGP Add-Path or to the other methods for Path Diversity that we will see in Chapter 12. It can be used alongside them to improve the "quality" of multiple advertisements to be propagated, by always adding the one that ensures the preservation of the optimal routing principles among them.

In conclusion, the BGP-ORR is a very simple and effective idea to virtualize the RR position, making it independent from its RR-Clients. This allows "retrieving" the optimal routing principles, which would otherwise be lost in many practical cases. The price to pay is a little extra work for the RR to store the matrix of the IGP distances among its RR-Clients and to complete the selection process, which becomes heavier, since a best-path needs to be determined for each RR-Client. However, using virtual RRs, which, according to the good design principles described in Section 8.3.4 above, are outside the forwarding path, this shouldn't be a problem. Modern servers have sufficient processing capacity to do this and much more.

8.3.6 Configuration aspects

The configuration of an architecture with RR is very simple, both in Cisco and Juniper technologies. In both cases, only the RRs require a bit of additional configuration. RR-Clients and Non-Clients only require standard iBGP session configurations.

In Cisco platforms, the configuration only requires two commands, with just the second one being mandatory:

- *Cluster ID* assignment:

  <u>IOS XE</u>
  RR(config)# **router bgp** *AS-number*
  RR(config-router)# **bgp cluster-id** *cluster-ID*

  <u>IOS XR</u>
  RP/0/RP0/CPU0:RR(config)# **router bgp** *AS-number*
  RP/0/RP0/CPU0:RR(config-bgp)# **bgp cluster-id** *cluster-ID*

  The *Cluster ID* value can be expressed both as decimal number and as IP address. Switching from one mode to the other can be done through standard binary arithmetic rules. Without this command, the RR creates the CLUSTER_LIST attribute anyway, using its own BGP-ID as *Cluster ID*.

  NOTE: In JUNOS, although the *Cluster ID* can be expressed as a decimal number, it is always shown in the IP address format in the views.

- *RR-Client* definition:

  <u>IOS XE</u>
  RR(config)# **router bgp** *AS-number*
  RR(config-router)# **neighbor** *IP-neighbor* ***route-reflector-client***

  <u>IOS XR</u>
  RP/0/RP0/CPU0:RR(config)# **router bgp** *AS-number*
  RP/0/RP0/CPU0:RR(config-bgp)# **neighbor** *IP-neighbor*
  RP/0/RP0/CPU0:RR(config-bgp-nbr)# **address-family {ipv4 | ipv6} unicast**
  RP/0/RP0/CPU0:RR(config-bgp-nbr-af)# **route-reflector-client**

In JUNOS, configuration is even easier, since it is sufficient to specify the *Cluster ID* value for each RR. The *Cluster ID* is assigned to a RR through the "**cluster** *value*" command, directly at global, group, or BGP Neighbor level. The *Cluster ID* value must be specified in the same format as the IP addresses.

If the command was given at global level, then all the BGP Neighbors specified (which must be necessarily iBGP) would become RR-Clients of the RR. In the same way, if the command was given at group level, then all the BGP Neighbors specified in the group (which must be necessarily iBGP) would become RR-Clients of the RR. Lastly, if the command was given at session level, then only the BGP Neighbor specified in the session (which must be necessarily iBGP) would become RR-Client of the RR.

Further interesting configurations are linked to the implementation of the Selective Route Download BGP function, mentioned in Section 8.3.4 above.

In Cisco platforms, the configurations to execute are:

IOS XE
RR(config)# **route-map** *RM-name* **deny**
!
RR(config)# **router bgp** *AS-number*
RR(config-router)# **address-family {ipv4 | ipv6} unicast**
RR(config-router-af)# **table-map** *RM-name* **filter**

IOS XR
RP/0/RP0/CPU0:RR(config)# **route-policy** *RP-name*
RP/0/RP0/CPU0:RR(config-rpl)# **drop**
RP/0/RP0/CPU0:RR(config-rpl)# **end-policy**
!
RP/0/RP0/CPU0:RR(config)# **router bgp** *AS-number*
RP/0/RP0/CPU0:RR(config-bgp)# **address-family {ipv4 | ipv6} unicast**
RP/0/RP0/CPU0:RR(config-bgp-af)# **table-policy** *RP-name*

These configurations prevent all the BGP best paths from being downloaded in the RIB (and therefore in the FIB). If you want to allow a partial download of the best paths, it would be sufficient to define some route-maps or routing policies to identify the prefixes to be exported into the RIB.

Differently from the different Cisco IOS types, in JUNOS, the BGP best paths are added directly to the RIB; in any case, their download from RIB to FIB can be adjusted through a routing policy. The configurations to execute are:

[edit policy-options policy-statement *RP-name***]**
from {
  protocol bgp;
  < *other conditions* **>;**
}
then reject;
[edit routing-options forwarding-table]
export *RP-name***;**

8.3.7 Case Study

To apply all that we said until now on Route Reflection, we've added two new routers RR-1 and RR-2 both acting as RR to our sample network in Figure 3.1. RR-1 is a Cisco router with IOS XE and RR-2 is a Juniper router with JUNOS. The resulting topology of AS 64501 is shown in Figure 8.12 below, which also highlights the IP addresses of the Loopback0 interfaces of the two new routers, used to establish the iBGP sessions. Let's assume that the two RRs and RR-Clients PE and GTW all belong to the same cluster, identified by *Cluster ID* = 1054 (which, in the typical IP address format, corresponds to 0.0.4.30).

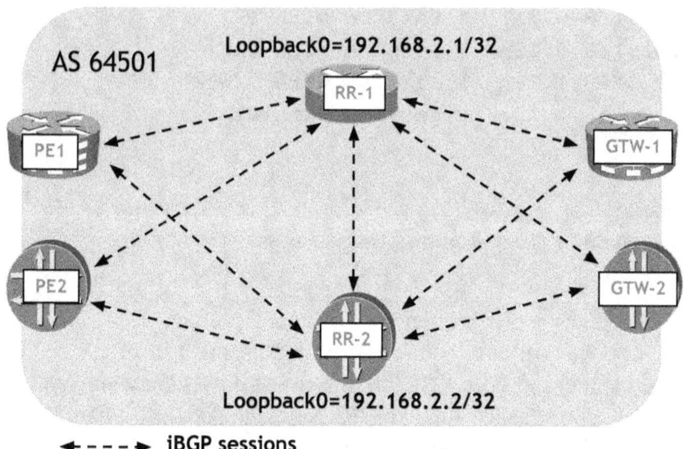

Figure 8.12 – Route Reflector in the sample network.

First, let's see the basic configurations on the two RRs. We will not show you any configuration on the RR-Clients, as it wouldn't add anything new to what we already know about iBGP session creation. Indeed, if you recall, RR-Client configurations are ordinary iBGP session configurations.

<u>RR-1</u> (IOS XE)

```
router bgp 64501
  template peer-policy RR-CLIENT
    route-reflector-client
  exit-peer-policy
  !
  template peer-session RR-CLIENT
    remote-as 64501
    update-source Loopback0
  exit-peer-session
  !
  bgp router-id 192.168.2.1
  bgp cluster-id 1054
  neighbor 192.168.0.11 inherit peer-session RR-CLIENT ! Session with PE1
  neighbor 192.168.0.11 inherit peer-policy RR-CLIENT
  neighbor 192.168.0.12 inherit peer-session RR-CLIENT ! Session with PE2
  neighbor 192.168.0.12 inherit peer-policy RR-CLIENT
  neighbor 192.168.1.11 inherit peer-session RR-CLIENT ! Session with GTW-1
  neighbor 192.168.1.11 inherit peer-policy RR-CLIENT
  neighbor 192.168.1.12 inherit peer-session RR-CLIENT ! Session with GTW-2
  neighbor 192.168.1.12 inherit peer-policy RR-CLIENT
  neighbor 192.168.2.2  inherit peer-session RR-CLIENT ! Session with RR-2
```

<u>RR-2</u> (JUNOS)
```
[edit protocols bgp]
local-address 192.168.2.2;
group RR-CLIENT {
    type internal;
    cluster 1054;
    neighbor 192.168.0.11;   # Session with PE1
    neighbor 192.168.0.12;   # Session with PE2
    neighbor 192.168.1.11;   # Session with GTW-1
    neighbor 192.168.1.12;   # Session with GTW-2
}
group TO-RR-1 {
    type internal;
    neighbor 192.168.2.1;   # Session with RR-1
}
```

RR-Client GTW-1 receives advertisements of different prefixes from eBGP Neighbor UP-1. For the sake of brevity, we will only consider the advertisement of prefix 203.0.113/24. GTW-1 propagates the advertisement to both RRs through the two iBGP sessions with them. Following the reflection rules described earlier, the two RRs reflect the advertisement between one another and to the other two RR-Clients. The advertisement is mutually reflected between the two RRs, since each one sees the other RR as a normal Non-Client. However, due to the presence of the CLUSTER_LIST containing in this example only the value *Cluster ID*=1054, the advertisements exchanged between RRs are rejected. For verification purposes, let's see how the detail of prefix 203.0.113/24 changes in the BGP Tables of RR-1 and PE1.

```
RR-1#show bgp ipv4 unicast 203.0.113.0/24
BGP routing table entry for 203.0.113.0/24, version 9
Paths: (1 available, best #1, table default)
  Advertised to update-groups:
     3          4          5          6
  Refresh Epoch 1
  65541 64496, (Received from a RR-client)
    192.168.1.11 (metric 2) from 192.168.1.11 (192.168.1.11)
      Origin IGP, metric 0, localpref 100, valid, internal, best
      rx pathid: 0, tx pathid: 0x0
RP/0/0/CPU0:PE1#show bgp ipv4 unicast 203.0.113.0/24
. . .
Paths: (2 available, best #1)
  Advertised to update-groups (with more than one peer):
    0.3
  Path #1: Received by speaker 0
  Advertised to update-groups (with more than one peer):
    0.3
  65541 64496
    192.168.1.11 (metric 2) from 192.168.2.1 (192.168.1.11)
      Origin IGP, metric 0, localpref 100, valid, internal, best, group-best
      Received Path ID 0, Local Path ID 0, version 176
      Originator: 192.168.1.11, Cluster list: 0.0.4.30
  Path #2: Received by speaker 0
```

```
Not advertised to any peer
65541 64496
  192.168.1.11 (metric 2) from 192.168.2.2 (192.168.1.11)
    Origin IGP, metric 0, localpref 100, valid, internal
    Received Path ID 0, Local Path ID 0, version 0
    Originator: 192.168.1.11, Cluster list: 0.0.4.30
```

It is interesting to notice that RR-1 has only one advertisement of prefix 203.0.113/24, since the one coming from RR-2 – as we mentioned earlier – is rejected, due to the presence of the CLUSTER_LIST attribute. Instead, PE1 has two advertisements of the same prefixes, coming from the two RRs. Between the two, the one coming from RR-1 is chosen as the best path, due to the lower BGP Neighbor address (last point of the modified selection process). The same occurs on PE2, which we will omit for the sake of brevity.

Let's assume we want to use the two routers RR-1 and RR-2 as simple servers, and keep them out of the forwarding path. Therefore we don't need to download all the BGP best paths in the FIB. In order to prevent this, since it is an automatic router process, we apply the BGP Selective Route Download, whose configuration aspects we saw in Section 8.3.5 above. The additional configurations to execute are:

RR-1 (IOS XE)
```
route-map NO-FIB deny
!
router bgp 64501
  address-family ipv4
    table-map NO-FIB filter
```

RR-2 (JUNOS)
```
[edit policy-options policy-statement NO-FIB]
from protocol bgp;
then reject;
[edit routing-options forwarding-table]
export NO-FIB;
```

To check its operation, let's check the presence of prefix 203.0.113/24 in the FIBs of the RRs, before the BGP Selective Route Download is applied:

```
RR-1#show ip cef 203.0.113.0/24
203.0.113.0/24
    nexthop 172.16.1.11 GigabitEthernet1

aft@RR-2>show route forwarding-table matching 203.0.113.0/24
. . .
Destination         Type RtRef Next hop      Type Index      NhRef Netif
203.0.113.0/24      user    0                indr 1048574     10
                                172.16.1.11  ucst     588      5 ge-0/0/1.0
```

After applying then BGP Selective Route Download, the prefix disappears from both FIBs:

```
RR-1#show ip cef 203.0.113.0/24
%Prefix not found

aft@RR-2>show route forwarding-table matching 203.0.113.0/24
Routing table: default.inet
Internet:
Enabled protocols: Bridging,
```

8.4 BGP CONFEDERATION

Today, the Route Reflection function is the most used by the ISPs to solve the issue of the quadratic growth of iBGP sessions. Another method has been standardized by the IETF (RFC 5065 – *Autonomous System Confederations for BGP*, August 2007), based on an equally simple idea: dividing the entire AS into a certain quantity of sub-ASes interconnected by eBGP sessions with slightly different characteristics from conventional eBGP sessions. The set of sub-ASes is called BGP Confederation.

An AS number (or rather, a sub-AS number) is assigned to each sub-AS, and, for best practice reasons, it should be a private AS number. Within each sub-AS, there must be a complete mesh of iBGP sessions, which can be avoided by using the Route Reflectors.

The sub-AS topology is invisible to the eBGP sessions between the AS and the other external ASes. In particular, the AS_PATH attribute is modified within a BGP Confederation, but presented outside in the same way, without the division into sub-ASes. So, with respect to the other ASes, the BGP Confederation appears as a single AS.

8.4.1 Intra-confederation eBGP sessions

Updating the AS_PATH attribute within the BGP Confederation is perhaps the main aspect of its operation. Before going over how this happens, we need to define the properties of the eBGP sessions between routers belonging to any two sub-ASes. We will call them intra-confederation eBGP sessions and we will indicate them with cBGP henceforth.

cBGP sessions have the following properties:

- same behavior as eBGP sessions to establish a connection. By default, cBGP Neighbors must be directly connected, or, otherwise, multihop cBGP sessions must be configured;

- same behavior as iBGP sessions to propagate certain BGP attributes; in particular, LOCAL_PREF, MED and NEXT_HOP attributes are left unchanged.

Since the entire BGP Confederation usually employs a single IGP to determine the optimal internal paths, it is best to use loopback interfaces also to establish the cBGP sessions (and therefore multihop cBGP sessions must be used). This is done to exploit any other path available between the two end routers of a session.

NOTE: For scalability reasons of the IGP protocol, theoretically it would be possible to use an independent routing process within each sub-AS. What's more (still theoretically), it would be possible to adopt different routing protocols for each sub-AS. In order to prevent unpleasant nightmares, we strongly advise against this practice, because, in latest-generation routers, on correctly designed networks, it is virtually impossible to have scalability issues in IGP.

In BGP's selection process, advertisements coming from cBGP sessions are treated at the same level as iBGP advertisements. This is very important in step 5 of the standard selection process (see Section 2.5.1), where iBGP and eBGP advertisements are compared, with the latter being the favorites.

8.4.2 Updating the AS_PATH

Let's see how the AS_PATH attribute is updated in a BGP Confederation. For this purpose, two other types of segments have been defined:

- AS_CONFED_SEQUENCE (*Path Segment Type* = 3): is a sorted list of Sub-ASes. AS_CONFED_SEQUENCE type segments are used by BGP Speakers to update the sorted list of sub-ASes crossed by a BGP advertisement that propagates within a Confederation.

- AS_CONFED_SET (*Path Segment Type* = 4): is an unsorted list of sub-ASes. AS_CONFED_ SET type segments are used by BGP Speakers belonging to sub-ASes that aggregate the prefixes to memorize the sub-ASes crossed by the prefixes being aggregated. In this case the sub-AS order doesn't matter.

In BGP's selection process, both types of segments are ignored, meaning that they do not contribute to determining the AS_PATH length in any way.

NOTE: Another important aspect about the impact on the selection process concerns the MED comparison mode. By default, both AS_CONFED_SET and AS_CONFED_SEQUENCE segments are not considered when determining the adjacent ASes. Only Cisco routers, through the BGP process "**bgp bestpath med-confed**" command, allow comparing the MED of advertisements that contain only AS_CONFED_SEQUENCE segments (provided that the first sub-AS matches).

The rules that govern the AS_PATH update in case of a BGP Confederation are the following:

- iBGP sessions (within a sub-AS): the AS_PATH doesn't change.

- cBGP sessions:

  - ➤ If the first segment of the AS_PATH belongs to the AS_CONFED_SEQUENCE type, the router that forwards the advertisement adds its own sub-AS on top of the AS_CONFED_ SEQUENCE segment list.

  - ➤ If the first segment of the AS_PATH does not belong to the AS_CONFED_SEQUENCE type, or if the AS_PATH is empty, the router forwarding the advertisement adds a new AS_CONFED_SEQUENCE segment containing only its own sub-AS number to the AS_PATH.

- Ordinary eBGP sessions (with ASes outside of the Confederation): all AS_CONFED_SET and AS_CONFED_SEQUENCE segments are removed from the AS_PATH, therefore:

  - ➤ If the first segment in the resulting AS_PATH belongs to the AS_SEQUENCE type, the AS number that identifies the BGP Confederation is added on top of the segment.

  - ➤ If the first segment of the AS_PATH does not belong to the AS_SEQUENCE type or the AS_PATH is empty, an AS_SEQUENCE segment containing the AS number that identifies the BGP Confederation is added on top of the list.

In case of locally-originated prefixes, the same rules apply, starting from an empty AS_PATH.
The use of AS_CONFED_SET segments follows the same rules as for AS_SET segments, with the only difference being that they are used in aggregation processes with "memory" of the prefixes, carried out by routers within a BGP Confederation.
Both Cisco IOS and JUNOS include AS_CONFED_SEQUENCE AS_PATH segments between brackets.

With the help of the example in Figure 8.13, let's see how the AS_PATH is updated within a BGP Confederation and when propagating the advertisements outside the Confederation. The BGP Confederation, identified by the AS number 64501, comprises three sub-ASes with numbers 65001, 65002 and 65003 respectively.

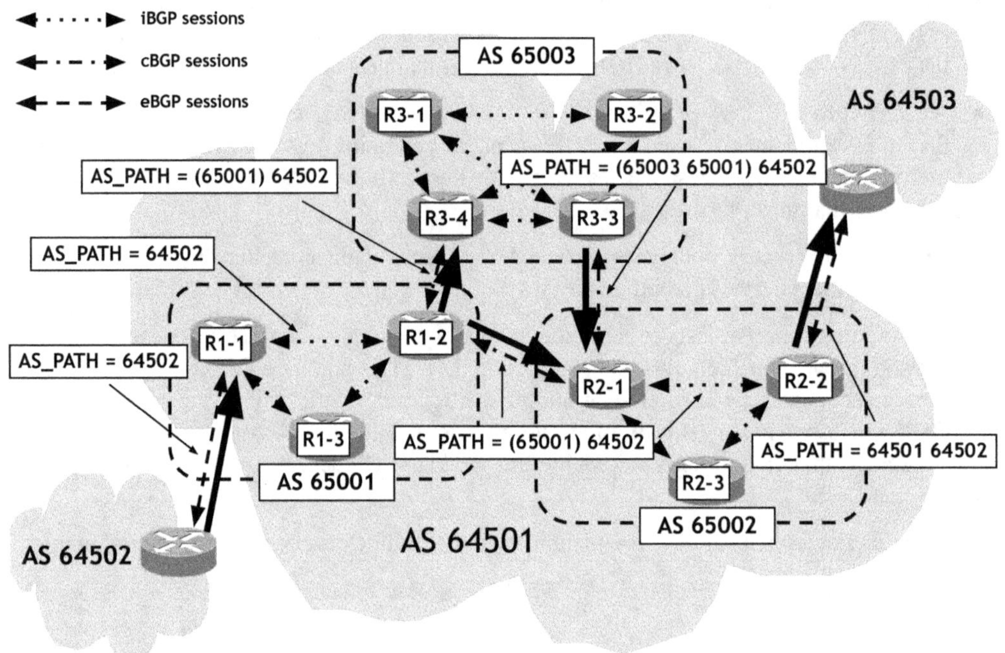

Figure 8.13 – Example of AS_PATH update within a BGP Confederation.

Let's assume that PE router R1-1 receives an advertisement of a local prefix of AS 64502. According to the standard BGP rules, the advertisement will only have one AS_SEQUENCE AS_PATH segment containing AS number 64502 within the AS_PATH. R1-1 propagates the advertisement on its iBGP sessions within sub-AS 65001 without changing the AS_PATH. Router R1-2, which has two cBGP sessions with routers R3-4 and R2-1, of sub-AS 65003 and 65002 respectively, propagates the advertisement on them, adding a AS_CONFED_SEQUENCE AS_PATH segment on top, containing sub-AS number 65001 (included between brackets, to indicate that it is a sub-AS number). When router R3-3 propagates the advertisement on the cBGP session with router R2-1 of sub-AS 65002, the AS_PATH is updated once again. The update consists in adding, on top of the AS_CONFED_SEQUENCE AS_PATH segment already containing sub-AS number 65001, sub-AS number 65003. When propagating to the iBGP sessions inside sub-AS 65002, the AS_PATH remains the same. When the advertisement reaches router R2-2, which has an eBGP session with a router of AS 64503, this is propagated (provided that it is the best path) toward AS 64503 and the AS_PATH is updated, by removing the AS_CONFED_SEQUENCE AS_PATH segment, and adding the AS number that identifies the BGP Confederation on top.

8.4.3 Configuration aspects

The configuration of a BGP Confederation is very simple, both in Cisco and Juniper technologies. In both cases, the configuration of BGP sessions (iBGP, cBGP, eBGP) is standard. Obviously, we should remember that a router within the Confederation belongs to a sub-AS, therefore its AS number is the related sub-AS number.

There are two data that should be provided to each router within the BGP Confederation:

- The Confederation identification number, that is, the AS number seen by external ASes (e.g., in Figure 8.13, AS number 64501).

- The sub-AS numbers of the BGP Confederation required by the router to understand whether the BGP sessions with the routers of another sub-AS or AS are cBGP or ordinary eBGP.

In Cisco platforms, configuring a BGP Confederation requires the following steps:

- Removing any existing BGP process from the router.

- Restoring the BGP process with AS number equal to the relevant sub-AS.

- Configuring (on all BGP Confederation routers) the Confederation identification number. This is done through the following commands:

  <u>IOS XE</u>
  router(config)# **router bgp** *AS-number*
  router(config-router)# **bgp confederation identifier** *conf-ID*

  <u>IOS XR</u>
  RP/0/RP0/CPU0:router(config)# **router bgp** *AS-number*
  RP/0/RP0/CPU0:router(config-bgp)# **bgp confederation identifier** *conf-ID*

- Defining, on each cBGP session end router, the list of all the sub-AS numbers of the BGP Confederation, except for the router number.

  NOTE: Actually, it would be sufficient to specify only the numbers of the sub-ASes with which you want to open a cBGP session; however, in practice, to prevent any configuration errors, network administrators often prefer to add them all, and on all routers of the BGP Confederation, even when this is not necessary.

  This is done through the following commands:

  <u>IOS XE</u>
  router(config)# **router bgp** *AS-number*
  router(config-router)# **bgp confederation peers** *sub-AS-1 sub-AS-2 ...*

  <u>IOS XR</u>
  RP/0/RP0/CPU0:router(config)# **router bgp** *AS-number*
  RP/0/RP0/CPU0:router(config-bgp)# **bgp confederation peers** *sub-AS-1*
  RP/0/RP0/CPU0:router(config-bgp)# **bgp confederation peers** *sub-AS-2*

  ...
  RP/0/RP0/CPU0:router(config-bgp)# **bgp confederation peers** *sub-AS-N*

NOTE: In IOS XR, cBGP sessions do not require any routing policy to allow the exchange of advertisements (as you may remember, this is mandatory for ordinary eBGP sessions, see Section 3.1.3).

Juniper implementations follow the same configuration rules as Cisco IOS, with a few minor differences.

In JUNOS, a BGP Confederation is configured only at hierarchical configuration level [**edit routing-options**]. At these level, for each router of a sub-AS, we need to specify:

- The relevant sub-AS, through the "**autonomous-system** *sub-AS*" command.

- The BGP Confederation identification and the list of sub-AS number (including one's own) through the "**confederation** *Conf-ID* **members** [*sub-AS-1 sub-AS-2* ...]" command (Note: Actually, as for Cisco IOS, only those of the sub-AS with which you want to open a cBGP session would be enough). Configuration of iBGP, eBGP and cBGP sessions follows ordinary BGP configuration rules. In particular, the configuration of cBGP sessions follows the same configuration rules as for eBGP sessions.

8.4.4 Case Study

Let's consider the topology of Figure 8.14 below. The network is divided into three sub-ASes, each one with a single-technology router:

- sub-AS 65001: Cisco IOS XE;

- sub-AS 65002: Cisco IOS XR;

- sub-AS 65003: Juniper JUNOS.

The BGP Confederation identification number is AS 64501. There is a complete mesh of cBGP sessions between routers P1, P2 and P3, and (as mandatory requirement) there is a complete mesh of iBGP sessions within each sub-AS. There is a single IGP protocol for the entire BGP Confederation (the type of which is completely irrelevant).

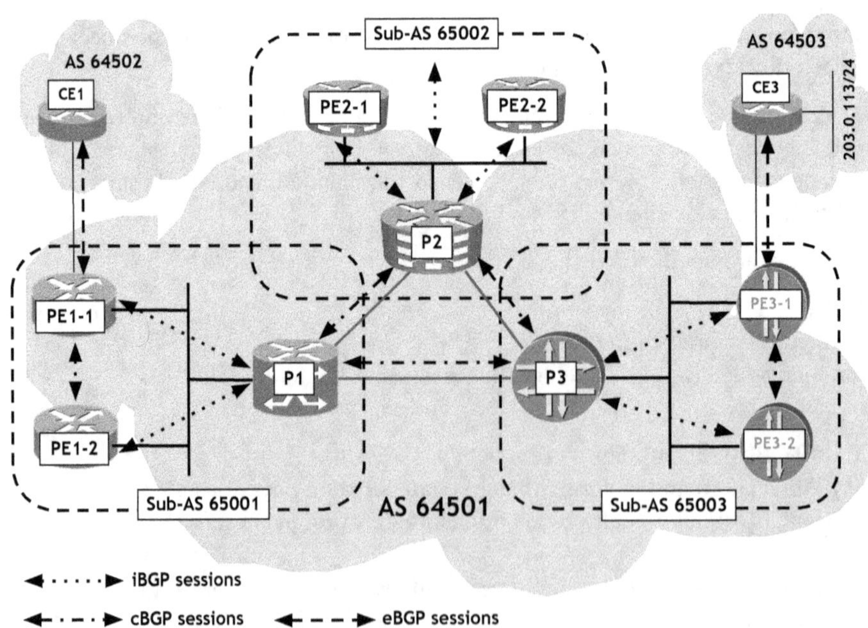

Figure 8.14 – Sample network to configure a BGP Confederation.

The configuration of the part concerning the BGP Confederation (including outbound eBGP sessions) only for routers PEX-1 and PX (X=1, 3) is shown below.

NOTE: The routers with IOS XR have similar configurations, omitted for the sake of brevity. The Confederation end routers have ordinary configuration that see the BGP Confederation as a normal AS. For instance, on router CE3, assuming it to be a Cisco router with IOS XE, the configuration of the eBGP session is:
```
router bgp 64503
  neighbor 10.3.3.1 remote-as 64501  ! SESSION WITH PE3-1
```

PE1-1 (IOS XE)
```
router bgp 65001
  peer-policy template IBGP
    next-hop-self
  exit-peer-policy
  !
  template peer-session IBGP
    remote-as 65001
    update-source Loopback0
  exit-peer-session
  !
  bgp confederation identifier 64501
  neighbor 10.1.1.2 remote-as 64502 ! SESSION WITH CE1
  neighbor 192.168.1.1 inherit peer-session IBGP ! SESSION WITH P1
  neighbor 192.168.1.1 inherit peer-policy IBGP
  neighbor 192.168.0.12 inherit peer-session IBGP ! SESSION WITH PE1-2
  neighbor 192.168.0.12 inherit peer-policy IBGP
```

NOTE: The list of sub-ASes is not required, since PE1-1 does not have any cBGP neighbor.

P1 (IOS XE)
```
router bgp 65001
  bgp confederation identifier 64501
  bgp confederation peer 65002 65003
  template peer-session IBGP
    remote-as 65001
    update-source Loopback0
  exit-peer-session
  template peer-session cBGP
    ebgp-multihop
    update-source Loopback0
  exit-peer-session
  !
  neighbor 192.168.0.11 inherit peer-session IBGP ! SESSION WITH PE1-1
  neighbor 192.168.0.12 inherit peer-session IBGP ! SESSION WITH PE1-2
  !
  neighbor 192.168.1.2 remote-as 65002
  neighbor 192.168.1.2 inherit peer-session cBGP ! SESSION cBGP WITH P2
  neighbor 192.168.1.3 remote-as 65003
  neighbor 192.168.1.3 inherit peer-session cBGP ! SESSION cBGP WITH P3
```

<u>PE3-1</u> (JUNOS)

```
[edit routing-options]
autonomous-system 65003;
confederation 64501;

[edit policy-options policy-statement NHS]
then
  next-hop self;
}
[edit protocols bgp]
  group IBGP {
  type internal;
  local-address 192.168.0.13;
  export NHS;
  neighbor 192.168.1.3;
  neighbor 192.168.0.32;
}
group EBGP {
  type external;
  neighbor 10.3.3.2 {
    peer-as 64503;
  }
}
```

NOTE: The list of sub-ASes is not required, since PE3-1 does not have any cBGP neighbor.

<u>P3</u> (JUNOS)

```
[edit routing-options]
autonomous-system 65003;
confederation 64501 members [ 65001 65002 65003 ];

[edit protocols bgp]
local-address 192.168.1.3;
group IBGP {
  type internal;
  neighbor 192.168.0.31;
  neighbor 192.168.0.32;
}
group cBGP {
  type external;
  multihop;
  neighbor 192.168.1.1 {
    peer-as 65001;
  }
  neighbor 192.168.1.2 {
    peer-as 65002;
  }
}
```

For verification purposes, let's see the basic information of prefix 203.0.113/24 in the BGP Table of P1.

```
P1# show bgp ipv4 unicast 203.0.113.0
... < output omitted > ...
  Advertised to update-groups:
     1
  (65002 65003) 64503
    192.168.0.31 (metric 2) from 192.168.1.2 (192.168.1.2)
      Origin IGP, metric 0, localpref 100, valid, confed-external, best
  (65003) 64503
    192.168.0.31 (metric 2) from 192.168.1.3 (192.168.1.3)
      Origin IGP, metric 0, localpref 100, valid, confed-external
```

From the view, we can see that P1 receives two advertisements of prefix 203.0.113/24 coming from the two cBGP sessions (**confed-external**) with P3 (**from 192.168.1.3**) and P2 (**from 192.168.1.2**). The BGP Next-Hop is, for both advertisements, **192.168.0.31** (address of PE3-1's lo0.0 interface), due to the NHS routing policy on router PE3-1 and to the fact that the NEXT_HOP attribute is not changed in cBGP sessions. You can easily verify if the AS_PATHs and the best path are correct (lowest BGP-ID).

8.5 INTERCONNECTION BETWEEN SERVICE PROVIDERS

One of the most debated topics among ISPs in the last few years is what interconnection model should be adopted. The interconnection issues were well known in the telephone world. Indeed, interconnection between the various telephone networks allowed considering this set of networks as a single network (a "network of networks"), where, from any phone terminal, you could reach any other phone terminal all over the world.

NOTE: the interconnection model adopted in the telephone world was very simple: the minutes of telephone traffic that the users of Provider A carried out towards users of Provider B and vice versa were counted, and at the end a difference was made between the minutes of traffic, with the consequent income statement. By way of example, if during one year, the users of Provider A made one million minutes of traffic toward the users of Provider B, and, vice versa, in the same period, the users of Provider B made 800,000 minutes of traffic toward the users of Provider A, Provider A paid a difference of 200,000 minutes of traffic to Provider B, according to a contractually-defined interconnection fee.

Unfortunately, in the IP world, the concept of connection does not exist, therefore defining an interconnection model is way more complex. Moreover, to keep the comparison with telephone interconnection, there is no concept of caller and callee. This led to the definition of a very simple interconnection model, where the bilateral relation between ISPs belongs to the supplier-client kind, meaning that one ISP acts as provider of the Internet access service, while the other ISP acts as service user.

The role of supplier is covered by Upstream Providers, as defined in Section 1.3.1. A bilateral supplier-client agreement is called transit relationship (or agreement), also defined in Section 1.3.1. The result of adopting this model is the definition of a tiered model, where local ISPs are clients of regional ISPs, which in turn are clients of national ISPs, which in turn are clients of transit ISPs, i.e. ISPs which can reach any Internet prefix. This tiered model has been described in Section 1.3.1. The ISPs of a certain tier act as Upstream Providers for lower tier ISPs.

In the real world, this tiered model is not always observed, and rather than a sorted set of supplier-client relationships, we often have ISPs using two or more ISPs as suppliers. And there is another aspect that lies outside the basic model. In the classic supplier-client model, clients pay their suppliers for a service. However, ISPs tend to use a *sender keep all* peering model, that is, an interconnection form where both ISPs involved in the interconnection determine that the benefit is the same for both ends, and so no ISP can take on the role of supplier.

This model can occur at any level of the interconnection hierarchy, and it is usually based on the principle that an equal agreement is better than paying a service supplier. This kind of agreement is defined as peering relation (or agreement) (see Section 1.3.1). In a peering relation between ISPs, each ISP provides access to its own IP prefixes to the other ISP free of charge. Henceforth, we will define the ISPs that establish a peering relation as local peers.

From a technical standpoint, an interconnection between ISPs requires the definition of inbound and outbound traffic management policies with each one of the interconnecting ISPs. As mentioned several times, the protocol that supports the definition of these traffic management policies is BGP, and it is the sum of the different ASes and the BGP sessions between ASes that forms the entire Internet.

We don't want to go over the economic aspects of ISP interconnection, because it is a complex matter that lies outside the scope of this book. Rather, we will focus on some types of interconnection, and, specifically, on the possible traffic management policies via BGP.

8.5.1 Interconnection between local peers

Interconnection between local peers is done either through direct connections – and in this case we talk about private peering – or through the Fabrics of the IXPs (Internet eXchange Points, see Section 1.3.2) – and in this other case we talk about public peering.

NOTE: As we specified in the first Chapter of this book, Internet eXchange Points are physical infrastructures that facilitate the interconnection between Autonomous Systems. They allow the establishment of both private (private peering) and public (public peering) relations. Private interconnections (achieved through PNIs, Private Network Interconnections), usually occur on passive infrastructures (Meet-Me-Room) of the IXPs, while public ones occur through the Fabrics (peering LAN). It should be noted that private interconnections between ASes can also be established outside an Internet eXchange Point.

Choosing one over the other mode depends on economic and technical factors. Usually, choosing an interconnection through the Fabric of an IXP is less expensive, since the costs related to the physical communication infrastructure are divided between several ISPs, however, if the bandwidth is not suitably sized, there could be performance issues. Vice versa, direct interconnection is costlier, but it ensures better performance, because it is simpler to provide a sufficient bandwidth connection to ensure a suitable service quality, by continuously monitoring traffic.

Concerning the BGP policies to adopt, private and public peering are equivalent. Private peering can be considered in the same way as bilateral and multilateral peering usually established on the Fabrics of the IXP (see Section 1.3.2). In particular, filtering policies should only allow the exchange of the local prefixes used by the ISPs to assign IP addresses to its own customers, and prevent the prefixes learned from a local peer from being propagated to other local peers and Upstream Providers.

A peculiar aspect of the interconnection to the Fabric of an IXP is the presence of Route Servers (RS), which can be seen as "facilitators" of the interconnection process. Indeed, without adopting the RS, an ISP connecting to other ISPs through the Fabric should establish many bilateral peerings with the other ISPs (not necessarily all of them). By using the RSes, instead, an ISP can establish just a couple of eBGP sessions toward the RSes (usually at least two, for reliability purposes), to exchange routing information with all the other connected ISPs.

There are many benefits related to the introduction of RSes, such as:

- reducing the configuration complexity – ISP routers only need a couple (or slightly more) eBGP sessions, instead of hundreds of them;

- reducing CPU and router memory use – ISP routers receive all the necessary routing information for traffic interexchange, without having to establish hundreds of eBGP sessions;

- reducing the administrative aspects related to the definition of bilateral peering agreements;

- reducing the filters to be implemented, many of which can be demanded to the RSes, which already implement filtering policies to prevent the ISPs from exchanging incorrect routing information;

- BGP advertisement validation. The RSes implement the RPKI architecture (see Chapter 10), which allows validating the correct origin of BGP advertisements;

- possibility of becoming immediately operative, once physically connected to the Fabric of an IXP, by establishing minimal configurations of the eBGP sessions toward the RSes;

- possibility of using the RSes as backup, if a bilateral peering session drops. Backup routing information are guaranteed by the RSes;

- possibility of receiving prefixes from large Content Providers. In some cases, this is the only solution: below a certain level of traffic, Content Providers do not allow the establishment of bilateral sessions.

The RSes operating logic is similar to that of the Route Reflectors (RRs) described in Paragraph 8.3, with an essential difference: while the RRs reflect iBGP advertisements, the RSes reflect eBGP advertisements. However, when reflecting eBGP advertisements, the RSes follow different rules than standard eBGP advertisement propagation rules. Indeed, since a RS is a tool to facilitate peering relations between ISPs, it must behave in a transparent manner. Specifically, a RS, differently from standard eBGP sessions, never changes the following attributes: NEXT_HOP, AS_PATH, LOCAL_PREF and COMMUNITY.

NOTE: A RS is never part of the forwarding path; its only purpose is providing routing information to the routers of the ISPs connected to the Fabric of an IXP. For this reason, like we saw for Route Reflectors (see Section 8.3.4), since a RS needs minimal forwarding hardware, it can be instantiated on commercial servers in bare metal mode, or instanced as VNF (Virtual Network Function) in an NFV (Network Function Virtualization) system.

The fact that the AS_PATH is not changed by a RS could entail, in certain implementations (e.g. on Cisco platforms) an issue related to the advertisements acceptance by the routers of the ISPs, as shown in Figure 8.15 below. The issue derives from the following rule:

A BGP Speaker refuses the advertisements coming from an AS different from the first AS value contained in the AS_PATH.

Let's consider the example in Figure 8.15. ISP-1, with AS number 64501, advertises its local prefix 192.0.2/24 on the eBGP session with the RS. The AS_PATH, as per standard rules, is [64501]. The RS, which belongs to AS 65541, "reflects" the advertisement on all eBGP sessions, including the one toward ISP-2. As we said earlier, the RS does not change the AS_PATH attribute, which remains [64501]. ISP-2 will receive the advertisement on its session with the RS, however, since the AS number of the RS (=65541) is not ranked first in the AS_PATH (actually, it is not even present), due to the rule mentioned above, the router of ISP-2 rejects the advertisement. And this makes traffic exchange between the two ISPs impossible.

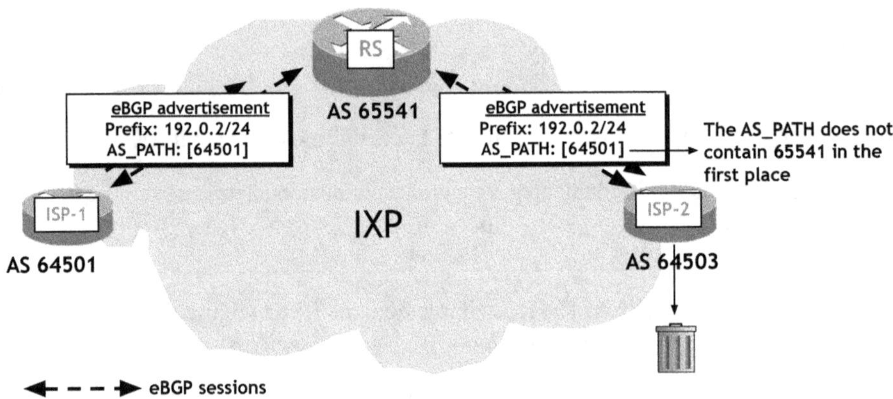

Figure 8.15 – Potential issue with the AS_PATH when using the RSes.

Concerning the technologies used in this book, only Cisco platforms follow this rule, while Juniper platforms with JUNOS do not. To address this issue, Cisco platforms provide the following configuration commands, to be executed on the routers of the ISPs with multilateral eBGP sessions.

<u>IOS XE</u>
ISP(config)# **router bgp** *AS-number*
ISP(config-router)# **no bgp enforce-first-as**

<u>IOS XR</u>
RP/0/RP0/CPU0:ISP(config)# **router bgp** *AS-number*
RP/0/RP0/CPU0:ISP(config-bgp)# **bgp enforce-first-as disable**

NOTE: In platforms with JUNOS, the default setting is to accept the advertisements anyway. If necessary, this rule could be forced via the "**enforce-first-as**" configuration command, to be executed under the [**edit protocols bgp**] hierarchy, or at global, group or session level.

The configuration of a Route Server requires only the addition of the command that allows defining whether the eBGP advertisements should be reflected to a certain eBGP Neighbor, according to the transparency rules above.

<u>IOS XE</u>
RS(config)# **router bgp** *AS-number*
RS(config-router)# **neighbor** *IP-* **route-server-client**

<u>JUNOS</u>
[**edit protocols bgp group** *group-name*]
route-server-client;

NOTE: When this book was published, IOS XR did not support the command that allows it to become a RS.

Let's see an example of configuration in the IXP environment, both for a RS and for an ISP router. The example refers to Figure 8.16 below.

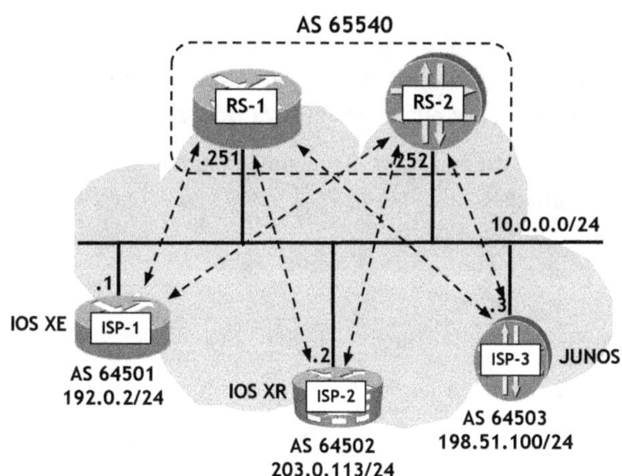

Figure 8.16 – Test network to configure a RS and ISP router in an IXP.

The numbering of the peering LAN is 10.0.0.0/24; the numbering of the interfaces on the peering LAN of the ISP routers and of the RSes are shown in the figure.
Let's see the relevant RSes configurations first.

RS-1 (IOS XE)
```
router bgp 65540
  bgp router-id 192.168.3.1
  neighbor 10.0.0.1 remote-as 64501
  neighbor 10.0.0.2 remote-as 64502
  neighbor 10.0.0.3 remote-as 64503
  !
  address-family ipv4
    neighbor 10.0.0.1 activate
    neighbor 10.0.0.1 route-server-client
    neighbor 10.0.0.2 activate
    neighbor 10.0.0.2 route-server-client
    neighbor 10.0.0.3 activate
    neighbor 10.0.0.3 route-server-client
  exit-address-family
```

RS-2 (JUNOS)
```
[edit routing-options]
router-id 192.168.3.2;
autonomous-system 65540;

[edit protocols bgp]
group RS-CLIENT {
  route-server-client;
  neighbor 10.0.0.1 {
    peer-as 64501;
  }
```

```
  neighbor 10.0.0.2 {
    peer-as 64502;
  }
  neighbor 10.0.0.3 {
    peer-as 64503;
  }
}
```

Now, let's see the configurations on the ISP routers. For the sake of brevity, we will only include the relevant configurations, and leave out any ordinary eBGP session configuration.

NOTE: The configuration of ISP-3 (JUNOS) is not included, since it does not require any specific command for multilateral sessions toward the RSes. As you may recall, JUNOS does not check the first value of the AS_PATH.

ISP-1 (IOS XE)
```
router bgp 64501
  bgp router-id 192.168.0.1
  no bgp enforce-first-as
  network 192.0.2.0
  neighbor RS peer-group
  neighbor RS remote-as 65540
  neighbor 10.0.0.251 peer-group RS
  neighbor 10.0.0.252 peer-group RS
```

ISP-2 (IOS XR)
```
router bgp 64502
  bgp enforce-first-as disable
  address-family ipv4 unicast
    network 203.0.113.0/24
  !
  af-group RS address-family ipv4 unicast
    route-policy ALL in
    route-policy ALL out
  !
  neighbor 10.0.0.251
    remote-as 65540
    address-family ipv4 unicast
      use af-group RS
  !
  neighbor 10.0.0.252
    remote-as 65540
    address-family ipv4 unicast
      use af-group RS
```

NOTE: In practical applications, these configurations should always be accompanied by suitable filters. Filtering aspects between local peers will be covered in Section 8.6.3.

To conclude the example, here is the content of the BGP table on ISP-2:

```
RP/0/RP0/CPU0:ISP-2#show bgp
. . .
    Network              Next Hop          Metric LocPrf Weight Path
*> 192.0.2.0/24         10.0.0.1               0             0 64501 i
*                       10.0.0.1               0             0 64501 i
*> 198.51.100.0/24      10.0.0.2               0             0 64503 i
*                       10.0.0.2                             0 64503 i
*> 203.0.113.0/24       0.0.0.0                0         32768 i
```

As expected, for each IP prefix advertised by the ISPs (except the one local to ISP-2), there are two eBGP advertisements received respectively from the two RSes. For instance, for prefix 192.0.2/24, the detail of the two advertisements is:

```
RP/0/RP0/CPU0:ISP-2#show bgp 192.0.2.0/24
. . .
Paths: (2 available, best #1)
Not advertised to any peer
  Path #1: Received by speaker 0
  Not advertised to any peer
  64501
    10.0.0.1 from 10.0.0.251 (192.168.3.1)
    Origin IGP, metric 0, localpref 100, valid, external, best, group-best
      Received Path ID 0, Local Path ID 1, version 9
      Origin-AS validity: (disabled)
  Path #2: Received by speaker 0
  Not advertised to any peer
  64501
    10.0.0.1 from 10.0.0.252 (192.168.3.2)
      Origin IGP, metric 0, localpref 100, valid, external
      Received Path ID 0, Local Path ID 0, version 0
      Origin-AS validity: (disabled)
```

We'll leave the analysis of this view to you.

8.5.2 Interconnection with Upstream Providers

A typical configuration, for a medium-small ISP – asides from having private and/or public peering with other similarly-sized ISPs – is to use the transit service toward the Internet, for higher reliability reasons, from at least two Upstream Providers.

The Upstream Provider side routing policies are more complex, compared to those applied toward a local peer, where, as we saw in Section 8.5.1 above, we just need simple filters to prevent Lateral ISP-ISP-ISP route leaks (see Section 8.6.1). Since the ISP has two or more exit points toward two or more Upstream Providers, apart from applying suitable filtering policies, it needs to establish how to manage traffic to/from them.

Concerning outbound traffic management, there are basically three options to choose from:

- Ask the Upstream Providers to send only the default route. As an alternative to request the default route only, an ISP could:

  ➢ apply a deny any filter and reject all BGP advertisements received from the Upstream Providers;

  ➢ configure a default route toward each Upstream Provider on its own edge router, with the connection interface to the Upstream Provider as Next-hop;

  ➢ redistribute the default route in the IGP protocol (OSPF, IS-IS) or using iBGP sessions.

- Ask for the default route and a set of selected prefixes, including those where the ISP generates more traffic (e.g. Content Providers, Cloud Providers, Social Networks, etc.).

- Ask for the FIRT.

An interesting issue of this last strategy is if and what addresses should be rejected from the FIRT received from the Upstream Providers, to prevent flooding the routers with mostly useless routing information. We will go over this aspect in Section 8.6.4.

Another aspect to take into account is that, if an ISP – as it often occurs – receives the advertisement of the same prefix from all Upstream Providers, it would be best to make the outbound traffic transit through the geographically closer AS (optimal routing). For instance, assuming that an ISP and its Upstream Provider UP-1 are in Europe, and the other Upstream Provider UP-2 is in the US, it may occur that the prefix of AS Z located in Europe but closer to UP-2 than to UP-1 according to the AS_PATH length, is reached through UP-2 rather than through UP-1, which is geographically closer. And this affects the end-to-end delay and round-trip-time – basic performance indexes for applications. Unfortunately, in BGP advertisements, the concept of geographical proximity does not exist; therefore, in order to solve the optimal routing issue, we need to adopt a few tricks. A very simple idea is for the Upstream Providers to associate COMMUNITY attributes to BGP advertisements, based on their geographical localization. One example of this issue was described at the end of Section 2.4.6, where we saw a possible solution based on wise use of the COMMUNITY attribute.

Lastly, still concerning outbound traffic, it is always best to configure some backup strategy, in case the connections toward the Upstream Providers are out of service. A very simple strategy is to create default routes toward the inside of the ISP's AS, conditioned by the operation of the respective connections toward the Upstream Providers. For instance, assuming that an ISP has two Upstream Providers UP-1 and UP-2 reached through the two gateways GTW-1 and GTW-2, two default routes conditioned via IGP (e.g. via OSPF) could be generated from them. In this case, with the same outbound traffic distribution we've seen until now in standard conditions, if the connection toward one of the two Upstream Providers is out of service, traffic following the default route will be routed through the other Upstream Provider.

NOTE: A recommendation to follow, when propagating a default route via IGP in the AS of an ISP, is to avoid installing it in routers with private or public peering. This should be avoided because the BGP Neighbors could configure on their router a default route toward the router of the ISP, and therefore use it as transit toward other destinations (thus violating the peering agreement, which entails only the exchange of traffic to/from its own customers). To avoid this issue, you should configure, in routers with private or public peerings, a default route with a bit bucket as Next-Hop (e.g., in Cisco routers with IOS or IOS XE: **ip route 0.0.0.0 0.0.0.0 Null0**).

To conclude this section, let's go over the possible strategies for inbound traffic. The strategies affect the way ISP prefixes are advertised toward the Upstream Providers. For the sake of simplicity, we will assume that the ISP has the option of aggregating all the subnets assigned to its customers in a single prefix (provider aggregatable prefix). If the connection bandwidth toward the Upstream Providers is identical, a possible strategy is to advertise the aggregate to all Upstream Providers, and, possibly, for a better distribution of inbound traffic, advertise the aggregate subnets on the different connections, chosen based on the volume of downstream traffic or on the services supplied.

For instance, assuming that an ISP has two Upstream Providers UP-1 and UP-2, for the connection toward UP-1 to be used by the traffic directed to residential customers, it is sufficient to number them with the same subnet part of the provider aggregatable prefix, and then to advertise it to UP-1, along with the aggregate. Similarly, for the connection toward UP-2 to be used by the traffic directed to business customers, it is sufficient to number these prefixes with the same subnet, and then advertise it to UP-2, along with the aggregate. If one of the two connections goes out of service, the aggregate advertisement, along with the specific subnets, ensures that the other connection acts as backup.

NOTE: When advertising the aggregate subnets, pay attention not to advertise subnets with a mask length greater than 24 bit for IPv4 or 48 bit for IPv6, as they are usually rejected by Upstream Providers.

If the connection bandwidth toward the Upstream Providers is different, the following strategy can be adopted:

- advertising the aggregate on a higher bandwidth connection toward the Upstream Providers;

- advertising on the other connections:

  - ➤ the aggregate with a suitable AS Path Prepending;

  - ➤ subnets of the aggregate chosen based on the volume of traffic drawn or the services provided.

8.6 FILTERING BEST PRACTICES

As we mentioned in Chapter 6, filtering policies are essential for the correct operation of the Internet's ecosystem, and they help to limit damage to one's own and other networks. Without suitable filtering, incidents such as route leaks and prefix hijacking (see Chapter 10) would be very frequent, and they would have greater impact within the entire ecosystem. Moreover, suitable filtering increases the scalability and stability of the entire Internet, preventing the proliferation of the amplitude of routing tables and the circulation of prefixes that should not be included in the RIBs of the routers, either because they can only be used in private networks (e.g. IP prefixes specified by RFC 1918), or because reserved to specific applications or documentation.

Before going over the filtering policies, we should classify the route leaks, so as to design the filters to prevent them.

8.6.1 Route leak classification

One of the weaknesses of BGP is that an incorrect application of the interconnection policies with the other ISPs can cause several issues, such as non-optimal routing, traffic black-holes, fraudulent traffic interception, and much more.

The RFC 7908 – *Problem Definition and Classification of BGP Route Leaks*, June 2016, defined a complete series of these issues, known as route leaks. Some of them refer to variations of BGP's default behavior, as introduced by RFC 8212.

RFC 7908, in Section 2, defines a route leak as follows:

A route leak is the propagation of routing announcement(s) beyond their intended scope.

To clarify this phenomenon, let's see a couple of significant examples. The examples are taken from the classification introduced by RFC 7908. For other examples, see the RFC. Some of the examples correspond to incidents that have occurred several times in real applications.

Example 1

Let's consider the classic case of an enterprise customer that, in order to access the Internet, has a multi-homed connection to two different ISPs (Upstream Providers), ISP-A and ISP-B. The scenario is described in Figure 8.17 below.

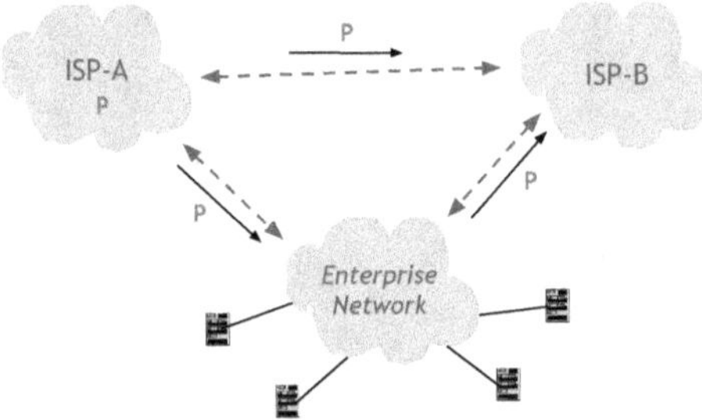

Figure 8.17 – Example of type 1 route leak.

Let's assume that Upstream Provider ISP-A advertises one of its own local prefixes (P) both directly to ISP-B, with which it has a peering relation, and to the enterprise network, to which it offers a transit service. If the administrator of the enterprise network applies BGP's default policies (i.e., does not apply any outbound filtering policy), the advertisement received by ISP-A is automatically propagated to ISP-B. If ISP-B – which currently receives two advertisements of prefix P – chose as best path the advertisement coming from the enterprise network, the latter would become a transit for the traffic sent by ISP-B toward prefix P. With two negative effects. The first, that the enterprise network would be deprived of the bandwidth that it pays to its Upstream Providers, and the second, that usually the resources of the enterprise network are not sufficient to handle the large volumes of traffic that the ISPs exchange directly. Therefore, most of the traffic between ISPs would be lost due to a lack of resources.

This type of route leak is classified by RFC 7908 as type 1 – *Hairpin Turn with Full Prefix*.

Example 2

Let's consider the case of three ISPs, with ISP-A having a peering relation with ISP-B, and ISP-B having a peering relation with ISP-C (see Figure 8.18).

In this case, the default policies include that an ISP should never propagate the advertisements it receives from an ISP with which it has a peering relation with to another ISP (not even to possible Upstream Providers offering a transit service). By way of example, referring to the figure, ISP-B should never propagate to ISP-C the advertisement of prefix P-A received from ISP-A, and, vice versa, ISP-B should never propagate to ISP-A the advertisement of prefix P-C received from

ISP-C. Otherwise, ISP-B would become a transit ISP between ISP-A and ISP-C, thus breaching the rules of the peering relation, which is only bilateral. As you may recall, a peering relation only entails the exchange of direct traffic, and never of transit traffic.

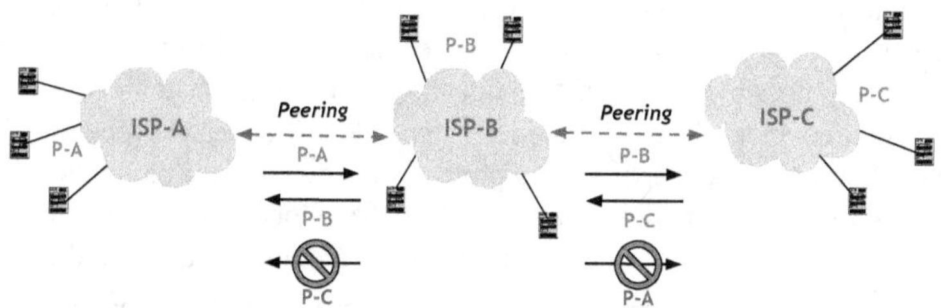

Figure 8.18 – Example of type 2 route leak.

This type of route leak is classified by RFC 7908 as type 2 – *Lateral ISP-ISP-ISP Leak*. Other two examples of this type described by RFC 7908 are:

- type 3: the propagation of advertisements that an ISP receives from an Upstream Provider toward an ISP with which it holds a peering relation;

- type 4: the opposite of type 3, that is, an ISP propagates to an Upstream Provider the advertisements coming from ISP with which it holds a peering relation.

All the types mentioned have the same root issue: automatic propagation of BGP advertisements on eBGP sessions. However, this is exactly what RFC 1771 and its review RFC 4271 say. And this automatic propagation has been covered by RFC 8212 (see Sections 2.1.2 and 3.1.3), which "requires" to implement both inbound and outbound filters.

8.6.2 Non-routable prefix filtering

There are prefixes that shouldn't circulate in the Internet (non routable prefixes), and therefore should never be included in the FIRT. For this reason, all the edge routers of an ISP – i.e. routers with BGP sessions with other ISPs – should apply standard filters to block these prefixes. We went over the list of non routable prefixes in Paragraph 6.2 (and Sections 6.2.1, 6.2.2 and 6.2.3 specifically), where we described the configurations in Cisco (IOS, IOS XE/XR) and Juniper (JUNOS) platforms. Please remember that the list is not static, and it should be updated every time IANA allocates routing spaces to the RIRs. There are several Internet websites that can be consulted for this purpose, such as *https://team-cymru.com/community-services/bogon-reference/*. Moreover, the IANA features web pages with the allocation of all IPv4 and IPv6 prefix blocks.

As mentioned in Paragraph 6.2, in Cisco routers with IOS or IOS XE, filters are usually created through prefix-lists, while in those with IOS XR through prefix-sets used in the routing policy conditions. Juniper routers have preset Martian Lists that can be updated. See Paragraph 6.2 for some sample configurations.

Control plane filters should always be accompanied by data plane filters (Access Control List (ACL) in Cisco routers and Firewall Filter (FF) in Juniper routers). The decision to install filters on the data plane depends on the edge routers' power, and on the traffic they handle. Indeed, data plane filters engage a lot of the router's forwarding capacity. Typically, small ISPs tend to implement very aggressive filters, while large ISPs – due to the fact that they have to handle a lot more traffic – tend to implement on the data plane only those filters deemed strictly necessary by the network administrator.

8.6.3 Filters in peering relations

In peering relations, the main filtering purpose is to avoid type 2 route leaks. This implies that, in the outbound direction, an ISP must advertise only its local prefixes to the local peers, possibly suitably aggregated, and it shouldn't propagate the advertisements received from the local peers to other local peers and to any possible Upstream Providers, but only to its customers, if strictly required. If an ISP has customers that advertise provider independent prefixes and perhaps have their own public AS, the ISP must also advertise these prefixes. In the inbound direction, filters must only allow the reception of advertisements of public prefixes from local peers, and block everything else (non routable prefixes, default routes, etc.). There are two methods to define a filter:

- Using a database (IRR, Internet Routing Registry), usually managed by RIRs or by third-parties, and checking if the prefixes advertised by the local peers comply with IRR declarations.

- Creating it manually, upon agreement between the local peers on the local prefixes to be exchanged, without any query to external databases.

NOTE: In the case of public peering, usually the compliance of prefixes advertised by local peers is checked by the route servers, which, through suitable scripts, query the IRRs, and block the propagation of any unauthorized prefixes.

As an example, let's consider the three local peers in Figure 8.16 with a multilateral peering between them achieved through the two route servers RS-1 and RS-2. For the sake of simplicity, let's focus only on router ISP-1 (IOS XE). The others, except for the different command syntax, have identical logic. Inbound/outbound filters applied on router ISP-1, in the two sessions toward the RSes are:

```
ip prefix-list AS64501 permit 192.0.2.0/24
ip prefix-list AS64502 permit 203.0.113.0/24
ip prefix-list AS64503 permit 198.51.100.0/24
!
router bgp 64501
  aggregate-address 192.0.2.0/24 summary-only
  neighbor RS peer-group
  neighbor RS remote-as 65540
  neighbor RS prefix-list AS64501 out
  neighbor RS prefix-list AS64502 in
  neighbor RS prefix-list AS64503 in
  neighbor 10.0.0.251 peer-group RS
  neighbor 10.0.0.252 peer-group RS
```

This configuration mode is the most accurate one, even if it has some scalability issues. Indeed, the ISPs should know all the prefixes of all the other local peers, and therefore establish many prefix-lists, one for each local peer, with each prefix-list comprising dozens of lines (as many as the prefixes advertised by the local peers). Moreover, adding/removing a prefix by a local peer or by the ISP, or the arrival of a new ISP connected to the Fabric of the IXP, entails an update of the prefix-lists. A solution to this issue is not possible with the ordinary configurations we've seen until now. There are two possible ways: either the ISP defers this task to the IXP's route servers, which usually filter the prefixes based on the information supplied by the ISPs and validated in the IRRs, or it does the same task itself, through suitable automation tools.

NOTE: Consistently with the scalability issues we've just described, it is best to implement manual filters also in the case of external databases, since they sometimes could return non-reliable information. Or at least in bilateral peering relations, which usually do not include all the ISPs present in the IXP.

8.6.4 Filters in transit relations

According to current best practices, specified by RFC 7454 – *BGP Operations and Security*, February 2015 (document known also as BCP-194), it is best for an ISP, in its transit relations, to apply inbound filters to block the following prefixes (with the possible exception of the default route, if the ISP does not request its Upstream Provider to send the FIRT):

- non routable prefixes (see Section 8.6.2);

- prefixes not allocated by IANA;

- prefixes with mask length greater than /24 (from /25 to /32) for IPv4 and greater than /48 for IPv6;

- prefixes belonging to your own AS;

- the default route.

Moreover, if the ISP is located within an IXP, it is best to block also the inbound advertisements of the prefix of the peering LAN and its possible more specific networks.

In the same way, an ISP should apply outbound filters to block the advertisement of the prefixes of the peering LAN to the Upstream Providers, except, of course, for its own local prefixes and the prefixes of its customers.

An interesting issue that occurs when an ISP receives the FIRT from one of its Upstream Providers is if and which prefixes to reject, apart from those mentioned above, to avoid flooding the routers with mostly useless routing information. A possible choice could be accepting only the local prefixes of the ISP with which it holds the eBGP session, and the local prefixes of the AS "close" to it. How close can be determined based on subsequent attempts. For instance, we could choose to accept the local prefixes up to two or three ASes away. For traffic toward all the other prefixes, we can use a simple default route. To achieve this type of filters, we must resort to the RegExp (see Paragraph 4.4). By indicating with AS-UP the AS number of the Upstream Provider, in Cisco and in Juniper platforms, the RegExp to be used are:

- Cisco platforms:
  - ➣ **^(AS-UP_)+([0-9]+)?$:** if we want to accept the advertisements of local prefixes of the Upstream Provider and of local prefixes of the ASes adjacent to it, that is, one hop from the Upstream Provider;
  - ➣ **^(AS-UP_)+([0-9]+)?_([0-9]+)?$:** if we want to accept the advertisements of local prefixes of the Upstream Provider and of local prefixes of the ASes up to two hops from the Upstream Provider.

- Juniper platforms:
  - ➣ **AS-UP.{0,1}:** if we want to accept the advertisements of local prefixes of the Upstream Provider and of local prefixes of the ASes adjacent to it, that is, one hop from the Upstream Provider;
  - ➣ **AS-UP.{0,2}:** if we want to accept the advertisements of local prefixes of the Upstream Provider and of local prefixes of the ASes up to two hops from the Upstream Provider.

In this way, we are fairly certain that we can route most of the outbound traffic in an optimal way. The reason is that, in modern networks, Content Providers, Cloud Providers, etc., use caching systems co-located in the IXPs or within the networks of the major Upstream Providers. This means that, if an ISP has one of its routers inside an IXP infrastructure, several Content/Cloud Providers are seen as adjacent. If the same ISP had a transit relation with an Upstream Provider, several Content/Cloud Providers would be seen as two or three hops away, at most.

8.6.5 Filters in customer side BGP sessions

The general rule in this case is to implement inbound filters on the eBGP sessions with the customers, which accept only those prefixes that the customers are authorized to advertise. These may include Provider Independent or Provider Aggregatable prefixes (see Section 9.2.1 for the definitions).

The same rule applies if the customer is an ISP, e.g., a Tier-3 ISP using a Tier-2 ISP as transit. However, this case falls into the one previously treated in Section 8.6.4, since there is a transit relation between the ISPs.

In any case, it is better not to accept prefixes that are too specific from a customer (e.g. with mask length greater than /24 for IPv4 or /48 for IPv6). A few exceptions are allowed, if the customer requests the option of doing BGP Traffic Engineering. For instance, a multi-homed customer (connected to two or more ISPs), could advertise a /24 prefix and the two /25 subnets, to divide its AS inbound traffic over several connections. In this case, the NO_EXPORT BGP Community should be linked to the IP subnets, to prevent these advertisements from being propagated upstream toward the other Upstream Providers (which would very likely reject them).

Outbound filtering depends on the prefixes requested by the customer. The customer could be happy with a simple default route and in this case the outbound filter must allow sending the default route and nothing else. If the customer (which must be multi-homed, otherwise it wouldn't make sense) requests the FIRT, outbound filters should be applied, to block the sending of:

- non routable prefixes (see Section 8.6.2);

- prefixes with mask length greater than /24 (from /25 to /32) for IPv4 or /48 for IPv6;

- the default route.

Lastly, the customer could also request to send the default route and some specific prefixes toward which it propagates a lot of traffic. In this case, the outbound filter should allow the default route and only those prefixes requested by the customer.

8.7 USING THE COMMUNITY ATTRIBUTE

The COMMUNITY attribute is used very often, especially by large transit ISPs, to make the routing policies simpler and more flexible.

The first public document on the use of the COMMUNITY attribute to define the routing policies was the aforementioned (see Section 7.3.1) RFC 1998 – *An Application of the BGP Community Attribute in Multi-home Routing*, August 1996, which describes how, one of the major US ISPs used the COMMUNITY attribute to allow its customers with multi-homed access to its network, to define their own routing policies on inbound traffic independently.

The principle behind RFC 1998 is very simple: making the Upstream Providers' life easier, by standardizing the configurations on edge routers, and giving their own (ISP and non-ISP) customers the option of defining their own inbound traffic management policies, without any additional configuration in the edge router of the Upstream Provider. In Section 7.3.4, we saw how to apply the mechanism suggested by RFC 1998 and the related configurations in Cisco and Juniper environments.

RFC 1998 was written a long time ago (August 1996), and since then, the ISPs have expanded and refined the use of the COMMUNITY attribute, making it a very powerful management tool. There are several real-life examples of its application, some of which are public, and some other not visible from the outside. The COMMUNITY attribute is used in several situations, such as:

- defining the Local Preference value;

- managing the AS_PATH Prepending;

- for advertisement propagation purposes;

- for prefix geographic localization;

- for packet coloring to differentiate their data plane treatment;

- ...

The configuration tools that allow implementing the policies based on the COMMUNITY attribute are those we saw in Chapter 4. Their application in the different real-life cases is conceptually easy, therefore we won't include any other examples, apart from the one in Section 7.3.4. Rather, we want to show the real-life case of how a European ISP uses this tool.

8.7.1 Case Study

This Case Study concerns one of the major global transit ISPs, and, for privacy reasons, we will call it **EuroISP** since it is based in Europe. Also for privacy reasons, we will indicate its AS number as AAAAA.

The COMMUNITY values accepted by customer ISPs are basically used for two purposes: defining a Local Preference value and the propagation scope of the advertisements received.

This is the list of accepted value, with a short description of their use:

Community	Action
AAAAA:40	*Propagate my advertisements only to EuroISP clients*
AAAAA:666	*Block traffic to this prefix on the edge router (COMMUNITY only valid for /32 prefixes)*
AAAAA:1090	*Set the Local Preference value to 90 (same value used in advertisements from ISPs with whom you have peering agreements)*
AAAAA:1070	*Set the Local Preference value to 70 (same value used in advertisements from ISPs with which you have transit agreements)*
AAAAA:1050	*Set the Local Preference value to 50 (path of last resort).*
AAAAA:200XX	*Do not advertise this prefix to... (see below)*

Use of value **AAAAA:40** narrows the propagation of an advertisement down to **EuroISP** customers, that is, it treats the advertisement as a peer of **EuroISP**, rather than one of its customers.

Value **AAAAA:666** blocks traffic from **EuroISP** to the customer, directed toward a specific *Host* (/32). This is very useful during DDoS (Distributed Denial of Service) attacks.

The three values **AAAAA:10xy** (xy = 50, 70, 90) allow customers that are multi-homed to **EuroISP** to divide the inbound traffic over several connections, using the Local Preference value (defined based on the COMMUNITY value by **EuroISP** routers). Obviously, the three COMMUNITY values are mutually exclusive.

Values **AAAAA:200XX** allow customers to block the propagation of their advertisements toward major global ISPs. Value **XX** defines the ISP to which the advertisement shouldn't be propagated. The following table defines some of the values of **XX** allowed and the related ISP.

XX	AS Number	ISP
01	701	Verizon
02	6453	TATA Communications
03	1239	Sprint
04	3320	Deutsche Telekom
05	5511	Orange
06	1299	Telia
07	3491	PCCW Global
08	2914	NTT GIN
...	...	...

The same COMMUNITY scheme is used to block the propagation of advertisements toward the IXPs to which *EuroISP* is connected. Value **XX** defines the IXP to which the advertisement shouldn't be propagated. The following table defines some of the values of **XX** allowed and the related IXP.

XX	IXP
99	LINX
98	AMSIX
97	DECIX
94	Equinix Singapore
93	EQUINIX Ashburn
96	PAIX Palo Alto

Concerning the BGP advertisements that *EuroISP* propagates to its customers, they contain at least one of the following COMMUNITY values, with the corresponding meaning described in the following table.

Community	Meaning
AAAAA:30	*Advertisement received from a European ISP*
AAAAA:31	*Advertisement received from a North American ISP*
AAAAA:32	*Advertisement received from a South American ISP*
AAAAA:33	*Advertisement received from an Asian ISP*
AAAAA:40	*Advertisement received from a EuroISP customer*

These COMMUNITY values help determine the optimal paths and are also useful if the customer wants to narrow down the traffic propagation to a single geographic area.
The determination of the origin geographic area of the advertisement is based on the advertisement entry point into the network (global coverage) of *EuroISP*. This means that the advertisement coming from a customer ISP based in South America could be labeled with the North American COMMUNITY value, because the BGP session is physically established with edge routers of the *EuroISP* network located in North America.

8.8 USE OF THE ROUTE FLAP DAMPING

One of the most dangerous phenomena in the entire Internet is the possible instability generated by the continuous prefix withdrawal and advertising (called route flapping), caused by the loss and consequent reestablishment of BGP sessions. The loss of a BGP session can be caused by several events, such as, out-of-service routers and/or physical connections, faulty hardware, software bugs, router software and/or hardware updates, etc.

When one of these events occurs, the BGP Neighbors of the BGP Speaker that caused the loss of BGP session (which, for the sake of simplicity, we will define as router R1), receive a BGP NOTIFICATION message indicating the reasons why the sessions has been lost, or do not receive any KEEPALIVE messages any longer. In both cases, the BGP session ends. This entails, on BGP Neighbors' side, the removal of all the advertisements received from router R1 from their Adj-RIB-in table (and therefore from the BGP advertisement table), and sending of UPDATE messages to withdraw all the best paths with Next-Hop R1 previously advertised to all their BGP Neighbors. Meanwhile, before recalculating any possible best paths, R1's BGP Neighbors reject direct traffic toward the prefixes advertised by R1. This process of sending UPDATE message to withdraw the best paths with Next-Hop R1 is repeated also by the BGP Neighbors of R1's BGP Neighbors, and so on, affecting a large number of ASes.

If, after some time, the BGP sessions between R1 and its BGP Neighbors are restored, R1 would resend all its best paths to its BGP Neighbors, which would have to choose the best paths again, and so on.

The constant flapping of BGP sessions entails a flooding of UPDATE messages that increase the processing load of the routers' CPU. When the quantity of prefixes to be advertised or withdrawn is very big, the number of UPDATE messages to process grows significantly, with possibly destructive consequences for the entire system. Moreover, there are more chances that traffic is blocked somewhere within the network, due to the temporary lack of suitable paths to reach its destination.

To mitigate the instability generated by route flapping, the Route Flap Damping (RFD) was developed by the IETF; this mechanism standardized by RFC 2439 – *BGP Route Flap Damping*, November 1998, has three main objectives:

- reducing the CPU load caused by unstable advertisements;

- preventing persistent advertisement oscillations;

- providing a greater advertisement stability, without sacrificing convergence time for advertisements not subject to route flapping.

8.8.1 RFD operation

The RFD is based on a "memory" mechanism, which allows the BGP process of a router to build a history of the instability of a prefix, based on which it will undertake temporary advertisement suppression actions, in order to prevent its participation to the selection process for a (limited) period of time.

In order to prevent traffic losses for long times within an AS, the RFD does not apply to the advertisements received on iBGP sessions, but only and exclusively to the advertisements received from eBGP sessions.

To define an unstable advertisement, a penalization mechanism based on a penalty value is used (described in RFC 2439 as *figure of merit*), and assigned to each advertisement subject to route flapping. The penalty is increased by a constant value (usually 1,000) after each advertisement withdrawal

NOTE: This is what RFC 2439 says. Not all manufacturers are aligned on this criteria; for instance, see Juniper's implementation below.

Within the interval between two subsequent withdrawals of the same advertisement, the penalty value decreases exponentially. The trend of the penalty value over time is similar to a typical "sawtooth", with the value increasing by a constant quantity when the UPDATE messages withdrawing an advertisement arrive, and decreasing exponentially between two subsequent increases. The constant that regulates the exponential decay is called half-life (*decay half life* in RFC 2439), and it represents the time spent by the BGP process to halve the current penalty value.

NOTE: Actually, RFC 2439 foresees two different constants: *decay half life while reachable*, to be used when the advertisement is present, and *decay half life while unreachable*, to be used when the advertisement has been withdrawn. Current implementations usually employ a single constant.

After a certain threshold, called suppress threshold (*cutoff threshold* in RFC 2439), the advertisement is "frozen" (suppressed), i.e. it is no longer considered in the selection process to determine the best path. The advertisement may be reused to determine the best path if and only if at least one of the following conditions is met:

- the penalty value drops below a configurable value called *reuse limit*;

- the time spent between the instant when the advertisement has been declared suppressed exceeds the configurable value called *max-suppress-time* (*maximum hold down time* in RFC 2439).

Based on the parameters above, each router determines a maximum penalty value (MAX_PENALTY) that can never be exceeded. The formula specified by RFC 2439 is the following:

$$MAX_{PENALTY} = RL \cdot \exp\left(\frac{MST}{HL}\right) \cdot \log(2)$$

where *RL=reuse limit, MST=max-suppress-time, HL=half-life* e *exp(x)=e^x*. This formula is extremely important, as it allows preventing inconsistent configuration values. Indeed, it is clear that the condition : $ST \leq MAX\_PENALTY$ where ST is the suppress threshold should always be valid, therefore, should the definition of the *RL, MST, HL* and *ST* values prove otherwise, the *ST* value could never be reached, making the RFD useless. For instance, values: $RL = 750$, $MST = 60$ min and $HL = 15$ min, entail a *MAX_PENALTY* value equal to:

$$MAX_{PENALTY} = 750 \cdot \exp\left(\frac{60}{15}\right) \cdot \log(2) \approx 12,326.76$$

therefore, ST configuration value should always be lower than – or equal to – 12,326.

Let's see the detailed operation of the penalization mechanism, with the help of an example. We will use the following parameters:

- Fixed penalty increment following the withdrawal of an advertisement: 1,000;

- ST: 2,500;

- RL: 750;

- HL = 15 min;

- MST = 60 min;

Figure 8.19 shows the trend of the penalty assigned to an advertisement over time, following repeated route flaps (coincident with the arrival of UPDATE messages withdrawing a prefix). At first, the penalty value is null. Following the first route flap, the penalty value increases to 1,000, and then it starts decreasing exponentially. Between the first and the second route flap, the advertisement is received again, and participates in the selection process regularly. The penalty value in this period drops exponentially, and, immediately before the second route flap, reaches a value determined by decay constant *HL*. By assuming the following penalty values, immediately subsequent to each route flap:

- 1° route flap: 1,000;

- 2° route flap: 1,650;

- 3° route flap: 2,200;

- 4° route flap: 2,800;

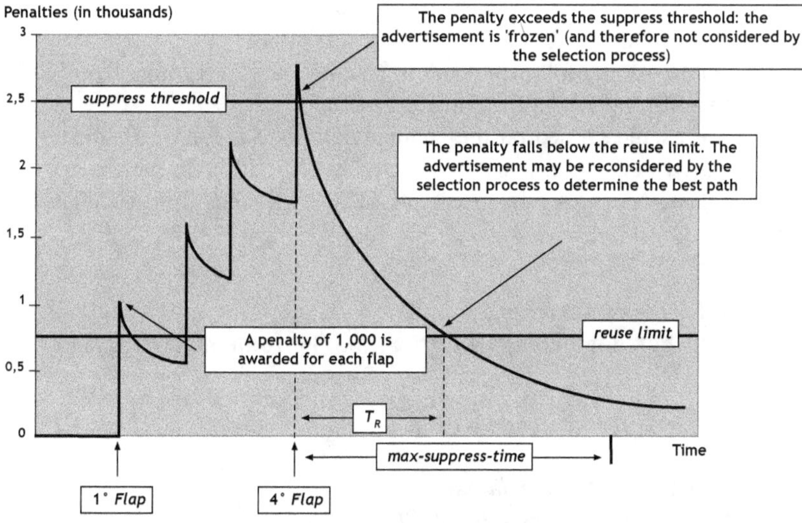

Figure 8.19 – Example of penalty time evolution in the RFD.

At the fourth route flap, the penalty exceeds the *ST* value, therefore the advertisement, once received again, is "frozen", i.e. is not considered within the selection process. Let's now assume that no more route flaps occur, that is, that the system stabilizes. The advertisement will still remain frozen until instant: $T_{Reuse} = \min\{T_R; MST\}$, where T_R is the interval between the beginning of the advertisement freezing period and the instant when the penalty – due to the exponential decay – reaches the *RL* value (see Figure 8.19). From this instant onward, the advertisement may be reconsidered in the selection process. In our example, $T_{Reuse} = T_R$. Indeed, since the *HL* value assumed is 15 min and, in the instant immediately following the fourth route flap, the penalty is equal to 2,800, after approx. 15 min from this, the penalty will drop to 1,400 and then, after another 15 min, it will drop to approx. 700, therefore below the *RL*. So, the T_R value can be estimated around 25 min, hence $T_{Reuse} = \min\{25; 60\} = 25 = T_R$.

8.8.2 Configuration aspects

Implementing the RFD mechanism both in JUNOS and in Cisco IOS XE/XR requires the configuration of the following four parameters: ST, RL, HL, MST. In both implementations, the penalty value for each route flap increased by a fixed value equal to 1,000; also, a penalty of 500 points is assigned, if an attribute is changed. The two implementations differ in two aspects: in defining the route flap and in the formula to calculate the MAX_PENALTY value.

For both implementations, a selective RFD implementation is possible, meaning that, at the user's discretion, more or less aggressive RFD parameters can be used, based on the importance given to the prefixes advertised. For instance, different parameters can be applied, based on the advertisements origin, type of prefixes contained, etc.

In Cisco implementations, the first aspect to consider is the route flap definition, which complies with RFC 2439: a route flap coincides with the arrival of an UPDATE message withdrawing a prefix. For each route flap, the penalty is increased by a value of 1,000. However, the MAX_PENALTY value is determined with a different formula, as suggested by RFC 2439. Based on the configuration parameters, the MAX_PENALTY value is calculated through the following relation:

$$MAX\_PENALTY = RL \cdot 2^{\left(\frac{MST}{HL}\right)}$$

All types of Cisco IOS use the following default parameters: HL=15 min, RL=750, ST= 2,000, MST=60 min, with a MAX_PENALTY value of 12,000.

The RFD should be enabled based on the configuration, and it can be enabled with the same parameters for all active eBGP sessions, or selectively, with different parameters, based on the different attributes contained in the advertisements, in the NLRI and other fields. The configuration commands are:

IOS XE
router(config)# **router bgp** *AS-number*
router(config-router)# **bgp dampening [[***HL RL ST MST***] | [route-map** *RM-name***]]**

router(config)# **route-map** *RM-name*
router(config-route-map)# **match** *condition*-1
...
router(config-route-map)# **match** *condition-N*
router(config-route-map)# **set dampening** *HL RL ST MST*

IOS XR
RP/0/RP0/CPU0:router(config)# **router bgp** *AS-number*
RP/0/RP0/CPU0:router(config-bgp)# **address-family ipv4 unicast**
RP/0/RP0/CPU0:router(config-bgp-af)# **bgp dampening [[***HL RL ST MST***] |**
                                       [route-policy *RP-name***]]**

RP/0/0/CPU0:R1(config)# **route-policy** *name*
RP/0/0/CPU0:R1(config-rpl)# **if destination in (***prefix/mask***) then**
           set dampening halflife *HL* **suppress** *SL* **reuse** *RL* **max-suppress** *MST* **endif**
RP/0/0/CPU0:R1(config-rpl)# **end-policy**

Route-maps and (optional) routing policies allow applying the selective RFD by choosing configuration parameters based on a set of conditions.

NOTE: Applying the simple "**bgp dampening**" command, without any option, enables the RFD with default parameters for all the advertisements received from any eBGP session. If you want to change the default parameters, you just need to specify them at the end of the command. For instance, if you want to use, for all eBGP advertisements, the set of parameters HL = 15 min, RL = 500, ST = 3,000 and MST = 45 min, you just need to execute the "**bgp dampening 15 500 3000 45**" command.

In JUNOS implementations, the route flap definition does not comply with RFC 2439. Indeed, a penalty of 1,000 points is assigned, in the case of UPDATE messages withdrawing a prefix, and in the case of UPDATE messages advertising a prefix. However, the MAX_PENALTY value is determined with the formula recommended by RFC 2439 and indicated above, in Section 8.8.1. Default parameters are: HL=15 min, RL=750, ST= 3,000, MST=60 min, with a MAX_PENALTY value of 12,326.78.

The RFD should be enabled based on the configuration, both at global, group or single session level, through the "**damping**" command. If the RFD is enabled at global level only, the command is applied only to eBGP sessions, and ignored for iBGP sessions. With the "**damping**" command only, the RFD is applied with default parameters.

To apply the selective RFD, first you need to define a parameter profile at "**policy-options**" level, and then apply the profile to a routing policy, which, in turn, should be applied, along with the "**damping**" command, at BGP protocol level as "**import**" or at global, group or single session level.

The RFD parameter profile is configured through the following commands:

```
[edit policy-options]
   damping profile-name {
   half-life value-in-minutes;
   max-suppress value-in-minutes;
   reuse value;
   suppress value;
   [disable];
}
```

NOTE: The "**disable**" option, when used, allows preventing the RFD application to a certain set of prefixes. Its application does not require the definition of the RFD parameter profile.

The routing policy to apply the profile to a defined prefix set – as specified in the conditions defined in the routing policy – is configured as such:

```
[edit policy-options]
policy-statement RP-name {
  from {
    various conditions
  }
  then {
    damping profile-name;
  }
}
```

Appendix A.7 shows a detailed Case Study of the RFD application. Here, we just want to provide a few guidelines for its practical application.

8.8.3 Guidelines for RFD application

In the past, the RFD and its use were a very controversial topic. Recommendations have been reviewed several times in the last two decades, and the value recommended by use parameters differ from the default values of the main implementations.

Document RIPE-229 – *Recommendations for Coordinated Route-flap Damping Parameters*, October 2001, was the first to provide interesting guidelines in RFD application, by suggesting parameters that have given good results in field applications, and, above all, by suggesting application methods, such as:

- not applying the RFD to important prefixes (e.g. DNS server, Global Top Level Domain server);

- applying the RFD selectively, based on the length of the prefix mask. In particular, it suggests to treat the prefixes with mask length ≥ 24 more aggressively, by defining for them an *MST* value=60 min, the prefixes with mask length 22 and 23 in an intermediate way, by defining for them an *MST* value=45 min, and, lastly, to treat the prefixes with mask length ≤ 21 in a non-aggressive way, by defining for them an *MST* value=30 min.

Moreover, RIPE-229 suggests not to "freeze" an advertisement before the fourth route flap. The parameters documented in the recommendation were adopted by many ISPs, and were considered almost as a best practice to observe for a long time.

Unfortunately, some subsequent studies have proven a few serious issues with the RFD as it is applied today. In particular, a few articles presented in 2002 by Zhuoqing Mao, Randy Bush and colleagues have highlighted an issue of the RFD when an advertisement is withdrawn. Indeed, when an advertisement is withdrawn, all BGP speakers receiving the UPDATE message signaling the withdrawal, use, in the event that the best path has been withdrawn, the selection process to decide the new best path, which is advertised to all BGP neighbors, according to the known propagation rules. In turn, since the advertisement has changed, they see a change of attributes in it, which entails an increase of the penalty, even if the advertisement is perfectly valid and the prefix has never been removed from the RIB.

And this, also through different BGP timers used by routers (and the MRAI timer in particular, see Paragraph 12.1), is propagated on the entire Internet. Therefore, a simple prefix withdrawal may result in a route flap a few ASes away from the one that executed the withdrawal, with the result that the prefix may be marked as suppressed, even without any sort of instability. Field tests were carried out, with the outcome that the simple withdrawal of an advertisement by an AS resulted in 41 BGP events a few ASes away.

Zhuoqing Mao, Randy Bush and colleagues suggested a few solutions to bypass this issue. But the ISPs did not take them into account and the manufacturers did not implement them. Actually, as the routers power grows and the transmission connections become more stable, the need to resort to the RFD – created in the mid-90s, when the routers' power was limited and transmission connections were fairly unstable – has become lower and lower. The ISPs are more worried with the RFD's fault, rather than appreciating its benefits. In light of this, Recommendation RIPE-229 has been replaced by RIPE-378 – *Recommendations on Route-flap Damping*, May 2006, which basically advises against the use of the RFD.

However, the controversy was resumed in 2011, with Cristel Pelsser's studies that brought to the definition of a set of parameters that make the RFD applicable. These studies were transposed both in the RIR framework (see the new Recommendation RIPE-528 – *Recommendations on Route Flap Damping*, January 2013, which rendered RIPE-378 obsolete) and in the IETF framework (see RFC 7196 – *Making Route Flap Damping Usable*, May 2014). Also, they are already recommended by the aforementioned RFC 7454. The same thing cannot be said about the various current BGP implementations that use the same default values as the configuration parameters. The following table compares the default parameters used by Cisco and Juniper to those recommended by Recommendations RIPE-528 and BGP-194.

RFD settings	Cisco	Juniper	BCP-194/RIPE-528
Penalties for withdrawing advertisements	1000	1000	1000
Penalties for sending advertisements	0	1000	0/1000
Penalties for attribute changes	500	500	500
Suppress-threshold	2000	3000	6000
Half-life (min)	15	15	15
Reuse-limit	750	750	750
Max suppress time (min)	60	60	60

SUMMARY

This chapter can be seen as a guide to practical BGP applications in medium-large ISP networks. In particular, it describes the interactions between the BGP and the IGP routing protocol, and the role they have in the global routing architecture of medium-large ISP networks.

The BGP protocol in itself is very scalable, and ideal to manage large volumes of routing information. However, some of its applications require further scalability mechanisms, such as when the BGP is used to import routing information external to the AS inside the AS. In this specific case, the use of BGP requires the establishment of a number of iBGP sessions that increases quadratically as the number of routers increases. In this chapter, we went over the two standard mechanisms that allow mitigating the quadratic growth issue: Route Reflection and BGP Confederation.

Another important aspect we covered is the interconnection between ISPs, where we introduced the best practices for interconnection between local peers and between an ISP and the Upstream Providers. In particular, we saw how to implement the filtering policies and the possible uses of the COMMUNITY attribute to obtain scalable configurations, and help obtain optimal routing.

Lastly, since BGP is subject to the instability generated by the constant prefix withdrawal and advertisement (known as route flapping), caused by the loss and subsequent re-establishment of BGP sessions, we described the standard Route Flap Damping mechanism. The Route Flap Damping helps to mitigate the route flap effect, by assigning penalties for each route flap and, after exceeding a certain penalty threshold, it prevents the advertisement of a certain prefix to take part in the selection process. The use of the Route Flap Damping is very much debated, and, in the past, there have been contradictory studies, until a set of operating parameters that make its application useful has been defined.

Worth remembering:

1. ISP network architecture and BGP role.

2. Interactions between IGP and BGP, with particular reference to the issues and solutions related to the different convergence rate.

3. The BGP/MPLS routing architecture, its practical implementation and the configuration best practices.

4. iBGP session reduction mechanisms: Route Reflection and BGP Confederation.

5. The role of Route Servers in IXP infrastructures.

6. The different types of interconnection between ISPs, Upstream Providers and local peers.

7. Standard filters used by ISPs.

8. Use of the COMMUNITY attribute.

9. The Route Flap Damping mechanism.

9 – BGP IN ENTERPRISE NETWORKS

In the past, enterprise networks have preferred to use exclusively IGP protocols (including, among the most widespread, RIP, OSPF and Cisco's proprietary EIGRP) to manage routing information on their network. BGP has never been taken into account, since it is considered an inter-domain routing protocol, and therefore too complex to be used in small enterprise networks.

This scenario has changed since the beginning of the 2000s, due to two important factors:

- networks' growth in size, which has highlighted important issues in terms of scalability of the routing architectures based exclusively on IGP;

- the diffusion of the Virtual Private Network service, based on the BGP/MPLS model. In this model, which will be treated in Chapter 11, routing information is transported within the network of the ISP providing the service, through the MP-BGP extension. Therefore, it is convenient to make customers access to service through BGP sessions, so as to avoid any potential complex issues of redistribution between routing protocols and exploit all the important properties of BGP, such as flexible traffic management and its loop prevention mechanism based on the AS_PATH attribute.

NOTE: From now on, we will indicate the Virtual Private Network service as VPN.

BGP's main applications in enterprise networks are basically two:

- as routing protocol between the enterprise network and an ISP for Internet access service;

- as PE-CE routing protocol for access to the VPN service, based on the BGP/MPLS model.

The PE-CE notation indicates the connection between routers PE (Provider Edge) of the network of the ISP that provides the service, and routers CE (Customer Edge) of the enterprise network. This classification, even if typical of the language of the VPN service based on the BGP/MPLS model, will be freely used also in this chapter.

In medium-large enterprise networks, BGP is applied also at transit network level, along with an IGP (usually IS-IS or OSPF). The implementation issues and the resulting routing architecture are in any case very similar to those of the large ISP networks we saw in Chapter 8. For this reason, we will not treat this aspect of BGP application to an enterprise network in this chapter.

In this chapter, we will see the possible BGP applications as routing protocol between the enterprise network and an ISP for Internet access service, by analysing in detail the possible solutions and best project and configuration practices. Everything we see is also valid if BGP is applied as PE-CE routing protocol, even if, in this case, some additional functions that we will see in Chapter 11 would be useful.

9.1 GENERAL CONSIDERATIONS

Today, access to IP services and to the Internet is vital for a company, insomuch that it is considered a mission critical service. Therefore, companies require highly reliable (fault tolerant) access services and flexible traffic management.

For these services, enterprise networks take advantage of the experience, service quality and capillarity offered by large ISP networks, to which they are connected through two different modes:

- single-homed connectivity: characterized by a single or redundant connection toward a single ISP;

- multi-homed connectivity: characterized by a single or redundant connection toward more than one ISP.

As mentioned in Paragraph 1.2, in technical literature, the terminology is not always compliant. Indeed, very often, redundant connectivity toward a single ISP is also defined as multi-homed. For the sake of clarity, in this textbook, we prefer to use the term "home" for an ISP, hence our classification.

9.1.1 Connection types: pros and cons

Choosing the connection type (single-homed/multi-homed) offers advantages and disadvantages that should be accurately weighted in order to gain a more robust and efficient access.

The advantage of connecting to a single ISP is the simplicity due mainly to the fact that the customer has a single technical and commercial interface, and a single billing centre. Customer requests, such as the implementation of specific routing policies, the activation of additional connections to increase the bandwidth, and the increase of the fault tolerance level, are met more quickly.

The main disadvantage of connecting to a single ISP is having a lower level of reliability, since a regional outage of the ISP network at regional and global level, causes a loss of connection to IP services and of Internet access. Loss of connectivity issues could also be worsened by the lack of physical redundancy in PE-CE transmission connections. Indeed, even in the case of connections that seem redundant at layer 3, it may occur that the ISP uses, in its transmission network, a single physical cable to route the two connections, or that it bundles the connections together in a single transmission flow (e.g. 2 x 1 Gbit/s flow bundled together in the same 10 Gbit/s flow). Therefore, if this kind of physical connection or a device bundling transmission flows together goes out of service, at layer 3, it causes the loss of both PE-CE connections. The concept of physical diversity of transmission connections is well known among network designers, and it holds the same importance, in a correct project, as the connections' logical diversity (at layer 3).

NOTE: In technical literature, two or more connections sharing the same physical resources (e.g. cable ducts, transmission devices, signal amplifiers, etc.), are said to belong to an SRLG (Shared Risk Link Group). By definition, an SRLG is a set of logical connections that share all or part of the physical resources of the transport network.

On the one side, connecting to two or more ISPs significantly increases the level of reliability of the connections, and on the other side, it increases the technical and managerial complexity, as well as the economic cost. For instance, the block of public IP addresses that a customer uses to number its hosts, cannot be aggregated in one of the macro-blocks made available to ISPs. Moreover, if BGP is used as PE-CE routing protocol (strongly recommended), what AS number should the Customer side CE use? All these issues, regardless of the choices made, have technical solutions that nevertheless increase the complexity of the configurations implemented.

From what we have said, we cannot draw a general best practice on the connection method. Every situation must be evaluated based on the company's needs. In any case, we believe that, if the ISP has a very reliable network, high-quality competencies and transparency in the solutions adopted, a single-homed connection should be preferred for an enterprise network.

9.1.2 Use of BGP

The basic solution for CE routers that must send traffic toward PE routers of the ISPs, is installing static default routes, very easy to configure, yet not very flexible in terms of traffic management. In the same way, the easiest solution for an ISP sending traffic from its own network to the enterprise network, is configuring static routes on the PE, and then propagate them within their own network through redistribution processes on the routing protocol used.

In some situations, using BGP is preferable, because, even though more complex, it offers the option of implementing more flexible routing policies, of preventing loops more easily, and of compensating for some layer-2 network deficiencies in detecting an outage, through the native KEEPALIVE message mechanism. Moreover, the BGP implementation gives customers greater autonomy in managing advertisements. For instance, if a customer needs to add a new prefix to its network, it can advertise it to the ISP network, without involving the ISP, differently from static routing, where the ISP is required to add the configuration of a static route on the PE where the customer connection ends.

Use of BGP between PE and CE also makes the distribution of routing information within the backbone of the ISPs using iBGP sessions for this scope (usually achieved through a route reflection or BGP Confederation architecture) easier.

Use of BGP on the CE side poses the issue of what AS number to choose to establish the sessions toward the ISP(s). For this purpose, the related best practices will be detailed in the following sections.

9.1.3 IP prefix propagation from PE to CE

The set of IP prefixes that the CE of an enterprise network accepts from the ISP affects the quality of its outbound routing policies. A good compromise between the different alternatives is that the more prefixes are accepted from the ISP, the higher the chance of routing outbound traffic optimally. On the other hand, however, the consumption of CE's internal resources increases, in terms of memory and CPU or traffic forwarding device use.

There are three possible alternatives:

- accepting only a default route from the ISPs;

- accepting a default route and a selected set of prefixes from the ISPs;

- accepting the entire Full Internet Routing Table from the ISPs.

In the first case, the PEs propagate to the CEs, via BGP, a default route, which is then redistributed by the CEs, in their own IGP, or propagated internally through iBGP sessions (see Figure 9.1). This is the less costly solution in terms of CE's internal resource consumption; however, it entails a non-optimal routing of outbound traffic.

The second alternative is a fair compromise between CE's resource consumption and the possibility of optimizing the routing of outbound traffic. The set of prefixes sent by PEs to CEs can be defined by the enterprise network administrator or by the ISP. In the first case, PEs send the entire FIRT, which is filtered by CEs through inbound filters. In the second case, PEs generally send the local prefixes of the ISP, to allow to CEs an optimal routing of the traffic toward other customers of the

ISP, and perhaps even prefixes two or three ASes far. The default route is still sent, to reach all the other Internet prefixes.

Lastly, the third alternative provides all the information for an optimal routing of outbound traffic, at the price of a high consumption of CE internal resources, which must, in any case, be routers that can manage large FIBs. In this case, using the default route is (obviously) not required.

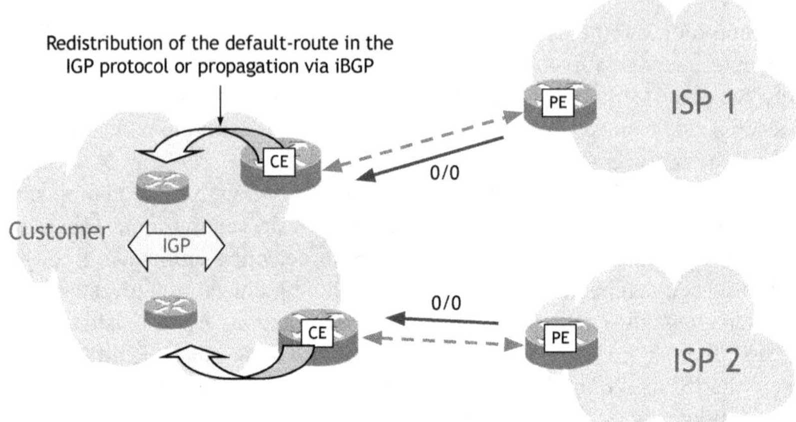

Figure 9.1 – Propagation of just the default route from PE to CE.

9.2 CUSTOMERS CONNECTED TO A SINGLE ISP

When a customer connects to a single ISP, there are three possible connection types:

- (possibly redundant) connection to a single PE;

- redundant connection with single CE to two different PEs;

- redundant connection with double CE to two different PEs.

In the case of a single connection, BGP is often not necessary (see Section 9.2.2 below). The most interesting issues are related to redundant connections, where BGP is almost always applied. Indeed, with BGP, we can define different routing policies (e.g. primary/backup, load balancing, load sharing), both inbound and outbound, and solve the issue of possible routing and/or forwarding loops – always lurking where there are redundant connections – in an effective way.

NOTE: Since, quite often, the terms load balancing and load sharing are considered to have the same meaning, we would like to point out that, actually, the term load balancing refers to the tendency to divide traffic equally on several paths toward the same destination (host or prefix), while the term load sharing refers to the (even unbalanced) traffic division on several paths toward the same destination (host or prefix).

9.2.1 Numbering plans

Once the (redundant or non-redundant) connection toward the ISP network has been established, the issue of what IP prefixes should be used for the network numbering plan arises, and, if BGP is used as PE-CE routing protocol, what AS number should be used on the CE(s).

Concerning IP prefixes, theoretically a customer could request the prefixes required to one of the

5 Regional Internet Registries (RIR). These prefixes are called Provider Independent (PI), as they are not assigned by an ISP, but rather directly by a RIR. In reality, however, it is hard for a private customer to obtain public IP prefixes from the different RIRs. The current policy of RIRs is to provide large blocks of IP prefixes only to ISPs (also called LIR, Local Internet Registries).

NOTE: Considering the endemic shortage of public IPv4 addresses available, major RIRs no longer assign blocks of PI addresses (for instance, see document RIPE – *IPv4 Address Allocation and Assignment Policies for the RIPE NCC Service Region*, sec. 5.1).

In turn, ISPs divide the prefix in many subnets with variable mask length, based on the numbering needs of their customers. These prefixes are called Provider Aggregatable (PA).

Sometimes, it happens that the subnets assigned to customers are a lot less, in terms of addresses available, than the routing needs, therefore it is necessary to resort to NAPT (Network Address and Port Translation) mechanisms on CE routers.

The address block assigned to the customer will not be propagated in detail to the entire Internet, because, apart from being insufficient for the entire system, due to the abnormal growth of RIBs and FIBs on the different Internet routers, it would run the risk of not being propagated on the entire Internet, as many ISPs reject the advertisements of prefixes with a too big mask (usually, large ISPs do not accept prefixes with mask greater than 24 bit for IPv4 and 48 for IPv6). The ISPs propagate the entire aggregate to the rest of the Internet (hence the name Provider Aggregatable), usually with mask smaller than /24 (IPv4) or /48 (IPv6).

The RIRs, upon request, also assign public AS numbers; however, in a single-homed scenario, a public AS number is not required (in any case, in order to obtain it, the adhesion to the reference RIR is required, in order to become a LIR). Here too, the RIR policy is to assign public AS numbers only to LIR/NIR. The best practice is to use, on the CE side, the private AS numbers assigned by the ISP providing the interconnection service. RFC 2270 – *Using a Dedicated AS for Sites Homed to a Single Provider*, January 1998, recommends choosing the same (public or private) AS number for all the customers of an ISP that access via BGP (see Figure 9.2).

This AS number assignment criteria can cause some issues linked to the anti-loop property of the AS_PATH. In particular, customers cannot exchange IP prefixes between them. This, on one side, could be positive, as it prevents connectivity between two customers, increasing the level

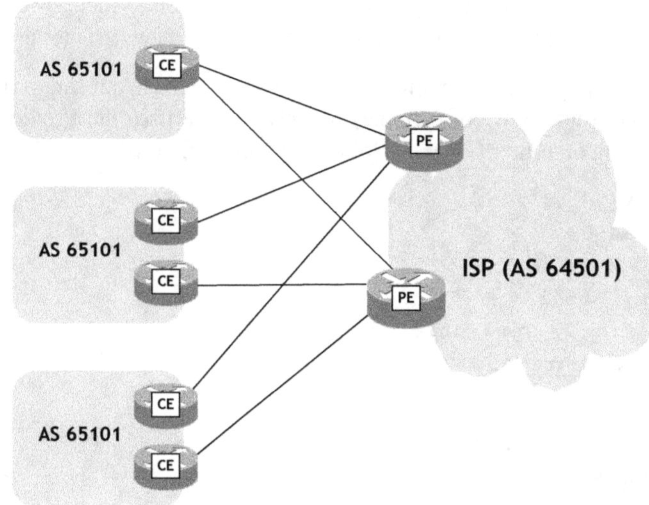

Figure 9.2 – Assigning of AS number to private customers, according to the RFC 2270 recommendation.

of security; however, it may also be negative, as it prevents traffic exchange between customers. The issue can be solved in different ways. The most immediate – and adopted more often, for its simplicity and scalability – is not propagating external IP prefixes on enterprise networks, and propagating a default route toward the CE via BGP instead. In Chapter 11, we will see another possible solution to this issue, with VPN BGP/MPLS (AS override function).

Another interesting issue linked to the use of private AS numbers on CEs, is their removal from the AS_PATH when the advertisement of a prefix is propagated toward other public ASes. Since, as per RFC, private AS numbers cannot circulate on the Internet, the ISPs must remove them from the AS_PATH (we are talking only about eBGP sessions). Both Cisco and Juniper routers support the private AS removal function. In Cisco and Juniper platforms, the configurations to execute are:

IOS XE
router(config)# **router bgp** *AS-number*
router(config-router)# **neighbor** *IP-neighbor* **remove-private-as [all]**

IOS XR
RP/0/RP0/CPU0:router(config)# **router bgp** *AS-number*
RP/0/RP0/CPU0:router(config-bgp)# **neighbor** *IP-neighbor*
RP/0/RP0/CPU0:router(config-bgp-nbr)# **address-family ipv4 unicast**
RP/0/RP0/CPU0:router(config-bgp-nbr-af)# **remove-private-as**

JUNOS (Note: the command can be given at global, group or session level)
[edit protocols bgp]
remove-private {
  < all >;
}

The default behaviour is different in the three operating systems. The default IOS XR removes all private ASes, while JUNOS and IOS XE remove only the private ASes present before a public AS. To uniform their behaviour, it is sufficient to use the "**all**" option, both in IOS XE and in JUNOS.

NOTE: The issue of removing private ASes does not apply, if the customer uses Provider Aggregatable prefixes. In this case, the ISP advertises the aggregate and, unless it doesn't use the option of memorizing the ASes of the most specific components (which, as we saw in Paragraph 5.3, is not recommended), the ASes of the more specific components are not propagated.

Figure 9.3 shows an example of command application taken from our sample network in Figure 3.1. Let's assume that router CE1 of (private) AS 65101 advertises the Provider Independent prefix 195.31.1/24. Using on router GTW the following configurations:

GTW-1 (IOS XR)
```
router bgp 64501
  neighbor 172.20.1.1
    remote-as 65541
    address-family ipv4 unicast
      remove-private-AS
```

GTW-2 (JUNOS)
```
[edit protocols bgp group EXT]
remove-private;
neighbor 172.20.2.1 {
    peer-as 65542;
```

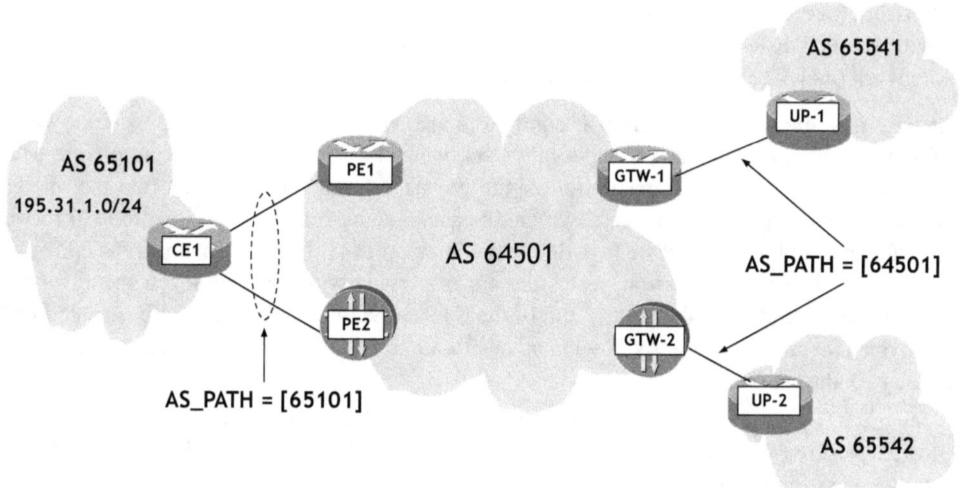

Figure 9.3 – Example of Private AS removal.

on the BGP tables of routers UP-1 and UP-2, the prefix will be seen with AS_PATH=[64501]. For instance, on UP-1 (IOS XR), we have:

```
RP/0/0/CPU0:AS-65541#show bgp | i 195
. . .
*> 195.31.1.0/24        172.20.1.0        4294967295          0 64501 i
```

9.2.2 Single connection

In the single connection type, whose diagram is shown in Figure 9.4, router CE of the enterprise network is connected through a single connection to a router of the network of an ISP. The connection is done through a layer-2 network, usually a Metro Ethernet. In such a scenario, using BGP is not necessary, even if it is sometimes used anyway. It is easier and more convenient to use simple static routes in the following way (see Figure 9.4):

- a default route with router PE as Next-Hop is configured on router CE, and redistributed within the customer's network through the selected IGP;

- a static route is configured on router PE toward the block of addresses used in the enterprise

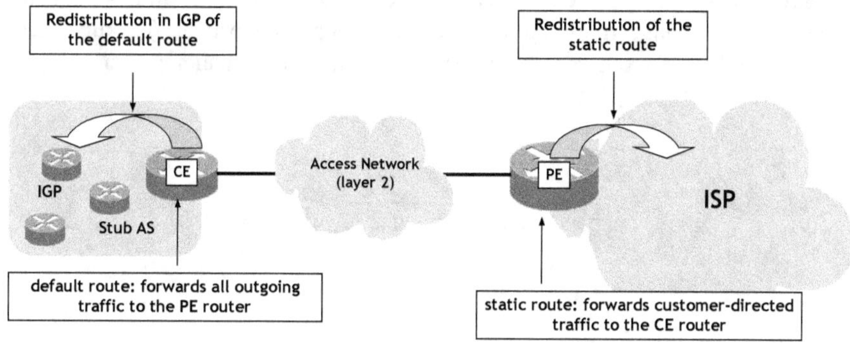

Figure 9.4 – Single PE-CE connection.

network (or more than one static route, if the prefixes are more than one and not aggregatable), with router CE as Next-Hop. Then, the static route must be redistributed within the ISP network (usually via BGP, see Chapter 8).

In the past, in some scenarios, BGP was configured also with single connections, when it was not possible to detect a line out of service at physical or layer-2 level. A typical example are Metro Ethernet networks, where an interruption of the physical connection between two intermediate switches is not detected by the routers, which, in case of static routes, would continue to forward traffic, which would in any case be lost, due to the interrupted path. STP (Spanning Tree Protocol, IEEE 802.1D), in its basic version, resets the out of service within a few dozen seconds (about 50), during which traffic is lost. At the end of the STP convergence period, traffic is routed on an alternative connection and it starts flowing again. To make up for this very high convergence time, there are two alternatives:

- using RSTP (Rapid Spanning Tree Protocol, IEEE 802.1w) on the Metro Ethernet network, which ensures a convergence time shorter than 6 s, and continuing to implement the static routes as specified above;

- configuring, in place of the static routes, an eBGP session between PE and CE, to exploit the function of the KEEPALIVE messages, by setting a low period (e.g. 2 seconds) and a consequent holdtime (e.g. 6 seconds). This would allow activating a possible backup connection in less than 6 seconds, the time needed to detect the loss of BGP session.

By introducing the BFD (RFC 5880 – *Bidirectional Forwarding Detection*, June 2010), this issue has been solved in a much more efficient manner. Therefore, activating a PE-CE eBGP session would not be needed, even if some network administrators prefer it, to avoid static route updates if prefixes are added/changed/removed on the customer side.

NOTE: We will go back to the BFD and its use with BGP in Chapter 12.

9.2.3 Redundant connections

Despite its frequent use, using a single connection does not offer a high level of reliability, as the one required by mission critical applications.
In practical implementations, in order to increase the connection's reliability, it is best to use redundant connections. The most common types of redundant connection in practical applications are the following:

- Single CE – Single PE: this connection mode, whose diagram is shown in Figure 9.5, is used to execute two or more connections between a CE and the same PE (multi-link connection). The two (or more) connections could be used according to the primary/backup scheme, or by dividing the traffic between them, more or less equally (load balancing/sharing).

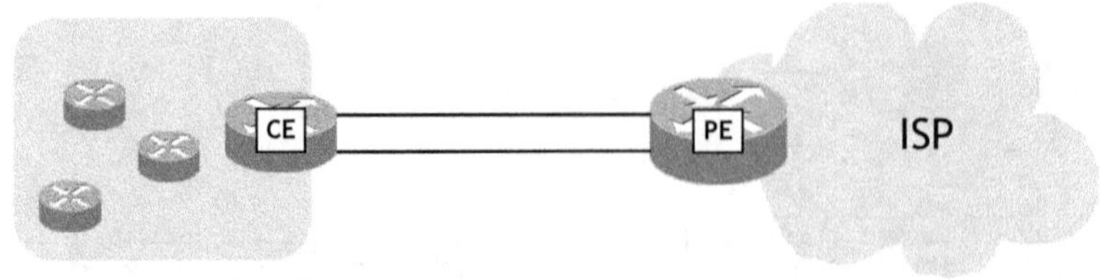

Figure 9.5 – Single CE – Single PE redundant connection.

- Single CE – Double PE: with this connection method, the diagram of which is shown in Figure 9.6, two connections are created between a CE and two different PEs. Just like in the previous case, the two connections could be used according to the primary/backup scheme, or by dividing the traffic between them, more or less equally (load balancing/sharing). However, in this instance, inbound/outbound traffic management issues are more complex, since it could be necessary to choose also the PE where to route the outbound traffic, and the PE that sends traffic toward the CE.

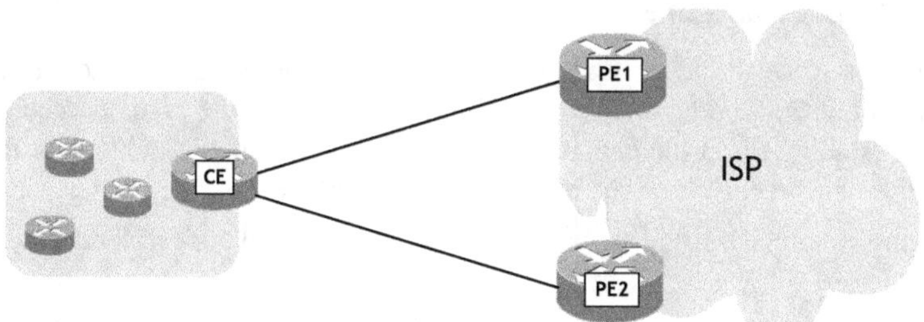

Figure 9.6 – Single CE – Double PE redundant connection.

- Double CE – Double PE: this connection mode, whose diagram is shown in Figure 9.7, is used to create two connections between two CEs and two different PEs. This is the mode that ensures the highest level of reliability, and, at the same time, the costlier, since a double CE is required on the customer side. It is used for websites where the most important corporate resources are stored (server farms, storage systems, general management, etc.). Traffic management issues are more complex than the previous case, especially on the enterprise network side, since it could be necessary, within the enterprise network, to choose the CE where to route the inbound/outbound traffic.

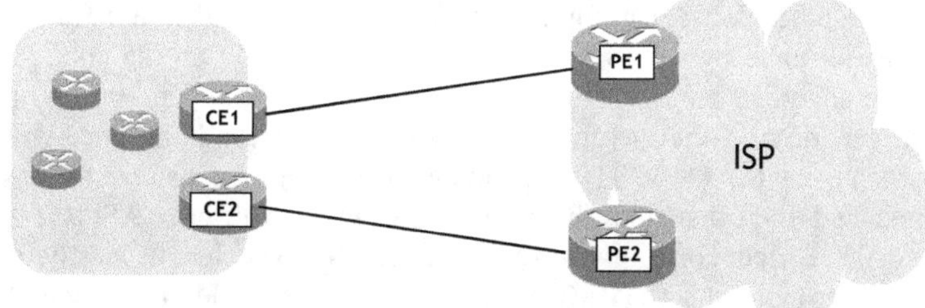

Figure 9.7 – Double CE – Double PE redundant connection.

Actually, there are also mixed configurations, apart from the three basic ones we just saw. For instance, in the double CE – double PE connection, it is possible that one of the single CEs has a double connection with one or two PEs. Traffic management issues are all easily defined and configured, starting from three basic cases.

In the following sections, we will see, for each type of redundant connection described, how all BGP tools can be used to define the two routing policies implemented in practical applications: primary/backup and load balancing/sharing.

9.2.4 Redundant connections: primary/backup routing policies

The primary/backup configuration is typical, in practical applications, of connections with a very different bandwidth from one another, such as a primary 100 Gbit/s Ethernet connection and a secondary 10 Gbit/s Ethernet connection.

Regardless of the type of redundant connection we saw in Section 9.2.3 above, we can define, when using BGP between PE and CE, best configuration practices to execute the primary/backup routing policy, both for managing outbound and inbound traffic (with reference to CE).

For outbound traffic management:

- assigning a Local Preference value lower to the value assigned by default (which, as you may recall, is 100, both for Cisco and Juniper routers) to the prefixes received on the eBGP session established on the backup connection. Leaving the default Local Preference on the advertisements received on the eBGP session established on the primary connection.

For managing inbound traffic, we can use one of the methods described in Paragraph 7.3, as follows:

- Via MED attribute: assigning a MED value higher than the default value assigned by router PE (which, according to RFC 4271, is 0 both for Cisco and Juniper routers), to the advertisements sent on the eBGP session established on the backup connection. Avoiding the use of the MED in the advertisements sent on the eBGP session established on the primary connection.

- Via AS_PATH prepending: executing an AS_PATH prepending for just one AS to the prefixes sent on the eBGP session established on the backup connection. Leaving the default AS_PATH on the advertisements sent on the eBGP session established on the primary connection.

- Via COMMUNITY attribute: assigning a specific value of the COMMUNITY attribute to the advertisements sent on the eBGP session established on the backup connection, so that the ISP, based on this, may assign a lower Local Preference value than the default value.

To manage inbound traffic, when opting for the MED, you need to ascertain the management policies of this attribute by the ISP. Indeed, many ISPs, based on the configuration, reset the MED of all the advertisements received, making it useless as inbound traffic management tool. Therefore, as general rule, the use of the MED should be agreed in advance with the ISP. In the same way, when using the AS_PATH prepending mechanism, you need to make sure that the ISP does not implement filters that block the advertisements with a different AS_PATH than the default one, or that define certain configurations to limit the AS_PATH length. Lastly, if you opt for the COMMUNITY attribute, the COMMUNITY value to be assigned to outbound advertisements must be agreed with the ISP.

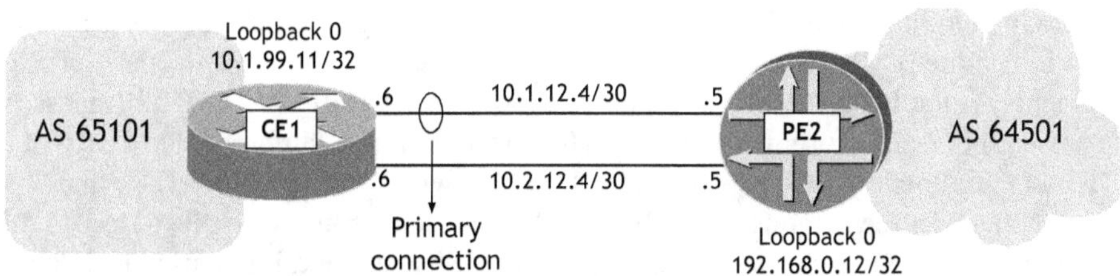

Figure 9.8 – Single CE – Single PE redundant connection with a single eBGP session.

Single CE – single PE connection

In the case of a single CE – single PE connection, the primary/backup policy can be used without resorting to BGP, with the help of floating static routes on both the CE and the PE side, that is, static routes with different degree of preference (or administrative distance, in Cisco routers' language). We will not include any configuration of this solution here, since it is not relevant for this book. If you deem appropriate to adopt BGP, there are several possible configuration alternatives. The first solution is to create a single multihop eBGP session and configure floating static routes toward the BGP Next-Hop. As configuration example, let's consider the mixed Cisco/Juniper scenario shown in Figure 9.8, where CE1 and PE2 are two routers belonging to the sample network in Figure 3.1 to which we added a connection between CE1 and PE2.

The relevant configurations are:

CE1 (IOS XE)
```
router bgp 65101
  neighbor 192.168.0.12 remote-as 64501
  neighbor 192.168.0.12 update-source loopback 0
  neighbor 192.168.0.12 ebgp-multihop 2
!
ip route 192.168.0.12 255.255.255.255 10.1.12.5 10
ip route 192.168.0.12 255.255.255.255 10.2.12.5 20
```

PE2 (JUNOS)
```
[edit protocols bgp group CE]
multihop;
local-address 192.168.0.12;
neighbor 10.1.99.11 {
  peer-as 65101;
}
[edit routing-options]
static {
  route 10.1.99.11/32 {
    qualified-next-hop 10.1.12.6 {
      preference 10;
    }
    qualified-next-hop 10.2.12.6 {
      preference 20;
    }
  }
}
```

For the sake of simplicity, we will assume that PE2 sends a single default route to CE1 via BGP (configuration omitted). CE1 will install it in its RIB (provided that there are no other default route advertisements with a better degree of preference), with Next-Hop 192.168.0.12 (that is, the IP address present in the advertisement's NEXT_HOP attribute). In addition, router CE1 will install in its RIB a (static) path toward prefix 192.168.0.12/32 with Next-Hop 10.1.12.5, thanks to the lowest (i.e. better) degree of preference (10, vs 20 of the static route with Next-Hop 10.2.12.5). When CE1 receives an IP packet toward any host outside its network, it will use the default route and execute a recursive lookup to identify the Next-Hop which is 10.1.12.5. Traffic will then flow on the primary connection.

A similar situation occurs on router PE2 for traffic toward hosts that can be reached through CE1, with the only difference that CE1 sends to PE2 a BGP advertisement of the prefix(es) used for the numbering plan of the enterprise network hosts. Therefore, both outbound and inbound traffic will flow on the primary connection. If the latter is out of service, CE1 will install in its RIB the second static route (with a higher degree of preference), and so will PE2. Going over what we said, we can immediately infer that traffic will flow on the backup connection in both directions. On the way back, based on the primary connection, both CE1 and PE2 will reinstall in their RIB the static route with the lowest degree of preference (hence the name floating static routes), and traffic will resume flowing on the primary connection.

Another alternative to the use of BGP – useful for the reasons mentioned in Section 9.2.2, for instance, when one of the two connections is achieved through a Metro Ethernet network – is to establish two different eBGP sessions, one for each connection. In this case, in order to manage both outbound and inbound traffic, we can follow the best practices described at the beginning of this section. We leave the development of the simple configurations for the scenario in Figure 9.8 to you.

Lastly, a practical consideration. The solution with double eBGP session should only be used when necessary, as it leads to a greater router CPU use (with the need to manage two eBGP sessions instead of one), and to twice the memory used by BGP advertisements, since two advertisements are received for each prefix, instead of one, as in the case of a single eBGP session. Therefore, when adopting the solution with a double eBGP session, it would be best that PE does not propagate the entire FIRT to CE, but either only the default route, or the default route and a few other prefixes.

Single CE – double PE connection

In the case of a single CE – double PE connection, it is still convenient to implement the primary/backup policy through BGP, even though, theoretically – and especially to manage traffic from CE to PE – we could use the static routes.

The configuration best practices to implement the primary/backup policy are the general ones we saw at the beginning of this section. As configuration example, let's assume the scenario in Figure 9.9 – from our sample network – with the following assumptions:

- PEs propagate only the default route to CE;

- router CE2 propagates to the two PEs only aggregate prefix 195.31.1/24 and accepts from the two PEs only the default route;

- the primary connection is the one between CE2 and PE2.

For the sake of brevity, we will include the relevant part of the configurations of routers PE1, PE2 and CE2, and leave the rest as exercise.

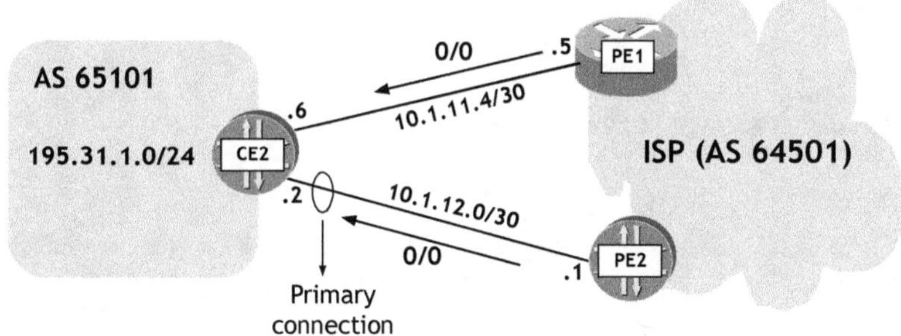

Figure 9.9 – Example of redundant single CE – double PE connection.

<u>PE1</u> (IOS XR)

```
route-policy ONLY-DR
  if destination in (0.0.0.0/0) then
    pass
  endif
end-policy
!
route-policy FILTER-CE2
  if destination in (195.31.1.0/24) then
    pass
  endif
end-policy
!
router bgp 64501
  bgp router-id 192.168.0.11
  address-family ipv4 unicast
  !
neighbor-group CUSTOMERS-INTERNET-v4
  remote-as 65101
  address-family ipv4 unicast
    route-policy ONLY-DR out
    route-policy FILTER-CE2 in
  !
neighbor 10.1.11.6  ! eBGP SESSION WITH CE2
  use neighbor-group INTERNET-CUSTOMERS-v4
```

<u>PE2</u> (JUNOS)

```
[edit policy-options policy-statement ONLY-DR]
term DR {
  from {
    route-filter 0.0.0.0/0 exact;
  }
  then accept;
}
term REJECT {
  then reject;
}
```

```
[edit policy-options policy-statement FILTER-CE2]
term PFX-CE2 {
  from {
    protocol bgp;
    route-filter 195.31.1.0/24 exact;
  }
  then accept;
}
term REJECT {
  then reject;
}
[edit protocols bgp group CUSTOMERS-INTERNET-v4]
export ONLY-DR;
import FILTER-CE2;
peer-as 65101;
neighbor 10.1.12.2; # eBGP SESSION WITH CE2
```

<u>CE2</u> (JUNOS)

```
[edit policy-options policy-statement ONLY-DR]
term DR {
  from {
    protocol bgp;
    route-filter 0.0.0.0/0 exact;
  }
  then {
    accept;
  }
}
term REJECT {
  then reject;
}
[edit policy-options policy-statement ONLY-DR-BK]
term DR {
  from {
    protocol bgp;
    route-filter 0.0.0.0/0 exact;
  }
  then {
    local-preference 50;
    accept;
  }
}
term REJECT {
  then reject;
}
[edit policy-options policy-statement SET-MED-PRI]
term PFX-CE2 {
  from {
    route-filter 195.31.1.0/24 exact;
  }
```

```
    then {
      metric 10;
      accept;
    }
}
term REJECT {
  then reject;
}
[edit policy-options policy-statement SET-MED-BK]
term PFX-CE2 {
  from {
    route-filter 195.31.1.0/24 exact;
  }
  then {
    metric 20;
    accept;
  }
}
term REJECT {
  then reject;
}
[edit protocols bgp group AS64501]
peer-as 64501;
neighbor 10.1.12.2 {
  import ONLY-DR;
  export SET-MED-PRI;
}
neighbor 10.1.11.5 {
  import ONLY-DR-BK;
  export SET-MED-BK;
}
```

It is interesting to notice that, both in CE2 configuration, and in PE1 and PE2 ones, we have introduced filters that only allow exchanging the prefixes agreed between the customer and the ISP: the default route from PE1 and PE2 to CE2 and aggregate prefix 195.31.1/24 from CE2 to PE1 and PE2. This is a good configuration practice to always follow, in any connection context between an enterprise network and an ISP.

Double CE – double PE connection

In the case of a double CE – double PE connection, it is still convenient to implement the primary/backup policy through BGP, even though, theoretically – and especially to manage outbound traffic from CE to PE – we could use the static routes.

Compared to the previous case of single CE-double PE, the configuration problems on the CE side are more complex, since it is necessary to ensure that the internal routers of the enterprise network also choose as exit point of the traffic towards the ISP network, the CE on which the primary link is connected. This requires greater focus on the default route propagation criteria in IGP or through iBGP sessions. One aspect we should also focus on is the possibility of generating forwarding loops within the enterprise network.

In order to better assess this last aspect, let's consider the example in Figure 9.10, where CE routers do not have a physical connection between them, and establish an iBGP session using router C as transit for BGP messages. CE routers both propagate a default route within the enterprise network, through a redistribution in the IGP protocol (e.g. OSPF).

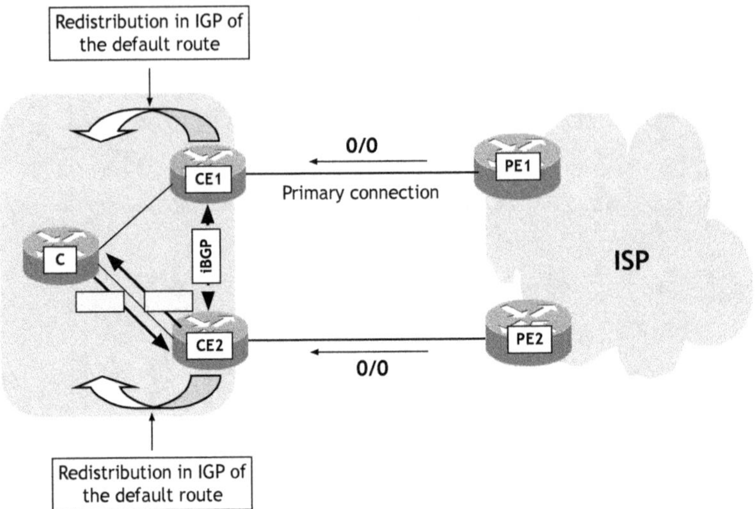

Figure 9.10 – Example of forwarding loop in a redundant double CE – double PE connection.

Let's assume that the primary connection is the one between PE1 and CE1, and that, in order to reach this objective, CE1 assigns a higher Local Preference value to the default route received from PE1, compared to the Local Preference value that CE2 assigns to the default route received from PE2. Consequently, CE2 will prefer the default route received from CE1 via iBGP, due to the higher Local Preference. By assuming this, both CE1 and CE2 can redistribute the default route in IGP, therefore C will receive two IGP advertisements of the default route. If, for any reason, C prefers the default route received from CE2 and installs it in its RIB, a forwarding loop is generated. And this is what happens when C receives a packet to be forwarded to the ISP:

- C uses the default route and sends the packet to CE2;

- CE2 has the default route with Next-Hop CE1 in its RIB, and so it attempts to forward the packet toward CE1;

- since the only available path toward CE1 passes through C, CE2 sends the packet to C.

In conclusion, the packet travels between C and CE2 until the TTL expires.
There are several options to solve this issue:

1. Making sure that CE2 redistributes the default route in IGP only when the primary connection is out of service, that is, inhibiting, in normal operating conditions, the default route propagation in IGP by CE2. CE2 should redistribute the default route in IGP only when it detects that the primary connection is out of service. However, this approach would require the redistribution of the IP subnet with which the primary connection is numbered in IGP.

2. Making sure that CE2 does not route traffic toward an internal router that uses it as Next-Hop for the default route. This can be achieved by adding a direct connection between CE-1 and CE-2, so as to create a path from CE2 to CE1 that doesn't have to transit on router C.

3. Creating a complete mesh of iBGP sessions between all the routers of the enterprise network, possibly using – in case of a medium-large network – Route Reflectors or a BGP Confederation.

4. Editing the metrics with which the default route is redistributed in IGP, so that any router inside the enterprise network chooses router CE1 as exit point for traffic toward the ISP. For instance, if IGP is OSPF, the default route can be injected by CE1 as E2 type with external metric 10, and by CE2 as E2 type with external metric 20.

In any case, you should be aware of the issues that may arise if the default route redistribution in IGP is incorrectly configured.

Referring to Figure 9.7 and assuming that the primary connection is the one between CE1 and PE1, the best configuration practice on router CE to implement the primary/backup policy is basically the same as the one we saw for the single CE – double PE connection case:

- assigning a Local Preference value lower to the value assigned by default (which, as you may recall, is 100, both for Cisco and Juniper routers) to the prefixes received on the eBGP session, established on the backup connection;

- forcing inbound traffic to enter from router CE1, using one of the three methods described earlier; using the prepending AS_PATH, the MED attribute or the COMMUNITY attribute.

Moreover, it is best, for security reasons, to apply inbound/outbound filters that allow only the relevant prefixes, and block all the others.

As configuration example, let's take the scenario in Figure 9.11, with the following assumptions:

- PEs propagate only the default route to CEs;

- CE routers advertise to the two PEs only aggregate prefix 195.31.1/24 and accept from the two PEs only the default route;

- both CE routers propagate the default route within IGP (OSPF);

- the primary connection is the one between CE1 and PE1.

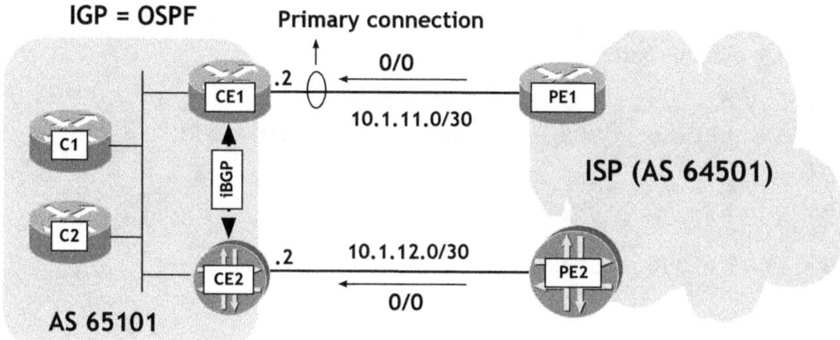

Figure 9.11 – Example of redundant double CE – double PE connection.

For the sake of simplicity, we will only include the relevant configurations of routers CE1 and CE2, and leave the others as exercise. For the sake of brevity, we will omit the configurations to force inbound traffic on the primary connection, since they are identical to the ones we saw earlier.

CE-1 (IOS XE)
```
ip prefix-list DEFAULT-ROUTE seq 5 permit 0.0.0.0/0
!
route-map SET-LP-IN permit 10
  match ip address prefix-list DEFAULT-ROUTE
  set local-preference 150
!
router bgp 65101
  bgp router-id 10.1.99.11
  neighbor 10.1.11.1 remote-as 64501
  neighbor 10.1.99.12 remote-as 65101
  neighbor 10.1.99.12 update-source Loopback0
  !
  address-family ipv4
    neighbor 10.1.11.1 activate
    neighbor 10.1.11.1 route-map SET-LP-IN in
    neighbor 10.1.99.12 activate
    neighbor 10.1.99.12 next-hop-self
  exit-address-family
!
!OSPF CONFIGURATIONS
!
interface Loopback0
  ip ospf 1 area 0
!
interface GigabitEthernet3  ! INTERNAL SIDE LAN INTERFACE
  ip ospf 1 area 0
!
router ospf 1
  router-id 10.1.99.11
  default-information originate metric 10
```

Route-map SET-LP-IN has the dual function of assigning the Local Preference and of filter, since it only allows the default route.

CE2 (JUNOS)
```
[edit policy-options policy-statement RED-DR-TO-OSPF]
term DR {
  from {
    protocol bgp;
    route-filter 0.0.0.0/0 exact;
  }
  then {
    metric 20;
    external {
      type 2;
    }
    accept;
  }
}
```

```
term REJECT {
  then reject;
}

[edit protocols ospf]
export RED-DR-TO-OSPF;
area 0.0.0.0 {
  interface ge-0/0/3.0;    /* INTERNAL LAN SIDE INTERFACE  */
  interface lo0.0 {
    passive;
  }
}

[edit protocols bgp]
group PE {
  import ONLY-DR-v4;
  neighbor 10.1.12.1;
}
group IBGP {
  type internal;
  local-address 10.1.99.12;
  export NHS;
  neighbor 10.1.99.11;
}
```

In nominal operating conditions – i.e. with the primary connection working – due to the higher Local Preference value – CE1 installs in its RIB the default route learned from the eBGP session with PE1, while CE2 installs the one learned from the iBGP session with CE1.

The OSPF process "**default-information originate**..." command, generates two default routes in the OSPF process, the first from CE1 with E2 metric (External type 2) equal to 10, and the second from CE2 with E2 metric equal to 20. Both routers C1 and C2 prefer the default route received from CE1, since it has a lower external metric.

If the primary connection is out of service, the eBGP session between CE1 and PE1 is dropped, the default route advertised by PE1 is withdrawn from CE1's BGP table (and therefore from its RIB), and also is the default route injected by CE1, since the OSPF process "**default-information originate**..." command is effective if and only if there is a default route in the RIB. Consequently, CE2 automatically installs in its RIB the default route learned via eBGP from PE2. The routing policy RED-DR-TO-OSPF on CE2 is effective, and generates a default route in the OSPF process, which is received by CE1, C1 and C2, making them capable of sending traffic outside their AS through router CE2.

On the way back, based on the connection, the reverse procedure occurs. We will leave the details to you, as a useful exercise. The result is that traffic once again flows on the primary connection.

9.2.5 Redundant connections: load balancing/sharing

In practical applications, it is rare for a primary/backup configuration like the one described in the previous paragraph to be employed. Indeed, ISP customers try to use the backup connection somehow, considering its fixed cost due to the application of flat fees that do not depend on traffic and usage time by transmission capacity providers.

The idea is to make traffic flow in the two directions on both connections, in a balanced way (load balancing) when the connections have the same bandwidth, or in an unbalanced way (load sharing), in the opposite case.

When we talk about load balancing/sharing, it is important not to consider traffic like a single entity, but as two separate entities: inbound and outbound traffic. Distributing inbound traffic over two (or more) connections is completely independent from the outbound traffic division.

In any case, you should keep in mind that perfect balancing is very difficult – if not impossible – to achieve. Distributing the load between two (or more) connections is an iterative process that depends on many factors. However, we can still define some general best practices, which should always be adapted to each situation.

We will now discuss two cases of single CE – single PE and double CE – double PE connection, since the issues of the single CE – double PE connection are similar.

NOTE: Traffic is distributed between connections by the data plane (forwarding). In practice, two methods can be used:

- Per-packet load balancing/sharing: the forwarding algorithm sends each packet on a different path, based on the distribution level.

- Per-flow load balancing/sharing: the forwarding algorithm sends all packets with identical source and target IP addresses – and possibly other layer 3 and 4 fields (e.g.. TOS, TCP/UDP ports, etc.), on the same path.

Packet-based traffic distribution is easier to implement and ensures the best traffic balancing. On the other hand, one of its disadvantages is losing the packets' sequence, which must be retrieved at upper protocol levels, worsening the application performance.

Flow-based traffic distribution is more complex to implement; however, it preserves the packets' sequence. The greater implementation complexity is due to the algorithm used to choose the path. A hash function is used, which, based on the source and target IP addresses, and possibly on other layer 3 and 4 Level fields, generates an integer number that indexes the path. The forwarding algorithm is implemented via dedicated ASICs, and characterizes the router's performance.

Single CE – single PE connection

In Section 9.2.4 above, we saw that, in the single CE – single PE scenario, it was possible to configure a single eBGP (multihop) session and two different eBGP sessions.

When the connection bandwidth is the same, it is best to distribute traffic more or less identically between the connections (load balancing). This can be done both with a single and a double BGP session.

In the first case, the load balancing is fairly easy to obtain, by following the same configuration shown in Figure 9.8, and eliminating the degree of preference (administrative distance) from the static routes.

In the case of a double eBGP session, the load balancing can be obtained through the Multipath BGP mechanism described in Paragraph 7.1, both for Cisco and Juniper routers. By way of example, here is the configuration for the Cisco and Juniper routers of Figure 9.8.

<u>CE1</u> (IOS XE)
```
router bgp 65101
  neighbor 10.1.12.5 remote-as 64501
  neighbor 10.2.12.5 remote-as 64501
  maximum-paths 2
```

PE2 (JUNOS)
```
[edit protocols bgp group CE]
multipath;
peer-as 65101;
neighbor 10.1.12.6;
neighbor 10.2.12.6;
```

When the connection bandwidth is different, traffic should be balanced proportionally to the connection bandwidth (load sharing). For instance, in the case of two connections, one at 10 Gbit/s and the other at 2 Gbit/s, it is best to implement a configuration that distributes traffic in a 10/12 and 2/12 ratio (approx. 83% and 17%) respectively on the two connections.

In this case, a load balancing would easily cause congestion in the lower bandwidth connection. Obtaining a load sharing with a single eBGP session is not convenient. Theoretically, it would be possible, by using the EIGRP protocol or the Traffic Engineering MPLS in place of the static routes. However, it is easier and more convenient, in a different bandwidth scenario, to use parallel eBGP sessions.

Establishing parallel eBGP sessions is the most versatile way to obtain load balancing or load sharing. Differently from the case with a single BGP session, it is not necessary to use static routing or dynamic routing protocols or other tricks, such as the multilink PPP, to balance traffic. Moreover, it allows managing the load sharing easily, with a distribution proportional to the connections' bandwidth. However, as mentioned in Section 9.2.4, the solution with dual eBGP sessions has also some disadvantages, in terms of memory space taken up and router CPU use.

We saw that, in order to obtain a load balancing with a dual eBGP session, it is sufficient to use the BGP Multipath. In order to obtain a load sharing, we need to resort to different techniques, which are similar for all kinds of connection, therefore we will only see them in the following case of double CE – double PE connection below.

Double CE – double PE connection: outbound traffic

Theoretically, obtaining a load balancing/sharing for outbound traffic is possible by adopting the BGP Multipath inside the enterprise network. However, this requires the extension of BGP within the enterprise network, which is not always possible, due to the higher complexity introduced by the protocol, and further measures that are not so easy to implement, and which we will discuss shortly. Without using the BGP Multipath, it is virtually impossible to obtain a load balancing, since we would have to make all the routers within the enterprise network "see" the CEs with identical IGP cost. In theory, this would be possible by manipulating the metrics used by IGP accordingly; however, practically speaking, it is very complex to do, especially with medium-large networks.

Not even propagating a default route in IGP from both CEs solves the issue. Without manipulating IGP metrics correctly, each router within the enterprise network would send its own traffic toward the ISP to the closest CE, based on the total IGP cost. This, obviously, does not ensure a load balancing for outbound traffic, but is nonetheless a reasonable solution. The risks are related to the possible congestion of a connection, perhaps when the other is not very much burdened, due to the lack of control of traffic distribution.

Figure 9.12 shows an example that clarifies how this solution works. Routers CE1 and CE2 propagate a default route within the IGP used by the enterprise network. Routers C1 and C2 will receive two advertisements of the default route and will install the one received from the closest router CE – based on the total IGP cost – on their RIB. C1, with an IGP cost of 10 to reach CE1 and an IGP cost of 20 to reach CE2, will install the default route received from CE1. Similarly, C2 will install the default route received from CE2. So, traffic from the enterprise network toward the ISP will flow partially on the CE1↔PE1 connection, and partially on the CE2↔PE2 connection.

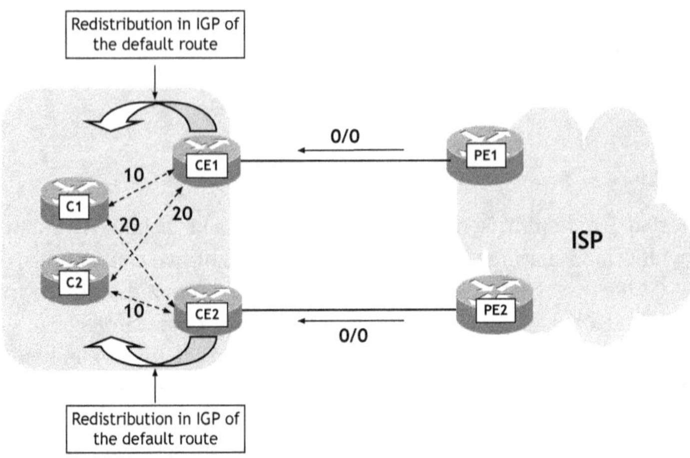

Figure 9.12 – Outbound traffic load balancing in the case of double CE – double PE.

This criterion does not always allow balancing the outbound traffic. Indeed, just think about the case in which the enterprise network comprises the two CEs and only router C1: all outbound traffic would flow on the CE1-PE1 connection.

The simpler technique to obtain any unbalanced distribution (load sharing) for outbound traffic is to ask the ISP to send, apart from the default route, also a selected set of significant prefixes – i.e. IP prefixes toward which the customer sends a substantial share of traffic (e.g. content provider, cloud provider, OTT prefixes, etc.) – and use a complete mesh of iBGP session within the enterprise network, so as to propagate the information on the Local Preference assigned within the enterprise network. This allows setting an outbound traffic distribution on the CEs, by assigning a suitable Local Preference value to each prefix received.

By way of example, let's consider the scenario in Figure 9.13, assuming that the enterprise network develops a lot of traffic toward the two prefixes 192.0.2/24 and 198.51.100/24. The administrator of the enterprise network wants traffic to flow toward prefix 192.0.2/24 on the CE1↔PE1 connection, and wants traffic toward prefix 198.51.100/24 to flow on the CE2↔PE2 connection. In order to obtain this distribution, the enterprise network administrators asks the ISP to send the default route and the two prefixes on both eBGP sessions, and executes a configuration on two routers CE, so as to assign a Local Preference (LP) value to eBGP advertisements in the following way:

- CE1 assigns LP=150 to prefix 192.0.2/24, leaving the default value (=100) for prefix 198.51.100/24;

- CE2 assigns LP=150 to prefix 198.51.100/24, leaving the default value (=100) for prefix 192.0.2/24.

The result is that all outbound traffic toward prefix 192.0.2/24 will use the CE1↔PE1 connection, while all outbound traffic toward prefix 198.51.100/24 will use the CE2↔PE2 connection. Direct traffic toward the other prefixes is randomly distributed over the CEs, through the default route.

Double CE – double PE connection: inbound traffic

Theoretically, for inbound traffic, it would be possible to obtain load balancing using the BGP Multipath mechanism on the ISP network. In order to see how, let's consider the example shown in Figure 9.14. Both routers CE1 and CE2 advertise local prefix 195.31.1/24 on the two eBGP

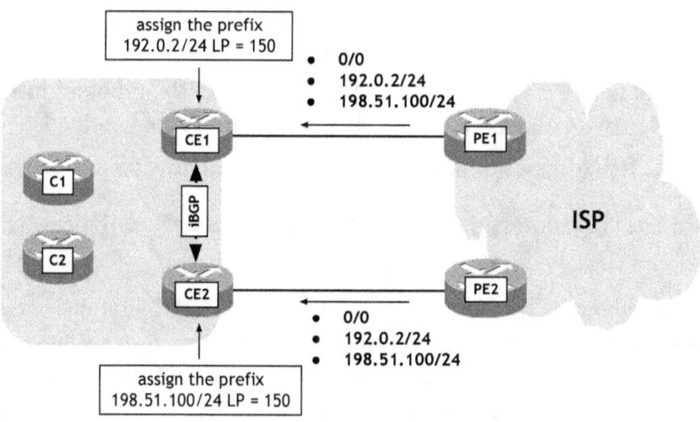

Figure 9.13 – Outbound traffic load sharing in the case of double CE – double PE.

sessions with the ISP's routers PE1 and PE2. Let's assume that the prefix is propagated within the ISP network without changing any default attribute (AS_PATH, MED and Local Preference). As is common in ISP networks (see previous Chapter 8), let's assume that there is a complete mesh of iBGP sessions between the routers; router PE3 will receive two advertisements of prefix 195.31.1/24, from PE1 and PE2 respectively. Now, if the total IGP cost of PE2 toward the BGP Next-Hop PE1 and PE2 was the same (as in the figure, where it is equal to 10), router PE3 could apply the BGP Multipath mechanism and install two identical paths toward the prefix in its RIB, and balance traffic equally between them. However, although theoretically simple, this procedure is very hard to reach in practice, as it is necessary to manipulate the IGP metrics, to make the total IGP cost of PE3 toward BGP Next-Hop PE1 and PE2 the same.

It is unlikely for an ISP to meet such requirements, which would significantly complicate its network configuration. Also, because there are other technical issues related to the use of Route Reflector to complicate the issue even further.

An alternative way to distribute inbound traffic is to do it based on the destination, i.e. sending traffic toward certain prefixes of the enterprise network on a connection, and traffic toward other prefixes on another connection.

A very simple technique is to divide the prefix used for the enterprise network numbering plan into two or more subnets, and then advertise the subnets separately on the two (or more) eBGP sessions toward the ISP.

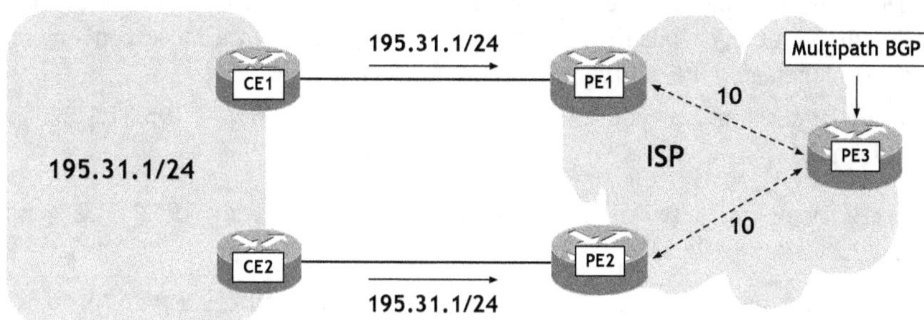

Figure 9.14 – Inbound traffic balancing in the case of a double CE – double PE connection via BGP Multipath.

By way of example, let's consider the scenario in Figure 9.15. Router CE1 advertises prefix 195.31.1/24 and its subnet 195.31.1.0/25 to PE1. Similarly, router CE2 advertises prefix 195.31.1/24 and its subnet 195.31.1.128/25 to PE2. Consequently, inbound traffic into AS 65101 will be distributed over two connections, available based on the destination:

- traffic toward the IP addresses of prefix 195.31.1.0/25 will flow on the CE1↔PE1 connection;

- traffic toward the IP addresses of prefix 195.31.1.128/25 will flow on the CE2↔PE2 connection.

It is also necessary to advertise the entire address block 195.31.1/24 on the two sessions, in order to ensure a backup if one of the connections goes out of service. For instance, if the CE1↔PE1 connection goes out of service, traffic toward the addresses of subnet 195.31.1.0/25 will flow on the CE2↔PE2 connection, thanks to the advertisement of block 195.31.1/24 on the eBGP session between CE2 and PE2. Without its advertisement, all traffic toward the addresses of subnet 195.31.1.0/25 would be lost.

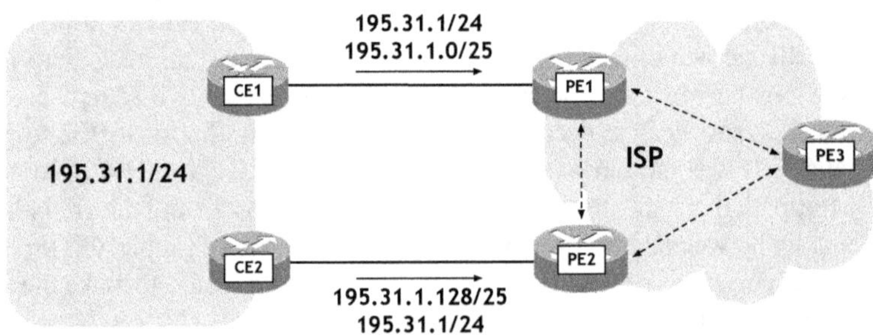

Figure 9.15 – Inbound traffic balancing in the case of a double CE – double PE connection via local prefix distribution between subnets.

Usually, the trick of advertising two equally big subnets of the prefix used by the customer for its numbering plan does not ensure an equal traffic distribution. The actual distribution depends on how much traffic is routed toward the two subnets. If, after a certain time, the traffic distribution is not suitable (e.g. one connection is overloaded, while the other is underloaded), the process can be repeated, by attempting to use several subnets, instead of just two. For instance, if, after a series of traffic measurements, it is detected that about 50% of the traffic is directed toward addresses of subnet 195.31.1.0/26, perhaps because this subnet has been used to number servers that are important for the company's business, traffic can be distributed in a more convenient way, by advertising the subnets and the entire prefix in the following way:

- on the eBGP session between CE1 and PE1, advertising prefix 195.31.1/24 and subnet 195.31.1.0/26;

- on the eBGP session between CE2 and PE2, advertising prefix 195.31.1/24 and subnets 195.31.1.128/25 and 195.31.64.0/26.

This way, in nominal operating conditions, traffic toward subnet 195.31.1.0/26 (50% of the total) will flow on the CE1↔PE1 connection, while the rest of the traffic (50% of the total), will flow on the CE2↔PE2 connection.

A traffic disaggregation done by dividing a prefix between subnets causes an increase in the RIB and FIB size on the ISP network routers, but it has no impact on the Internet, since the ISP advertise aggregate prefixes that contain the prefixes assigned to customers. Sometimes, to prevent an abnormal RIB and FIB growth, ISPs accept only the prefix assigned from their customers, therefore this method may not be effective. A good rule to follow is, before adopting any inbound traffic distribution strategy, to check the policies that the ISP applies to its customers, and maybe attempt a negotiation to reach a mutually satisfying agreement.

An alternative technique to carry out load balancing/sharing by destination, is to use the techniques described in Paragraph 7.3 based on AS_PATHs prepending (Section 7.3.2) or the MED (Section 7.3.3) and COMMUNITY (Section 7.3.4) attributes. This is very useful, especially when the enterprise network uses two or more prefixes that cannot be aggregated together for its numbering plan. By way of example, let's assume a scenario like the one shown in Figure 9.16, where the AS of the enterprise network has the two prefixes 192.0.2/24 and 203.0.113/24 available. The figure shows a MED allocation, allowing inbound traffic to be distributed as follows:

- traffic toward the IP addresses of prefix 192.0.2/24 flows on the CE1↔PE1 connection;

- traffic toward the IP addresses of prefix 203.0.113/24 flows on the CE2↔PE2 connection.

If one of the connections goes out of service, since each prefix is advertised on both connections, all traffic flows on the working connection. For both Cisco and Juniper platforms, the configurations to execute are basically the same shown in Section 7.3.3.

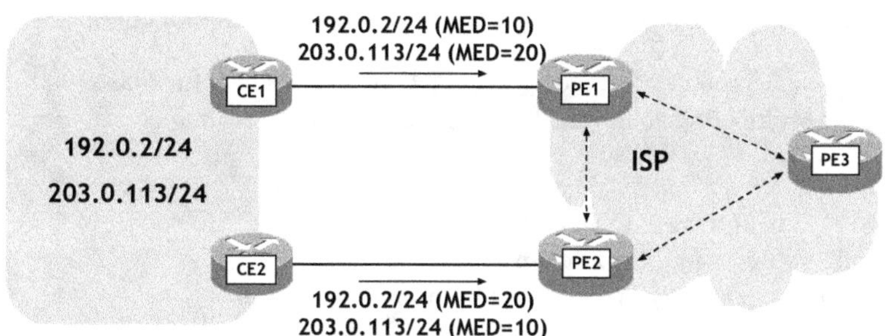

Figure 9.16 – Inbound traffic destination-based balancing, in case of double CE – double PE connection, through the use of the MED attribute.

9.2.6 Distribution of outbound traffic on connections with different bandwidth

When the connection bandwidth is different – as we saw for the single CE – single PE case, it is best to balance traffic in a directly proportional way to the connections' bandwidth (load sharing). However, in order to do this, the routers within the enterprise network (e.g. routers C1 and C2 in Figure 9.12), must be somewhat informed about the bandwidth of the connections on which the eBGP sessions with the ISP are established, i.e. the connections between routers CE and routers PE. A new Extended Community has been defined exactly for this purpose. Once linked to the iBGP advertisements propagated by the CEs within the enterprise network, it allows internal routers C to know the bandwidth of the CE-PE connections, and thus, thanks to forwarding-level load sharing techniques, to distribute traffic proportionally to the bandwidth. Actually, this new Extended Community has never become a standard, but it is anyway supported both by Cisco and Juniper routers (see draft-ietf-idr-link-bandwidth – *BGP Link Bandwidth Extended Community*, expired in March 2018). For the sake of simplicity, in compliance with the document we just mentioned, hereinafter we will refer to it as Bandwidth Extended Community.

In Cisco routers, support to the Bandwidth Extended Community can be configured as follows:

1. Configure the addition of Bandwidth Extended Communities on inbound eBGP advertisements:

    <u>IOS XE</u>
    router(config)# **router bgp** *AS-number*
    router(config-router)# **neighbor** *IP-neighbor* **dmzlink-bw**

    <u>IOS XR</u>
    RP/0/RP0/CPU0:RR(config)# **router bgp** *AS-number*
    RP/0/RP0/CPU0:RR(config-bgp)# **neighbor** *IP-neighbor*
    RP/0/RP0/CPU0:RR(config-bgp-nbr)# **dmz-link-bandwidth**

    NOTE: The Bandwidth Extended Community value added is exactly the value of the bandwidth parameter associated to the physical interface that receives the advertisements.

2. Configure the propagation of the Extended Communities toward iBGP sessions (IOS XE only, since in IOS XR, COMMUNITY attributes in iBGP sessions are propagated by default):

    <u>IOS XE</u>
    router(config)# **router bgp** *AS-number*
    router(config-router)# **neighbor** *IP-neighbor* **send-community extended**

3. Activate, on the AS routers deemed appropriate, the load distribution based on the bandwidth, and the BGP Multipath through the following commands:

    <u>IOS XE</u>
    router(config)# **router bgp** *AS-number*
    router(config-router)# **bgp dmzlink-bw**
    router(config-router)# **maximum-paths ibgp** *number-of-path*

    <u>IOS XR</u>
    RP/0/RP0/CPU0:RR(config)# **address-family (ipv4 | ipv6) unicast**
    RP/0/RP0/CPU0:RR(config-bgp-af)# **maximum-paths ibgp** *number-of-path*

Let's see a practical example of application of this procedure. We will refer to the topology of the network shown in Figure 9.17 where two PE routers of AS 64501 (ISP) send a default route to two CEs of AS 65101 (enterprise network). Each CE – PE connection has its own eBGP session. The figure shows the bandwidth values of each connection to the ISP, where the eBGP sessions are activated.

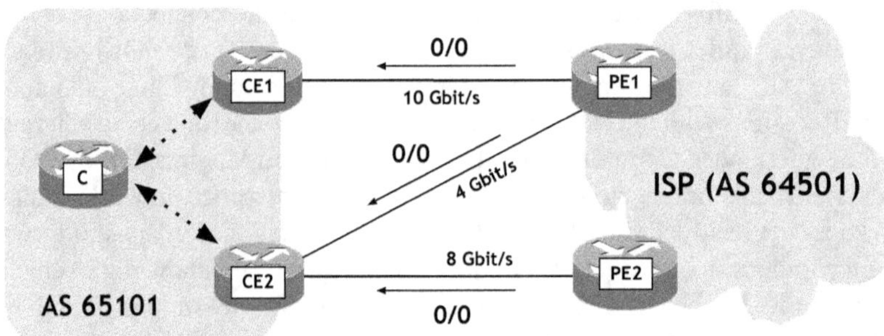

Figure 9.17 – Sample network for outbound traffic load sharing application, with distribution based on the bandwidth of the connections with the ISP.

Assuming that CE1, CE2 and C are Cisco routers with IOS XE, the relevant configurations are those of the BGP processes of routers CE1, CE2 and C:

CE1
```
router bgp 65101
neighbor 10.1.11.1 description "eGBP SESSION with PE1"
neighbor 10.1.11.1 remote-as 64501
neighbor 10.1.11.1 dmzlink-bw
neighbor 10.1.9.3 description "iGBP SESSION with C"
neighbor 10.1.9.3 remote-as 65101
neighbor 10.1.9.3 update-source Loopback0
neighbor 10.1.9.3 next-hop-self
neighbor 10.1.9.3 send-community extended
```

NOTE: Router CE1, with a single connection toward the ISP, cannot distribute traffic in any way, hence the absence of the "**bgp dmzlink-bw**" and "**maximum-paths**..." commands.

CE2
```
router bgp 65101
bgp dmzlink-bw
neighbor 10.1.11.5 description "eBGP SESSION WITH PE1"
neighbor 10.1.11.5 remote-as 64501
neighbor 10.1.11.5 dmzlink-bw
neighbor 10.1.12.1 description "eBGP SESSION WITH PE2"
neighbor 10.1.12.1 remote-as 64501
neighbor 10.1.12.1 dmzlink-bw
neighbor 10.1.9.3 description "iGBP SESSION with C"
neighbor 10.1.9.3 remote-as 65101
neighbor 10.1.9.3 update-source Loopback0
neighbor 10.1.9.3 next-hop-self
neighbor 10.1.9.3 send-community extended
maximum-paths 2
```

C
```
router bgp 65101
bgp dmzlink-bw
neighbor 10.1.9.1 description "iBGP SESSION WITH CE1"
neighbor 10.1.9.1 remote-as 65101
neighbor 10.1.9.1 update-source Loopback 0
neighbor 10.1.9.2 description "iBGP SESSION WITH CE2"
neighbor 10.1.9.2 remote-as 65101
neighbor 10.1.9.2 update-source Loopback 0
maximum-paths 2
```

In order to check that traffic is actually distributed, let's see the detailed forwarding information of the default route on CE2's RIB:

```
CE2#show ip route 0.0.0.0
Routing entry for 0.0.0.0/0, supernet
  Known via "bgp 65101", distance 20, metric 0, candidate default path
  Tag 64501, type external
```

```
Last update from 10.1.15.5 00:43:34 ago
Routing Descriptor Blocks:
* 10.1.12.1, from 10.1.12.1, 00:43:34 ago
  Route metric is 0, traffic share count is 2
  AS Hops 1
  Route tag 64501
  10.1.11.5, from 10.1.11.5, 00:43:34 ago
  Route metric is 0, traffic share count is 1
  AS Hops 1
  Route tag 64501
```

From the view, we notice that router CE2 executes a load sharing for traffic using the default route, with a 1/2 ratio on the connections toward PE1 (Next-Hop = 10.1.11.5) and toward PE2 (Next-Hop = 10.1.12.1), respectively. This ratio results from the fact that the bandwidth ratio of the connections from CE2 toward PE1 and PE2 is 4/8 = 1/2.

Let's now see the traffic distribution data on router C:

```
C#show ip route 0.0.0.0
Routing entry for 0.0.0.0/0, supernet
  Known via "bgp 65101", distance 200, metric 0, candidate default path
  Tag 64501, type internal
  Last update from 10.1.9.1 00:52:50 ago
  Routing Descriptor Blocks:
  * 10.1.9.2, from 10.1.9.2, 00:52:51 ago
      Route metric is 0, traffic share count is 6
      AS Hops 1
      Route tag 64501
    10.1.9.1, from 10.1.9.1, 00:52:51 ago
      Route metric is 0, traffic share count is 5
      AS Hops 1
      Route tag 64501
```

From the view, we notice that router C executes a load sharing for traffic using the default route, with a 5/6 ratio on the connections toward CE1 (Next-Hop = 10.1.9.1) and toward CE2 (Next-Hop = 10.1.9.2), respectively. This ratio results from the fact that the bandwidth ratio of the connections from routers CE1 and CE2 toward routers PE1 and PE2 respectively is $10/(4+8) = 10/12 = 5/6$.

Juniper routers also support load sharing based on the Bandwidth Extended Community. The configuration entails the following steps:

1. Define the Bandwidth Extended Community values. The Bandwidth Extended Communities must be expressed in the "**bandwidth**:*AS*:*bandwidth-value*" format, where *AS* is an AS number, and the bandwidth value must be specified in byte/s.

2. Define a routing policy that assigns the Bandwidth Extended Community value. Then, the routing policy should be applied to the desired direction (import or export). Remember that, in Juniper routers, differently from Cisco routers, the propagation of (extended and ordinary) Communities is automatic.

3. Activate, on the AS routers deemed appropriate, the load distribution and the BGP Multipath.

As application example, let's consider the topology in Figure 9.17, where we will only consider the connections between CE2 and the two PEs of AS 64501. For the sake of brevity, we will only see router CE2's configuration.

CE2

```
[edit policy-options]
policy-statement SET-BW {
  term SLOW-PEER {
    from {
      neighbor 10.1.11.5;
      route-filter 0.0.0.0/0 exact;
    }
    then {
      community add SLOW-BW;
      accept;
    }
  }
  term FAST-PEER {
    from {
      neighbor 10.1.12.1;
      route-filter 0.0.0.0/0 exact;
    }
    then {
      community add HIGH-BW;
      accept;
    }
  }
  term REJECT-ALL {
    then reject;
  }
}
community SLOW-BW members bandwidth:65101:500000000;
community HIGH-BW members bandwidth:65101:1000000000;

[edit protocols bgp group PE]
import SET-BW;
multipath;
peer-as 64501;
neighbor 10.1.11.5;
neighbor 10.1.12.1;

[edit policy-options policy-statement LB]
then {
  load-balance per-packet;
}

[edit routing-options forwarding-table]
export LB;
```

With this configuration, router CE2 assigns to the advertisements from BGP peers 10.1.11.5 (PE1) and 10.1.12.1 (PE2), the Bandwidth Extended Communities 65101:500000000 and 65101:1000000000, where the two values 500000000 and 1000000000 represent the speed of the two low and high-speed connections, expressed as byte/s. They are automatically propagated to router C, which, similarly to router CE2, will use them to implement the load sharing with a bandwidth-based distribution. Just like on router C, on router CE2 we also need to enable both the BGP Multipath and the load distribution. The latter is enabled by applying the routing policy **LB** at hierarchical level **[edit routing-options forwarding-table]**.

In order to check that, on CE2, the load sharing has been correctly activated, let's go over the detail of the default route advertisements:

```
aft@CE2> show route protocol bgp 0.0.0.0/0 exact detail
inet.0: 11 destinations, 12 routes (11 active, 0 holddown, 0 hidden)
0.0.0.0/0 (2 entries, 1 announced)
   *BGP    Preference: 170/-101
           ... < output omitted > ...
           Source: 10.1.11.5
           Next hop: 10.1.12.1 via ae0.0 balance 67%, selected
           Session Id: 0x0
           Next hop: 10.1.11.5 via ae1.0 balance 33%
           ... < output omitted > ...
           AS path: 64501 I
           Communities: bandwidth:65101:500000000
           Accepted Multipath
           Localpref: 100
           Router ID: 192.168.0.11
    BGP    Preference: 170/-101
           ... < output omitted > ...
           Source: 10.1.12.1
           Next hop: 10.1.12.1 via ae0.0, selected
           ... < output omitted > ...
           Inactive reason: Not Best in its group - Router ID
           ... < output omitted > ...
           AS path: 64501 I
           Communities: bandwidth:65101:1000000000
           Accepted MultipathContrib
           Localpref: 100
           Router ID: 192.168.0.12
```

From the view, we can see that CE2 carries out a load distribution with a ratio of 33% on the connection toward PE1 (4 Gbit/s), and 67% on the connection toward PE2 (8 Gbit/s). The distribution results directly from the bandwidth ratios. Indeed, the bandwidth ratio of the connection toward PE2, with respect to the total available, is: 8/(4+8) = 66.66%, and Juniper routers round it up to value 67%. In other words, out of 100 traffic flows, 67 on average are routed on the higher speed connection (toward PE2) and 33 on the lower speed connection (toward PE1).

9.3 MULTI-HOMED CUSTOMERS

When a customer, for reliability reasons, chooses to use the IP services from two (or even more) different ISPs, only two types of connection are possible (both redundant):

- redundant connection with single CE;

- redundant connection with double CE.

For each type of connection, there are also further types of redundancy, such as, for the first type, multilink PE-CE connections, for the second type, single CE – double PE connections, etc. In all these scenarios, even if not theoretically mandatory, BGP is normally used as PE-CE routing protocol. Here too, just like in the connection to a single ISP we saw in the previous paragraph, we can use the options provided by BGP to define different routing policies (e.g. primary/backup, load balancing, load sharing), both inbound and outbound, and solve the issue of possible routing and/or forwarding loops – always lurking where there are redundant connections – in an effective way. The configuration best practices are basically the same we saw for connection to a single ISP, with a few exceptions.

9.3.1 Numbering plans

In this case, the issue of the prefix(es) to use for the numbering plan of the enterprise network, and the AS number to use to establish eBGP sessions with the ISPs, is much more complex than the one we saw for the connection to a single ISP.

To get an idea of the greater difficulty, let's consider the case of a customer that initially uses the IP services of an ISP – which we'll call ISP-A. ISP-A provides prefix 192.0.2.0/25 – part of its prefix 192.0.2/24 – to its customer. As is commonly practised, ISP-A advertised to the rest of the Internet only aggregate prefix 192.0.2/24. Let's assume that the customer connects to another ISP – which we'll call ISP-B – to use its IP services. The customer advertises its prefix 192.0.2.0/25 also to ISP-B, but this ISP cannot aggregate it, therefore it propagates it as is to the entire Internet. A possible ISP-C, connected via eBGP to both ISPs – ISP-A and ISP-B – will receive two advertisements, the first of aggregate prefix 192.0.2/24 from ISP-A, and the second of prefix 192.0.2.0/25 from ISP-B. Figure 9.18 summarizes what we just said.

This approach generates two kinds of issues:

- Prefix 192.0.2.0/25 may not be accepted by the different ISPs on the Internet, since its mask is too big. As you may recall, a common policy for large ISPs is not accepting prefixes with a mask greater than /24.

- If ISP-C does not set any limitation to prefix acceptance, due to the longest match prefix algorithm, all the traffic that ISP-C routes toward the customer will transit via ISP-B, leaving the connection between the customer and ISP-A empty. Paradoxically, ISP-A will serve as backup ISP, even if, being the provider of the prefix used for the numbering plan, it should theoretically have the role of primary ISP.

One possible solution to solve the second issue (but not the first!) is for the customer to ask ISP-A to advertise to the other ISPs – and therefore also to ISP-C – apart from aggregate 192.0.2/24, also the more specific prefix 192.0.2.0/25. Actually, this might not be sufficient, as the path following by inbound traffic depends on ISP-C's decisions. If it chose to transit on ISP-B as best path for 192.0.2.0/25, we would be back to the previous situation. However, since both ISP-A and ISP-B have sessions with other ISPs, and not just with ISP-C, it is likely that, statistically speaking,

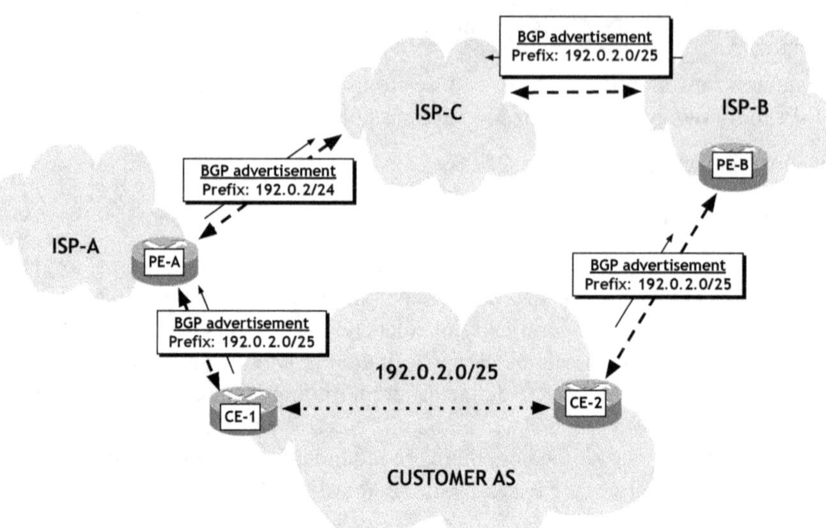

Figure 9.18 – Example of advertisement propagation in a multi-homing scenario.

traffic would be distributed on the two available connections. In any case, it is hard to foresee the actual distribution of inbound traffic on them.

Besides not solving the first issue, the suggested solution has also the problem of abnormally increasing the RIBs/FIBs of Internet routers. And it is precisely to avoid this that large ISPs do not accept prefixes with too big a mask.

Theoretically, there are two possible solutions to solve the issue of the prefix(es) the customer should use for the numbering plan of its enterprise network, but they both have their own shortcomings:

- The customer uses its own Provider Independent prefix (see Section 9.2.1) with a sufficiently small mask. In theory, this would be a simple solution, yet difficult to implement, since, as we said in Section 9.2.1, the current policy of RIRs is to provide large blocks of IP prefixes (e.g. /32 or /29 in IPv6) only to ISPs.

- The customer uses two different prefixes, provided by the two ISPs, both aggregatable by ISPs into a larger supernet (Provider Aggregatable prefixes). In this case, the issue is that the customer could be forced to renumber part of its network.

Between these solutions, however, the second one is more feasible.

Concerning the AS number to be used for the eBGP sessions toward the ISPs, it would be ideal to use a public AS number. Here too, however, there may be allocation issues (unless the customer is a LIR/NIR). Therefore, in the vast majority of situations, it is necessary to resort to private AS numbers. And this poses the issue of what private AS number to use. Indeed, as we saw in Section 9.2.1, the best practice for ISPs is to use, on the CE side, private AS numbers, following the recommendations by RFC 2270, i.e. using a single AS number for all customers accessing via BGP.

Let's see what problems this may cause. Let's assume that the customer uses the IP services of ISP-A, and only then decides to use the IP services of ISP-B. ISP-A will assign to the customer a private AS number, which will be used to activate the BGP sessions (eBGP and possibly also iBGP) on the customer's routers. Once it has acquired the customer, ISP-B could theoretically use the number already assigned by ISP-A as the customer's AS number. However, this would entail a customized customer configuration, which ISPs are reluctant to activate. Indeed, usually ISPs have configuration templates they will use for all customers. Therefore, ISP-B will assign one of its own private AS numbers to the customer, usually different from the one assigned by ISP-A.

NOTE: We need to think about the uniqueness of numeral resources within the Internet, and, even more, within a single autonomous system. In the case we just described, we cannot expect ISP-B is to connect to the customer's enterprise network by configuring the same autonomous system number previously decided by ISP-A, since, in ISP-B's network, that number could already have been assigned for other purposes.

Since it is not possible to activate more than one BGP process on the routers, the issues of what AS number to use, and, also, of how to activate the eBGP sessions toward the ISP that does not provide the AS number used, arise. Leading manufacturers provide a solution to this issue through the AS Translation function. The idea is to ensure that, even though the AS number used to activate the BGP process is, for instance, AS = X, the My Autonomous System field of the OPEN message shows the AS value = Y used by the BGP Neighbor to activate the BGP session. Both Cisco and Juniper routers support the AS Translation function.

In Cisco and Juniper routers, the command is the following:

<u>IOS XE</u>
router(config)# **router bgp** *AS-number*
router(config-router)# **neighbor** *IP-neighbor* **remote-as** *AS-neighbor*
router(config-router)# **neighbor** *IP-neighbor* **local-as** *private-AS*

<u>IOS XR</u>
RP/0/RP0/CPU0:router(config)# **router bgp** *AS-number*
RP/0/RP0/CPU0:router(config-bgp)# **neighbor** *IP-neighbor*
RP/0/RP0/CPU0:router(config-bgp-nbr)# **remote-as** *AS-neighbor*
RP/0/RP0/CPU0:router(config-bgp-nbr)# **local-as** *private-AS*

<u>JUNOS</u> (Note: the "**local-as**" command can be given at global, group or session level)

[edit routing-options]
autonomous-system *AS-number*;

[edit protocols bgp]
local-as *private-AS*;

A consequence of these commands is that in the OPEN messages sent to the BGP Neighbor, the My Autonomous System field shows, in place of their own AS number (= *AS-number*), the AS number indicated in the configuration as *private-AS*.

NOTE: Cisco and Juniper routers differ for one detail, when implementing the AS Translation function. Indeed, in Cisco's implementation, in the UPDATE messages, the AS_PATH contains both AS number, its own and the one specified in the "**local-as**..." command. In Juniper's implementation, the AS_PATH contains only the AS number specified in the "**local-as**" command.

Let's see an example of application of the "**local-as…**" command, with reference to the topology shown in Figure 9.19.

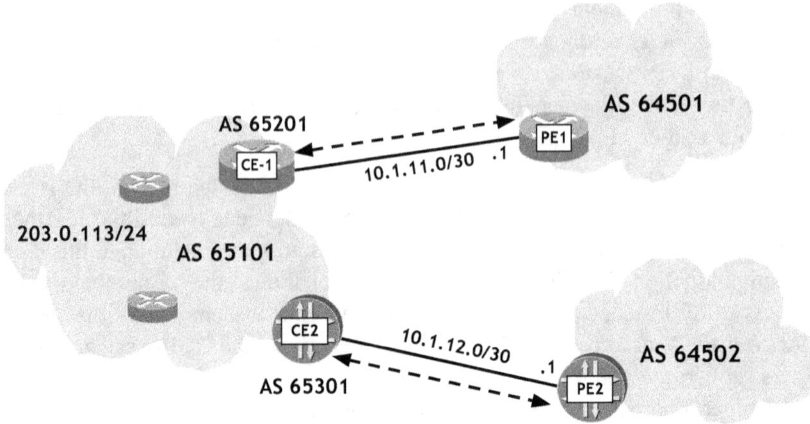

Figure 9.19 – Example of application of the AS Translation mechanism.

In the scenario shown in the figure, the customer uses AS number AS 65101 internally. The ISP with AS number AS 64501 uses, for its customers, AS number AS 65201, while the other ISP (AS 64502), uses an AS number for the eBGP session toward CE2, AS number 65301. In short, in CEs, the BGP process uses AS 65101, but it presents itself to AS 64501 with AS number 65201 and to AS 64502 with AS number 65301.

The relevant configurations executed are:

<u>CE1</u> (IOS XE)

```
router bgp 65101
  neighbor 10.1.11.1 remote-as 64501
  neighbor 10.1.11.1 local-as 65201
```

<u>PE1</u> (IOS XR)

```
router bgp 64501
  bgp router-id 192.168.0.11
  address-family ipv4 unicast
  !
  neighbor 10.1.11.2
    remote-as 65201
    address-family ipv4 unicast
      route-policy ALL in
      route-policy ALL out
```

<u>CE2</u> (JUNOS)

```
[edit routing-options]
autonomous-system 65101;

[edit protocols bgp group PE]
neighbor 10.1.12.1 {
    peer-as 64502;
    local-as 65301;
}
```

<u>PE2</u> (JUNOS)
```
[edit routing-options]
autonomous-system 64502;

router-id 192.168.0.12;

[edit protocols bgp group PE]
neighbor 10.1.12.1 {
    peer-as 65301;
}
```

The detailed view of the advertisement of prefix 203.0.113/24 on PE1 shows that, in Cisco's implementation, the AS_PATH is composed by the AS number of the BGP process on CE1 (=65101) and the local AS (= 65201).

```
RP/0/0/CPU0:PE1#show bgp 203.0.113.0/24
BGP routing table entry for 203.0.113.0/24
. . . < output omitted > . . .
Paths: (1 available, best #1)
  Not advertised to any peer
  Path #1: Received by speaker 0
  Not advertised to any peer
  65201 65101
    10.1.11.2 from 10.1.11.2 (10.1.99.11)
      Origin IGP, metric 0, localpref 100, valid, external, best,
group-best, import-candidate
```

The view of the same prefix on PE2 shows that, in Juniper's implementation, the AS_PATH comprises only the local AS (= 65301).

```
aft@PE2> show route protocol bgp 203.0.113.0/24
. . . < output omitted > . . .
203.0.113.0/24     *[BGP/170] 02:04:33, localpref 100
                      AS path: 65301 I, validation-state: unverified
                   >  to 10.1.12.2 via ge-0/0/2.0
```

9.3.2 Routing policies

The best practices to be used for primary/backup routing policies are basically the same as the ones we saw in Section 9.2.4 for redundant connections, when connecting to a single ISP. The only difference is that, when managing the inbound traffic, it is not possible to use the MED, because, as you may recall, the MED is not propagated outside an AS, and, moreover, the MED is compared by default only when the advertisements come from the same AS. Theoretically, by using additional configuration commands, it would be possible to use the MED, but in this scenario it is not recommended.

In place of the MED, to manage inbound traffic, we could use the AS_PATH prepending mechanism. The idea, already described in Sections 7.3.2 and 9.2.4, is to increase, on a configuration basis, the length of the AS_PATH of the advertisements sent on the eBGP session established on the backup connection, and leaving the default AS_PATH on the advertisements sent on the eBGP session established on the primary connection. It is not easy to establish how many ASes should be added. Basically, this process is iterative, by increasing the ASes added by one unit a time, until no more traffic flows on the backup connection. One thing to keep in mind when using the AS_PATH prepending mechanism is that it should be agreed with the ISPs. Indeed, they could have inbound filters that allow advertisements only with the customer's AS number (and not with the copies), and they could have outbound policies that change the AS_PATH, eliminating any additional ASes due to the AS_PATH prepending mechanism.

A primary/backup policy per se, in a scenario with a customer multi-homed to different ISPs, is not ideal. Indeed, by taking the example in Figure 9.19 and assuming AS 64501 as primary, with a primary/backup policy per se, traffic sent by AS 65101 to the local prefixes of AS 64502 would still transit only through AS 64501.

A better routing policy should entail the following:

- traffic toward the local prefixes of AS 64502 uses the connection between CE2 and PE2;

- the rest of the traffic uses primary AS 64501.

One example of configuration in a Cisco environment that allows using a primary routing/backup policy has already been described in Section 7.2.1. The same example, in a Juniper environment, can be found in Section 7.2.2.

In the case of load balancing/sharing policies, the best practices to use to distribute traffic (in a more or less equivalent way) on the connections toward the two ISPs are basically the same we saw in Section 9.2.5 for redundant connections, when connecting to a single ISP, with the difference that, when managing inbound traffic, it is not possible to use the MED, for the reasons explained earlier.

SUMMARY

This chapter does not introduce any new concepts; rather, it can be seen as a guide to practical BGP applications in medium-large enterprise networks. It explains the different redundant connection methods, both when the network is connected to a single ISP, and when it is connected to different ISPs. For each type of connection, we analysed several aspects, such as the numbering plans and the related routing policies. It also includes some practical tips and best application practices.

Worth remembering:

1. Advantages and disadvantages of the different connection methods (single-homed/multi-homed).

2. Numbering plan management in the case of customers connected to a single ISP, different types of redundant connections (single CE – single PE, single CE – double PE, double CE – double PE) and the routing policies (primary/backup, load balancing/sharing).

3. Numbering plan management in the case of customers connected to different ISPs, the different types of redundant connections and the routing policies (primary/backup, load balancing/sharing).

10 – SECURITY ASPECTS

With the Internet switching from a limited-use network, in a "trusted" environment, to a network with strong commercial motivations, in the last years, it became necessary to study and implement security measures for all routing protocols. This is especially true for BGP, since the entire Internet is based on it, and since the exchange of routing information for which BGP is responsible occurs between many different entities, over which it is utterly impossible to make assumptions of complete reliability and "ethical" conduct.

Due to this, the original standard – both RFC 1771 and its updated RFC 4271 – did not include a security function. Over the years, some operative mechanisms – such as prefix filtering – have been introduced, and, even if they were not initially intended as security functions, they can still be used as tools that help to build a safe BGP architecture.

Speaking of security in general is very difficult, since it is evident that there can be no absolute security. Therefore, in this chapter, we will only describe the main BGP security issues, and focus on those few consolidated operative aspects, useful for correctly configuring and administering network devices.

Lastly, although it is obvious, it is best to stress out that the techniques covered in this chapter concern eBGP sessions, even though they could be theoretically applied also to iBGP sessions. Indeed, only in eBGP sessions the counterpart should be considered "untrusted" from a security-standpoint, since it is administered by a different entity.

10.1 TYPES OF ATTACKS AND VULNERABILITY

Any discussion on security aspects cannot prescind from starting with a description of the possible types of attacks and a vulnerability analysis. Clearly, the entire Internet is vulnerable to attacks to its routing protocols. And BGP is no exception; moreover, being the most important protocol, it is the one where protection-related attention should be focused.

The areas of main concern can be summarized as follows:

- authentication – checking that the identity of the BGP Neighbor is certain;

- integrity – checking that the BGP messages received by a BGP Neighbor have not been illegally manipulated;

- availability – protecting a BGP Speaker against attacks that tend to saturate its processing resources and make it unusable (DoS, Denial of Service attacks);

- advertisement origin validation – implementing mechanism to check whether an AS is authorized or not to advertise a certain IP prefix to the Internet ecosystem;

- AS_PATH validation – making sure that the AS_PATH has not been manipulated during the path between the origin AS and the destination AS.

There are multiple attack methods. A broad classification identifies the following two main types:

- Session attacks – they include attacks that attempt to alter the flow of BGP messages, such as message modification, insertion, cancellation; attacks that attempt to knock down the session between two BGP Neighbors; attacks that attempt to infer confidential information by intercepting BGP messages. Among session attacks, we can also include all typical TCP protocol attacks.

- Denial of Service (DoS) attacks – attacks that attempt to deny the operation of a service, e.g. by fraudulently terminating BGP sessions, or, as it often happens, saturating the resources of a router (memory, CPU), or saturating the capacity of the transmission media. Another classic example is the prefix hijacking, which entails hijacking traffic toward specific points where it can be analyzed or rejected.

Then, there are some unethical behaviors by network administrators, which can be considered the same as an attack. These include the possibility of "stealing" bandwidth from an AS, by making traffic transit between two routers of their own AS, for instance, and using the resources of another (unaware) AS.

In this section, we will describe those that are deemed the most critical attacks to BGP and its weaknesses (that is, its main vulnerabilities). For a more detailed description of the types of attacks and vulnerabilities of BGP, see RFC 4272 – *BGP Security Vulnerabilities Analysis*, January 2006.

10.1.1 Session attacks

Let's consider the case of a "minimal" BGP operation, i.e. two routers that established a BGP session. According to a widespread practice in security literature, we will name the two routers Alice and Bob (actually, we should name the two router administrators Alice and Bob!). There are three potential fraudulent entities in this "minimal" system: Alice, Bob and possibly a third entity that gets into the communication (man-in-the-middle), which we will name Charlie. Let's assume that at least one between Alice and Bob operates correctly, otherwise any possible protocol would be completely vulnerable.

And let's go over some of the main session attack types:

- Inference of confidential information: generally, the information exchanged on a BGP session is not confidential. However, in certain situations – and especially in commercial agreements between big ISPs – they don't want to reveal the content of the agreements and routing policies adopted. By intercepting BGP messages (and UPDATE messages in particular), it would be possible to easily reconstruct this information. Intercepting could be done by Charlie, which somehow manages to intercept the flow of BGP messages exchanged between Alice and Bob, and to obtain confidential data through them.

- Attacking the message integrity: an additional risk to the previous one occurs when Charlie, besides intercepting the messages, becomes an active (yet hidden) part of the data exchange. For instance, Charlie could add false BGP messages in the communication between Alice and Bob, with the purpose of altering the routing information. Charlie could also eliminate some of the messages – e.g. KEEPALIVE messages – with the aim of taking down the BGP session. Lastly, Charlie could also intercept and modify a message "on the fly", altering its content.

- Unwanted session termination: one of the consequences of adding and/or editing and/or changing BGP messages – or even TCP segments – is the possibility for Charlie (or for any fraudulent end between Alice or Bob) to terminate the session beforehand. There are multiple fraudulent actions that can lead to terminate a BGP session, including, by way of example, sending a TCP reset segment, adding incorrect events that entail machine transitions to finite BGP states toward Idle or Active states, the aforementioned block of KEEPALIVE messages, the creation of NOTIFICATION messages – whose consequence is terminating the session.

Moreover, as mentioned earlier, among session attacks, we should include all typical TCP protocol attacks, such as Syn flooding, TCP reset, Session Desynchronization, etc. To know more about them, refer to the broad literature on this topic. In any case, contrarily to popular belief, attacking a BGP session is not that easy. Indeed, since BGP messages are transported on TCP connections, we need to know:

- Neighbor Address of the BGP Neighbors: the IP addresses of the packets transporting BGP messages can be discovered through simple traceroutes, and then simulated (spoofing). There are at least two ways to "hide" the IP addresses used in the session: using Loopback interfaces (i.e. multihop eBGP sessions) for eBGP sessions, or using secondary addresses as BGP Neighbor Addresses; in both cases, IP addresses are not visible through traceroutes. In BGP sessions for IPv6, we can also use link-local IPv6 addresses (to this end, see the second note in Section 3.1.6).

- Connection TCP ports: as we saw in Chapter 2, the BGP session is initialized by one of the two BGP Neighbors (acting as client) that chooses a casual port from a set interval (the interval depends on the specific implementation). The other port is well-known port 179. Since it is not possible to know who started the session beforehand (and therefore which side of the session uses port 179), we need to catch a packet or do some trial and error.

- TCP sequence number: as you know, the TCP sequence number allows sorting the byte flow sent by a source. It also holds a security function, since it ensures that the incoming TCP segment has its own expected sequence number; otherwise, the segment is rejected. There are some well-known techniques to predict the sequence number; however, improved pseudo-casual number generation algorithms have made discovering the correct sequence number of a session incredibly harder. With these new techniques, hackers are forced to directly connect to a router or intercept the BGP messages.

However, this should not lead network administrators to ignore the issue, without implementing suitable countermeasures.

10.1.2 Denial of Service (DoS) attacks

Some of the aforementioned attacks – such as those leading to a fraudulent termination of a BGP session – can be considered as attempts to deny the service (DoS attacks).
There are many other types of attacks that prevent the performance of the services offered by BGP. It is hard to compile an exhaustive list, therefore we will only mention a few examples.
One first example is denying a "prefix reachability service" (prefix hijacking). Prefix hijacking is one of the most popular "malicious" practices to divert traffic to a black-hole, or – even worse – analyze it for unethical purposes (e.g. industrial espionage, military espionage, etc.).
The idea is very simple. Let's assume that we want to divert traffic to a certain prefix toward our router, and then reject it. We just need to advertise the prefix via BGP, and, if a BGP Neighbor chooses the advertisement sent as best-path, traffic to the prefix will be diverted by the BGP Neighbor toward the "non-ethical" router, creating a "black hole", that is, a point within the network where this traffic is rejected due to a lack of a valid path.
In the past – and now still – there have been hundreds of cases of prefix hijacking, some of

which has made history, just like the one describe in Section 10.1.5 below, which occurred on 24 February 2008, when Pakistan Telecom (AS 17557) injected a BGP advertisement of prefix 208.65.153/24, part of prefix 208.65.152/22, assigned by a Regional Internet Registry, to the popular YouTube, without authorization. One of the Upstream Providers of Pakistan Telecom, PCCW Global (AS 3491), propagated the prefix to the rest of the Internet, allowing Pakistan Telecom to attract part of the global traffic directed toward YouTube.

The cause of this is one of BGP's intrinsic vulnerabilities: the fact that there is no control over the identity of those who input prefixes into the Internet. In other words, no one checks if the entity originating a prefix is authorized to do so, if it has received that prefix from a Regional Internet Registry.

The example in Figure 10.1 below exemplifies this phenomenon. AS 64501 received prefix 192.0.2/24 from a Regional Internet Registry, therefore it is the only one authorized to advertise it to the Internet. Let's assume that AS 64505, which doesn't have this authorization, advertises the same prefix, whether for a configuration error or due to a "malicious" behavior. A generic AS in the Internet will receive two advertisements of prefix 192.0.2/24, and, if the BGP selection process chooses the advertisement originated by the unauthorized AS as the best path, traffic toward that prefix would be hijacked in a black-hole and perhaps analyzed. For instance, AS 64504 in the figure, due to the shorter AS_PATH, will choose the path toward AS 64505 that originated the advertisement (without authorization) as the best path for prefix 192.0.2/24.

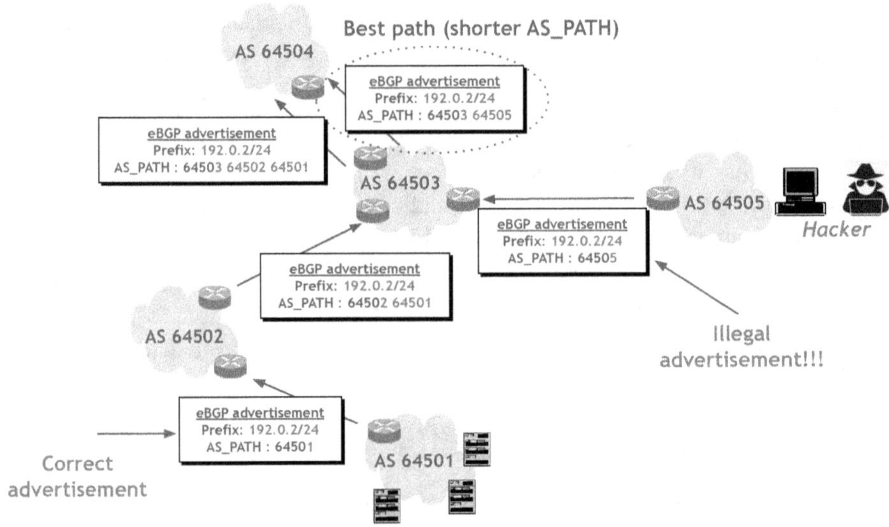

Figure 10.1 – Example of prefix hijacking.

What we just described is not the only Prefix Hijacking method, even if it is one of the most common ones. In Figure 10.2 below, you can see a variant that is actually the one that originated the incident above concerning YouTube. In this variant, whether for an (improbable) configuration error or due to a "malicious" behavior, an unauthorized AS advertises the subnet of a prefix that a Regional Internet Registry assigned to another AS.

Just like the case in Figure 10.1, AS 64501 received prefix 192.0.2/24 from a Regional Internet Registry, therefore it is the only one authorized to advertise it to the Internet. With AS 64501's authorization, the subnets of this prefix could be advertised by other ASes, but an AS could advertise a subnet even without authorization.

For instance, in the figure, AS 64505 advertises subnet 192.0.2.0/25 without any authorization. One AS in the Internet, shown as AS 64504 in the figure, will receive two advertisements, one of the entire prefix 192.0.2/24, originated by AS 64501, and one of subnet 192.0.2.0/25, originated by AS 64505. BGP considers these two prefixes different, and it will elect two best paths; they will both end up in the IP routing table of AS 64504 border router. According to the longest match prefix rule, a portion of the traffic directed toward prefix 192.0.2/24 – the one directed toward subnet 192.0.2.0/25 – will be hijacked toward AS 64505, ending up in a black-hole.

The cause of this issue is the fact that BGP does not check the identity of those who input prefixes on the Internet. The only available tools are filters, but not everyone uses them, and they would significantly increase the configuration complexity, without solving the issue. For example, how can an intermediate AS know whether a remote AS is authorized to advertise a prefix or not?

The only possible solution to avoid prefix hijacking issues is to implement an authorization system, managed by one or more central entities (e.g. Regional Internet Registries), which, through digital certificates, allow checking whether an AS is authorized to advertise a certain prefix in the Internet or not, with reasonable certainty. Those aspects will be treated further in Paragraph 10.6.

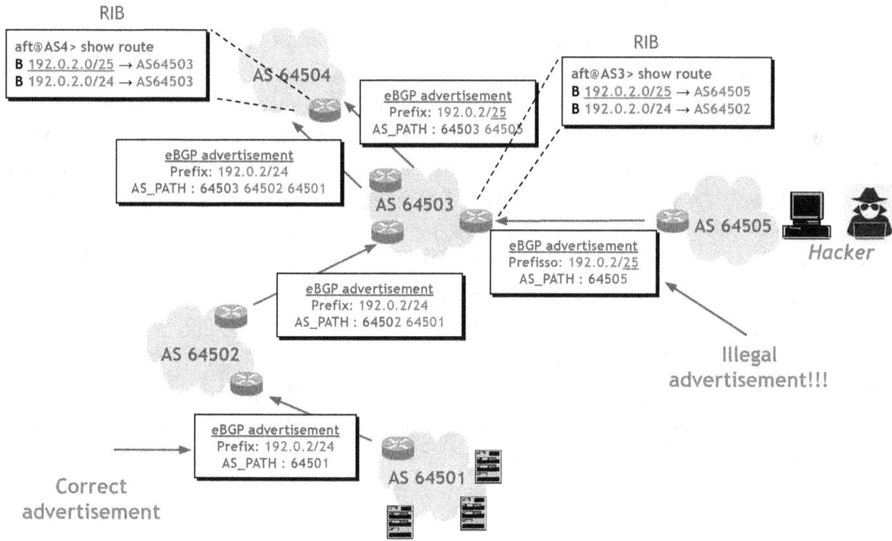

Figure 10.2 – Another example of prefix hijacking.

We can find another example of DoS attack in those routers that implement the Route Flap Damping. By simulating the route flaps, we can keep an advertisement frozen for a long time, alternating the correct traffic routing.

Lastly, classic DoS attacks are also those that attempt to saturate the memory and/or CPU resources of a router. For instance, by flooding a router with BGP advertisement, we can saturate its memory; or, during the three-way-handshake phase of the TCP connection, a hacker could send a large quantity of TCP Syn (Syn flooding), without ever sending the following TCP ACK (i.e., the third segment of the three-way-handshake), leading to an intensive use of the memory and of the CPU, until the router goes out of service.

In addition to these, there are volumetric DoS attacks, which consist in conveying large traffic flows toward a specific target, such as a DNS server, a web server, etc. And even more dangerous are Distributed DoS (DDoS) attacks, where hackers, in order to expand the traffic volume toward the victim, add a malicious code (trojan horse) to thousands of hosts of any kind. This set of hosts is called botnet, and the bigger the botnet, the greater the attack's effect. At a preset instant, all these thousands of hosts in the botnet will start sending traffic toward the server(s) attacked, until their processing and/or memory resources are saturated. This type of attack is even more devastating, in an Internet of Things (IoT) scenario, where the botnet comprises thousands of small devices connected to the Internet, typically used as sensors or function actuators. In Paragraphs 10.4 and 10.5, we will see how to contrast DDoS attacks.

NOTE: There are many different types of DoS/DDoS attacks (amplification and reflection, application attack, multivectorial, etc.). In the cases described, we only considered those for which a countermeasure via BGP is possible.

10.1.3 Unethical behavior

As mentioned many times, BGP is a protocol with a lot of metrics and functions. These features are its strength, but they are also its Achilles heel, since this wealth of metrics and functions can be used by network administrators for unethical purposes.

A typical unethical behavior is using an (unsuspecting) AS as transit, thus allowing an actual "bandwidth theft". To get a sense of how such a fraud can be achieved, let's consider the example in Figure 10.3, where two ISPs have a double connection on two different peering points (IXP-1 and IXP-2) between them. Let's assume that ISP-2 naively redistributes the two prefixes 172.16.1/24 and 172.16.2/24 used for the peering LANs of the two IXPs on its IGP, to propagate the BGP advertisements received from the eBGP Neighbors correctly within its network, through iBGP sessions. This way, the option of a layer-3 connection is given to the two routers RF and RE of ISP-1, using ISP-2 as transit. The layer-3 connection between the two routers RF and RE allows ISP-1 to create an IP tunnel (e.g. a GRE tunnel) between them, by establishing a (virtual) connection where traffic can transit, while using ISP-2's resources (bandwidth).

Actually, this unethical behavior can be easily countered: it is sufficient to change the default management of the NEXT_HOP attribute, according to Section 2.4.3, and avoid the redistribution of the prefixes with which the peering LANs of the two IXPs are numbered in IGP. This is just an example of what BGP can cause, when incorrectly configured. In this specific case, the countermeasure is simple, but it may not always be so.

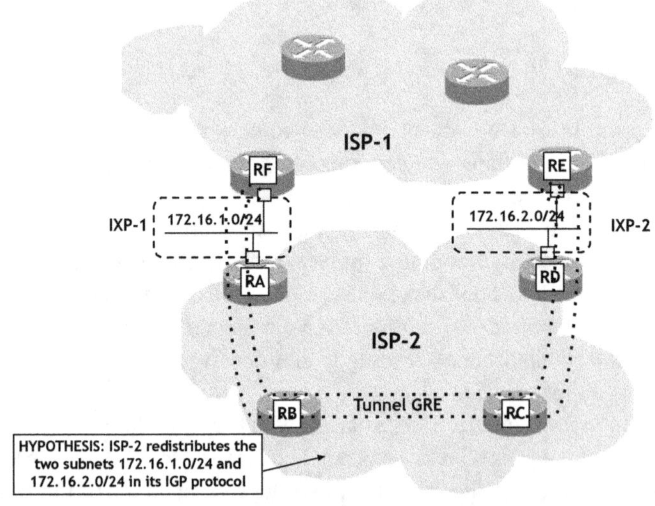

Figure 10.3 – Bandwidth theft via GRE tunnel.

10.1.4 Vulnerability

RFC 4272 highlights the main vulnerabilities of BGP in terms of security. In particular, it describes the following three main limits:

- BGP has no mechanism to protect the integrity and "freshness" of messages and identify their origin. Integrity ensures that the message has not been altered, "freshness" ensures that those who receive the message have actually received a new message, and not one replicated by a man-in-the-middle, and, lastly, origin authentication ensures that those who originate the message are entitled to do so.

- BGP does not offer any AS validation tool. In other words, BGP has no tools to ensure the ASes' reliability in terms of authorization to spread correct routing information. As stated in Section 10.1.2, when talking about the prefix hijacking phenomenon, an AS can generate any prefix, even one not belonging to its AS. Or, an AS could propagate the routing information received from another AS, thus changing some BGP attributes in a fraudulent manner. BGP does not check the correctness of these operations.

- BGP has no tools to ensure the authenticity of the AS_PATH attribute advertised by an AS. Altering the AS_PATH is one of the many mechanisms that an unethical administrator can resort to damage or manipulate the routing infrastructure.

Awareness of these vulnerabilities has led to the search for various types of countermeasures that we will go over in the next sections, and which are applied by honest administrators to avoid serious damages to their routing infrastructure and hold an ethical and responsible behavior toward the entire Internet ecosystem.

10.1.5 Real Case Study of Prefix Hijacking

In this section, as real example, we will see the timeline of a real prefix hijacking incident, documented in the European Regional Internet Registry RIPE NCC "YouTube Hijacking: A RIPE NCC RIS case study", and the countermeasures adopted to mitigate the effect and restore the previous situation.

On 24 February 2008 (Sunday), Pakistan Telecom (AS 17557) injected an unauthorized BGP advertisement of prefix 208.65.153/24, part of prefix 208.65.152/22, assigned by a Regional Internet Registry to the popular YouTube. One of the Upstream Providers of Pakistan Telecom, PCCW Global (AS 3491), propagated the prefix to the rest of the Internet, allowing Pakistan Telecom to attract part of the global traffic directed toward YouTube.

Here is the event timeline registered by the RIPE NCC Routing Information Service:

- **before Sunday 24 February 2008**: AS 36561 (YouTube) advertises, along with other prefixes not involved in the event, prefix 208.65.152/22;

- **Sunday, 24 February 2008, 18:47 (UTC)**: AS 17557 (Pakistan Telecom) advertises prefix 208.65.153/24. AS 3491 (PCCW Global) propagates the advertisement. Global Internet routers receive the advertisement, and part of the traffic directed toward YouTube is redirected toward Pakistan, where it ends on a "black hole", i.e. is rejected;

- **Sunday, 24 February 2008, 20:07 (UTC)**: AS 36561 (YouTube) starts, as initial countermeasure, to advertise prefix 208.65.153/24. With the two identical prefixes within the Internet, the selection process rules that bases the choice of the best-path on the shortest AS_PATH does not allow to bring all traffic back in the correct direction. This means that AS 17557 (Pakistan Telecom) continues to attract traffic directed toward YouTube;

- **Sunday, 24 February 2008, 20:18 (UTC)**: AS 36561 (YouTube) advertises prefixes 208.65.153.0/25 and 208.65.153.128/25. Due to the longest prefix match rule used by routers to forward IP traffic, every router that receives the advertisements of these two prefixes, forwards traffic toward YouTube. (However, this measure is not very effective, since, in the FIRT, prefixes longer than 24 bit are usually filtered);

- **Sunday, 24 February 2008, 20:51 (UTC)**: AS 3491 (PCCW Global) applies a Prepending AS_PATH to all advertisements originated by AS 17557 (Pakistan Telecom), including prefix 208.65.153/24, adding a copy of AS number 17557. This can be used to choose YouTube advertisements with the shortest AS_PATH;

- **Sunday, 24 February 2008, 21:01 (UTC)**: AS 3491 (PCCW Global) withdraws all prefixes originated by AS 17557 (Pakistan Telecom), thus stopping the prefix hijacking against YouTube. AS 17557 has not been completely disconnected from AS 3491. The prefixes originated by other ASes in Pakistan, accepted by AS 17557, were regularly propagated by AS 3491.

As the story shows, this event occurred in a very short period of time. YouTube's first reaction occurred 80 minutes after the unauthorized advertisement by Pakistan Telecom and the correct situation was restored after a little over two hours. While the incident, on one hand, showed the need for ISPs to equip tools that can detect anomalous situations and make the required corrections, on the other hand, it highlighted the need for a correct BGP Speaker configuration by AS administrators, which should at least implement filters to reject any unauthorized advertisement. Since this is not always possible, a security tool that allows advertising IP prefixes only to those ASes to which they were assigned by the different Regional Internet Registries becomes necessary. In Paragraph 10.6 below, we will mention some of the security architectures to prevent these issues.

10.2 PROTECTING A BGP SESSION

Just like all routing protocols, BGP is constantly enriched with functions that are usually related to operative needs. The security countermeasures described in this section are no exception.
However, security is still an object of study, therefore it quickly becomes obsolete. For this reason, we will only describe the consolidated countermeasures often used by network administrators and which we can say are the minimum measures to implement.
The first aspect to consider is how to secure BGP sessions, which, as we saw in Section 10.1.1, are subject to several types of attacks.

10.2.1 Authenticating BGP messages

Protecting the TCP connection is the easiest way to mitigate all attacks to a BGP session. A very popular and inexpensive (from a CPU usage standpoint) measure among network administrators, supported by all major device manufacturers (e.g. Cisco and Juniper), is to implement a MD5 hash function to protect TCP segments. RFC 4271 establishes that all BGP implementations must support the authentication mechanism specified by RFC 2385 – *Protection of BGP Sessions via the TCP MD5 Signature Option*, August 1998.
Authentication through an MD5 hash function does not protect the content of the messages, which travels unencrypted; its only purpose is to check who sent the message.

The operating mechanism is based on a password that should be the same for both TCP connection ends. The password must be configured in advance on both machines (in our case, on the routers) at both ends of the connection, and, for security reasons, it should be changed periodically (for a guide on how to select the passwords and manage security, see RFC 3562 – *Key Management Considerations for the TCP MD5 Signature Option*, July 2003).

Every router uses the password – together with various fields of the IP, TCP and transported data headers – to generate a 128 bit (=16 byte) number, through a mathematical algorithm. The mathematical algorithm, known as hash function, cannot be reversed, that is, even by knowing the 128 bit number, we cannot trace it back to the secret key. The number obtained is added as a TCP option in the segment sent and used by the recipient to check the message validity. The recipient, having the same secret key, carries out the same operations as the source to determine the 128 bit number, and then compares it to the one received. If they do not match, the segment is rejected. Since it is not specific to BGP, the use of the MD5 hash function is not negotiated during the session initialization; it is only a matter of router configuration, instead. In order to transport the 128 bit number obtained through the MD5 hash function, a TCP option defined by the Type (Kind)=19 value is used (see Figure 10.4 below). The 128 bits are directly added to the TCP header.

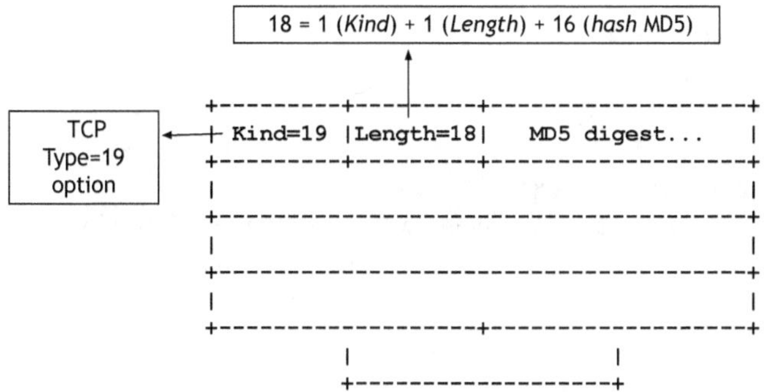

Figure 10.4 – TCP option format for transporting the 128 bits resulting from the application of the MD5 hash function (by RFC 2385).

NOTE: Initially, RFC 1771 entailed the authentication negotiation, and, for transporting the result of the hash function, the use of the 16 bytes of the Marker field, in the common header of BGP messages.

The MD5 hash function uses the following fields:

- TCP pseudo-header, comprising:
  - ➢ source IP address;
  - ➢ target IP address;
  - ➢ protocol type (Protocol Type field of the IP header):
  - ➢ packet length.
- TCP header (except the options and the checksum term).
- Data transported by the TCP segment (i.e., the BGP message).
- Secret key.

From a configuration standpoint, implementing an MD5 authentication is very easy: it is sufficient, through a suitable configuration command, to assign the secret key to both routers at the end of the BGP session (the same secret key).

Let's see how Cisco and Juniper routers implement the mechanism.

IOS XE
router(config)# **router bgp** *AS-number*
router(config-router)# **neighbor** *IP-neighbor* **password** *pwd*

IOS XR
RP/0/RP0/CPU0:router(config)# **router bgp** *AS-number*
RP/0/RP0/CPU0:router(config-bgp)# **neighbor** *IP-neighbor*
RP/0/RP0/CPU0:router(config-bgp-nbr)# **password** {**clear** | **encrypted** } *pwd*

JUNOS
[edit protocols bgp]
authentication-key *pwd*;
group *group-name* {
  authentication-key *pwd*;
  neighbor *IP-neighbor* **<peer-as** *remote-AS***>** {
    authentication-key *pwd*;
  }
}

The only configuration parameter is the secret key (pwd).

Here is an example of how to apply the commands we saw to the eBGP session between routers CE1 (IOS XE) and PE2 (JUNOS) of sample network in Figure 3.1, using the following password: ^rEi$$N@mEx!$.

CE1 (IOS XE)
```
router bgp 65101
  neighbor 10.1.12.5 remote-as 64501
  neighbor 10.1.12.5 password ^rEi$$N@mEx!$
```

PE2 (JUNOS)
```
[edit protocols bgp group CE]
peer-as 64501;
neighbor 10.1.12.6 {
    authentication-key ^rEi$$N@mEx!$;
}
```

NOTE: When applying the MD5 authentication of BGP messages, you should pay attention to the behavior of any possible firewall present between the BGP Neighbors. For instance, some firewalls, for each TCP connection that crosses them, use a random number as an offset of the TCP sequence number. This could cause issues to the MD5 authentication, since the hash function is also based on the TCP header, and a variation of the sequence number introduced in the BGP message path, entails that the target hash function will generate a different value than the one contained in the TCP option, making the mechanism unusable. Another important aspect to keep in mind is that certain default firewalls may not allow TCP options. All these aspects should be carefully evaluated, based on the firewalling technology adopted.

The authentication mode based on RFC 2385 has been significantly improved by introducing the TCP-AO (TCP-Authentication Option), described in RFC 5925 – *The TCP Authentication Option,*

June 2010. TCP-AO is a new TCP option with value Kind=29, which offer significant benefits compared to the simple MD5 authentication we saw earlier, such as:

- The option of dynamically changing the secret key. While RFC 2385 entails the use of a single key.

- The option of using more than one algorithm to determine the hash function (e.g. AES-128-CMAC-96, HMAC-SHA-1-96). Use of these algorithms is described in RFC 5926 – *Cryptographic Algorithms for the TCP Authentication Option (TCP-AO)*, June 2010, which describes, in addition to the ones we mentioned, the rules to observe for future use of any other algorithms. Contrarily, RFC 2385 entails only the use of the MD5 hash algorithm, much less strong than those mentioned earlier.

The TCP-AO option is supported by all recent versions of IOS XE/XR and JunOS. Configurations are based on the key-chain mechanism, which allows defining more than one secret key and their use interval. If you are interested, you can explore these configurations further in the manufacturers' documents.

As best practice, when applying the BGP message authentication mechanisms, you should always prioritize the authentication based on the TCP-AO option (Kind=29), rather than the one based on the classic option (Kind=19).

10.2.2 TCP level filters

Let's go back to the basics of the transport protocol – TCP – to reiterate an aspect most of you already know, but that cannot be missing in a complete discussion on security. Since the IPv4/v6 addresses of the neighbors with which we want to establish a BGP session are known, it is possible (and recommended) to implement a filter on the packets received from the BGP Neighbor. In other words, we can establish a few simple access control rules (Access Control List (ACL) in Cisco IOS language, Firewall Filter (FF) in JUNOS language) allowing the transit of TCP packets on another source or target port 179, if and only if coming from the IPv4/v6 address of the neighbor. This way, we can easily obtain a good protection against attackers that want to disturb our router with unauthorized BGP messages. Here are a few configuration examples on Cisco and Juniper platforms, which can be adapted to the most common scenarios.

Cisco (IOS e IOS XE)

```
ip access-list extended BGP_179
 permit tcp host 192.0.2.1 neq bgp host 192.0.2.2 eq bgp
 permit tcp host 192.0.2.1 eq bgp host 192.0.2.2 neq bgp
 deny   tcp any neq bgp any eq bgp
 deny   tcp any eq bgp any neq bgp
 permit ip any any
!
interface GigabitEthernet0/0
  description *** Local interface for BGP sessions ***
  ip address 192.0.2.1 255.255.255.252
  ip access-group BGP_179 in
```

NOTE: Cisco platform configurations that use IOS XR are basically the same, except for a few minimal syntax differences.

<u>JUNOS</u>

```
[edit firewall family inet filter BGP_179]
term ACCEPT {
    from {
        address {
            192.0.2.0/30;
        }
        protocol tcp;
        port bgp;
    }
    then accept;
}
term REJ {
    then {
        reject;
    }
}
[edit interfaces lo0 unit 0]
family inet {
    filter {
        input BGP_179;
    }
    address 203.0.113.1/32;
}
```

These configurations allow accepting all TCP/IP packets incoming from the BGP Neighbor with IPv4 address 192.0.2.1, with source or target TCP port 179.

10.2.3 Secure TTL management

As mentioned earlier, one of the greatest vulnerabilities of BGP is using TCP as Transport Level. This implies the option of launching attacks to BGP sessions from any part of the Internet, since TCP segments are transported by IP packets.

A very simple, yet effective countermeasure to contrast these remote attacks is to change the TTL management in IP packets that transport BGP messages. Indeed, as we saw in Section 2.1.2, in eBGP sessions, IP packets have TTL=1 by default. When a BGP Speaker receives from a BGP Neighbor an IP packet with TTL higher than 1, it rejects the packet. An attacker, by going on a hunch, or knowing the number of routers that the packet crosses (which could be determined with a traceroute), can still easily simulate a packet reaching the BGP Speaker with TTL=1.

Let's consider the situation in Figure 10.5 and assume that two attackers, after knowing the IP addresses of the BGP sessions, the TCP ports and the sequence numbers, want to send TCP segments or false BGP messages (e.g. TCP reset, false UPDATEs, etc.), to router RA.

Router RA has an ordinary eBGP session with RB, and a multihop eBGP session with RC. For the two attackers to send IP packets that can reach RA with TTL=1, it is sufficient for the attacker directly connected to RB to generate them with TTL=2, while for the attacker directly connected to RC to generate them with TTL=3.

Let's suppose to vary the TTL management by RA on ordinary eBGP sessions as follows: an IP packet of the BGP session is accepted if and only if its TTL is equal to 255. If this was the rule,

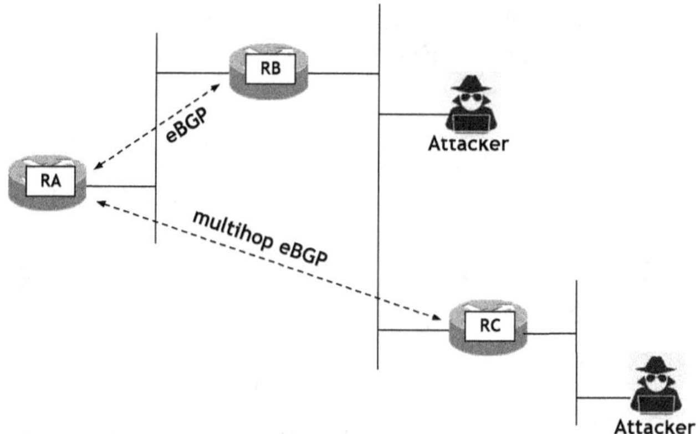

Figure 10.5 – Example of remote attack to a BGP Speaker.

the attacker directly connected to RB couldn't send false packets to RA, unless it was directly connected to RA. Even more so, this applies to the attacker connected to RC.

In multihop eBGP sessions, this rule should be changed, to keep the "distance" (in terms of hops) between the routers at the session ends into account. Assuming that, between the two eBGP peers, there are N hops of distance, the rule becomes the following: an IP packet of the BGP session is accepted if and only if its TTL is greater than or equal to (255-N+1). For instance, in the case of multihop eBGP between RC and RA in Figure 11.5, is N=2, therefore RA accepts packets with TTL=254 or 255. This makes it impossible for the attacker directly connected to RC to send false packets to RA, unless it was directly connected to RB.

The last rule described, which contains as peculiar case the first, since, for BGP Neighbors directly connected is N=1, is the basis of the Generalized TTL Security Mechanism (GTSM), standardized in RFC 5082 – *The Generalized TTL Security Mechanism (GTSM)*, October 2007, and applicable to any routing protocol in general.

The GTSM is not a mechanism negotiated during the session opening with any BGP Capability; it must be enabled in the configuration. Also, it is obvious that the configuration is necessary on both sides of the BGP session, because, on one side, the BGP Neighbor must encapsulate the TCP segments that transport the BGP messages into IP packets with TTL=255, and on the other side, the rule above must be applied.

The mechanism is currently implemented both on Cisco and on Juniper routers. When this book was published, it was supported in IOS XR only in the specific case of N=1.

<u>IOS XE</u>
router(config)# **router bgp** *AS-number*
router(config-router)# **neighbor** *IP-neighbor* **ttl-security hops** *N*

<u>IOS XR</u>
RP/0/RP0/CPU0:router(config)# **router bgp** *AS-number*
RP/0/RP0/CPU0:router(config-bgp)# **neighbor** *IP-neighbor*
RP/0/RP0/CPU0:router(config-bgp-nbr)# **ttl-security**

Once the command has been executed, the BGP Speaker accepts on the BGP session only IP packets with TTL≥(255–N+1).

NOTE: This command, in the configuration of multihop eBGP sessions, becomes mutually exclusive with the "**neighbor** *IP-neighbor* **ebgp-multihop** [*TTL*]" command, as we already saw in Section 3.1.5.

In JUNOS, the configuration requires two steps. The first is a command to redefine the TTL value with which TCP/IP packets transporting BGP messages are transmitted.

<u>JUNOS</u>
[edit protocols bgp]
ttl *value;*
group *group-name* {
  ttl *value;*
  neighbor *IP-neighbor* {
    ttl *value;*
  }
}

The second step is defining a filter on the data plane (which, in JUNOS jargon, is called Firewall Filter), which allows receiving only those BGP messages with a preset TTL (e.g. TTL=255) or within a preset interval (see the following example).

Here is an example of how to apply the commands we saw to the eBGP session between routers CE1 (IOS XE) and PE2 (JUNOS) of the sample network in Figure 3.1.

<u>CE1</u> (IOS XE)
```
router bgp 65101
  neighbor 10.1.12.5 remote-as 64501
  neighbor 10.1.12.5 ttl-security hops 1
```

<u>PE2</u> (JUNOS)
```
[edit protocols bgp group CE]
peer-as 64501;
neighbor 10.1.12.6 {
    ttl 255;
}
[edit firewall filter GTSM]
term DISCARD {
    from {
        source-address {
            10.1.12.5/32;
        }
        protocol tcp;
        ttl-except 255;
        port 179;
    }
    then {
        discard;
    }
}
term ACCEPT {
    then accept;
}
```

```
[edit interfaces ge-0/0/2 unit 0 family inet]
filter {
    input GTSM;
}
address 10.1.12.5/30;
```

Notice that the GTSM is less burdensome to apply, compared to BGP message authentication we saw in Section 10.2.1 above. Indeed, the TTL check is much easier than the MD5 hash function check, which can be CPU intensive. However, since there is always a possibility that the GTSM may be bypassed, it is best to implement both countermeasures. And this is a general rule when it comes to security: the more countermeasures are applied, the lower the system vulnerability becomes.

10.3 PROTECTION AGAINST DOS ATTACKS

In Section 10.1.2, we showed two types of DoS/DDoS attacks. Here, we will go over some useful countermeasures that will help limit the damage, if applied. There are many countermeasures, and some of them, given their complexity, will require an entire section. Here we will just describe two very simple ones, which, being so minimally invasive, should always be implemented. And in the following sections, we will see how to tackle volumetric and prefix hijacking attacks.

10.3.1 Limiting the number of prefixes received

A poorly configured (or intentionally poorly configured) BGP Speaker could send to one of its BGP Neighbors a great number of advertisements of different prefixes, until its memory is overloaded. This is a classic DoS attack attempting to overload the resources of a router. There are many incidents of this kind reported on the Internet.

The countermeasure that should be adopted for this kind of issues is very simple, and it consists in limiting the number of prefixes that a BGP Speaker can receive from a BGP Neighbor.

When this limit is exceeded, the following advertisements are rejected and, based on the implementation, this may entail the closure and possible restart of the BGP session.

From a configuration standpoint, the command is usually one, with some option to manage the events after the number of prefixes allowed has been exceeded, in a flexible way.

Let's see how Cisco and Juniper routers implement the mechanism.

<u>IOS XE</u>
router(config)# **router bgp** *AS-number*
router(config-router)# **neighbor** *IP-neighbor* **maximum-prefix** *value* [*warning-threshold-%*] [**warning-only** | **restart** *interval*]

<u>IOS XR</u>
RP/0/RP0/CPU0:router(config)# **router bgp** *AS-number*
RP/0/RP0/CPU0:router(config-bgp)# **neighbor** *IP-neighbor*
RP/0/RP0/CPU0:router(config-bgp-nbr)# **address-family ipv4 unicast**
RP/0/RP0/CPU0:router(config-bgp-nbr-af)# **maximum-prefix** *value* [*warning-threshold-%*] [**warning-only** | **restart** *interval*]

The commands require as a single mandatory configuration parameter the maximum number of prefixes that can be received from the BGP Neighbor (indicated as *value*). The options have the following meaning:

- *warning-threshold*: is a value expressed as % that allows obtaining a warning message, once the % *warning-threshold* value of the number of prefixes allowed is exceeded (default: *warning-threshold*=75%). For instance, by setting *value*=6 and *warning-threshold*=80, we have, once value 6 is exceeded by 80% (rounded up), i.e. 5, of the number of prefixes received from the BGP Neighbor with Neighbor ID 172.16.1.12, a warning message such as:

  ```
  01:19:42: %BGP-4-MAXPFX: No. of prefix received from 172.16.1.12 (afi 0)
  reaches 5, max 6
  ```

- **warning-only**: by default, when the maximum number of prefixes that a BGP Speaker can receive from one of its BGP Neighbors is exceeded, the session is closed and a NOTIFICATION message is sent to the BGP Neighbor. For instance, by setting value=6, when the seventh prefix is received, the BGP Speaker closes the session and sends a NOTIFICATION message to the BGP Neighbor:

  ```
  01:33:43: %BGP-3-MAXPFXEXCEED: No. of prefix received from 172.16.1.12
  (afi 0): 7 exceed limit 6
  ```

  ```
  01:33:43: %BGP-5-ADJCHANGE: neighbor 172.16.1.12 Down BGP Notification
  sent
  ```

  The **warning-only** option allows not to close the BGP session, provided that the prefixes exceeding the configured value are rejected.

- **restart** *interval*: once (if) the BGP session is closed, due to the exceeding number of prefixes allowed, a manual operation is required to reactivate it. However, clearly before reactivating the session, you need to act on the BGP Neighbor to reduce the number of prefixes sent, otherwise the session will be immediately closed again. The "**restart** *interval*" option, where the interval value is expressed in minutes, allows reactivating the session automatically after a period equal to the interval value configured. During this period, it is necessary, as mentioned earlier, to act on the BGP Neighbor to reduce the number of prefixes sent, otherwise the session will be immediately closed again.

<u>JUNOS</u>

```
[edit protocols bgp]
family inet {
  (any | unicast | multicast | labeled-unicast) {
    prefix-limit {
    maximum value;
    teardown <threshold-log-%> <idle-timeout
                (forever | minutes)>;
    }
  }
}
```

The command can be given at global, group or session. The only mandatory configuration parameter is the maximum number of prefixes that can be received from the BGP Neighbor (always indicated as *value*).

Without specifying any option, however, this command does not hold much value, since the default behavior – much different from the same Cisco IOS command – entails, once the maximum number of prefixes configured is exceeded – only the issuance of a log message such as:

```
Jun 10 19:31:24 P2 rpd[2254] 172.16.12.2 (External AS 64501): Configured
maximum prefix-limit (20) exceeded for inet unicast nlri:21
```

The BGP session remains active and the BGP Speaker continues to accept any excess prefixes. By applying the "**teardown** *<log-threshold-%>*" option, once the maximum number of prefixes allowed is exceeded, the session is closed and a log message like the one above is issued. By specifying also the (%) "*log-threshold-%*" value, a log message is issued, once the "*log-threshold-%*" value of the number of prefixes allowed is exceeded (Note: with the "**teardown 75**" option, the default behavior of Cisco routers is exactly replicated).

Unfortunately, by using only this option, we end up in a dead end. Once the session is closed, the two routers attempt to reactivate it immediately. However, if, in the meantime, nothing is done on the BGP Neighbor exceeding the number of prefixes sent, the session is closed again, and so on (in Cisco routers, on the other hand, once the session is closed, it must be reactivated manually, after solving the situation). To prevent this vicious cycle, the "**idle-timeout** (**forever** | *minutes*)" option is used. With this option, the session is automatically reactivated after a period equal to the *minutes* configuration value (the same as the "**restart** *interval*" option in Cisco routers). If, instead of an automatic restart after a certain interval, a manual restart is preferred, the "**forever**" option is used instead of the *minutes* value. Reactivation is done manually, through the **clear bgp neighbor** *neighbor-ID*" command.

By way of example, let's consider the following configuration:

```
[edit protocols bgp group EBGP]
family inet {
  unicast {
    prefix-limit {
      maximum 10;
      teardown 80 idle-timeout 30;
    }
  }
}
```

The rest of this configuration is that, for all eBGP sessions of the EBGP group, the maximum number of IPv4 prefixes that the router can receive is 10. When the router receives the eighth IPv4 prefix on a session, a log message is issued. When the eleventh IPv4 prefix is received on a session, the session is closed and then automatically reactivated after 30 min.

10.3.2 Limiting the length of the AS_PATH

BGP advertisements on the Internet have an average AS_PATH length of a few ASes. For instance, studies completed by RIPE NCC (https://labs.ripe.net/author/mirjam/update-on-as-path-lengths-over-time/), have shown that the average length of the AS_PATH has remained fairly stable over time for the IPv4 Internet, and equal to 4.3, while for the IPv6 Internet, after an initial decrease, a fairly stable tendency around 3.6 has arisen. Without considering the AS_PATH prepending, the same values drop to 3.9 and 3.5, respectively.

However, several IPv4/v6 researchers and observers have noticed, from time to time, cases in which some ISPs issue BGP advertisements with a very long AS_PATH, resulting from AS_PATHs prepending made by entering dozens if not hundreds of times their own AS number. It is not completely clear why, probably due to an operator error, a poor knowledge of the AS_PATH prepending mechanism, or malicious intentions. In any case, this causes several issues to the Internet, including security-related ones. An actual example can help us describe one of the possible security issues that may result from an excessive AS_PATH prepending. An Eastern Europe operator (AS 197158) advertised prefix 95.47.142/23 with the following AS_PATH:

... 3255 197158

executing an AS_PATH prepending with 23 times its own AS number. A malicious user could intercept or manipulate traffic toward this prefix, by using an ISP with loose morals that allows advertisements of the same prefix with an AS_PATH type "ASxxxx ASyyyy 197158". Here, the fictional ASxxxx represents the ISP's AS number, while the AS indicated as ASyyyy represents the attacker's AS. This simple example shows how dangerous it is to use the prepending AS_PATH incorrectly.

As we were saying, we do not know why all these excessive prepending AS_PATHs are used. Sometimes, they are caused by configuration errors, or oversights of network administrators who used the prepending AS_PATH correctly and then, after closing the BGP session, end up with advertisements sent with a useless prepending AS_PATH. For instance, let's assume an ISP with three Upstream Providers, doing AS_PATH prepending with two out of three to affect inbound traffic. When the ISP closes the session with the Upstream Provider without AS_PATH prepending, and forgets to update the configurations of the sessions toward the other two, it sends advertisements with artificially extended AS_PATHs toward the Internet, perhaps ignoring the risk this poses.

Another issue caused by excessive AS_PATH prepending has occurred in the past with Cisco platforms. Due to a software bug, an excessive AS_PATH prepending caused the entire router to go out of service. To solve this issue, leading manufacturers provide a command that allows rejecting those advertisements with AS_PATH length greater than a configuration value.

IOS XE configuration is based on the following command:

router(config)# **router bgp** *AS-number*
router(config-router)# **bgp maxas-limit** *value*

where value is the maximum AS_PATH length allowed.

In Cisco platforms with IOS XR and in Juniper platforms with JUNOS, the limitation is set through a routing policy. By way of example, let's assume, on a BGP Speaker, that we want to accept only those advertisements of prefixes with AS_PATH length smaller or equal to two from the eBGP Neighbor of AS 65541, with IP address IP 172.20.1.1. The configurations to execute are:

```
route-policy MAX_AS_PATH_LENGTH
  if as-path length le 2 then
    pass
  endif
end-policy
!
router bgp 64501
  neighbor 172.20.1.1
    remote-as 65541
    address-family ipv4 unicast
      route-policy MAX_AS_PATH_LENGTH in
```

```
[edit policy-options]
policy-statement MAX_AS_PATH_LENGTH {
    term NO-AS_PATH-GE3 {
        from as-path GE-3;
        then reject;
    }
}
as-path GE-3 ".{3,}";


[edit protocols bgp group ISP]
neighbor 172.20.1.1 {
    import MAX_AS_PATH_LENGTH;
    peer-as 65541;
}
```

Considering the statistics we've mentioned at the beginning of this section, a recommended value for the AS_PATH length limit, which also considers any AS_PATHS prepending executed by an ISP, could be around 10.

10.4 PROTECTION AGAINST DDoS ATTACKS: RTBH

A very interesting security function for ISP networks is the RTBH (Remote-Triggered Black-Hole) mechanism. RTBH is not a countermeasure to protect BGP, but it uses BGP to contrast DDoS attacks toward a customer of the ISP, by blocking the attacker's traffic at the network edge. The first countermeasure against this kind of attacks is identifying the attacker, and especially the IP address from which the attack tool packets originate, and the attacked host. Once the attacker and attacked unit have been identified via a centralized controller (usually a specific router called signaling router), the edge routers – hereinafter referred to as PE routers – are warned that incoming traffic from the attacker (or attackers), and/or traffic directed to the attacked unit must be rejected (black-holed). In this way, the traffic used for the attack does not enter the ISP network. Information from the controller to the PEs is conveyed through BGP UPDATE messages. The idea is summarized in Figure 10.6 below.

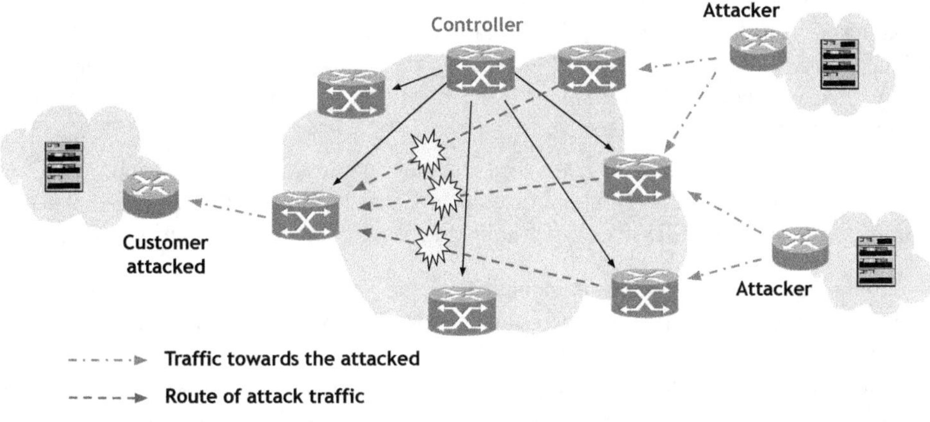

Figure 10.6 – Black-holing of traffic to contrast DDoS attacks.

There are two different versions of RTBH:

- Destination-based: in this version, traffic toward the attacked customer's IP address is rejected by PE routers. Notice that this approach somewhat plays into the attacker's hands, whose purpose is to cause problems to the customer (and not the ISP). This mechanism only protects the ISP network. In any case, once the source of the attack has been identified, the ISP can investigate it further, and implement other countermeasures.

- Source-based: in this version, traffic from the attacker's IP address is rejected by PE routers. Unfortunately, in many DDoS attacks, it is hard to understand the source of the attack, as it changes constantly, due to the great number of attacking hosts. As we will see in Section 10.4.2, this version of the RTBH also requires the use of the uRPF (unicast Reverse Path Forwarding) command.

Both these versions are based on standard BGP functions, and do not require any additional features; only a smart application of routing policies.

The benefits of the source-based RTBH with respect to the destination-based version, is that legitimate traffic toward the target of the attack can continue to flow regularly. The disadvantage is that, unfortunately, in many DDoS attacks, it is hard to understand where the attack comes from, since there are many, constantly changing sources.

The operation of RTBH has been described, for the destination-based version, by RFC 3882 – *Configuring BGP to Block Denial-of-Service Attacks*, September 2004, while for the source-based version, by RFC 5635 – *Remote Triggered Black Hole Filtering with Unicast Reverse Path Forwarding (uRPF)*, August 2009. In the latter RFC, you can also find a short story and some configuration examples of Cisco and Juniper routers.

NOTE: RFC 3882 describes an interesting approach based on the BGP Community attribute, which we will see in the Case Study of Section 10.4.3.

10.4.1 Destination-based RTBH

The idea behind the destination-based version is rejecting traffic toward the host attacked on PE routers. In order to achieve this goal, the ISP carries out preliminary configurations both on the signaling router and on PE routers. Once the attack has been detected, an action (trigger) is executed only on the signaling router to communicate to the PEs to block all traffic directed to the attacked host. Unfortunately, this has an unavoidable side effect: both "illegitimate" and "legitimate" traffic is blocked.

There are three main configuration steps, of which one (trigger) is carried out only on the signaling router, once the attack has been detected.

1. First, all routers must be configured with a static route toward a certain prefix, with the bit bucket virtual interface as Next-Hop (null0 in Cisco IOS, discard in JUNOS). This target prefix, which we will refer to as black-holing, is usually (but not necessarily) a bogon prefix.

2. A router must be configured as signaling router. This router, once the attack has been detected, i.e. once the target IP address being attacked is detected, will warn the other routers to block the traffic. For this reason, a routing policy is defined on this router, which, applied to the BGP process, allows creating BGP advertisements of the attacked prefix (or simple host routes of the attacked server), with any IP address of the black-holing prefix as BGP Next-Hop. Furthermore, the Local Preference value should be set to a very large value, so that the advertisement generated is preferred over other advertisements of the same prefix.

Then, it is best to associate also the NO_EXPORT well-known Community, to prevent the advertisement from being exported outside the ISP's AS.

3. Once the attack has been detected, an action should be executed on the signaling router to allow the BGP process to create advertisements of the attacked prefix (or of the simple host route of the attacked server), with the values of the BGP attributes described in the previous point.

After the action has been configured, the signaling router sends the advertisements created to all PE routers. When a PE router receives traffic directed toward the attacked host, it will perform a first lookup of the RIB; which will show an address of the black-holing prefix as BGP Next-Hop. In order to find a path toward this address, the router will perform a second lookup, which will show the bit bucket virtual interface as Next-Hop. Consequently, all packets directed towards the host being attacked will be rejected.

Once the attack has ended, in order to restore the pre-existing situation, it is sufficient to cancel the action on the signaling router. Therefore, the signaling router sends a BGP UPDATE message to withdraw the advertisement previously sent.

Figure 10.7 below shows an example of how to apply the above in a Cisco environment with IOS XR. Similar configurations with IOS XE and JUNOS are very simple. We will leave them to you to figure out.

As black-holing prefix, we used prefix 192.0.2/24, which is one of the (non routable) prefixes reserved by IANA for documentation. The attacked host's IP address is 203.0.113.1.

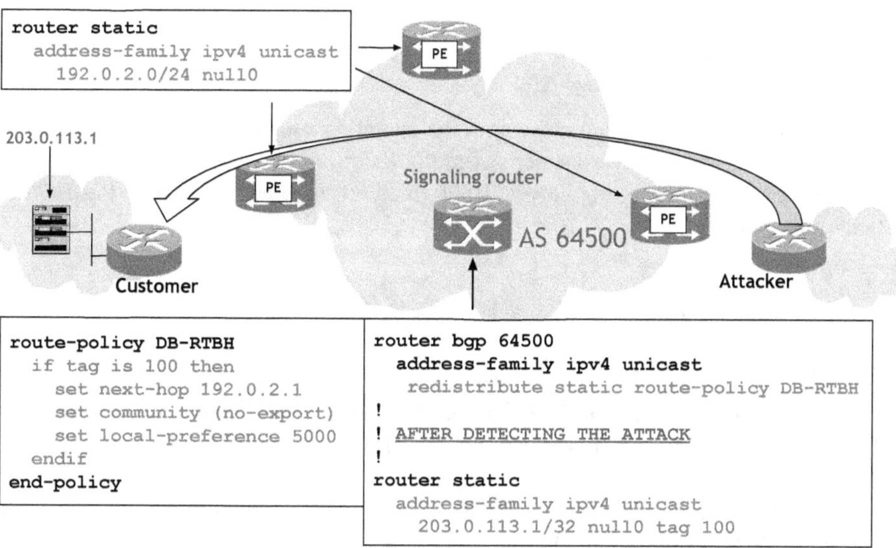

Figure 10.7 – Example of application of the destination-based RTBH.

NOTE: Instead of prefix 192.0.2/24, it is also possible to use any Martian prefix or the (private) prefixes of RFC 1918. IANA has defined a similar prefix for IPv6, to be used for the RTBH. This prefix is 0100::/64 (see RFC 6666 – *A Discard Prefix for IPv6*, August 2012).

By going over the steps above, first we have configured a static route on all PE routers toward black-holing prefix 192.0.2/24 with the bit bucket (null0) as Next-Hop:

```
router static
  address-family ipv4 unicast
    192.0.2.0/24 null0
```

Then, we configured the following routing policy on the signaling router:

```
route-policy DB-RTBH
  if tag is 100 then
    set next-hop 192.0.2.1
    set community (no-export)
    set local-preference 5000
  endif
end-policy
```

and then, we activated a static route redistribution in the BGP process using route policy DH-RTBH:

```
router bgp 64500
  address-family ipv4 unicast
    redistribute static route-policy DB-RTBH
```

At first, this last configuration has no effect. When the attacked customer communicates that it is under attack to the ISP's NOC, the following static route (action) is configured on the signaling router:

```
router static
  address-family ipv4 unicast
    203.0.113.1/32 null0 tag 100
```

After this last static route has been configured, the signaling router redistributes the static route to all PE routers, creating an advertisement of prefix (host route) 203.0.113.1/32, with the BGP attributes specified by routing policy DB-RTBH (which is triggered due to the "**tag 100**" clause in the static route), that is:

- BGP Next-Hop=192.0.2.1;

- Local preference=5,000;

- Community=NO_EXPORT.

This advertisement will be sent to all PEs through iBGP sessions (possibly achieved through Route Reflectors). When this advertisement is received, each PE will install a path toward prefix 203.0.113.1/32 in its RIB, with Next-Hop=192.0.2.1. So, when a PE router receives traffic directed toward host route 203.0.113.1/32, it will perform a first lookup of its RIB, which will show address 192.0.2.1 as Next-Hop. In order to find a path toward address 192.0.2.1, router PE will execute a second lookup on the RIB, which will show the null0 (bit bucket) virtual interface as Next-Hop. Consequently, all packets directed towards host 203.0.113.1 being attacked will be rejected, at the ISP network edges.

10.4.2 Source-based RTBH

Configuring the source-based RTBH requires the same steps as the destination-based RTBH, with two substantial differences:

- once the attack has been detected, a static route toward the attack source must be configured on the signaling router, with the bit bucket virtual interface as Next-Hop, and a tag value allowing to apply the routing policy;

- on every interface where an attack is expected (e.g. on all PE routers interfaces toward the outside of the AS), the uRPF check in loose mode is implemented.

NOTE: The uRPF check in loose mode consists in executing a RIB lookup based on the source IP address, and accepting a packet if and only if the source IP address can be reached through any RIB entry. If there is no entry in the RIB that allows reaching the source IP address, or if there is an entry with the bit bucket as Next-Hop, the uRPF check fails and the packet is rejected.

Since the uRPF check allows rejecting those packets with a source IP address that can be reached from the RIB through an entry with the bit bucket as Next-Hop, in order to reject traffic coming from a certain source (attacker), it is sufficient to add to the RIB of PE routers an entry with the attack source as target, and the bit bucket as Next Hop.

Figure 10.8 below shows an example of how to apply the source-based RTBH, in a Cisco environment with IOS XR. Here too, as black-holing prefix, we used 192.0.2/24. Attacker hosts have as IP address part of the IP subnet 198.51.100/24. In the example in the figure, the uRPF check is implemented via the interface-level "**ipv4 verify unicast source reachable-via any**" command, on all the interfaces outside the AS of routers PE, including the one where traffic generated by the attacker comes in. Consequently, this traffic is rejected because the uRPF check is negative. Indeed, in the RIBs of PE routers, there is an entry with target 198.51.100/24 and Next-Hop 192.0.2.1. However, on PEs, a static route toward black-holing prefix 192.0.2/24 with the bit bucket (null0) as Next-Hop has already been configured, therefore the actual Next-Hop for prefix 198.51.100/24 is the null0 interface.

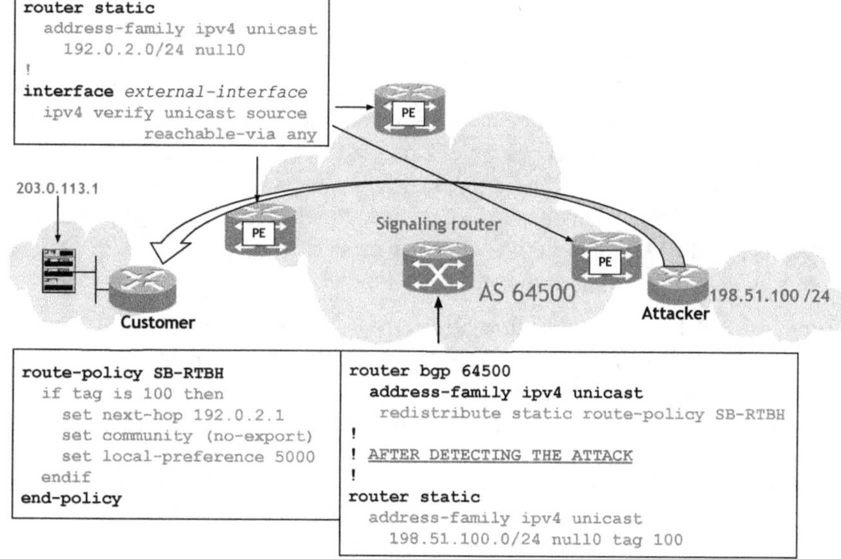

Figure 10.8 – Example of application of the source-based RTBH.

10.4.3 Case Study: RTBH in an IXP

In this Case Study, we will analyze a possible application of the RTBH in an IXP scenario. The network topology used is shown in Figure 10.9 below.

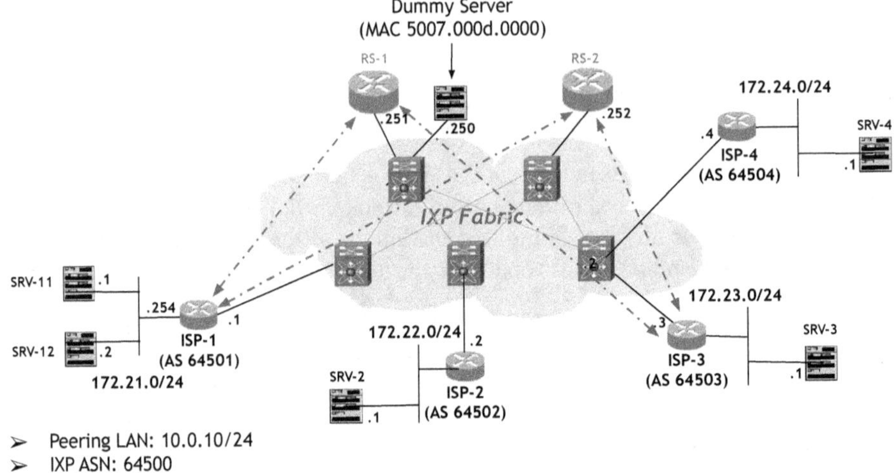

Figure 10.9 – RTBH application scenario in an IXP.

Three routers of three different ISPs (all Cisco with IOS XE) are connected to the IXP Fabric. And also two Route Servers (RS-1 and RS-2) are connected to it, and used for exchanging routing information between ISPs. In this scenario, the Route Servers act as a signaling router. The figure shows also the numbering plan adopted.

Connected to the IXP Fabric there is also a dummy server that we'll use for traffic black-holing. This server, which could be a simple virtual machine defined on a physical server, has IP address 10.0.10.250 and MAC address 5007.000d.0000. It doesn't require anything else; it just needs to be capable of responding to a classic ARP request.

The goal of this test is to check RTBH's validity in blocking a DDoS attack toward server SRV-11 with IP address IP 172.21.0.1 and positioned on a LAN directly connected to the router of ISP-1. To this end, the idea is to block all traffic directed toward the attacked server, that is, all IP traffic with target address 172.21.0.1, directly at layer 2 on the ISP routers connected to the switches. In order to do this, we will use a layer 2 filter applied to the access interfaces of the switches of the IXP fabric where the ISP routers are positioned, which allows blocking all traffic with the dummy server address as target MAC address (we will see why shortly).

In broad terms, the DDoS attack is contrasted as follows:

- As soon as ISP-1 detects the attack toward its own server 172.21.0.1, it advertises host route 172.21.0.1/32 to the Route Servers via BGP. Community 65535:666 will be added with this advertisement, which IANA reserved for RTBH applications (see RFC 7999 – *BLACKHOLE Community*, October 2016).

- Upon receiving the advertisement, the Route Servers will propagate it to the other ISPs, changing the BGP Next-Hop to IP address IP 10.0.10.250 of the dummy server, and overwriting Community 65535:666 with the well-known Community NO_EXPORT, to prevent the other ISPs from propagating the advertisement of the host route outside their AS.

- As soon as the other ISPs receive this advertisement, they will start sending traffic toward IP address 172.21.0.1 of the server being attacked, using the new BGP Next-Hop 10.0.10.250. Then, the IP packets will be encapsulated in Ethernet frames with destination MAC address corresponding to IP 10.0.10.250 of the dummy server – which is 5007.000d.0000. This MAC address is learned through standard ARP procedures.

- Due to the preconfigured layer 2 filter, traffic is blocked upon entering the switches of the IXP Fabric.

Below are the relevant preliminary configurations for router ISP-1, which allow, once the attack has been detected, to apply the RTBH mechanism.

ISP-1
```
router bgp 64501
  bgp router-id 192.168.0.1
  no bgp enforce-first-as
  network 172.21.0.0 mask 255.255.255.0
  redistribute static route-map RTBH
  neighbor RS peer-group
  neighbor RS remote-as 64500
  neighbor RS description "SESSION WITH RS-1/2"
  neighbor RS send-community
  neighbor 10.0.10.251 peer-group RS
  neighbor 10.0.10.252 peer-group RS
!
ip prefix-list IP-RTBH seq 5 permit 0.0.0.0/0 ge 32
!
route-map RTBH permit 10
 match ip address prefix-list IP-RTBH
 set community 65535:666  ! BLACKHOLE COMMUNITY RESERVED FOR RTBH
```

Let's go over the main command for the RTBH application. The idea behind the configurations executed is very simple: through the **redistribute static route-map RTBH** command, the static routes are redistributed, and, during the redistribution, route-map RTBH is applied, which allows applying BGP Community 65535:666 (BLACKHOLE Community) to all the advertisements of the prefixes allowed by the prefix-list IP-RTBH. Prefix-list IP-RTBH only allows the host routes, i.e. /32 prefixes.

This configuration implies that, when an attack toward server 172.21.0.1 is detected, it is sufficient to add a dummy static route in the router of ISP-1 toward the host route of the server attacked, with the bit bucket as Next-Hop. Downstream of this addition and of the configurations, prefix 172.21.0.1/32 will be advertised via BGP to the two Route Servers, with the related BLACKHOLE Community.

NOTE: The meaning of the **no bgp enforce-first-as** command has been described in Section 8.5.1.

Let's now see the preliminary configurations on the Route Servers. For the sake of brevity, we will only go over RS-1's configuration, since RS-2's is basically the same (except for the BGP router ID). The RTBH application consists of adding the route-map RTBH in the outbound direction, on all sessions toward the ISPs.

<u>RS-1</u>

```
router bgp 64500
 bgp router-id 172.20.0.1
 neighbor RS-C peer-group
 neighbor 10.0.10.1 remote-as 64501
 neighbor 10.0.10.1 peer-group RS-C
 neighbor 10.0.10.2 remote-as 64502
 neighbor 10.0.10.2 peer-group RS-C
 neighbor 10.0.10.3 remote-as 64503
 neighbor 10.0.10.3 peer-group RS-C

 !
 address-family ipv4
  neighbor RS-C route-server-client
  neighbor RS-C route-map RTBH out
  neighbor 10.0.10.1 activate
  neighbor 10.0.10.2 activate
  neighbor 10.0.10.3 activate
 exit-address-family
!
ip prefix-list HOST-ROUTES seq 5 permit 0.0.0.0/0 ge 32
ip community-list 666 permit 65535:666  ! BLACKHOLE COMMUNITY
!
route-map RTBH permit 10
 description *** RTBH ROUTES OUT ***
 match ip address prefix-list HOST-ROUTES
 match community 666
 set community no-export
 set ip next-hop 10.0.10.250
route-map RTBH permit 20
```

The route-map RTBH acts on the advertisements of host routes with the BLACKHOLE Community and executes two actions:

- overwrites all BGP Communities present (including the BLACKHOLE Community) with the BGP Community NO_EXPORT;

- adds the IP address of dummy server 10.0.10.250 to the BGP NEXT_HOP attribute.

NOTE: The other commands in the Route Server configuration are more or less standard. Worthy of mention is the "**neighbor … route-server-client**" command, similar to the "**neighbor … route-reflector-client**" command we saw in Section 8.3.5, when talking about Route Reflector configuration. The basic difference is that, in this case, eBGP advertisements are reflected, and this changes some of BGP's basic rules. One example is how the AS_PATH attribute is managed, with the Route Server leaving it unchanged, differently than standard eBGP sessions.

As mentioned earlier, in order to block the traffic toward the attacked unit, a layer 2 filter is applied to the edge of the IXP Fabric, to block all traffic with the dummy server as target MAC. The filter must be pre configured on all those switches where the ISPs are positioned, and then applied to all interfaces where the ISPs are positioned.

The reason why this filter is sufficient for this purpose is easy. The IP packets directed toward the attacked server, with target IP address 172.21.0.1, thanks to the advertisement of the host route of the attacked server, have BGP Next-Hop 10.0.10.250, to which corresponds the MAC address of the dummy server, which is 5007.000d.0000, learned through standard ARP procedures. IP packets with destination address 172.21.0.1 will be encapsulated in Ethernet frames with destination MAC 5007.000d.0000. However, these Ethernet frames are blocked on the ISP access ports to the IXP Fabric by the layer 2 filter. For instance, assuming that the switches of the IXP Fabric are Cisco, the configurations to be executed would be:

```
mac access-list extended RTBH
  deny any host 5007.000d.0000
  permit any any
!
interface number type
  mac access-group RTBH in
```

Let's see what happens as soon as ISP-1 detects the attack to server 172.21.0.1. ISP-1 carries out a simple operation: it configures a static route toward the server, with the bit bucket as fictitious Next-Hop:

```
ip route 172.21.0.1 255.255.255.255 null0
```

The static route is installed in the RIB and then redistributed in BGP, with the **redistribute static route-map RTBH** command we saw earlier. The BGP advertisement, as shown by the following view, reaches the Route Servers with the BLACKHOLE Community:

```
RS-1# show ip bgp 172.21.0.1/32
. . . < output omitted > . . .
  64501
    10.0.10.1 from 10.0.10.1 (192.168.0.1)
      Origin incomplete, metric 0, localpref 100, valid, external, best
      Community: 65535:666
      rx pathid: 0, tx pathid: 0x0
```

and is then reflected to the other ISPs, including ISP-3. As shown in the following view, by applying the route-map RTBH in the outbound direction, ISP-3 will receive two advertisements (from the two Route Servers), both with BGP Next-Hop 10.0.10.250 (IP address of the dummy server) and BGP Community NO_EXPORT:

```
ISP-3# show ip bgp 172.21.0.1/32
. . . < output omitted > . . .
  64501
    10.0.10.250 from 10.0.10.252 (192.168.2.2)
      Origin incomplete, metric 0, localpref 100, valid, external
      Community: no-export
      rx pathid: 0, tx pathid: 0
  64501
    10.0.10.250 from 10.0.10.251 (192.168.2.1)
      Origin incomplete, metric 0, localpref 100, valid, external, best
      Community: no-export
      rx pathid: 0, tx pathid: 0x0
```

As a final check, we executed a ping repeated 500 times, from server SRV-3 (simulated by a Cisco router) toward the server attacked.

```
SRV-3# ping 172.21.0.1 rep 500
Type escape sequence to abort.
Sending 1000, 100-byte ICMP Echos to 101.1.0.1, timeout is 2 seconds:
!!!!!!!!!!!!!!!!!!!!!!!!!!!!!!!!!!!!!!!!!!!!!!!!!!!!!!!!!!!!!!!!!!!!!!!!!!!
!!!!!!!!!!!!!!!!!!!!!!!!!!!!!!!!!!!!!!!!!!!!!!!!!!!!!!!!!!!!!!!!!!!!!!!!!U.
.............................................................
Success rate is 66 percent (138/208), round-trip min/avg/max = 3/17/26 ms
```

From the outcome view, we see that the ping suddenly stops working. The instant when it happens coincides with the instant when ISP-3 receives the advertisement of host route 172.21.0.1/32. Indeed, after this is installed in ISP-3's RIB:

```
ISP-3#show ip route bgp
. . . < legend omitted > . . .
        172.21.0.0/16 is variably subnetted, 2 subnets, 2 masks
B          172.21.0.0/24 [20/0] via 10.0.10.1, 00:43:41
B          172.21.0.1/32 [20/0] via 10.0.10.250, 00:36:20
. . .
```

the BGP Next-Hop changes and becomes 10.0.10.250, which – as we stated earlier – corresponds to the MAC address of the dummy server. ICMP Echo request packets directed to 172.21.0.1 will be blocked by the switch to which ISP-3 router is connected, via the preconfigured layer 2 filter, since they have the dummy server address as MAC address.

Often, it may occur that traffic toward the server attacked only comes from some ISPs belonging to the IXP. Therefore, it makes sense to act selectively, and block malicious traffic only from those ISPs sending it, while letting legitimate traffic from other ISPs through.

In our Case Study, we are going to assume that ISP-1, through its tools (e.g. a Netflow traffic analyzer), identifies only ISP-2 and ISP-4 as malicious traffic generators. The idea is to block traffic toward the attacked server (SRV-11) from those ISPs, and let traffic from ISP-3 through.

In order to reach this objective, we can use the BGP Community values that the IXP provides to its connected ISPs. In particular, one of these, in our Case Study, is the following: "1:ASN", indicates that the BGP advertisements received with this BGP Community value must be propagated only to the ISP with AS number=ASN. For instance, if one of the two Route Servers received a BGP advertisement with BGP Community 1:64502 and 1:64504, it would propagate the advertisement only to AS 64502 (ISP-2) and 64504 (ISP-4).

BGP Community 64500:100 is used by the Route Server to distinguish the RTBH routes from the global prefixes advertised by the ISPs. This BGP Community could be assigned both by the Route Server through a special inbound route-map, or directly by the ISP. Alternatively to the BGP Community, the Route Server could use the prefix(es) of the ISPs directly.

The Community Lists to be used when applying the selective RTBH mechanism and the route-maps adopting it are:

```
ip community-list 1 permit 1:64501 65535:666
ip community-list 2 permit 1:64502 65535:666
ip community-list 3 permit 1:64503 65535:666
ip community-list 4 permit 1:64504 65535:666
ip community-list 11 permit 64500:100
!
```

```
route-map RTBH-6450X permit 10  ! X = 1, 2, 3, 4
 description *** RTBH ROUTES OUT ***
 match ip address prefix-list HOST-ROUTES
 match community X
 set community no-export
 set ip next-hop 10.0.10.250
!
route-map RTBH-6450X permit 20
  match community 11
```

Notice that the Community Lists allow all the advertisements containing at least both the BGP Communities specified. For instance, for route-map RTBH-64502, the match condition is met by all the advertisements with at least both BGP Community 1:64502 and 65535:666.

The configuration of the two Route Servers uses these outbound route-maps, as shown below.

```
router bgp 64500
 neighbor 10.0.10.1 remote-as 64501
 neighbor 10.0.10.2 remote-as 64502
 neighbor 10.0.10.3 remote-as 64503
 neighbor 10.0.10.4 remote-as 64504
 !
 address-family ipv4
  neighbor 10.0.10.1 activate
  neighbor 10.0.10.1 route-server-client
  neighbor 10.0.10.1 route-map RTBH-64501 out
  neighbor 10.0.10.2 activate
  neighbor 10.0.10.2 route-server-client
  neighbor 10.0.10.2 route-map RTBH-64502 out
  neighbor 10.0.10.3 activate
  neighbor 10.0.10.3 route-server-client
  neighbor 10.0.10.3 route-map RTBH-64503 out
  neighbor 10.0.10.4 activate
  neighbor 10.0.10.4 route-server-client
  neighbor 10.0.10.4 route-map RTBH-64504 out
 exit-address-family
```

Let's see what happens as soon as ISP-1 detects the attack to server 172.21.0.1. Let's assume that, using a tool, ISP-1 verifies that the malicious traffic only comes from ISP-2 and ISP-4. ISP-1 performs two operations:

- adds the relevant BGP Communities that allow propagating host route 172.21.0.1/32 only to the ISPs from where malicious traffic comes from (ISP-2 and ISP-4) to the RTBH route-map. The two BGP Communities to add are 1: 64502 and 1:64504;

- configures a static route toward the server, with the LAN side interface as Next-Hop (Gi0/0). In this case, it is not possible to use the bit bucket as dummy Next-Hop (we will leave the explanation to you).

```
ip route 172.21.0.1 255.255.255.255 gi0/0
!
route-map RTBH permit 10
```

```
   match ip address prefix-list IP-RTBH
   set community 1:64502 1:64504 65535:666
```

The static route is installed in the RIB and then redistributed in BGP, with the **redistribute static route-map RTBH** command we saw earlier. The BGP advertisement reaches the Route Servers with the BLACKHOLE Community and the other two BGP Communities 1:64502 and 1:64504, as shown in the following view:

```
RS-1# show ip bgp 172.21.0.1/32
. . . < output omitted > . . .
  64501
    10.0.10.1 from 10.0.10.1 (192.168.0.1)
      Origin incomplete, metric 0, localpref 100, valid, external, best
      Community: 1:64502 1:64504 65535:666
      rx pathid: 0, tx pathid: 0x0
```

and is therefore reflected only to ISP-2 and ISP-4, and not to ISP-3. The following view shows that ISP-2 receives host route 172.21.01/32 with BGP Next-Hop 10.0.10.250 (IP address of the dummy server) and with BGP Community NO_EXPORT. We will have a similar view for ISP-4 (omitted, for the sake of brevity).

```
ISP-2# show ip bgp 172.21.0.1/32
. . . < output omitted > . . .
  64501
    10.0.10.250 from 10.0.10.251 (192.168.2.1)
      Origin incomplete, metric 0, localpref 100, valid, external
      Community: no-export
      rx pathid: 0, tx pathid: 0
  64501
    10.0.10.250 from 10.0.10.252 (192.168.2.2)
     Origin incomplete, metric 0, localpref 100, valid, external, best
      Community: no-export
      rx pathid: 0, tx pathid: 0x0
```

On the other hand, the following view shows – as expected – that ISP-3 does not receive the advertisement of host route 172.21.01/32.

```
ISP-3# show ip bgp 172.21.0.1/32
% Network not in table
```

As a final test, we executed a ping from the two servers SRV-2 and SRV-4 connected to ISP-2 and ISP-4, respectively. Indeed, traffic from servers SRV-2 and SRV-4 directed to the server under attack is blocked.

```
SRV-2# ping 172.21.0.1
Type escape sequence to abort.
Sending 5, 100-byte ICMP Echos to 172.21.0.1, timeout is 2 seconds:
.....
Success rate is 0 percent (0/5)
```

```
SRV-4# ping 172.21.0.1
Type escape sequence to abort.
Sending 5, 100-byte ICMP Echos to 172.21.0.1, timeout is 2 seconds:
```

```
. . . . .
Success rate is 0 percent (0/5)
```

Instead, traffic from the SRV-3 server regularly reaches the server under attack.

```
SRV-3# ping 172.21.0.1
Type escape sequence to abort.
Sending 5, 100-byte ICMP Echos to 172.21.0.1, timeout is 2 seconds:
!!!!!
Success rate is 100 percent (5/5), round-trip min/avg/max = 4/7/19 ms
```

10.5 PROTECTION AGAINST DDoS ATTACKS: BGP FLOWSPEC

As mentioned in the previous paragraph, following a DDoS attack, the RTBH only executes one action: it rejects the packets, both directed toward the host attacked (destination-based RTBH) or incoming from the attacker (source-based RTBH).

The evolution of the RTBH is the BGP FlowSpec, standardized by RFC 8955 – *Dissemination of Flow Specification Rules*, December 2020. The extension to IPv6 is specified by RFC 8956 – *Dissemination of Flow Specification Rules for IPv6*, December 2020.

NOTE: The first RFC to define the BGP FlowSpec was RFC 5575 – *Dissemination of Flow Specification Rules*, August 2009. RFC 8955 is its evolution, including also the specifications contained in RFC 7674 – *Clarification of the Flowspec Redirect Extended Community*, October 2015.

The BGP FlowSpec has three basic differences with the BGP RTBH:

- it requires the support of a new address-family, while the RTBH does not require any additional BGP function, being based only on standard BGP features;

- it can include contrast actions at a much more granular level, not only on the attacker's source IP addresses, and on the attacked unit's target IP addresses, differently from the RTBH. The contrast action can be done also on single micro-flows (hence the name FlowSpec, an abbreviation of Flow Specification);

- it has more actions to counter DDoS attacks, beside packet rejection.

The basic architecture of the BGP FlowSpec is the same as the RTBH: starting from a centralized controller, BGP UPDATE messages are sent to PE routers (not necessarily all of them); the messages contain a description of the flows to be controlled and the actions to implement on them. The actions are then implemented directly on the forwarding hardware, similarly to standard rules that allow controlling an interface's inbound/outbound traffic (i.e., access lists for Cisco and firewall filters for Juniper).

NOTE: It is possible that the traffic flow to be controlled and the actions to be implemented on it are described directly by the customer to the ISP network. This solution helps to react to DDoS attacks more quickly, since the customer does not have to communicate the flows to be controlled and any actions to be implemented to the NOC (Network Operations Center), and does it himself. Obviously, in this case the customer must have a router that supports the BGP FlowSpec. We will not cover this case, which is a simple extension of what we will see, based on a centralized controller managed by the ISP's NOC.

10.5.1 Traffic flow coding

The key aspects of the BGP FlowSpec theory are basically the codification of the traffic flow where to act, and the actions implemented on them. The first aspect is coded through NLRIs of a new address-family, while the second, shown in the following Section 10.5.2, uses new BGP Extended Communities.

The aforementioned RFC 8955 and 8956 define new address-families, identified by the following AFI/SAFI codes:

- AFI/SAFI=1/133 (2/133): indicates the address-family for use with IPv4 (IPv6) unicast;

- AFI/SAFI=1/134 (2/134): indicates the address-family for use with L3VPN IPv4 (IPv6) unicast.

In this book, we will not cover the IPv6 extension, as it doesn't add anything to the concept; the only thing that changes are the flow coding types.

Flow coding is done by defining a new NLRI, transported by a standard MP_REACH_NLRI attribute (and MP_UNREACH_NLRI in case of withdrawal). This attribute does not use the Network Address of Next Hop field, as it is not significant. The new NLRI does not transport reachability info on the prefixes, and this is why no information on the Next-Hop is required. Therefore, the related field is not added to the MP_REACH_NLRI attribute (the trick is to set the value of the **Length of Next Hop Network Address** field to zero). The generic format of the new NLRI is shown in Figure 10.10 below, taken from RFC 8955.

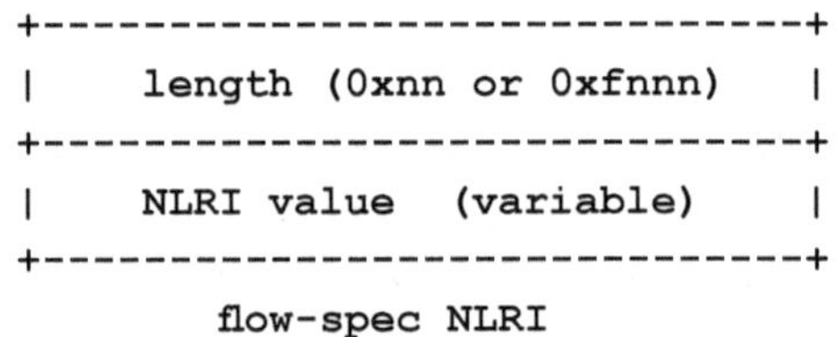

Figure 10.10 – Generic NLRI format for traffic flow coding.

The **length** value indicates the length of the entire NLRI, expressed as 1 or 2 bytes. If the NLRI length was (strictly) lower than 240 byte, the single byte coding would be adopted (e.g. if the NLRI was 160 byte long, the **length** field would only be one byte long, and have hexadecimal value of 0xa0). If the length was greater than 239 byte, the two byte coding would be used, with the first nibble of the hexadecimal notation fixed and equal to "f", and the remaining three equal to the length value (e.g., if the NLRI was 241 byte long, the **length** value would be two byte long and have hexadecimal value of 0xf0f1). Consequently, the maximum length of an NLRI is 4,095 bytes.

The NLRI value, i.e. the Flow Specification, consists of various optional components. A packet belongs to the specified flow if and only if it belongs to all the components specified in the NLRI (logical AND). Each component has a coding in which the first byte is the type of component, and the rest is the content. RFC 8955 defined the 12 following components.

Type	Content
1	Destination prefix
2	Source prefix
3	IP Protocol
4	Port
5	Destination port
6	Source port
7	ICMP Type
8	ICMP Code
9	TCP Flags
10	Packet Length
11	DSCP
12	Fragment

Here, we will only explain the entire coding for the most significant ones. For the others, see RFC 8955. An important note is that, in an NLRI, components are optional, but they should be listed according to a specific order, based on the type numerical value.

<u>**Type 1/2**</u>: Destination/Source prefix

Scope: coding of IP subnets to which the packets' destination (Type 1) or source (Type 2) IP addresses belong.

General format:

Type (1 byte)	Prefix Length (1 byte)	Prefix (variable)

Example: 198.51.100.0/24

0x01/0x02	0x18 (= /24)	0xc6336400

Hexadecimal representation 0xc63364 corresponds to decimal representation 198.51.100.

<u>Type 3</u>: Protocol ID

Scope: coding Protocol ID values present in the packets.

General format:

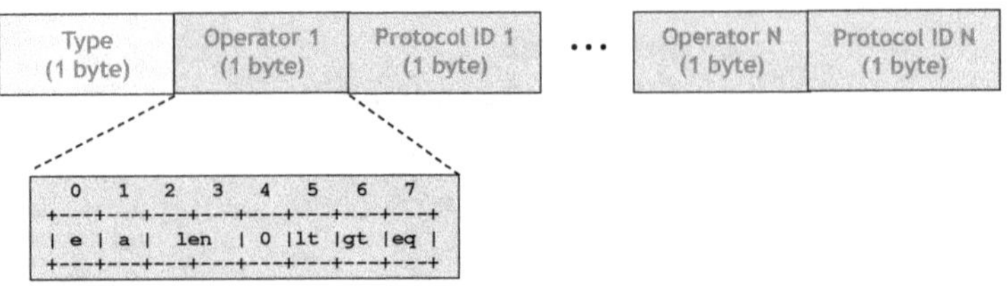

Type 3 coding uses several <operator, value> pairs, used to specify the Protocol ID field. The operator field comprises several flags, with the following meaning:

- **e**: equal to 1 in the last operator, and 0 in the previous ones;

- **a**: if unset, the result of the previous <operator, value> pair is logically ORed with the current one. If set, the operation is a logical AND;

- **len**: if **len**=0 the following value is coded with 1 byte, if **len**=1 with two bytes. For Type 3 coding, **len**=0.

- **lt**: "less than" operator;

- **gt**: "greater than" operator;

- **eq**: "equal" operator.

Example: coding of a Protocol ID with TCP (Protocol ID=6=0x06) or UDP (Protocol ID=17 =0x11).

0x03	0x01	0x06	0x81	0x11

<u>Type 4/5/6</u>: Port/Destination port/Source port

Scope: coding port values of the transport protocol. Type 4 (Port) indicates a general source or destination port.

General format: same format as Type 3, with port values in place of Protocol ID values. The port value length can be 1 or 2 byte.

Example: coding the source or target port number 53 (Type 4).

0x04	0x81	0x35

Let's see two examples of how these coding types can be used to identify specific traffic flows.

Example 1: coding of the traffic flow comprising IP packets with destination IP address belonging to IP subnet 203.0.113/24 and TCP destination port 23.

NLRI:

Length	Destination	Protocol	Port
0x0b	01 18 cb 00 71	03 81 06	05 81 17

Decoding:

0x0b	NLRI Length	11 byte
0x01	Type	1 (Destination prefix)
0x18	Prefix Length	24
0x(cb 00 71)	IP Prefix	203.0.113/24
0x03	Type	3 (Protocol ID)
0x81	Operator	e=1; eq=1
0x06	Protocol ID	TCP
0x05	Type	5 (Destination Port)
0x81	Operator	e=1; eq=1
0x17	source/dest. Port	23

Example 2: coding of the traffic flow comprising IP packets with source and target IP address belonging to subnets 192.0.2/24 and 203.0.113/24 respectively, and source or target port equal to 8080 or within the interval [100, 150].

NLRI:

Length	Destination	Source	Port
0x12	01 18 cb 00 71	02 18 c0 00 02	04 03 64 45 96 91 1f 90

Decoding:

0x12	NLRI Length	18 *byte*
0x01	Type	1 (Destination prefix)
0x18	Prefix Length	24
0x (cb 00 71)	Destination IP Prefix	203.0.113/24
0x02	Type	2 (Source prefix)
0x18	Prefix Length	24
0x (c0 00 02)	Source IP Prefix	192.0.2/24
0x04	Type	4 (Port)
0x03	Operator	gt=1, eq=1 (>=)
0x64	Minimun Port	100
0x45	Operator	a=1 (AND); lt=1, eq=1 (<=)
0x96	Maximum Port	150
0x91	Operator	e=1, len=1; eq=1
0x1f90	Port	8080

10.5.2 Defining the actions

The second fundamental aspect of the BGP FlowSpec is the action coding. Actions are added to BGP UPDATE messages through Extended Communities, whose type is specified in the first column of Figure 10.11 below, taken from RFC 8955 (e.g., for the traffic marking action, the Extended Community type is 0x8009).

```
+=====================+========================+=========================+
| community 0xttss    | action                 | encoding                |
+=====================+========================+=========================+
| 0x8006              | traffic-rate-bytes     | 2-octet AS, 4-octet     |
|                     |                        | float                   |
+---------------------+------------------------+-------------------------+
| 0x800c              | traffic-rate-packets   | 2-octet AS, 4-octet     |
|                     |                        | float                   |
+---------------------+------------------------+-------------------------+
| 0x8007              | traffic-action         | bitmask                 |
+---------------------+------------------------+-------------------------+
| 0x8008              | rt-redirect AS-        | 2-octet AS, 4-octet     |
|                     | 2 octet                | value                   |
+---------------------+------------------------+-------------------------+
| 0x8108              | rt-redirect IPv4       | 4-octet IPv4 address,   |
|                     |                        | 2-octet value           |
+---------------------+------------------------+-------------------------+
| 0x8208              | rt-redirect AS-        | 4-octet AS, 2-octet     |
|                     | 4 octet                | value                   |
+---------------------+------------------------+-------------------------+
| 0x8009              | traffic-marking        | DSCP value              |
+---------------------+------------------------+-------------------------+
```

Figure 10.11 – Format of BGP Extended Communities for action coding.

Traffic-rate actions, which differ only for their unit of measurement, are used to limit the flow traffic to a preset value (expressed as byte/s or packet/s, using the floating point representation IEEE.754.1985 – Standard for Binary Floating-Point Arithmetic). A null traffic-rate value indicates the packet rejection. Out of curiosity, you can see the complete format below, and an example related to a traffic-rate of 1 kbyte/s.

General format:

Example:

where "0x45fa0000" is the hexadecimal coding of the traffic-rate, which, according to RFC 8955, should be based on the floating point representation IEEE.754.1985. The traffic action is used to sample traffic, and it can be used by an ISP to gather more information on the attack.

Redirect actions are very useful to convey traffic toward devices that can clean it (scrubbing center). Redirection is done through a VRF (Virtual Routing and Forwarding, sometimes indicated as "dirty VRF"), which uses a certain Route Target in its import policy. There are three formats of the Extended Community that specifies this kind of action, which differ for the Route Target coding (which is 6 byte long):

- 0x8008: 2 byte ASN + 4 byte arbitrary;

- 0x8108: 4 byte IP + 2 byte arbitrary;

- 0x8208: 4 byte ASN + 2 byte arbitrary.

NOTE: If you are not familiar with the Route Target concept, a Route Target is a value transported through BGP Extended Community attributes and used to filter BGP advertisements, usually in scenarios related to MPLS services (e.g. L3VPN). Based on the Route Targets, the following types of filters can be created: if the BGP advertisement contains a certain Route Target value, then accept the advertisement, otherwise reject it. More details on this in Chapter 11.

Lastly, the traffic-marking action can be used to change the value of the DSCP (Differentiated Services Code Point) field in the IP packet header. Usually, the change consists of downgrading a packet, i.e. the value of the DSCP is redefined so as to assign a new, less prized service class to the packet. This can be used to assign a service class that entails a higher rejection probability in case of congestion to a packet. In this way, traffic is not rejected in nominal conditions, but only when congestion occurs.

10.5.3 Advertisement validation

An important aspect of the BGP FlowSpec is validating the advertisements sent by the controller, i.e. checking that it is legitimated to send that specific advertisement. Otherwise, an ill-intentioned user could send a BGP FlowSpec advertisement for a prefix owned by somebody else, and execute a new type of DoS attack.

The validation process described by RFC 8955 uses unicast (AFI=1/2) advertisements of the address-family with the same AFI and with:

- SAFI=1 for BGP FlowSpec advertisements with SAFI=133;

- SAFI=128 for BGP FlowSpec advertisements with SAFI=134.

Without an explicit configuration disabling the validation, a BGP FlowSpec advertisement is considered valid if all the following conditions are met:

1. The flow description contains a Destination Prefix component (Type 1) in the NLRI.

2. The advertisement originator is the same as the originator of the best-path for the target prefix contained in the Destination Prefix component of the previous point. In other words, if a controller originates a BGP FlowSpec advertisement with a Destination Prefix a.b.c.d/M, those who receive the advertisement must have as best-path toward the a.b.c.d/M prefix the advertisement received from the controller.

3. There are no paths toward prefixes more specific than the Destination Prefix, received from a eBGP Speaker belonging to an AS different than the one specified in the previous point. In other words, if there was a path toward a more specific component than the Destination Prefix coming from a different AS, the BGP FlowSpec advertisement would be considered invalid.

NOTE: The originator of a BGP FlowSpec advertisement means either the neighbor address of the BGP Neighbor, or, if present, the IP address contained in the ORIGINATOR_ID attribute (see Section 8.3.3).

The idea on which the validation is based is that only one adjacent best path AS for a prefix is authorized to send BGP FlowSpec advertisements with the prefix or one of its subnets as Destination Prefix. Figure 10.12 below shows an example that clarifies the concept. AS 64500 has, as best path for prefix 192.0.2/24, originated by AS 64501, the unicast advertisement (AFI/SAFI=1/1) sent by AS 64501. The BGP FlowSpec advertisement sent by AS 64501, with subnet 192.0.2.1/32 of prefix 192.0.2/24 as Destination Prefix, is deemed valid by the router of AS 64500, because it comes from the AS that is the best path for prefix 192.0.2/24. Vice versa, the BGP FlowSpec advertisement coming from AS 64502 is deemed invalid, because it comes from an AS that is not the best path for prefix 192.0.2/24.

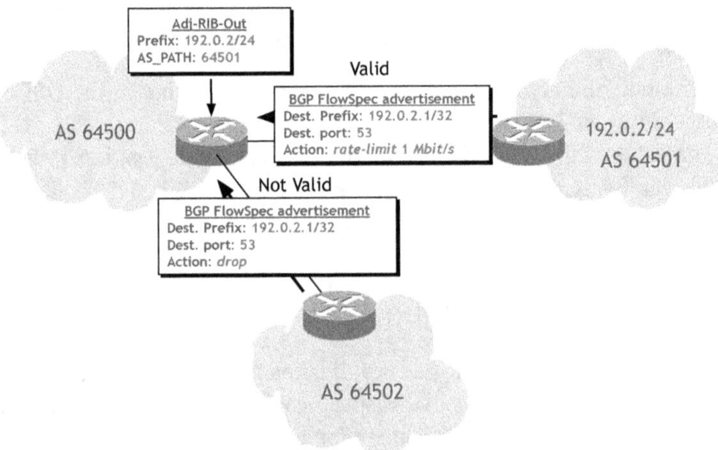

Figure 10.12 – Example of BGP FlowSpec advertisement validation.

There are some situations in which the validation process, as defined by RFC 8955, does not allow sending BGP FlowSpec advertisements. A classic case is a centralized controller, managed for instance by the NOC of an ISP, which, upon a customer's request, sends advertisements to perform actions on certain traffic flows. Another case is that of an ISP that has a portal, or showcases some APIs (Application Programming Interface), through which a customer can add flow and action descriptions, which are then translated into BGP FlowSpec advertisements.

In both cases, the second validation condition cannot be met. For this reason, RFC 8955 states that all BGP FlowSpec implementations must include the option of disabling the validation process.

10.5.4 Configuration aspects

For configuration purposes, we should divide routers into controllers and clients, where clients are the BGP Speakers that receive the actions to adopt for the different flows (via BGP). As a general rule, the controller function can be performed by any server with a BGP implementation that supports the address-family BGP FlowSpec (e.g. ExaBGP, BIRD).

The controller configuration requires three steps:

1. enabling the address-family BGP FlowSpec support;

2. defining the flow and actions;

3. transferring the actions on flows to clients through BGP UPDATE messages.

While the client configurations are:

1. enabling the address-family BGP FlowSpec support;

2. transferring the action on the flows to the hardware;

3. (optional) disabling the validation process.

The first step is pretty common, and is done through the following commands, which must be executed both at client and server level:

<u>IOS XE</u>:
router(config)# **router bgp** *AS-number*
router(config-router)# **neighbor** *IP-neighbor* **remote-as** *AS-neighbor*
router(config-router)# **address-family { ipv4 | ipv6 | vpnv4 | vpnv6 } flowspec**
router(config-router-af)# **neighbor** *IP-neighbor* **activate**

<u>IOS XR</u>:
RP/0/RP0/CPU0:router(config)# **router bgp** *AS-number*
RP/0/RP0/CPU0:router(config-bgp)# **address-family { ipv4 | ipv6 | vpnv4 | vpnv6 } flowspec**
RP/0/RP0/CPU0:router(config-bgp-af)# **exit**
RP/0/RP0/CPU0:router(config-bgp)# **neighbor** *IP-neighbor*
RP/0/RP0/CPU0:router(config-bgp-nbr)# **remote-as** *AS-neighbor*
RP/0/RP0/CPU0:router(config-bgp-nbr)# **address-family { ipv4 | ipv6 | vpnv4 | vpnv6 } flowspec**

<u>JUNOS</u>
[edit protocols bgp]
family inet {
  flow;
}
to be executed at global, group or neighbor level.

The flow definition only concerns the routers used as controllers. Concerning Cisco platforms, only those that use IOS XR support the controller function. They use an object widely known among those who are familiar with QoS IP configurations in Cisco environments: the class-maps. The configuration to execute is the following:

RP/0/RP0/CPU0:router(config)# **class-map type traffic [match-all | match-any]** *class-map-name*
RP/0/RP0/CPU0:router(config-cmap)# **match** < *condition* 1 >

. . .

RP/0/RP0/CPU0:router(config-cmap)# **match** < *condition N* >
RP/0/RP0/CPU0:router(config-pmap-c)# **end-class-map**

NOTE: If there is more than one match condition, and if the match-all clause is present, they are treated according to a logical AND, while, if the match-any clause is present, they are treated according to a logical OR.

The match conditions supported include all those defined by RFC 8955 and its IPv6 extension. We will include some of them as an example; for the others, you can refer to Cisco documentation:

- **match {destination-address | source-address} {ipv4 | ipv6}** *prefix/mask* ;

- **match protocol** {*protocol ID |min-value - max-value*};

- **match {destination-port | source-port}** {*port | min-value - max-value*};

- **match redirect nexthop route-target** *route-target;*

- . . .

The action definition uses another command widely known among those who are familiar with QoS IP configurations in Cisco environments: the policy-maps. The configuration to execute is the following:

```
RP/0/RP0/CPU0:router(config)# policy-map type pbr policy-map-name
RP/0/RP0/CPU0:router(config-pmap)# class type traffic class-map-name
RP/0/RP0/CPU0:router(config-pmap-c)# < action 1 >

. . .

RP/0/RP0/CPU0:router(config-pmap-c)# < action N >
RP/0/RP0/CPU0:router(config-pmap-c)# end-policy-map
```

In JUNOS, the conditions and related actions are configured under the **[routing-options]** configuration hierarchy, with the following commands:

```
[edit routing-options]
flow {
  route flow-name {
    match {
     < condition 1 > ;

      ...
     < condition N > ;
    }
    then {
     < action 1 > ;

      ...
     < action N > ;
    }
  }
}
```

Based on this simple configuration, JUNOS controller generates a BGP FlowSpec advertisement that installs locally into the "inetflow.0" table.

Lastly, the actions on the flows are transferred to the client in Cisco controllers with the following configurations:

```
RP/0/RP0/CPU0:router(config)# flowspec
RP/0/RP0/CPU0:router(config-flowspec)# address-family { ipv4 | ipv6 | vpnv4 | vpnv6 }
RP/0/RP0/CPU0:router(config-flowspec-af)# service-policy type pbr policy-map-name
```

In JUNOS, the transfer is done after defining a routing policy that allows exporting the content of the "inetflow.0". table into the BGP process.

The configurations to execute are:

```
[edit policy-options policy-statement policy-name]
from {
   rib inetflow.0;
}
then {
   accept;
}

[edit protocols bgp]
export policy-name;
group group-name {
   export policy-name;
   neighbor IP-neighbor <peer-as remote-AS> {
      export policy-name;
   }
}
```

With these configurations, the controllers generate a BGP FlowSpec advertisement, which is propagated according to standard BGP rules. Upon receiving the advertisement, the clients program their hardware to control the flows according to the actions specified in the advertisements. This last aspect is automatic in Juniper routers, while in Cisco routers it is done through the following commands:

```
RP/0/RP0/CPU0:router(config)# flowspec
RP/0/RP0/CPU0:router(config-flowspec)# address-family { ipv4 | ipv6 }
RP/0/RP0/CPU0:router(config-flowspec-af)#  local-install interface-all
```

valid both for IOS XE and for IOS XR. If the validation process on the client side or in a Route Reflector propagating the BGP FlowSpec advertisements received from a controller needs to be disabled, the following commands can be used:

IOS XE:
```
router(config)# router bgp AS-number
router(config-router)# address-family { ipv4 | ipv6 | vpnv4 | vpnv6 } flowspec
router(config-router-af)# neighbor IP-neighbor validation off
```

IOS XR:
```
RP/0/RP0/CPU0:router(config)# router bgp AS-number
RP/0/RP0/CPU0:router(config-bgp)# neighbor IP-neighbor
RP/0/RP0/CPU0:router(config-bgp-nbr)# address-family { ipv4 | ipv6 } flowspec
RP/0/RP0/CPU0:router(config-bgp-nbr-a)# flowspec validation disable
```

JUNOS
```
[edit protocols bgp]
family inet {
  flow;
  no-validate routing-policy-name;
}
```

where the routing policy defines the characteristics of the BGP FlowSpec advertisements for which we want to disable the validation.

10.5.5 Case Study: redirecting a flow to a scrubbing center

A typical application scenario of the BGP FlowSpec is the one that allows redirecting the traffic flows toward an attacked server, to a specific device called scrubbing center, which attempts to eliminate malicious traffic and safeguard legitimate traffic in real time. The overall idea is simple: once the target of the attack has been identified, all traffic toward the server, or the application attacked, is sent to the scrubbing center, which returns only legitimate traffic to the network.

Its practical application is not so obvious. Indeed, there is an important aspect to keep in mind: when the scrubbing center returns the legitimate traffic back to the network, it must prevent it from returning to the scrubbing center, that is, from generating a forwarding loop. Traffic could return to the network on an interface that applies the action on the flow defined by the BGP FlowSpec advertisement, which redirects it to the scrubbing center.

To avoid this issue, all traffic toward the attacked unit is conveyed toward a specific VRF, often called "dirty VRF", and then sent to the scrubbing center. Return traffic is then sent to a router on a connection linked to the global RIB (or GRT, Global Routing Table), and from here it will follow the normal path toward its destination. An important aspect to check is that, when traffic returns to the network, the interface receiving it must not apply the redirection action toward the scrubbing center.

NOTE: A VRF (VPN Routing and Forwarding) is just a virtual router with interfaces, a RIB and routing contexts associated to it, through which the RIB is populated. The use of VRF is very common in L3VPN based on the BGP/MPLS model (see Chapter 11).

The scenario of our Case Study is summarized in Figure 10.13 below. The ISP network AS number is AS 64500, and it is an IP/MPLS network. The controller comprises a Cisco router with IOS XR. The PEs are Juniper routers. The scrubbing center, connected to router PE1, is simulated by a router that receives the traffic from the dirty VRF and returns it on a second interface associated to the GRT (also known as default VRF). Address Target 64500:1 is used to route the VRF. Various traffic flows toward the attacked server (host 203.0.113.1) arrive from the Internet, some of which legitimate and many of which malicious, originated by many hosts (botnet).

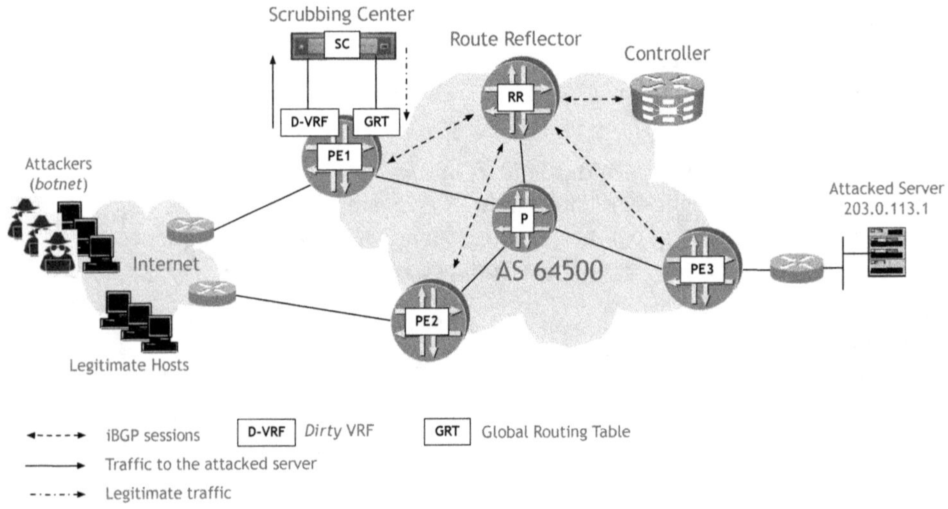

Figure 10.13 – BGP FlowSpec application network scenario.

We will only include the relevant configurations.

Controller (Cisco IOS XR)
```
! iBGP FLOWSPEC SESSION TOWARD THE ROUTE REFLECTOR
router bgp 64500
address-family ipv4 flowspec
 !
neighbor 192.168.2.1
  remote-as 64500
  update-source Loopback0
  address-family ipv4 flowspec
! TRAFFIC FLOW DEFINITION
class-map type traffic match-all FLOW
  match destination-address ipv4 203.0.113.1 255.255.255.255
end-class-map
! ACTION DEFINITION (REDIRECTING TOWARD DIRTY VRF)
policy-map type pbr ACTION
 class type traffic FLOW
  redirect nexthop route-target 64500:1
end-policy-map
! TRANSFER TO CLIENTS (PE) OF THE ACTIONS ON FLOWS VIA BGP
flowspec
 address-family ipv4
  service-policy type pbr ACTION
```

NOTE: The equivalent configuration in JUNOS to define the traffic and action flow is the following:

```
[edit routing-options flow route FLOW]
match {
   destination 203.0.113.1/32;
}
then routing-instance target:64500:1;
```

Client <u>PE1</u> (JUNOS)
```
# iBGP SESSION TOWARD RR (IP=192.168.2.1)
[edit protocols bgp group TO-RR]
type internal;
local-address 192.168.0.1; #ADDRESS LO0.0 DI PE1=192.168.0.1
family inet {
   flow {
      no-validate FROM-RR;
   }
}
family inet-vpn {
   unicast;
}
neighbor 192.168.2.1;

[edit policy-options policy-statement FROM-RR]
term 1 {
```

```
    from {
        rib inetflow.0;
    }
    then accept;
}
term 2 {
    then reject;
}
```

The "**family inet-vpn unicast**" command is used to enable the address-family L3VPN (AFI/SAFI=1/128) required to transfer to the "dirty VRF" of the other PE routers a default route that allows redirecting traffic toward the "dirty VRF" of the PE where the scrubbing center (PE1) is located. We will go over more details on this address-family in Chapter 11. The "**family inet flow no-validate FROM-RR**" command is used to disable the validation of the BGP FlowSpec advertisements accepted by the routing policy **FROM-RR**. In this case, the routing policy accepts all the BGP FlowSpec advertisements (present in the "inetflow.0" table), therefore the validation is disabled for all BGP FlowSpec advertisements.

```
# CREATION OF THE "DIRTY VRF"
[edit routing-instances DIRTY-VRF]
instance-type vrf;
interface ge-0/0/1.0;
route-distinguisher 64500:1;
vrf-target target:64500:1;
routing-options {
    static {
        route 0.0.0.0/0 next-hop 172.20.1.2;
    }
}
```

The configurations shown are the standard ones to create a VRF in JUNOS, and we will see them more in detail in Chapter 11. Notice the Route Target value 64500:1 used to redirect all traffic directed to host 203.0.113.1 toward the "dirty VRF". The (logic) interface "ge-0/0/1.0" associated with the "dirty VRF" is the PE1 interface toward the scrubbing center.
Within the VRF, a default route with the IP address of the other end of the connection toward the scrubbing center (IP=172.20.1.2/30) as Next-Hop has been configured. This default route, following the rules of L3VPN, is propagated to the other "dirty VRFs" on routers PE. For instance, the following view shows the presence of the default route in PE2's "dirty VRF":

```
aft@PE2> show route table DIRTY-VRF.inet.0 0.0.0.0/0 exact
. . . < output omitted > . . .
0.0.0.0/0 *[BGP/170] 01:28:58, localpref 100, from 192.168.2.1
            AS path: I, validation-state: unverified
        > to 172.16.2.22 via ge-0/0/3.0, Push 299840, Push 299792(top)
```

NOTE: Configuring the "dirty VRFs" on the other PEs does not require configuring the default route or associating any interface. These configurations are only necessary on the PE where the scrubbing center is located.

Lastly, there is one last very important configuration to execute. To avoid forwarding loops, we need to exclude all interfaces of the PEs on the backbone side from the flow actions. Without a similar configuration, traffic returning from the scrubbing center would end up on an interface that takes the redirection action toward the "dirty VRF" on this traffic, thus creating a forwarding loop. For instance, in our Case Study, PE1 interface toward the scrubbing center associated to the GRT (ge-0/0/3) must be excluded from the redirection action. In the same way, PE3's backbone side interface must be excluded from the redirection action. This is because traffic toward the attacked host reaches PE3 as simple IP traffic, and if the interface that receives it from the redirection action is not excluded, it would be sent again to the "dirty VRF", creating another forwarding loop. The configurations to be executed on PE1 are the following (those on the other PEs are the same, except for the interface numbering):

```
[edit interfaces ge-0/0/3.0 family inet]
filter {
  group 1;
}

[edit routing-options flow]
interface-group 1 exclude;
```

NOTE: The equivalent configuration in Cisco platforms with IOS XR is the following:

RP/0/RP0/CPU0:router(config)# **interface** *number type*
RP/0/RP0/CPU0:router(config-flowspec)# **{ ipv4 | ipv6 } flowspec disable**

Based on the configurations executed, the controller generates a BGP FlowSpec advertisement that installs locally in the BGP table associated with the address-family BGP FlowSpec, and from here the advertisement is propagated according to standard BGP rules.

NOTE: If the controller is a Juniper router, the BGP FlowSpec advertisement is added to the "inetflow.0" table.

By way of example, here is the detail of the BGP FlowSpec advertisement on the controller and on router PE1.

```
RP/0/0/CPU0:CONTROLLER# show bgp ipv4 flowspec Dest:203.0.113.1/32
. . .
BGP routing table entry for Dest:203.0.113.1/32/48
. . .
Paths: (1 available, best #1)
  Advertised to peers (in unique update groups):
    192.168.2.1
  Path #1: Received by speaker 0
  Advertised to peers (in unique update groups):
    192.168.2.1
  Local
    0.0.0.0 from 0.0.0.0 (192.168.2.2)
      Origin IGP, localpref 100, valid, redistributed, best, group-best
      Received Path ID 0, Local Path ID 0, version 3
      Extended community: FLOWSPEC Redirect-RT:64500:1

aft@PE1> show route table inetflow.0 extensive
inetflow.0: 1 destinations, 1 routes (1 active, 0 holddown, 0 hidden)
203.0.113.1,*/term:2 (1 entry, 1 announced)
```

```
TSI:
KRT in dfwd;
Action(s): routing-instance DIRTY-VRF,count
        *BGP      Preference: 170/-101
                  Next hop type: Fictitious, Next hop index: 0
                  . . . < output omitted > . . .
                  AS path: I  (Originator)
                  Cluster list:  192.168.2.1 # IP ADDRESS RR
                  Originator ID: 192.168.2.2 # IP CONTROLLER ADDRESS
                  Communities:  redirect:64500:1
                  Accepted
                  Localpref: 100
                  Router ID: 192.168.2.1
```

In this second view, there are two things to highlight. The first is that the **Next-Hop type** is
Fictitious, (see Section 10.5.1). The second is the Extended Community that transports information
on the action to be executed on the specified flow. It indicates that it is a redirect action toward a
VRF with Route Target (import) 64500:1.

Below is the wireshark analysis of the BGP UPDATE message that the controller sends to the
RR, containing the MP_REACH_NLRI attribute of the address-family BGP FlowSpec, and the
Extended Community where the action to be performed is contained.

```
Border Gateway Protocol - UPDATE Message
    Marker: ffffffffffffffffffffffffffffffff
    Length: 64
    Type: UPDATE Message (2)
    Withdrawn Routes Length: 0
    Total Path Attribute Length: 41
    Path attributes
      Path Attribute - MP_REACH_NLRI
        Flags: 0x90, Optional, Extended-Length, Non-transitive, Complete
        Type Code: MP_REACH_NLRI (14)
        Length: 12
        Address family identifier (AFI): IPv4 (1)
        Subsequent address family identifier (SAFI): Flow Spec Filter (133)
        Next hop network address (0 bytes)
        Number of Subnetwork points of attachment (SNPA): 0
        Network layer reachability information (7 bytes)
          FLOW_SPEC_NLRI (7 bytes)
            NRLI length: 6
            Filter: Destination prefix filter (203.0.113.1/32)
              Filter type: Destination prefix filter (1)
              203.0.113.1/32
                Destination IP filter prefix length: 32
                Destination IP filter: 203.0.113.1
      Path Attribute - ORIGIN: IGP
      Path Attribute - AS_PATH: empty
      Path Attribute - LOCAL_PREF: 100
      Path Attribute - EXTENDED_COMMUNITIES
```

```
Flags: 0xc0, Optional, Transitive, Complete
Type Code: EXTENDED_COMMUNITIES (16)
Length: 8
Carried extended communities: (1 community)
  Flow spec redirect AS 2 bytes: RT 64500:1 [Transitive Experimental]
    Type: Transitive Experimental (0x80)
    Subtype (Experimental): Flow spec redirect AS 2 bytes (0x08)
    2-Octet AS: 64500
    4-Octet AN: 1
```

When receiving the advertisement, router PE1 automatically creates a filter on the data plane (Firewall Filter) to which JUNOS assigns the name "**__flowspec_default_inet__**":

```
aft@PE1> show firewall filter __flowspec_default_inet__
Filter: __flowspec_default_inet__
Counters:
Name                                              Bytes              Packets
203.0.113.1,*                                         0                    0
```

To conclude the Case Study, let's check that traffic directed toward the attacked host actually passes through the scrubbing center and, if deemed legitimate, reaches its destination. In order to do this, we will execute a traceroute from a router connected to a router gateway of an Internet AS, assuming that the traffic generated is legitimate:

```
Router> traceroute 203.0.113.1
Type escape sequence to abort.
Tracing the route to 203.0.113.1
VRF info: (vrf in name/id, vrf out name/id)
  1 198.51.100.254 3 msec 2 msec 1 msec
  2 10.1.12.1 3 msec 3 msec 3 msec
  3 172.16.2.22 [MPLS: Labels 299792/299840 Exp 0] 9 msec 7 msec 5 msec
  4 172.16.1.1 [MPLS: Label 299840 Exp 0] 41 msec 27 msec 26 msec
  5 172.20.1.2 5 msec 6 msec 5 msec
  6 172.20.1.5 24 msec 12 msec 8 msec
  7 172.16.1.11 [MPLS: Label 299808 Exp 0] 8 msec 8 msec 13 msec
  8 172.16.3.3 7 msec 7 msec 12 msec
  9 203.0.113.1 17 msec 9 msec 10 msec
```

where IP addresses are:

1. **198.51.100.254**: IP address of the default gateway for the router where the traceroute command has been executed;

2. **10.1.12.1**: IP address of PE2, Internet side;

3. **172.16.2.22**: IP address of the PE2↔P connection, router P side. If you are familiar with MPLS services, label 299840 is the service label associated to the default route configured in the "dirty VRF", and 299792 is the transport label;

4. **172.16.1.1**: IP address of the PE1↔P connection, router PE1 side;

5. **172.20.1.2**: IP address of the PE1↔SC flow connection, scrubbing center side;

6. **172.20.1.5**: IP address of the PE1↔ SC return connection, PE1 side;

7. **172.16.1.11**: IP address of the PE1↔P connection, router P side. Label MPLS 299808 is a transport label;

8. **172.16.3.3**: IP address of the PE3↔P connection, router PE3 side;

9. **203.0.113.1**: IP address of the target host.

And this concludes the practical section. As usual, for further implementation details, you can refer to the official documents of the different manufacturers.

10.6 ROUTE ORIGIN VALIDATION

Many incidents on the Internet are caused by the propagation of incorrect routing information. The most common threats (or errors), such as prefix hijacking or route leak, exploit a basic vulnerability of BGP: the impossibility of checking if the ASes propagating the advertisements are legitimated to do so. Indeed, information on Internet resource properties (AS numbers and prefixes) are contained in public databases called Internet Routing Registries (IRR), managed and serviced by Regional Internet Registries. They are not located within BGP.

BGP has no native tool to check if an AS advertising a certain prefix in the Internet is authorized to do so, that is, if the prefix advertised has actually been assigned by a Regional Internet Registry. Since every prefix can be advertised and originated by any AS, regardless of its right to do so, an out-of-band mechanism is necessary to help BGP check which AS can advertise what prefix.

This mechanism exists, and is part of the IRR system. As mentioned earlier, there are public databases containing information on the prefix properties, some of which are managed by big operators, and others managed by Regional Internet Registries. Generating filters starting from information within the IRRs is now a widespread practice. But is there a limit to this system: can we trust this information? Unfortunately, the IRR system is far from being complete; the objects representing information <Prefixes; authorized ASes> are not entirely reliable, because often they are not updated, or they contain incorrect information.

To overcome this problem, IETF's SIDR (Secure Inter Domain Routing) working group has developed in RFC 6481 – *A Profile for Resource Certificate Repository Structure*, February 2012, a framework based on a public structure (RPKI, Resource Public Key Infrastructure) with distributed databases (RPKI repository) containing the associations <Prefixes; authorized ASes>. Each pair is associated with a Digital Certificate that allows those who consult the databases to check if the declarations are correct. The pairs with a Digital Certificate associated with them are called ROA (Route Origin Authorization).

To facilitate the architecture implementation, known and tested security tools are used, such as the X.509 digital certificate format, with the extension defined by RFC 3779 – *X.509 Extensions for IP Addresses and AS Identifiers*, June 2004, the new encryption standard and the digital object signature, defined by RFC 3852 – *Cryptographic Message Syntax* of July 2004.

Also, the certificate issuance functions are assigned to the bodies in charge of assigning the IP address blocks and the AS numbers, that is, the five Regional Internet Registries (ARIN, RIPE NCC, APNIC, LACNIC, AfriNIC), and, if present, the National Internet Registries and/or the Local Internet Registries (e.g. ISP). Therefore, these bodies act as Certification Authorities (CA). The main purpose of digital certificates is to validate public keys and the legitimacy of an AS to inject a certain block of prefixes into BGP and use a certain AS number.

10.6.1 RPKI architecture

The general architecture of the RPKI framework is summarized in Figure 10.14 below. This is based on databases (RPKI repository) containing information on the ROA, which can then be directly input by Regional Internet Registries or by Local Internet Registries (verified by Regional Internet Registries) through a specific Publication Protocol. Usually, for this purpose, Regional Internet Registries provide simplified web interfaces to hide all the complexities related to Digital Certificates from end users, focusing only on the creation and publication of ROA.

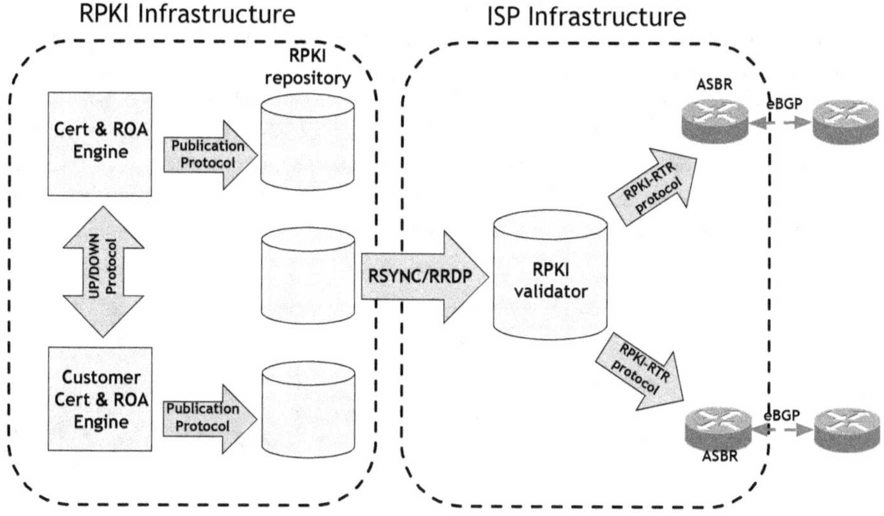

Figure 10.14 – Block scheme of the RPKI architecture.

Each RPKI repository, apart from the ROAs, also keeps a list of sub-RPKI repositories (also called Trust Anchors) used to synchronize the information on the ROAs and then achieve a single virtual RPKI repository at global level. Based on the ROAs contained in the RPKI repositories, an AS can validate the correctness of the advertisements received and select those it wants to accept.

In order for this to be effective, an AS needs to be sure that the information of the RPKI repositories are correct and synchronized at global level. The RPKI architecture entails a RPKI repository hierarchy, and therefore Digital Certificates following the same hierarchy for assigning IP addresses, simplified as follows: IANA→ Regional Internet Registry → Local Internet Registry. The five global Regional Internet Registries have the task of managing the RPKI repository of the ROAs of their area, and of making this information available to the other Regional Internet Registries and the ISPs all over the world.

On the ISP side, the architecture entails the use of servers called RPKI Validators, usually based on open source software. In turn, RPKI Validators have interfaces with the RPKI repositories of the different Regional Internet Registries to carry out a local download of the ROAs. For the download, the known RSYNC (Remote SYNChronization) protocol or RRDP – specifically defined for the RPKI architecture and specified by RFC 8182 – *The RPKI Repository Delta Protocol (RRDP)*, July 2017 – can be used.

NOTE: RSYNC is an open source software for file synchronization, capable of performing this operation in a unidirectional way, through a single data transmission for each communication direction (source server - target server).

The Edge router of the ISP (ASBR), through standard protocol RPKI-to-Router Protocol (RFC 8210 – *The Resource Public Key Infrastructure (RPKI) to Router Protocol, version 1*, September 2017), download the ROAs present in the RPKI Validator locally, adding them to a RPKI Table. When a BGP advertisement arrives, a router can infer the validity of the advertisements it receives, by comparing the content of the advertisements with that of the ROA in its RPKI Table.

10.6.2 RPKI and prefix hijacking

In Section 10.1.2, we described the issue of prefix hijacking, behind which there is the failure to control the legitimacy of an AS to advertise an IP prefix.

Figure 10.15 below shows a classic example of prefix hijacking, which occurs without any check on the origin of the prefixes advertised. In the figure, AS 64502, without any authorization, advertises subnet 192.0.2/24 of prefix 192.0.2/23 that a Regional Internet Registry (RIPE NCC, in the figure), assigned to AS 64501. One AS in the Internet, shown as 64500 in the figure, will receive two advertisements, one of the entire prefix 192.0.2/23, originated by AS 64501, and one of the more specific subnet 192.0.2/24, originated illegally by AS 64502, which is not authorized to advertise prefix 192.0.2/23 nor any of its subnets.

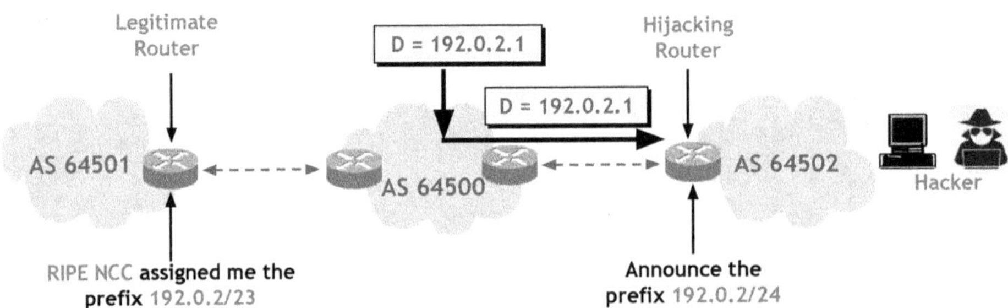

Figure 10.15 – Example of prefix hijacking.

BGP considers these two prefixes different, and it will elect two best paths that will both end up in the IP routing table of AS 64500 routers. According to the Longest Match Prefix rule, a portion of the traffic directed toward prefix 192.0.2/23 – the one directed toward subnet 192.0.2/24 – will be hijacked toward AS 64502, ending up in a black-hole, or, even worse, giving AS 64502 the possibility to spy on traffic.

Here too, the cause of this issue is the fact that BGP does not check the identity of those who input prefixes on the Internet. The only available tool is implementing suitable filters to block the advertisements of unauthorized prefixes, but not everyone uses them; and this process would significantly increase the configuration complexity, without solving the issue. For example, how can an intermediate AS know whether a remote AS is authorized to advertise a prefix or not? The best solution to solve this issue is to use RPKI architecture.

Figure 10.16 refers to the example of Figure 10.15 above, with a substantial difference that AS 64500 checks if the advertisement received is legitimate, through one of its RPKI Validators. Since the RPKI Validator declares that the advertisement received is not valid, the router of AS 64500 rejects the advertisement, thus avoiding the issue of the prefix hijacking (which has no impact on AS 64500, but on AS 64501). Actually, the type of decision that AS 64500 makes could be different, even if rejection makes more sense.

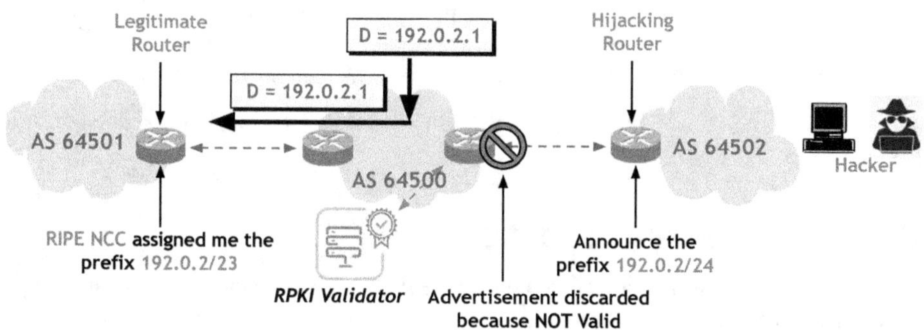

Figure 10.16 – Example of prefix hijacking solved by using an RPKI validator.

10.6.3 Route Origin Authorization (ROA)

ROAs are the key element of the RPKI architecture. They can be seen as objects that provide a way to check if an AS is authorized to advertise a certain IP prefix. Every ROA has four components:

1. an IPv4 or IPv6 prefix, with a certain mask length. Usually, it is a prefix assigned by a Regional Internet Registry to a Local Internet Registry;

2. a maximum mask length that specifies what IP subnets of the prefix originated can be advertised;

3. the AS number originating the IP prefix or one of its authorized subnets, with mask length lower than or equal to the one specified in the previous point;

4. a digital signature, based on the public/private key system.

Figure 10.17 below shows examples of ROA for an IPv4 prefix and for an IPv6 prefix.

NOTE: The ROA format and their use is described by RFC 6811 – *BGP Prefix Origin Validation*, January 2013.

AS number=0 is indicated in IANA registries as reserved. RFC 6491 – *Resource Public Key Infrastructure (RPKI) Objects Issued by IANA*, February 2012, specifies that the value AS=0 in a ROA should be used to identify prefixes that do not have to be advertised in the Internet, and therefore not used for packet routing. This allows those who have a certain IP prefix to indicate that the prefix – and possibly all its IP subnets – cannot be used for IP packet routing.

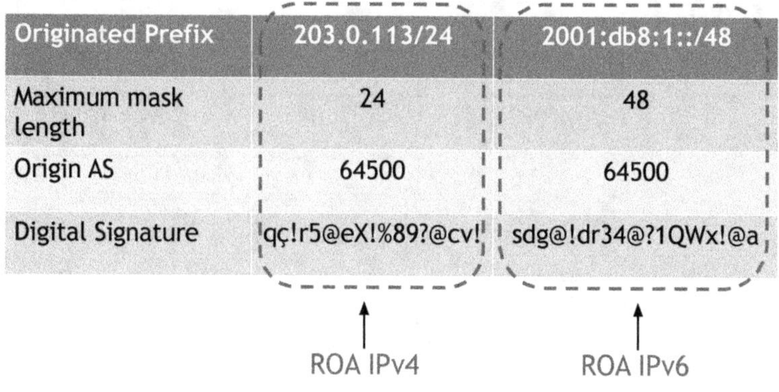

Originated Prefix	203.0.113/24	2001:db8:1::/48
Maximum mask length	24	48
Origin AS	64500	64500
Digital Signature	qç!r5@eX!%89?@cv!	sdg@!dr34@?1QWx!@a

Figure 10.17 – Examples of IPv4 and IPv6 ROA.

When defining a ROA with AS=0, it is best to define the maximum mask length, equal to that of the prefix object of the ROA, even if some network administrator prefers to define a maximum mask length equal to 32 for IPv4 ROA and 128 for IPv6 ROA. But the final result does not change.

NOTE: The use of AS=0 was specified in RFC 7607 – *Codification of AS 0 Processing*, August 2015.

10.6.4 Advertisement validation

The validation process of a BGP advertisement of the IPv4 or IPv6 unicast address-family is based on the comparison between the information contained in the advertisement and the ROA in the router database (RPKI table) downloaded from the RPKI Validator.

The possible results of the validation process, as described by, are three: **Valid**, **Invalid** and **NotFound**.

To see the meaning, let's assume to validate a BGP advertisement of the IPv4 or IPv6 unicast address-family, which contains the following information:

- NLRI = Pfx/M (Pfx=prefix; M=prefix length);

- AS Origin = AS-X.

The possible results of the validation process are the following:

- **Valid**: in RPKI Validator, there is a ROA=<Pfx-ROA/M-ROA; Max-Mask; AS-ROA> with AS-X=AS-ROA, where Pfx/M matches Pfx-ROA/M-ROA or is one of its subnets and M≤Max-Mask;

- **Invalid**: in RPKI Validator, there is a ROA=<Pfx-ROA/M-ROA; Max-Mask; AS-ROA>, with Pfx/M matching Pfx-ROA/M-ROA or is one of its subnets, but AS-X≠AS-ROA and/or M>Max-Mask;

- **NotFound**: in RPKI Validator, there is no ROA=<Pfx-ROA/M-ROA; Max-Mask; AS-ROA> for which Pfx/M matches Pfx-ROA/M-ROA or is one of its subnets.

Figure 10.18 below shows an example that helps to understand the RPKI validation states of a BGP advertisement better. The advertisements are compared with a ROA characterized by:

- Pfx-ROA/M-ROA=79.140.80.0/20;

- Max-Mask=24;

- AS-ROA=6762.

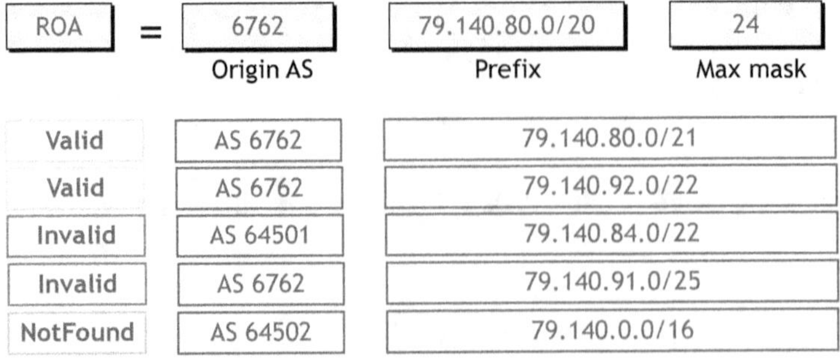

Figure 10.18 – Examples of prefix validation states.

Compared to this ROA, the first two advertisements have a **Valid** validation state, since they are both originated by AS 6762, and they both contain an IPv4 prefix that is a subnet of prefix 79.140.80.0/20; plus, both prefixes have a mask length equal to 21 and 22, respectively, lower than the Max-Mask value of the ROA, equal to 24.

The third advertisement of prefix 79.140.84.0/22, originated by AS 64501, has an **Invalid** validation state, since, although it is a subnet of prefix 79.140.80.0/20 with mask length lower than the Max-Mask value of the ROA, it is originated by another AS than the one present in the ROA (AS-ROA =6762≠64501).

The fourth advertisement of prefix 79.140.91.0/25, originated by AS 6762, has an **Invalid** validation state, since, although it is a subnet of prefix 79.140.80.0/20 originated by the same AS present in the ROA (AS-ROA=6762), it has a mask length greater than the Max-Mask value of the ROA.

Lastly, the last advertisement of prefix 79.140.0.0/16, originated by AS 64502, has a **NotFound** validation state, since it is not a subnet of prefix 79.140.80.0/20. It would have had a **NotFound** validation state even if AS 6762 had originated the advertisement.

10.6.5 Best implementation practices

This section describes the RPKI architecture, with particular reference to the two key elements characterizing it: ROA objects and advertisement validation. A network operator should keep in mind, when implementing the RPKI architecture, the certification of its prefixes (and thus the creation of ROA objects), as well as the treatment of prefixes with an **Invalid** validation state.

ROA creation, even if made simple by the RIRs, which provide a web-based user-friendly interface that hides all encryption issues to the users, such as the key rollover and related publishing, requires particular attention to the Max-Mask parameter (i.e. the maximum mask length, described in Section 10.6.3). The IETF document, RFC 9319 – *The Use of maxLength in the Resource Public Key Infrastructure*, October 2022 contains a good description of the aspects to consider when creating the ROAs. Among the various recommendations, we want to highlight the following:

- always create ROAs for the aggregate and the single subnets routed in BGP;

- avoid creating ROAs for the subnets of an aggregate, unless they are actually advertised;
  - if the ROA exists, but the subnet is not advertised, this gives attackers the possibility to originate the subnet using the origin AS, with consequent prefix hijacking;
- whenever possible create ROAs with a minimum Max-Mask equal to the prefix mask;

- protect the routing space not advertised on the Internet using ROAs with AS=0.

Concerning prefix validation, there are some simple recommendations also for the Validator deployment:

- use at least two geographically distributed Validators; in case of maintenance or failure of one of them, the other can be used as backup instance;

- implement at least two different softwares for validation cache, for diversity and independence;

- configure the Validator both on IPv4 and IPv6 and configure the routers on both TCP sessions;

- securing the Validator: allow only the routers with an eBGP session to access the validation instances.

10.6.6 Configuration aspects: Cisco platforms (IOS XE/XR)

The configurations to execute on a Cisco router to connect to an RPKI Validator are very simple, with only three parameters to specify:

- IP address of the RPKI Validator;
- the TCP port to use. Usually, the port used by the RPKI Validator is 3323, but it can also be different. For instance, in our Case Study (see Section 10.6.8), the RPKI Validator uses port 8282;
- the query period toward the RPKI Validator (refresh time) for downloading the VRPs (VRP=Validated ROA Payload). A typical value used in practical applications is 600 seconds.

The commands to be executed are the following:

IOS XE:
router(config)# **router bgp** *AS-number*
router(config-router)# **bgp rpki server tcp** *IP-Validator* **port** *Validator-port* **refresh** *seconds*

If, for reliability purposes, we have two or more RPKI validators, it is sufficient to repeat the "**bgp rpki ...**" command two or more times, changing the IP address of the server where the RPKI validator is located.

IOS XR:
RP/0/RP0/CPU0:router(config)# **router bgp** *AS-number*
RP/0/RP0/CPU0:router(config-bgp)# **rpki server** *IP-Validator*
RP/0/RP0/CPU0:router(config-bgp-rpki-server)# **transport tcp port** *Validator-port*
RP/0/RP0/CPU0:router(config-bgp-rpki-server)# **refresh-time** *seconds*

Using the BGP advertisement validation via RPKI modifies the BGP selection process that no longer considers all the advertisements (of the same prefix) to determine the best-path. Indeed, by default, the advertisements with an **Invalid** validation state are not used (or they shouldn't be) in the BGP selection process. An **Invalid** advertisement can never get into the RIB, which, ultimately, is the main purpose of the RPKI architecture.

In any case, even **Invalid** advertisements can participate to the BGP selection process, by using the following commands:

IOS XE:
router(config)# **router bgp** *AS-number*
router(config-router)# **address-family ipv4 unicast**
router(config-router-af)# **bgp bestpath prefix-validate allow-invalid**

IOS XR:
RP/0/RP0/CPU0:router(config)# **router bgp** *AS-number*
RP/0/RP0/CPU0:router(config-bgp)# **address-family ipv4 unicast**
RP/0/RP0/CPU0:router(config-bgp-af)# **bgp bestpath origin-as allow invalid**

If one or more advertisements of a same IP prefix, of which at least one **Valid**, the **Valid** advertisement has precedence, and is elected best-path, regardless of BGP metrics. For instance, let's assume to have two eBGP advertisements of prefix 79.140.80/20, with the first **Valid** and the second **Invalid**, and let's also assume that the first has a Local Preference=100 and the second a Local Preference=200. Not considering the RPKI validation states, the second advertisement would become the best-path; however, with the RPKI enabled, it is the first advertisement to become the best-path, because it is **Valid**.

Sometimes, for test reasons, it may be useful to disable the use of information on validation states in the selection process. This can be done with the following commands:

<u>IOS XE</u>
router(config)# **router bgp** *AS-number*
router(config-router)# **address-family ipv4 unicast**
router(config-router-af)# **bgp bestpath prefix-validate disable**

<u>IOS XR</u>
RP/0/RP0/CPU0:router(config)# **router bgp** *AS-number*
RP/0/RP0/CPU0:router(config-bgp)# **address-family ipv4 unicast**
RP/0/RP0/CPU0:router(config-bgp-af)# **bgp origin-as validation disable**

These commands, whose use should be temporary and only in specific situations, disable the use of validation state information in the selection process, without disconnecting the router from the RPKI Validator.

NOTE: You should be aware that the use of the commands both for disabling the use of information on the validation states in the selection process, and for the use in the selection process of advertisements declared **Invalid**, is not a good practice, since undermines the very basis of using the RPKI architecture.

Lastly, we can use the results of the validation process to apply policies through which execute actions on the advertisements, based on the validation state. These policies can be configured through standard route-map (IOS XE) and route policy (IOS XR) tools. New "match" conditions referring to the validation states have been defined for them.

Below is an example in an IOS XE environment, where **Valid** advertisements are assigned a value of Local Preference=200, **NotFound** advertisements are assigned a value of Local Preference= 100, and **Invalid** advertisements are assigned a value of Local Preference=50. Notice that, if we want to execute any action on **Invalid** advertisements, it would be necessary to execute the command we saw earlier, which allows these advertisements to take part in the BGP selection process.

```
route-map RPKI permit 10
 match rpki invalid
 set local-preference 50
!
route-map RPKI permit 20
 match rpki not-found
 set local-preference 100
!
route-map RPKI permit 30
 match rpki valid
 set local-preference 200
!
router bgp AS-number
  bgp bestpath prefix-validate allow-invalid
  neighbor IP-neighbor route-map RPKI in
```

Here is another example, for IOS XR. The only difference with the one we just saw is that, in this case, **Invalid** advertisements are rejected.

```
route-policy RPKI
 if validation-state is valid then
    set local-preference 200
 elseif validation-state is not-found then
    set local-preference 100
 else
    drop
!
router bgp AS-number
  neighbor IP-neighbor
     address-family ipv4 unicast
       route-policy RPKI in
```

With RPKI enabled, the default behavior of a Cisco router is to not propagate on the iBGP sessions the RPKI validation state of the eBGP advertisements received. To allow their propagation, the following commands are used.

<u>IOS/IOS XE</u>
router(config)# **router bgp** *AS-number*
router(config-router)# **address-family ipv4 unicast**
router(config-router-af)# **neighbor** *IP-iBGP-neighbor* **announce rpki state**
router(config-router-af)# **neighbor** *IP-iBGP-neighbor* **send-community extended**

<u>IOS XR</u>
RP/0/RP0/CPU0:router(config)# **router bgp** *AS-number*
RP/0/RP0/CPU0:router(config-bgp)# **address-family ipv4 unicast**
RP/0/RP0/CPU0:router(config-bgp-af)# **bgp origin as validation signal ibgp**

Notice that the validation state information is propagated using a specific BGP Extended Community. The format of the Extended Community is:

- 1st byte = 0x43 – indicates Extended Community of the Non-Transitive Opaque type (see RFC 7153, sect. 5.2.9);

- 2nd byte = 0x0 – indicates BGP Origin Validation State (see RFC 7153, sect. 5.2.9);

- 3rd-8th byte = 0x0/0x1/0x2 for **Valid/NotFound/Invalid** states, respectively (see RFC 8097, sect. 2).

Upon receiving the iBGP advertisement containing the BGP Extended Community, the iBGP peer can infer the advertisement validation state, without connecting to the RPKI Validator.

10.6.7 Configuration aspects: Juniper platforms (JUNOS)

The configurations to execute on a Juniper router with JUNOS are a little bit more complex (at least basic ones) and much more manual than Cisco's. On the other hand, they allow for broader freedom of **Valid/Invalid/NotFound** advertisement management. This greater freedom stems from the fact that JUNOS implementation of the RPKI architecture requires the implementation of a routing policy, through which decide whether a type of advertisement is accepted or not, associate specific Local Preference or Community values to the validation states, etc.

The configuration is divided into two parts. The first part establishes the connection to the server, where the RPKI validator lies. The commands to be executed are:

[edit routing-options validation group *name* **]**
 session *IP-Validator* {
    <refresh-time *seconds*;**>**
    <hold-time *seconds*;**>**
    <record-lifetime *seconds*;**>**
    <preference *value*;**>**
      port *Validator-port*;
      local-address *local-IP*;
}

Within each group, we can define up to two sessions toward two different RPKI validators. With respect to Cisco configuration, there are two additional timers:

- Hold Time: the time after which, if no activity with the server is recorded, the TCP session is closed. This timer must be longer than the refresh-time value.

- Record Lifetime: time of validity of the ROAs learned from the Validator. If the session with the Validator drops, the ROA expires, unless the session is restored within a preset value. The default value is 3,600 sec.

Moreover, through the "**preference**" parameter, we can define a «degree of preference» of the Validator. This is useful if more than one Validator is present (up to two), to establish which has the primary role and which has the backup role. The default value is 100.

The second part of the configuration concerns the validation check and the policies to be applied to the advertisements, based on their validity state; there is a lot of freedom regarding the policies. Moreover, within the same policy, we can assign the Extended Community values mentioned in the previous section, which can be used on iBGP sessions to propagate the advertisement validation state. The general policy configuration is:

[edit policy-options]
policy-statement *RPKI-Policy-Name* {
   term VALID {
     from {
       protocol bgp;
       validation-database valid;
     }
     then {
       validation-state valid;
       community add COMM-V;
       accept;
     }
   }
   term INVALID {
     from {
       protocol bgp;
       validation-database invalid;
     }
     then {

```
        validation-state invalid;
        community add COMM-I;
        accept/reject;
      }
    }
    term NOTFOUND {
      from {
        protocol bgp;
        validation-database unknown;
      }
      then {
        validation-state unknown;
        community add COMM-U;
        accept/reject;
      }
    }
}
community COMM-I members 0x4300:0:2;
community COMM-U members 0x4300:0:1;
community COMM-V members 0x4300:0:0;
```

NOTE: Theoretically, it would be possible to use the "**reject**" clause also for **Valid** advertisements, but we did not include it, since it makes no sense from a practical standpoint.

This routing-policy must be applied to the BGP process in the "import" direction, on all eBGP sessions for which we want to validate the prefixes received:

```
[edit protocols bgp]
group eBGP {
   import RPKI-Policy-Name;
. . .
}
```

NOTE: With the RPKI enabled, the default behavior of a Juniper router is to automatically propagate on iBGP sessions, without any additional command, the RPKI validation state of the eBGP advertisements received, using the BGP Extended Community COMM-X (X=V, I, U) defined above.

Now, we just need to apply all the configurations we have seen, and go over the main show commands that allow us to check the RPKI architecture operation.

10.6.8 Case Study

After seeing the main elements of the RPKI architecture and their basic operation, it is now time to put what we said into practice. In this section, we will describe the RPKI implementation, both in a Cisco (IOS XE) and Juniper (JUNOS) environment.

NOTE: In the following scenario, random AS numbers have been used (we hope the rightful owners won't mind!). The prefixes advertised by each AS have been taken by the RPKI repository of RIPE NCC, so that their actual validity, invalidity or impossibility to verify their state can be assessed.

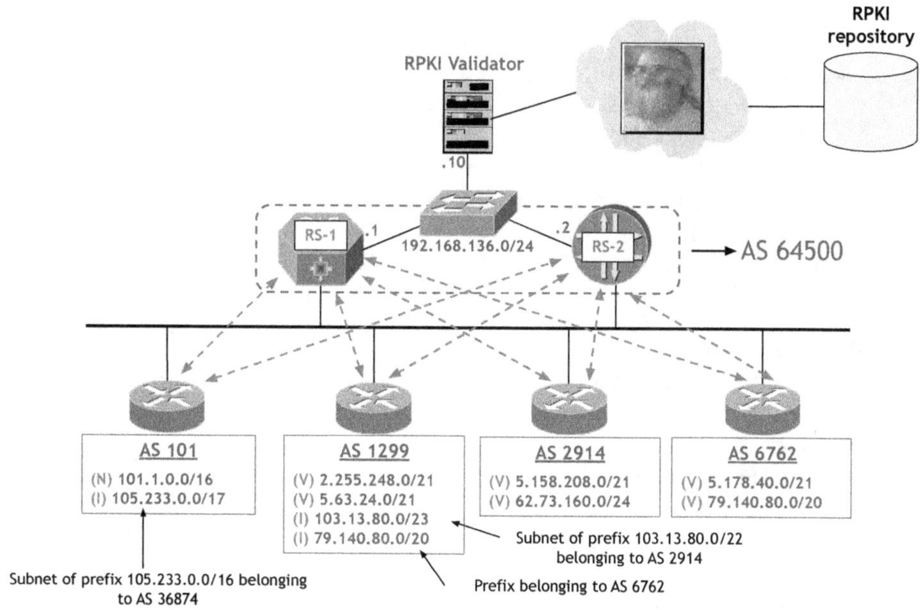

Figure 10.19 – Case Study scenario for RPKI architecture implementation.

Figure 10.19 shows the scenario of the Case Study we will use to implement the RPKI architecture and check its operation.

The scenario is that of an IXP (AS 64500) that, through its Route Servers (RS-1 and RS-2) provides the validation service for the advertisements exchanged to its members (in this Case Study, ASes 101, 1299, 2914 and 6762).

In order to do this, the two Route Servers use an RPKI Validator installed on a COTS server, with IP address 192.168.136.10. The TCP port used by the RPKI Validator is 8282. In turn, the RPKI Validator is connected via Internet to an RPKI repository. The two Route Servers are realised with two routers, a Cisco router using IOS XE (RS-1) and a Juniper router using JUNOS (RS-2).

NOTE: in an IXP infrastructure, prefix validation on the Route Servers is recommended by MANRS (Mutually Agreed Norms for Routing Security), which on the IXP page, under section "Action 1. Prevent propagation of incorrect routing information. (Mandatory)", reads: "IXPs using a Route Server to facilitate multilateral peerings should use it to validate received route announcements from a peer and subsequently filter them to other peers."

Each AS advertises the prefixes shown in the figure. To make the Case Study more interesting, we made ASes 101 and 1299 advertise three prefixes belonging to other ASes (see figure) and therefore not valid. The figure shows the validation states we should expect, downstream of the validation process (**V=Valid**; **N=NotFound**; **I=Invalid**).

The relevant basic configurations executed are:

RS-1 (Cisco IOS XE)

```
router bgp 1234
 bgp rpki server tcp 192.168.136.10 port 8282 refresh 600
```

RS-2 (Juniper JUNOS)

```
[edit routing-options]
autonomous-system 64500;
```

```
validation {
    group RPKI-VAL {
        session 192.168.136.10 {
            refresh-time 600;
            hold-time 1500;
            port 8282;
            local-address 192.168.136.2;
        }
    }
}

[edit policy-options]
policy-statement VALIDATION {
    term VALID {
        from {
            protocol bgp;
            validation-database valid;
        }
        then {
            validation-state valid;
            community add COMM-V;
            accept;
        }
    }
    term INVALID {
        from {
            protocol bgp;
            validation-database invalid;
        }
        then {
            validation-state invalid;
            community add COMM-I;
            reject;
        }
    }
    term NOTFOUND {
        from {
            protocol bgp;
            validation-database unknown;
        }
        then {
            validation-state unknown;
            community add COMM-U;
            accept;
        }
    }
}
community COMM-I members 0x4300:0:2;
community COMM-U members 0x4300:0:1;
```

```
community COMM-V members 0x4300:0:0;

[edit protocols bgp]
group eBGP {
    import VALIDATION;
. . .
}
```

Notice that, in RS-2 configuration, the routing policy VALIDATION rejects **Invalid** advertisements. What really happens, as we will see shortly, is that JUNOS places them in a hidden part of RIB "inet.0".

Let's see how we can check if the configurations are working correctly. The first thing to do is to check if the TCP connection toward the RPKI Validator is active. Let's see it for RS-1 first:

```
RS-1# show bgp ipv4 unicast rpki servers
BGP SOVC neighbor is 192.168.136.10/8282 connected to port 8282
Flags 64, Refresh time is 600, Serial number is 22, Session ID is 36388
InQ has 0 messages, OutQ has 0 messages, formatted msg 17
Session IO flags 3, Session flags 4008
 Neighbor Statistics:
  Prefixes 253843
  Connection attempts: 46
  Connection failures: 39
  Errors sent: 124
  Errors received: 0

Connection state is ESTAB, I/O status: 1, unread input bytes: 0
Connection is ECN Disabled, Minimum incoming TTL 0, Outgoing TTL 255
Local host: 192.168.136.1, Local port: 11109
Foreign host: 192.168.136.10, Foreign port: 8282
Connection tableid (VRF): 0
Maximum output segment queue size: 50
. . . < rest of the output omitted > . . .
```

The view result shows that the TCP connection has been established correctly (**Connection state is ESTAB**) and the 4 components identifying the TCP connection (IP addresses and source/destination ports):

- **Local host**: 192.168.136.1, **Local port**: 11109;

- **Foreign host**: 192.168.136.10, **Foreign port**: 8282.

It also shows other, less relevant data. Among these, we can also see the overall number of VRPs (IPv4 and IPv6) downloaded (**Prefixes 253843**). The view has been truncated, for the sake of brevity.

The same check for RS-2 can be done with the following command:

```
aft@RS-2> show validation session detail
Session 192.168.136.10, State: up, Session index: 2
  Group: RPKI-VAL, Preference: 100
  Local IPv4 address: 192.168.136.2, Port: 8282
  Refresh time: 600s
  Hold time: 1500s
  Record Life time: 3600s
```

```
 Serial (Full Update): 22
 Serial (Incremental Update): 22
   Session flaps: 0
   Session uptime: 1d 16:13:36
   Last PDU received: 00:00:01
   IPv4 prefix count: 213924
   IPv6 prefix count: 39919
```

NOTE: Differently from Cisco's, the view shows the number of IPv4 and IPv6 VRPs downloaded separately. IPv4 VRPs are 213924 (**IPv4 prefix count: 213924**) while IPv6 VRPs are 39919 (**IPv6 prefix count: 39919**). The sum coincides with the overall value shown in Cisco's view (213.924+33.919=253.843).

The following commands can be used to view the IPv4/IPv6 RPKI Tables, that is, the list of IPv4 and IPv6 VRPs that the router downloads from the RPKI Validator and inputs in the local memory. Since the list of VRPs is very long (as we've seen above, they were 253,843 in total, when this Case Study was completed, and they will be much more in the future), it is best to view only the relevant part. For instance, assuming we want to view, on RS-1's local database, all IPv4 and IPv6 VRPs of AS 6762, the commands to be executed are:

```
RS-1# show bgp ipv4 unicast rpki table | section _6762_
5.178.40.0/21         24        6762        0         192.168.136.10/8282
78.138.4.0/22         22        6762        0         192.168.136.10/8282
78.138.36.0/22        22        6762        0         192.168.136.10/8282
. . . < output omitted > . . .

RS-1# show bgp ipv6 unicast rpki table | section _6762_
2001:41A8::/32        32        6762        0         192.168.136.10/8282
```

The view above shows the RPKI Table of IPv4 VRPs, and the one below the RPKI Table of IPv6 VRPs. The first column contains the ROA prefix, the second column the maximum mask length, and the third column the prefix origin AS. Lastly, the second to last column is always null, and the last one contains the IP address of the RPKI Validator (=192.168.136.10) and the TCP port (=8282). The view of the RPKI Tables on RS-2, always related to the origin AS 6762, is obtained through the following command:

```
aft@RS-2> show validation database origin-autonomous-system 6762
RV database for instance master

Prefix                Origin-AS  Session           State     Mismatch
5.178.40.0/21-24         6762 192.168.136.10       valid
78.138.4.0/22-22         6762 192.168.136.10       valid
78.138.36.0/22-22        6762 192.168.136.10       valid
. . . < output omitted > . . .
2001:41a8::/32-32        6762 192.168.136.10       valid

  IPv4 records: 21
  IPv6 records: 1
```

Now we just need to check the validation state of the eBGP advertisements. On RS-1, we have:

```
RS-1#show ip bgp
. . . < output omitted > . . .
RPKI validation codes: V valid, I invalid, N Not found
```

```
        Network                Next Hop              Metric LocPrf Weight Path
V*>   2.255.248.0/21      10.0.0.2                              0 1299 i
V*>   5.63.24.0/21        10.0.0.2                              0 1299 i
V*>   5.158.208.0/21      10.0.0.3                              0 2914 i
V*>   5.178.40.0/21       10.0.0.4                              0 6762 i
V*>   62.73.160.0/24      10.0.0.3                              0 2914 i
V*>   79.140.80.0/20      10.0.0.4                              0 6762 i
I*                        10.0.0.2                      200     0 1299 i
N*>   101.1.0.0/16        10.0.0.1                              0 101 i
I*>   103.13.80.0/23      10.0.0.2                              0 1299 i
I*    105.233.0.0/17      10.0.0.1                              0 101 i
```

We leave the task of proving that the validation states are correct to you, by comparing these advertisements to the scenario described in Figure 10.19. An interesting aspect to notice concerns the advertisements of prefix 79.140.80.0/20, (legitimately) originated by AS 6762 and (illegitimately) by AS 1299. One of these two advertisements has a **Valid** state, and the other an **Invalid** state. Despite the latter having a greater Local Preference value (=200), the BGP selection process chooses the **Valid** advertisement as the best path. This wouldn't have changed, even if we allowed **Invalid** advertisements in the selection process, with the command:

```
router bgp 1234
 address-family ipv4
  bgp bestpath prefix-validate allow-invalid
```

To conclude, let's see the BGP advertisement table on RS-2 (Note: in this case, we left all Local Preference values at their default value).

```
aft@RS-2> show route table inet.0 protocol bgp

inet.0: 13 destinations, 14 routes (11 active, 0 holddown, 3 hidden)
+ = Active Route, - = Last Active, * = Both
2.255.248.0/21      *[BGP/170] 00:44:10, localpref 100
                        AS path: 1299 I, validation-state: valid
                    >  to 10.0.0.2 via ge-0/0/0.0
5.63.24.0/21        *[BGP/170] 00:44:10, localpref 100
                        AS path: 1299 I, validation-state: valid
                    >  to 10.0.0.2 via ge-0/0/0.0
5.158.208.0/21      *[BGP/170] 00:44:10, localpref 100
                        AS path: 2914 I, validation-state: valid
                    >  to 10.0.0.3 via ge-0/0/0.0
5.178.40.0/21       *[BGP/170] 00:44:10, localpref 100
                        AS path: 6762 I, validation-state: valid
                    >  to 10.0.0.4 via ge-0/0/0.0
62.73.160.0/24      *[BGP/170] 00:44:10, localpref 100
                        AS path: 2914 I, validation-state: valid
                    >  to 10.0.0.3 via ge-0/0/0.0
79.140.80.0/20      *[BGP/170] 00:45:08, localpref 100
                        AS path: 6762 I, validation-state: valid
                    >  to 10.0.0.4 via ge-0/0/0.0
101.1.0.0/16        *[BGP/170] 00:44:10, localpref 100
                        AS path: 101 I, validation-state: unknown
                    >  to 10.0.0.1 via ge-0/0/0.0
```

As you can notice, the table only shows **Valid** and **NotFound** advertisements (which JUNOS calls **Unknown**). **Invalid** advertisements are in the hidden part of the table (**3 hidden**). The view them, you can use the following command:

```
tt@RS-2> show route table inet.0 hidden

inet.0: 13 destinations, 14 routes (11 active, 0 holddown, 3 hidden)
+ = Active Route, - = Last Active, * = Both

79.140.80.0/20        [BGP] 00:49:15, localpref 100
                        AS path: 1299 I, validation-state: invalid
                      >  to 10.0.0.2 via ge-0/0/0.0
103.13.80.0/23        [BGP] 00:10:48, localpref 100
                        AS path: 1299 I, validation-state: invalid
                      >  to 10.0.0.2 via ge-0/0/0.0
105.233.0.0/17        [BGP] 00:49:15, localpref 100
                        AS path: 101 I, validation-state: invalid
                      >  to 10.0.0.1 via ge-0/0/0.0
```

NOTE: If you are not familiar with JUNOS, we would like to remind you that hidden advertisement do not take part in BGP selection process, and cannot become best-paths.

JUNOS behavior in the BGP selection process differs from Cisco's, since it does not take the prefix validation state into account. For instance, by accepting **Invalid** prefixes in the routing policy VALIDATION, or defining the Local Preference for prefix 79.140.80.0/20 as per RS-1, the selection process chooses the **Invalid** advertisement as the best path, as you can see in the following view:

```
aft@RS-2> show route 79.140.80.0/20

inet.0: 13 destinations, 14 routes (13 active, 0 holddown, 0 hidden)
+ = Active Route, - = Last Active, * = Both

79.140.80.0/20       *[BGP/170] 00:00:11, localpref 200
                        AS path: 1299 I, validation-state: invalid
                      >  to 10.0.0.2 via ge-0/0/0.0
                      [BGP/170] 01:01:21, localpref 100
                        AS path: 6762 I, validation-state: valid
                      >  to 10.0.0.4 via ge-0/0/0.0
```

Therefore, to avoid situations that are contrary to the spirit of the RPKI architecture, we recommend to reject **Invalid** advertisements, as best practice.

10.7 VALIDATING SOURCE IP ADDRESSES

If, until now, we have followed the certification logic that the resources on the Internet must have, to be accepted by autonomous systems, now we will complete the argument by showing the measures we should implement so that our AS does not become an accomplice in global level attacks against third parties. For this purpose, we need to accurately define from which IP address the packets originated by our AS can depart.

This is important to prevent situations in which an attacker can create an IP packet *ad hoc*, with the address of a victim as source (IP spoofing). A classic example is the so-called amplification attack on a DNS query, that is, sending a packet with only a few bytes to the DNS server with address

203.0.113.53, while pretending it comes from IP 192.0.2.2, so that 203.0.113.53 provides a hefty reply with many bytes to the unaware 192.0.2.2.

Usually, the victim is targeted by many different angles, and many different autonomous systems that, on average, are not fully aware of what is happening. The result expected by the attacker is putting the victim out of service.

10.7.1 IP Spoofing

Without going into detail of the subspecies of IP Spoofing, for the purposes of our discussion it is sufficient to know how it works, so as to better understand the countermeasures we can adopt.

Let's start with a few points of reference: the attacker acts from a host with address 198.51.100.100 belonging to AS 64496; the attack target system has address 192.0.2.2 and is part of AS 65536; the server that unknowingly helps the malicious operation has address 203.0.113.53 and belongs to AS 65550.

In a pacific scenario, host 198.51.100.100 can send a query to nameserver 203.0.113.53 and receive a reply, whatever it is. Everything is OK, since AS 64496 lets traffic flow legitimately from network 198.51.100/24; the same goes for AS 65550, which has the right to originate IP packets from prefix 203.0.113/24.

However the attacker can tamper with the message coming from AS 64496 and destined to AS 65550, by arranging for the Source Address field in the IP packet header to no longer be 198.51.100.100, and to become 192.0.2.2 (belonging to AS 65536). Now, nameserver 203.0.113.53 will send a message (most of the times, amplified) to victim 192.0.2.2 to reply to a query the latter never generated.

The method is simple, almost trivial, insomuch so that, in the last years, we've observed dozens of thousands of attacks based on spoofing other IPs, every single day. A study conducted by CAIDA (Center for Applied Internet Data Analysis), also thanks to a software called Spoofer that can analyze whether an autonomous system lets IP packets with a falsified source, both on IPv4 and to IPv6, through.

date	IPv	client address	ASN	outbound private	outbound routable	inbound private	inbound internal	report ▶
2021-06-22 12:34:24	4	185.5.200.251	59715	✓ blocked	✓ blocked			report
2021-06-19 19:21:30	4	151.37.170.22	1267	✓ blocked	✓ blocked			report
2021-06-18 14:55:35	4	95.245.153.225	3269	✓ blocked	✓ blocked			report
2021-06-17 10:36:35	4	185.5.200.251	59715	✓ blocked	✓ blocked			report
2021-06-11 17:45:04	4	151.47.175.53	1267	✓ blocked	✓ blocked			report
2021-06-10 22:23:13	4	95.245.153.225	3269	✓ blocked	✓ blocked			report
2021-06-10 09:31:07	4	185.5.200.251	59715	? unknown	✓ blocked			report
2021-06-09 15:43:52	4	185.5.200.251	59715	✓ blocked	✓ blocked			report
2021-06-09 15:21:11	4	95.251.71.163	3269	✓ blocked	✓ blocked			report
2021-06-03 09:44:45	4	185.5.200.251	59715	✓ blocked	✓ blocked			report
2021-06-02 21:26:45	4	151.46.209.212	1267	✓ blocked	✓ blocked			report
2021-06-02 10:58:02	4	185.5.200.251	59715	✓ blocked	✓ blocked			report

Figure 10.20 – Screenshot of CAIDA's Spoofer software.

10.7.2 SAV and BCP 38

Once we know that our autonomous system can originate attacks based on IP spoofing, and that we are being accomplices of malpractices, how can we remedy this? First of all, let's clarify that (unfortunately) we are not alone, and that this phenomenon has been studied in all its facets, and this has generated recommendations and effective solutions.

The scope is making only legitimate packets pass through the AS, that is, those with source IP addresses belonging to prefixes assigned by the relevant RIR, and consequently blocking all illegitimate ones.

The technique developed for this purpose has been coded with the name Source Address Validation (SAV), which is an integral part of the Best Current Practice number 38 (RFC 2827 – *Network Ingress Filtering: Defeating Denial of Service Attacks which employ IP Source Address Spoofing*, May 2000). A milestone in the Internet literature, which is always brought to the ISPs' attention, but which, even now, does not seem to be largely observed.

The remedy lies in a check. Taking once again the example of the previous section, the edge router of AS 64496 (i.e. the attacker's), can analyze the traffic incoming on the inbound interface:

- IF the source IP address of the packet falls within 198.51.100/24 THEN forward it regularly;

- IF the source IP address of the packet is different than 198.51.100/24 THEN prevent its forwarding.

On Cisco platforms, you can also use standard ACLs:

```
ip access-list extended IPv4-LOCAL
    permit ip 198.51.100.0 0.0.0.255 any
!
interface Interface-name
    ip access-group IPv4-LOCAL in
```

In JUNOS, Firewall Filters are used:

```
[edit firewall family inet filter IPv4-LOCAL]
term ALLOWED-SOURCES {
  from {
     source-address {
        198.51.100.0/24;
     }
  }
  then accept;
}
[edit interfaces interface-name.unit family inet]
filter {
    input IPv4-LOCAL;
}
```

We will leave the implementation of the checks on IPv6 to you.

These checks can be done on multiple device interfaces, with the reminder of applying the rule as close to the source as possible. In the case of an ISP providing connectivity to a customer with a specific IPv4 or IPv6 prefix assigned (or more than one), it is reasonable for the ISP to apply inbound filters on the interface (or interfaces, depending on the context) connecting the customer.

This way, any spoofed IP generation attempts will be confined to the customer's network, and will not do damage on the Internet.

The effectiveness of SAV techniques for the Internet ecosystem is directly proportional to the quantity of ASes applying them; and this is why, on one hand, they should be applied always and everywhere (*cum grano salis*), and, on the other hand, the importance of BCP 38 should be widespread to all interested parties in the Internet ecosystem, and first and foremost among ISPs. Lastly, we should specify that there is no cure-all to contrast all attack vectors circulating right now; however, it is proven that the correct large-scale application of the techniques described in this chapter, suitably combined with one another, limit and significantly reduce the malicious effects.

10.7.3 SAV and BCP 84

A big step forward in the direction of a safest Internet, was done by publishing the Best Current Practice number 84, which groups two complementary RFCs: RFC 3704 – *Ingress Filtering for Multihomed Networks*, March 2004 and RFC 8704 – *Enhanced Feasible-Path Unicast Reverse Path Forwarding*, February 2020. This is an evolution of what we already described; let's go step by step and try to illustrate the recommended techniques to keep the network of our AS safe, in case it is targeted by an attacker.

First of all, we want to clarify that the terms are the same, as well as the AS scenario, which consists of a distributed Denial of Service attack. The methods to mitigate the attack are those described in the previous section; however, we need to explore them further, to consider specific types, especially that of a multi-homed or asymmetrical routing network.

The recommendation of filtering any packets entering the network is always valid, especially those coming from customers, so as to avoid the circulation of those with spoofed IPs. There are many manual or automatic techniques to reach this result, and they can be summarized by points:

- Inbound filters (ACL/Firewall Filter);

- Strict Reverse Path Forwarding;

- Feasible Path Reverse Path Forwarding;

- Loose Reverse Path Forwarding;

- Loose Reverse Path Forwarding ignoring default routes.

We already saw the filters applied to inbound traffic in the previous section. We will continue with the different types of packet forwarding on the reverse path (Reverse Path Forwarding).

The Strict RPF mode can be explained as simple inbound filters that, instead of being set manually from time to time, are dynamically applied to traffic: the source address of a packet is searched in the router's Forwarding Information Base (FIB) and, if the packet transits through the same interface the router would have used to forward traffic toward the source of that packet, it gets a green light, and data can flow through.

Here is an example of Strict RPF in unicast Cisco devices, both for IPv4 and IPv6 protocols (remember that you need to enable the CEF, Cisco Express Forwarding):

```
interface GigabitEthernet0/0
  ip verify unicast source reachable-via rx
  ipv6 verify unicast source reachable-via rx
```

On Juniper devices with JUNOS (family inet for IPv4, family inet6 for IPv6):

```
[edit interfaces interface-name unit 0]
family (inet | inet6) {
    rpf-check;
}
```

It seems a very rigid behavior, and it is; this technique should be implemented with care, because it could generate unreasonable malfunctions (i.e. false positives). For example, let's consider the asymmetrical routing case, where a packet enters from a router interface, but the best routing selection process decides that it should reply to the source of that packet through another interface, different from the entry one. In this case, the Strict RPF check gives a red light, since the packet enters from a different interface than the one used to reach the source. As you may have understood, the Strict RPF can be applied by the ISP toward those customers to which it provides only one access, but things get complicated in case of routing asymmetry, or in case of multi-homed customers.

One first measure to overcome this limit is the Feasible Path RPF, which has been devised as an extension of the Strict RPF. It consists in adding, among the routes to consider for packet forwarding, not just the optimal path, but also any possible alternative paths. Obviously, the device used for this purpose must have a software that supports this operating mode.

Among them, by scrolling down the initial list, we find Loose RPF, in two different types: one with and the other without a default routing check. The first consists of searching for the source IP of a packet in the router RIB, and of checking if there is any routing (including the default one) for the network that IP belongs to. If the outcome is positive (without any further checks on the outbound interface, as it occurs in the Strict RPF) the router allows the packet to transit; otherwise it rejects it. Let's think about all non routable addresses; it is easy to see how the presence of a default route undermines all benefits of this technique. Hence the reason for the second type of RPF, the Loose RPF ignoring default routes. All the above reasoning applies, with the exception that its basic algorithm does not take the presence of a default route in the FIB into account.

Sixteen years after the first formalizations of the RPF mechanism, following the many experiences and implementations that the Internet industry has brought along, the IETF found a way to broaden the good practices published in 2004, by launching the Enhanced Feasible-Path unicast Reverse Path Forwarding (EFP-uRPF), i.e. an advanced Feasible RPF. Here are the news on which the EFP-uRPF is based: when a prefix – e.g. 198.51.100/24 – is learned from an X interface of the router connecting a customer – e.g. with AS64496 – and, at the same time, other prefixes – e.g. 203.0.113/24 and 192.0.2/24 – are received on the other peering interfaces Y and Z, and share the same origin AS – e.g. number 64496 – then a sort of flexibility is granted, which allows the three prefixes to be received rightfully on the X interface of the router. In conclusion, the principle is based on the possibility of expanding the legitimacy of the prefixes allowed on an interface (e.g. the customer's) to all those that have a single origin AS in common, regardless of the circumstance of them being learned by other interfaces.

When this document was drafted, there were no implementations of an EFP-uRPF algorithm by big vendors, despite a timid awareness-raising trend starting to manifest in international conventions.

10.8 NOTES ON THE BGPsec ARCHITECTURE

Another piece of the puzzle in the direction of a safer Internet is represented by BGPsec, resulting from a 20-year commitment of the community, and transitioned through other attempts, such as S-BGP (Secure Border Gateway Protocol), soBGP (Secure Origin BGP), psBGP (Pretty Secure BGP). Different approaches and similar tools to reach the purpose of restricting BGP's area exposed to attacks as much as possible. Among published studies, only BGPsec has been legitimated by the

SIDR working group of the IETF: the standard was published as RFC 8205 – *BGPsec Protocol Specification*, September 2017.

10.8.1 The protocol

BGPsec was born as an extension of BGP capable of introducing a level of security in the AS_PATH. The focus is the UPDATE message, which is enriched with a new attribute (BGPsec_PATH, optional and non-transitive) with the digital signatures of all the autonomous systems involved in the path. These signatures ensure the explicit approval of each AS, so that a certain AS_PATH can be added to an UPDATE message. The capacity of managing this attribute is specified during the BGP capability negotiation phase.

In any case, this protocol is based on the RPKI infrastructure – crucial to certify that a certain AS number and certain IP resources have actually been assigned to the operator using them. Each router of an AS that wants to implement BGPsec (i.e., capable of sending UPDATE messages containing the BGPsec_PATH attribute), must have a private key associated to the certificate of an RPKI router belonging to the same AS (which is not required when the UPDATE is received). Within the BGPsec_PATH attribute, we find both the Secure_Path containing information related to the AS_PATH to be added to the BGPsec UPDATE message, and the Signature_Block (one or two) with a so-called Signature Segment for each AS number of the Secure_Path. This signature, in the UPDATE message, is placed on the AS number to which the UPDATE is destined; consequently, if there is more than one BGP Neighbor, the router dealing with BGPsec must generate a BGPsec UPDATE message for each recipient.

Obviously, if the router configured to manage BGPsec receives an UPDATE message without the BGPsec_PATH attribute (i.e. a traditional UPDATE), it will propagate that message to its neighbors without adding the BGPsec attribute. Moreover, when forwarding the BGPsec_PATH attribute to neighbors within the AS (iBGP), the BGPsec-speaking machine is free to not modify it; vice versa, when forwarding on eBGP sessions, it must follow precise instructions. First of all, it must generate a new Secure_Path Segment by adding its own AS number, which must match the one stated in the Object field of the certificate used by the router with RPKI functions, which will then be used to check the digital signature placed by the BGPsec machine.

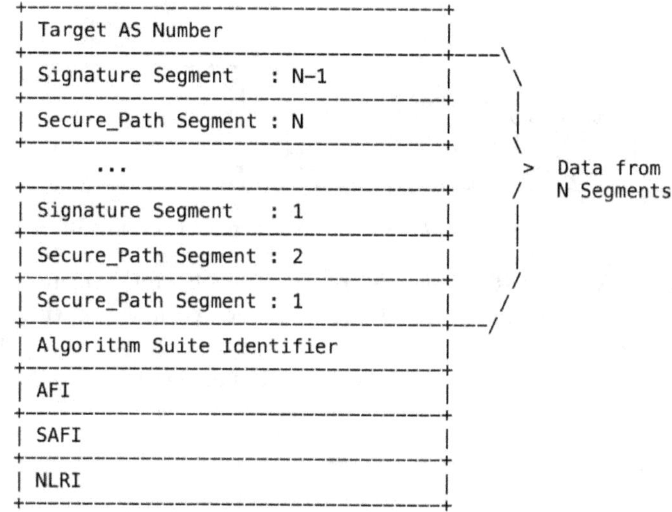

Figure 10.21 – Signature Block elements that need to be signed (from RFC 8205).

Right after, the latter generates the Signature_Block through a suite of algorithms that must be understood by the recipient of the UPDATE message, and adds a new Signature Segment that is added to the list of segments already present. The segment contains a digital signature coupling the prefix and the BGPsec_PATH attribute to the RPKI certificate of the router belonging to the same AS of the BGPsec machine.

All these elements must comply with a specific order, as shown in Figure 10.21, where:

- the Target AS Number is the AS we want to send the UPDATE message to;

- the Signature Segment and Secure_Path Segment are taken from the BGPsec_PATH attribute;

- the AFI, SAFI and NLRI values are taken from the MP_REACH_NLRI attribute.

When a router, capable of understanding BGPsec, receives an UPDATE message through an eBGP session, it has the option of validating the message to determine the authenticity of the information contained in the BGPsec_PATH attribute (as shown in Figure 10.22). This validation requires some data held by the router that manages the RPKI and, specifically, the AS number, the public key and the Subject Key Identifier of the RPKI certificate. In any case, after the validation process, there may be two outcomes: valid or invalid (alternatively). Therefore, this result will affect the BGP routing selection process, even after suitable local policies configured by the operators, when the UPDATE message is processed at the AS' edge.

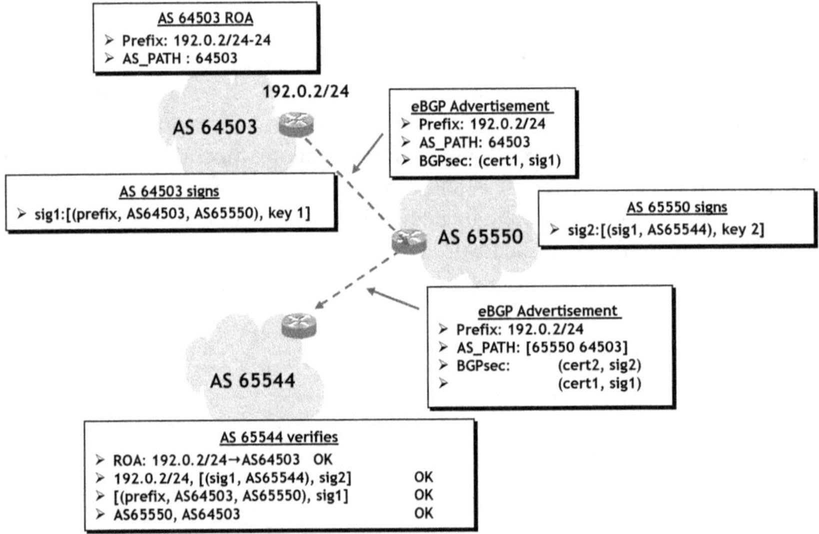

Figure 10.22 – Signature and verification within BGPsec.

When this book was published, the most recent software implementation of BGPsec was the one by the US NIST (National Institute of Standards and Technology), which modified the ExaBGP project by the UK company Exa Networks to create the open source code ExaBGPsec. There are also other experiences on GoBGP, Bird Internet Routing Daemon and Quagga Routing Suite.

10.9 ASPA

The proposed approach to address the AS_PATH integrity issue, without requiring widespread implementation of BGPsec, involves the utilization of Autonomous System Provider Authorization (ASPA) objects. This strategy leverages the RPKI to improve the security of BGP routing. The core concept revolves around each AS explicitly declaring its providers and upstream peers. This entails announcing the networks that are authorized to disseminate announcements regarding the AS's prefixes, as depicted in Figure 10.23. A broader participation of networks in this declaration increases the potential to identify misconfigurations and mitigate potential path disruptions.

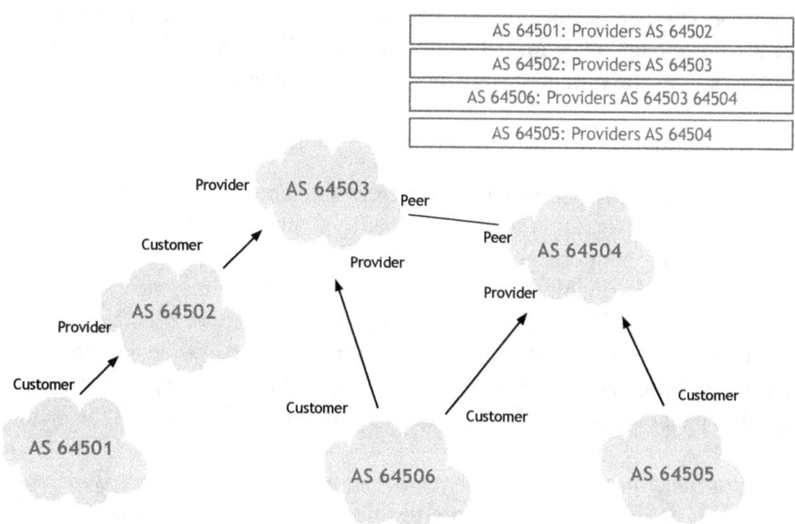

Figure 10.23 – Autonomous System Provider Authorization (ASPA).

ASPA is a digitally signed object that binds, for a selected AFI, a Set of Provider AS numbers to a Customer AS number (in terms of BGP advertisements not business), and are signed by the holder of the Customer AS. An ASPA object attests that a Customer AS Holder (CAS) has authorized Set of Provider ASes (SPAS) to propagate Customer's IPv4/IPv6 announcements onward, e.g. to the Provider's upstream providers or peers.

The primary distinction between ASPA objects and the RPKI framework lies in the types of objects considered. While ROAs in the RPKI indicate which AS numbers are permitted to advertise particular prefixes, ASPA objects focus on determining which AS numbers are authorized to broadcast the routes of a given AS number. Consequently, the goal is to provide a mechanism for specifying an AS's legitimate providers and publishing this information via the RPKI infrastructure. The ASPA implementation is still in development and has undergone testing within small networks to assess its efficacy. A global adoption timeline is anticipated around 2027. ASPA's primary emphasis is on averting route loss by ensuring that only approved providers can propagate routes associated with a specific AS.

10.10 CONFIGURATION VERIFIABILITY

The effectiveness of the measures described is directly proportional to the number of operators adhering to the application of routing security best practices. This is why, apart from a constant moral suasion by international organizations and a constant spreading and training for field professionals, it is essential to produce and distribute tools that can apply formal network configuration analysis and verification methods. In other words, especially in complex networks, we need an automatic device that formally checks configurations before they can be committed on BGP speakers.

In such a scenario, we need to define the policies to be observed in advance, that is, the cornerstones of the configuration that can never be in conflict with others within the same AS. This habit is very effective also when testing or implementing new installations, such as when expanding the borders of an AS, or consolidating new transit or peering relations.

10.10.1 The tools

Over the last twenty years, many tools have been created to check different BGP aspects.

Among them, Bagpipe allows autonomous systems to summarize their routing policies and to automatically check that these policies are correctly implemented in device configurations.

Just like FVR (Formally Verifiable Routing), which automatizes Internet routing configuration checks. Header Space Analysis checks the packet forwarding behavior on the data plane.

C-BGP is a simulator that establishes how traffic will be routed, based on a certain topology and set of configurations. Other studies cover the BGP convergence analysis, attempting to complete the technology frame that today still, despite its over thirty years of service, is the beating heart of the World Wide Web.

One of the most fortunate projects is Batfish, an actual network (and not just BGP) configuration analysis tool. Batfish holds an important role in this scientific field, as it is the basis for other studies that expanded its functions, such as Minesweeper and its successor, Plankton.

10.10.2 Batfish

Security, reliability and consistency summarize the work of Batfish in analyzing network device configurations. It can generate network models starting from the configurations, and looking for errors or inconsistencies with respect to previously defined network policies (including good practices). By way of example, without requiring any direct access to the routers, Batfish can be considered a link in the production chain that will lead to applying an error-free configuration.

Among Batfish functions, we can mention the configuration compliance check, e.g. the search for "defined but unused" or "undefined and used" parameters; MTU, AAA, NTP settings according to reference models; checking that the devices can be reached only through SSHv2 and that they do not have empty passwords.

Reliability can be ensured by checking that the devices' reachability is not undermined by single out-of-service connections or devices; and also by checking that some key services, such as the name resolution, is always working at global level. Security is also ensured by checking that some sensitive services can be reached only by specific networks or devices; that the connection between two specific points in the network complies with certain prerequisites, such as the existence of two different paths between them.

Another task is analyzing configuration changes to check that device reachability is always ensured, before and after the change; that modifications to access lists do not cause unexpected traffic damage; that the instructions from different vendors have equivalent functions.

10.10.3 How it works

Batfish is implemented according to a client-server architecture. The server (developed in java) is the actual check engine, and it can be installed via docker technology. On the other hand, a client software called pybatfish (developed in Python) is used to interact with the server and forward configurations and queries to it.

Today, the server supports many vendors, such as Arista, AWS, Cisco, Check Point, Cumulus, F5 BIG-IP, Juniper, Palo Alto Networks, Free-Range Routing (FRR), Fortinet. Indeed, Batfish can analyze multiple photos of a network – where 'network' means a set of devices, and 'photo' means a specific moment – allowing it to keep track of its changes over time.

The photos must be organized as text files in a certain way, within folders to which the pybatfish client will have access. Once the configurations have been submitted to Batfish via pybatfish, it is possible to execute queries to examine the network state and its parameters in detail.

Concerning the BGP analysis, it is possible to formulate queries to check the settings of each session, and look for problems and errors. By way of example, the INVALID_LOCAL_IP reply suggests that the local IP address configured for a certain neighbor does not belong to any active interface on the router; or NOT_ESTABLISHED refers to those sessions that, although configured correctly, have not been established due to a reachability issue, perhaps caused by a block introduced by an ACL.

Apart from checks on BGP, Batfish can work on multiple aspects: topology, routing table and forwarding table, packet forwarding, access lists and firewall rules, IPSEC tunnel, VXLAN, EVPN etc. For a monographic discussion on this topic, you can refer to the web resource, at https://www.batfish.org.

SUMMARY

Just like all routing protocols, BGP is subject to vulnerabilities that reduce its security against external attacks. In this chapter, apart from describing the most common types of attacks and vulnerabilities, we also covered a few simple countermeasures. Concerning session level attacks, we described MD5 authentication at TCP connection level, and a secure management of the IP TTL used to transport BGP messages. Concerning DoS/DDoS attacks, we saw how to set a limit to the number of prefixes received that a BGP Speaker receives from the different BGP Neighbors, and then a few advanced techniques, such as the traffic black-holing through the RTBH mechanism and the actions to undertake on traffic flows deemed harmful of the network, using the BGP FlowSpec. Another very important topic we saw is the RPKI architecture that allows validating the prefix origin. Lastly, we devoted a bit of space also to the validation of source IP addresses and to the BGPsec architecture. For all countermeasures, we saw the configuration aspects both in Cisco and in Juniper platforms, and a few actual Case Studies. Lastly, we included the state-of-the-art configuration verifiability aspects.

Worth remembering:

1. Attack types and the main vulnerabilities.

2. Possible countermeasures, such as MD5 authentication, limitation of the number of prefixes received, and secure management of the IP TTL used for BGP message transport.

3. RTBH and BGP FlowSpec mechanisms for protection against DDoS attacks.

4. RPKI architecture to validate the prefix origin.

5. Source IP address validation.

6. Countermeasure configuration in Cisco IOS and Juniper JUNOS environments.

7. Basic BGPsec architecture concepts.

8. Batfish and configuration verifiability.

11 – THE ROLE OF BGP IN MPLS SERVICES

The BGP/MPLS routing architecture – shortly described in Section 8.2.3 – is used by ISPs and in big Enterprise networks to provide several services. The best known and also the one that has had the greatest commercial success is the L3VPN (Layer 3 Virtual Private Network) service, that is, the option of connecting more sites of a single customer, emulating the operation of a private network. The L3VPN service is almost always offered in its unicast mode, but there are also IETF standards that allow exploiting the BGP/MPLS architecture for multicast L3VPN services.

NOTE: In this book, we will address the VPN service based on the BGP/MPLS model as L3VPN. To be precise, this is kind of stretching it, since the L3VPN name includes a broader range of technologies (e.g. GETVPN, DMVPN, etc.).

On the same routing architecture, we can also create L2VPN (Layer 2 Virtual Private Network) services, that is, services where the ISP directly transports the layer-2 frames of the customers (e.g. Ethernet, PPP, ATM, etc.), leaving the layer-3 control in the customer's hands. Among these, worthy of mention are circuit emulation services, which are used to achieve point-to-point (P2P) virtual connections to transport any kind of layer-2 frames, and Ethernet LAN emulation services, which are used to achieve layer-2 multipoint-to-multipoint (MP2MP) services, emulating the operation of an Ethernet switch.

Then, the same routing architecture can be used to transport IPv6 traffic. In this case, there are two relevant services:

- the 6PE service, used to transport IPv6 traffic through a BGP/MPLS transport architecture based on IPv4;

- the 6VPE service, which is an IPv6 extension of the L3VPN concept. In other words, with the 6VPE service, you can connect the IPv6 sites of a customer, emulating a private network service.

The key aspect of this architecture is that the configuration of all these services does not concern the inside of the IP/MPLS network in any way, thus making its implementation a lot simpler. The only service-specific configurations concern only the edge routers (PE routers, Provider Edge) i.e. those routers where the customer's connections (service users) end. Figure 11.1 below shows a summary diagram for BGP/MPLS services, and highlights the role of BGP, which carries out two fundamental control plane functions:

- signaling the MPLS service labels, that is, those labels a service corresponds to. A service label can be seen as an "instruction" for the outbound PE of the IP/MPLS network to execute a certain operation (e.g. do a lookup on a certain routing instance; forward the payload to a certain interface, etc.);

- auto-discovery, that is, determining the PEs where the sites of the same VPN instance are located.

Chapter 11

MPLS acts only on the data plane. The link between the control plane and the data plane are the service labels, which are advertised on the control plane, almost always via BGP, and used on the data plane as described earlier.

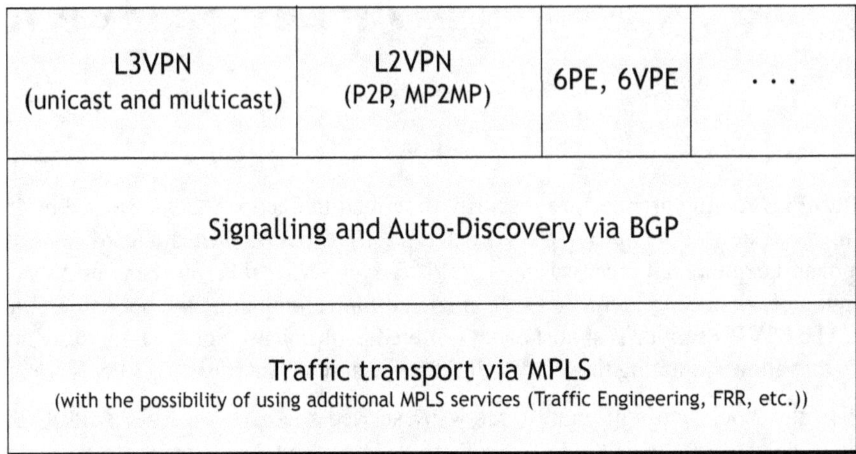

Figure 11.1 – MPLS services.

NOTE: Before reading this chapter, you need to be familiar with the MPLS standard and the related services.

11.1 BGP IN L3VPN SERVICES

As we mentioned in the introduction, in MPLS services, BGP plays a key role on the control plane. The reasons are essentially linked to the flexibility offered by BGP. In particular, BGP allows:

1. transporting routing information of non-IP prefixes, and also general info, using its multiprotocol extension (MP-BGP, see Paragraph 2.6);

2. associating parameters to the advertisements (e.g. several Community types);

3. associating one or more MPLS labels (service labels) to each advertisement.

These are BGP's characteristics that allow its use in L3VPN MPLS services (and not just there). In particular, BGP can be applied to the following contexts related to unicast L3VPN services:

- in the control plane, to exchange IPv4/v6 routing info between L3VPN sites, and for signaling the service labels;

- as routing protocol, to exchange information between the customers' sites and the Service Provider network (routing PE-CE);

- as an auto-discovery mechanism, to increase the service's scalability.

Then, BGP also plays another key role in the multicast L3VPN service, for which a new specific address-family has been defined, which we will only mention briefly, given its complexity.

11.1.1 Preface: L3VPN services

The idea of a L3VPN service based on the BGP/MPLS model, is basically a generalization of the BGP/MPLS routing architecture concept. The generalization consists of creating, within the edge router – which, in L3VPN jargon, are called PE (Provider Edge) routers – several routing instances, commonly called VRF (VPN Routing and Forwarding).

NOTE: Some manufacturers (e.g. Juniper) use the general "routing instance" name, of which VRFs are a specific type.

Routing information contained in a VRF is completely separate from that of the other VRFs. In a way, each PE router can be seen as a set of "virtual routers", each one of them dedicated to a L3VPN instance (although, it is not always like that, but these considerations go beyond the scope of this book). Traffic separation is physically ensured by associating a specific VRF to each physical interface of the PE accessed by customers, during the configuration phase.
The RIBs associated to the VRFs are populated:

- on one side, directly by the customer's routers – which, in L3VPN jargon, are called CE (Customer Edge) routers – which, as in a classic peer-to-peer model, exchange routing info with PE routers, using any kind of (static or dynamic) routing;

- on the other side, by the other PE routers, which exchange routing information to be installed on the relevant VRFs. The exchange of routing information between PEs is done through iBGP sessions between the different pairs of PEs.

NOTE: Actually, when it comes to exchanging routing information between PEs, it would be best – as we will see later on – to talk about MP-iBGP sessions, since they are internal BGP sessions that use its multi-protocol extension.

The general operation is summarized in Figure 11.2 below, which highlights two L3VPNs, VPN-A and VPN-B, with 3 sites each, located on 4 different PEs. Even if, for the sake of simplicity, in the figure all CEs have single-homed connections to the related PEs, in practice they are usually linked through multiple connections to more than one PE (usually two).

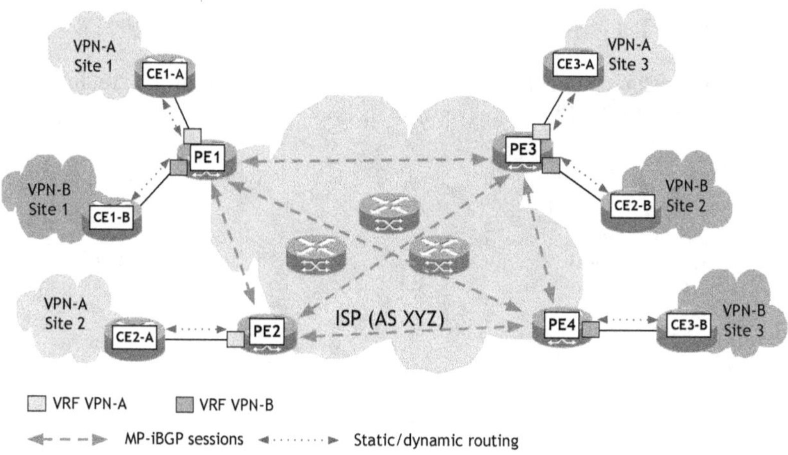

Figure 11.2 – Basic components of a L3VPN service.

Figure 11.3 below shows the logical diagram, from which we can see that the L3VPN service logically corresponds to a private network, with the routers connected to one another, with a complete mesh, in this example (any-to-any L3VPN service); however the service is very flexible, and also allows achieving different topologies (e.g. Hub-and-Spoke, Centralized Services, etc.) Some of the advantages of the L3VPN models include:

- L3VPN are simple and flexible to create (e.g. option of creating several topologies);

- option for customers to use arbitrary numbering plans;

- standard architecture (RFC 4364 – *BGP/MPLS IP Virtual Private Networks (VPNs)*, February 2006).

For these reasons, the L3VPN solution is the favorite one by the different ISPs.

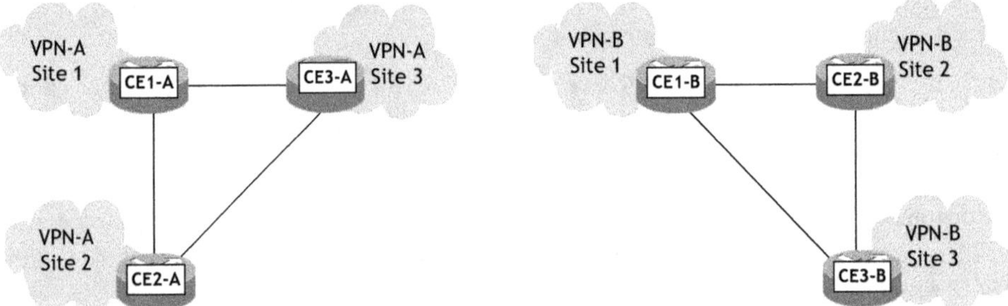

Figure 11.3 – Logical vision of an any-to-any L3VPN service.

11.1.2 The role of BGP in populating the VRFs

The key aspect that makes the entire L3VPN BGP/MPLS model work, is the VRF population, that is, which routing information to add. The VRF population issue must be tackled extremely carefully, because an IP subnet input error in a VRF compromises traffic separation between the L3VPNs, with severe impact on the service logic.

The RIBs/FIBs associated to the VRFs contain two types of IP subnets (Figure 11.4):

- Local: the subnets input locally through the routing protocol active on the PE-CE connection.

- Remote: the subnets received from the other PE routers, which distribute the IP subnets learned locally, using a PE-PE routing protocol.

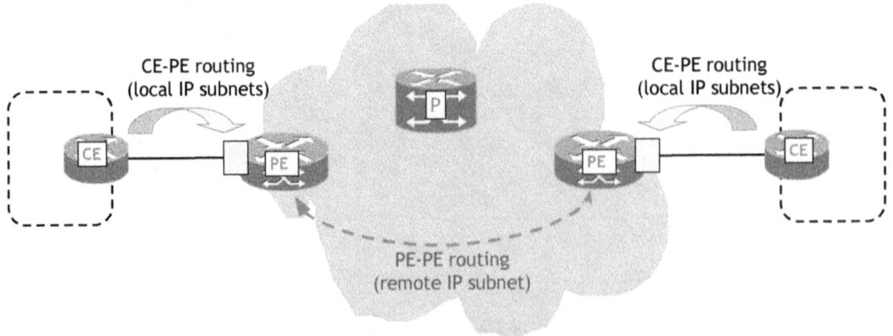

Figure 11.4 – VRF population.

Each PE router distributes its local routing info to the other PEs through the IP/MPLS backbone, using BGP's multiprotocol version (or, more correctly, iBGP, since the advertisement distribution between PEs occurs within the same AS). Since the IP subnets must be made known only to PE routers (and not to P routers, which, in the BGP/MPLS routing architecture, only connect PE routers between one another), the advertisements are exchanged through MP-iBGP sessions between each pair of PEs (or using Route Reflectors).

Remember that the option of using the BGP multiprotocol version – see Paragraph 2.6 – is negotiated between the two BGP Neighbor during the session initialization phase, using the optional Capabilities field in BGP's OPEN message. The Capability value field contained in the optional Capabilities field contains the two AFI and SAFI values. In the L3VPN BGP/MPLS model, it is AFI=1/2 (indicates IPv4/IPv6 prefixes) and SAFI=128 (indicates VPN-IPv4/VPN-IPv6 prefixes with MPLS label associated to them).

The input of local IP subnets into the VRFs does not require particular care, apart from the simple configuration of a routing protocol or static routes on the PE-CE connection. For reasons we will cover in the next section, the best protocol is BGP; in simpler cases, we can also use a static routing.

The most complex issues occur when managing remote IP subnets. In order for everything to work correctly, we need to solve two important issues:

- how to solve possible ambiguities, resulting from the use of overlapped numbering plans?

- How to determine in which VRFs we should input the remote IP subnets?

NOTE: L3VPN customers, since the service is an emulation of a private network, have the option of using arbitrary numbering plans. It is therefore possible for two or more customers to use overlapped numbering plans.

To solve the first issue, we need a tool that allows distinguishing identical IP subnets elonging to different L3VPN, which may occur due to L3VPN customers using arbitrary numbering plans. The need for some tricks to distinguish identical IP subnets from different L3VPNs arises from the fact that, if a PE router received two or more BGP advertisements related to the same IP subnet, they would all be treated by the BGP process as multiple advertisements of the same IP subnet, which is not true, since the advertisements refer to IP subnets belonging to different L3VPNs: consequently, BGP selects the best path only toward one of the IP subnets advertised, removing connectivity toward one or more L3VPN sites.

The trick used by the BGP/MPLS model to solve this issue is very simple: it adds an 8 byte code, called Route Distinguisher (RD), to the IP subnet. The association between RD and IP subnet forms a VPN-IPv4/v6 prefix. If two or more L3VPNs used the same IP subnet in their numbering plan, the PE, by adding the RD – which must be different for the two L3VPNs – transforms these IP prefixes into different VPN-IPv4/v6 prefixes. This ensures that, if two or more L3VPNs use the same IP subnet, it is possible to install more than one (different) path, one for each L3VPN, toward these prefixes.

The RD does not dictate any semantics to the IP subnet; actually, it does not contain any information on the origin of the advertisement of the IP subnet or on the set of L3VPNs to which the advertisement is distributed. The only purpose of the RD is to allow the BGP process to distinguish identical IP subnets belonging to different L3VPNs (and therefore to allow the creation of different paths toward L3VPN sites with the same IP subnet).

The RD's 8 bytes are divided into two fields: Type (2 bytes) and Value (6 bytes). RFC 4364 entails three RD formats, identified by the value of the Type field (comprising the two most significant bytes).

- Type=0: Value=Administrator (2 byte)+Assigned Number (4 byte), where:
    - Administrator=2 byte AS number (usually that of the ISP providing the service).
    - Assigned Number=Numbering space managed by the ISP.

- Type=1: Value=Administrator (4 byte)+Assigned Number (2 byte), where:
    - Administrator=IP address (usually PE's BGP RID).
    - Assigned Number=Numbering space managed by the ISP.

- Type=2: Value=Administrator (4 byte)+Assigned Number (2 byte), where:
    - Administrator=4 byte AS number (usually that of the ISP providing the service).
    - Assigned Number=Numbering space managed by the ISP.

In this book, unless otherwise specified, we will use the coding with Type=0. The RD value will always be indicated by two numbers, separated by ":", with the first number representing a 2 byte AS number, and the second one an arbitrary value managed by the ISP. For instance, RD=64500:1 represents an RD defined by an ISP with AS=64500. A VPN-IPv4/v6 prefix will be indicated by "RD:subnet-IPv4/v6" (e.g. 64500:1:198.51.100.0/24).

NOTE: When representing a VPN-IPv6 prefix, in order not to mistake the RD with a part of the IPv6 prefix, the RD is represented between square brackets. For instance, to represent the VPN-IPv6 prefix comprising the association of RD=64500:1 to IPv6 prefix 2001:db8:a::/48, we use the notation "[64500:1]:2001:db8:a::/48".

Figure 11.5 below summarizes how the VPN-IPv4 prefixes are generated (Note: the generation of IPv6 prefixes follows the same logic). They are created during the distribution of MP-iBGP advertisements. This usually occurs by manually configuring an RD value for each VRF (step 1 in the figure). Every time a PE receives from a CE the advertisement of a local IPv4 subnet (step 2 in the figure), the VPN-IPv4 prefix is created and advertised via MP-iBGP (step 3 in the figure). The PEs receiving the MP-iBGP advertisement, after the BGP selection process has been completed, and knowing which VRF(s) the advertisement will be imported into, remove the RD and add only the IPv4 prefix with the IP address used by the PE that sent the advertisement as Next-Hop to the VRF(s), to open the MP-iBGP session (step 4 in the figure).

Another issue is linked to BGP advertisement "filtering". Indeed, a PE, after receiving a BGP advertisement and executing the selection process, must decide in which VRF the <subnet IP; Next-Hop> pair would be stored, or, if the advertisement will not be added to any VRF, i.e. whether to reject it or not.

To this end, special parameters associated with each advertisement are used: the Route Targets (RT). The RT are parameters associated to each VPN-IPv4/v6 prefix exported by a PE. They are transported as BGP Extended Community attributes. The format of the BGP Extended Community attributes is specified by RFC 4360 – *BGP Extended Communities Attribute*, February 2006, and is similar to that of the Route Distinguishers. The attribute, with a total length of 8 bytes, is divided into two parts:

- Type: 1 or 2 byte.

- Value: 6 or 7 byte.

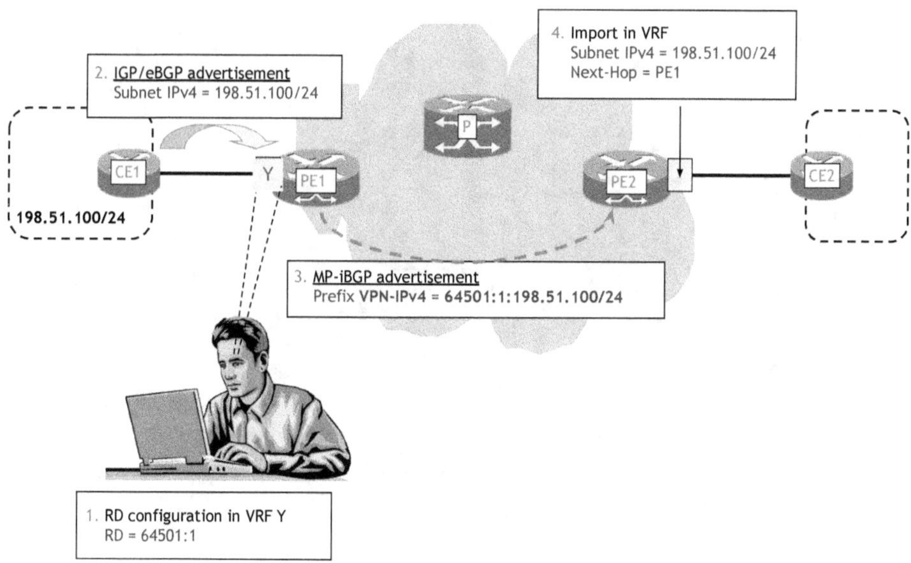

Figure 11.5 – VPN-IPv4 prefix generation.

RT-type BGP Extended Community attributes have a two byte Type field (see RFC 4360), with the second always equal to 0x02. The Value field has three possible formats:

- Type=0x00-02: Number-AS-2byte:nn format (e.g. 64501:123).

- Type=0x01-02: IP-address:nn format (e.g. 192.0.2.1:123).

- Type=0x02-02: Number-AS-4byte:nn format (e.g. 65540:123).

where nn is an arbitrary number available to the ISP. The last format is specified by RFC 5668 – *4-Octet AS Specific BGP Extended Community*, October 2009.

In this book, the RT value, unless otherwise specified, will always be indicated by two numbers, separated by ":", with the first number representing a 2 byte AS number (usually the ISP's), and the second one an arbitrary value managed by the ISP. For instance, RT=64501:1 represents an RT defined by an ISP with AS=64501.

The RT is the key element for a PE to filter the advertisements. Every VPN-IPv4/v6 prefix exported by a PE toward other PEs can contain more than one RT value, as needed. Furthermore, zero or more RT imports and zero or more RT exports can be configured in each VRF, with the following purpose:

- RT import: used to determine which prefixes to import into the VRF.

- RT export: used to determine which RT to associate to the advertisements exported by a VRF.

The fundamental rule that allows advertisement filtering by a PE is the following:
An advertisement exported by a PE is imported into a VRF of another PE if and only if at least one of the "RT import" values configured matches at least one RT present in the MP-iBGP advertisement received.

The advertisement filtering mechanism based on the RT is very powerful and flexible, and allows creating L3VPNs with different topologies. A classic, very common example is a completely

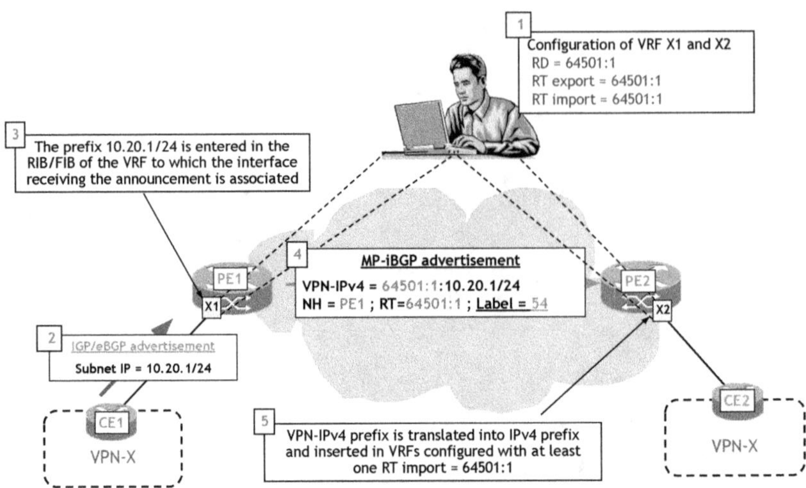

Figure 11.6 – Summarizing example of the control plane operation.

meshed topology. In order to achieve this service, it is sufficient to configure all the VRFs containing CEs from the same L3VPN with identical RT imports and RT exports. We will leave this test to you.

To conclude this session on the role of BGP in the control plane of the L3VPN BGP/MPLS service, let's see a summarizing example, shown in Figure 11.6 below. This example will also include a MPLS label.

In the example, the logical steps of the control plane are:

1. Configuring the VRFs of VPN-X with the RD values, RT import and RT export. In the figure: RD=64501:1, RT import=RT export=64501:1.

2. Router CE1, through a routing protocol (or static routing) configured on the PE-CE connection, advertises IP subnet 10.20.1/24.

3. In the RIB of VRF X1 on PE1, to which the (physical or logical) interface receiving the advertisement is associated, the new entry is created: <subnet IP=10.20.1/24; Next-Hop=CE1>.

4. The IP subnet is then exported via MP-iBGP to all the PEs within the network, and PE2 in particular. Actually, prefix VPN-IPv4=64501:1:10.20.1/24 is advertised. The MP-iBGP UPDATE message sent by PE1 has, as BGP Next-Hop attribute, the address used by PE1 as its own endpoint for the MP-iBGP session; moreover, it has RT=64501:1, configured in VRF X1 as RT export, associated to it and transported in a BGP Extended Community attribute. In the NLRI field of the MP-REACH_NLRI attribute, a MPLS label (Service Label, in the example equal to 54), associated to the VPN-IPv4 prefix, is also advertised, and its use is essential for correctly forwarding the packets at egress PE.

5. When the MP-iBGP advertisement reaches PE2, after executing the selection process, the latter cancels the RD and adds the triplet <subnet IP; Next-Hop; Label MPLS> (in the example <10.20.1/24; PE1; 54>) to all VRFs configured with at least a RT import=64501:1. Now, concerning this prefix, in the VRF, we will find the following info:

   - prefix: 10.20.1/24;

   - BGP Next-Hop: address used by PE1 as its own endpoint for the MP-iBGP session;

   - MPLS label (Service Label): 54.

With this information, and the information on the MPLS PE-PE paths, traffic can flow from one site to the other, within the same L3VPN. The data plane operation, although simple, lies outside the scope of this book, and will not be covered.

NOTE: Although the example shown in Figure 11.6 concerns a VPN-IPv4 prefix, the logic followed for VPN-IPv6 advertisements is the same. However, there is an important detail worthy of consideration, and concerning the BGP Next-Hop format. The BGP Next-Hop is transported in the Network Address of Next Hop field of the MP_REACH_NLRI attribute, rather than in the standard BGP NEXT_HOP attribute, which is not even added to the advertisement. This generates a very interesting question: the BGP Next-Hop is an IPv4 address, while, according to standard MP-BGP rules, in the Network Address of Next Hop field of the MP_REACH_NLRI attribute, the BGP Next-Hop should be added in the same format defined by the AFI code, that is, in the IPv6 format, for this specific case. To solve this issue, a specific IPv6 address format, compatible with the IPv4 format, is used: "**::ffff:IP-address**", i.e., the first eighty bits null, the sixteen following bits all set to '1', and the last thirty-two matching the IPv4 address. They are often represented with a mixed hexadecimal/decimal notation. For instance, IP address 192.168.0.1 is represented as "**::ffff:192.168.0.1**". The format is called IPv4-Mapped IPv6 Address and is shown in RFC 4291 – *IP Version 6 Addressing Architecture*, February 2006.

11.1.3 BGP as PE-CE routing protocol

To complete the framework of L3VPN service creation, we must go over the PE-CE routing implementation. Both Cisco and Juniper routers support several routing methods and protocols. In particular, routing can be static or dynamic.

Static routing is preferably used for single connections, where it is possible to quickly detect when the connection is out of service, and therefore uninstall the static route from the RIB and activate a possible backup. In those cases, detecting when a connection is out of service quickly and in a completely independent way from the underlying technology is paramount. And the BFD (Bidirectional Forwarding Detection) protocol – a quick Hello mechanism, specified by RFC 5880 – *Bidirectional Forwarding Detection (BFD)*, June 2010 – can help.

Concerning dynamic routing, Cisco and Juniper support all the main protocols, such as RIPv2, EIGRP (Cisco only), OSPF, IS-IS e BGP. Dynamic routing is usually preferred in the case of multi-homed connections. Among these protocols, the most used in practical applications is surely BGP, for at least three reasons:

- it has a very effective native anti-loop function, based on the AS_PATH check;

- thanks to its wealth of metrics (Local Preference, AS_PATH, MED, etc.), it allows implementing several routing policies, both for inbound and outbound traffic;

- continuity with the MP-iBGP protocol used in the ISP network, which prevents annoying redistribution issues from the PE-CE routing protocol into MP-iBGP.

If we want to implement BGP as a PE-CE routing protocol, the first thing to do is to choose whether to use eBGP or iBGP sessions. In the vast majority of practical cases, ISPs prefer the eBGP sessions; however, under certain situations, using iBGP is more convenient. We will see both solutions, and try to highlight their advantages and disadvantages.

If we decide to use eBGP sessions, the first thing to do is assigning an AS number to the CEs. The current best practice is to use private AS numbers. The private AS numbers defined by the IANA (Internet Assigned Numbers Authority) are contained within the interval [64.512, 65.534] for 2 byte AS number, and within the interval 4200000000, 4294967294 for 4 byte AS numbers (see RFC 6996 – *Autonomous System (AS) Reservation for Private Use*, July 2013).

Usually, CE's AS numbers are assigned by the ISP providing the L3 VPN service. The management of these numbers is completely arbitrary. RFC 2270 – *Using a Dedicated AS for Sites Homed to a Single Provider*, January 1998, recommends, for all sites of private customers of an ISP accessing via BGP, a single AS number. And this practice, which streamlines the management of AS numbers, is currently adopted by many operators.

The BGP PE-CE session is of the external (eBGP) type, since the two AS numbers PE and CE belong to are different. And, according to standard BGP rules, the IP addresses used for the sessions are those at the endpoints of the PE-CE connection.

Now, let's see the configurations on Cisco platforms:

<u>IOS XE</u>
PE(config)# **router bgp** *ISP-AS*
PE(config-router)# **address-family ipv4 vrf** *vrf-name*
PE(config-router-af)# **neighbor** *CE-IP-address* **remote-as** *CE-AS*
PE(config-router-af)# **neighbor** *CE-IP-address* **activate**

<u>IOS XR</u>
RP/0/RP0/CPU0:PE(config)# **router bgp** *ISP-AS*
RP/0/RP0/CPU0:PE(config-bgp)# **vrf** *VRF-name*
RP/0/RP0/CPU0:PE(config-bgp-vrf)# **address-family ipv4 unicast**
RP/0/RP0/CPU0:PE(config-bgp-vrf-af)# **exit**
RP/0/RP0/CPU0:PE(config-bgp-vrf)# **neighbor** *CE-IP-address*
RP/0/RP0/CPU0:PE(config-bgp-vrf-nbr)# **remote-as** *CE-AS*
RP/0/RP0/CPU0:PE(config-bgp-vrf-nbr)# **address-family ipv4 unicast**
RP/0/RP0/CPU0:PE(config-bgp-vrf-nbr-af)# . . .

And here are the configurations in JUNOS environment:

[edit routing-instances *VRF-name* **protocols bgp]**
group *group-name* {
  neighbor *CE-IP-address* {
    peer-as *CE-AS*;
  }
}

However, the choice of using eBGP sessions, following the recommendation by RFC 2270, poses an IP subnet distribution issue to the CEs. Indeed, according to BGP rules, in order to avoid the formation of routing information loops, the advertisements should never be distributed to routers belonging to ASes corresponding to the AS that generated the advertisement, or with an AS through which the advertisement has transited. Therefore, if two L3 VPN sites use the same AS number, and access via BGP to the IP/MPLS network, it is not possible to distribute the prefixes generated by one CE to another CE, since they would have the same AS number.

Figure 11.7 below summarizes this phenomenon. CE2 of VPN-X advertises to PE2, via eBGP, the reachability of network 10.12.2/24. The advertisement will have an AS_PATH attribute containing the AS number CE2 belongs to (=65501).

Now, according to the rules of the BGP protocol once the BGP selection process has been executed, and after ascertaining that the advertisement received has been chosen as the best path, this is automatically propagated on all MP-iBGP sessions (and also on eBGP ones, if applicable). During propagation via MP-iBGP, the AS_PATH attribute does not change.

When the advertisement reaches PE1, the latter executes the BGP selection process and, if the new advertisement is the new best path, it automatically propagates it on all eBGP sessions (and not on MP-iBGP ones). According to BGP's standard rules, when an advertisement is propagated on an eBGP session, the AS_PATH attribute contained in the BGP advertisement is updated, by adding its own AS number (=64501, the AS number of the ISP) on top of the list.

The AS_PATH of the advertisement sent to CE1 will contain values 64501 and 65501. Router CE1, upon receiving the advertisement, checks the AS_PATH field and applies the following BGP's standard rule: if the AS_PATH attribute contains at least one AS value matching its own AS number, the advertisement is rejected. In the example in the figure, the AS_PATH field contains values 64501 and 65501, and one of them (65501) matches CE1's value, which will therefore reject the advertisement. So CE1 won't see IP subnet 10.12.2/24.

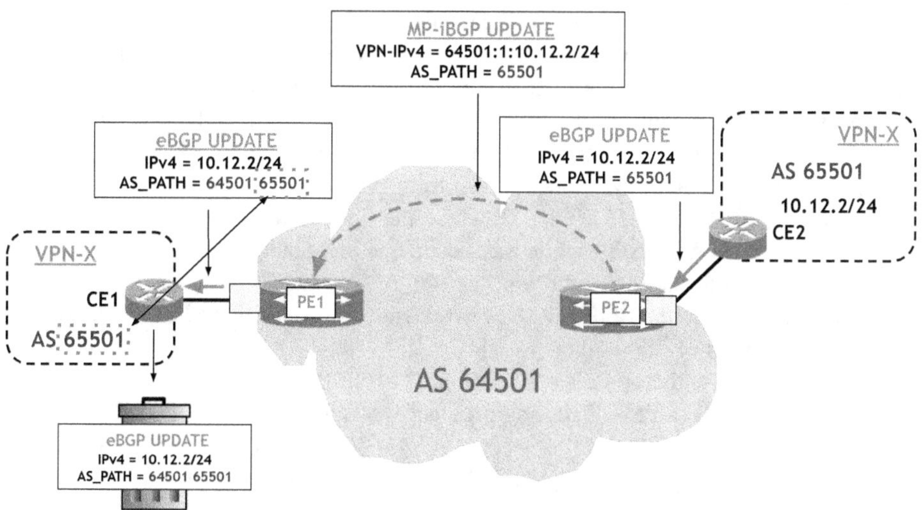

Figure 11.7 – Issue when using identical AS numbers.

There are several ways to solve this issue. The first, very simple method, is to equip CE with a default route, possibly propagated by the PE via eBGP, thus making transferring routing info from PE to CE unnecessary. However, sometimes CEs use the default route for other purposes, such as accessing an Internet gateway, so this solution may not be feasible.

The alternative is a function known as AS override, which does exactly what it says: it overwrites an AS. After enabling this function in the configuration, it allows a router to put its own AS number in place of the AS number of the BGP Neighbor in the current AS_PATH.

This function is configured on PE routers, and it should be activated any time the PE-CE routing is configured via eBGP, unless propagating the remote prefixes learned on the MP-iBGP sessions is considered superfluous, or the CEs use different AS numbers. The additional configurations to execute in Cisco and Juniper platforms are:

<u>IOS XE</u>
PE(config)# **router bgp** *ISP-AS*
PE(config-router)# **address-family ipv4 vrf** *vrf-name*
PE(config-router-af)# **neighbor** *CE-IP-address* <u>**as-override**</u>

IOS XR
RP/0/RP0/CPU0:PE(config)# **router bgp** *ISP-AS*
RP/0/RP0/CPU0:PE(config-bgp)# **vrf** *VRF-name*
RP/0/RP0/CPU0:PE(config-bgp-vrf)# **neighbor** *CE-IP-address*
RP/0/RP0/CPU0:PE(config-bgp-vrf-nbr)# **address-family ipv4 unicast**
RP/0/RP0/CPU0:PE(config-bgp-vrf-nbr-af)# <u>**as-override**</u>

JUNOS
[edit routing-instances *VRF-name* **protocols bgp group** *group-name* **neighbor** *CE-IP-address*]
<u>**as-override**</u>;

With these configurations, the PE router checks every eBGP advertisement, before sending it to the CE router, overwrites the CE's AS number in the AS_PATH with its own, and then, according to standard BGP rules, adds its own AS number to the AS_PATH field.

Going back to the example in Figure 11.7 above, the AS override function enabled in the eBGP session between PE1 and CE1, allows PE1 to rewrite the AS number contained in the AS_PATH of the advertisement received from PE2 (=[65501]), changing it from 65501 (i.e. the common AS number used by the L3VPN customers in the two sites with CE1 and CE2) into 64501 (i.e. the ISP's AS number). Router CE1 will then receive from PE1 an eBGP advertisement of IP subnet 10.12.2/24, with AS_PATH=[64501, 64501], where the first value 64501 is due to normal BGP procedures to update the AS_PATH, while the second one has changed from 65501 to 64501.

In conclusion, we would like to remind you that the AS override function is necessary only in those cases where access to the BGP/MPLS network is done via eBGP, and two or more sites use the same (public or private) AS number.

Even if used more rarely, there is also the option of using BGP in its iBGP version as PE-CE routing. The use of iBGP as PE-CE routing protocol was standardized by RFC 6368 – *Internal BGP as the Provider/Customer Edge Protocol for BGP/MPLS IP Virtual Private Networks (VPNs)*, September 2011, at first supported only by JUNOS, and much later (with a few limitations) by Cisco.

The characterizing aspect of the solution described by RFC 6368, apart from the option of using iBGP PE-CE sessions, is the possibility of transporting the BGP attributes locally defined by a CE on the IP/MPLS backbone, in a transparent manner. This means that it is possible to transport a Local Preference, Community, etc. values from a CE to another CE.

NOTE: This is analogous to what occurs when using OSPF as PE-CE routing protocol, where, through suitable Extended Communities, it is possible to preserve some of the characteristics of OSPF's Link State Advertisements.

The BGP attributes defined by a CE are transported in MP-iBGP advertisements through the new BGP ATTR_SET attribute (Attribute Type=128) defined by RFC 6368. Moreover, another important aspect is the fact that the BGP Next-Hop of the advertisements sent by the outbound PE to the target CE, is the PE side IP address of the PE-CE interface. And this is similar to what happens in standard eBGP sessions.

Using iBGP as PE-CE routing protocol requires some variations, with respect to standard BGP operation. The first is that CE's iBGP advertisement, when received by a PE, must be propagated to the other PEs, possibly through one or more Route Reflectors. In addition, the advertisements received by a PE from another PE, possibly through one or more Route Reflectors, must be propagated to the target CE (see RFC 6368, Section 3). In both cases, the Split Horizon principle – which prohibits the propagation of iBGP advertisements on other iBGP sessions – is violated. The second variation is that the BGP Next-Hop must match the outbound PE's, as in the eBGP sessions. And this goes against the basic rules for iBGP sessions, which never change the BGP Next-Hop (see RFC 6368, Section 6).

The advantage of using iBGP as PE-CE routing protocol is that there is no need for the AS override function, simply because the advertisements are generated by a CE with an empty AS_PATH, according to BGP's standard behavior, and therefore reach the target CE still with an empty AS_PATH.

The configuration of iBGP as PE-CE routing protocol differs slightly between JUNOS and IOS XE/XR. While in JUNOS, on the CE side, it is possible to use one's own AS number, in IOS XE/XR the same AS number as the ISP must be used on the CE side.

In IOS XE/XR, the additional command on the PEs is the following:

IOS XE

PE(config)# **router bgp** *ISP-AS*
PE(config-router)# **address-family ipv4 vrf** *vrf-name*
PE(config-router-af)# **neighbor** *CE-IP-address* **remote-as** *ISP-AS*
PE(config-router-af)# **neighbor** *CE-IP-address* **internal-vpn-client**
PE(config-router-af)# **neighbor** *CE-IP-address* **next-hop-self**

IOS XR

RP/0/RP0/CPU0:PE(config)# **router bgp** *ISP-AS*
RP/0/RP0/CPU0:PE(config-bgp)# **vrf** *VRF-name*
RP/0/RP0/CPU0:PE(config-bgp-vrf)# **neighbor** *CE-IP-address*
RP/0/RP0/CPU0:PE(config-bgp-vrf-nbr)# **remote-as** *ISP-AS*
RP/0/RP0/CPU0:PE(config-bgp-vrf-nbr)# **internal-vpn-client**
RP/0/RP0/CPU0:PE(config-bgp-vrf-nbr)# **address-family ipv4 unicast**
RP/0/RP0/CPU0:PE(config-bgp-vrf-nbr-af)# **next-hop-self**

Remember that the AS number of the BGP Neighbor (i.e. the CE) must match the AS number of the ISP, otherwise the iBGP sessions will not switch to the Established state. In IOS XR, if the AS is different, the configuration cannot even be executed. Also, notice the presence of the "**neighbor ... next-hop-self**" command. This command is necessary because Cisco's implementation does not follow the provisions of RFC 6368 (Section 6), which states that the BGP Next-Hop must match the outbound PE's. Indeed, by default, Cisco's implementation leaves as BGP Next-Hop the one of the PE originating the advertisement, which, since it cannot be reached by the target CE, would prevent the advertisement from being included in BGP's selection process.

In JUNOS, the additional commands are:

```
[edit routing-instances VRF-name]
routing-options {
    autonomous-system CE-AS independent-domain;
}
protocols {
    bgp {
        group group-name {
            type internal;
            neighbor CE-IP;
        }
    }
}
```

where CE's AS number can even be different from the ISP's AS number.

11.1.4 The auto-discovery function

In the original version of the L3VPN BGP/MPLS service, when a PE router sends a MP-iBGP UPDATE message to advertise an IP subnet of a L3VPN sites, the message is sent to all the other PEs within the network, even those with no sites of the L3VPN customer. This way of working generates a substantial waste of resources, both in terms of router CPU usage – due to the useless processing of a large quantity of MP-iBGP messages – and in terms of uselessly occupied bandwidth (even if this is less of a problem).

NOTE: The function introduced in this section is not just applicable to L3VPN services, but also more generally, to all VPN services based on the BGP/MPLS architecture (e.g. L3VPN IPv4 and IPv6 unicast and multicast, BGP-based VPLS, EVPN, etc.).

Figure 11.8 below highlights this issue. Usually, even in smaller networks, MP-iBGP UPDATE messages are sent through Route Reflectors (RR), which, as you may recall, propagate (reflect) the messages to their clients. In the example shown in the figure, PE1 has the VRFs of the 4 L3VPN instances A, B, C, D, while PE2 and PE3 have the VRFs of the L3VPN instances C, D and A, B, respectively. Every time PE1 sends an advertisement of a VPN-IPv4/v6 prefix, it will always be sent to PE2 and PE3, which will reject the L3VPN advertisements for which they have no sites connected. For instance, when PE1 sends an advertisement of a VPN-IPv4/v6 prefix of L3VPN A, it will be reflected by Route Reflector RR-1 both to PE2 and PE3. However, since PE2 does not have a VRF to import the advertisements of L3VPN A, it will reject the advertisement.

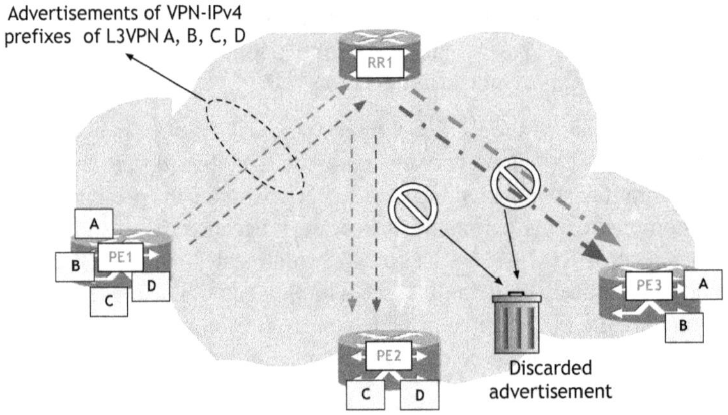

Figure 11.8 – Propagating MP-iBGP advertisements in a L3VPN BGP/MPLS service.

This way of operating poses a critical scalability issue. Think about an ISP with 10,000 L3VPN customers, and each one of them with 100 IP subnets on average, for a total of 1,000,000 IP subnets. Let's assume that, at a certain point, a new PE is added to the network, with the VRF associated with a new site of an existing L3VPN configured on it. Once the configuration is completed, the BGP process of the new PE sends to the RR(s) a BGP Route Refresh message to request the L3VPN routes, from which it will filter out anything that does not concern the new VRF. Since a PE often has two MP-iBGP sessions toward two RRs, it will receive a total of 2,000,000 VPN-IPv4 prefixes, when the PE is actually interested in a lot less – about one hundred.

The solution to this scalability issue is simple, and is known as BGP Constrained Route Distribution, standardized by RFC 4684 – *Constrained Route Distribution for Border Gateway Protocol/ MultiProtocol Label Switching (BGP/MPLS) Internet Protocol (IP) Virtual Private Networks (VPNs)*, November 2006. The basic idea is simple: every time a new VRF is created on a PE, the PE advertises all the RTs configured in the VRF as RT Imports to the RRs, via BGP. Obviously, these are peculiar advertisements that require the definition of a new BGP Address Family, which we will call RT Address Family, and hence the use of BGP's Multi-Protocol extension.

The new RT Address Family, as specified by RFC 4684, is characterized by AFI/SAFI values=1/132, and the NLRI field of the MP_REACH_NLRI and MP_UNREACH_NLRI attributes is coded as follows:

```
+-----------------------------------+
| origin as          (4 octets)     |
+-----------------------------------+
| route target       (8 octets)     |
+                                   +
|                                   |
+-----------------------------------+
```

where the "**origin as**" field contains the AS number of the router generating the advertisement, and the "**route target**" field the RT value advertised. Notice that the "**origin as**" field is preset to support 4 byte AS numbers.

With this information, the RRs create a PE↔RT Import map, which defines, for each PE, what RT Imports are configured on the different VRFs of the PE. We have finally reached the solution to our issue: when an RR receives an advertisement of a VPN-IPv4/v6 prefix, it compares the RTs contained in the advertisement with the PE↔RT Import map, and then propagates the advertisement only to the relevant PEs, that is, those that have at least one RT Import matching at least one RT contained in the advertisement.

NOTE: This solution can be applied also without RRs, by enabling the RT Address Family on each MP-iBGP session, between each pair of PEs.

In the most common use of RR, to further optimize the advertisement distribution of the RT Address Family, it is possible to avoid any advertisement reflection. Indeed, with a similar topology, only the RRs need to know the PE↔RT Import map. In order to achieve this goal, it is sufficient for the RRs to advertise the equivalent of a default route, obtained by setting all fields of the NLRI to zero (Note: later on, we will refer to this peculiar default route with the notation "RT default route", which has a "0:0:0/0" structure). In a way, it is like if the RRs told all the PEs: send me all your L3VPN advertisements, and we will optimize the distribution.

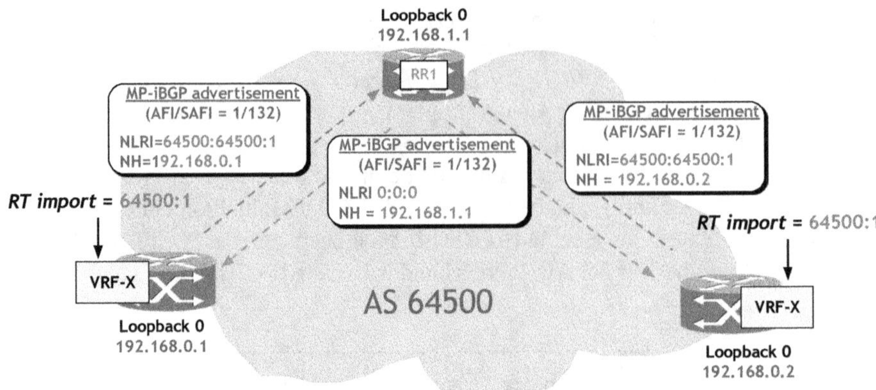

Figure 11.9 – RT Address Family advertisements with Route Reflector.

Figure 11.9 shows the exchange of advertisements of the new RT Address Family, with a RR. Obviously, this function must be supported both by PE and RR, and is negotiated when the MP-iBGP session is opened, through the BGP Capabilities. In any case, when dealing with an RR that does not support this function and others that do, you can make both L3VPN advertisement propagation methods – the standard (inefficient) one and the optimized one covered in this section – coexist.

There are many benefits to this optimization of the L3VPN BGP/MPLS control plane:

- lower number of MP-iBGP advertisements propagated by the RRs;

- less PE's CPU use and lower bandwidth usage, due to the lower number of MP-iBGP advertisements received;

- lower BGP convergence times.

Cisco and Juniper routers have been supporting this function for quite some time.

In Cisco IOS XR, the RT Address Family is enabled via the "**address-family ipv4 rt-filter**" command, within the BGP configuration. This command can be complemented with the "**default-originate**" option, to advertise the RT default route. (Note: in some IOS XR versions, no specific command to generate the RT default route is required, as it is automatically generated by the RRs). Remember that, by default, in Cisco IOS XR, the RRs do not reflect the advertisements of the RT Address Family.

NOTE: In Cisco platforms, the command to enable the RT Address Family uses the "**ipv4**" keyword, since the AFI of the RT Address Family is equal to 1, and identifies the IPv4 address family. However, this is misleading, since the BGP Constrained Route Distribution function – as mentioned in the note at the beginning of this section – applies to any kind of VPN services, as long as they are based on a BGP control plane. Therefore, the use of the "**ipv4**" word is a little ambiguous (at least in our opinion!).

In JUNOS, the RT Address Family is enabled via the "**set family route-target**" command, within the BGP configuration. This command can be complemented with the "**advertise-default**" option, to advertise the RT default route. Remember that the advertisement of the RT default route, automatically implies that the advertisements of the RT Address Family are not reflected by the Route Reflectors.

11.1.5 Notes on BGP's role in multicast L3VPN services

Next-generation multicast L3VPN services – from now on indicated as MVPN (Multicast VPN) – follow a model similar to unicast L3VPN: they use BGP on the control plane and MPLS in the data plane.

The control plane of a MVPN model must perform three important functions:

- Auto-Discovery. In unicast L3VPN, there is no need for any auto-discovery mechanism: a PE learns about the existence of a remote website when it receives, from the PE where the site is located, MP-iBGP advertisements of networks within the site. The auto-discovery mechanism – as we have seen in Section 11.1.4 above – is only implemented to optimize the distribution of the advertisements of VPN-IPv4/v6 prefixes. MVPNs, on the other hand, need to know the position of multicast traffic sources and receivers in advance.

- Signaling of PIM JOIN/PRUNE messages between MVPN websites: the new MVPN model uses MP-iBGP sessions. On the other hand, the (old) Draft-Rosen model used PIM adjacencies between PEs. (Note: RFC 6037 – *Cisco Systems' Solution for Multicast in BGP/MPLS IP VPNs*, October 2010, which formalized the so-called Draft-Rosen, has been moved to the "Historic" category).

- Signaling of LSP MPLS type to be used on the data plane (P-Tunnel): the new MVPN model supports P-Tunnels MPLS-based. This choice is deemed better, thanks to the wealth of functions supported by the MPLS protocol (Traffic Engineering, Fast ReRouting, QoS support, etc.). In any case, the model includes the option of using P-Tunnels based on the PIM protocol, as in the Draft-Rosen. This is possible because, in the new MVPN model, there is a clear separation between control plane and data plane.

In order to exchange routing (multicast) information required for the new MVPN model to work, the new Address Family BGP MCAST-VPN has been defined, with code SAFI=5 associated with it. The AFI code is still 1 for the IPv4 address family, and 2 for the IPv6 address family.

For the MVPN model operation, 7 new types of NLRI have been defined, whose general format is shown in Figure 11.10 below (TLV coding), and whose meaning is not relevant for the purposes of this book.

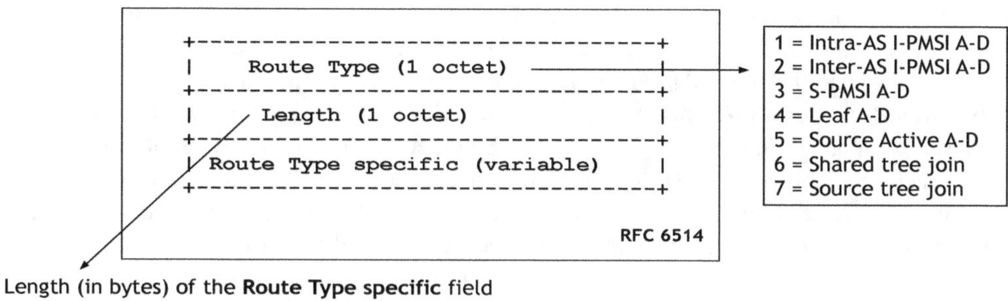

Figure 11.10 – General NLRI format for the Address Family MCAST-VPN.

11.2 BGP IN L2VPN SERVICES

In L2VPN services, BGP plays a role only in LAN emulation services, i.e. multipoint-multipoint services (MP2MP), allowing to emulate the operation of an Ethernet switch (see the next section). LAN emulation services are basically executed in two ways – the standard way, known as VPLS (Virtual Private LAN Service), and the more modern and efficient way, known as EVPN (Ethernet VPN) model. BGP plays a crucial role in both models.

The interesting aspect of BGP in this context, is that, differently from what we have seen until now, BGP advertisements do not contain layer-3 routing information (e.g. advertisements of IPv4/v6, VPN-IPv4/v6 prefixes), but rather layer-2 (and also layer-3) information, or data on MPLS labels to be used, or simple auto-discovery and other parameters. This is another aspect that highlights BGP's versatility, which is far from a simple protocol to advertise routing information; it is a protocol that can also advertise general information.

11.2.1 Preface: L2VPN services

A layer-2 VPN (L2VPN) is an overlay VPN, where the shared network is (almost always) IP/MPLS.

Basically, the IP/MPLS network just transports layer-2 frames in a "transparent" manner, from a customer device to the other, using MPLS's multiprotocol property. For those customers using the system, it is like having their own layer-2 private network where they have complete control over the layer 3.

There are two variants offered by L2VPN services:

- circuit emulation: they are point-to-point (P2P) services that allow emulating a virtual channel on an IP or IP/MPLS network;

- LAN emulation: they are multipoint-to-multipoint (MP2MP) services that allow emulating the operation of an Ethernet switch.

Circuit emulation services can be applied to different layer-2 types: Ethernet, ATM, Frame Relay, PPP, etc. Just to get a "physical" vision of the service, let's assume that a customer with two branches geographically distant from one another, wants to connect the two CE routers of its two branches using two Ethernet interfaces. The circuit emulation service allows to do this, by emulating an Ethernet connection between the two routers. In a way, from a connection standpoint, it is as if the two routers were one next to the other, connected by a crossover Ethernet cable.

On the other hand, LAN emulation services allow emulating an Ethernet LAN on an IP/MPLS network. Just like point-to-point services, the IP/MPLS network only transports layer-2 frames in a transparent manner (in this case, they must be Ethernet) from one router to another.

For those customers using the system, it is like having their own layer-2 private network where they have complete control over the layer 3. Just to get a "physical" vision of the service, let's assume that a customer with several branches geographically distant from one another, wants to connect the CE routers of its branches using several Ethernet interfaces. Multipoint-to-multipoint services allow this, by emulating an Ethernet switch that connects the routers via LAN. In a way, from a connection standpoint, it is as if all the routers were one next to the other, connected by a straight Ethernet cable to an Ethernet switch.

11.2.2 BGP in the VPLS model

The VPLS model is the standard model used to create LAN emulation L2VPN services. Despite a few drawbacks – the main being the lack of a multihoming function – it is very much used in practical applications, since it has been the first introduced in production networks.

The VPLS model Control Plane carries out the two following functions:

- discovery process: used to determine in which PE the VSI (Virtual Switch Interface) of the same VPLS instance is present;

- pseudowire signaling: used to establish the VC Labels associated with the pseudowires.

NOTE: VC label – where VC stands for Virtual Circuit – is the name used for service labels in L2VPN services. They have the same role as in L3VPN services, that is, they are instructions on how to execute the service for PEs.

A PE can discover the other PEs taking part in the same VPLS instance either through a manual configuration, or through an automatic discovery process (auto-discovery).

The manual configuration is a configuration-intensive approach, especially if there are many PEs taking part in the same VPLS instance, due to the need for a complete mesh of pseudowires between the PEs. Then, when a PE is added/removed, the configuration on all PEs must be changed. Through the auto-discovery process, each PE automatically determines – through a certain protocol – what other PEs take part in the same VPLS instance.

For the VPLS model Control Plane, the IETF defined two alternative standards:

- RFC 4761 – *Virtual Private LAN Service (VPLS) Using BGP for Auto-Discovery and Signaling,* January 2007: uses BGP for both functions – discovery and pseudowire signaling;

- RFC 4762 – *Virtual Private LAN Service (VPLS) Using Label Distribution Protocol (LDP) Signaling,* January 2007: uses LDP for signaling, and leaves complete freedom on the auto-discovery protocol used (BGP, RADIUS server, etc.).

Cisco and Juniper implementations support both standards, but they can also adopt mixed solutions, such as BGP for auto-discovery and LDP for signaling.

One of the distinctive elements for using BGP in VPLS's control plane is the support of the auto-discovery function. The mechanism defined by RFC 4761 is very similar to that used in L3VPNs, which uses Route Targets (RT), with the same semantic used for L3VPNs. Every PE discovers to take part in a certain VPLS instance by comparing the RT contained in MP-iBGP advertisements, with the RT configured in their own VSI (Virtual Switch Interface – analogous to VRFs in L3VPN services). Since the PEs taking part in the same VPLS instance have a full mesh of pseudowires, a single RT for each VPLS is enough. Therefore, the RT is actually an identifier of the VPLS instance.

A PE advertises (via MP-iBGP) its belonging to a VPLS instance, including the RT in the BGP UPDATE messages. Just like in L3VPN BGP/MPLS, the RT is used to accept or reject the BGP UPDATE message. Moreover, a PE that no longer takes part in a VPLS instance, withdraws all the advertisements sent with the RT identifying that VPLS.

To signal the VC labels of the pseudowires, BGP uses specific BGP UPDATE messages sent on MP-iBGP sessions. Based on BGP's use – if used only as auto-discovery tool or both as auto-discovery and signaling tool – two different Address Families are used, identified by the same AFI/SAFI codes=25/65: BGP-AD and VPLS-BGP.

The BGP-AD and VPLS-BGP Address Families are activated through the following configuration commands:

<u>IOS XE</u>
PE(config)# **router bgp** *AS-number*
PE(config-router)# **address-family l2vpn vpls**
PE(config-router-af)# **neighbor** *peer-IP-address* **activate**
PE(config-router-af)# **neighbor** *peer-IP-address* **send-community extended**

<u>IOS XR</u>
RP/0/RP0/CPU0:PE(config)# **router bgp** *ISP-AS*
RP/0/RP0/CPU0:PE(config-bgp)# **address-family l2vpn vpls-vpws**
RP/0/RP0/CPU0:PE(config-bgp)# **neighbor** *peer-IP-address*
RP/0/RP0/CPU0:PE(config-bgp-nbr)# **address-family l2vpn vpls-vpws**

<u>JUNOS</u>
[edit protocols bgp group *group-name*]
family l2vpn {
    signaling;
}

The structure of the information contained in the NLRI field – which, as you may recall, in BGP's multiprotocol version, is contained in the MP_REACH_NLRI attribute – is shown in Figure 11.11.

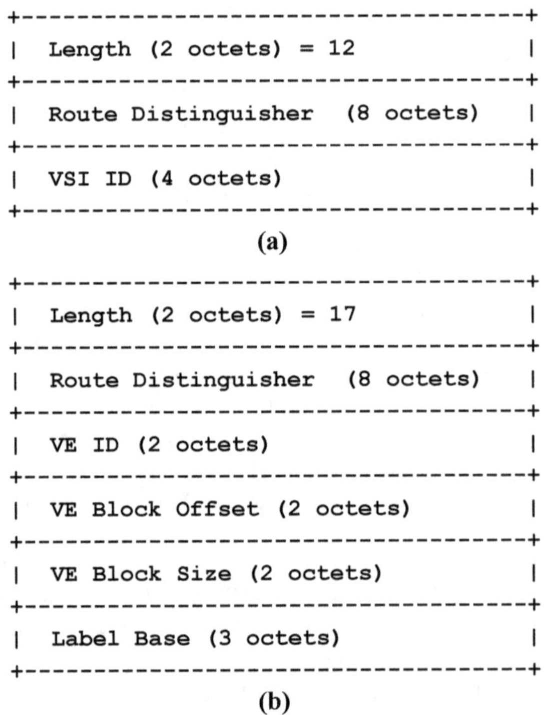

Figure 11.11 – NLRI of the BGP-AD (a), and VPLS-BGP (b) Address Families.

The BGP Neighbor receiving the BGP UPDATE message recognizes if it belongs to one or the other Address-Family from the value of the "**Length**" field, which can only be 12 for the BGP-AD Address Family, and 17 for the VPLS-BGP Address Family.

Both types of NLRI contain a Route Distinguisher (RD), with the same format and use as the one we saw for L3VPN.

For the BGP-AD Address Family, the NLRI, apart from the RD, also contains a specific router VSI-ID, which differs for each router. Usually, in major manufacturers' implementations, the BGP RID is used as VSI-ID.

In the case of the VPLS-BGP Address Family, the NLRI structure is more complex. In particular, it conveys two kinds of information:

- the VE ID (VPLS Edge ID), which is an identifier associated with the PE taking part in the VPLS instance. The VE ID must be established based on the configuration, after correctly planning the service;

- three fields, VE Block Offset (VBO), VE Block Size (VBS) and Label Base (LB), which are used to manage the VC Labels that remote PEs can use to send traffic toward the PE sending the advertisement.

For signaling the VC Labels, each PE should send a different advertisement to each remote PE, part of the same VPLS instance. For instance, if the VSIs of a certain VPLS were present in 10 PEs, each PE should send 9 BGP advertisements to all the other 9 PEs, each one containing a different VC Label. To save on the quantity of BGP advertisements and on CPU time, BGP-based VPLS signaling uses a method based on sending blocks of labels, giving each remote PE the option of determining the VC label to be used for traffic toward the PE issuing the BGP advertisement. This allows drastically reducing the quantity of BGP advertisements. For instance, in the case of a VPLS instance with VSI on 10 PEs, it would be sufficient to send only one BGP advertisement, replicated 9 times, to reduce CPU usage times. In the case of a Route Reflector, the advertisement becomes only one per each Route Reflector, thus reducing also the quantity of BGP advertisements. The calculation method to determine the VC Label by the remote PEs must ensure that there are no overlaps, meaning that each remote PE must determine, within the block received, a different VC Label.

For greater flexibility, a PE has the option of advertising more than one block with different length. The VBO is used to identify the first label of each block. The length of each block is based on the number of sites of the VPLS instance. In practice, it is often oversized, to take future extensions into accounts. If the VC Labels of a block are no longer sufficient, a PE advertises also another block.

Each block of VC Labels advertised by a PE is identified by three parameters (contained in the three VBO, VBS and LB fields of the NLRI, respectively):

- VBO: identifies which block should be used.

- VBS: the number of MPLS labels of the block.

- LB: the value of the first MPLS label.

After receiving this information, a remote PE determines the VC Label to use to send the Ethernet frames toward the PE that sent the advertisement, in the following way:

- Based on its own VE ID, it determines the block to use, by comparing $VBO \leq VE\ ID \leq VBO + VBS - 1$.

- It determines the output VC Label through the following calculation: $VC\ Label = LB + VE\ ID - VBO$.

Also, a PE determines the VC Label on which to expect the arrival of the frames from a remote PE, through the following calculation: Remote LB + local VE ID - remote VBO. To clarify this mechanism, let's see an example. Figure 11.12 below shows the first part of an example of a VPLS instance with three sites, identified by VE ID 1, 2 and 3. Notice that the website located on PE1 has two CEs, with a single VE ID. The VE ID identifies the entire site, and not the single CE.

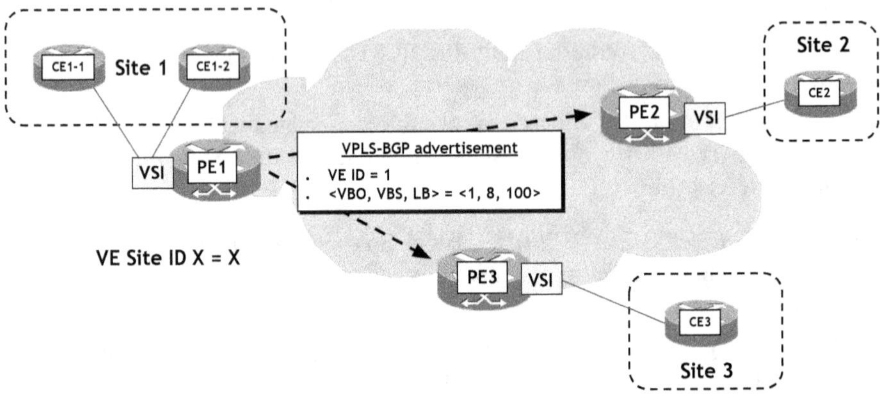

Figure 11.12 – Example of how to use the MPLS label block mechanism.

Router PE1, connected to site 1, sends a MP-iBGP advertisement of the VPLS-BGP Address Family to the other PEs taking part in the VPLS instance (in the figure, PE2 and PE3). The advertisement contains the VE ID in the NLRI field, and the triple: <VBO, VBS, LB>=<1, 8, 100>. Upon receiving the advertisement, the two remote PEs – PE2 and PE3 – determine the VC Label to use for the frames sent to PE1. For instance, PE2 executes the following operations:

- identifies the block to use. Since 1 (=VBO) ≤ 2 (=VE ID) ≤ 1 (=VBO) + 8 (=VBS) - 1, uses the block with VBO=1 (currently the only one available);

- determines the VC Label toward PE1: VC Label=remote LB+local VE ID-remote VBO=100 +2–1=101.

The same operations executed by PE3 lead to VC Label=102 used by PE3 for the frames sent toward PE1. Figure 11.13 below shows the MP-iBGP advertisements of the VPLS-BGP Address Family sent by PE2 and PE3. Following the same steps we saw for PE2, you can easily determine the VC Labels that PE1 uses to send frames to PE2 and PE3.

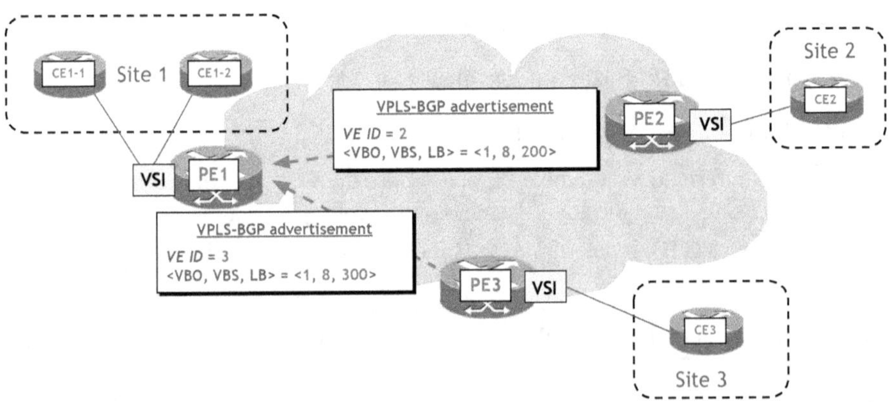

Figure 11.13 – MP-iBGP advertisements of the VPLS-BGP Address Family sent by PE2 and PE3.

Figure 11.14 below shows all the VC labels determined by each PE after the advertisements of the VPLS-BGP Address Family sent by PE1, PE2 and PE3 (shown in the two previous figures) have been exchanged. We will leave checking their correctness to you.

Notice that the length of the label block advertised (in the example, equal to 8), is sufficient to create a VPLS with up to 8 sites. Let's assume that the VPLS grows to 12 sites. What would happen? All PEs advertise another block, with length=8. This new block will have VBO=9, to indicate that the second block starts from the ninth label, out of a total of 16 labels.

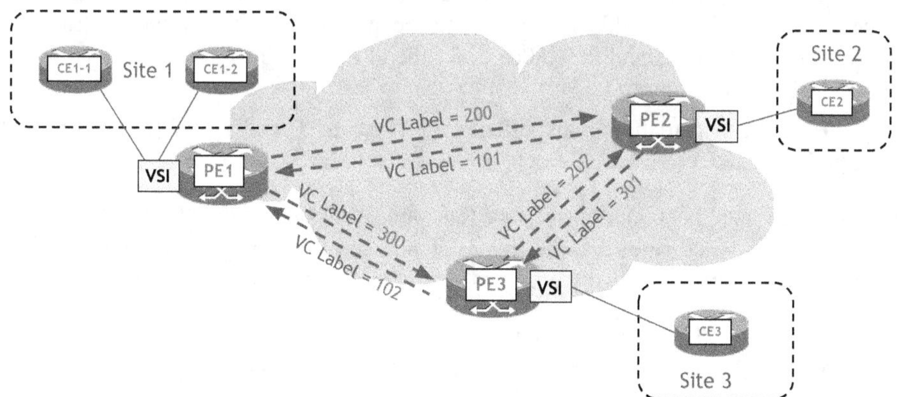

Figure 11.14 – VC labels used to forward traffic on the pseudowires.

Let's now see how a new site – for instance that with VE ID=10 – connected to PE10, determines the VC Label to use for the frames toward PE1. Let's assume that PE1 and PE10 advertise the two following blocks, respectively:

- PE1: 1st block <VBO, VBS, LB>=<1, 8, 100>; 2nd block <VBO, VBS, LB>=<9, 8, 150>;

- PE10: 1st block <VBO, VBS, LB>=<1, 8, 1,000>; 2nd block <VBO, VBS, LB>=<9, 8, 1,050>.

PE10 executes the following operations:
- identifies the block to use. Since 9 (=VBO) ≤ 10 (=VE ID) ≤ 9(=VBO)+8 (=VBS)-1, it uses the block with VBO=9 (the second block advertised by PE1);

- determines the VC Label toward PE1: VC Label=remote LB+local VE ID-remote VBO=150 + 10- 9=151.

Following the same logic, PE1 determines the VC label to use for the frames toward PE10 as follows:

- identifies the block to use. Since 1 (=VBO) ≤ 1 (=VE ID) ≤ 1 (=VBO) + 8 (=VBS) - 1, uses the block with VBO=1;

- determines the VC Label toward PE10: VC Label=remote LB+local VE ID– VBO=1,000 + 1- 1=1,000.

The pseudowire between PE1 and PE10 will have VC Labels 1,000 for the frames sent by PE1 to PE10, and 151 for the frames sent by PE10 to PE1.

Using this data, you can practice and determine, for instance, the VC labels between PE12 (VE ID=12) and PE2, between PE9 (VE ID=9) and PE12, etc.

The BGP UPDATE messages used in the VPLS model, apart from the MP_REACH_NLRI attributes, and standard BGP attributes (e.g. AS_PATH, NEXT_HOP, ORIGIN, etc.), contain two Extended Community attributes, one of which conveys information on the RT, and the other depends on the specific Address-Family.

In the case of the BGP-AD Address Family, the second Extended Community attribute, with Type field (first 2 bytes) equal to 0x000a, transports a value of L2VPN-ID (called "Two-octet AS specific Layer 2 VPN Identifier "in RFC 6074 – *Provisioning, Auto-Discovery, and Signaling in Layer 2 Virtual Private Networks (L2VPNs)*, January 2011) with the "AS:number" format.

In the case of the VPLS-BGP Address Family, the second Extended Community attribute, with the Type field (first 2 bytes) equal to 0x800a and called "Layer 2 info", transports some service information, such as (see Figure 11.15):

- Type of layer-2 encapsulation, transported in the "**Encaps Type**" field. For the VPLS model, "**Encaps Type**"=19.

- Two Control Flags, contained in the two less significant bits of the "**Control Flags**" field. Flag C, if set to 1, indicates that the frames sent to the PE must contain the Control Word. Flag S, if set to 1, indicates that the frames sent to the PE must be in sequence.

- The MTU of the PE interface facing CE side, contained in the "**Layer-2 MTU**" field. Remember that, for a pseudowire to be created, the MTUs of the endpoint ACs (Attachment Circuit) must match.

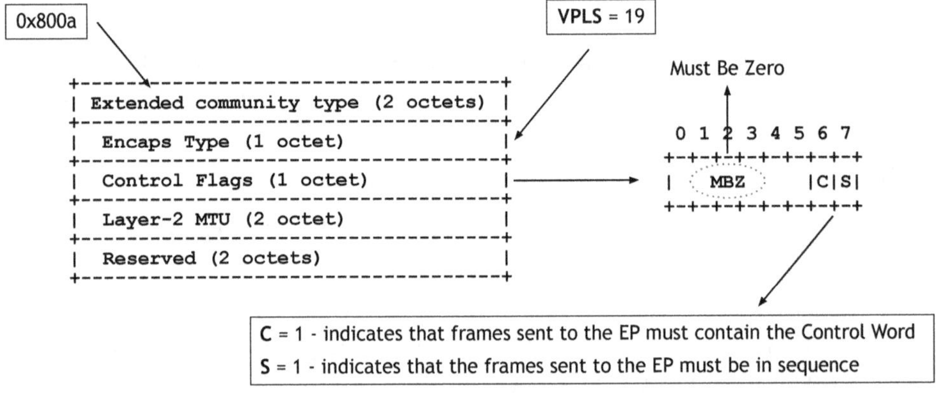

Figure 11.15 – Format of the Extended Community associated to MP-iBGP VPLS-BGP advertisements.

What control plane should we use? There are no specific rules, it all comes down to scalability. In very small networks, with less than 10 PEs and few VPLS instances (say, less than 5), it may be convenient to use the LDP (Label Distribution Protocol) for manual signaling and discovery.

Using BGP both for signaling and auto-discovery is convenient in medium-large networks, with many VPLS instances – the typical ISP network scenario.

In this kind of networks, BGP scalability is ensured by the presence of the Route Reflectors, which are usually employed also for other MPLS services (e.g. L3VPN), and that can be exploited also to create VPLS instances.

The mixed solution – LDP for signaling and BGP for auto-discovery – is not widely employed, because it does not offer advantages compared to the BGP-only solution, and it also adds another protocol (LDP).

11.2.3 BGP in the EVPN model

When it comes to LAN emulation services, the VPLS model has many drawbacks that prevent its use in advanced scenarios of major interest, such as the interconnection of Data Centers (a service often called DCI, Data Center Interconnection). This is why a new model for LAN emulation services – known as EVPN (Ethernet VPN) has been developed, and its purpose is making service implementation more suitable to meet the DCI's needs.

The EVPN model was standardized by RFC 7432 – *BGP MPLS-Based Ethernet VPN*, February 2015. The title of the RFC already indicates the main idea – using BGP to advertise MAC addresses, with the same operating model as L3VPNs. In other words, MAC learning does not occur only on the data plane, as in the VPLS model, but partially on the data plane (local MAC learning), and partially on the control plane, using BGP. Do not be misled by the fact that even the VPLS model can use BGP for its operation; the EVPN model uses BGP in a very different way (similar, for the auto-discovery portion, and completely different for the signaling one).

And this is not the only new aspect introduced by the EVPN model. The standard focuses particularly on the implementation of multihoming connections, load balancing, loop prevention and other aspects we will not cover here, since they lie outside the scope of this book. All these aspects are not treated (or only marginally treated) in the VPLS model, while RFC 7432 introduced many clever solutions for them.

The importance of the EVPN model is due to two reasons: the first, that it is a very well-designed standard, and the second that, thanks to the complete separation between control plane and data plane, it can be used as control plane for several kinds of data plane. There are currently three standards with the EVPN control plane:

- RFC 7432 (mentioned above): MPLS data plane.

- RFC 7623 – *Provider Backbone Bridging Combined with Ethernet VPN (PBB-EVPN)*, September 2015: MAC-in-MAC data plane, also known as PBB (Provider Backbone Bridge), defined by IEEE standard 802.1ah.

- RFC 8365 – *A Network Virtualization Overlay Solution Using Ethernet VPN (EVPN)*, March 2018: general data plane used in the Overlay Virtual Networks in a Data Center environment. In particular, the document deals with EVPN integration with the two most used standards – VXLAN and NVGRE (between the two, it is the first one that became a *de facto* standard in latest-generation Data Centers).

The EVPN control plane is based on the BGP MAC routing concept. The idea is similar to the control plane in L3VPN service, with the difference that, instead of the IP prefixes of VPN sites, the MAC addresses learned locally by PEs (and, optionally, also the IP addresses of the hosts with that MAC address) are the ones advertised via MP-iBGP. Since MAC addresses, differently from IP addresses, cannot be aggregated, a BGP advertisement for each MAC address is required.

Another idea similar to L3VPNs is the auto-discovery mode, which occurs through the standard Route Target filtering mechanism, also used – as we have seen extensively in Section 11.2.2 – in the VPLS model, with auto-discovery via BGP.

What makes EVPN and VPLS models very different is the MAC learning mode. Just like in the VPLS model (and in L3VPN for IP prefixes), in EVPN, MAC learning is achieved in two steps – one local and one remote. The local phase is identical to VPLS's: through it, a PE learns about the existence of MAC addresses, and, optionally, with a few tricks (e.g. GARP, Gratuitous ARP) also about the corresponding IP addresses associated with them.

Then it creates, in its own MAC table, indicated in the EVPN model as MAC-VRF, a <MAC; local port> association. However, the remote learning phase is quite different. After learning a MAC address, it is communicated to all the other PEs within the same EVPN instance, via MP-iBGP advertisements. The process is summarized in Figure 11.16 below, where we assumed – as it almost always occurs in practical applications – to use Route Reflectors to minimize the number of MP-iBGP sessions.

NOTE: In the EVPN standard, the set of connections between CEs and PEs is called Ethernet Segment (ES). In the case of a multi-homed connection of one CE to several PEs, it represents the set of connections. In the case of a single-homed connection to a single PE, it represents the only connection. Each ES is identified by an ESI (Ethernet Segment Identifier), which, in the case of multi-homed PE-CE connections, is a non-null identifier (10 byte long). In the case of single-homed PE-CE connections, ESI=0.

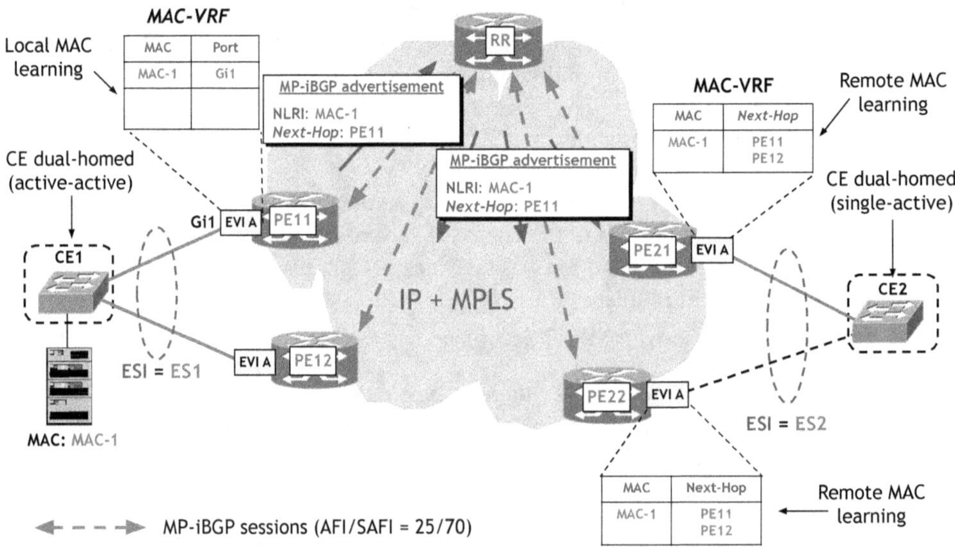

Figure 11.16 – Local and remote MAC learning in the EVPN model.

What happens when BGP is used in the control plane, when a MAC address learned from a PE is removed from the MAC-VRF table, because the MAC aging timer has expired (or the table has been cleared)? One of the advantages of using BGP is that, through a BGP UPDATE message, the advertisement previously sent is withdrawn. This causes the cancellation on the remote PEs of the entry related to the MAC address on the MAC-VRFs, thus allowing an automatic synchronization of the MAC-VRF tables on all the PEs. The advertisement and withdrawal of a MAC address are particularly important in the case of MAC mobility, that is, when a MAC address moves from one ES to another.

MP-iBGP advertisements are very peculiar, and, similarly to what occurred for other services, the new BGP EVPN address-family has been defined, with new NLRIs within them. Then, new BGP Extended Community attributes, specific for the EVPN model, have also been defined. IANA defined for the new BGP EVPN address-family the AFI code equal to 25 (identical to the VPLS model) – and the SAFI code equal to 70.

The BGP EVPN Address Family is activated through the following configuration commands:

<u>IOS XE</u>
PE(config)# **router bgp** *AS-number*
PE(config-router)# **address-family <u>l2vpn evpn</u>**
PE(config-router-af)# **neighbor** *IP-neighbor* **activate**

<u>IOS XR</u>
RP/0/RP0/CPU0:PE(config)# **router bgp** *ISP-AS*
RP/0/RP0/CPU0:PE(config-bgp)# **address-family <u>l2vpn evpn</u>**
RP/0/RP0/CPU0:PE(config-bgp)# **neighbor** *IP-neighbor*
RP/0/RP0/CPU0:PE(config-bgp-nbr)# **address-family <u>l2vpn evpn</u>**

<u>JUNOS</u>
[edit protocols bgp group *group-name***]**
<u>family evpn</u> {
    <u>signaling</u>;
 }

The general NLRI format is the standard TLV (Type-Length-Value) type shown below, with the "**Route Type**" field representing the type of coding in the "**Route Type Specific**" field, the "**Length**" field representing the length of the following field in byte, and the "**Route Type Specific**" field the actual coding of the NLRI.

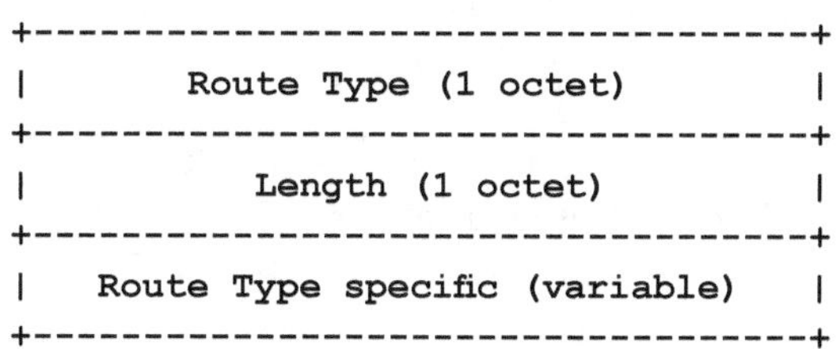

```
+-----------------------------------+
|         Route Type (1 octet)      |
+-----------------------------------+
|          Length (1 octet)         |
+-----------------------------------+
|    Route Type specific (variable) |
+-----------------------------------+
```

RFC 7432 defined 4 different types of NLRIs, shown in the following table (Type 1, ..., 4). Subsequently, type 5 has also been defined (see: RFC 9136 – *IP Prefix Advertisement in EVPN*). The following table shows the most important fields and their use. Moreover, in all NLRI types, there is a Route Distinguisher (RD) value, whose format and meaning are the same as those of the L3VPNs, i.e. they are values used to distinguish any possible identical NLRIs, generated by different EVPN instances.

Type	Name	Main fields	Use
1	Ethernet Auto-Discovery (A-D) route	• ESI • Ethernet tag • MPLS Label	• Fast convergence • Aliasing • Label advertisement for Split-Horizon
2	MAC/IP Advertisement route	• ESI • Ethernet tag • MAC address • IP address • MPLS Label	• MAC advertisements • Advertisement of MAC/IP associations
3	Inclusive Multicast Ethernet Tag route	• Ethernet tag • IP address of the router generating the advertisement (*)	Auto-discovery of PEs where CEs of the same EVI are attested
4	Ethernet Segment route	• ESI • IP address of the router generating the advertisement (*)	• Discovery of PEs multi-homed to the same ES • DF election
5	IP Prefix route	• ESI • Ethernet tag • IP prefix • GW IP address • MPLS Label	IP prefixes advertisement

(*) Typically a Loopback Address

The use of the different NLRI types depends on the type of PE-CE connections. For instance, if all connections were single-homed, we would only need types 2 and 3. Types 1 and 4 are used (along with types 2 and 3) only in multi-homed connections, while type 5 is used both within an EVPN domain, and in the interconnection with external IP/MPLS networks.

As you may have understood in these few lines, the EVPN standard is very complex, and covering it completely would require a lot of time. Therefore, if you want to explore the concepts further, see the already cited RFC 7432.

11.3 BGP IN IPv6 TRANSPORT ON IPv4/MPLS NETWORKS

Between the Tunneling techniques to transport IPv6 packets, the one that has become a de facto standard among the ISPs is based on IPv4 backbones implementing the BGP/MPLS routing architecture. This technique – which Cisco initially called 6PE – has become a standard with RFC 4798 – *Connecting IPv6 Islands over IPv4 MPLS Using IPv6 Provider Edge Routers (6PE)*, February 2007.

Among the advantages of 6PE, we can mention:

- reuse of an existing and broadly tested infrastructure: it does not require any additional configuration on the BGP/MPLS backbone side, except for a minimum update of BGP PE-PE (or PE-RR) sessions. 6PE can be considered an additional BGP/MPLS service;

- scalability: differently from other Tunneling mechanisms, it does not require the Tunnel configuration on the customer's routers; the specific 6PE configuration only concerns the PE routers of the ISP network;

- same services offered by the other Tunneling mechanisms (access to the IPv6 Internet, connection of native IPv6 sites, etc.).

The control plane of the 6PE service is the same as the BGP/MPLS architecture's, and it therefore comprises three basic components:

- BGP's multiprotocol extension (MP-iBGP) for the advertisement, by PE routers of the IPv6 prefixes, and the MPLS labels (service label) associated to them;

- an IGP in IPv4 environment (IS-IS or OSPF) to create optimal paths between PEs, and especially between IPv4 addresses of the PE Loopback interfaces, used to create the MP-iBGP sessions;

- LDP or Segment Routing to associate the MPLS labels to the paths created through IGP (or, alternatively, although very rarely the RSVP-TE protocol).

Just like in every other network based on the BGP/MPLS architecture, a complete mesh of MP-iBGP sessions is required, possibly created using Route Reflection functions, as well as a complete mesh of MPLS LSP between PEs. Theoretically, in order to create a complete mesh of MPLS LSP (Label Switched Path), alternatively to LDP or Segment Routing, we could use the RSVP-TE protocol; however, in practical applications, this is not recommended, due to the significant overload of configuration requirements. MP-iBGP advertisements transport both the information on the IPv6 prefix, and a MPLS label associated to the prefix (IPv6 address family+Label, AFI/SAFI=2/4). Figure 11.17 below shows an example of both MP-iBGP and LDP advertisements allowing IPv6 traffic entering any PE of the IPv4/MPLS backbone and directed toward IPv6 prefix 2001:db8:1::/48, to reach the PE that advertised the prefix, and from here the CE router that advertised the prefix to the IPv4/MPLS backbone.

IPv6 prefix 2001:db8:1::/48 is advertised by router CE-X to router PE2 of the IPv4/MPLS backbone, through any IPv6 routing (e.g. BGP for IPv6) or static routing protocol. Router PE2, starting from the advertisement received, creates a MP-iBGP advertisement where it adds the association <IPv6 prefix; MPLS label>=<2001:db8:1::/48; 54>. The BGP Next-Hop is set equal to an IPv6 address with the special format "::ffff:IPv4-PE2", where IPv4-PE2 is the IPv4 address used by PE2 for the MP-iBGP session (see note at the end of Section 11.1.2).

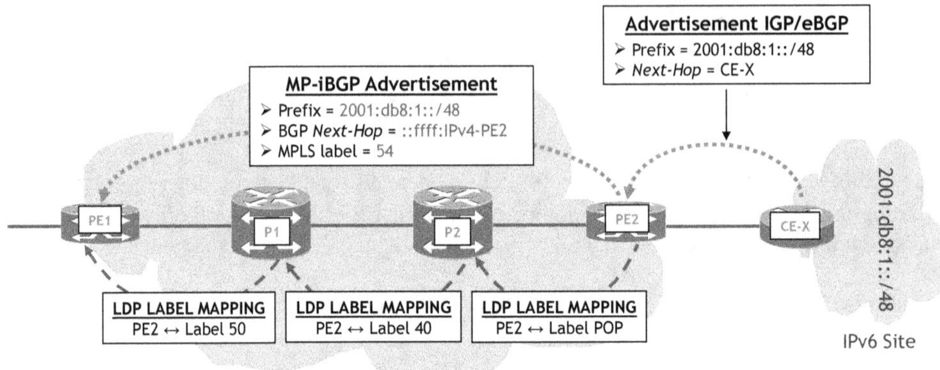

Figure 11.17 – Control plane of the 6PE service.

The data plane uses two MPLS labels:

- LSP Labels: the labels distributed by LDP (or RSVP-TE or Segment Routing) and identifying the PE-PE MPLS LSP. They are simple Transport Labels;

- IPv6 Labels: the labels distributed via MP-iBGP, associated to IPv6 prefixes. These are actual service labels.

Theoretically, it would be possible to use only one MPLS label rather than two, but in this case, the P routers adjacent to the PEs should be Dual Stack, that is, they should be capable of routing also IPv6 packets. Indeed, due to the (automatic) Penultimate Hop Popping mechanism, typical of the MPLS standard, the penultimate router of the MPLS path – which is usually a P router – eliminates the LSP Labels, therefore, without the second label, it would have to route an IPv6 packet. To avoid this, the 6PE service entails the use of a second label (IPv6 Label).

Figure 11.18 below shows an example of data plane that refers to the example of control plane shown in Figure 11.17. We will leave checking the correctness of the MPLS labels used to you.

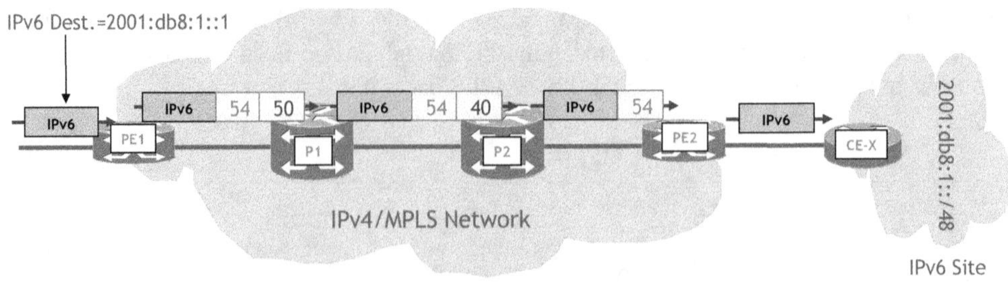

Figure 11.18 – Data plane of the 6PE service.

Concerning the value of the MPLS label advertised via MP-iBGP (IPv6 Label), Cisco platforms use a "subnet-based" allocation by default, while Juniper platforms use a "CE-based" allocation. In IOS XR, you can choose the allocation mode, through the following commands:

RP/0/RP0/CPU0:PE(config)# **router bgp** *ISP-AS*
RP/0/RP0/CPU0:PE(config-bgp)# **address-family ipv6 unicast**
RP/0/RP0/CPU0:PE(config-bgp)# **label mode {per-ce | per-vrf}**

In JUNOS, you can choose the "VRF-based" mode (which, in this case, would be more correct calling "table-based", since no VRF is configured for the 6PE service on the PEs!), with the following command:

[edit protocols bgp group *group-name***]**
family inet6 {
  labeled-unicast {
    explicit-null;
  }
}

Notice that, for both JUNOS and IOS XR, once the "VRF-based" mode is enabled, all IPv6 prefixes are advertised with the reserved MPLS label "2" (IPv6 Explicit Null).

The general configuration procedure for the 6PE requires, as a preliminary step, the implementation of a BGP/MPLS backbone. This consists in the configuration of the IGPv4 protocol (usually OSPFv2 or IS-IS), of LDP or Segment Routing, and lastly of the complete mesh of MP-iBGP sessions, usually logically achieved through the Route Reflection mechanism. So, nothing new so far, compared to the unicast IPv4 L3VPN service.

Concerning the MP-iBGP session, the configuration procedure is the standard one for iBGP sessions and for the Route Reflection mechanism, with the only difference – which is the only peculiar aspect of the 6PE service – that the transport of IPv6 routing+label (AFI/SAFI=2/4) needs to be activated, and its configuration requires the following additional commands:

IOS XE
PE(config)# **router bgp** *ISP-AS*
PE(config-router)# **address-family ipv6**
PE(config-router-af)# **neighbor** *IPv4-neighbor* **activate**
PE(config-router-af)# **neighbor** *IPv4-neighbor* **send-label**

IOS XR
RP/0/RP0/CPU0:router(config)# **router bgp** *ISP-AS*
RP/0/RP0/CPU0:PE(config-bgp)# **address-family ipv6 unicast**
RP/0/RP0/CPU0:PE(config-bgp-af)# **allocate-label {route-policy** RP-name | **all}**
RP/0/RP0/CPU0:PE(config-bgp-af)# **exit**
RP/0/RP0/CPU0:PE(config-bgp)# **neighbor** *IPv4-neighbor*
RP/0/RP0/CPU0:PE(config-bgp-nbr)# **address-family ipv6 labeled-unicast**

where the IPv4-neighbor is the IPv4 address of the MP-iBGP Neighbor (another PE or, more commonly, a Route Reflector). These are the only specific commands to enable the 6PE. It is important to remember that the commands must be executed in both BGP Neighbors, otherwise the BGP Capability "Multiprotocol BGP" is not negotiated.

NOTE: the IOS XR **"allocate-label {route-policy** RP-name | **all}"** command allows associating the MPLS labels to all the BGP advertisements of the address-family IPv6 unicast (**"all"** clause), or to part of them, controlled by a route-policy.

<u>JUNOS</u>
[edit protocols bgp group *group-name***]**
family inet6 {
   labeled-unicast;
}

A very subtle side in JUNOS is that an IPv6+label advertisement, in order to be deemed valid, must have a BGP Next-Hop that can be solved through the "inet6.3" table. Otherwise, the advertisement would be added as hidden in the "inet6.0" table, and the "**show route table** *VRF-name.inet6.0* **hidden detail**" command would show the message "**Next hop type: Unusable**". The logic behind this rule is that IPv6 traffic on the data plane necessarily uses PE-PE MPLS LSP, and the presence of a path toward the BGP Next-Hop in the "inet6.3" table ensures the existence of a PE-PE MPLS LSP.

NOTE: This rule does not apply to normal IPv4 prefix advertisements (exported from the "inet.0" table). Indeed, for these, it is sufficient for the BGP Next-Hop to be solvable either through the "inet.3" table or through the "inet.0" table. The reason behind this is that, in this case, traffic does not necessarily need a LSP MPLS to be carried to its destination.

Lastly, an important – yet not peculiar – aspect of the 6PE service, is the activation of a IPv6 PE-CE or static routing protocol. For this part, all the considerations made for routing protocols in the IPv6 environment apply (see, for instance, Section 2.6.3 on BGP for IPv6).

SUMMARY

Nowadays, MPLS is a very important part of modern IP networks. Many providers have implemented it in their networks and offer services based on this paradigm. Thanks to its flexibility and extension and use potential, MPLS has become one of the most important standards in modern IP networks.

The real strength of MPLS, the actual reason why it is used, is the possibility of providing new network services. One of the most popular, and surely the most important one, which has made MPLS a commercial success, is the L3VPN service, that is, the option of creating an actual (virtual) private network, using a shared IP/MPLS backbone.

BGP plays a crucial role in MPLS services, since it is the "smart" component, with basically two tasks: advertising routing information and auto-discovery functions. In addition, in certain scenarios (see multicast L3VPN services, LAN emulation services), BGP – in its multiprotocol version – is used to allocate general information, required for several service aspects.

In this chapter, without any claim to completeness, we highlighted how BGP is used in the different MPLS services, and specified the Address Families for each one of them.

Worth remembering:

1. The role of BGP in MPLS services.

2. The Address Families used in the different services.

3. The role of BGP in signaling the MPLS service labels and for auto-discovery.

12 – CONVERGENCE ASPECTS

There are many myths surrounding BGP. One of them – which we'll try to debunk here – is linked to the convergence speed, which everyone deems very slow. Actually, this was the case in BGP's first implementations, but today, thanks to the new functions introduced by the main manufacturers, and to others according to IETF standards, things have radically changed, and BGP's convergence speed is becoming comparable with some of the most important IGPs, such as OSPF and IS-IS.

In the early days of BGP, given its role as inter-domain routing protocol, developers focused more on its capacity to manage high quantities of advertisements, at the expense of the convergence aspects, not deemed important in its original role. Things radically changed when BGP became the smart element of the services based on the BGP/MPLS model. Since these services are dedicated to business customers (of any size), suddenly convergence speed issues became primary.

In this chapter, we will focus on the different aspects that help to drastically improve BGP's convergence issues, starting with classic elements – such as timer tuning, TCP parameter optimization, and depth adjustment of the queues where BGP messages are stored, waiting to be processed – and then switching to BGP session drop detection times and the techniques to reduce them, and ending with all path diversity functions – that is, those functions that allow, apart from a primary Next-Hop (the Next-Hop defined by the selection process), also a backup Next-Hop to be added directly to the FIB, which can be used immediately, once the primary Next-Hop becomes unreachable.

12.1 PARAMETERS OPTIMIZATION

Just like all routing protocols, BGP has a series of parameters to optimize its performance, both in terms of convergence speed, and of use of the internal memory and the CPU.

The parameters that can be configured, based on the specific implementation, fall within three defined areas:

- timers: they regulate aspects related to sessions, to sending UPDATE messages, etc.;

- TCP connections: they regulate some typical TCP connection parameters, such as, for instance, the TCP window and the Maximum Segment Size (MSS);

- queue size: they regulate the size of inbound queues, to tackle any BGP signaling traffic peaks, such as the TCP ACK received after sending BGP messages.

A good parameter regulation brings many benefits to the overall BGP operation, reducing the quantity of messages that the routers must process, and – especially – convergence times.

12.1.1 BGP timers

According to RFC 4271, BGP uses 5 timers. The three following timers are linked to the sessions:

- ConnectRetryTimer: the time after which, after a failed attempt, another attempt to open the TCP connection is repeated. The value recommended by RFC 4271 is 120 s.

- HoldTimer: the Hold Time of the BGP session that, as you may recall, is negotiated when the session is opened, via OPEN messages. The lowest value between those suggested by the two BGP Neighbors is chosen as common value. The value recommended by RFC 4271 is 90 s.

- KeepaliveTimer: the period of KEEPALIVE messages. The value recommended by RFC 4271 is 1/3 of the HoldTimer value.

While the ConnectRetryTimer is generally a non-configurable value, current implementations allow configuring the HoldTimer and/or KeepaliveTimer. The configurations to execute in Cisco devices are:

<u>IOS XE</u>:
router(config)# **router bgp** *AS-number*
! To change the timers of all sessions
 router(config-router)# **timers bgp** *KT HT*
! Or, to change the timers only in a specific session
 router(config-router)# neighbor *IP-neighbor* **timers** *KT HT*

<u>IOS XR</u>:
RP/0/RP0/CPU0:router(config)# **router bgp** *AS-number*
! To change the timers of all sessions
RP/0/RP0/CPU0:router(config-bgp)# **timers bgp** *KT HT*
! Or, to change the timers only in a specific session
RP/0/RP0/CPU0:router(config-bgp)# **neighbor** *IP-neighbor*
RP/0/RP0/CPU0:router(config-bgp-nbr)# **timers** *KT HT*

where KT=KeepaliveTimer and HT=HoldTimer, with both values expressed as seconds. Default values are: HoldTimer=180 s and KeepaliveTimer=60 s.
Remember that, when initializing a BGP session, downstream of the OPEN message exchange, a single HoldTimer value is negotiated, equal to the minimum value between the two suggested. While the KeepaliveTimer is not negotiated.
Cisco IOS, based on the configuration values, determines HoldTimer and KeepaliveTimer as follows. With (KTA; HTA) and (KTB; HTB) as the values configured in the two BGP Neighbors, which we will call RA and RB, and HTN=min{HTA; HTB} as the HoldTimer value negotiated, common to both BGP Neighbors. The KeepaliveTimer is determined using the following relations:

- on RA: $\min\{KTA; \text{trunc}[HTN/3]\}$;

- on RB: $\min\{KTB; \text{trunc}[HTN/3]\}$.

where trunc[x] indicates the integer part of x.
JUNOS, in line with its configuration philosophy, provides many less configurable timers. The three session timers are all supported.
Concerning the HoldTimer and the KeepaliveTimer, only the first one can be configured, while the second one is determined automatically through the relation KT=trunc[HTN/3], where HTN=min{HTA; HTB} is the HoldTimer negotiated value common to both BGP Neighbors.

JUNOS entails a common KeepaliveTimer value (and obviously HoldTimer value), used by both BGP Neighbors of a session. The command to change the HoldTimer is "**hold-time** *value-in-seconds*", and it can be executed at global, group or session level. The default value is HoldTimer = 90 s, and consequently KeepaliveTimer = 30 s.

BGP also has two other timers, linked to the generation of UPDATE messages:

- MinRouteAdvertisementIntervalTimer (MRAI): the minimum time between two UPDATE messages sent to a BGP Neighbor, advertising or withdrawing a certain prefix.

- MinASOriginationIntervalTimer (MAOI): the minimum time between two UPDATE messages advertising a local prefix.

Both these last two timers set an upper limit to the UPDATE message generation frequency, and have a very important impact on convergence speed. For this reason, there is still a lot of debate on their use, among the scientific community. Also, the practical implementation of these timers is anything but easy, because, if we'd follow RFC 4271 to a T, it would require a separate timer for each prefix, and this is certainly not scalable, for routers that have dozens if not hundreds of thousands of BGP advertisements stored, such as those routers with the entire FIRT.

This is why not all BGP implementations support these two timers, and not all of them are compliant with standard specifications. Any changes to default values must be carefully evaluated, by taking actual implementation into account.

Between all these timers, the one that most affects convergence is the MRAI timer.

To better understand the meaning of the MRAI, let's consider BGP Speaker RA, receiving UPDATE messages from several BGP Neighbors, and propagating the best paths toward another BGP Neighbor RB. When the first UPDATE message arrives, RA determines the best path, propagates the best path toward RB and starts the MRAI timer. Any best path determined before the MRAI expires is not immediately propagated, but only once it expires, then the MRAI is restarted and so on (see Figure 12.1 below). In other words, the UPDATE messages containing the best paths of the same prefix are sent once the MRAI expires. This requires a sort of rate limiting when the best paths of the same prefix are sent, so as to not overload the BGP Neighbor.

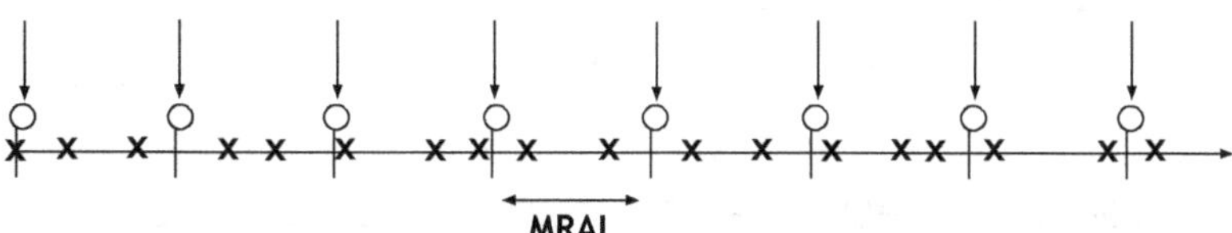

X   UPDATE Message Arrival

O   Sending UPDATE messages (best path)

Figure 12.1 – The MRAI timer.

Cisco IOS supports the MRAI timer, albeit in a different way than described by RFC 4271. Indeed, in Cisco IOS, the MRAI timer sets a minimum distance between generations of UPDATE groups toward the same BGP Neighbor, rather than between UPDATE messages containing the same NLRI.

In IOS XE, the MRAI is configured through the following command:

router(config)# **router bgp** *AS-number*
router(config-router)# **neighbor** *IP-neighbor* **advertisement-interval** *value-MRAI*

with the following default values:

- 5 *s* for iBGP sessions;

- 30 *s* for eBGP sessions.

In IOS XR, the command is the same:

RP/0/RP0/CPU0:router(config)# **router bgp** *AS-number*
RP/0/RP0/CPU0:router(config-bgp)# **neighbor** *IP-neighbor*
RP/0/RP0/CPU0:router(config-bgp-nbr)# **advertisement-interval** *value-MRAI*

but default values change:

- 0 *s* for iBGP sessions and for eBGP sessions toward CE routers, i.e. for eBGP sessions in a VRF;

- 30 *s* for eBGP sessions not in a VRF.

The actual MRAI value used by the router can be controlled through the standard show command **"show bgp ipv4 unicast neighbors"**. The following view shows an example of the command being executed on a router of AS 64500, which has an iBGP session and an eBGP session with AS 65000:

```
PE1-1# show bgp ipv4 unicast neighbors

BGP neighbor is 10.1.1.2,  remote AS 65000, external link
. . . < output omitted > . . .

Default minimum time between advertisement runs is 30 seconds
. . . < output omitted > . . .

BGP neighbor is 192.168.0.31,  remote AS 64500, internal link
. . . < output omitted > . . .

Default minimum time between advertisement runs is 5 seconds
```

JUNOS supports the MRAI timer, albeit in a different way than described by RFC 4271 and Cisco IOS implementation.

Before showing how MRAI is implemented by JUNOS, let's go over how it works when it receives an UPDATE message. In JUNOS, the BGP process, for each UPDATE message received, stores the information contained in the message in the IP RIB (NLRI, attributes, etc.), activates the selection process, then immediately exports the best path to the BGP process, which prepares a new UPDATE message to propagate it to its BGP Neighbors.

This immediate exchange of routing information between the IP RIB and the BGP process can cause instability, especially in case of route flapping, and it is also a source of inefficiency when forming UPDATE messages, as it does not allow fully exploiting the concept of update packing. The MRAI allows delaying the immediate exporting of each best path from the RIB to the BGP process, by a configurable quantity, thus mitigating any instability due to route flaps, while allowing the BGP process to optimize the sending of UPDATE messages, using the update packing concept. JUNOS implementation of the MRAI is summarized in Figure 12.2 below.

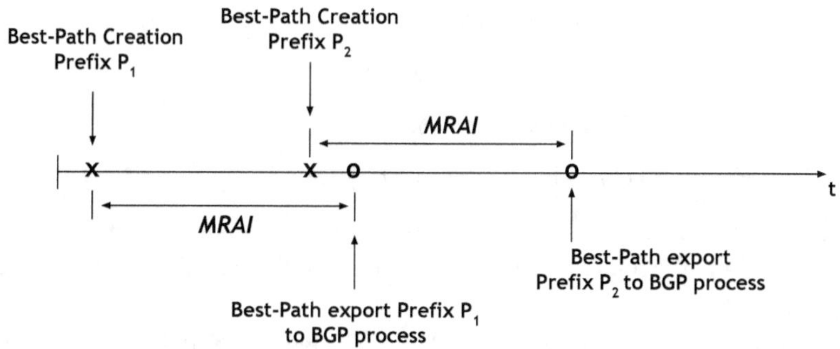

Figure 12.2 – JUNOS implementation of the MRAI timer.

The command to implement the MRAI is "**out-delay** *value-in-seconds*", and it can be executed at global, group or session level. The default value is 0 s, that is, the MRAI is disabled by default.

12.1.2 The MRAI timer and BGP path hunting

As we mentioned several times in the previous chapters, BGP uses the "triggered updates" mechanism, that is, it only propagates the news it gets, without sending periodical updates.

When BGP must advertise a new prefix, it propagates pretty quickly in the AS ecosystem, insomuch so that it is visible by the entire Internet, in just a few seconds. In this case, the MRAI timer is not even triggered, since the advertisement travels fairly quickly along the optimal path (intended as the minimum number of ASes it crosses).

The situation is different when a prefix previously advertised is withdrawn. This requires a lot more time, and the MRAI timer plays a key role. Basically, in BGP, "good news " (newly advertised prefixes) travel fast, while "bad news" (withdrawn prefixes that are no longer reachable) travel a lot more slowly.

Let's see what happens when we withdraw a prefix, with an example. Let's assume the scenario of Figure 12.3 below.

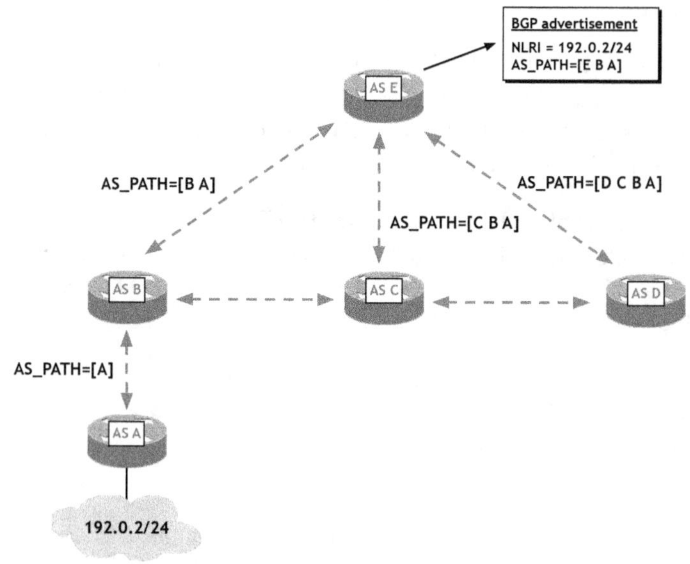

Figure 12.3 – Prefix propagation between ASes.

The router of AS E has three paths available for prefix 192.0.2/24 advertised by AS A:

- P(B) → AS_PATH = [B A] (advertisement by B);

- P(C) → AS_PATH = [C B A] (advertisement by C);

- P(D) → AS_PATH = [D C B A] (advertisement by D).

Assuming that the router of AS E does not apply any BGP attribute manipulation, the best path will be path P(B). Then, the router of AS E will advertise prefix 192.0.2/24 toward the outside with AS_PATH = [E B A].
Let's now see what happens when AS A loses its reachability to prefix 192.0.2/24. The event sequence is the following:

1. The router of AS A sends an UPDATE message to withdraw prefix 192.0.2/24, previously advertised.

2. Having no alternatives left, the router of AS B sends a BGP message to its BGP Neighbors (routers of ASes C and E) to also withdraw prefix 192.0.2/24, previously advertised.

3. When it receives the UPDATE message, the router of AS E activates the selection process and elects path P(C) as the best path, which has AS_PATH = [C B A]. Then, it installs the best path in its RIB and FIB and advertises the new best path to the BGP Neighbor, which will have AS_PATH = [E C B A].

4. The router of AS E continues to send traffic to prefix 192.0.2/24 using the router of AS C as Next-Hop, being oblivious to the fact that the prefix is actually unreachable. Indeed, it does not know that the router of AS C has also received the UPDATE message withdrawing prefix 192.0.2/24.

5. In the meantime, the router of AS C activates the selection process and, having no alternatives left, sends an UPDATE to its BGP Neighbors (routers of ASes D and E) to also withdraw prefix 192.0.2/24, previously advertised.

6. When it receives the BGP UPDATE message, the router of AS E activates the selection process and elects path P(D) as the best path, which has AS_PATH = [D C B A]. Then, it installs the best path in its RIB (and FIB) and advertises the new best path to the BGP Neighbor, which will have AS_PATH = [E D C B A].

7. Like before, the router of AS E continues to send traffic to prefix 192.0.2/24 using the router of AS D as Next-Hop, being oblivious to the fact that the prefix is actually unreachable. Indeed, it does not know that the router of AS D has received the UPDATE message withdrawing prefix 192.0.2/24.

8. The router of AS D activates the selection process and, having no alternatives left, sends a BGP message to its BGP Neighbors (router of AS E) to also withdraw prefix 192.0.2/24, previously advertised. Notice that it does not send the UPDATE message to the router of AS C (why?).

9. Lastly, the router of AS E, having no alternatives left, sends a BGP message to its BGP Neighbors to withdraw prefix 192.0.2/24, previously advertised. And BGP convergence process ends here.

The one we just described is a phenomenon known in BGP literature as BGP path hunting, since the BGP process of the router of AS E hunts a path to reach prefix 192.0.2/24, and explores all the alternatives available, starting from the one with the shortest AS_PATH, until reaching the one with the longest AS_PATH.

The path hunting phenomenon has a close link with the MRAI timer, and hence with BGP convergence. Indeed, as you may notice from the sequence of events we just described, the router of AS E first sends a new UPDATE message with AS_PATH=[E C B A] (point 3), then a new UPDATE message with AS_PATH=[E D C B A] (point 6), and then the UPDATE message to withdraw prefix 192.0.2/24 (point 9). Now, a time equal to at least the MRAI must elapse between the two consecutive UPDATE messages of the same prefix. And so, in our example, at least twice the MRAI. For instance, using the default values of Cisco routers, 60s. And other MRAIs should be added to this, since the router of AS E could be connected to many other ASes. However, using the default value of Juniper routers (**out-delay**=0), the convergence would become very fast, at the cost of possibly greater network instability. Think for instance about the case of a route flapping of prefix 192.0.2/24, where UPDATE messages would be sent continuously to withdraw and advertise the prefix.

We can easily prove that the quantity of best path hunting, and therefore the convergence time, increases as the meshing of the AS topology increases. In a tree topology, there is only one path possible, therefore the path hunting does not occur. The addition of a single connection in this topology creates a cycle in the graphic, and so maximum two possible paths to the BGP. The subsequent connections can add many alternative paths to search for the best path, depending on where they are placed in the graphic.

There is a lot of debate on the optimal MRAI value to use in practical applications. The 30s value recommended by RFC 4271 is universally deemed an obstacle to the BGP convergence speed, insomuch so that, for instance, some manufacturers use null MRAI by default (e.g. Juniper, which uses the default value 0s, the same as in some versions of Cisco IOS, as mentioned earlier). On the other hand, studies have been carried out according to which a mix of different MRAI values can worsen BGP's convergence speed by a lot. Therefore, the issue of choosing an optimal value is still open, and its practical implementation is not easy.

12.1.3 TCP connection parameter adjustment

Convergence speed – especially after restarting the BGP process – can be improved also by suitably adjusting the TCP parameters, since this allows us to significantly reduce the traffic of UPDATE messages, and therefore the number of TCP ACKs to be processed.

The TCP has two adjustable parameters:

- Maximum Segment Size (MSS): represents the maximum size of TCP segments;

- TCP window size: represents the number of bytes that can be sent, without feedback (ACK) from the receiver.

The MSS is negotiated during the TCP connection opening phase (Three-way Handshake). The lowest between the two suggested by the connection endpoints is chosen as common value. The influence of MSS on BGP is that, the higher this value, the lower is the number of UPDATE messages required to send their best paths to the BGP Neighbors. The number of UPDATE messages, based on the MSS, can be determined through the ratio:

$$Number\ of\ messages\ UPDATE\ =\ \frac{(BP) \cdot (BBP)}{MSS}$$

where BP is the number of best paths to be sent, and BBP the average quantity of bytes for each best path (a typical value is 250 byte). By way of example, switching from a 536 byte MSS (default value used in old Cisco IOS versions) to a 1,460 byte MSS (default value used in current Cisco IOS and JUNOS versions), leads to a 272% reduction of UPDATE messages, with consequent identical TCP ACK reductions.

In practice, it is best to use the maximum value allowed by the interfaces crossed by BGP messages as MSS. For this reason, the Path MTU Discovery (PMTUD) mechanism – described in RFC 1191 – which allows determining the minimum MTU (min-MTU) of the interfaces crossed, on a path, could be useful. The MSS value is calculated by subtracting 40 to the min-MTU, to take IP and TCP headers into account. The PMTUD mechanism can be enabled, in Cisco routers, through the global-level command: **ip tcp path-mtu-discovery** [**age-timer** {*minutes* | **infinite**}], where the "**age-timer**" option, allows defining a value to periodically recalculate the min-MTU value (default=10 min), while the "**infinite**" option in place of the number of minutes, allows disabling the periodical min-MTU recalculation.

In Juniper routers, the same command is: "**path-mtu-discovery**", where there are no options. The command should be executed within the configuration hierarchy [**edit system internet-options**]. The size of the TCP window, as we will see in the next Section 12.1.4, has an important role to size interface inbound queues. Typically, this is a non-configurable value, managed by the router internally. Cisco routers use a fixed value equal to 16 kbytes, while Juniper routers use an initial value of 16.384 kbytes.

12.1.4 Queue length adjustment

There are scenarios where restarting the BGP process causes very consistent bursts of inbound TCP ACKs, due to the sending of many UPDATE messages to the different BGP Neighbors. TCP ACKs must be processed by the router CPU, which may not have sufficient processing capacity, thus causing a consistent TCP ACK queueing in interface inbound queues, up to the congestion limit. The congestion of inbound queues causes a consistent TCP ACK rejection, and therefore a significant increase in the retransmission of UPDATE messages, thus increasing the CPU load. Hence, the need to correctly size the inbound queues related to each interface, to avoid a significant loss of TCP ACKs (due to congestion issues).

In order to have an idea of the quantity of how many TCP ACKs received by a router could be, let's consider the case of Route Reflector (RR) BGP process restart in a large network, with 100 RR-Clients. Let's assume that, from its Non-Client Neighbors, the RR receives 600,000 advertisements, resulting in 200,000 best paths. The 200,000 best paths are sent to 100 RR-Clients, which observe that each UPDATE message has been received with a TCP ACK. Therefore, as worst-case scenario, avoiding any update packing optimization, we are talking about 20 million TCP ACKs received in a short time. This does not mean that the 20 million TCP ACKs are received from RR at the same time. They are distributed over time.

In order to estimate the TCP ACKs that the RR receives at the same time (in a very short time frame), we need to take into account the TCP window mechanism. The window mechanism, along with the MSS, limits the number of TCP segments that a router can send, on a single TCP connection, without waiting for a TCP ACK. For instance, with a MSS=536 byte, and window size W at 16 kbytes, this number of segments is equal to 29, while with MSS=1,460 bytes and W always equal to 16 kbytes, the number of segments is equal to 10.

The router receiving TCP segments could, in a worst-case scenario, once the window is completed, send a TCP ACK for each segment received. For instance, with MSS=1,460 bytes and W=16 kbytes, the receiving router sends 10 TCP ACKs at the same time, every 10 segments received. The BGP Speaker sending UPDATE messages therefore receives 10 TCP ACKs at the same time from each BGP Neighbor, which must be queued and processed. A more accurate estimate of the number of TCP ACKs that a BGP Speaker would receive from its BGP Neighbors at the same time, in a worst-case scenario like the one we described, can be obtained through the relation:

$$Number\ of\ ACK\ TCP\ =\ \frac{(W) \cdot (N)}{K \cdot MSS}$$

where W is the size of the TCP window in bytes, N is the number of BGP Neighbors, MSS the Maximum Segment Size (in bytes) and K a reduction factor that depends on how many UPDATES are acknowledged by each TCP ACK.

Using a Cisco router as an example, it would be K=2 (that is, every TCP ACK acknowledges two UPDATE messages), and, as we have seen in the previous section, W=16,000 byte. When N and MSS vary, the following table is obtained:

MSS (byte)	W (byte)	N	Number of ACK TCP
536	16,000	50	*700*
1,460	16,000	50	200
4,430	16,000	50	50
536	16,000	100	1,400
1,460	16,000	100	400
4,430	16,000	100	199

which provides an estimate of the number of TCP ACKs that we can expect, in the worst-case scenario. This value may be considered as reference for a possible sizing of inbound queues. However, we won't specify any configuration command for it, since it is too much dependent on the technology used, and, within that technology, on the platform and on the scheduling mechanism used to process network control packets, such as the TCP ACKs.

12.2 BGP SESSION FAST FAILURE DETECTION

One of the most important aspects, which affects the convergence speed of any routing protocol, is the time required to detect when an adjacency/session drops. It is only after this step that a routing process starts all the operations required to end the convergence period, and define new paths to bypass any out-of-service network elements.

To detect when an adjacency/session drops, routing protocols have three alternatives:

- Using the physical layer: a router, after detecting that an interface is down, notifies the affected routing protocols, which take any required action. However, this alternative cannot be applied when the interface is the endpoint of a connection that crosses one or more active elements (e.g. an Ethernet switch). Indeed, in this case, it may occur that a router sees the interface from one side of the connection in the down state, while the router on the other end of the connection sees its interface in the up state. In the next section, we will see what happens to a BGP session in this specific case.

- Using HELLO (e.g. OSPF, IS-IS) or KEEPALIVE (e.g. BGP) messages: the issue in this case is the slow rate at which the adjacency/session drop is detected, since the Hold time value associated to these messages is usually very high, such as dozens of seconds, or even a few minutes (e.g. default Hold time of BGP sessions in Cisco and Juniper platforms).

- Using the BFD protocol (Bidirectional Forwarding Detection): BFD is based on a quick Hello mechanism, which allows detecting if a connection is down regardless of the underlying technology.

NOTE (on BFD): BFD is a standard protocol, initially suggested by Juniper and then developed by IETF (RFC 5880 – *Bidirectional Forwarding Detection (BFD)*, June 2010), which allows quickly detecting if a connection and/or path is out of service, regardless of the protocol used and of layer 1 or 2. It is based on a standard very small BFD HELLO message mechanism, in RFC 5880 called BFD Control Packets (24 bytes, encapsulated in an UDP+IP header). From this standpoint, BFD is very similar to an adjacency determination mechanism used by latest-generation routing protocols (e.g. EIGRP, OSPF, IS-IS), albeit with two fundamental differences:

1) BFD HELLO messages are used exclusively for the bidirectional communication test. Differently from HELLO messages used by routing protocols, they do not contain any information on protocol operation (for instance, the HELLO messages of OSPF protocol contain several protocol operation information, such as, for instance, the priority for DR and BDR election, Hello/Dead intervals, Area-ID, etc.).

2) BFD HELLO, in routers with distributed architecture (that is, with a clear separation between the control plane and the data plane), can be directly processed at data plane level, without triggering the CPU, or causing its minimal triggering. On the other hand, HELLO messages used by routing protocols are always processed by the CPU (Routing Engine).

First, we will analyze the typical scenario where a router loses a session with a BGP Neighbor. Although the RIB indicates that the BGP Neighbor is no longer reachable, BGP does not start the convergence process until the BGP session drops. This occurs either because the Holdtime has expired (whose default value is very high, 180 sec in Cisco routers and 90 sec in Juniper routers), or because the TCP connection drops, due to the TCP ACK timeouts.

BGP often relies on an IGP to determine the best path. If the path toward the BGP Neighbor is lost, for instance, even if IGP quickly detects the loss of BGP Neighbor, there is no guarantee that the BGP process will react quickly to this change. For instance, in the "historical" implementation of Cisco BGP the presence of the BGP Neighbor in the RIB was verified every 60 sec (BGP Scan Time).

There are many, less important, variables that regulate BGP's reaction speed. In this paragraph, we will focus on a primary issue: how is it possible to speed up BGP's determination of a dropped session. In following paragraphs, we will see how BGP can speed up the determination of the new Next-Hop to use for traffic forwarding. This last issue is more complex and interesting, and there are several functions covered by RFCs.

12.2.1 The fast external fall-over function

The first "turbo" to BGP convergence speed occurred many years ago, with the fast external fall-over function, introduced, for instance, by Cisco, in release 10.0, and has always been present in Juniper platforms.

When using only basic BGP functions to detect the failure of a BGP session, we rely on timers associated to BGP KEEPALIVE messages, period and Hold time, which are generally very high (remember that default values are 60/180 sec in Cisco implementation, and 30/90 sec in Juniper implementation). It is possible to change these two timers and bring them to very low values, but this would increase CPU usage by a lot, due to the higher frequency of BGP KEEPALIVE messages.

The fast external fall-over function that applies only to eBGP sessions between directly connected routers, with the endpoints of the TCP connection matching the IP addresses of the interfaces at the connection endpoints, starts from an elementary observation: the eBGP session is disconnected (with all relevant consequences, elimination of the advertisements received from the BGP Neighbor and recalculation of the best paths), as soon as the router realizes that the IP subnet (directly connected) used to number the interfaces at the connection endpoints, disappears from the RIB.

To make an example, let's consider two Cisco routers connected directly with a point-to-point link, whose endpoint interfaces are part of subnet IP 10.1.11.0/30.

It is possible to quantify the action of the fast external fall-over function, simply by analyzing the console messages.

With the fast external fall-over function disabled:

```
*Sep 29 09:28:31.127: %LINK-5-CHANGED: Interface GigabitEthernet0/0,
changed state to administratively down

*Sep 29 09:28:32.127: %LINEPROTO-5-UPDOWN: Line protocol on Interface
GigabitEthernet0/0, changed state to down

*Sep 29 09:30:32.371: %BGP-5-ADJCHANGE: neighbor 10.1.11.2 Down BGP
Notification sent

*Sep 29 09:30:32.371: %BGP-3-NOTIFICATION: sent to neighbor 10.1.11.2 4/0
(hold time expired) 0 bytes

*Sep 29 09:30:32.371: %BGP_SESSION-5-ADJCHANGE: neighbor 10.1.11.2 IPv4
Unicast topology base removed from session  BGP Notification sent
```

With the fast external fall-over function enabled:

```
*Sep 29 09:26:33.255: %BGP-5-ADJCHANGE: neighbor 10.1.11.2 Down Interface flap

*Sep 29 09:26:33.255: %BGP_SESSION-5-ADJCHANGE: neighbor 10.1.11.2 IPv4
Unicast topology base removed from session  Interface flap

*Sep 29 09:26:35.255: %LINK-5-CHANGED: Interface GigabitEthernet0/0,
changed state to administratively down

*Sep 29 09:26:36.255: %LINEPROTO-5-UPDOWN: Line protocol on Interface
GigabitEthernet0/0, changed state to down
```

As you may notice by analyzing the instants of the events, without the fast external fall-over function, the BGP session drops shortly after 2 minutes, when the Hold time expires. With the fast external fall-over function enabled, the session drop is detected almost in real time (in the example, Cisco IOS immediately notifies that the interface is down to the BGP process, and the session is immediately dropped, even before it is signaled that the interface is down).

The fast external fall-over function is enabled by default, and in Cisco routers it can be disabled via the BGP process level "**no bgp fast-external-fallover**" command (in IOS XR, the equivalent command is "**bgp fast-external-fallover disable**").

It is important to notice that the function does not apply in case of multihop eBGP sessions. This is why another mechanism is necessary, which applies also to iBGP sessions and that we will see soon.

The fast external fall-over function described has a problem, it only works with back-to-back connections achieved without intermediate devices. To understand this problem and how to solve it, consider the situation in Figure 12.4 below, where the point-to-point connection between routers PE1 and PE2 is achieved through a simple VLAN on an Ethernet switch.

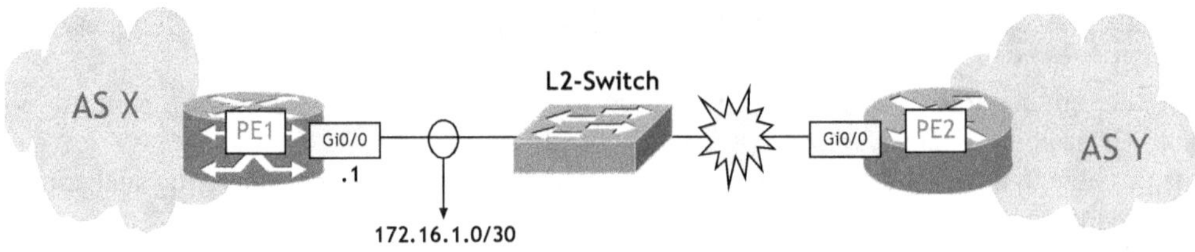

Figure 12.4 – Example of eBGP session with a non back-to-back connection.

What happens when the connection between the Ethernet switch and router PE2 drops? Well, in this case, the fast external fall-over function activates only on PE2, but not on PE1, which sees the connection interface to the Ethernet switch in the up/up state. In other words, while PE2 immediately closes the session, PE1 closes the session after the Holdtime has expired (for instance, in Cisco routers, in a worst-case scenario, after almost three minutes!) This is the sequence of what happens, after a connection between PE2 and L2-Switch drops (simulated by a shutdown of PE2's Gi0/0 interface):

On router PE2

```
*Sep 29 12:29:59.803: %BGP-5-ADJCHANGE: neighbor 172.16.1.1 Down Interface flap

*Sep  29  12:30:01.695:  %LINK-5-CHANGED:  Interface  GigabitEthernet0/0,
changed state to administratively down

*Sep 29 12:30:01.699: %ENTITY_ALARM-6-INFO: ASSERT INFO GigabitEthernet0/0
Physical Port Administrative State Down

*Sep  29  12:30:02.695:  %LINEPROTO-5-UPDOWN:  Line  protocol  on  Interface
GigabitEthernet0/0, changed state to down
```

On router PE1

```
*Sep  29  12:32:39.475:  %BGP-5-ADJCHANGE:  neighbor  172.16.1.2  Down  BGP
Notification sent

*Sep 29 12:32:39.479: %BGP-3-NOTIFICATION: sent to neighbor 172.16.1.2
4/0 (hold time expired) 0 bytes
```

As you may notice, PE1 closes the session about three minutes after PE2 closes it. During this period, a traffic black-holing from PE1 to PE2 occurs, for all IP prefixes for which PE2 address 172.16.1.2 is the BGP Next-Hop.

To solve the issue, we can use the aforementioned BFD protocol, supported by both Cisco and Juniper platforms. The different Cisco IOS versions support BFD for BGP only on single-hop eBGP sessions. Only some platforms support the multihop version. Juniper routers support both versions.

Going back to the example in Figure 12.4, the configurations to be executed are the following:

PE1 (IOS XR)
```
router bgp 64500
  bfd minimum-interval 300
  bfd multiplier 5
  neighbor 172.16.1.2
    remote-as 64510
    bfd fast-detect
```

PE2 (IOS XE)
```
interface GigabitEthernet 0/0
  bfd interval 300 min_rx 300 multiplier 5
!
router bgp 64510
  neighbor 172.16.1.1 remote-as 64500
  neighbor 172.16.1.1 fall-over bfd
```

In IOS and IOS XE, the configuration entails that the BFD is enabled first at interface level. The command requires three parameters:

- **interval**: the period of BFD HELLO messages sent (expressed as msec).

- **min_rx**: the minimum interval between two BFD HELLO messages coming from the BFD Neighbor. Usually, it is set equal to the "**interval**" value.

- **multiplier**: is the number of BFD HELLO messages that can be lost, before declaring the connection down. The recommended value in practical applications ranges from 3 to 5.

Then, the BFD supporting BGP needs to be enabled, through the "**neighbor** *IP-neighbor* **fall-over bfd**" command.

In IOS XR, the configuration only occurs within the BGP process, where the period of BFD HELLO messages ("**minimum-interval** *period-in-msec*") and the "**multiplier**" value (with the same meaning we saw for IOS and IOS XE) are defined. Within a single BGP Neighbor, we need to enable the BFD with the "**bfd fast-detect**" command.

The following is an example of configuration in JUNOS, assuming the same scenario of Figure 12.4.

PE1 (JUNOS)
```
[edit protocols bgp]
traceoptions {
    file bgp.log;
    flag state;
}
group eBGP {
    bfd-liveness-detection {
        minimum-interval 300;
        multiplier 5;
    }
    neighbor 172.20.1.2 {
        peer-as 64510;
    }
}
```

NOTE: the configuration of the "**traceoptions**" section is required only to analyze the events dynamics, and has no relation with the BFD.

PE2 configuration is the same, and will be omitted. Now, let's see what happens if the connection between PE2 and switch L2 goes out of service. As we mentioned earlier, without the BFD, PE2 immediately closes the session, while PE1 closes the session once the Hold time expires. On the other hand, with the BFD enabled, as you may notice from the results of the following "**show log bgp.log**" commands, both PE1 and PE2 close the BGP session, almost at the same time, PE1 closes it shortly after 1.5 sec, being the time needed to detect the out of service 5*300 =1,500 msec:

```
aft@PE2> show log bgp.log

Nov 25 08:22:41.982350 bgp_ifachange: interface 172.20.1.2(ge-0/0/0.0)
went down, state <Broadcast Multicast>, chng <UpDown>, instance master,
checking who this bothers

Nov 25 08:22:41.982372 bgp_affected2: peer 172.20.1.1 (External AS 64501)
idled, shared interface went down

Nov 25 08:22:41.982392 bgp_ifachange_group:6289: NOTIFICATION sent to
172.20.1.1

(External AS 64501): code 6 (Cease) subcode 6 (Other Configuration Change),
Reason:Interface change for the peer-group

. . .

aft@PE1> show log bgp.log

Nov 25 08:22:43.820435 bgp_peer_close: closing peer 172.20.1.2 (External
AS 64502), state is 7 (Established)

Nov 25 08:22:43.821347 bgp_event: peer 172.20.1.2 (External AS 64502) old
state Established event Restart new state Idle
```

12.2.2 The fast peering deactivation function

The fast external fall-over function described above cannot be applied to iBGP sessions or to multihop eBGP sessions. What alternatives are there, apart from the standard BGP KEEPALIVE and Hold time tuning? In Cisco platforms, there is the fast peering deactivation function support, which can be applied both to iBGP and multihop eBGP sessions. The idea is simple: as soon as the IP address of the BGP Neighbor can no longer be reached by the RIB, the session is immediately deactivated. In Cisco routers, the fast peering deactivation function is activated via the IOS/IOS XE "**neighbor** *IP-neighbor* **fall-over**" command. There is no similar command in the IOS XR. For example, consider router PE11 of AS 64501, which has two iBGP sessions with routers PE21 and PE22. The address of the Loopback0 interface of router PEXY is 192.168.2.XY/32. iBGP sessions, as per best practice, are established using the IP addresses of the Loopback0 interfaces. The BGP configuration of router PE11 is the following:

```
router bgp 64501
  template peer-session iBGP
    remote-as 64501
    update-source loopback0
    fall-over
 !
```

```
neighbor 192.168.2.21 inherit peer-session iBGP
neighbor 192.168.2.22 inherit peer-session iBGP
```

Let's assume that the entire router PE21 goes out of service. By activating the "**debug ip routing**" command on PE11, we obtain:

```
*Sep 29 16:36:38.527: RT: NET-RED 192.168.2.21/32
```

```
*Sep 29 16:36:38.531: RT: del 192.168.2.21/32 via 172.20.13.12, ospf
metric [110/21]
```

```
*Sep 29 16:36:38.535: RT: delete subnet route to 192.168.2.21/32
```

```
*Sep 29 16:36:38.535: RT: NET-RED 192.168.2.21/32
... < output omitted > ...
```

```
*Sep 29 16:36:38.567: RT: Try lookup less specific 192.168.2.21/32, default 1
```

```
*Sep 29 16:36:38.571: RT: Failed found subnet on less specific
```

```
*Sep 29 16:36:38.571: RT: return NULL
```

```
*Sep 29 16:36:38.611: %BGP-5-ADJCHANGE: neighbor 192.168.2.21 Down Route
to peer lost
```

As you may have noticed, as soon as router PE11 is missing the path toward BGP Neighbor 192.168.2.21/32, the iBGP session between PE11 and PE21 is deactivated.

Obviously, this approach is strongly affected by the convergence speed of IGP (in the example, we used OSPF).

However, the fast peering deactivation function has a downside: the prefix aggregation or the presence of a default route in the RIB makes the function inapplicable. In other words, if, in the RIB, router PE11 has a default route, perhaps advertised via OSPF by PE21, connectivity toward BGP Neighbor 192.168.2.21/32 would not be considered lost, and therefore the mechanism would not work (meaning that the BGP session would only be deactivated once the Holdtime expires).

There are two possible "escape ways". The first is to advertise the default route via BGP, rather than via OSPF, since BGP routes are not considered among the possible alternatives to reach the BGP Neighbor.

The second "escape way" is to use the extended selective address tracking for bgp fast session deactivation function, which consists in adding, to the "**neighbor** *IP-neighbor* **fall-over**" command, a route-map to select what IP prefixes should be monitored to determine if the iBGP session drops.

Going back to our example, the Loopback0 interfaces used as endpoints of iBGP sessions are all /32 subnets of IP prefix 192.168.2/24. So, we can add a route-map to the configuration that allows all /32 subnets of prefix 192.168.2/24 to solve the issue. The additional configurations are:

```
ip prefix-list LOOPB seq 5 permit 192.168.2.0/24 ge 32
!
route-map BGP-NEIGHBOR permit 10
  match ip address prefix-list LOOPB
  match source-protocol ospf 1
!
router bgp 1
  template peer session iBGP
    remote-as 1
```

```
    update-source loopback 0
    fall-over route-map BGP-NEIGHBOR
!
neighbor 192.168.2.21 inherit peer-session iBGP
neighbor 192.168.2.22 inherit peer-session iBGP
```

NOTE: The configuration above shows a clear example of configuration scalability allowed by using, in Cisco platforms, BGP peer-templates (see Section 3.2.2), which are currently recommended over the old BGP peer-groups (a similar configuration in IOS XR is comprised by BGP configuration templates, see Section 3.2.3).

12.3 RECALCULATING THE BGP NEXT-HOP

In the previous paragraph, we have highlighted how it is possible to close a BGP session, without waiting for the Holdtime negotiated between the two BGP Neighbors to expire. In this paragraph, we will focus on what happens when the BGP Next-Hop becomes unreachable.

12.3.1 From the time-driven BGP to the event-driven BGP

In order to understand how this problem started and why it can considerably extend convergence times, let's see what happened in the first BGP implementations in Cisco routers.

For each BGP prefix, the BGP Next-Hop resolution is usually recursive. This means that often (but not always) the BGP Next-Hop is not directly connected, therefore the router must execute a new lookup on the RIB to find a new path toward it. This path is determined by an IGP (OSPF, IS-IS, etc.), or even (only in particularly elementary situations) via static routing.

In Cisco routers, this interaction between BGP and IGP protocols was implemented by the special process known as BGP scanner. The BGP scanner process executes a periodical scanning of the BGP table, through which several checks and updates are carried out on all the advertisements present, including BGP Next-Hop reachability (if not, the advertisement is removed from the BGP table, and, if it is a best path, the selection process is executed again to determine the new best path), Route Flap Damping mechanism updates, conditioned advertisements check, etc. The default value of the scanning process period is 60 sec, and it can be varied through the command (valid for all IOS types):

router(config)# **router bgp** *AS-number*
router(config-router)# **bgp scan-time** *value-in-seconds*

where the interval of permitted values is [5, 60]. You should keep in mind that a low value entails several benefits in terms of convergence speed, despite a greater CPU commitment. The actual value of the scanning process period used by the router can be controlled through the standard show command "**show bgp (ipv4 | ipv6) unicast summary**".

The reason why the BGP scanner process extends convergence times is easy. Think for a moment that, once a process cycle ends, a BGP Next-Hop becomes unreachable after a few seconds. IGP realizes this pretty quickly, however, due to the BGP scanner, the BGP process realizes it after approx. 60 sec (statistically, mid the default scanning period of 60 sec, after about 30 sec). This entails that, for a certain period (up to almost 60 sec, using the default value), traffic is very likely to run into a forwarding loop and/or black-hole.

The convergence speed difference between IGP and BGP is now very evident. While IGP detects the loss of a prefix very quickly – usually in less than one second, and, if the main timers are suitably tuned and the LFA (Loop Free Alternate) function is active, even less than a few dozen msec – in Cisco implementation of BGP, convergence times to a new BGP Next-Hop are around dozens of seconds (up to almost 60).

The ideal would be to have an immediate (or near-immediate) communication from IGP to BGP, that the BGP Next-Hop has become unreachable. In particular, it would be best to switch from a time-driven BGP Next-Hop validation management (based on the BGP scanner process), to an event-driven management, based on a communication from IGP to BGP about the BGP Next-Hop reachability.

12.3.2 The BGP Next-Hop Tracking function

In its evolution, Cisco's BGP implementation, after the introduction of the BGP Next-Hop Tracking (BGP NHT) function, went from a time-driven to an event-driven management. On the other hand, this function has always been implemented in JUNOS, which has used an event-driven approach since the beginning.

Let's see how the BGP NHT function is implemented in Cisco routers. The idea is to allow the BGP process to register any BGP Next-Hop (through a process called RIB watcher), and then request a sort of warning every time the BGP Next-Hop reachability is changed (actually, not just its reachability, but any change concerning the BGP Next-Hop, such as the IGP cost to reach it, which, as you may remember, affects BGP's selection process).

Notice that the number of BGP Next-Hops is much smaller than the number of prefixes learned via BGP, therefore the BGP NHT function is not very heavy for the CPU, nor for memory consumption (for instance, think about the router of an ISP receiving the FIRT from two Upstream Providers; there are approximately hundreds of thousands prefixes, but the BGP Next-Hops are just two).

Let's go over some configuration aspects in Cisco routers. First of all, in all new IOS versions (IOS, IOS XE, IOS XR, etc.) the BGP NHT function is implemented by default. It can only be disabled (e.g. in the case of BGP Next-Hop flap not solved by damping mechanisms) with the following command:

router(config)# **router bgp** *AS-number*
router(config-router)# **address-family ...**
router(config-router-af)# **no bgp nexthop trigger enable**

There are two other configuration aspects we should dwell on. The first concerns the delay with which the BGP process uses information on the BGP Next-Hop received from IGP. By default, BGP uses this information with a 5 sec delay, to allow the BGP process to collect more events communicated by IGP, and thus optimize their processing. Usually, this delay should be configured at a value slightly higher than IGP's convergence speed; however, it can also be configured as null, so that every event communicated by IGP is processed immediately (but beware that this could lead to possible BGP route oscillations, caused by BGP Next-Hop oscillations (status changes)). To change this delay, the following command is used:

router(config)# **router bgp** *AS-number*
router(config-router)# **address-family ...**
router(config-router-af)# **bgp nexthop trigger delay** *value-in-sec*

The other interesting configuration aspect concerns an issue we've already seen in the previous paragraph, when talking about the "**neighbor ... fall-over**" command: prefix aggregation or the presence of a default route in the RIB make the BGP NHT function ineffective. Indeed, if a router has a default route in its RIB, or an aggregate prefix containing a BGP Next-Hop, a possible state change of the BGP Next-Hop is not reported to the BGP process, since nothing about its reachability changes in the RIB.

The "escape way" to use is the BGP selective address tracking extended NHT function, which allows selecting the IP prefixes to which the BGP Next-Hops to be monitored belong to. The command that allows activating this function is:

router(config)# **router bgp** *AS-number*
router(config-router)# **address-family ...**
router(config-router-af)# **bgp nexthop route-map** *route-map-name*

where the route-map allows defining the set of BGP Next-Hops that should be monitored. If a BGP Next-Hop does not belong to a prefix allowed by the route-map, it is considered unreachable. Consequently, all prefixes learned via BGP that have this BGP Next-Hop do not take part in BGP's selection process.

> **NOTE**: The only two "match" conditions allowed in the route-map are "**match ip address** ..." and "**match source-protocol** ...".

Let's see how the BGP selective address tracking works with an example. Consider the scenario in the figure below:

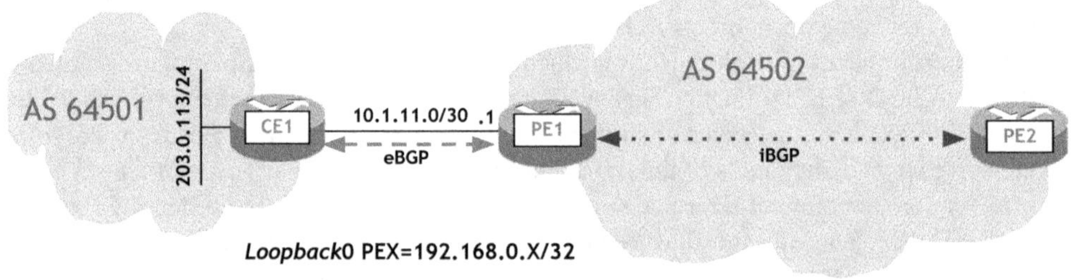

Figure 12.5 – Network scenario for checking the BGP selective address tracking.

The eBGP session between routers CE1 and PE1 is standard, and uses the addresses of the interfaces at the point-to-point connection endpoints as IP addresses. Moreover, the next-hop-self function has not been configured on router PE1, and subnet 10.1.11.0/30 has not been redistributed on IGP of AS 64502. As a consequence, on PE2, the advertisement of prefix 203.0.113/24 does not take part in the selection process, since, for PE2, BGP Next-Hop 10.1.11.2 is not reachable:

```
PE2# show bgp ipv4 unicast 203.0.113.0 255.255.255.0
BGP routing table entry for 203.0.113.0/24, version 7
Paths: (1 available, no best path)
Flag: 0x820
  Not advertised to any peer
  64501
    10.1.11.2 (inaccessible) from 192.168.0.1 (192.168.0.1)
      Origin IGP, metric 0, localpref 100, valid, internal
```

Now, suppose that a dummy static router with Next-Hop=null0 is configured on PE2, toward an IP prefix that is a supernet of prefix 10.1.11.0/30:

```
PE2(config)# ip route 10.1.0.0 255.255.0.0 null0
```

As you can see in the following view, even if it may seem incorrect, the advertisement of prefix 203.0.113/24 takes part in the selection process (even if BGP Next-Hop 10.1.11.2 remains unreachable to PE2):

```
PE2# show bgp ipv4 unicast 203.0.113.0 255.255.255.0
BGP routing table entry for 203.0.113.0/24, version 8
Paths: (1 available, best #1, table Default-IP-Routing-Table)
Flag: 0x820
  Not advertised to any peer
  64501
    10.1.11.2 from 192.168.0.1 (192.168.0.1)
      Origin IGP, metric 0, localpref 100, valid, internal, best
```

Now, with the help of the BGP selective address tracking, let's see how we can put things back in place. Often a BGP Next-Hop comes from a /32 prefix (a typical example is using Loopback interfaces for BGP sessions) or /30 or /31 prefixes (a typical example is using the IP addresses of the physical interfaces of point-to-point connections for BGP sessions). With the BGP selective address tracking function, we can narrow down the set of valid BGP Next-Hops, for instance, by allowing only those BGP Next-Hops belonging to prefixes in the RIB, with mask length 30, 31 or 32. This is the configuration to execute:

```
ip prefix-list GE-30 seq 5 permit 0.0.0.0/0 ge 30
!
route-map TEST permit 10
 match ip address prefix-list GE-30
!
router bgp 64502
 bgp nexthop route-map TEST
```

The BGP advertisement of prefix 203.0.113/24, with this configuration, no longer takes part in BGP's selection process, since the only prefix in the RIB containing the BGP Next-Hop is prefix 10.1.0.0/16 (added with a dummy static route), whose mask is not greater than or equal to 30, therefore it is not considered to define the BGP Next-Hop reachability:

```
PE2# show bgp ipv4 unicast | i 203.0.113.0
* i203.0.113.0/24     10.1.11.2                 0    100      0 64501 i
```

12.3.3 Case study

In order to check the BGP NHT operation, we executed a lab test showing the difference in convergence times between the time-driven BGP (with the NHT function disabled) and the event-driven BGP. The scenario of this test is shown in the following figure.

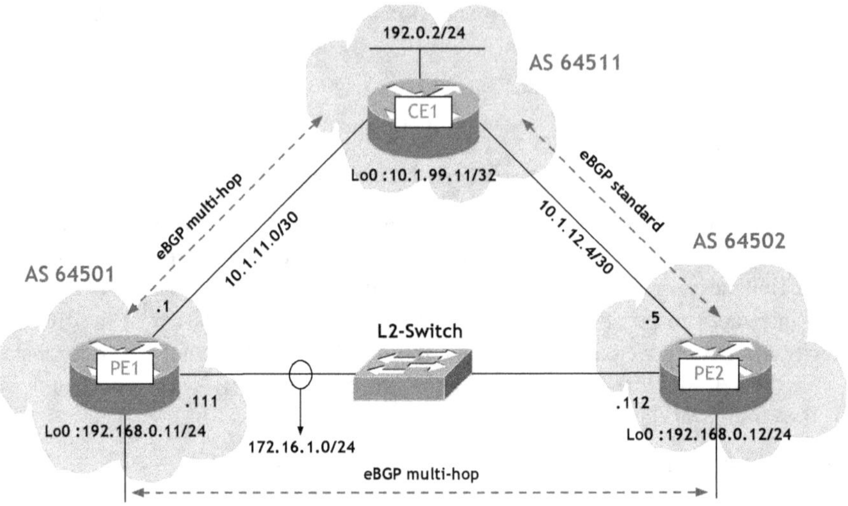

Figure 12.6 – Case study scenario.

Basic BGP configurations on the three routers are:

```
hostname PE1
!
router bgp 64501
 neighbor 10.1.99.11 remote-as 64511
 neighbor 10.1.99.11 ebgp-multihop 255
 neighbor 10.1.99.11 update-source Loopback0
 neighbor 192.168.0.12 remote-as 64502
 neighbor 192.168.0.12 ebgp-multihop 255
 neighbor 192.168.0.12 update-source Loopback0

hostname PE2
!
router bgp 64502
 neighbor 10.1.12.6 remote-as 64511
 neighbor 192.168.0.11 remote-as 64501
 neighbor 192.168.0.11 ebgp-multihop 255
 neighbor 192.168.0.11 update-source Loopback0

hostname CE1
!
router bgp 64511
 network 192.0.2.0 mask 255.255.255.0
 neighbor 10.1.12.5 remote-as 64502
 neighbor 192.168.0.11 remote-as 64501
```

```
 neighbor 192.168.0.11 ebgp-multihop 255
 neighbor 192.168.0.11 update-source Loopback0
```

At first, let's assume we have disabled the BGP NHT function on router PE1:

```
router bgp 64501
 address-family ipv4
  no bgp nexthop trigger enable
```

and we have activated the "**debug ip routing**".

Then, we shutdown CE1's Loopback0 interface, which is used for the multihop eBGP session with PE1, and let's see what happens on PE1. First of all, with IGP convergence times (which, in our case, is the basic OSPF, with non-optimized timers), PE1 cancels prefix 10.1.99.11/32 (address of CE1's Loopback0 interface) from its RIB:

```
*Oct 14 13:59:37.407: RT: del 10.1.99.11 via 10.1.11.2, ospf metric [110/65]

*Oct 14 13:59:37.407: RT: delete subnet route to 10.1.99.11/32
```

Then, we immediately checked PE1's BGP table, from which you can see that PE1 still believes that its BGP Next-Hop is 10.1.99.11:

```
PE1# show bgp ipv4 unicast

. . . < output omitted > . . .

     Network          Next Hop       Metric LocPrf  Weight    Path
*    192.0.2.0/24     192.168.0.12                      0     64502 64511 i
*>                    10.1.99.11          0              0     64511 i
```

However, address 10.1.99.11 can no longer be reached:

```
PE1# ping 10.1.99.11
Type escape sequence to abort.
Sending 5, 100-byte ICMP Echos to 10.1.99.11, timeout is 2 seconds:
.....
Success rate is 0 percent (0/5)
```

What is happening? Easy, the BGP scanner process on PE1 (which has a default period of 60 sec that we haven't changed), still hasn't checked the BGP Next-Hop's reachability, which therefore remains the initial one. After a while, the process resumes the BGP Next-Hop reachability check, and, when it realizes it can no longer be reached by the RIB, it reruns the BGP selection process and converges on the alternative Next-Hop 192.168.0.12.

```
*Oct 14 14:00:32.487: RT: updating bgp 192.0.2.0/24 (0x0): via 192.168.0.12

*Oct 14 14:00:32.487: RT: closer admin distance for 192.0.2.0, flushing 1
routes

*Oct 14 14:00:32.487: RT: add 192.0.2.0/24 via 192.168.0.12, bgp metric
[20/0]

PE1# show bgp ipv4 unicast

. . . < output omitted > . . .
```

```
       Network           Next Hop      Metric LocPrf  Weight  Path
 *>  192.0.2.0/24        192.168.0.12                      0   64502 64511 i
 *                       10.1.99.11         0              0   64511 i
```

How long did BGP take to converge on the new best path? From the outputs of the debugs, it appears it takes a little over 55 sec! And we were lucky! It could take longer, since the scanning period is 60 sec.

Now, let's enable the BGP NHT. To be fair, we should say let's "re-enable" the BGP NHT, since, as we mentioned earlier, the BGP NHT is enabled by default in recent IOS versions.

```
router bgp 64501
 address-family ipv4
  bgp nexthop trigger enable
```

If we repeat the previous procedure, here is what happens on PE1:

```
*Oct 14 14:10:32.843: RT: del 10.1.99.11 via 10.1.11.2, ospf metric
[110/65]

*Oct 14 14:10:32.843: RT: delete subnet route to 10.1.99.11/32

*Oct 14 14:10:37.843: RT: updating bgp 192.0.2.0/24 (0x0): via 192.168.0.12

*Oct 14 14:10:37.843: RT: closer admin distance for 192.0.2.0, flushing 1
routes

*Oct 14 14:10:37.843: RT: add 192.0.2.0/24 via 192.168.0.12, bgp metric
[20/0]
```

As you may notice, now BGP converges on the alternative best-path 192.168.0.12 after just 5 sec, which is the default value of the BGP NHT trigger delay. We executed the test again, after setting this value to zero:

```
router bgp 64501
 address-family ipv4
  bgp nexthop trigger delay 0
```

Here is the result:

```
*Oct 14 14:13:48.591: RT: del 10.1.99.11 via 10.1.11.2, ospf metric
[110/65]

*Oct 14 14:13:48.591: RT: delete subnet route to 10.1.99.11/32

*Oct 14 14:13:48.595: RT: updating bgp 192.0.2.0/24 (0x0): via 192.168.0.12

*Oct 14 14:13:48.595: RT: closer admin distance for 192.0.2.0, flushing 1
routes

*Oct 14 14:13:48.595: RT: add 192.0.2.0/24 via 192.168.0.12, bgp metric
[20/0]
```

The convergence time has become 4 ms! However, this is just the time it took router PE1 to converge to the new best path. The overall convergence time depends on the time it takes IGP to communicate that CE1's Loopback0 interface is out of service to PE1. And this opens an interesting consideration, BGP's convergence time to the new BGP Next-Hop strongly depends on IGP's convergence time. We will go back to this aspect in the next paragraphs.

12.3.4 BGP fast external fall-over and BGP NHT: differences

Sometimes, there is a suspicion (or doubt) that the BGP fast external fall-over function, introduced in the previous paragraph, has the same purpose of the BGP NHT function, and therefore that one of the two is useless. To prevent any doubt and confusion, we want to end this paragraph by highlighting the differences between these two functions.

As we saw in the previous paragraph, the BGP fast external fall-over is used to close an eBGP session(s), after the BGP Neighbor address is no longer reachable, that is, when no path to reach the IP address of the BGP Neighbor is available in the RIB.

As we have extensively seen in this paragraph, the BGP NHT is an event-driven criteria, used to check the BGP Next-Hop reachability (which does not necessarily coincide with the BGP Neighbor address; a typical example concerns the presence of Route Reflectors, where the BGP Next-Hop and the BGP Neighbor address usually does not match). If the BGP Next-Hop is no longer reachable, the BGP session won't necessarily be closed (unless the BGP Next-Hop coincides with the BGP Neighbor address, as when using the "**neighbor ... next-hop-self**" command, or when a router adds a prefix to propagate locally, in the BGP table); the BGP process just withdraws the prefix, recalculates the best path and readvertises the new best path. If there is no new best path available, the prefix is just withdrawn.

12.4 CONVERGENCE ON THE CONTROL PLANE AND DATA PLANE

In the two previous paragraphs, we talked about two topics: the speed at which the loss of a BGP session is detected, and how to quickly check if the Next-Hop is reachable.

In this paragraph, we will cover two other topics, one that is basically invisible, i.e. it has (almost) no impact on configurations, and another one concerning a function activated based on the configuration.

Before covering these two additional topics, however, we need to make a premise. Through which criteria does BGP's control plane allow converging on a new best path?

12.4.1 Convergence on the control plane

In a standard IP backbone using a routing architecture as the one described in Paragraph 8.2 (it doesn't matter if by adding MPLS or not), we can identify three out-of-service scenarios, entailing BGP's convergence on a new best path:

1. Out of service of elements within the backbone (routers and/or connections).

2. Out of service of an edge router, which, from now on, with a tiny abuse of notation, we will call PE (Provider Edge) router.

3. Out of service of PE↔CE, connections, where CE (Customer Edge routers, here too by stretching the notation a bit), are routers outside the backbone, which, in our example, exchange routing information with the backbone via eBGP.

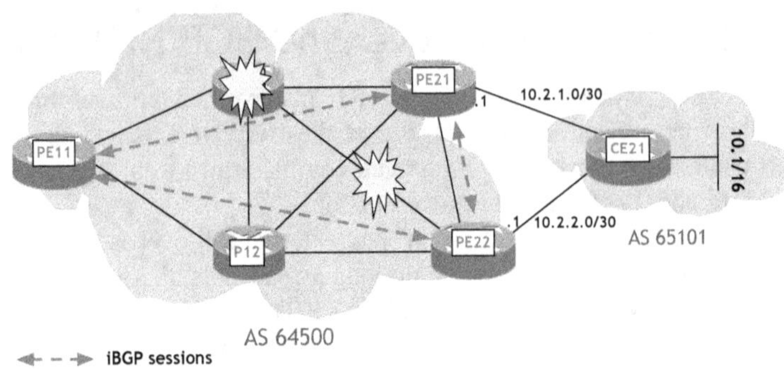

Figure 12.7 – Scenario 1: out of service of elements inside the backbone.

The first scenario is shown in Figure 12.7. Let's see how the convergence toward a new best path occurs, in a similar scenario, after router P11 goes out of service. The network comprises Cisco routers with IOS. As the figure shows, between the three PE routers there is a full mesh of iBGP sessions, while router CE21 has two eBGP sessions toward the two routers PE21 and PE22, to which it advertises prefix 10.1/16. Also, on the two routers PE21 and PE22, we activated the "**next-hop self**" function on the iBGP sessions toward PE11. To make the test more interesting, we set the IGP metrics of router P12 interface on the connection toward router PE21 to 1,000. All other metrics are set to 10, except for those associated to the Loopback0 interfaces, which are set to 1. Lastly, the IP addresses of the Loopback0 interfaces of routers PEXY are 192.168.0.XY/32, and the iBGP sessions, as per best practice, are established using the IP addresses of the Loopback0 interfaces.

First, let's see PE11's BGP table:

```
PE11# show bgp ipv4 unicast 10.1.0.0
BGP routing table entry for 10.1.0.0/16, version 2
Paths: (2 available, best #2, table Default-IP-Routing-Table)
  Not advertised to any peer
  65101
    192.168.0.22 (metric 21) from 192.168.0.22 (192.168.0.22)
      Origin IGP, metric 0, localpref 100, valid, internal
  65101
    192.168.0.21 (metric 21) from 192.168.0.21 (192.168.0.21)
      Origin IGP, metric 0, localpref 100, valid, internal, best
```

As you can see, PE11 chooses Next-Hop 192.168.0.21 as the best path; due to the lowest BGP router-ID value (we will leave the details to you, as useful practice).

Now, after activating the "**debug ip routing**" and "**debug ip bgp updates**" commands on router PE11, we turned off router P11 completely. As expected, the BGP Next-Hop changes (and you can figure out the details yourself):

```
PE11# show bgp ipv4 unicast 10.1.0.0
BGP routing table entry for 10.1.0.0/16, version 3
Paths: (2 available, best #1, table Default-IP-Routing-Table)
Flag: 0x800
  Not advertised to any peer
  65101
    192.168.0.22 (metric 21) from 192.168.0.22 (192.168.0.22)
      Origin IGP, metric 0, localpref 100, valid, internal, best
```

```
65101
  192.168.0.21 (metric 31) from 192.168.0.21 (192.168.0.21)
     Origin IGP, metric 0, localpref 100, valid, internal
```

This is the interesting part of the debugs activated on PE11:

```
*Nov 16 16:59:06.263: RT: del 192.168.0.21/32 via 172.20.11.11, ospf
metric [110/21]
*Nov 16 16:59:06.279: RT: add 192.168.0.21/32 via 172.20.13.12, ospf
metric [110/31]
*Nov 16 16:59:06.299: RT: del 192.168.0.22/32 via 172.20.11.11, ospf
metric [110/21]
*Nov 16 16:59:11.331: BGP(0): Revise route installing 1 of 1 routes for
10.1.0.0/16 -> 192.168.0.22(main) to main IP table
*Nov 16 16:59:11.335: RT: 10.1.0.0/16 gateway changed from 192.168.0.21
to 192.168.0.22
```

As you may notice, the BGP convergence time toward the new BGP Next-Hop 192.168.0.22 (PE22's Loopback0 interface) is slightly more than 5 sec (of which 5 sec due to the BGP NHT Trigger Delay). As you can easily verify, if we hadn't changed the value of the IGP metrics of router P12 interface on the connection toward router PE21 to 1,000, the BGP Next-Hop wouldn't have changed.

In short, the sequence of the operations on router PE11 is the following:

1. IGP detects that the adjacencies established by router P11 are out of service, and determines, through a new execution of the SPF algorithm, new optimal paths toward the new possible BGP Next-Hops PE21 and PE22.

2. If the path toward the optimal BGP Next-Hop changes, IGP notifies it to the BGP process, otherwise nothing happens.

3. PE11 identifies all BGP advertisements with the BGP Next-Hop whose path has changed, and thus immediately executes a new best path selection process. In general, this period is proportional to the number of IP prefixes advertised via BGP, and may be fairly long.

4. After determining the new best path, PE11 updates both the RIB and the FIB, and traffic continues to flow, on a different path.

The second scenario, as shown in Figure 12.8 below, entails an out-of-service of a PE router.

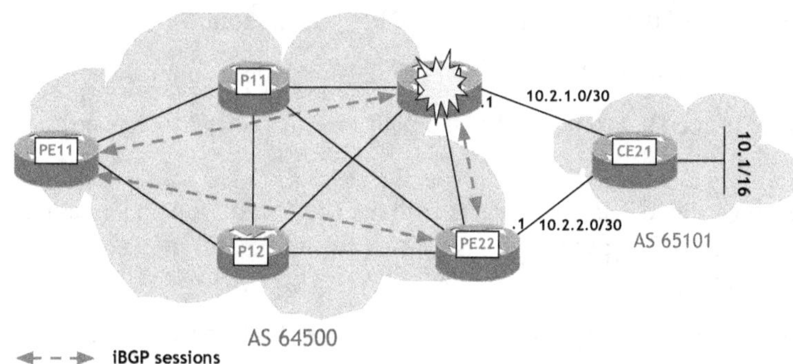

Figure 12.8 – Scenario 2: out of service of a PE router.

Here too, we did a lab test, with the same network configuration, after setting the IGP metric of the P12↔PE21 connection back to 10. At first, the best path for prefix 10.1/16 is router PE21 (for the same reason of the previous setting; the change in the P12↔PE21 connection metrics does not affect the best path determination):

Now, after activating on router PE11 the same debugs as in the previous setting, we shut down router PE21 – i.e. the optimal BGP Next-Hop – completely (if we switched off router PE22 instead of router PE21, nothing would have happened in terms of BGP convergence). As expected, on PE11 the BGP Next-Hop changes and the BGP control plane converges to the new (and only) BGP Next-Hop 192.168.0.22:

```
PE11# show bgp ipv4 unicast 10.1.0.0
BGP routing table entry for 10.1.0.0/16, version 7
Paths: (2 available, best #1, table Default-IP-Routing-Table)
  Not advertised to any peer
  65101
    192.168.0.22 (metric 21) from 192.168.0.22 (192.168.0.22)
      Origin IGP, metric 0, localpref 100, valid, internal, best
  65101
    192.168.0.21 (inaccessible) from 192.168.0.21 (192.168.0.21)
      Origin IGP, metric 0, localpref 100, valid, internal
```

To see how long it took, let's analyze the interesting part about the debugs activated on PE11:

```
*Nov 16 17:49:37.023: RT: del 192.168.0.21/32 via 172.20.11.11, ospf
metric [110/21]

*Nov 16 17:49:37.031: RT: del 192.168.0.21/32 via 172.20.13.12, ospf
metric [110/21]

*Nov 16 17:49:37.035: RT: delete subnet route to 192.168.0.21/32

*Nov 16 17:49:42.059: BGP(0): Revise route installing 1 of 1 routes for
10.1.0.0/16 -> 192.168.0.22(main) to main IP table

*Nov 16 17:49:42.063: RT: 10.1.0.0/16 gateway changed from 192.168.0.21
to 192.168.0.22
```

As you may notice, in this case too, the BGP convergence time toward the new BGP Next-Hop 192.168.0.22 (PE22's Loopback0 interface) is slightly more than 5 sec (of which 5 sec due to the BGP NHT Trigger Delay).

In short, the sequence of the operations on router PE11 is the following:

1. IGP detects that router PE21 (the optimal BGP Next-Hop) is not reachable;

2. IGP notifies to the BGP process that the path toward router PE21 is no longer valid (BGP NHT function);

3. PE11 identifies all BGP advertisements with the BGP Next-Hop no longer reachable, and so, after the BGP NHT Trigger Delay has elapsed (default 5 sec), it executes a new process for best path selection;

4. After determining the new best path, PE11 updates both the RIB and the FIB, and traffic continues to flow, on a different path.

Before switching to the third scenario, let's point out a key aspect: the convergence time toward the new BGP Next-Hop, in both scenarios we described, depends on IGP's convergence speed. BGP's control plane only intervenes with the BGP NHT Trigger Delay. By resetting the BGP NHT Trigger Delay in both these scenarios, BGP's convergence speed is basically the same as IGP's convergence speed (which, if suitably configured, converges within a few dozen or hundred msec). The third and last scenario, as shown in Figure 12.9 below, entails an out-of-service of a PE↔CE connection:

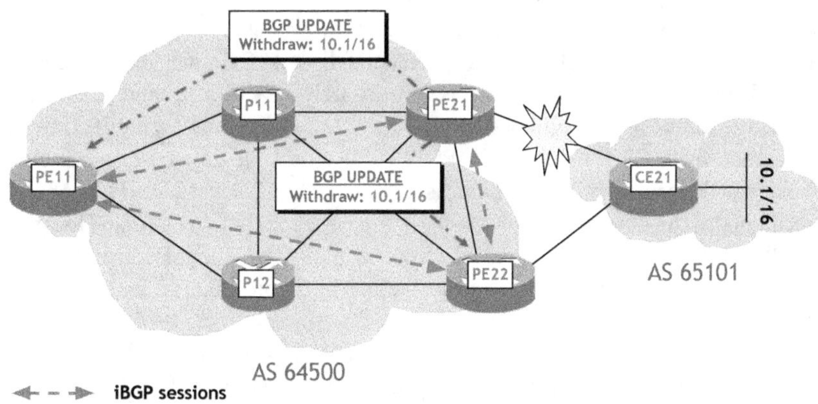

Figure 12.9 – Scenario 3: out of service of a PE↔CE connection.

Here too, we did a lab test, with the same network configuration as in previous scenarios. Remember that, on routers PE21 and PE22, the "**neighbor 192.168.0.11 next-hop-self**" command is active. At first, the best-path for prefix 10.1/16, as we saw in the tests of the previous scenarios, is router PE21.

Now, after activating the usual debugs, on router PE11, we shutdown the PE21 side interface of the PE21↔CE21 connection (notice that, if we had instead shutdown the PE22 side interface of the PE22↔CE21 connection, nothing would have happened in terms of BGP convergence). As expected, on PE11, the BGP Next-Hop changes and the BGP control plane converges to the new BGP Next-Hop 192.168.0.22:

```
PE11# show bgp ipv4 unicast 10.1.0.0
BGP table version is 3, local router ID is 192.168.0.11
. . . < legend omitted > . . .

  Network          Next Hop          Metric    LocPrf    Weight  Path
*>i10.1.0.0/16     192.168.0.22           0       100         0   65101 i
```

As usual, to see how long it took, let's analyze the interesting part about the debugs activated on PE11:

```
*Nov 16 19:08:12.355: BGP(0): 192.168.0.21 rcv UPDATE about 10.1.0.0/16
- withdrawn
*Nov 16 19:08:12.367: BGP(0): Revise route installing 1 of 1 routes for
10.1.0.0/16  -> 192.168.0.22(main) to main IP table
*Nov 16 19:08:12.371: RT: 10.1.0.0/16 gateway changed from 192.168.0.21
to 192.168.0.22
```

When analyzing the debug, we can make a first, very important observation: the convergence speed, differently from the two previous scenarios, does not depend on IGP's convergence speed, but only on BGP's control plane, due to the presence of the **"neighbor 192.168.0.11 next-hop-self"** command on routers PE21 and PE22. Indeed, this entail that router PE11 sees as BGP Next-Hop addresses 192.168.0.21 (PE21) or 192.168.0.22 (PE22), rather than the CE side addresses of the PE↔CE point-to-point connection, therefore the PE↔CE connections out-of-service has no impact on the BGP Next-Hops seen by PE11. The convergence only occurs thanks to the exchange of BGP messages.

In particular, what happens is that, following the shutdown of the PE21 side interface of the PE21↔CE21 connection, through the fast external fall-over function seen in Section 12.2.1, the BGP session between PE21 and CE21 is immediately deactivated, and PE21 sends a BGP UPDATE message to its BGP Neighbors PE11 and PE22 to withdraw prefix 10.1/16 (in general, all prefixes learned from CE21). After this, PE11 recalculates the new best path (notice that, for PE22, the best path does not change!), which, as we saw earlier, is Next-Hop 192.168.0.22 (PE22). PE21 too recalculates the new best path, which, in this case too, becomes Next-Hop 192.168.0.22 (PE22). On PE11, it all occurs in 20 msec! (Note: actually, we should add the BGP UPDATE message generation time by PE21, and its propagation time from PE21 to PE11 to it, but they are quite short).

Such a short convergence time is misleading, because it usually depends on the number of prefixes that CE21 advertises to AS 64500. If CE21, instead of being the router of a customer of AS 64550, would be one of its Upstream Providers advertising the entire FIRT, things would be different, because PE21 would have to withdraw hundreds of thousands of prefixes, and thus re-execute the selection process for each one of them!

Let's repeat the key concept: convergence only occurs at BGP level, and the BGP NHT function is no help in this case, since, for PE11, the BGP Next-Hop regularly remains in its RIB.

What would happen if we removed the handy **"neighbor 192.168.0.11 next-hop-self"** command on routers PE21 and PE22? First of all, we would have to redistribute the IP subnets used to number the PE↔CE point-to-point connections, in the protocol, or make them participate in the IGP process (possibly with a passive-interface on the PE side interface!), or PE11 would see its BGP Next-Hops unreachable. After doing so, the BGP Next-Hops become the CE side IP addresses of the PE↔CE point-to-point connections. In this case, the out of service of the PE21↔CE21 connection entails that the IGP protocol withdraws the IP subnet with which the PE21↔CE21 connection is numbered from PE11 routing table, and the BGP NHT comes into play.

In general, in topologies with a large number of BGP advertisements, this undoubtedly entails a significant benefit in terms of convergence. If, on the other hand, the number of BGP advertisements is low, the benefits in terms of convergence speed are compensated by the disadvantages of IP subnet redistribution of PE↔CE connections in IGP (increase of the memory necessary to LSDB, of the RIB size, possible security issues, etc.).

However, the problem with this approach is that it is not always applicable. Indeed, for instance, in the case of L3VPN MPLS service, every time a BGP advertisement is exported from a VRF, there is an automatic, non-removable **"next-hop self"**. And the same goes also for the other MPLS services using BGP on the control plane.

Summarizing what we have seen until now, in two out of the three scenarios described (the first and the second one), BGP's convergence speed basically depends on IGP's convergence speed (and this debunks the old myth that BGP is much slower to converge than IGPs), while in the third scenario it depends on BGP's control plane. In all scenarios, BGP is warned about a change, and must scan the BGP table to identify all the prefixes affected by the change. Although event-driven, this scanning process entails a period proportional to the number of IP prefixes. The process could be optimized (e.g. see scoped walks in IOS XR), but the time still depends on the number of prefixes advertised. The ideal would be to have a process independent of the number of prefixes, and this is what we will cover in the next paragraph.

12.4.2 Flat FIBs and hierarchical FIBs

A very important aspect for convergence, yet invisible from the outside, is how the FIB (Forwarding Information Base) is organized, that is, the table (usually hardware) that the router uses to switch packets.

NOTE: FIB construction starting from the information contained in the RIB, uses vendor-dependent algorithms (CEF Cisco, PFE Juniper, etc.). An algorithm – Openflow – was suggested, that would make the RIB-FIB communication protocol standard, that is, make the "control plane – data plane" dialogue standard; however, when this book was published, it was not very widespread.

The FIB can have a flat or hierarchical architecture. In a flat architecture, every prefix within the FIB (both learned via BGP or IGP) has the forwarding info associated to it (output interface, MAC rewrite, MPLS labels, and others, if necessary, see Figure 12.10 below). Forwarding information are often also called Direct Next-Hop.

However, a flat architecture is not very efficient, because any change concerning the Direct Next-Hop, requires the update of all prefixes associated to that Direct Next-Hop.

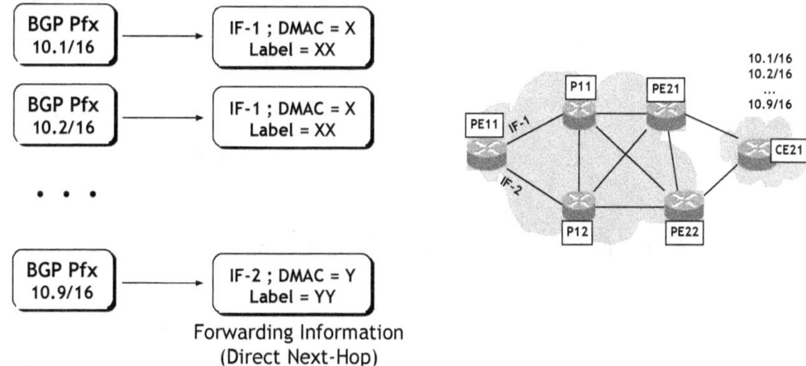

Figure 12.10 – Logical structure of a FIB with a flat architecture.

Obviously, with this kind of architecture, the FIB update time depends on the number of prefixes within it, and it can become very high.

If the FIB only had one hundred prefixes, even if a flat architecture would be OK, if the number of prefixes was hundreds of thousands, the update could require very high times, even in the order of minutes. The FIBs with a flat architecture could be OK 20 years ago, when the FIRT had less than 10k prefixes. In the 21st century IP networks, where it exceeds a million lines, we need to adopt a different approach.

So, the FIB architecture has been redesigned by the different manufacturers, to make its update faster. The idea is to organize it over three hierarchical levels:

Prefix → Pointer → Forwarding info

where the pointer, also called Indirect Next-Hop, in our case is just a BGP Next-Hop, as shown in Figure 12.11 below (actually, some manufacturers use a number chosen internally by the router as Indirect Next-Hop; however, in order to better understand the concepts we are explaining, it is easier to consider it as a BGP Next-Hop).

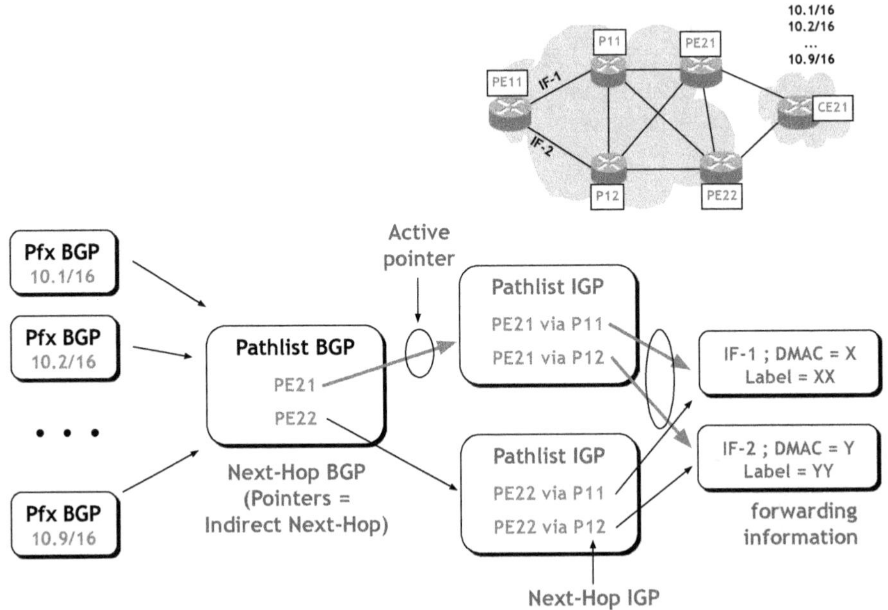

Figure 12.11 – Logical structure of a FIB with a hierarchical architecture.

One (or more, in the case of multipath BGP enabling) of these pointers – called active pointer – is the one actually used to determine the forwarding info. The "**Pointer → Forwarding info**" association is usually determined by an IGP routing.

In order to understand why this simple idea improves the FIB's convergence property by a lot, we will see what happens in the case of the three scenarios described in Section 12.4.1 above. For all scenarios, we will assume that router CE21 advertises prefixes 10.X/16, X=1, ..., 9, and, without loss of generality, we will assume that all prefixes 10.X/16 can be reached by PE11, through the same BGP Next-Hop PE21, which is the initially active pointer.

Let's consider the first scenario, assuming that router P11 is out of service. Figure 12.12 below summarizes what happens in the hierarchical FIB. On router PE11, IGP quickly determines the new optimal paths toward routers PE21 and PE22, and so the FIB updates the IGP Pathlist. The pointers (BGP Next-Hop) do not change. The only thing that could change at pointer level is their use, which depends on the new IGP costs toward the BGP Next-Hops. However, the actual pointer change can only occur downstream of a new BGP selection process, which is BGP's control plane task.

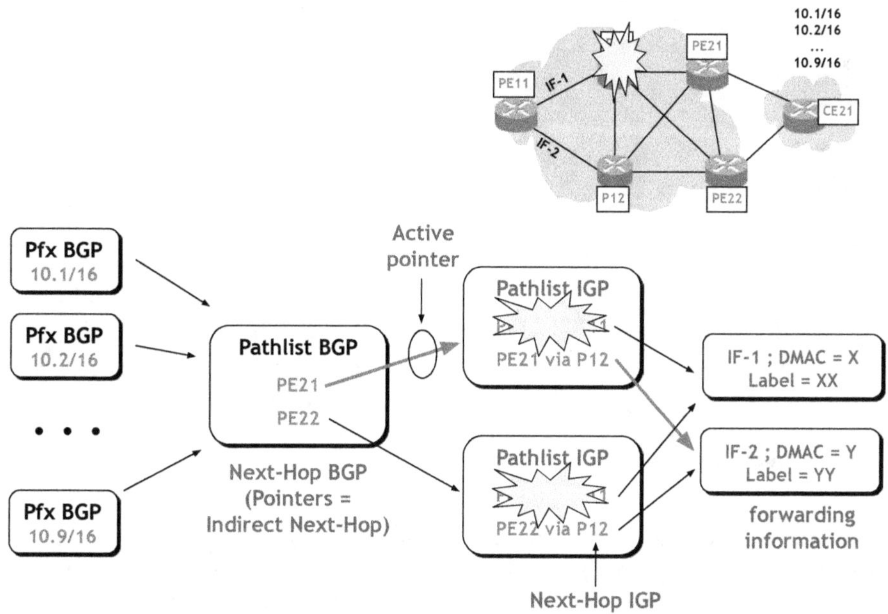

Figure 12.12 – Scenario 1: behavior of a FIB with a hierarchical architecture.

If, before router P11 went out of service, PE21 was used as active pointer, after the convergence of BGP's control plane, the FIB could use PE22 as active pointer, if the new IGP cost toward PE22 was lower than that toward PE21. But, during the convergence of BGP's control plane, the FIB continues to use the previous pointer (PE21). Convergence is immediate and – a very important aspect – it does not depend on BGP's control plane in any way, nor on the number of BGP prefixes, but only on IGP's convergence speed.

NOTE: In this scenario, the presence of an alternative pointer is not actually necessary. Indeed, if there isn't, traffic would continue to flow always toward the only BGP Next-Hop, just using a different internal path.

Let's now consider the second scenario, assuming that edge router PE21 is out of service. Figure 12.13 summarizes what happens in the hierarchical FIB.

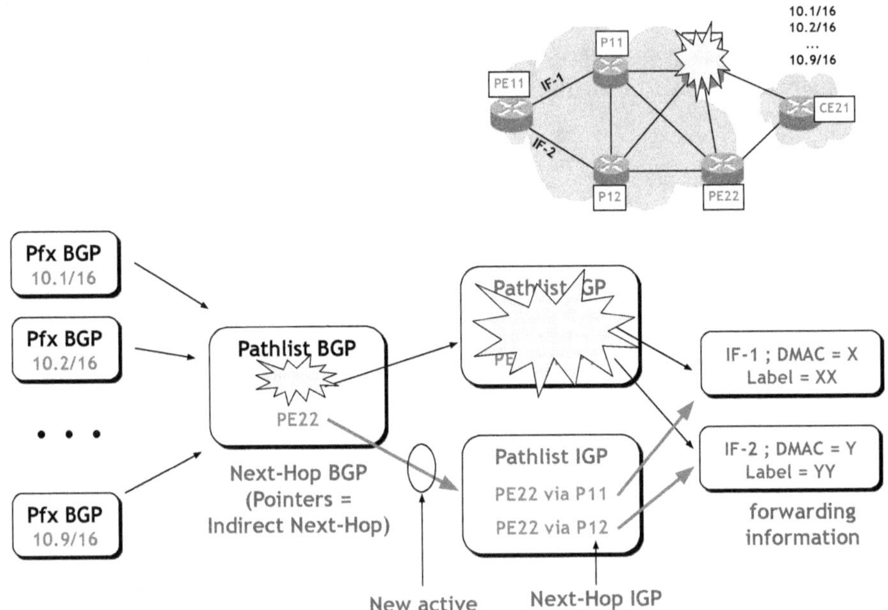

Figure 12.13 – Scenario 2: behavior of a FIB with a hierarchical architecture.

The IGP protocol, according to its convergence times, quickly informs edge routers PE11 and PE22 that PE21 is no longer reachable. In view of this new situation, the FIB eliminates the pointer toward PE21 and redirects traffic immediately, using the second pointer available, which therefore becomes active. In this case, differently from the previous one, even the BGP NHT function becomes operational, and it activates the convergence on BGP's control plane. And even if this was long, traffic would continue to flow regularly, thanks to the availability of the second pointer, which, as we mentioned earlier, activates immediately. In this scenario, convergence to the new active pointer is immediate, and directly occurs on the data plane, without the intervention of BGP's control plane. Moreover, convergence times do not depend on the number of prefixes, but only on IGP's convergence speed.

Lastly, let's consider the third scenario, assuming that the PE21↔CE21 connection is out of service. In this scenario, we will assume that the two edge routers PE21 and PE22 use the **"neighbor 192.168.0.11 next-hop-self"** command, and that the address used for iBGP sessions is the IP address of the Loopback0 interface. As we already saw in Section 12.4.1 above, this is a different case from the two previous ones, since the out-of-service of the PE21↔CE21 connection has no impact on the pointers or on the IGP Pathlists. However, edge router PE21 can exploit its hierarchical FIB and immediately change its pointer from CE21 to PE22. Traffic from PE11 toward the prefixes advertised by CE21 will follow the path PE11→PE21→PE22→CE21, as shown in Figure 12.14 below.

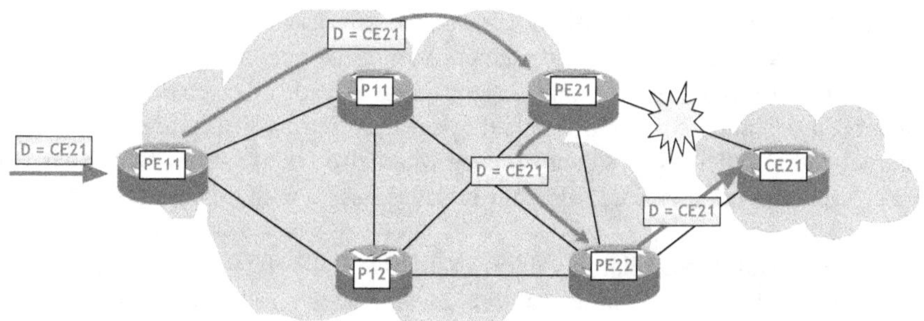

Figure 12.14 – Scenario 3: path followed by traffic

Here too, on PE21 and not on PE11, the BGP NHT comes into operation, and it activates BGP's control plane and PE11 reconvergence on the second BGP Next-Hop available. And even if this convergence was long, traffic would continue to flow regularly, thanks to the availability of the second pointer on router PE21, which, as we mentioned earlier, activates immediately. Once the convergence of BGP's control plane is over, traffic would continue to flow, following the more "natural" path PE11→PE22→CE21.

In all the three scenarios shown, using a hierarchical FIB allows reducing the convergence time – or rather, the LoC, Loss of Connectivity time, to a few dozen msec.

In modern routing platforms, the use of FIB with hierarchical architectures is pervasive, and it often does not require special configuration commands. This is why, as we mentioned earlier, this aspect is often invisible from the outside.

We need some essential pieces to complete the puzzle. Unless multipath BGP is enabled, should it be possible, in the second and third scenario, how can the FIB management algorithm know the alternative BGP Next-Hop? And also, are we sure that the alternative BGP Next-Hop is always available? Without an alternative BGP Next-Hop, the FIB must resort to BGP's control plane to have another one. And this would make the convergence much longer, making the use of hierarchical FIB basically pointless.

12.4.3 BGP Prefix Independent Convergence (BGP PIC)

For now, let's assume that an alternative BGP Next-Hop is available. However, we will have to circle back to this issue, because, in many cases, our assumption is not true (in the meantime, you can think about the cases where this does not apply), so we need to come up with something new (or some trick that can be done using "standard" functions) for this to happen, and this will be the main subject of our next section, because there are many methods available.

We already know that the BGP NHT can quickly detect the loss of a BGP Next-Hop, and that this information activates a local switchover to the new BGP Next-Hop.

If we use a hierarchical FIB architecture, this switchover does not require any BGP RIB scanning, and no best path re-election; it only requires a pointer change. Therefore, the switchover does not depend on the number of prefixes within the FIB. It is a simple operation at FIB (i.e. data plane) level. For this reason, this function is called Prefix Independent Convergence (PIC).

NOTE: The term 'BGP PIC' is typically used in Cisco's literature. In Juniper's literature, the term Indirect Next-Hop or its variant Chained Composite Next-Hop are used. Hereinafter, we will use Cisco's term.

In the first scenario we described in the previous section, we talked about BGP PIC Core function, and in this scenario, having an alternative BGP Next-Hop is not strictly necessary (even if it often occurs, for fault-tolerance reasons). This is because, in any case the BGP Next-Hop currently being used is always available, since if an element within the network goes out of service, this has no impact on its reachability, but only on the internal path to reach it (assuming that the backbone has been designed correctly, with sufficient meshing to ensure a good availability of multiple internal paths). Then, BGP's control plane could also choose a new BGP Next-Hop, if it deems more convenient, but this is a BGP control plane's issue, with no impact on the data plane convergence.

In the other two scenarios, the availability of an alternative BGP Next-Hop is crucial, because, if the current BGP Next-Hop became unreachable, we would need one "ready for use", or we would have to resort to BGP's control plane to find an alternative one, thus extending the convergence times. In these two scenarios, we talk about BGP PIC Edge operation.

This idea of the BGP PIC Edge is nothing new, and it has already been applied in the past, for the first time in Cisco's proprietary routing protocol EIGRP, where, together with the primary Next-Hop (Successor), an alternative loop-free Next-Hop (Feasible Successor) was added to the FIB.

NOTE: Today, the option of adding an alternative Next-Hop in addition to the primary Next-Hop in the FIB, is a function present also in Link-State (OSPF and IS-IS) routing protocols, known as LFA (Loop Free Alternate).

However, this does not mean that the normal convergence on BGP's control plane does not occur, but only that it is possible to use an alternative Next-Hop (already installed in the FIB) immediately, therefore drastically reducing the loss of traffic during the control plane convergence.

There are two BGP PIC Edge modes: multipath and unipath. The multipath mode – which occurs in an active/active scenario, that is, when both the available BGP Next-Hops are used to forward traffic – does not require any specific configuration, besides the standard multipath BGP activation. The unipath mode in an active/standby scenario – i.e. when, out of the two available BGP Next-Hops, one is used as primary (active) and the other as backup – requires a configuration that allows the installation of the second best path in the FIB.

NOTE: If you are familiar with the way the MPLS-TE Fast-ReRoute service works, this is similar to what happens when a node or connection part of the main MPLS-TE tunnel goes out of service: the important traffic that needs to be protected momentarily runs on a pre-installed backup MPLS-TE tunnel that avoids the out-of-service node or connection. However, the backup MPLS-TE tunnel is used until the Edge-LSR originating the main MPLS-TE tunnel determines an alternative path, signals it (via RSVP-TE) and forwards traffic toward it.

As tangible proof of the BGP PIC Edge function, in a presentation in 2006, Clarence Filsfils from Cisco showed the results of an interesting lab test, showing how, in a scenario where an AS has two eBGP sessions with another AS, and receives the FIRT from it (which, back then, was approx. 350k prefixes), thanks to the BGP PIC Edge function, a series 12k Cisco router connected with two BGP sessions to the two edge routers to the other AS, took only 180 msec to converge on the alternative Next-Hop, while, without the PIC function, the convergence time was in the range of hundreds of seconds.

12.4.4 Some design aspects

When we talk about BGP PIC, we talk about convergence on the data plane, rather than on the control plane. So we might think that no engineering aspect should be taken into consideration. In truth, this is not the case, because, in order to reach a convergence time of dozens of msec, we surely need to do something:

1. Since, in the different scenarios described above (and in the first two in particular), BGP's convergence time is strictly related to IGP's convergence time, we need to tune up IGP, by implementing all the functions that allow us to obtain a fast convergence.

2. We need to pay attention to any possible forwarding (micro-)loops that can occur in a non-BGP core-free scenario (i.e., without the use of MPLS).

3. In the BGP PIC Edge, we need to make sure that a backup (alternative) BGP Next-Hop is present.

We already mentioned this last aspect, and we will go over it in the next sections. Concerning the first, it is not the topic of this book. However, for the sake of completeness, we will include a few tips:

1. Use only mechanisms that allow detecting the loss of a routing adjacency as quickly as possible (e.g. BFD, Carrier-delay). Do not rely on fast-hello mechanisms that could overload the router's CPU.

2. Perform an efficient tuning of the LSA/LSP generation timers and of the optimal paths determination (via SPF). This measure alone, along with the previous one, will allow you to take the convergence time below one second.

3. Starting from the consideration that not all prefixes are equally important (e.g. a prefix /32 of a PE router used to establish iBGP sessions is more important than a subnet used to number a point-to-point connection), we should implement "spf per-prefix prioritization" mechanisms, so that the most important prefixes are treated before the less important ones (and end up in the RIBs and in the FIB first).

4. Keep your IGP lean and clean, do not redistribute any unnecessary IP subnets within it, and avoid any function without added value.

5. If the network topology allows it, evaluate the introduction of LFA (Loop Free Alternate) functions and its variants (R-LFA, TI-LFA) into the network.

Concerning the second aspect, we want to show you how forwarding micro-loops could be generated, and what counter-measures you should adopt. Let's consider the network we used in Section 12.4.1 for lab tests, and let's assume we want to activate also iBGP sessions (with an active "**next-hop self**") between each PE router and internal transit routers P – for instance, between PE21 and the two routers P11 and P12 (see Figure 12.15 below, where, for the sake of brevity, we only included the iBGP sessions that have PE21 as common endpoint). With this network design, router P12 will also receive the iBGP advertisements from PE21 and PE22 for the prefixes originated by CE21. We will assume that P12 chooses PE21 as the best path, and that the PE21↔CE21 connection goes out of service. As we saw earlier, router PE21 redirects the traffic directed toward CE21 using router PE22 as (remote) Next-Hop, presumably by passing through P12 (possible, due to IGP metrics). If P12 did not yet receive the withdrawal of the prefix originated by CE21 from BGP's control plane, and hence did not determine the new best path – which is very likely, since PE21 can exploit the PIC function, but P12 can't, and P12 can't even exploit the BGP NHT function (why?) – P12 would send traffic back to PE21, generating a micro-loop.

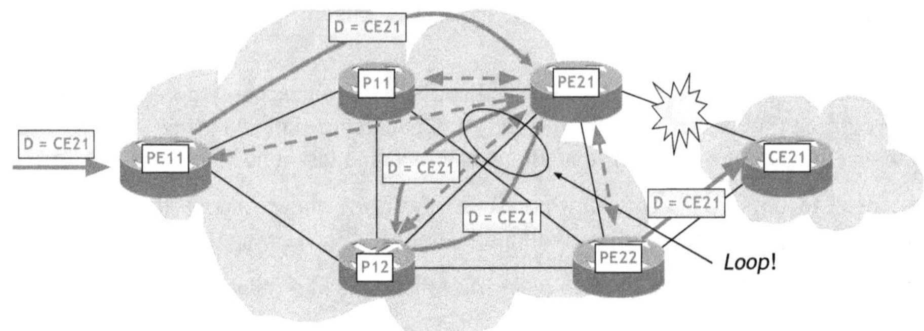

Figure 12.15 – Scenario 3: possible micro-loop formation.

The micro-loop stops as soon as P12 also receives the withdrawal of the prefix originated by CE21 from BGP's control plane.

How can we prevent these micro-loops? The advice is to always design a core-free BGP backbone, using MPLS inside it (because, as you may remember, a core-free BGP means that internal routers do not need BGP, see Section 8.2.3). In this way, P routers only act as connecting tools between the PE routers, do not have access to the content of the MPLS payload, and therefore cannot send the packets back. Other tunneling types, such as GRE tunnels, are not recommended, even if, theoretically, they could be used.

12.4.5 BGP PIC configuration in Cisco platforms

To enable the installation of a backup Next-Hop in the FIB – assuming that it is available (and for now we are assuming it is) – we need a suitable configuration.

Let's see the Cisco environment first. First of all, we need to check whether the platform we are configuring has a hierarchical FIB enabled or not. As it often occurs in Cisco environments, we need to pay attention to the platform type. In certain platforms, the hierarchical FIB is enabled by default (e.g. CRS, ASR9k, NCS, NX-OS), so there is no need for a special configuration command for them; while in other platforms, the hierarchical FIB must be enabled via the **"cef table output-chain build favor convergence-speed"** global command.

For the BGP PIC core function, we don't need anything else, while for the BGP PIC Edge function, we need to enable the installation of another BGP Next-Hop in the FIB. The two BGP Next-Hops installed in the FIB – as we saw in Section 12.4.3 – can be managed in active/active (BGP PIC Edge multipath) or in active/standby (BGP PIC Edge unipath) mode.

The BGP PIC Edge multipath mode does not require any specific configuration, except for the standard enabling of the multipath BGP through the **"maximum-paths ..."** command at global address-family level, with all its options (see Section 7.1.1).

In IOS and in IOS XE, the unipath requires the following command:

router(config)# **router bgp** *AS-number*
router(config-router)# **address-family ...**
router(config-router-af)# **bgp additional-paths install**

NOTE: In some cases, the unipath mode is automatically enabled, after another function is enabled, as, for instance, in the case of the BGP best-external function, which we will see in the next section (see Section 12.5.1).

In IOS XR, the configuration is a little more tricky, and it requires a routing policy:

RP/0/RP0/CPU0:router(config)# **route-policy** *RP-name*
RP/0/RP0/CPU0:router(config-rpl)# **set path-selection backup 1 install [...** *options omitted...*]
RP/0/RP0/CPU0:router(config-rpl)# **end-policy**
!
RP/0/RP0/CPU0:router(config)# **router bgp** *AS-number*
RP/0/RP0/CPU0:router(config-bgp)# **address-family ...**
RP/0/RP0/CPU0:router(config-bgp-af)# **additional-paths selection route-policy** *RP-name*

NOTE: In the "**set path-selection backup 1 ...**" command, value 1 indicates the installation of only one alternative backup BGP Next-Hop in the FIB.

To show the effect of these commands, we performed a lab test with a router (PE1) belonging to AS 64500, which uses IOS XR. Through a standard configuration, we made sure that this router received, from two Route Reflectors with addresses 192.169.2.1 and 192.168.2.2, two advertisements of two different paths toward prefix 10.1.99.12/32, the first with (remote) BGP Next-Hop 192.168.0.11 (which ended up being the best-path) and the second one with (remote) BGP Next-Hop 192.168.0.12. Then, we enabled the BGP PIC Edge function through the following commands:

```
route-policy PIC-EDGE
  set path-selection backup 1 install
end-policy
!
router bgp 64500
 address-family ipv4 unicast
   additional-paths selection route-policy PIC-EDGE
!
neighbor-group RR
  remote-as 64500
  update-source Loopback0
  address-family ipv4 unicast
!
neighbor 192.168.2.1
  use neighbor-group RR
  description *** IBGP SESSION WITH RR-1 ***
!
neighbor 192.168.2.2
  use neighbor-group RR
  description *** IBGP SESSION WITH RR-2 ***
```

Here are the views obtained through standard commands, which allow us to check if the BGP PIC Edge function has been enabled. The first concerns the detail of the BGP advertisements of prefix 10.1.99.12/32, included in PE1's BGP table:

```
RP/0/1/CPU0:PE1# show bgp 10.1.99.12/32
. . .
```

```
Paths: (2 available, best #1)
  Not advertised to any peer
  Path #1: Received by speaker 0
  Not advertised to any peer
  65012
    192.168.0.11 (metric 32) from 192.168.2.1 (192.168.0.11)
     Origin IGP, metric 0, localpref 100, valid, internal, best, group-best
      Received Path ID 0, Local Path ID 1, version 7
      Originator: 192.168.0.11, Cluster list: 192.168.2.1
  Path #2: Received by speaker 0
  Not advertised to any peer
  65012
    192.168.0.12 (metric 32) from 192.168.2.2 (192.168.0.12)
     Origin IGP, metric 0, localpref 100, valid, internal, backup, add-path
      Received Path ID 0, Local Path ID 2, version 8
      Originator: 192.168.0.12, Cluster list: 192.168.2.2
```

Obviously, the backup path is the "non best" one. The word "**backup**" in the third to last line of
the view shows that the BGP PIC Edge function has been correctly enabled.

The second view concerns the detail of the information related to prefix 10.1.99.12/32 in the RIB:

```
RP/0/1/CPU0:PE1# show route 10.1.99.12/32

. . .
   Routing Descriptor Blocks
      192.168.0.11, from 192.168.2.1
        Route metric is 0
      192.168.0.12, from 192.168.2.2, BGP backup path
        Route metric is 0
  No advertising protos.
```

From the view, we can see that there are two paths toward prefix 10.1.99.12/32, and the backup path
is the one with BGP Next-Hop 192.168.0.12 (highlighted by "**BGP backup path**").

Lastly, the third view – which is also the most important one – concerns the CEF table:

```
RP/0/1/CPU0:PE1# show cef 10.1.99.12/32
. . .
10.1.99.12/32, version 43, internal 0x14000001 (ptr 0xae3523d0) [1], 0x0
. . .
  local adjacency 172.16.2.21
  Prefix Len 32, traffic index 0, precedence routine (0), priority 4
    via 192.168.0.11, 2 dependencies, recursive [flags 0x6000]
     path-idx 0 [0xae352010 0x0]
     next hop 192.168.0.11 via 192.168.0.11/32
    via 192.168.0.12, 2 dependencies, recursive, backup [flags 0x6100]
     path-idx 1 [0xae352088 0x0]
     next hop 192.168.0.12 via 192.168.0.12/32
```

From the view, we can see that there are two paths toward prefix 10.1.99.12/32 in the FIB, and the
backup path is the one with BGP Next-Hop 192.168.0.12 (highlighted by "**backup**").

12.4.6 BGP PIC configuration in Juniper platforms

Concerning JUNOS, almost all latest-generation platforms support hierarchical FIBs, enabled by default (e.g. MX series platforms). If a specific platform requires it, the FIB hierarchical architecture can be enabled via the following command:

```
[edit routing-options forwarding-table]
indirect-next-hop;
```

To check if the command was effective, we can use the (hidden) "**show krt indirect-next-hop**" command:

```
aft@PE2> show krt indirect-next-hop
Indirect Nexthop:
Index: 262142 Protocol next-hop address: 192.168.1.12
  RIB Table: inet.0
  Policy Version: 0                         References: 1
  Locks: 2                                  0x165c0e8
  Flags: 0x1
  Ref RIB Table: unknown
        Next hop: 172.30.2.1 via ge-0/0/0.0
```

The FIB hierarchical architecture enabling is marked by the flag 0x1 (Flags: 0x1). When the "**indirect-next-hop**" command is deleted or disabled via the following command (if allowed by the platform):

```
[edit routing-options forwarding-table]
no-indirect-next-hop;
```

the flag value changes from 0x1 to 0x0.

The efficiency of the hierarchical FIB can be improved, in a scenario where a backbone offers different kinds of MPLS services, such as those treated in Chapter 11. In this kind of scenarios, Juniper has improved the hierarchical architecture to apply to the PE router, by moving the MPLS service label from the last level of the hierarchy to the first. This allows reducing the Next-Hops in the last level of the hierarchy by a lot, improving the performance if the backbone elements go out of service. This version – which Juniper calls Chained Composite Next Hop – must be enabled via configuration for each BGP address-family, through the following command (Note: in our example, the architecture has been configured for address-families "**l2vpn**" and "**l3vpn**", already mentioned in Chapter 11):

```
[edit routing-options forwarding-table]
chained-composite-next-hop {
    ingress {
        l2vpn;
        l3vpn;
    }
}
```

For BGP PIC Core functions, nothing else is required, while for the BGP PIC Edge function, a suitable configuration is needed. JUNOS supports the BGP PIC Edge both for the L3VPN service and for IPv4/IPv6 Internet access services. There are two different commands, based on the protection type. The first concerns the protection against the out-of-service of another PE router (scenario 2 of Section 12.4.1). In this case, the BGP PIC Edge function is enabled through the following command:

```
[edit <routing-instances RI-NAME> routing-options]
protect core;
```

> **NOTE**: The command's syntax is a little misleading. Even though it indicates "**protect core**", it is actually the command that allows installing two BGP Next-Hops – a primary one (best path) and a backup one – in the FIB of a router (usually PE).

The second type of protection concerns the out-of-service of a PE↔CE connection (scenario 3 of Section 12.4.1). JUNOS uses a different name than Cisco, by differentiating the case in which a connection is used for a network directly connected to the PE (e.g. an Ethernet LAN), from when a prefix is advertised through a routing protocol (e.g. eBGP). In the first case, JUNOS uses the name Link Protection with Host Fast ReRoute (HFRR), while in the second one simply PE Link Protection. Both HFRR and PE Link Protection are supported only for connections ending on a VRF (that is, VRF type routing instances, in JUNOS jargon).

The HFRR is enabled through the following command:

[edit routing-instances *RI-name* **routing-options]**
interface *number type* **link-protection;**

while in order to enable the PE Link Protection function, assuming to use eBGP as PE-E routing protocol, the following configurations should be executed:

[edit routing-instances *RI-name* **protocols bgp group** *group-name*]
family (inet|inet6) {
  unicast {
    protection;
  }
}

For further details, see JUNOS documents.

12.5 PATH DIVERSITY FUNCTIONS

In the previous paragraph, we saw that the BGP PIC function could be used to speed up BGP's convergence, by installing a backup path in the FIB. In order for this to happen, the existence of a backup BGP path is obviously required.

In many cases, this occurs by default; however, in many other important practical applications, this does not occur. Pay attention to a key point: the backup path must have a different BGP Next-Hop than the primary path (best path). In technical jargon, this property is called Path Diversity. We can see that the Path Diversity is not always guaranteed, through a simple example.

Let's consider the network in Figure 12.16, where, as it often happens in practice, the ISP network, in order to reduce the number of iBGP sessions, uses two Route Reflectors. Let's also assume that router PE1 is "closer" than PE2 (according to the IGP costs) both to RR-1 and to RR-2.

Router CE1 advertises prefix Px to routers PE1 and PE2, via eBGP. Routers PE1 and PE2 propagate the advertisement to the two RRs, which execute the selection process on the two advertisements received. With the same standard BGP attributes, the selection process of both RRs chooses as the best path the advertisement received from the PE which is the "closest", according to the IGP cost – i.e. PE1. So, both RRs will advertise to PE3 prefix Px with the IP address used by PE1 for the iBGP sessions toward the two RRs as BGP Next-Hop (Note: remember that RRs do not change the NEXT_HOP attribute). And this does not allow to obtain the Path Diversity, because both advertisements that PE3 receives have the same BGP Next-Hop.

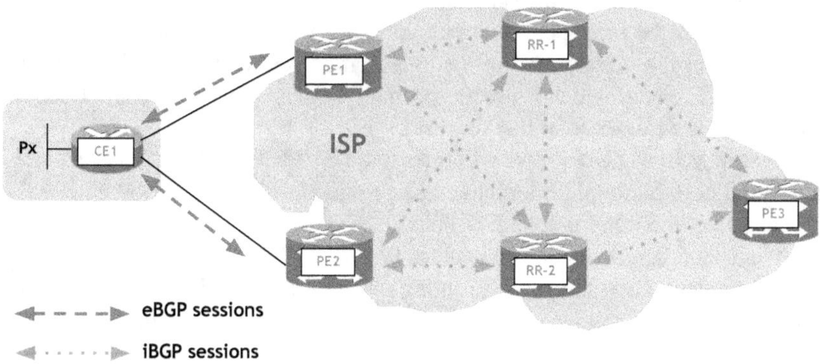

Figure 12.16 – Typical ISP network with Route Reflector.

In any case, with a simple trick, we can still reach the Path Diversity in the scenario in Figure 12.16. Indeed, let's assume to alter the internal metrics of IGP so that RR-1 is closer to PE1 than to PE2, and, vice versa, that RR-2 is closer to PE2 than to PE1. Going over the previous case, the result is that RR-1 elects as the best path the advertisement received from PE1, and RR-2 elects as the best path the advertisement received from PE2.

PE3 will receive two advertisements of prefix Px, one from RR-1 with PE1 as BGP Next-Hop, and one from RR-2 with PE2 as BGP Next-Hop. In PE3's BGP table there will be two advertisements with a different BGP Next-Hop, and so we have reached the purpose of having the Path Diversity. Although the solution to reach the Path Diversity may seem elementary, the reality is quite different. In large networks, thinking of acting on IGP metrics to make the two RRs see the PEs with different distances is absolutely impractical. Moreover, we may incur into sub-optimal routing issues, as the one described in the example of Figure 8.9, in Section 8.3.5. And, if the two RRs were co-located, the IGP distance from each RR toward the same PE would be identical, and this would mean that the same advertisement will always be reflected. For instance, if RR-1 and RR-2 were co-located, the IGP distance of RR-1 and RR-2 from PE1 would be identical, e.g. equal to 10. Similarly, also the IGP distance of RR-1 and RR-2 from PE2 would be identical, e.g. equal to 20. The result is that RR-1 would choose as the best path the advertisement coming from PE1 (shorter IGP distance), and RR-2 would do the same. Therefore, even though PE3 would get two BGP advertisements of prefix Px, they would both have PE1 as BGP Next-Hop, and the Path Diversity would not be achieved.

Specific functions to reach the Path Diversity have been developed and suggested. We will describe the most popular and widespread in the following sections: BGP Best External, BGP Add-Path and BGP Diverse Path. For each one of these functions, we will try to highlight their operation, Cisco and Juniper implementations and a few lab tests.

12.5.1 BGP Best External function

Out of the three, the BGP Best External function is the easiest one. It can be implemented alone or together with the other two we will see. It does not require any modification to BGP messages, nor any negotiation between BGP Neighbors. It only requires a modification of the advertisements sent. As you know, the BGP process, by default, only sends the best path to the BGP Neighbors, according to well-known rules described in Section 2.1.2 and 2.1.3; in the BGP Best External function (and in the other two functions we will see later on), this rule is extended, allowing to advertise also paths other than the best path.

Before we go over how the BGP Best External works, it is important to understand what happens in BGP by default, in the classic case of a single-homed AS, with a double connection to two routers of another AS, one of which is used as primary, and the other as backup. Because the BGP Best External finds its natural use in this scenario.

To better contextualize the scenario, we will refer to a L3VPN BGP/MPLS service; however, this applies also in the case of simple Internet access provided to a customer by an ISP. The overall reference scenario is shown in Figure 12.17 below.

Router CE1 has a double connection to routers PE1 and PE2. As it often happens in practical applications, let's assume that the PE-CE routing protocol is BGP. The desired routing policy is for the CE1↔PE1 connection to be used as primary (indicated in the figure by the letter **P**), and the other as backup (indicated by the letter **B**).

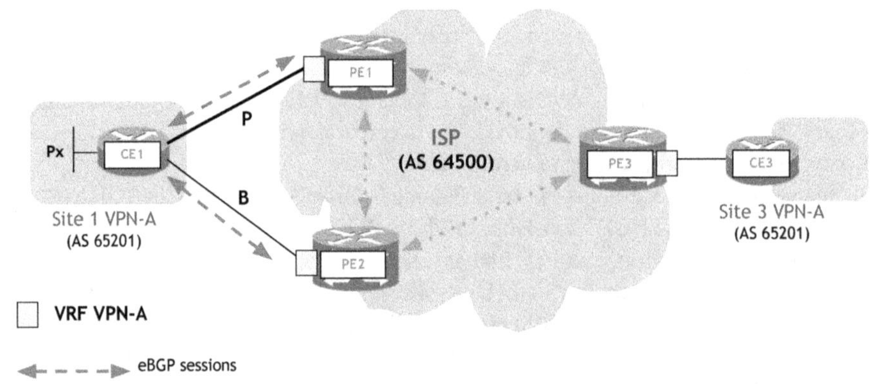

Figure 12.17 – Typical redundant PE-CE connection in a L3VPN service.

As we extensively described in Chapter 7 (see Sections 7.2 and 7.3), standard BGP tools are used to achieve this policy. Concerning outbound traffic (from site 1 of VPN-A toward the ISP network), we can use the standard Local Preference attribute. And for inbound traffic, there are several alternatives, including the use of the MED or the AS_PATH Prepending on the CE side, or the Local Preference (LP) on the PE side.

Let's see what happens in practice in the scenario we just described. Let's assume that, based on a certain value of the BGP Community attribute received, the advertisements of prefix Px sent by CE1 are assigned by router PE1 LP=200 and by router PE2 LP=150 (Note: Actually, we could simplify the procedure by assigning only an LP value, and exploiting the default value LP=100, which almost all manufacturers use; however, for clarity reasons, we will use explicit assignments in both PEs). Moreover, let's assume that the eBGP session between CE1 and PE1 is established first, and then the one between routers CE1 and PE2. The final result would be the same if we assumed the opposite.

According to the rules of the LP attribute, eBGP advertisements propagate within the ISP network (AS 64500) through the MP-iBGP sessions, leaving LP values unchanged.

NOTE: Actually, as we saw in Chapter 11, in a L3VPN scenario, the advertisement of prefix VPN-IPv4 "RD:Px" are propagated, where RD is the Route Distinguisher value set via manual configuration.

In particular, the advertisement received from PE1, to which the value LP=200 is assigned, will be propagated to PE2 and PE3 with LP=200. Both these routers will choose the only path advertised as BGP's best path.

Then, after the eBGP session between CE1 and PE2 reaches the Established state, PE2 receives the eBGP advertisement of prefix Px from CE1. Therefore, PE2 will have two advertisements available, and will execute the BGP selection process. Since the eBGP advertisement is assigned a value LP=150 and the MP-iBGP advertisement received from PE1 has LP=200, the path with PE1 as BGP Next-Hop is elected as the best path. According to the split horizon rule, this best path is not advertised to router PE3, which will only have one MP-iBGP advertisement for prefix Px.

Now, let's see what happens if the primary CE1↔PE1 connection goes out of service. The convergence toward the backup connection for PE1 and PE3 occurs entirely on the control plane, while, by enabling the BGP PIC Edge function, for PE2, it can also occur on the data plane. The sequence of the event is as usual, and we already saw it in the previous paragraph; in any case, we will repeat it, for the sake of completeness. As soon as it detects that the primary connection is out of service, router PE1, through the BGP fast external fall-over function, immediately closes the eBGP session with CE1, and sends a BGP UPDATE message to PE2 and PE3 to withdraw prefix Px, which can no longer be reached (see Figure 12.18 below).

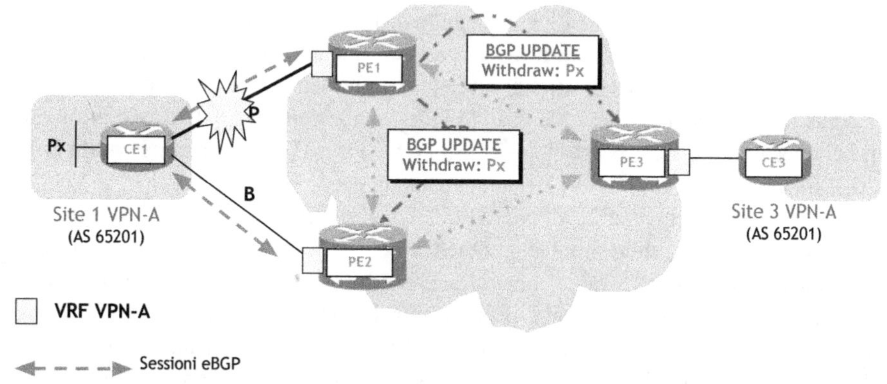

Figure 12.18 – Withdrawal of prefix Px after the PE1↔CE1 connection goes out of service.

The message reaches PE2, which, having a second advertisement saved (e.g. the eBGP advertisement received from CE1), immediately converges on the eBGP path. The convergence occurs on the data plane, if the BGP PIC Edge function is enabled on PE2, or on the control plane if it is not enabled. In any case, PE2 elects the new BGP best path and advertises it to PE1 and PE3. Now, both PE1 and PE3 will have the new path available, and traffic from the ISP AS toward site 1 of the VPN-A will use the backup connection.

All is well that ends well, then. Actually, the movie ending was good... but it lasted too long! It would have been different if PE1 and PE3 had a backup path available. Regardless of whether BGP PIC Edge was enabled or not, convergence would have been faster. With BGP PIC Edge enabled, even faster.

In order for PE1 and PE3 to have the backup path available too, it would be sufficient to change BGP's default behavior a little, as follows: allow router PE2 to advertise the eBGP path in any case, even if it isn't the best path. In this way, both PE1 and PE3 would have, apart from the best path chosen by PE1, also a second (backup) path – the eBGP path propagated by PE2 – stored. So PE1, as soon as it detects that the eBGP session with CE1 has been lost, can immediately use this second path and PE2 as BGP Next-Hop. With the BGP PIC Edge function enabled, the switchover to the new path occurs on the data plane, and is immediate. Even if the BGP PIC Edge function was not enabled, the convergence toward the new Next-Hop would in any case be faster, since PE1 would have a backup path available, and so the BGP selection process would be able to determine the new best path immediately, without having to wait for a new advertisement from PE2.

This variation in BGP's default behavior is called BGP Best External and it concerns non-best path eBGP advertisements. For this reason, it cannot be applied in a scenario with Route Reflectors. If a Route Reflector is present, we need to resort to other techniques (Add-Path, Diverse Path), as we will see in the two following sections.

NOTE: Curiously, in the original specifications of BGPv4 (RFC 1771), this behavior had already been foreseen, but it has never been implemented by manufacturers, which, in order to avoid possible routing and forwarding loops and an excessive memory consumption due to the higher quantity of advertisements, only advertise the best path by default. In our scenario, the application of the original rule, from a loop standpoint, is innocuous, as it can generate micro-loops at worst, with a negligible memory consumption.

Actually, in a L3VPN BGP/MPLS scenario like the one we are considering, not even micro-loops are generated. There is a subtle reason for that, and we will explain it through an example. Let's assume that PE1 receives a packet directed to a Host of prefix Px, and that PE2 has not yet received the BGP UPDATE message sent by PE1 to withdraw prefix Px. After receiving the packet, PE1 routes it toward prefix Px, forwarding it to PE2, since it cannot route it on the direct PE1↔CE1 connection, which is out of service, and has already determined the new best path PE2. However, since PE2 has not yet received the BGP UPDATE message sent by PE1 to withdraw prefix Px, PE2 still believes that the BGP Next-Hop toward prefix Px is PE1, and so one would be tempted to think that PE2 sends the packet to PE1 again, causing a micro-loop.

Actually, this does not occur in a L3VPN BGP/MPLS scenario, and no micro-loop is generated. The reason for this is that, when the packet reaches PE2, it will not be routed toward prefix Px, based on a lookup on the VRF table, but rather based on the data contained in PE2's MPLS forwarding table (known as LFIB, Label Forwarding Information Base), since the IP packet is encapsulated in a MPLS label (the VPN Label!). If you are familiar with the way the L3VPN BGP/MPLS service's forwarding plane works, you know that the VPN Label is directly associated to the output interface, therefore the packet is directly forwarded on the interface between PE2 and CE2, and reaches its destination.

NOTE: Apart a few tiny differences, this operating mode is adopted both by Cisco and Juniper; the IETF standard of the L3VPN BGP/MPLS service, RFC 4364 – *BGP/MPLS IP Virtual Private Networks (VPNs)*, February 2006, successor of the famous RFC 22547bis with the same title, doesn't say anything in this regard.

In a purely (non-L3VPN) IP scenario, however, the micro-loop is generated, because PE2 executes a lookup on the IP routing table, and sends the packet to PE1 again. This occurs until PE2 receives the BGP UPDATE message, withdrawing prefix Px from PE1.

To conclude this section, let's go over some configuration aspects. In Cisco routers, the BGP Best External function is activated in IOS/IOS XE and IOS XR, through the following configurations:

IOS XE:
router(config)# **router bgp** *AS-number*
router(config-router)# **address-family ...**
router(config-router-af)# **bgp advertise-best-external**

IOS XR:
RP/0/RP0/CPU0:router(config)# **router bgp** *AS-number*
RP/0/RP0/CPU0:router(config-bgp)# **address-family ...**
RP/0/RP0/CPU0:router(config-bgp-af)# **advertise best-external**

In Juniper routers, the configuration to execute is the following:

[edit protocols bgp group *group-name*]
 advertise-external <**conditional**>;

where the **conditional** option allows advertising the second path if and only if the selection process, when determining the best path, reaches a point where the MED attribute is compared. Consequently, with the use of the **conditional** option, an external non best path advertisement, with an AS_PATH longer than the best path, is not propagated.

Let's see a configuration example. The network scenario is the one in Figure 12.17, where PE1 is a Cisco router with IOS XR and PE2 and PE3 are Juniper routers. The IP addresses of the Loopback0 interfaces of routers PEX are 192.168.0.X (X=1, 2, 3) and prefix Px=10.1/16.

For the sake of brevity, we will only show the relevant configurations of router PE2, which is the only one, in our example, which requires the enabling of the BGP Best External function (even if, in practice, the command is set on all PEs).

```
[edit protocols bgp]
group IBGP {
    type internal;
    local-address 192.168.0.2;
    advertise-external;
    family inet-vpn {
        unicast;
    }
    neighbor 192.168.0.1;
    neighbor 192.168.0.3;
}

[edit routing-instances VPN-A]
instance-type vrf;
interface ge-0/0/1.0;
route-distinguisher 64500:1;
vrf-target target:64500:1;
protocols {
    bgp {
        group CE {
            type external;
```

```
        peer-as 65201;
        as-override;
        neighbor 10.1.12.2;
    }
  }
}
```

On router PE1, we assigned LP=200 to all the advertisements coming from CE1, in order for the PE1↔CE1 connection to be used as primary connection (we will leave this configuration to you, as useful practice). Let's see the paths in the routing table associated to VRF VPN-A on PE3, toward the network 10.1/16 advertised by CE1, before and after applying the BGP Best External function.

<u>Before</u> applying the BGP Best External function:

```
aft@PE3> show route table VPN-A.inet.0 10.1/16 exact

. . .

10.1.0.0/16  *[BGP/170] 00:06:23, localpref 200, from 192.168.0.1
                AS path: 65201 I
              > to 172.30.1.1 via ge-0/0/1.0, Push 300000, Push 299808(top)
```

<u>After</u> applying the BGP Best External function:

```
aft@PE3> show route table VPN-A.inet.0 10.1/16 exact

. . .

10.1.0.0/16 *[BGP/170] 00:08:14, localpref 200, from 192.168.0.1
               AS path: 65201 I
             > to 172.30.1.1 via ge-0/0/1.0, Push 300000, Push 299808(top)
              [BGP/170] 00:00:06, localpref 100, from 192.168.0.2
               AS path: 65201 I
             > to 172.30.1.2 via ge-0/0/2.0, Push 300016, Push 299824(top)
```

As you can see, before applying the BGP Best External function, PE3 has only one path in its memory, the one advertised by PE1. After the application, apart from the path advertised by PE1, PE3 also finds a path advertised by PE2, which is not the best path for PE2. For PE2, this is the best eBGP path.

12.5.2 BGP Add Path function

In the example in the previous section, we avoided using any Route Reflectors (RR), because, as explained earlier, the BGP Best External function does not work if the RRs are present. However, in practical application, this scenario is realistic only with very few PEs.

In the case of L3VPN BGP/MPLS, with RRs, we can still achieve the Path Diversity through a very simple trick: by assigning two different Route Distinguishers (RD) to the two VRFs where the two connections of the VPN site are located. In this way, we "trick" BGP into thinking of being in front of two different NLRIs. Actually, the only thing that differs is the RD component of the VPN-IPv4 prefix, while the IP component is the same.

What happens is obvious. Referring to the scenario in Figure 12.16, each one of the two RRs will receive two advertisements of prefix Px, one from PE1 and one from PE2. Actually, the advertisement received from PE1 is the advertisement of the VPN-IPv4 prefix "RD1:Px", and the one received from PE2 is the advertisement of the VPN-IPv4 prefix "RD2:Px" (with RD1 different from RD2). Each RR, it will see two different NLRI, and each path will be elected the best path. And so each RR will reflect two different best paths to its RR-Clients. On all VRFs of instance VPN-A, we will have two different paths toward the VPN prefix Px, one with BGP Next-Hop PE1 and the other with BGP Next-Hop PE2, thus achieving the Path Diversity.

This trick has a limited validity within L3VPN BGP/MPLS services, although it has serious scalability (management) issues on ISP networks with dozens/hundreds of thousands of VPN customers' redundant sites. We only explained it because the Add-Path function treated in this section is based on a very similar logic.

In the IETF framework, a simpler, more general solution to this issue has been suggested. This (standard) solution, known as BGP Add-Path function, was defined by RFC 7911 – *Advertisement of Multiple Paths in BGP*, July 2016, and is supported by all the main vendors.

The solution to the issue described in the introduction to this paragraph (see Figure 12.16), could be achieved by making the two RRs advertise, apart from the best path, also the alternative best path. A sort of "Columbus' Egg". In doing so, on router PE3, we would have, apart from the advertisements with BGP Next-Hop PE1, also those with BGP Next-Hop PE2, thus achieving the Path Diversity. However, RRs do not behave like this by default.

The possibility that the RRs advertise both the best path and the alternative best path can be obtained through a trick similar to that we›ve seen in the L3VPN scenario, with two different RDs. However, in a general scenario, we cannot rely on the RDs.

The BGP Add-Path function is based on a similar idea, and expands on the standard NLRI definition. The idea of the BGP Add-Path is described in Figure 12.19 below.

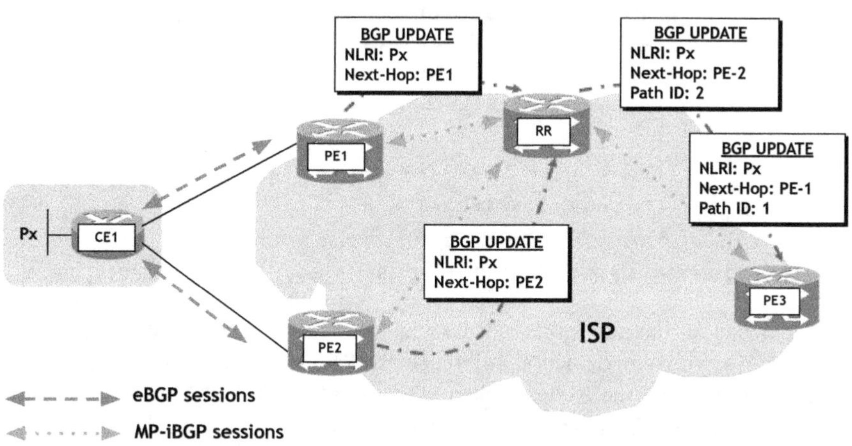

Figure 12.19 – BGP Add-Path function.

The RR advertises both the best path and the alternative best path (Note: actually, it could advertise even the other available paths, and not just 2). Moreover, it associates an ID (Path ID) generated automatically by the BGP process to each advertisement. The ID is added to the NLRI and makes the <Path ID; Px> pair unique. The BGP Speaker receives the two advertisements and installs them both in the BGP RIB, because it considers them different. The key element is the presence of the Path ID, which plays the same role as the RD in the L3VPN service. Without the Path ID, due to BGP's implicit withdraw mechanism, the second advertisement would replace the first, and we would only have one advertisement in the BGP RIB.

The BGP Add-Path function is based on a very simple idea, to advertise several paths toward the same prefix, and preventing the advertisements after the first one to implicitly replace the previous one. This is how the Path Diversity is reached, instead of the Path Hiding.

As you may certainly have noticed, the BGP Add-Path function required a change to BGP's basic code. Indeed, the two BGP Speakers at the ends of the BGP sessions must be capable of generating advertisements with modified NLRI (i.e. with the addition of the Path ID) and also be capable of interpreting them.

RFC 7911's suggestion is to change the NLRI field in BGP UPDATE messages, described by RFC 4271, by adding a Path ID, as shown in Figure 12.20 below.

```
+----------------------------------+
| Path Identifier (4 octets)       |
+----------------------------------+
| Length (1 octet)                 |
+----------------------------------+
| Prefix (variable)                |
+----------------------------------+
```

Figure 12.20 – New NLRI for the IPv4 unicast address-family (from RFC 7911).

In the same way, RFC 7911 suggests changing the coding of the NLRI field of RFC 3107 – *Carrying Label Information in BGP-4*, May 2001, as shown in Figure 12.21 below.

```
+----------------------------------+
| Path Identifier (4 octets)       |
+----------------------------------+
| Length (1 octet)                 |
+----------------------------------+
| Label (3 octets)                 |
+----------------------------------+
| ...                              |
+----------------------------------+
| Prefix (variable)                |
+----------------------------------+
```

Figure 12.21 – New NLRI for the VPN-IPv4 unicast address-family (from RFC 7911).

In both cases, the key difference is the Path ID addition, which, in this context, acts as the RD in the L3VPN scenario, with a fundamental difference: the Path ID is not subject to configuration, and is selected automatically by the BGP Speaker, which sends multiple advertisements of the same prefix, thus removing any RD assignment management issues.

The BGP Add-Path function must be supported by both BGP Neighbors at the endpoints of a BGP session, and they must negotiate its support. Also, remember that additional functions must be negotiated through BGP Capabilities in the OPEN message (see Section 2.3.1). RFC 7911 suggests using the ADD-PATH BGP Capability, to which IANA has assigned the Capability Code 69, with the format shown in Figure 12.22 below.

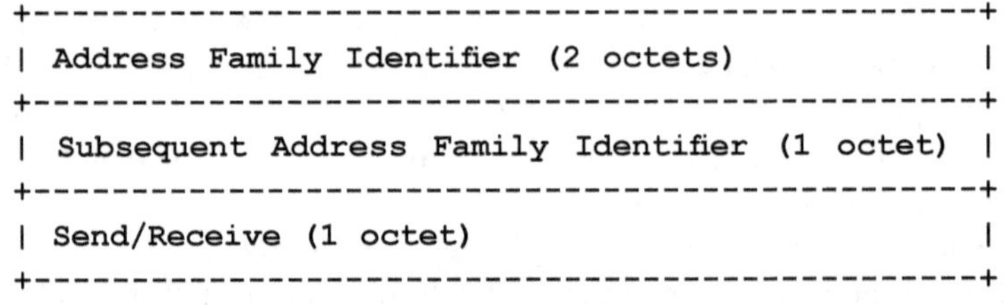

```
+------------------------------------------------------+
| Address Family Identifier (2 octets)                 |
+------------------------------------------------------+
| Subsequent Address Family Identifier (1 octet)       |
+------------------------------------------------------+
| Send/Receive (1 octet)                               |
+------------------------------------------------------+
```

Figure 12.22 – ADD-PATH BGP Capability format (from RFC 7911).

As you recall, the AFI/SAFI fields identify the address family. The Send/Receive field establishes the role of the BGP Speaker. Possible values (in decimal) are 1, 2 and 3:

1. The BGP Speaker can receive advertisements.

2. The BGP Speaker can send advertisements.

3. The BGP Speaker can send and receive advertisements,

with NLRI extended with the Path ID, for the address family specified by the AFI/SAFI codes. This is sufficient for our purposes. If you want to know more also about the operating aspects, then read the two following IETF drafts (that never became RFC):

- draft-ietf-idr-add-paths-guidelines – Best Practices for Advertisement of Multiple Paths in IBGP;

- draft-retana-idr-add-paths-implementation – Advertisement of Multiple Paths in BGP: Implementation Report.

The first draft is especially interesting, as it defines the possible selection methods for multiple advertisements.

To conclude this section, let's go over some configuration aspects. In Cisco routers, the general steps to undertake are 3:

1. specifying whether the BGP Speaker must negotiate the ADD-PATH Capability or not, and the method (send, receive, send/receive);

2. selecting the set of paths to advertise (apart from the best path) according to a certain criterion;

3. specifying, for each BGP Neighbor, the set of paths to advertise (which can also be a subset of those specified in the previous step).

As usual, the configurations differ in the different IOS versions. In IOS and IOS XE, the command to execute to negotiate the ADD-PATH Capability is the following:

```
router(config)# router bgp AS-number
router(config-router)# address-family ...
router(config-router-af)# bgp additional-paths {send [receive] | receive}
```

The same command can be executed at BGP Neighbor-level, as follows:

```
router(config)# router bgp AS-number
router(config-router)# neighbor IP-neighbor additional-paths {send [receive] | receive}
```

NOTE: In IOS XE, the BGP Add-path function is supported only on iBGP sessions.

In IOS XR, the ADD-PATH Capability is negotiated through the following commands:

```
RP/0/RP0/CPU0:router(config)# router bgp AS-number
RP/0/RP0/CPU0:router(config-bgp)# address-family ...
RP/0/RP0/CPU0:router(config-bgp-af)# additional-paths send | receive
```

! in addition to or as an alternative

```
RP/0/RP0/CPU0:router(config-bgp-af)# additional-paths receive | send
```

The criterion to define the set of paths to advertise, in IOS and IOS XE, is configured as follows:

router(config)# **router bgp** *AS-number*
router(config-router)# **address-family . . .**
router(config-router-af)# **bgp additional-paths select { best** *number* | **all** | **group-best}**

The "**best** *number*" option, where "*number*" in IOS/IOS XE can be 2 or 3. If *number* =2, it allows advertising, apart from the best path, also an alternative best path (obtained from a new BGP selection process, where the primary best path is eliminated). If *number*=3, it allows advertising two additional alternative best paths. The "**all**" option allows selecting all the advertisements with a different BGP Next-Hop. Lastly, the "**group-best**" option is a little more complex, and we will explain how it works through an example. Let's assume that the BGP Speaker has three BGP sessions with the routers of three different ASes, AS 64501, AS 64502 and AS 64503. Each one of them sends three advertisements of the same prefix X. For the sake of brevity, we will call them Xnm, where n is the last digit of the AS number, and m the advertisement sequence number. For instance, the three advertisements of AS 64501 will be X11, X12 e X13.

In order to choose which ones to send, the router executes the selection process on all the advertisements coming from the same AS. We will assume that the best paths are X11, X21 and X31, respectively. The **group-best** option will select exactly the three advertisements X11, X21 and X31 to be sent.

In IOS XR, the selection criterion is defined through a routing policy:

RP/0/RP0/CPU0:router(config)# **router bgp** *AS-number*
RP/0/RP0/CPU0:router(config-bgp)# **address-family . . .**
RP/0/RP0/CPU0:router(config-bgp-af)# **additional-paths selection route-policy** *RP-name*

Within the routing policy, the command that allows choosing the criterion is: "**set path-selection {backup** *number* | **group-best** | **all** | **best path} advertise**", where the "**group-best**" and "**all**" options have the same meaning we saw for IOS/IOS XE. The "**backup** *number*" option, where currently number can only take on value 1, allows advertising only one alternative best path, in addition to the best path. While the "**best path**" option allows advertising only the best path.

Lastly, to conclude the configuration, IOS and IOS XE (but not IOS XR) required the third step described above, which uses the command "**neighbor** *IP-neighbor* **advertise additional-paths [best** *number*] **[group-best] [all]**".

In JUNOS, the commands to use are the following (Note: we have omitted some of the less-used options):

```
[edit protocols bgp group group-name family ...]
add-path {
  receive;
  send {
    path-count number;
    prefix-policy RP-name;
  }
}
```

where, as in the case of Cisco's platforms, the "**send**" and "**receive**" options can be used separately. When you choose the "**send**" option, you must specify the "**path-count** ..." which is the number of advertisements selected, including the best path (for this reason, the minimum number value is equal to 2). The "**prefix-policy** *RP-name*" option allows defining the prefixes for which the BGP Add-Path function applies. Without this option, the function is applied to all prefixes.

Let's now see an example that allows checking the BGP Add-Path function. The scenario used is the one in Figure 12.19, with prefix Px=10.1.99.11/32. Routers PEX (X=1,2,3), all Cisco with IOS XR, have the IP address of the Loopback0 interface equal to 192.168.0.X. While the RR has the IP address of the Loopback0 interface equal to 192.168.2.1. All iBGP sessions are established using the IP addresses of the Loopback0 interfaces. The BGP Add-Path function has been configured between the RR (send mode) and router PE3 (receive mode).

We left all BGP attributes to their default value. Without applying the BGP Add-Path, RR receives two advertisements of prefix 10.1.99.11/32, respectively from routers PE1 and PE2. RR executes the selection process and advertises the only resulting best path. On PE3, we will have only one advertisement of prefix 10.1.99.11/32:

```
RP/0/4/CPU0:PE3# show bgp ipv4 unicast
 . . .  < output omitted > . . .
    Network            Next Hop       Metric    LocPrf     Weight      Path
*>i 10.1.99.11/32      192.168.0.1         0       100          0      65201  i
Processed 1 prefixes, 1 paths
```

These are the BGP process' configurations on routers RR and PE3. For the sake of brevity, we will only include the commands to enable the BGP Add-Path function:

RR
```
router bgp 64500
 address-family ipv4 unicast
  additional-paths send
  additional-paths selection route-policy ALLROUTES
!
route-policy ALLROUTES
  set path-selection all advertise
end-policy
```

PE3
```
router bgp 64500
 address-family ipv4 unicast
  additional-paths receive
 !
```

To check the result, let's see how many BGP advertisements of prefix 10.1.99.11/32 are included in PE3's BGP table:

```
RP/0/4/CPU0:PE3# show bgp ipv4 unicast 10.1.99.11/32
 . . .
Paths: (2 available, best #1)
  Not advertised to any peer
  Path #1: Received by speaker 0
  Not advertised to any peer
  65201
    192.168.0.1 (metric 4) from 192.168.2.1 (192.168.0.1)
    Origin IGP, metric 0, localpref 100, valid, internal, best, group-best
      Received Path ID 1, Local Path ID 1, version 9
      Originator: 192.168.0.1, Cluster list: 192.168.2.1
  Path #2: Received by speaker 0
```

```
Not advertised to any peer
65201
   192.168.0.2 (metric 4) from 192.168.2.1 (192.168.0.2)
     Origin IGP, metric 0, localpref 100, valid, internal
     Received Path ID 2, Local Path ID 0, version 0
     Originator: 192.168.0.2, Cluster list: 192.168.2.1
```

As the view shows, on PE3 there are two advertisements of prefix 10.1.99.11/32, with a different BGP Next-Hop (192.168.0.1 and 192.168.0.2, respectively). In this view, it is interesting to notice the value of the Path ID received, equal to 1 for the first advertisement, and 2 for the second one. These values have been dynamically selected by the RR and added to the NLRI. You can see it well in the following view, which shows the detail of the advertisements sent by RR and PE3:

```
RP/0/0/CPU0:RR# show bgp ipv4 unicast advertised neighbor 192.168.0.3
. . .
10.1.99.11/32 is advertised to 192.168.0.3
  Path info:
    neighbor: 192.168.0.1    neighbor router id: 192.168.0.1
    (Received from a RR-client)  valid  internal  best
Received Path ID 0, Local Path ID 1, version 3
  Attributes after inbound policy was applied:
    next hop: 192.168.0.1
    MET ORG AS LOCAL
    origin: IGP  neighbor as: 65201  metric: 0  local pref: 100
    aspath: 65201
  Attributes after outbound policy was applied:
    next hop: 192.168.0.1
    MET ORG AS LOCAL
    origin: IGP  neighbor as: 65201  metric: 0  local pref: 100
    aspath: 65201
    originator: 192.168.0.1    cluster list: 192.168.2.1


10.1.99.11/32 is advertised to 192.168.0.3
  Path info:
    neighbor: 192.168.0.2    neighbor router id: 192.168.0.2
    (Received from a RR-client)  valid  internal
Received Path ID 0, Local Path ID 2, version 3
  Attributes after inbound policy was applied:
    next hop: 192.168.0.2
    MET ORG AS LOCAL
    origin: IGP  neighbor as: 65201  metric: 0  local pref: 100
    aspath: 65201
  Attributes after outbound policy was applied:
    next hop: 192.168.0.2
    MET ORG AS LOCAL
    origin: IGP  neighbor as: 65201  metric: 0  local pref: 100
    aspath: 65201
    originator: 192.168.0.2    cluster list: 192.168.2.1
```

The BGP Add-Path function can be used together with or alternatively to the BGP Best External function described in the previous section. For instance, in a scenario where the CE1↔PE1 connection is selected as primary (e.g., by setting on PE1 a value of Local Preference higher than 100 to the advertisements received from CE1), as we saw in the previous section, by applying the BGP Best External function on PE2, we can make two advertisements reach the RR, and through the BGP Add-Path function configured as earlier between RR and PE3, PE3 will receive both advertisements, one with BGP Next-Hop PE1 and the other with BGP Next-Hop PE2.

Alternatively, we could use only the BGP Add-Path function on PE2, RR and PE3. On router PE2 in send mode, on RR in send/receive mode and on PE3 in receive mode.

If you are interested, the equivalent JUNOS configurations on RR and PE3 are included below.

RR

```
[edit protocols bgp group PE]
type internal;
local-address 192.168.2.1;
cluster 192.168.2.1;
neighbor 192.168.0.3 {
  family inet {
    unicast {
      add-path {
        send {
          path-count 2;
        }
      }
    }
  }
}
```

PE3

```
[edit protocols bgp group TO-RR]
type internal;
local-address 192.168.0.3;
neighbor 192.168.2.1 {
  family inet {
    unicast {
      add-path {
        receive;
      }
    }
  }
}
```

12.5.3 BGP Diverse Path function

In the previous section, dedicated to the BGP Add-Path function, we saw how, by changing the structure of the BGP UPDATE messages, a BGP Speaker can advertise more than one path to the same IP prefix, beside the best path. The change to BGP UPDATE messages concerns the structure of the NLRI field (or MP_REACH_NLRI for MultiProtocol-BGP), to which a 4 byte element – the Path ID – is added.

The BGP Add-Path function provides a final solution to the issue of multiple advertisements of a same prefix; however, its downside – as we just explained – is to require a modification of the BGP UPDATE messages, and, also, it must be negotiated between BGP Neighbors, therefore it requires the routers at the endpoints of the BGP session to have a version of the operating system supporting it.

For the transition period during which not all routers will have the BGP Add-Path function available, within the IETF framework, a simpler solution has been suggested, which does not require any modification of the BGP messages, and which can therefore be broadly applied. This solution, known as BGP Diverse Path, is the topic of RFC 6774 – *Distribution of Diverse BGP Paths*, November 2012. This type of solution applies in a standard scenario, with redundant Route Reflectors, but currently it is not supported by all manufacturers.

In order to obtain a stable Path Diversity on router PE3 of our usual scenario with redundant RRs, we can resort to a very simple solution, also a sort of "Columbus' Egg": making one RR behave as "usual", and advertise the best path, and the other RR advertise the backup best path, i.e., the one obtained from a selection process where the primary best path is eliminated.

The idea is described in Figure 12.23 below.

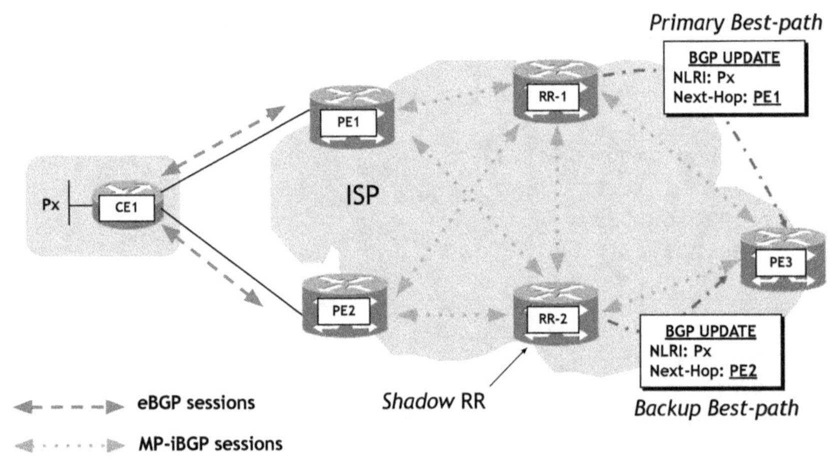

Figure 12.23 – BGP Diverse Path function.

RR-1 behaves as usual, and advertises the best path, while RR-2, which is called shadow RR, advertises only the backup best path. In this way, on PE3, we have two different paths for prefix Px, the best path (advertisement with BGP Next-Hop PE1) received from RR-1, and a backup best path (the one with BGP Next-Hop PE2) received from RR-2, thus achieving the Path Diversity.

The idea is extremely simple and effective. However, there are a few implementation details we should take into account. The most important is the following. Let's assume that RR-1 chooses as the best path the path with BGP Next-Hop PE1, because it is closer, according to IGP metrics.

In the same way, let's assume that RR-2 (the shadow RR!) chooses as the best path the path with BGP Next-Hop PE2, and as the backup best path the path with BGP Next-Hop PE1. The result is that PE3 will have only one path available – the one with best path PE1, and the Path Diversity would not be achieved. Obviously, the issue does not arise, if both RRs choose the same path as the primary best path. Since this issue, with the same standard BGP metrics (Local Preference, AS_PATH, ORIGIN, MED) can be caused by the different IGP "distance" between RRs and the PE router, it is best to disable the IGP cost check in BGP's selection process (if this specific control is available, and the main vendors provide it). In this way, RR-1 and RR-2 will have the same primary best path, and RR-2 will have a different backup best path (which is what we are interested in).

In Cisco platforms, support of the BGP Diverse Path was introduced both by IOS and in IOS XE, but not in IOS XR. JUNOS does not support the BGP Diverse Path.

In Cisco platforms with IOS and IOS XE, the general configuration steps are:

1. Disabling the IGP metric check from the BGP selection process. The command to execute under the BGP process is "**bgp bestpath igp-metric ignore**". If both RRs have identical IGP distances from the PEs, the command would not be needed; however, we still recommend its execution.

2. Allowing the backup best path calculation on the shadow RRs.
   router(config)# **router bgp** *AS-number*
   router(config-router)# **address-family ...**
   router(config-router-af)# **bgp additional-paths select backup**

3. Allowing the advertisement of the backup best path to RR-Clients on the shadow RR.
   router(config)# **router bgp** *AS-number*
   router(config-router)# **address-family ...**
   router(config-router-af)# **neighbor** *IP-Client* **advertise diverse-path {backup | mpath}**

In the following lab test, we will show how to use the two "**backup**" and "**mpath**" options. Only if the RR is in the forwarding path (not very frequent in practical applications), the BGP PIC Core should be enabled with the commands we saw in Section 12.4.5.

On the primary RR, it is best to configure only the command in point 1. Everything else requires only ordinary configurations.

Now, we will see a lab test that will help us check the BGP Diverse Path function. The scenario used is the one in Figure 12.23, with Px=10.11.32/24, AS(CE)=65101 and AS(ISP)=64500. The shadow RR is RR-2. All BGP attributes were left to their default value.

First, let's see what happens with the basic configurations, without applying the BGP Diverse Path. RR-1 and RR-2 each received two advertisements of prefix 10.11.32/24, from routers PE1 and PE2 respectively. The two RRs execute the selection process to determine the best path, which, as you can see in the following views, is the path with BGP Next-Hop PE1 (we will leave the reason to you, as useful practice):

```
RR-1# show bgp ipv4 unicast
. . .
     Network          Next Hop       Metric     LocPrf       Weight      Path
*>i 10.11.32.0/24 192.168.0.1          0          100            0       65101 i
*  i                192.168.0.2          0          100            0       65101 i
```

```
RR-2# show bgp ipv4 unicast
. . .
     Network        Next Hop      Metric    LocPrf      Weight     Path
*>i 10.11.32.0/24 192.168.0.1       0         100          0      65101 i
*  i               192.168.0.2       0         100          0      65101 i
```

On PE3, we will have two advertisements of prefix 10.11.32/24:

```
PE3# show bgp ipv4 unicast
. . .
     Network        Next Hop      Metric    LocPrf      Weight     Path
*>i 10.11.32.0/24 192.168.0.1       0         100          0      65101 i
*  i               192.168.0.1       0         100          0      65101 i
```

As you can see, the two advertisements have the same BGP Next-Hop (=192.168.0.1), and, as we mentioned multiple times, the Path Diversity requires two different BGP Next-Hops.

And here is where the BGP Diverse Path comes into play. We will use RR-2 as shadow RR. The configuration of the BGP process on RR-2 is the following (Note: in this test, we are using the default IPv4 unicast address family):

```
router bgp 64500
  template peer-policy RRC-POLICY
    route-reflector-client
    advertise diverse-path backup
  exit-peer-policy
 !
  template peer-session RRC-SESSION
    remote-as 64500
    update-source Loopback0
  exit-peer-session
 !
  bgp additional-paths select backup
  bgp bestpath igp-metric ignore
  neighbor 192.168.0.1 inherit peer-session RRC-SESSION
  neighbor 192.168.0.1 inherit peer-policy RRC-POLICY
  neighbor 192.168.0.2 inherit peer-session RRC-SESSION
  neighbor 192.168.0.2 inherit peer-policy RRC-POLICY
  neighbor 192.168.0.3 inherit peer-session RRC-SESSION
  neighbor 192.168.0.3 inherit peer-policy RRC-POLICY
```

RR-1's configuration is the standard Route Reflector configuration. Basically, it is identical to RR-2's, we just need to remove the specific BGP Diverse path commands, which are "**advertise diverse-path backup**" within the peer-policy template and "**bgp additional-paths select backup**".

First, let's see if and what changes in the BGP Tables of the two RRs:

```
RR-1# show bgp ipv4 unicast
. . .
     Network        Next Hop      Metric    LocPrf      Weight     Path
*>i 10.11.32.0/24 192.168.0.1       0         100          0      65101 i
*  i               192.168.0.2       0         100          0      65101 i
```

```
RR-2# show bgp ipv4 unicast
. . .

    Network          Next Hop       Metric     LocPrf       Weight     Path
*>i 10.11.32.0/24 192.168.0.1         0          100            0      65101 i
*bi                 192.168.0.2        0          100            0      65101 i
```

The only thing that differs compared to the two previous BGP tables is the presence of code "**b**" in the non best path advertisement of RR-2's BGP table, which indicates the backup-path. This means that the non best path advertisement has been selected for the advertisement to RR-Clients. For instance, with the following view, it is clear that RR-2 advertises this non best path to PE3:

```
RR-2# show bgp ipv4 unicast neighbor 192.168.0.3 advertised-routes
. . .

     Network         Next Hop       Metric     LocPrf       Weight     Path
*bia 10.11.32.0/24 192.168.0.2         0          100            0     65101 i
```

Notice the presence of the three "**bia**" codes. The additional code "**a**" stands for additional-path, that is, that the path advertised is not the best path, but rather an "additional" path.
Lastly, let's see what happens on PE3. In the BGP table, we find two advertisements coming from the two Route Reflectors RR-1 and RR-2:

```
PE3# show bgp ipv4 unicast
. . .

    Network          Next Hop       Metric     LocPrf       Weight     Path
*>i 10.11.32.0/24 192.168.0.1         0          100            0      65101 i
*bi                 192.168.0.2        0          100            0      65101 i
```

As you can see, this time the two advertisements have a different BGP Next-Hop, therefore we achieve the Path Diversity. For the sake of completeness, let's see also how the BGP PIC Edge (unipath) function is enabled on PE3:

```
router bgp 64500
   bgp additional-paths install
```

The FIB entry (CEF table) related to prefix 10.11.32/24, shows that both paths are included in the FIB:

```
PE3# show ip cef 10.11.32.0/24 detail
10.11.32.0/24, epoch 0, flags rib only nolabel, rib defined all labels
   recursive via 192.168.0.1
       nexthop 172.30.1.11 GigabitEthernet0/0
       nexthop 172.30.1.12 GigabitEthernet0/0
   recursive via 192.168.0.2, repair
       nexthop 172.30.1.11 GigabitEthernet0/0
       nexthop 172.30.1.12 GigabitEthernet0/0
```

Each one of the BGP Next-Hops has two IGP Next-Hops. The second BGP Next-Hop (=192.168.0.2), as indicated in the key word "**repair**", is used on the forwarding plane as backup. In some situations, especially in small networks, the RRs can be used also on the data plane, i.e. the forwarding path. In these situations, it may be useful to enable the multipath BGP on the RRs. What happens in this case on the shadow RR? Since both paths available have been used, the router advertises only the the best path and ignores the BGP Diverse Path specific commands. Therefore, on PE3, we go back to a situation as if the BGP Diverse Path was not enabled.

NOTE: Remember that, if the multipath BGP is enabled, the BGP selection process is still completed, and the resulting best path is advertised to the BGP Neighbors, according to standard BGP rules (see Section 7.1.1, point 8 of the selection process).

To enable the BGP Diverse Path, if the multipath BGP is enabled on the RRs, we need to use the "**mpath**" option of the "**neighbor** *IP-Client* **advertise diverse-path** ..." command. In this case, RR-2's configuration becomes (Note: the "**bgp additional-paths select backup**" command is no longer necessary):

```
router bgp 64500
 template peer-policy RRC-POLICY
   route-reflector-client
   advertise diverse-path mpath
 exit-peer-policy
 !
 template peer-session RRC-SESSION
   remote-as 64500
   update-source Loopback0
 exit-peer-session
 !
 bgp bestpath igp-metric ignore
 maximum-paths ibgp 2
    . . .  < neighbor commands omitted > . . .
```

In this way, PE3 will receive from RR-1 the path with BGP Next-Hop PE1 (best path for PE1, despite the multipath BGP being enabled), and from RR-2, the path with BGP Next-Hop PE2, thanks to the "**mpath**" clause, which allows advertising a non best path marked in RR-2's RIB BGP as multipath (indicated in the RIB BGP with code "**m**").

SUMMARY

In the past, one of BGP's Achilles heels was a fairly slow convergence time, especially in scenarios where hundreds of thousands of IP prefixes are involved. Over the years, as technology moved forward, several techniques were introduced to reach acceptable convergence times.

Obviously, this entails the use of functions such as BGP fast external fall-over, BGP NHT, BFD protocols, an accurate IGP tuning, the implementation of FIB with hierarchical structure, and the application of the BGP PIC Core/Edge. The main equipment vendors, such as Cisco and Juniper, provide all the tools to do this, you just need to apply them!

In addition, new Path Diversity functions have been developed, allowing to store both a primary Next-Hop and a backup Next-Hop in the FIB, in order to speed up the convergence on an alternative Next-Hop. We described three of them, each one with their pros and cons, and different reference scenarios.

Perhaps, the BGP Best External is the simplest one, but it also has a limited application scenario. However, it can complement the other two. The BGP Add-Path function is very general, and allows advertising several paths of the same prefix. However, it requires an update of the operating systems, since its application requires changes to BGP UPDATE messages. Therefore, this function needs to be negotiated between BGP Neighbors. On the other hand, the BGP Best External function does not require modifications to BGP messages, but its applicability is rather limited. Among other things, this does not allow advertising a number of paths higher than 2, while the BGP Add-Path function does not set limits.

The BGP Diverse Path function is less general than the BGP Add-Path function; however, it has the advantage of not requesting modifications to BGP UPDATE messages, nor does it need to be negotiated between BGP Neighbors. Therefore, it could be broadly applicable, in the transition period until which all the network routers (and PE and RR in particular) support the BGP Add-Path function. The application scenario is often found in practical applications, where usually the RRs are always redundant (or at least they should be!).

Worth remembering:

1. BGP timers (and MRAI in particular) and their impact on the convergence speed.

2. TCP connection and queue parameter regulation.

3. The methods to speed up the detection of a BGP session drop (BFD, BGP fast external fall-over, BGP fast peering deactivation).

4. The difference between BGP time driven and event driven.

5. The BGP Next-Hop tracking function and its BGP selective address tracking variant.

6. Convergence on the data plane and control plane.

7. The BGP PIC Edge/Core function.

8. Path Diversity methods: BGP Best External, BGP Add-Path and BGP Diverse Path.

This chapter does not introduce any new concept; it is rather a collection of references and operational guidelines, a useful hands-on "manual" and a set of rules to follow, to help network administrators achieve a good operation and a correct protocol configuration within their network infrastructure. And also about an ethical and responsible use of BGP, to make the entire Internet ecosystem more efficient and – above all – safer. In short, a sort of "BGP etiquette".

Out of the many functional aspects of this protocol, we would like to dwell on a few of them that we deem more significant and important to keep in mind. In particular, we will refer to three macro areas of interest: BGP session establishment, prefix filtering and security.

We invite you to explore the best practices mentioned here further in the related chapters, indicated from time to time.

13.1 ESTABLISHING AND PROTECTING THE SESSIONS

We have covered the rules that govern the BGP sessions in Chapter 2. Concerning the operational best practices, we can classify them, on one side, as the rules that should be followed to correctly establish the sessions, and, on the other side, as the protection tools. The latter have been mainly covered in Chapter 10.

13.1.1 Best practices to establish a session

Best practice #1 – Always specify the BGP-ID manually

When establishing a BGP session, for the BGP process to be activated, the router needs to elect a BGP-ID, which can be any IP address, not necessarily associated to a physical or logical interface. The only limit to observe, to avoid interaction issues between routers using different operating systems, is that the BGP-ID should not match the endpoint BGP Neighbors of a session.

Even if each platform usually has an automatic BGP-ID selection criterion, we recommend to specify manually, as best practice. This ensures an easier reading of "**show …**" commands, where the Neighbors' BGP-ID is always present, and also to immediately identify the BGP-ID, by simply viewing the configuration file.

In order to avoid duplicates, it is best (although not necessary) for the BGP-ID to match the IP address of a Loopback interface.

[Reference: Section 3.1.1 – Basic configurations]

Best practice #2 – In eBGP sessions between directly connected routers, you should use the IPv4/IPv6 addresses of the connection's physical interfaces as the session endpoints

The reason for this is that, in any case, if one of the two interfaces at both endpoints of the connection is out of service, this entails the loss of connectivity at layer 3, and therefore of the eBGP session, which, after a certain time, is closed, since the Hold Time has expired. Actually, many developers, in this situation, have BGP implementations that allow to close the BGP session by default, as soon as the router detects that the interface is out of service at layer 2 or physically. Sometimes, due to security reasons, some network administrators use Loopback interfaces as endpoints, since they are not visible to traceroutes. And this should also be done in the case of multilink connections between the two endpoint routers in the connection.

Another advantage is that adding a new connection between the two routers does not entail any additional configuration at BGP level. While the downside is a more complex configuration, as it requires a layer-3 connection between the Loopback interfaces used, and the activation of a multihop eBGP session (see Figure 2.7, Section 2.1.2). One more best practice is to always use a LAG (Link Aggregation Group) even in the case of single port connection. The rationale behind this is to ease future bandwidth expansion: For instance, if you have a single 100 Gbit/s Ethernet connection to your upstream provider or peer, adding a new 100 Gbit/s Ethernet, to expand bandwidth no new IPs are needed and no BGP changes. As an example, Google's peering policy states that "Link aggregation via LACP is required for all links, including single links"

[Reference: Section 2.1.2 – Rules in eBGP Sessions].

Best practice #3 – In iBGP sessions and in multihop eBGP sessions, you should use the IPv4/IPv6 of Loopback interfaces as the session endpoints

This is because Loopback interfaces, being virtual, never go out of service, thus allowing the e/iBGP session to remain active as long as there is a layer 3 connection between the two BGP Neighbors.

[Reference: Section 2.1.2 and 2.1.3 – Rules in e/iBGP Sessions].

Best practice #4 – You should avoid transporting IPv6 routing information on sessions using IPv4 addresses

In order to avoid situations that prevent connectivity, it is advisable to avoid transporting IPv6 routing information on sessions using IPv4 addresses as endpoints of the BGP session. This is because some manufacturers do not support the transport of IPv6 routing info on IPv4 sessions, or have a code that does not work correctly.

[Reference: Section 3.1.6 – BGP sessions for IPv6]

Best practice #5 – In BGP sessions for IPv6, it is best not to use link-local addresses

Theoretically, when defining directly connected BGP Neighbors, it would be possible to use link-local addresses. However, in this case, we need to indicate what IPv6 link-local address we are using to open the TCP connection, through suitable configuration.

[Reference: Section 3.1.6 – BGP sessions for IPv6]

13.1.2 Best practices to protect a session

Best practice #6 – Protect the BGP Speaker by implementing filters on the data plane, to block any packets with source or destination port 179, except for those related to any configured session

Since the IPv4/v6 addresses of the Neighbors we want to establish a BGP session with are known, it is a good practice to implement some filters on the packets received from the BGP Neighbors, allowing the transit of TCP packets on the source or destination port 179, only if they come from the IPv4/v6 address of a Neighbor (Access Control List (ACL), in Cisco IOS language, Firewall Filter (FF) in JUNOS language).

Operational experience has proven that the native protections of TCP are not sufficient, because, without more stringent blocks, a BGP Speaker can be attacked by simply sending a high volume of connection requests.

If the platform supports it, it is best to apply the filters directly on the control plane. For instance, in Juniper platforms, the filters should be applied to the lo0.0. interface, in the inbound direction, while in Cisco platforms, based on the platform type, we can use Control-Plane Policing, receive-ACLs, etc.

In addition to filters, for greater protection of the control plane, we should also apply rate-limiting (policing) mechanisms to the BGP message traffic. This allows us to protect the router's control plane, if the traffic of BGP messages exceeds the platform CPU's processing limits.

> **NOTE:** The issue of control plane protection goes well beyond the use of BGP; however, it is part of a broader plan to protect the processing capacity of the entire router, whose CPU is not engaged only for BGP. Reaching the maximum usage limits of the CPU leads to an overall router – and consequently BGP's – disservice. For more detailed guidelines concerning the protection of a router control plane, you can read RFC 6192 – *Protecting the Router Control Plane*, March 2011.

[Reference: Section 10.2.2 – TCP-level filters]

Best practice #7 – Limit the number of prefixes received from a BGP Neighbor

Limiting the number of prefixes that a BGP Neighbor can receive from one of its BGP Neighbors is useful to avoid classic DoS attacks, whose aim is to saturate the router's resources, by sending a very high quantity of advertisements of different prefixes.

The value of the limit is based on the type of peering relation. From a BGP Neighbor with which you have a peering relation, the limit should be set a little higher than the estimate of the number of prefixes that the BGP Peer can (legitimately) advertise. Once the maximum threshold is exceeded, the BGP Speaker should be set to drop the BGP session, in order to avoid the risk that, due to some configuration error, the BGP Peer sends the FIRT and the router is not sized to support it.

From an Upstream Provider you have a transit relation with, and which provides the entire FIRT, the limit must be set to a higher value than the total number of Internet prefixes, while taking into account the scalability limits of the platform available.

> **NOTE:** In this case, we believe that putting the entire FIRT in the memory of your router – unless it is a Tier-1 ISP – is not a good practice. This is because, due to consolidated statistics, the majority of traffic is directed toward directly connected ASes, or to those distant two or three hops at most. The rest of the traffic destined to the other hundreds of thousands of prefixes should be left to the destiny of the default route.

[Reference: Section 10.3.1 – Limiting the number of prefixes received]

Best practice #8 – Use authentication based on the TCP-AO option, rather than that based on option 19 of the TCP

If you want to apply the BGP messages authentication mechanisms, it is always best to use authentication based on the TCP-AO option (Kind=29) option, rather than on the standard option (Kind=19). And, if the vendor supports it, implement automatic password change mechanisms (e.g. key-chain in Cisco and Juniper platforms), and more sophisticated cryptographic algorithms to determine the hash function.

[Reference: Section 10.2.1 – BGP message authentication]

Best practice #9 –Apply the GTSM mechanism to eBGP sessions between directly connected BGP Neighbors

One of the greatest vulnerabilities of BGP is using the TCP as Transport layer. This implies the option of launching attacks to BGP sessions from any part of the Internet, since TCP segments are transported by IP packets.

A very simple, yet effective countermeasure to contrast these remote attacks is to use the GTSM (Generalized TTL Security Mechanism), which consists in changing the TTL management of IP packets transporting BGP messages. Indeed, in eBGP sessions, IP packets have TTL=1 by default. When a BGP Speaker receives an IP packet with TTL higher than 1 from a BGP Neighbor, it rejects the packet. A hacker, by attempting, or by knowing the number of hops that the packet crosses (which could be determined through a simple traceroute), could easily simulate a packet reaching the BGP Speaker with TTL=1.

In order to avoid the issue, the idea is very simple yet effective: changing the default value of the TTL from 1 to 255, and "instruct" the BGP Speaker to accept BGP messages only if transported by IP packets with TTL=255. And this is the GTSM mechanism. Since it is not possible to send IP packets with TTL=255 to a host not directly connected, the GTSM mechanism manages to contrast the issue, for eBGP sessions between BGP Neighbors.

The GTSM mechanism can also be applied to multihop eBGP sessions; in this case, the TTL should be adjusted based on an estimate of the network diameter, that is, the maximum distance between any two BGP Neighbors, in terms of hops. However, it is not as effective as in the case of sessions between directly connected BGP Neighbors, because anyone, in the route between the two BGP Neighbors, could simulate packets with a TTL adjusted so as to reach the destination, and thus tricking the GTSM. Therefore, the best practice is to use the GTSM only on eBGP sessions between directly connected BGP Neighbors.

[Reference: Section 10.2.3 – Secure TTL management]

NOTE: As you may recall, both the implementation of the BGP message authentication and of the GTSM mechanism, requires a configuration on both BGP Neighbors at the endpoints of the BGP session.

13.2 ROUTE FILTERING

As you already know, filtering policies are essential for the correct operation of the Internet's ecosystem, and they help to limit damage to one's own and other networks. Without suitable filtering, incidents such as route leak and prefix hijacking (which we covered extensively in Chapter 10) would be very frequent, and they would have greater impact within the entire ecosystem.

Moreover, suitable filtering increases the scalability and stability of the entire Internet, preventing the proliferation of the amplitude of routing tables and the circulation of prefixes that should not be included in the RIBs of the routers, either because they can only be used in private networks, or because reserved to specific applications or documentation.

The advertisement propagation best practices that every ISP should follow are summarized in the following table.

Type of advertisements	eBGP-out to customers	eBGP-out to BGP peers	eBGP-out to u.p. (*)
Received from a customer	Accept	Accept	Accept
Received from a BGP peer	Accept	Reject	Reject
Received from an u.p.	Accept	Reject	Reject
Local advertisements	Accept	Accept	Accept
Unclassified	Reject	Reject	Reject

(*) u.p. = Upstream Provider

Among other things, inbound and outbound filtering policies, in order to prevent route leak incidents, must comply with the advertisement propagation described in this table. And, if adopted correctly, they also help to prevent prefix hijacking incidents, by blocking the advertisements of prefixes that an ISP or client has no right to advertise.

13.2.1 General aspects

Best practice #10 – Register your numbering resources (ASes, IPv4/v6 prefixes) on the Internet Routing Registry (IRR)

An important aspect, vital to the security of the Internet ecosystem, is that everyone should advertise only what belongs to them, that is, the resources assigned by RIR/LIR. This is the foundation to create and maintain the filters.

Therefore, it is necessary to publish the information on one's own resources, to help the other participants within the ecosystem create and maintain suitable filters. The publication is done within the Internet Routing Registries (IRR), which are public databases where the resources assigned to the operators requesting them are specified.

Even if you can use any IRR available, it is recommended and preferable to use the one provided by your own RIR. Usually the RIRs provide, on their portal, after logging in, an area to create and manage Internet resources, a user interface that helps to handle the different objects within the IRR. If you acquire the resources from different RIRs, then you should work on more than one IRR.

Apart from the differences between the different registries and IRRs, the objects you should focus on and keep updated are the same (they will be the source of information from which the operators will create the filters). In particular, we can identify 3 of them:

aut-num: object that specifies the routing policies of an AS. Here is an example:

```
aut-num: AS64500
descr: Provider 64500
remarks: ++ Customers ++
mp-import: from AS64501 accept AS64501[AR2]
mp-export: to AS64501 announce ANY
mp-import: from AS64502 accept AS64502
mp-export: to AS64502 announce ANY
remarks: ++ Peers ++
```

mp-import: from AS64511 accept AS64511:AS-ALL
mp-export: to AS64511 announce AS64500:AS-ALL
remarks: ++ Transit ++
mp-import: from AS64510 accept ANY except FLTR-BOGONS
mp-export: to AS64510 announce AS64500:AS-ALL
mnt-by: MAINT-AS64500
created: 2012-10-27T12:14:23Z
last-modified: 2016-02-27T12:33:15Z
source: RIPE

NOTE: Routing policies are expressed using the RPSL language, Routing Policy Specification Language (RFC 4012 – *Routing Policy Specification Language next generation (RPSLng)*, March 2005) within the "mp-import" and "mp-export" attributes.

route/route6: these two objects, used for IPv4 and IPv6 respectively, are more common for filter generation. They contain the pair <prefix; prefix origin>, and tie an ASN to a prefix. These objects must include prefixes actually advertised within the Internet, and they provide a high-level representation of each advertisement. Here is an example of **route6** object:

route6: 2001:db8:1000::/36
descr: Provider 64500
origin: AS64500
mnt-by: MAINT-AS64500
created: 2012-10-27T12:14:23Z
last-modified: 2016-02-27T12:33:15Z
source: RIPE

as-set: another very important object that specifies, in the "members" attribute, the customer ASes (downstream) of an Upstream Provider. Here is an example:

as-set: AS64500:AS-CUSTOMERS
members: AS64501
members: AS64502
mnt-by: MAINT-AS64500
created: 2012-10-27T12:14:23Z
last-modified: 2016-02-27T12:33:15Z
source: RIPE

We would like to remind you that constantly updating the objects is a crucial best practice. Just think about the filtering usually performed in the Route Server infrastructures of an Internet Exchange Point, where the different BGP Peer filters are generated from the information contained within the as-set, route and route6 objects! Incorrect or non-updated objects cause the failure to announce the reachability information to all the other ISPs connected to the peering LAN.

NOTE: if you want to know more about the different objects available, you can refer to the websites of the RIRs. Such as: https://www.ripe.net/manage-ips-and-asns/db/support/documentation/ripe-database-documentation/rpsl-object-types.

Best practice #11 – Classify advertisements using BGP Communities

Usually, an ISP has three types of eBGP sessions: those toward the Upstream Providers, those toward ISPs with which they have peering relations, and those toward customers.

To simplify the filtering operations, a good practice is associating each type of advertisement to a BGP Community (standard, extended or large) and writing the filters using the Community values.

[Reference: Section 6.4.2 – Case Study]

13.2.2 Filtering on eBGP Sessions

Best practice #12 – Do not accept and do not propagate advertisements of non-routable prefixes on all eBGP sessions

The edge routers of an ISP, that is, the routers that have eBGP sessions with other ISPs, must apply standard filters to block the advertisements of prefixes that shouldn't circulate within the Internet (non routable prefixes) both inbound and outbound.

The list of non routable prefixes is available on several websites, such as:

https://team-cymru.com/community-services/bogon-reference/**.**

[Reference: Section 8.6.2 – Non-routable prefix filtering]

Best practice #13 – In eBGP sessions with customer, accept only those prefixes that the customers are authorized to advertise

In order to avoid prefix hijacking incidents, it is best to implement inbound filters on the eBGP sessions with the customers, which accept only those prefixes that the customers are authorized to advertise. These could be Provider Independent or Provider Aggregatable prefixes.

Even better, you should automate these inbound filters, by creating whitelists of the prefixes that every customer can advertise. Since the set of prefixes that a customer can advertise varies over time (e.g. a customer acquires the right to use a new public prefix), to keep the filters updated, you can use tools that, by interacting with the IRRs, can automatize filter writing (e.g. bgpq3/4, IRRToolSet).

[Reference: Section 8.6.5 – Filters in customer side BGP sessions]

Best practice #14 – In a peering relation, an ISP should advertise to local peers only its local prefixes and those of its customers

In the outbound direction, an ISP must advertise to the local peers only its local prefixes, possibly aggregated, and those received from its customers. It should not propagate the advertisements received from local peers to other local peers and to any Upstream Provider, but only to its customers, if required. If an ISP has customers that advertise Provider Independent prefixes and perhaps have their own public AS, the ISP must also advertise these prefixes. In the inbound direction, filters must only allow the reception of advertisements of public prefixes from local peers, and block everything else (non routable prefixes, default routes, etc.).

[Reference: Section 8.6.3 – Filters in peering relations]

Best practice #15 – In transit relations, apply a good filtering policy

A good rule of thumb is that an ISP, in its transit relations, applies inbound filters to block the following prefixes (with the possible exception of the default route, if the ISP does not require its Upstream Provider to send the FIRT, or if the Upstream Provider sends it and the ISP filters part of it):

- non routable prefixes (see Section 8.6.2);

- prefixes not allocated by IANA (only IPv6, the allocation of IPv4 prefixes has already been completed);

- prefixes with mask length greater than /24 (from /25 to /32) for IPv4 and greater than /48 for IPv6;

- prefixes belonging to your own AS;

- the default route.

Moreover, if the ISP is located within an IXP, it is best to block also the inbound advertisements of the prefix of the peering LAN and its possible more specific networks.

In the same way, an ISP should apply outbound filters to block the advertisement of the prefixes of the peering LAN to the Upstream Providers, except, of course, for its own local prefixes and the prefixes of its customers.

[Reference: Section 8.6.4 – Filters in transit relations]

Best practice #16 – Do not accept advertisements from customers and local peers transiting through OTT or Tier-1

As it is highly unlikely – not to say impossible – that an OTT (Over The Top), such as Google, Facebook, Amazon, etc. or a Tier-1 ISP (e.g. Telia, TI Sparkle, etc.) uses a customer or local peer as transit, a good rule of thumb is that an ISP does not accept advertisements that have transited through ASes of these big providers, from its customers or local peers. For instance, a filter (based on the AS_PATH) implementing this policy in a Cisco platform with IOS XR could be:

```
as-path-set BIGNETWORKS
  ios-regex '_(174|209|286|701|1299|6762| ...)_'
end-set
!
route-policy NO-BIGNETWORKS
   if as-path in BIGNETWORKS then drop
     else pass
   endif
 end-policy
```

where the AS numbers present in the regular expression belong to big providers (e.g. 1299 is Telia's AS number, 6762 is TI Sparkle's AS number, etc.).

NOTE: For an updated list of Tier-1 and OTT AS numbers, see: https://api.asrank.caida.org/v2/docs.

13.3 SECURITY

Best practice #17 – Do not accept advertisement with an AS_PATH longer than a configuration value

BGP advertisements on the Internet have an average AS_PATH length of a few ASes. Sometimes, in the Internet, there are abnormally long AS_PATHS, resulting from prepending AS_PATHS obtained by adding dozens if not hundreds of times their own AS number. This causes several issues to the Internet, including security problems, as an excessive AS_PATH prepending could cause the entire router to go out of service.

[Reference: Section 10.3.2 – Limiting the AS_PATH length]

Best practice #18 – Implement the validation mechanism on the advertisement origin (RPKI)

In order to avoid prefix hijacking incidents, a good practice is to implement the RPKI architecture that allows validating the origin of the prefixes input in the Internet ecosystem, that is, if an ISP can legitimately advertise a certain IPv4/v6 prefix. Therefore, it is good to create ROA objects for one's own prefixes, and reject any Invalid prefix on the router.

[Reference: Paragraph 10.6 – Prefix origin validation]

Best practice #19 – Define from which IP addresses the packets originated by our AS can depart

We should follow some precautions so that our AS does not become the accomplice of global attacks against third parties. The application and implementation of anti-spoofing mechanisms is necessary, in order to ward off any circumstances in which a hacker can create an IP packet with the address of a victim as source (IP spoofing). In order to prevent an attack from starting within our AS, we should apply filters on the data plane (ACL in Cisco platforms and FF in Juniper platforms) that allow rejecting traffic with a source IP address that is not part of the public routing plan of our AS.

[Reference: Section 10.7.2 – SAV and BCP 38]

Best practice #20 – Prevent IP spoofing implementing RPF on the interfaces toward external domains

In order to avoid IP spoofing phenomena on inbound packets, implement at least one of the different Reverse Path Forwarding versions available.

[Reference: Section 10.7.3 – SAV and BCP 84]

13.4 MANRS – Mutually Agreed Norms For Routing Security

As we mentioned in Chapter 10, many incidents on the Internet are caused by the propagation of incorrect routing information. The most common threats, such as prefix hijacking or route leak, take advantage of a basic vulnerability of BGP, that is the impossibility of checking whether the ASes propagating the advertisements are actually legitimated in doing so. Information on the ownership of Internet resources (ASN and prefixes) do not reside within the protocol; they are contained within public databases (IRRs), managed and maintained by the Regional Internet Registries and updated by users. Therefore, we need to activate control processes on what we receive, out-of-band mechanisms to help BGP check if the reachability information received by our Neighbors are correct.

And not just that. Beyond the technical aspects of the protocol, Internet's history taught us that a closer collaboration between the ecosystem's participants, and a greater shared responsibility, are the foundations that support the Internet's growth and success. So, if, on one side, we need to activate control mechanisms to protect the correct reachability of Internet destinations, on the other hand, we need to share reachability data ourselves, and avoid generating routing incidents in the ecosystem: the routing issues of a single operator could trickle-down on the others.

Today, the validation of the prefix origin is an extremely important topic, and good practices for BGP's responsible use are well consolidated. Over the years, several initiatives focused on collecting the best practices on routing security, and a lot has been done in terms of promoting a culture of collective responsibility toward the ecosystem's security. Among the different initiatives, we would like to highlight one, maybe the most important one today, that is MANRS (Mutually Agreed Norms For Routing Security). Launched in 2014 by the Internet Society (ISOC), in 2023 ISOC has reached a partnership agreement with the Global Cyber Alliance (GCA) for it to assume the day-to-day operational responsibility for MANRS effective 1st January 2024. As part of the partnership, the Internet Society will continue to financially support MANRS and provide training and global advocacy over the next five years, while GCA will provide the secretariat function and operate the MANRS Observatory.

This global initiative provides an effective solution to the reduction and mitigation of the main routing threats. Hundreds (when this book was written) of realities have adhered to the initiatives and are following and implementing the best practices suggested by it.

NOTE: MANRS website: https://www.manrs.org/. The updated list of operators participating in the initiative: https://www.manrs.org/isps/participants/.

For the first time, all the important and relevant pieces of information on routing security can be found in one place. And not just that: the actual added value is having structured all these data. Then, we need to consider another important aspect: MANRS is constantly updated, it follows the evolution of the defense mechanisms of the most common routing threats, and is therefore a guide for everyone who wants to improve and keep the security level of their infrastructure up-to-date. MANRS provides different programs, based on the network type and the activities carried out in the ecosystem. The actions suggested concern Internet Exchange Points, Content Providers, Content Delivery Networks, Vendors, and, above all, network operators, which we will go over soon.

The basic idea is to:

- increase the awareness of routing security issues and encourage the implementation of measures to contrast them;

- promote a culture of collective responsibility toward security;

- provide a framework so that operators can understand and tackle issues in the best way possible.

MANRS specifies important actions aimed at tackling three kinds of problems:

- wrong reachability information;

- traffic with spoofed source IP addresses (IP spoofing);

- coordination and collaboration between operators.

And, lastly, here are the 4 actions defined by the initiative, which, by the way, we have already covered and illustrated in the previous pages:

1. Preventing the propagation of incorrect routing information: we need to implement a system based on which an operator advertises only and exclusively its own prefixes and those of its customers to adjacent networks. In the same way, the operator must check that the prefixes advertised by its customers are actually owned by them.

2. Blocking traffic coming from spoofed IP addresses (IP spoofing): an operator should implement a system that enables Source Address Validation for its network and its customers. Therefore, it is necessary to include anti-spoofing filters to prevent packets with an incorrect source IP address from getting into or out of the network.

3. Facilitating coordination and collaboration with other operators: we need to keep contact info (such as the NOC email and telephone number) up-to-date inside the IRRs and peeringDB (https://www.peeringdb.com/).

NOTE: peeringDB is a network database available free of charge (on the initiative of volunteers) and managed by users, whose main purpose is facilitating peering coordinators in achieving the interconnections. Over the last years, it has evolved and it has expanded the information available: in it, apart from all the details concerning peering in Internet eXchange Point, you can also find information on data centers and the other interconnection facilities. Right now, it is a global point of reference for consulting operator data, with over 23K organizations, 40K users, 25K networks and 1K Internet eXchange Points taking part in it.

4. Publicly documenting your routing information: in order to make filtering easier for our BGP Neighbors, we should specify our reachability data, both inside the IRRs (through route and route6 objects), and the list of our Downstreams (in the as-set object), and create the ROAs for our prefixes.

As mentioned earlier, MANRS is constantly evolving. The best practices suggested are taken directly from the industry, and are constantly changing. You can view the guide on how to implement the actions at this link: https://www.manrs.org/isps/guide/.

APPENDIXES

A.1 AS4_PATH AND AS4_AGGREGATOR ATTRIBUTES

Both these Optional Transitive attributes were introduced in RFC 4893 – *BGP Support for Four-octet AS Number Space*, May 2007, for supporting the interworking between routers supporting the 2-byte and the 4-byte AS versions.

The AS4_PATH attribute (Attribute Type Code=17) is managed according to the basic rules we saw for the AS_PATH attribute, and its use is the same. The AS4_PATH attribute is also made up of ordered (AS_SEQUENCE) and non-ordered (AS_SET) segments, with the only difference being that the length of the Path Segment Value is Nx4 bytes. In the same way, the semantics of the AS4_AGGREGATOR attribute (Attribute Type Code=18) is the same as that of the AGGREGATOR attribute, with the only difference being that the AS number is 4 bytes.

The option to manage 4-byte ASes, and therefore the AS4_PATH and AS4_AGGREGATOR attributes, is negotiated by two BGP neighbors, when the BGP session is initialized, through a BGP Capability in the OPEN message, with the following characteristics:

- Capability Code = 65;

- Capability Length = 4;

- Capability Value = AS number of the router (4 byte).

The interesting aspect about these two attributes is the interwork between routers that support only 2-byte ASes – which we will call Old BGP Speakers (OBS), and routers that support 4-byte ASes instead – which we will call New BGP Speakers (NBS).

For easier interpretation, 4-byte AS numbers are often represented with the asdot+ notation, which is a representation with two 2-byte ASes, separated by a comma. For instance, AS 65,536,005 (65 millions, etc.), if represented in the binary code, generates the 32-bit sequence:

$$00000011111101000000000000000101$$

By dividing these 32 bits into two equal 16-bit parts, we have:

$$0000001111101000.0000000000000101$$

which, in the decimal notation, corresponds to 1000.5. Obviously, writing 1000.5 is much more convenient that writing 65,536,005! To obtain the asdot+ representation without the binary representation first, we can apply the following procedure. If AS4 is a 4-byte AS number and [x] the integer part of number "x", AS4's asdot+ representation will be X1.X2, where:

X1 = [AS4/65,536].

X2 = AS4 – (X1*65.536) (the rest of the division AS4/65,536).

We will leave verifying that the asdot+ notation of AS 65,536,005 is the one obtained using the binary representation to you.

NOTE: The routers of the main vendors allow both using the asdot+ notation and the notation as a simple decimal number (called asplain notation). For instance, in a Cisco platform, writing "**router bgp 65536005**" or "**router bgp 1000.5**" is perfectly equivalent. The same goes for Juniper platforms that use JUNOS.

Interwork rules between NBS and OBS, concerning the management of AS_PATH and AS4_PATH attributes, are:

- When an NBS sends an UPDATE message to an OBS, it adds both AS_PATH and AS4_PATH attributes. The AS_PATH attribute contains the 2-byte AS numbers (unchanged), while the 4-byte AS numbers are replaced by reserved AS number 23456 (in RFC 4893, called AS_TRANS). The AS4_PATH attribute contains the 4-byte AS numbers unchanged, and the 2-byte AS numbers coded as 4-byte AS with the first 2 bytes null.

- When an NBS sends an UPDATE message to an NBS, it only adds the AS_PATH attribute, with the AS numbers coded with 4 bytes.

Figure A1.1 shows these two rules graphically.

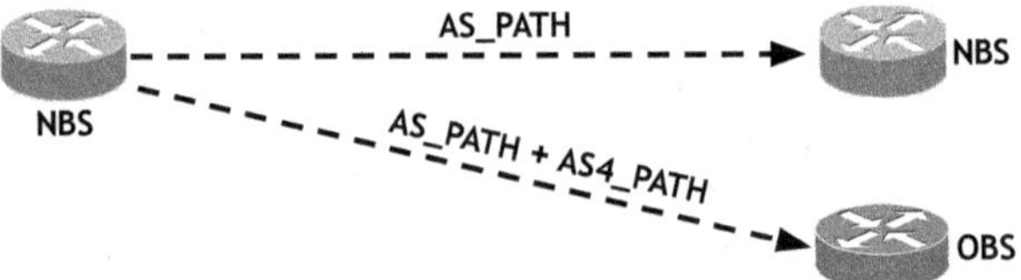

Figure A1.1 – AS_PATH and AS4_PATH in the UPDATE messages sent by NBS.

The other rules concern the processing of AS_PATH and AS4_PATH attributes received from NBS and OBS in UPDATE messages:

- When an OBS receives an UPDATE message from an NBS or an OBS, it updates the AS_PATH attribute according to the usual rules, and leaves the AS4_PATH attribute unchanged.

- When an NBS receives an UPDATE message from an OBS, which must propagate to a BGP Neighbor NBS, it adds an AS_PATH with 4-byte coded ASes, obtained from the two AS_PATH and AS4_PATH attributes received, to the UPDATE message. The new AS_PATH attribute is obtained from the current AS_PATH, by replacing the values 23456 within the AS_PATH with the corresponding 4-byte ASes within the AS4_PATH attribute (first value 23456 with the first AS in the AS4_PATH, and so on). For instance, let's assume that an NBS, belonging to AS 1.1 (asplain= 65537), receives from an OBS an UPDATE message with the following attributes:

  - AS_PATH = [64500 64510 64496 23456 23456 64505 23456 64506].

  - AS4_PATH = [1.2 1.3 64505 1.4 64506].

  The UPDATE message propagated toward a BGP neighbor will (only) contain the following AS_PATH attribute with 4-byte coded ASes:

  - AS_PATH = [1.1 0.64500 0.64510 0.64496 1.2 1.3 0.64505 1.4 0.64506].

Figure A1.2 shows this rule graphically.

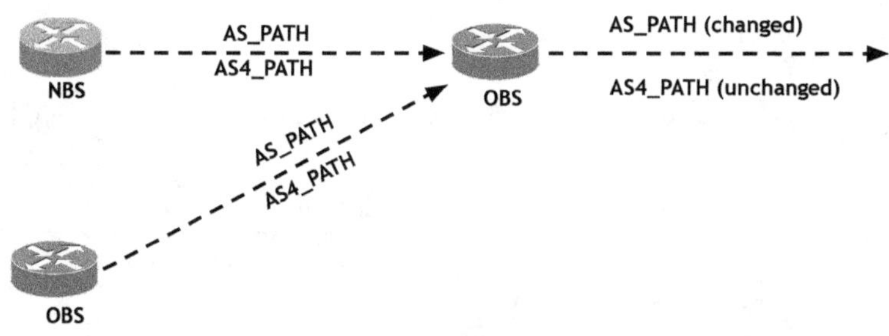

Figure A1.2 – AS_PATH and AS4_PATH processing by an OBS.

The following Figure A1.3 shows an example of how these rules are applied. We will leave verifying if the AS_PATH and AS4_PATH attributes shown are correct to you.

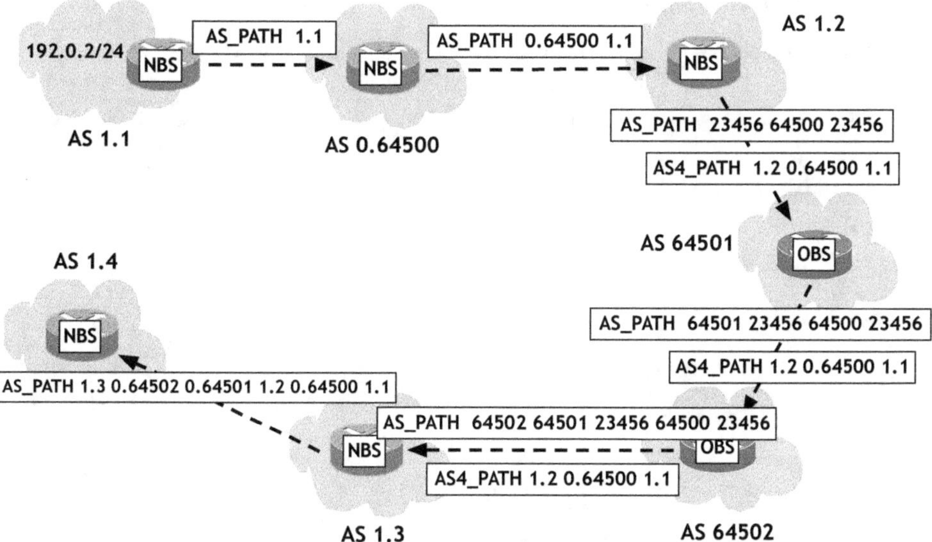

Figure A1.3 – Example of interwork between NBS and OBS of the AS_PATH and AS4_PATH attributes.

Interwork rules between NBS and OBS, concerning the way the AGGREGATOR and AS4_ AGGREGATOR attributes are managed, are similar to the ones we have seen above on AS_PATH and AS4_PATH attribute management, and are:

- An NBS aggregating prefixes, generates both AGGREGATOR and AS4_AGGREGATOR attributes toward an OBS. If the NBS belongs to a 4-byte AS, it adds dummy AS 23456 to the AGGREGATOR attribute.

- An NBS receiving both attributes from an OBS ignores the AGGREGATOR attribute.

- An NBS aggregating prefixes, generates the AGGREGATOR attribute toward an NBS, albeit with the AS field extended to 4 bytes.

The following Figure A1.4 shows an example of how these rules are applied.

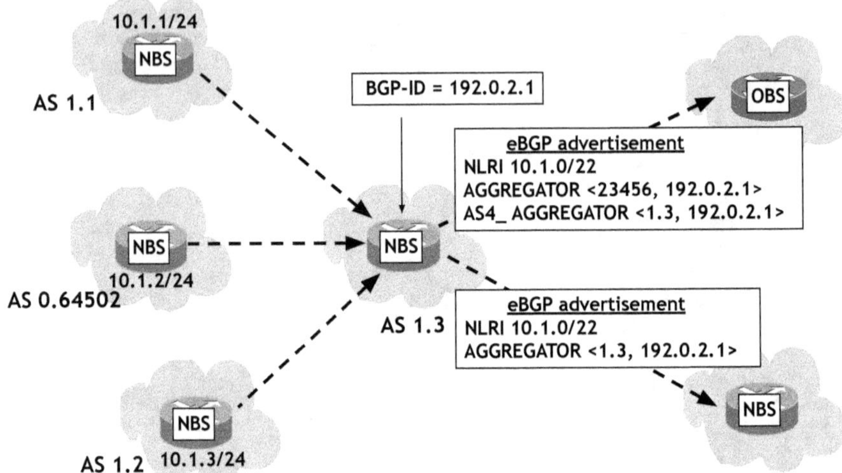

Figure A1.4 – Example of interwork between NBS and OBS of the AGGREGATOR and AS4_ AGGREGATOR attributes.

A.2 WIRESHARK ANALYSIS OF TCP AND BGP MESSAGES

Referring to the lab network in Figure 3.1, let's see a wireshark analysis of the exchange of TCP and BGP messages between CE1 and PE1, to establish eBGP session CE1↔PE1. For the sake of brevity, we will only display the messages exchanged, and leave out the details.

Three-way-handshake

Source	Destination	Protocol	Length	Info
10.1.11.1	10.1.11.2	TCP	62	49241 → **179 [SYN]** Seq=0 Win=16384 Len=0 MSS=1460 WS=1

Source	Destination	Protocol	Length	Info
10.1.11.2	10.1.11.1	TCP	60	**179** → 49241 **[SYN, ACK]** Seq=0 Ack=1 Win=16384 Len=0 MSS=1460

Source	Destination	Protocol	Length	Info
10.1.11.1	10.1.11.2	TCP	54	49241 → **179 [ACK]** Seq=1 Ack=1 Win=16384 Len=0

From the exchange of TCP messages, we can easily infer (as you can test out) that router PE1 (IP address=10.1.11.1) opened the TCP connection.

OPEN messages

Once the TCP connection is opened, OPEN messages are exchanged. The message sequence is shown below. Notice that every OPEN message is acknowledged by a TCP ACK.

Source	Destination	Protocol	Length	Info
10.1.11.1	10.1.11.2	**BGP**	107	**OPEN Message**

Source	Destination	Protocol	Length	Info
10.1.11.2	10.1.11.1	**TCP**	60	**179** → 49241 **[ACK]** Seq=1 Ack=54 Win=16331 Len=0

Source	Destination	Protocol	Length	Info
10.1.11.2	10.1.11.1	**BGP**	111	**OPEN Message**

Source	Destination	Protocol	Length	Info
10.1.11.1	10.1.11.2	**TCP**	54	49241 → **179 [ACK]** Seq=54 Ack=77 Win=24528 Len=0

We will not include a detailed analysis of the OPEN messages, since we've already seen it in Section 2.3.1.

UPDATE and KEEPALIVE messages

After the OPEN messages are exchanged, the two BGP Neighbors exchange UPDATE and KEEPALIVE messages, as shown in the following sequence. Here too, you can notice how each BGP message is acknowledged by a TCP ACK.

Source	Destination	Protocol	Length	Info
10.1.11.1	10.1.11.2	**BGP**	73	**KEEPALIVE** Message

Source	Destination	Protocol	Length	Info
10.1.11.1	10.1.11.2	**TCP**	54	[TCP Window Update] 49241 → **179 [ACK]** Seq=73 Ack=77 Win=32768 Len=0

Source	Destination	Protocol	Length	Info
10.1.11.2	10.1.11.1	**BGP**	73	**KEEPALIVE** Message

Source	Destination	Protocol	Length	Info
10.1.11.2	10.1.11.1	**BGP**	140	**UPDATE** Message, **UPDATE** Message

Source	Destination	Protocol	Length	Info
10.1.11.1	10.1.11.2	**TCP**	54	49241 → **179 [ACK]** Seq=73 Ack=182 Win=32663 Len=0

Source	Destination	Protocol	Length	Info
10.1.11.1	10.1.11.2	**BGP**	77	**UPDATE** Message

Source	Destination	Protocol	Length	Info
10.1.11.2	10.1.11.1	**TCP**	60	**179** → 49241 **[ACK]** Seq=182 Ack=96 Win=16289 Len=0

We will not include a detailed analysis of the UPDATE messages, since we've already seen it in Section 2.3.2. KEEPALIVE messages are empty, and therefore not very interesting. We will only include the analysis of one of them, for the sake of completeness.

Internet Protocol Version 4, Src: 10.1.11.1, Dst: 10.1.11.2
Transmission Control Protocol, Src Port: 49241, Dst Port: 179, Seq: 54, Ack: 77, Len: 19
Border Gateway Protocol - **KEEPALIVE** Message
   Marker: ffffffffffffffffffffffffffffffff
   Length: **19**
   Type: **KEEPALIVE** Message (**4**)

A.3 FINITE-STATE MACHINE

BGP is based on a clear, simple model, and the formalization of its operation, since the first draft of RFC 1105 – *A Border Gateway Protocol (BGP)*, June 1989, is a guarantee of interoperability and a *vade mecum* to solve any issue that arises during its use. The protocol was updated by RFC 1163 (1990), RFC 1267 (1991), RFC 1654 (1994), RFC 1771 (1995), RFC 4271 (2006), RFC 6608 (2012). This model is scientifically represented through a finite-state automaton, also called, as stated in the RFCs, Finite State Machine (FSM). In any case, the implementations produced over the years by the different vendors sometimes deviate from RFC descriptions.

A3.1 Events at the core of the FSM

FSM input data are called 'events', and they classify into two macro-categories: mandatory and optional. In order to make the discussion lighter, we will only describe the mandatory ones, and leave you the option of reading about the optional events in the RFCs directly.

Administrative events

- ManualStart: the local operator starts the connection with the neighbor manually.

- ManualStop: the local operator stops the connection with the neighbor manually.

Timer events

- ConnectRetryTimer_Expires: expiry of the ConnectRetryTimer session attribute (default after 120 sec).

- HoldTimer_Expires: expiry of the HoldTimer session attribute (default after 90 sec).

- KeepaliveTimer_Expires: expiry of the KeepaliveTimer session attribute (with value defined in KeepaliveTime, recommended by default at 1/3 of HoldTimer).

TCP connection-based events

- Tcp_CR_Acked: local system request to establish a TCP connection with the neighbor.

- TcpConnectionConfirmed: confirmation received by the local system that the TCP connection has been established with the neighbor.

- TcpConnectionFails: notification received by the local system on the impossibility of establishing a TCP connection with the neighbor.

BGP message-based events

- BGPOpen: reception of a valid OPEN message.

- BGPHeaderErr: reception of a BGP message with invalid header.

- BGPOpenMsgErr: reception of an OPEN message containing errors.

- NotifMsgVerErr: reception of a NOTIFICATION message containing a version error.

- NotifMsg: reception of a NOTIFICATION message containing any error other than a version error.

- KeepAliveMsg: reception of a KEEPALIVE message.

- UpdateMsg: reception of a valid UPDATE message.

- UpdateMsgErr: reception of an invalid UPDATE message.

A3.2 The finite state machine

A punctual description of the FSM for BGP goes beyond the purpose of this section, since the RFC provides everything that is useful to know to explore this topic. However, we deem that providing a "portable" diagram (not included in the RFC) can be helpful to understand the text, and consequently how the protocol works.

In a nutshell, the FSM figure can be described as follows:

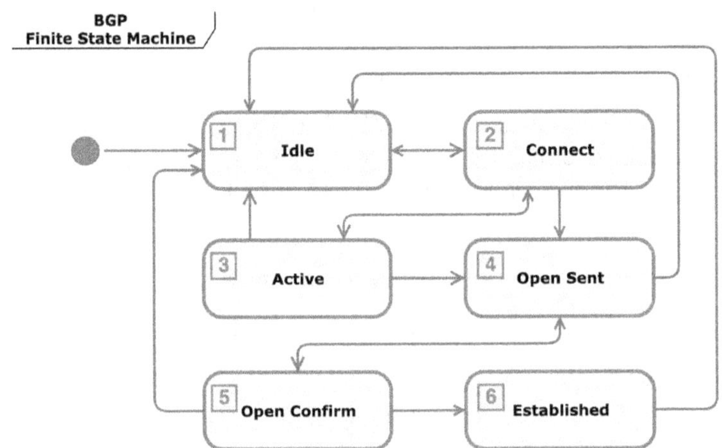

Figure A3.1 – Finite state machine.

- At first, the automaton is in the IDLE state, and does not accept BGP connections; it can be "woken up" through an administrative event, such as a ManualStart, that is, a concrete action undertaken by a local system administrator starting the process.

- The automaton switches to the CONNECT state, during which it waits for the TCP connection to be established. Now there are multiple options available; just remember that, in case of error, the automaton switches back to the IDLE state, and in case of success, it switches to the OPENSENT state.

- At this point, the BGP Neighbor could reply with an OPEN message, and the automaton would first send its own OPEN message, and then a KEEPALIVE message, before switching to the OPENCONFIRM state; or, the TCP connection could fail, and it would switch to the ACTIVE state, which, in the end, is the state in which the automaton attempts to connect to the BGP Neighbor through a TCP connection.

- From the ACTIVE state we can go back to the IDLE, CONNECT, or OPENSENT state, based on other events. As we mentioned earlier, when the automaton is in the OPENSENT state, it waits for an OPEN message from the BGP Neighbor, and, if all goes well, it switches to the OPENCONFIRM state, or, in the other possible cases, it switches back to the IDLE state or to the ACTIVE state.

- The OPENCONFIRM is the state in which it waits for the KEEPALIVE or NOTIFICATION message. If the KEEPALIVE is received, the system modifies the automaton state into ESTABLISHED, otherwise it switches back to IDLE.

- In the ESTABLISHED state, the system can exchange UPDATE and KEEPALIVE messages with its Neighbor, while remaining in the same state. It may also exchange NOTIFICATION messages, but in this case they would bring bad news that would make the automaton switch back to the IDLE state.

Lastly, you should always remember that every BGP Speaker must manage a finite state machine for every BGP session confirmed, and, obviously, every automaton follows its own rhythm and events.

A.4 REGULAR EXPRESSIONS FOR COMMUNITIES

In order to define the sets of Community values, as mentioned in Section 4.3.4, we could use Regular Expressions (RegExp). The structure of RegExp is identical to those we saw in Section 4.4, but in this context RegExp are applied to the definition of Community sets. Here, we only want to show some examples that can be a guide for future applications, if suitably processed. First, let's start with examples in Cisco platforms.

For the sake of simplicity, we will use the typical IOS and IOS XE Community-List construct; however, this can be easily applied also to routing policies in IOS XR.

By way of example, let's consider the following community-list:

```
ip community-list 100 deny _64500:1[0-9]_
ip community-list 100 permit .*
```

This extended Community-List rejects the advertisements that contain at least one Community value 64500:1x (x=0,1,...,9), while it allows all the others. Notice the RegExp in the second line: it allows the advertisements containing any set of Communities. It is essential because, without this line, due to the implicit deny all of Community-Lists, the application to a BGP Neighbor entails the rejection of all BGP advertisements, not just those with at least one Community value 64500:1x (x=0,1,...,9).

The same Community-List in IOS XR can be written as follows:

```
route-policy TEST-COMM1
  if community matches-any (ios-regex '_64500:1[0-9]_') then
    drop
  else
    pass
  endif
end-policy
```

or even by using a Community-set, in the following way:

```
community-set ABC
  ios-regex '_64500:1[0-9]'
end-set
!
route-policy TEST-COMM2
  if community matches-any ABC then
    drop
  else
    pass
  endif
end-policy
```

In JUNOS, RegExp can be of two types: simple and complex.
Simple RegExp use only two wildcard characters:

- "*****" : identifies any AS or number value. For instance, RegExp "***:300**" indicates all Community values characterized by any AS value and by number 300 (e.g. 64500:300, 64510:300, etc.).

- "**.**" : identifies any single numerical value within the AS number or the following number. For instance, RegExp "**64...:300**" indicates all Community values characterized by any AS value comprising 5 digits, with the first two equal to 64, and by number 300 (e.g. 64500:300, 64510:300, etc.).

The two characters can be used together, to create more complex RegExp. For example, RegExp "***:3..**" indicates all Community values characterized by any AS value, and by a three-digit number, with the first being 3 (e.g. 64500:313, 64499:320, etc.).
Complex RegExp use the same characters we saw for RegExp to define filters based on the AS_PATH attribute, therefore we will only make a few examples (Note: The use of delimitation characters "**^**" and "**$**" is optional; however, we recommend it for clarity purposes):

- **^64500:.{3,4}$** : indicates all Community values with AS=64500 and a 3 or 4 digit number (e.g. 64500:123, 64500:1111).

- **^64500:.*$** : indicates all Community values with AS=64500 and any number.

- **^64...:.{3,4}$** : indicates all Community values with a 5-digit AS, 64 as the first two digits, and a 3 or 4 digit number (e.g. 64500:123, 64501:1111).

- **^.*:.*$** : indicates any Community value.

The definition of Community values using the RegExp is made (just like for the explicit assignment of Community values) using the configuration:

[edit policy-options]
community *comm-name* **members** *RegExp*;

A.5 GRACEFUL RESTART OPERATION

Before seeing how the Graceful Restart mechanism can help to mitigate the route flap effect in BGP, let's see, with the aid of a simple example of a redundant connection between two ASes (see Figure A5.1), what happens in BGP's standard behavior. Router RC receives two advertisements for each (local or remote) prefix, reachable through AS 64500. Let's assume that the advertisement received from RA is always selected as the best path. If the BGP process in RA is re-initialized, for any reason (e.g., following a software update), router RC will continue to forward traffic toward RA, until, due to the KEEPALIVE messages failing to arrive, or to the reception of a BGP NOTIFICATION message, the BGP session with RA ends. Now, RC will recalculate the best paths for each prefix, and will forward traffic toward router RB. This is the default behavior, but not the desired one; indeed, if router RA cannot maintain the BGP session, then RC should recalculate its best paths as quickly as possible, in order to find an alternative path and avoid that the traffic sent to AS 64500 is lost. The situation would be different, if router RA was able to preserve its FIB even during the re-initialization of the BGP process, that is, if router RA was NSF-capable (NSF = Non Stop Forwarding). Indeed, if that were the case and the network topology did not undergo any changes during BGP's re-initialization period, it would be convenient for RC to continue to forward traffic toward AS 64500, using RA as transit. And this would also prevent the negative effect of route flaps, since RC wouldn't have to notify the withdrawal of the prefixes learned by RA to its BGP Neighbors. However, in order to reach this objective, we need to alter router RC's default behavior, (and, in general of the BGP Neighbors of the router that will re-initialize the BGP process), by preventing it, if RA is NSF-capable, from withdrawing the prefixes learned by RA.

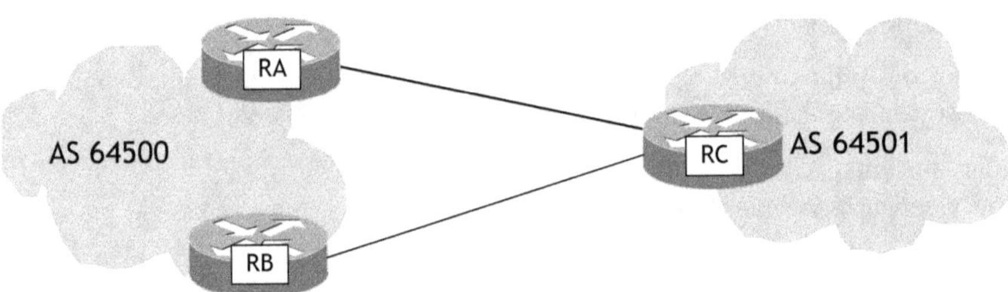

Figure A5.1 – Simple example of redundant connection between two ASes.

A.5.1 Description of the standard mechanism

The mechanism developed within the IETF, and introducing the changes necessary to modify BGP's default behavior if the BGP process is restarted, is described by RFC 4724 – *Graceful Restart Mechanism for BGP*, January 2007. There are two modifications introduced in BGP to support the Graceful Restart mechanism between two BGP Neighbors:

- A specific UPDATE message called End-of-RIB marker, used by a BGP Speaker to indicate to one of its BGP Neighbors that it has completed sending its routing information. The End-of-RIB marker is an UPDATE message with only the Withdrawn Routes Length and Total Path Attribute Length fields, both set to zero (the message is 23 bytes long).

- A new BGP Capability, used to notify the support of the Graceful Restart mechanism, or to notify that the router is capable of helping the BGP Neighbor in the Graceful Restart mechanism.

The End-of-RIB marker message can also be used outside the Graceful Restart mechanism context to reduce BGP's convergence times. Indeed, receiving an End-of-RIB marker can trigger the selection process and thus reduce the time employed by the BGP Speaker to forward the best paths to its BGP Neighbors.

The new Graceful Restart BGP Capability, defined by RFC 4724, has Capability Code=64, variable Capability Length and the content specified in Figure A5.2. The different fields have the following meaning:

- Restart Flags: a field where the only bit defined is the most significant one (bit R, Restart State); the other three bits are reserved and set to zero. Bit R is used by BGP Speakers supporting the Graceful Restart mechanism, which, from now on, we will call GR-capable BGP Speaker to indicate to its BGP Neighbors that it has re-initialized the BGP process (R=1).

- Restart Time: an estimate of the time (in seconds) used by the BGP Speaker sending the BGP Capability, to re-establish a BGP session with one of its own BGP Neighbors. For the Graceful Restart mechanism to work correctly, its value should not exceed the session Hold Time value, otherwise the BGP Neighbor would declare the BGP session dropped, due to Hold Time expiry.

- AFI/SAFI: used to specify the address families for which a BGP Speaker supports the Graceful Restart mechanism.

- Flags for Address Family: a field where the only bit defined is the most significant one (bit F, Forwarding State). A BGP Speaker, upon sending the BGP Capability, uses bit F to specify that it is capable of maintaining the FIB for a specific address family, specified by the pair <AFI, SAFI>, i.e., it is an NSF-capable router.

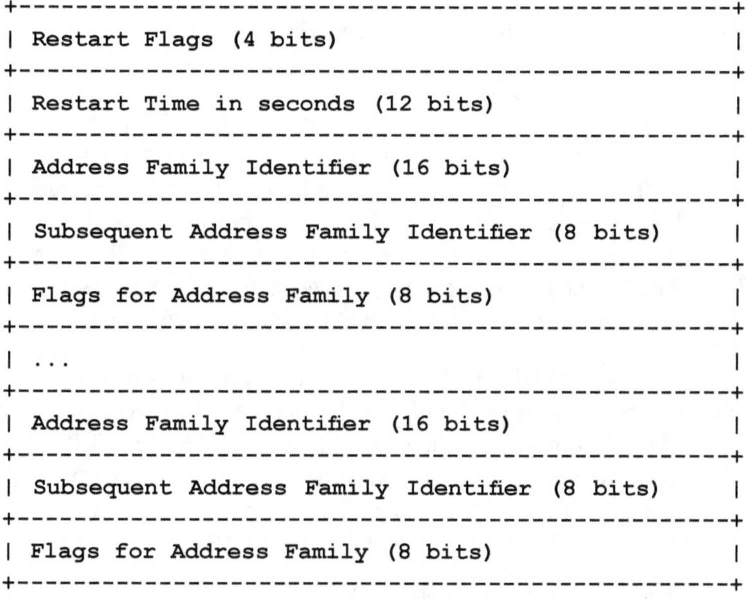

Figure A5.2 – Format of the BGP Capability Graceful Restart.

With the help of Figure A5.3, let's go over the sequence of events occurring between two GR-capable and NSF-capable routers, when one of the two (RB in the figure) re-initializes its BGP process. For the sake of simplicity, we will only consider the case of the IPv4 unicast address family (AFI/SAFI=1/1):

1. RA and RB establish a BGP session, exchanging the BGP Capability Graceful Restart to indicate that they support the Graceful Restart mechanism and that the FIB can be maintained operational during the BGP process restart period (i.e., that the BGP speakers are GR-capable and NSF-capable).

2. RA and RB exchange routing information according to BGP's standard procedures.

3. Let's assume that RB must re-initialize its BGP process, for whatever reason. All the prefixes learned via BGP and present in RB's FIB are marked locally as stale and a stale timer is started. The prefixes marked as stale continue to be regularly used to forward the packets.

4. RA realizes that its BGP session with RB has dropped. Since it knows that RB is GR-capable and NSF-capable, it starts the Restart Timer received by RB. The prefixes previously received from RB are not deleted, they are marked as stale. RA starts a stale timer and regularly uses the prefixes marked as stale to forward packets, until the Restart Timer expires. Now, RA waits for the BGP session to be restarted by RB. If this doesn't occur within the Restart Timer period, all prefixes marked as stale are deleted from the FIB.

5. After the restart period has ended, RB attempts to re-establish the BGP session, and sends a new OPEN message to RA, containing the BGP Capability Graceful Restart with R=1 and F=1 for the IPv4 address family (in general, for each address family for which RB has maintained the FIB).

6. As soon as the session state becomes Established, RA sends the content of its Adj-RIB-Out table and then an End-of-RIB marker to RB.

7. RB receives the UPDATE messages containing RA's Adj-RIB-Out table (in general, all its BGP Neighbors), and rebuilds its Adj-RIB-Out table. The selection process is delayed until the End-of-RIB marker message is received (in general, the selection process starts after receiving the last End-of-RIB marker), but not beyond a configurable time (Selection_Deferral_Timer), after which the selection process is executed in any case. After this, RB updates its Loc-RIB, FIB and Adj-RIB-Out and advertises the new best paths to all its BGP Neighbors, ending with an End-of-RIB marker message to mark the end of the UPDATE messages.

8. RA updates its Adj-RIB-in table with the new best path received from RB. Once it receives the End-of-RIB marker message from RB, RA deletes all prefixes marked as stale from its FIB, executes the selection process, updates its Loc-RIB, FIB and Adj-RIB-Out advertising the new best-paths to its BGP Neighbors (except for RB, of course!). In order to avoid maintaining prefixes marked as stale indefinitely in its FIB, RA uses the stale timer, after which the prefixes marked as stale are deleted from the FIB.

And BGP's normal operation is re-established.

NOTE: A minor variation to the procedure was introduced by RFC 8538 – *Notification Message Support for BGP Graceful Restart*, March 2019. However, when this book was published, it was not yet supported by BGP implementations, therefore we will not cover it.

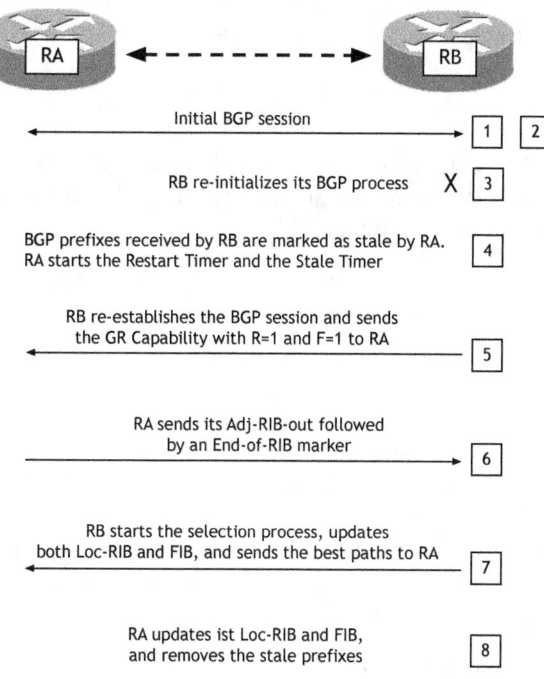

Figure A5.3 – Sequence of events between two GR-capable and NSF-capable routers, following a restart of the BGP process.

A.5.2 Implementation

In Cisco IOS, IOS XE and IOS XR. the Graceful Restart is not enabled by default; it can be enabled via the command:

router bgp *AS-number*
  bgp graceful-restart

Also, the Restart Time and Stale Timer can be defined via the commands:

router bgp *AS-number*
  bgp graceful-restart restart-time *value*
  bgp graceful-restart stalepath-time *value*

The default values recommended in practical applications are: Restart Timer=120 sec and Stale Timer=360 sec. Cisco platforms do not support the Selection_Deferral_Timer configuration.
To verify that the GR has been activated the "**show bgp** *afi safi* **neighbors**" command can be used. Here is an example in IOS XR:

```
RP/0/0/CPU0:AS-65542#show  bgp  ipv4  unicast  neighbors  172.20.2.0  |  i
Graceful Restart

. . .

    Graceful Restart (GR Awareness): received
    Graceful Restart capability advertised
    Graceful Restart capability received
```

In JUNOS, the Graceful Restart is supported for all the main routing protocols, and as such it must be enabled at the "**routing-options**" configuration hierarchy level:

[edit routing-options]
graceful-restart;

Moreover, the Graceful Restart can only be disabled at single protocol level, or its main timers can be changed. For BGP, timers can be disabled or changed directly at global, group or BGP Neighbor level, through the set of commands:

graceful-restart {
  [disable];
  [restart-time *seconds***];**
  [stale-routes-time *seconds***];**
}

Default values of the Restart Timer and Stale Timer are: Restart Timer=120 s and Stale Timer=300 sec. Just as Cisco IOS, IOS XE/XR, Junos does not support the Selection_Deferral_ Timer configuration.

The function operation can be verified via the standard "**show bgp neighbor**" command. For instance, by applying the command to an RTR router and assuming that Graceful Restart is enabled only with default timers, we have:

```
aft@RTR> show bgp neighbor 172.30.1.1
Peer: 172.30.1.1+179 AS 64501 Local: 172.30.1.3+1028 AS 64503
  Type: External    State: Established    Flags: <Sync>
. . . < output omitted > . . .

NLRI for restart configured on peer: inet-unicast
NLRI advertised by peer: inet-unicast
NLRI for this session: inet-unicast
Restart time configured on the peer: 120
Stale routes from peer are kept for: 300
Restart time requested by this peer: 120
NLRI that peer supports restart for: inet-unicast
NLRI peer can save forwarding state: inet-unicast
NLRI that peer saved forwarding for: inet-unicast
NLRI that restart is negotiated for: inet-unicast
NLRI of received end-of-rib markers: inet-unicast
NLRI of all end-of-rib markers sent: inet-unicast
  . . . < output omitted > . . .
```

Lastly, let's go over the (partial) wireshark analysis of a BGP OPEN message highlighting the Graceful Restart BGP Capability negotiated by two BGP Neighbors. In particular, the message was generated by a Juniper router.

```
Internet Protocol Version 4, Src: 172.20.2.0, Dst: 172.20.2.1
Transmission Control Protocol, Src Port: 62284, Dst Port: 179, Seq: 1, Ack: 1, Len: 67
Border Gateway Protocol - OPEN Message
    Marker: ffffffffffffffffffffffffffffffff
    Length: 67
    Type: OPEN Message (1)
```

Version: 4
My AS: 64501
Hold Time: 90
BGP Identifier: 192.168.1.12
Optional Parameters Length: 38
Optional Parameters
  Optional Parameter: Capability
  Optional Parameter: Capability
  Optional Parameter: Capability
  Optional Parameter: Capability
  Optional Parameter: Capability
    Parameter Type: Capability (2)
    Parameter Length: 8
    Capability: **Graceful Restart capability**
      Type: Graceful Restart capability (**64**)
      Length: 6
      Restart Timers: 0x4078
        0... .... = **Restart: No**
        .... 0000 0111 1000 = **Time: 120**
      AFI: **IPv4** (1)
      SAFI: **Unicast** (1)
      Flag: 0x80, **Preserve forwarding state**
        1... .... = **Preserve forwarding state: Yes**
  Optional Parameter: Capability
    Parameter Type: Capability (2)
    Parameter Length: 2
    Capability: Long-Lived Graceful Restart (LLGR) Capability
      Type: Long-Lived Graceful Restart (LLGR) Capability (71)
      Length: 0

NOTE: The wireshark analysis, apart from highlighting the BGP Capability Graceful Restart, also shows the Long-Lived Graceful Restart BGP Capability. When this book was published, this new BGP Capability was not yet standard; it is supported by a few vendors (e.g. JUNOS in version 15.1 and later, Cisco IOS XR only for BGP sessions for L3VPN BGP/MPLS services and for BGP Flowspec, open implementations like BIRD from version 1.6.3 and GoBGP from version 1.33). It allows extending the value of the Restart Timer from the max value of 4.095 sec (maximum value allowed, since the Restart Timer value is 12 bits, see Figure A5.2) to higher values. This could be useful in situations where false positives could occur when checking whether a BGP session is down or not. False positive means that the session is considered down when it actually isn't. A typical scenario is when BGP is implemented on a server and uses the BFD to check the state of physical links. Due to a strong CPU load, it may occur that the server is not able to temporarily process BFD HELLO, and thus it declares one or more links down, with all the BGP sessions defined on those links. If you are interested in this topic, you can find more details in the draft IETF draft-uttaro-idr-bgp-persistence-05 – *Support for Long-lived BGP Graceful Restart*, expired in May 2019.

A.6 ADVANCED MED MANAGEMENT

As shown in the Note in Section 7.3.3, in Cisco platforms using IOS XE, the best path selection, in the case of MED coming from different ASes, depends on the advertisements' arrival order. Since this could generate a bit of confusion, Cisco has provided the following command:

router(config)# **router bgp** *AS-number*
router(config-router)# **bgp deterministic-med**

which allows making the best path selection independent from the advertisements' arrival order.

NOTE: This command is by default in Cisco platforms with IOS XR and in JUNOS. In JUNOS, there is the option, through the global "**path-selection cisco-non-deterministic**" command, to use the MED with Cisco IOS/IOS XE routers' default mode.

Processing is done as follows:

1. group the advertisements coming from the same AS;

2. for each group, choose the best path;

3. choose the best path by comparing the best paths of each group.

The configuration of this command is recommended on all platforms using standard IOS and IOS XE.

Let's see through some examples how this command and the "**bgp always-compare-med**" command works (we have already seen the latter in Section 7.3.3). First, let's consider the case in which both commands are disabled (see Figure A6.1). We will assume that advertisement 1 is more recent, and advertisement 3 less recent (remember that the best path determination process is based on the comparison of advertisements of the same prefix, starting from the most recent one, see Section 7.1.1) and that the Local Preference, AS_PATH length and Origin values are the same.

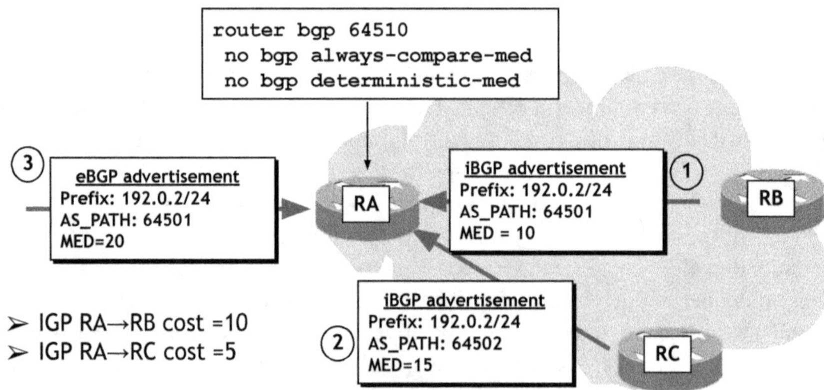

Figure A6.1 – Example of advanced MED configuration.

By applying Cisco router's selection process logic, advertisement 3 is selected as the best path (even though its MED is higher!). Indeed:

- When comparing advertisements 1 and 2, advertisement 2 is preferred (due to the lower IGP cost toward the Next-Hop). Notice that the MED cannot be compared, because the advertisements come from different ASes (64501 and 64502, respectively), and the "**bgp always-compare-med**" command is disabled.

- When comparing advertisements 2 and 3, advertisement 3 is preferred (eBGP advertisements are favored over iBGP ones).

As you can easily test out, the best path determination depends on the processing order (e.g., if we change the arrival – and processing – order of advertisements 2 and 3, the best path becomes advertisement 2).

With the same example in Figure A6.1, let's assume the following configuration on router RA:

```
router bgp 64510
  no bgp always-compare-med
  bgp deterministic-med
```

By applying the logic of the "**bgp deterministic-med**" command, advertisement 2 is selected as the best path (even though its MED is higher!). Indeed:

- We group the advertisements from the same AS. We have two groups: GR1 = {64501} and GR2 = {64502}.

- The best paths of the two groups are, advertisement 1 for group GR1 (lower MED), and advertisement 2 for group GR2 (one advertisement only).

- We compare the two best paths of the two groups. Since the MED comparison for advertisements coming from different ASes is disabled, advertisement 2 is the best path, because its IGP cost toward the Next-Hop is lower.

We will leave proving that the best path does NOT depend on the advertisements' processing order to you.

With the same example in Figure A6.1, we will assume that the router has the following configuration:

```
router bgp 64510
  bgp always-compare-med
  bgp deterministic-med
```

By going over the process of the first two cases, try to prove that the best path in this case is advertisement 1 (due to the lower MED) and that the best path does not depend on the advertisements' processing order.

A.7 CASE STUDY on RFD'S APPLICATION

The Route Flap Damping (RFD) is one of BGP's stability mechanisms, and we broadly covered it in Section 8.8. In this Appendix, we will describe two Case Studies, one in Cisco IOS XE environment and the second one in Juniper environment, in order to highlight further operational aspects.

A.7.1 Case Study in Cisco IOS XE environment

The different versions of Cisco IOS provide a set of show and debug commands to track the history of penalty values. Instead of going over them one by one, we will see how they are used, through the example of Figure A7.1 below.

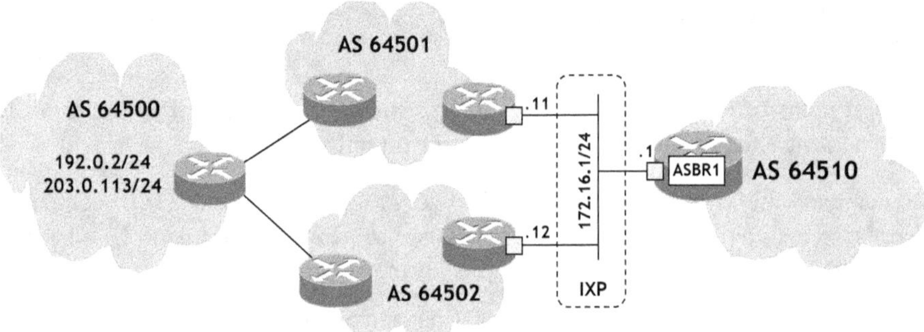

Figure A7.1 – Example of RFD application in Cisco IOS XE environment.

In the example in the figure, router ASBR1 of AS 64510 receives, for each prefix 192.0.2/24 and 203.0.113/24, originated by AS 64500, two advertisements, one from AS 64501 and the other from AS 64502. Let's assume that we want to apply the RFD only to prefix 192.0.2/24, and not to the other prefix, due to administrative reasons. The following configuration applies a selective RFD only to the advertisements of prefix 192.0.2/24, with the parameters specified in route-map SELECTIVE-RFD.

```
router bgp 64510
  neighbor 172.16.1.11 remote-as 64501
  neighbor 172.16.1.12 remote-as 64502
  bgp dampening route-map SELECTIVE-RFD
!
ip prefix-list P1 permit 192.0.2.0/24
route-map SELECTIVE-RFD permit 10
  match ip address prefix-list P1
  set dampening 20 750 2000 80
```

You can check the parameters through the following command:

```
ASBR1# show ip bgp dampening parameters

dampening 20 750 2000 80 (route-map SELECTIVE-RFD 10)
    Half-life time        : 20 mins      Decay Time          : 3095 secs
    Max suppress penalty: 12000          Max suppress time: 80 mins
    Suppress penalty      :  2000        Reuse penalty       : 750
```

Now, let's assume that the connection between ASes 64500 and 64501 is subject to frequent UP/DOWN transitions (link flapping) causing the constant drop and subsequent re-establishment of the BGP session between the routers of the two ASes. The advertisement of prefix 192.0.2/24 coming from AS 64501 will undergo the RFD mechanism. Before the first route flap, the BGP table on ASBR1 is the following:

```
ASBR1# show ip bgp
...
    Network            Next Hop      . . .    Path
*   203.0.113.0/24     172.16.1.12            64502 64500 i
*>                     172.16.1.11            64501 64500 i
*   192.0.2.0/24       172.16.1.12            64502 64500 i
*>                     172.16.1.11            64501 64500 i
```

From it, we see that the best path for prefix 192.0.2/24 is the transit on AS 64501. Let's suppose we want to activate a debug on ASBR1 to view the penalty variations:

```
ASBR1# debug ip bgp dampening
```

and, after activating the debug, that the first route flap – the withdrawal by AS 64501 of prefix 192.0.2/24 – occurs. The debug command enabled generates the following view:

```
6d00h: EvD: charge penalty 1000, new accum. penalty 1000, flap count 1
6d00h: BGP(0): charge penalty for 192.0.2.0/24 path 64501 64500 with
halflife-time 20 reuse/suppress 750/2000
6d00h: BGP(0): flapped 1 times since 00:00:00. New penalty is 1000
```

which indicates that a 1,000 penalty was assigned to the advertisement of prefix 192.0.2/24 with AS_PATH = [64501 64500]. The detail of prefix 192.0.2/24 in the BGP table shows that the new best path is the path with transit on AS 64502, and that the withdrawn advertisement currently has a penalty of 991, resulting from the exponential degradation, 17 sec after the route flap. Also, the view shows that the advertisement switches to a state called History (**history entry**).

```
ASBR1# show ip bgp 192.0.2.0
BGP routing table entry for 192.0.2.0/24, version 4
Paths: (2 available, best #2, table Default-IP-Routing-Table)
  Advertised to non peer-group peer:
  172.16.1.11
  64501 64500 (history entry)
    172.16.1.11 from 172.16.1.11 (192.168.0.11)
      Origin IGP, metric 0, localpref 100, external
      Dampinfo: penalty 991, flapped 1 times in 00:00:17
  64502 64500
    172.16.1.12 from 172.16.1.12 (192.168.0.12)
      Origin IGP, metric 0, localpref 100, valid, external, best
```

The debug continuously generates messages that highlight the penalty degradation:

```
ASBR1#
3d06h: EvD: accum. penalty decayed to 991 after 17 second(s)
3d06h: EvD: accum. penalty decayed to 985 after 11 second(s)
```

Let's see what happens after the third route flap. The penalty rises to 2,891, exceeding the Suppress Threshold, which is set to 2,000 in this configuration.

```
ASBR1#
6d00h: BGP(0): flapped 3 times since 00:02:52. New penalty is 2891
```

Then, let's assume that prefix 192.0.2/24 is re-advertised by AS 64501; router ASBR1 will not use the new advertisement in the selection process, since the penalty value has exceeded the Suppress Threshold value. The advertisement is marked as dampened and added to a list of paths marked as dampened, which can be viewed through the command:

```
ASBR1#show ip bgp dampening dampened-paths
. . .

   Network              From           Reuse      Path
*d 192.0.2.0/24        172.16.1.11    00:41:53 64501 64500   i
```

RFD statistics can be viewed as follows:

```
ASBR1# show ip bgp dampening flap-statistics
. . .

   Network              From           Flaps Duration Reuse      Path
*d 192.0.2.0/24        172.16.1.11    3       00:03:33 00:41:38 64501 64500
```

The view shows that 3 route flaps occurred in 3 min and 33 sec, and that the time necessary to reuse the advertisement is 41 min and 38 sec. The advertisement marked as dampened, is viewed in the BGP table as valid and damped (***d**):

```
ASBR1# show ip bgp
. . .

   Network              Next Hop       . . .   Path
*  203.0.113.0/24      172.16.1.12            64502 64500 i
*>                     172.16.1.11            64501 64500 i
*> 192.0.2.0/24        172.16.1.12            64502 64500 i
*d                     172.16.1.11            64501 64500 i
```

By viewing the prefix detail in the BGP table, the frozen path is indicated as "**suppressed due to dampening**", and the RFD statistics are also shown:

```
ASBR1# show ip bgp 192.0.2.0
BGP routing table entry for 192.0.2.0/24, version 4
Paths: (2 available, best #1, table Default-IP-Routing-Table)
  Advertised to non peer-group peer:
  172.16.1.11
  64502 64500
    172.16.1.12 from 172.16.1.12 (192.168.0.12)
      Origin IGP, metric 0, localpref 100, valid, external, best
  64501 64500, (suppressed due to dampening)
    172.16.1.11 from 172.16.1.11 (192.168.0.11)
      Origin IGP, metric 0, localpref 100, valid, external
      Dampinfo: penalty 2830, flapped 3 times in
      00:03:38, reuse in 00:41:15
```

The advertisement can be reused when the penalty drops below the Reuse Limit, within approximately over 41 min. If the advertisement needs to be reconsidered immediately in the selection process, without waiting for the penalty to drop below the Reuse Limit or the Max-Suppress-Time to be exceeded, because, for instance, the resolution of the issue that caused the route flapping is notified, this operation can be executed through the following clear command:

```
ASBR1# clear ip bgp dampening 192.0.2.0
```

which immediately takes us back to the initial situation.

A.7.2 Case Study in JUNOS environment

Now, with the help of Figure A7.2, let's see a very interesting example of RFD application, in a quite realistic scenario. The network only comprises Juniper routers using JUNOS.

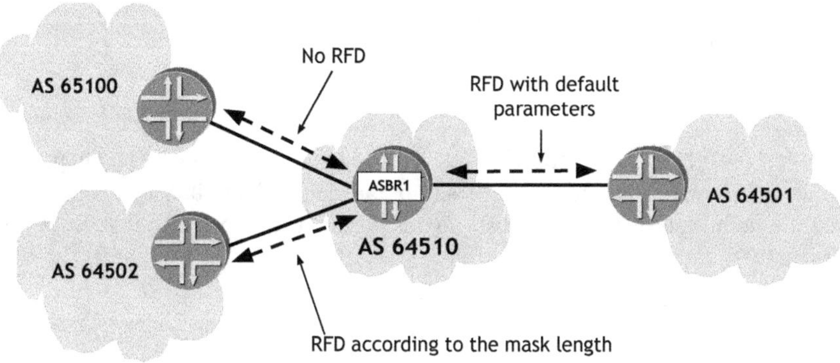

Figure A7.2 – Example of RFD application in JUNOS environment.

Router ASBR1 of AS 64510 has three eBGP sessions:

- eBGP session with a customer, with private AS number 65100; the advertisements received on this session are not subject to RFD.

- eBGP session with AS 64501; the RFD with default parameters is applied on this session.

- eBGP session with AS 64502; on this session, router ASBR1 receives the FIRT. The RFD is applied based on the mask length of the prefixes advertised, and is not applied to "important" prefixes, such as those used by Root Server DNS. The RFD parameters for each class of prefixes are specified in the following configuration.

Let's see all the configuration steps. First, we create the RFD parameter profiles:

```
[edit policy-options]
/* Min: 30 min, Max: 60 min, suppression after 3 "withdraw" */
damping RFD-LONG {
    half-life 30;
    reuse 1640;
    suppress 6000;
    max-suppress 60;
}
```

```
/* Min: 15 min, Max: 45 min, suppression after 3 "withdraw" */
damping RFD-MEDIUM {
    half-life 15;
    reuse 1500;
    suppress 6000;
    max-suppress 45;
}
/* Min: 10 min, Max: 30 min, suppression after 3 "withdraw" */
damping RFD-SHORT {
    half-life 10;
    reuse 3000;
    suppress 6000;
    max-suppress 30;
}
/* Do not apply RFD */
damping NO-RFD {
    disable;
}
```

Actually, the last profile is a "non-profile", since it is used to not apply the RFD. Then, we create the routing policy to apply the parameters profiles (Note: For the sake of brevity, in the configuration, we omitted the definition of the prefix-list identifying important prefixes that are not subject to the RFD):

```
[edit policy-options policy-statement RFD]
/* Do not apply RFD to "important" prefixes */
term 1 {
    from {
        prefix-list IMPORTANT-PREFIXES;
    }
    then {
        damping NO-RFD;
        /* skip to the next Routing Policy */
        next policy;
    }
}
/* Apply RFD based on the prefix length */
term 2 {
    from {
/* RFD parameters for prefixes with mask <= /21 */
        route-filter 0.0.0.0/0 upto /21 damping RFD-SHORT;
/* RFD parameters for prefixes with mask /22 or /23 */
        route-filter 0.0.0.0/0 upto /23 damping RFD-MEDIUM;
/* RFD parameters for prefixes with mask >= /24 */
        route-filter 0.0.0.0/0 orlonger damping RFD-LONG;
    }
    then {
        next policy;
    }
}
```

Lastly, in the last step, we enable the RFD (where required). For the eBGP session toward the BGP Neighbor of AS 65100, we do not need to enable the RFD, as it is not required. For the eBGP session toward the BGP peer of AS 64501, the "**damping**" command at session level is enough, since the RFD is requested with only the default parameters. Lastly, to apply the selective RFD to the eBGP session toward the BGP Neighbor of AS 64502, we need to apply (at session level) the routing policy "**RFD**" (and the "**damping**" command). The final configuration is the following:

```
[edit protocols bgp group EBGP]
type external;
neighbor 172.16.1.11 {
    description *** eBGP SESSION WITH AS 65100 ***
    peer-as 65100;
}
neighbor 172.16.1.12 {
    description *** eBGP SESSION WITH AS 64502 ***
    damping;
    import RFD;
    peer-as 64502;
}
neighbor 172.16.12.2 {
    description *** eBGP SESSION WITH AS 64501 ***
    damping;
    peer-as 64501;
}
```

JUNOS also provides a set of show and traceoptions commands (the equivalent of debug in Cisco platforms), to track the history of penalty values. With the example in Figure A7.2, let's see how to use them. We will assume that ASBR1 receives from AS 64502 the advertisements of the two prefixes 192.0.2/24 and 198.51/16, and also that the connection between the two ASes is unstable, and that there are continuous withdrawals and re-advertisements of the two prefixes. Both prefixes are not deemed important, therefore the related advertisements are subject to RFD. After the first prefix withdrawal, we can check the penalty assigned via the following view command:

```
aft@ASBR1> show route damping history detail
inet.0: 22 destinations, 22 routes (20 active, 0 holddown, 2 hidden)
192.0.2.0/24 (1 entry, 0 announced)
. . . < output omitted > . . .
            Merit (last update/now): 1000/996
                damping-parameters: RFD-LONG
            Last update: 00:00:11 First update: 00:00:11
                Flaps: 1
            History entry.  Expires in: 01:00:20
198.51.0.0/16 (1 entry, 0 announced)
. . . < output omitted > . . .
            Merit (last update/now): 1000/988
                damping-parameters: RFD-SHORT
            Last update: 00:00:11 First update: 00:00:11
            Flaps: 1
            History entry.  Expires in: 00:23:20

. . . < output omitted > . . .
```

The view highlights the profile of the parameters used (**RFD-LONG** for advertisements of prefix 192.0.2/24 and **RFD-SHORT** for those of prefix 198.51/16). If the RFD was configured to use the default profile, "**Default damping parameters used**" would be displayed. Also, the penalty value assigned when the advertisement is withdrawn (1,000), and the current one (996 for the advertisement of prefix 192.0.2/24 and 988 for that of prefix 198.51/16, both determined 11 sec after the route flap) are specified. We would like to point out that the second current value is lower, due to the higher decaying speed of the RFD-SHORT profile (Half-life=10 min), compared to that of the RFD-LONG profile (Half-life=30 min). The last timer (**Expires in:**) indicates after how long the advertisement will be removed from the RIB, without a re-advertisement. The two advertisements are marked as hidden in the RIB.

Let's assume that the two prefixes are re-advertised. We can check the new penalty through the following view command:

```
tt@ASBR1> show route damping decayed detail
inet.0: 22 destinations, 22 routes (22 active, 0 holddown, 0 hidden)
192.0.2.0/24 (1 entry, 1 announced)
. . . < output omitted > . . .
        Merit (last update/now): 1843/1835
             damping-parameters: RFD-LONG
        Last update: 00:00:16    First update: 00:07:32
             Flaps: 2

198.51.0.0/16 (1 entry, 1 announced)
. . . < output omitted > . . .
        Merit (last update/now): 1216/1202
             damping-parameters: RFD-SHORT
        Last update: 00:00:16    First update: 00:07:32
             Flaps: 2

. . . < output omitted > . . .
```

The view shows that, immediately before the re-advertisement (which, as you may remember, in Juniper routers, is considered a new route flap), the penalty was 843 for prefix 192.0.2/24 and 216 for prefix 198.51/16. Immediately after, the penalty increases by 1,000, and when the command is executed, 16 sec after the second route flap, it had already decayed to 1,835 for prefix 192.0.2/24 and 1,202 for prefix 198.51/16.

Lastly, let's assume to be at the tenth route flap (which is a re-advertisement of the two prefixes). In both cases, the penalty value exceeds the Suppress Threshold (= 6,000 for all profiles), therefore the advertisements are frozen (suppressed).

```
aft@ASBR1> show route damping suppressed detail
inet.0: 22 destinations, 22 routes (20 active, 0 holddown, 2 hidden)
192.0.2.0/24 (1 entry, 0 announced)
. . . < output omitted > . . .
        Merit (last update/now): 6577/6551
        damping-parameters: RFD-LONG
        Last update: 00:00:17 First update: 00:13:27
             Flaps: 10
        Suppressed. Reusable in: 01:00:00
             Preference will be: 170
```

```
198.51.0.0/16 (1 entry, 0 announced)
. . . < output omitted > . . .
                Merit (last update/now): 8116/8022
                   damping-parameters: RFD-SHORT
            Last update: 00:00:17 First update: 00:13:27
                   Flaps: 10
            Suppressed. Reusable in: 00:14:20
                   Preference will be: 170
```

Among other things, the view highlights that both advertisements are suppressed, and that they can be reused, the first after 1 h, while the second after 14 min and 20 sec. We will leave checking if these two values (and the first one in particular) are correct to you. Until they can be reused, the two advertisements are marked as hidden in the RIB.

If the advertisements need to be immediately reconsidered in the selection process, without waiting for the penalty to decay below the Reuse Limit, or the Max-Suppress-Time to be exceeded, because, for instance, the resolution of the issue that caused the route flapping has been notified in some way, the operation can be executed through the following clear command:

```
aft@ASBR1> clear bgp damping [prefix]
```

which immediately takes us back to the initial situation.

A.8 BGP MONITORING PROTOCOL (BMP)

Not a routing protocol, but rather a way to analyze a routing overview. This is the BMP, BGP Monitoring Protocol, formalized by RFC 7854, June 2016, which basically changes the paradigm to obtain information on the RIB of BGP in a router managing its sessions. Previously, we worked on the router output, by capturing at certain time intervals and feeding it to further analysis tools. Not really the easiest solution. The BMP optimizes these needs, by structuring a protocol that gives direct access to the routes learned by inbound UPDATE messages coming from the BGP Neighbors. In this chapter, we will briefly describe the protocol, and detail one of its widespread implementations – pmacct.

A.8.1 The protocol

First of all, let's begin by saying that BMP works on TCP, and that the information flow always goes from the monitored router toward the monitoring station, and never the other way around. So, the configuration options that can be read by multiple stations reside on the router. In any case, each router-station pair uses TCP connections, within which an active part and a passive one are identified by configuration. The passive part establishes the TCP listening port; in any case, the router can narrow down the number of simultaneous connections from a certain IP address. Once the connection is established, there is no phase preceding the message transmission, and messages flow directly until the monitoring station stops the connection. A router can be configured to send monitoring information to all its BGP Neighbors, or only to a subset of them. In any case, once the session has been set-up, the router starts transmitting an initiation message, followed by a Peer Up message. After this, it continues to communicate all the routings learned from a certain neighbor, and then it sends an End-of-RIB message to inform the monitoring station that the initial copy of the routing table is complete. Henceforth, any subsequent RIB update will be sent in incremental mode.

A.8.2 Router configuration

In Cisco applications, it is very easy to activate a BMP session with the external monitoring station:

IOS/IOS-XE
```
router bgp 64502
bmp server 1
address 198.51.100.11 port-number 1790
update-source GigabitEthernet1
initial-delay 60
failure-retry-delay 60
flapping-delay 60
stats-reporting-period 300
activate
exit-bmp-server-mode
!
neighbor Y.Y.Y.Y remote-as 64510
neighbor Y.Y.Y.Y bmp-activate all
neighbor Z.Z.Z.Z remote-as 64511
neighbor Z.Z.Z.Z bmp-activate all
```

```
bmp buffer-size 100
bgp log-neighbor-changes
```

To verify the session:

```
ROUTER# show ip bgp bmp
```

To monitor the session:

```
ROUTER# debug ip bgp bmp
ROUTER# show debugging
```

For a detailed synopsis of the session with a monitoring station:

```
ROUTER# show ip bgp bmp server 1
```

```
Print detailed info for 1 server number 1.
```

```
bmp server 1
address: 198.51.100.11       port 1790
description SERVER1
up time 00:06:22
session-startup route-refresh
initial-delay 20
failure-retry-delay 40
flapping-delay 120
activated
```

```
ROUTER# show ip bgp bmp server summary
```

```
Number of BMP servers configured: 1
Number of BMP neighbors configured: 12
Number of neighbors on TransitionQ: 0, MonitoringQ: 0, ConfigQ: 0
Number of BMP servers on StatsQ: 0
BMP Refresh not in progress, refresh not scheduled
Initial Refresh Delay configured, refresh value 30s
BMP buffer size configured, buffer size 2048 MB, buffer size bytes used 0 MB

ID   Host/Net          Port   TCB    Status   Uptime    MsgSent     LastStat
1    198.51.100.11     1790   0x0    Down               0
```

Here is the entire BMP section on Cisco routers:

```
ROUTER# show running-config | section bmp
bmp server 1
address 198.51.100.11 port-number 1790
description SERVER1
initial-delay 20
failure-retry-delay 40
flapping-delay 120
update-source GigabitEthernet1
set ip dscp 3
activate
exit-bmp-server-mode
bmp initial-refresh delay 30
bmp-activate all
```

Configuration on Cisco IOS XR:

```
router bgp 64510
neighbor Y.Y.Y.Y
bmp-activate server 1
neighbor Z.Z.Z.Z
bmp-activate server 1
!
bmp server 1
host 198.51.100.11 port 1790
description BMP TEST
update-source GigabitEthernet0/0/0/10
initial-delay 60
initial-refresh delay 60
stats-reporting-period 300
initial-refresh delay 10
```

And the configuration on JUNOS is equally intuitive:

```
routing-options {
    bmp {
            station FQDN {
                connection-mode active;
                monitor enable;
                route-monitoring {
                    pre-policy;
                    post-policy;
                    }
                station-address 198.51.100.11;
                station-port 1790;
                }
        }
}
```

To check the session state on JUNOS:

```
user@ROUTER> show bgp bmp
  BMP station address/port: 198.51.100.11+1790
  BMP session state: DOWN
   Statistics timeout: 15
```

A.8.3 Monitoring station based on pmacct

For the BMP monitoring station, the software we recommend is pmacct, written by the Italian developer Paolo Lucente, for its completeness and versatility, also when interacting with multiple external frameworks (http://www.pmacct.net/). Concerning the BMP, pmacct allows configuring the pmbmpd daemon as a single instance, and to receive data from routers, both in real time and at preset intervals.

The monitoring station based on the pmbmpd daemon can also export data, such as JSON or Avro messages. Lastly, here is an example of configuration to populate a text file with data from routers in real-time, and to create a file with such data in 60 seconds intervals:

```
bmp_daemon: true
!
bmp_daemon_msglog_file: /path/to/bmp-$peer_src_ip.log
!
bmp_dump_file: /path/to/bmp-$peer_src_ip-%H%M.dump
bmp_dump_refresh_time: 60
```

A.9 xBGP

Until now, we've explained all of BGP's faces, as it has been specified in RFCs and received – and interpreted – by vendors.

Now, let's try for a moment to abstract the plane of our discussion and explore new possibilities, like some talented researchers have done recently: T. Wirtgen, Q. De Coninck, R. Bush, L. Vanbever and O. Bonaventure. Their dissertation, published in 2020, was selected by the Internet Research Task Force (IRTF) among the winning ones for the 2021 edition of the Applied Networking Research Prize.

Their work lays the foundations for a new operator approach to routing protocols, by including the option of programming them through xBGP.

A.9.1 Beyond SDN

The characteristics of Software-Defined Networks, which have now been in use for about ten years, is, in a nutshell, going beyond the single switching and routing implementations of the different manufacturers, and let the devices display their forwarding tables through APIs (Application Programming Interface). Electronic manipulators use these APIs to allow operators a centralized, and carefully programmed management of switch and router devices.

Traffic engineering protocols reap the benefits resulting from these implementations, as they are improved, making convergence mechanisms faster, and protection against distributed DoS attacks more effective.

Also, if, on the one hand, SDN overcomes the critical issue of managing multiple devices manufactured by different companies, on the other hand, it pays the price of requiring a capillary network review on the control and data plane field.

This last aspect has prevented a widespread diffusion of the SDN model over the years, and today, the operators that remained anchored to the traditional multi-vendor approach, are waiting for something new.

To this end, it is worthy of mention what the operators should know about the standardization process that makes a technology being used in a production environment: first, someone has an idea that, however brilliant, must necessarily pass through the IETF; then, vendors come up with their version and follow specific testing, and lastly the machines are commissioned. As you can imagine, this process sometimes tasks quite a few years.

NOTE: According to the study edited in January 2021 by Christian Huitema in RFC 8963 – *Evaluation of a Sample of RFCs Produced in 2018*, January 2021, usually 3 years and 4 months pass between an idea and its publication: 2 years and 10 months in the working group, 3 months for the rough consensus and IESG's review, and 3 months for drafting a RFC.

Here is why, among the most innovative ideas, we can foresee an overcoming of SDN by the team of researchers guided by Wirtgen, who has come up with a new approach called xBGP, stemming from a series of reflections on the possibility of modifying the routing protocols with a virtual machine capable of doing plugins; and these plugins extend or modify the algorithms based on the protocols' operation.

The model is inspired by the extended Berkeley Packet Filter (eBPF), a virtual machine inside the GNU/Linux kernel that supports a set of customized instructions, with which one can safely and easily implement new programs, capable of accessing a subset of the kernel's functions and the memory. Just like eBPF, xBGP allows routing protocol to expose an API and a virtual machine inside the protocol to a set of customized instructions to access and modify the protocol functions and the memory (and these instructions and virtual machine must be adopted and employed by each vendor). In this way, the same code can be executed on different implementations of the routing protocol selected.

The protocol on which the researchers are focusing is BGP, given its key role for ISPs and in data centers, as a tool that provides access to the Internet and to other added-value services.

Right now, the proof of concept studied consists in adding xBGP to two different implementations: FRRouting and BIRD. Specifically, the work in question describes a new route reflection implementation, a new attribute coding a georeferentiation, the route origin validation (ROA) and an extension that shortens the paths within data centers, according to a so-called valley-free model.

A.9.2 Valley-free routing

First of all, we have to understand what a valley in a routing path is, and in order to do so, we will reference the hierarchical classification of autonomous systems, based on their size, position and interconnection to one another, and, consequently, we can observe how this classification can interfere with the AS_PATH attribute length.

In a standard scenario, the Tier-3 ISP-Z autonomous system can be interconnected to a Tier-2 ISP-B system, which, in turn, is connected to a Tier-1 ISP-A. The latter gives transit also to ISP-Y (Tier-3). If ISP-Z users want to use ISP-Y resources, they just need to follow the path

```
                  ISP-A
               /        \
          ISP-B          \
        /                  \
  ISP-Z               ISP-Y
```

that is, reflecting on their logical placement in the hierarchy, users would climb up to ISP-B and toward ISP-A, and then would go down to ISP-Y.

The graphic representation could be an inverted V, like the profile of a peak (Λ).

Let's add another element to this scenario: ISP-X, a Tier-3 autonomous system multihomed to ISP-B and ISP-A, and let's patiently place it in the center of our diagram. We should wonder right away what would happen if ISP-X inadvertently (or perhaps because it did not follow the advice we gave in this book!) became a transit AS between ISP-B and ISP-A.

We will help you out by integrating the previous example: ISP-Z users that want to reach ISP-Y, could follow the path

```
                              ISP-A
                            /       \
       ISP-B              /           \
     /       \          /               \
ISP-Z     ISP-X —— ISP-X           ISP-Y
```

The graphic representation taking into account the hierarchy is now clear: two inverted Vs, one next to the other ($\wedge\_\wedge$). Between the two peaks, there would be a valley that, it should be clear, could ruin the traffic flow efficiency between ISP-Z to ISP-Y, because, apart from being a non-optimal routing, it could also be subject to slowdowns caused by transit, for a small autonomous system with a business not oriented toward the interconnection of big ASes.

For these reasons, one should always tend to a so-called valley-free routing; however, the literature tells us that the presence of valleys is more widespread than one might expect. Indeed, a study conducted in 2007 proves that, already in that year, around 10 thousand advertisements of valleys were observed every day, with 11% of providers (mostly Tier-2) propagating those advertisements. The most frequent cause is the presence of transitory configuration errors, which, as we already explained, can be prevented by correctly implementing suitable filtering policies, by extensively using tools to formally check the configurations, and by adopting the Autonomous System Provider Authorization (ASPA) objects as we previously mentioned in the Paragraph 10.9.

[1] J. Doyle, J. Carrol, *Routing TCP/IP (Vol. 1)*, 2^ ed., Cisco Press, 2005.

[2] S. Halabi, D. McPherson, *Internet Routing Architectures*, 2^ ed., Cisco Press, 2000.

[3] D. Marschke, H. Reynolds, *JUNOS Enterprise Routing*, O'Reilly, 2008.

[4] C. Panigl , J. Schmitz , P. Smith, C. Vistoli, *Recommendations for Coordinated Route-flap Damping Parameters*, Document RIPE-229, October 2001.

[4] P. Smith, C. Panigl, *Recommendations on Route-flap Damping*, Document RIPE-378, May 2006.

[5] R. White, D. McPherson, S. Srihari, *Practical BGP*, Addison Wesley, July 2004.

[6] R. Zhang, M. Bartell, *BGP Design and Implementation*, Cisco Press, 2004.

[7] Kotikalapudi Sriram, Doug Montgomery, *Resilient Interdomain Traffic Exchange: BGP Security and DDoS Mitigation*, NIST Special Publication 800-189, December 2019.

[8] Melchior Aelmans, Niels Raijer, *Deploying BGP Routing Security*, Juniper Day One book, 2019.

[9] RIPE-580, *Recommendations on Route Flap Damping*, January 2013.

[10] Justin Ryburn, *Deploying BGP Flowspec*, Juniper Day One book, 2015.

C

D

E

L

L2VPN   73, 74, 166, 239, 307, 465, 482, 483, 488
L3VPN   62, 73, 74, 119, 166, 239, 274, 307, 422, 427, 432, 434, 465-469, 472-489, 495, 497, 530, 542-550, 591
LACNIC   13, 438
LAG   35, 564
LDP   84, 253, 279, 308, 483, 488, 493-495
LFA   518, 536, 537
Martin Libicki   18
Link State   13, 22, 185, 303, 307, 315, 476, 536
LIR   17, 357, 384, 567
Loc-RIB   24, 213, 231, 232, 588
Loopback   34-37, 40, 56, 78, 79, 84, 87, 101, 102, 105, 215, 302-307, 379, 393, 493, 521, 563, 564
Kirk Lougheed   9, 10, 29
LSA   316, 537
LSDB   37, 315, 530
LSP   306, 481, 493-496, 537
Paolo Lucente   605

M

MAC-VRF   490
MANRS   449, 571-573
Zhuoquing Mao   350
MAOI   505
Martian networks   137
MSS   509
Max-Mask   442, 443
MD5 authentication   400, 401, 464
Meet-Me-Room   21, 81, 330
Minesweeper   462
MP2MP   465, 482
MP-BGP   73-75, 77, 102, 104, 353, 466, 473
mp-export   567, 568
MP-iBGP   307, 467, 469-483, 486-495, 545
mp-import   567, 568
MPLS-TE   536
MP_REACH_NLRI   436
MRAI   350, 505-509, 561

N

NAP   19
NAPT   357
NBS   575-578
NFV   313, 331
NIR   17, 357, 384
NO_ADVERTISE   61, 141
NO_EXPORT   61, 141, 194, 226, 342, 411-417, 420
NO_EXPORT_SUBCONFED   61, 141
NSF   586-589
NVGRE   489

O

OBS   575-578
OLO   100
OLT   300
OpenBGPD   95, 313
Openflow   531
ORF   234-246
OSI   300
OSPF   13, 22, 25, 37, 39, 40, 84, 148, 185, 204, 207, 274-276, 299, 302, 303, 307, 315, 316, 336, 353, 368-371, 473, 476, 493, 503, 511, 512, 517, 518, 523, 536
OSPFv3   77
OTT   374, 570
Output Policy Engine   24

P

Pakistan Telecom   394, 397, 398
Path Vector   9, 22, 23, 28, 51
PCCW Global   394, 397, 398
peeringDB   573
Cristel Pelsser   350
Plankton   462
pmacct   602, 605
PNI   81, 224, 330
PPP   308, 373, 465, 482
prepending   169, 262- 265, 269, 271, 273, 297, 362, 369, 377, 387, 388, 407-409, 571
psBGP   458

Q

R

S

T

V

Validator   440, 442-452
VC   483-487
VLAN   514
VNF   313, 331
VPLS-BGP   483-488
VPN-IPv4   46, 62, 74, 103, 125, 469-473, 478-482, 545, 548, 550
VRF   95, 427, 432-437, 451, 467-472, 474-479, 490, 495, 496, 506, 530, 542, 546, 548
vRR   313
VSI   483-485
VXLAN   19, 463, 489

Y

YouTube   394, 397, 398